Introductory Econometrics

Longman Economics Series
Series editors: Robert Millward, Michael T. Sumner
and George Zis

Mathematics for economists

Introductory Econometrics: Theory and Applications

R. Leighton Thomas

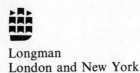
Longman
London and New York

Longman Group Limited
Longman House, Burnt Mill, Harlow
Essex CM20 2JE, England
Associated companies throughout the world

Published in the United States of America
by Longman Inc., New York

First published 1985

British Library Cataloguing in Publication Data
Thomas, R. Leighton
    Introductory econometrics (Longman
    economics series)
    I. Title
    330′.028

    ISBN 0-582-29634-X

Library of Congress Cataloging in Publication Data
Thomas, R. Leighton, 1942–
    Introductory econometrics, theory and applications.

    (Longman economics series)
    Bibliography: p.
    Includes index.
    1. Econometrics.   I. Title.   II. Series.
HB139.T52 1984   330′.028   84-932
ISBN 0-582-29634-X

Printed in Singapore by
Champion Office Supplies Pte Ltd.

Contents

Preface

The idea of writing this book arose out of my teaching of the final-year course in applied econometrics at the University of Salford during the late 1970s. Students on this course did not necessarily take a parallel course in introductory econometric theory so the course, although labelled 'applied', had to include a fairly extensive but mainly intuitive theoretical section. The students moreover were composed entirely of non-specialists in econometrics whose background in statistics consisted simply of a second-year course in 'quantitative methods' similar to that run in many British universities and polytechnics.

When searching for a suitable background text for the course, it was immediately clear that no precisely suitable textbook existed. Typical texts either consisted of a long theoretical section with one or two 'applied' topics tagged on at the end, or included a brief theoretical introduction followed by a series of applied chapters each written by a different author. The problem with the latter type of book was, not surprisingly, a lack of integration between the various sections. I have therefore attempted to write an integrated textbook for non-specialist students which includes a fair proportion both of theoretical material and of econometric applications, but in which the range of theoretical topics covered is, to some extent, determined by the applied topics included later. Ideally, students using the book will eventually be studying both theoretical and applied sections at the same time.

The book will, I hope, be of use both to students taking a single final-year course in econometrics and to those who take parallel non-specialist courses in both theory and applied. It may also be useful for non-specialist graduate courses in econometrics such as those appearing in the taught Master's programmes at most British universities. When used for a single theory/applied course it will probably be necessary to limit the applied chapters covered and possibly to concentrate on those theoretical topics specifically required for the applied topics chosen.

The typical quantitative methods course taught in the second year of most British university and polytechnic first-degree courses should be a perfectly adequate preparation for tackling this book. Students should have a working knowledge of the two-variable regression model, including its inferential aspects. However, a brief revision of some of the basic concepts of two-variable regression is included in Chapter 2. A limited knowledge of calculus, including partial differentiation, is also assumed as is some familiarity with matrix algebra (e.g. the meaning of an inverse matrix). However, use of matrix algebra is kept to a minimum and largely confined to Chapter 2.

An important feature of the applied econometrics course at Salford is the series of empirical exercises that students are expected to tackle during the year. Any student of econometrics should, at an early stage, get used to handling genuine data and using simple multiple regression packages. Such packages are, of course, now readily available at virtually all British universities and polytechnics. Accordingly, appendices based on the exercises used at Salford have been included at the end of each applied chapter in the book. These appendices are not meant just to be read. Students should use regression programmes to duplicate any estimated equations that are quoted and to follow up any suggestions made for further work. In using the book it is not necessary to wait until the applied section is reached before attempting the exercises. It is quite possible, for example, to tackle the early sections of any of the exercises once Chapter 2 has been read.

I owe a considerable debt to a number of friends and colleagues for making helpful comments on early drafts of various chapters in the book. In particular I must thank George Zis, Mike Sumner and Neil Thompson. For the painstaking job of actually typing both earlier and final drafts, I am most grateful to my wife, Margaret, and to Shirley Wooley. Thanks for typing are also due to Kath Bacon, Susan Mullins and Sharon Machin. None of the above, of course, are responsible for any errors and confusions that remain.

R.L.T. 18 October 1983.

Acknowledgements

We are indebted to the following for permission to reproduce copyright material:

Cambridge University Press for Tables 6.1 (Prais & Houthakker, 1955), 10.2 (Courakis, 1978), 10.3–10.5 (Hendry & Mizon, 1978); The Econometric Society for Table 7.1 (Zellner & Geisel. 1970); Elsevier Biomedical Press B.V. Amsterdam, for Table 10.1 from Table 1, p. 227 *Demand for Money in UK* by D. Laidler; International Statistical Institute & the author, Prof. H. Theil for fig. 11.1, Tables 11.2, 11.3 (Theil & Boot, 1962); National Institute of Economic & Social Research for Table 11.4, p. 27 *NIER*, Nov. 1981; Yale University Press for Table 11.1 (L.A. Klein 1950).

Abbreviations

AIDS	almost ideal demand system
AIH	absolute income hypothesis
APC	average propensity to consume
APC	'equilibrium' average propensity to consume
BLUE	best linear unbiased estimator
BB	*National Income and Expenditure Blue Book*
CE	Cambridge Econometrics
CEPG	Cambridge Economic Policy Group
CES	Constant elasticity of substitution
EIU	Economic Intelligence Unit
ETAS	*Economic Trends Annual Supplement*
FIML	full information maximum likelihood
GLS	generalised least squares
ILS	indirect least squares
LBS	London Business School
LCH	life-cycle hypothesis
LIML	limited information maximum likelihood
MLE	maximum likelihood estimation
MPC	marginal propensity to consume
MPS	marginal propensity to save
MRS	marginal rate of substitution
NI	National Institute
OLS	ordinary least squares
PIH	permanent income hypothesis
RIH	relative income hypothesis
SSE	explained sum or squares
SSR	residual sum of squares
SST	total sum of squares
TSLS	two-stage least squares
VES	variable elasticity of substitution

1 Introduction

Most economic theories have developed out of *a priori* reasoning based on relatively simple assumptions. However, different assumptions will lead to different theories. If we are to provide government with sensible policy prescriptions, we therefore require some way of distinguishing 'good' theories from 'bad' theories. The obvious way is to refer to 'the facts'. In the physical sciences a theory is judged by its ability to make successful predictions. Hypotheses are developed by a combination of *a priori* reasoning and empirical observations and are then used to generate predictions which can be tested against further data. If the predictions are judged 'correct', the hypothesis or theory still stands, while if the predictions are incorrect the hypothesis is either rejected or simply reformulated to take account of the new data. Such traditional 'scientific method' has served the physical sciences well over the past two centuries and one might hope that a similar approach was possible in economics. However, there are problems.

A major problem is that the economist can rarely, if ever, conduct a controlled laboratory experiment. Take two simple examples – one from physics and the other from economics. Suppose we were interested in the effect on the volume, V, of a gas of variations in its temperature, T, and the pressure under which it is kept, P. Specifically, we might wish to test the hypothesis that a given proportionate increase in the temperature of the gas, with pressure held constant, leads to a more than proportionate increase in its volume. That is, resorting to the terminology of economics, we ask the question – is the elasticity of volume with respect to temperature greater than unity? Suppose we assume that a relationship of the form

$$V = AT^\alpha P^\beta \qquad [1.1]$$

exists where A, α and β are constants. α measures the effect on volume of changes in temperature when pressure, P, is kept constant and β measures the effect on volume of changes in pressure when temperature, T, is held constant.[1]

Equation [1.1] is referred to as a *maintained hypothesis*. In hypothesis-testing situations, typically we make a number of assumptions not all of which are to be tested. Those assumptions we are prepared to accept and do not intend to test constitute the maintained hypothesis. We can never be certain that a maintained hypothesis is valid (e.g., a simpler linear formulation might be preferable to [1.1]), but some such assumptions are always necessary if hypothesis testing is to proceed at all. The form of equation [1.1] is, in fact, very suitable for the purpose at hand since α and β are, of course, elasticities. α is the elasticity of volume with respect to temperature under conditions of constant pressure. To measure α we would set up a laboratory experiment under which pressure is kept constant and we vary the temperature of the gas at will. We then observe, the relationship between temperature and volume under these conditions and come to some conclusion about the size of α. Similarly, β is the elasticity of volume with respect to pressure under conditions of constant temperature. A further controlled experiment would be set up if we wished to come to some conclusion about the size of β.

Now consider a situation in economics where we are interested in the effect on a household's consumption expenditure, C, of variations in its disposable income, Y, and its stock of liquid assets, L. Specifically we might be concerned whether, for a given stock of liquid assets, the relationship between consumption and income was one of proportionality. Suppose we specified the maintained hypothesis

$$C = AL^{\alpha}Y^{\beta} \qquad\qquad [1.2]$$

where α now measures the elasticity of consumption with respect to liquid assets when income is constant, and β measures the elasticity with respect to income when the liquid asset stock is constant. Given the maintained hypothesis [1.2], testing whether the relationship between C and Y is one of proportionality simply involves testing the hypothesis

$$\beta = 1.$$

Unfortunately, it is very unlikely that we will ever be able to set up controlled experiments in which, for example, we hold a household's liquid asset stock constant and observe the relationship between C and Y. In economics it is very rarely the case that we are able to collect data specifically generated for the purpose in hand. Rather, the economist has to make use of whatever data he can find. Such data can be classified into two kinds – *time series* data and *cross-sectional* data.

Time series data on an individual household would consist of observations on the income, consumption and liquid assets of the household for a series of successive periods, e.g. months or years. Although most published time series data on the consumption behaviour of households refers to aggregates (often economy-wide), of very many households, it would be quite feasible to collect data on an individual household. Unfortunately, there would be no way in which we could guarantee that the household's liquid asset stock remained constant while we observed the relationship between C and Y.

Cross-sectional data consist of observations on different households over the same period of time. For example, the Family Expenditure Surveys in the UK and general household surveys in other countries provide such data on many thousands of households. However, there would be no reason to expect household stocks of liquid assets to be constant over the cross-section. Moreover, as we are now dealing with different households, we would also be faced with the problem of variations in size, composition and background.

Clearly, whatever type of data is available for the investigation of [1.2] we are faced with the difficulty that both Y and L will be varying. This situation is, of course, the normal one in economics. Our data is almost invariably such that all variables we are interested in will be non-constant, the controlled experiment not being feasible.

A statistical technique exists that goes some way to overcoming the handicap of being unable to carry out controlled experiments. This technique, known as *multiple regression analysis*, enables us to 'estimate' quantities such as A, α and β in equation [1.2] simultaneously, without the need to hold variables constant artificially. Notice that if we take logarithms of equation [1.2] we obtain the linear equation

$$\log C = \log A + \alpha \log L + \beta \log Y \qquad\qquad [1.3]$$

The reader should be familiar with the *least squares technique* of estimating a simple linear relationship between two variables. This technique can, in fact, be extended to the estimation of linear relationships such as [1.3], although in the multiple regression case the estimated relationship cannot be depicted in a simple two-dimensional diagram. Multiple regression, then, is the economist's replacement for a controlled laboratory experiment. Often it may not be a very good replacement but it is normally the best we have and much *econometrics* involves its use in one form or another.

Equations [1.2] and [1.3] suggest that an exact or *deterministic* relationship exists between the left-hand side or dependent variable and the two right-hand side or explanatory variables. However, economic relationships are never exact – human beings are unpredictable in their behaviour, and for this reason a random *disturbance* is usually added to such relationships. For example, a household may receive exactly the same income and possess exactly the same liquid asset stock in one week as it does in another. Yet its consumption may well differ for purely random reasons. We therefore rewrite equations such as [1.3] which we wish to estimate as

$$\log C = \log A + \alpha \log L + \beta \log Y + \varepsilon \qquad\qquad [1.4]$$

where ε is a random disturbance which may take either a positive or a negative value.[2] This disturbance can also be regarded as reflecting all other factors apart from Y and L which have some (hopefully slight) effect on household consumption. One cannot expect Y and L to encompass all influences on C.[3]

The fact that a random disturbance is included in economic relationships means that we cannot expect to measure quantities such as A, α and β in [1.4] exactly. This would be the case even if we were able to set up controlled experiments and hold Y and L constant because we would have no control over ε, the random factor. For example, if we held L constant in order to investigate β, then our findings from one experiment might well differ from those in another because of the different random responses of the household, reflected in different values for ε. Similarly, when applying the multiple regression technique, we might obtain one set of estimates for A, α, and β from one sample of observations on Y, L and C and a rather different set from another sample. In other words, the estimators are subject to sampling variability and have sampling distributions.[4] We cannot therefore estimate A, α and β exactly but are reduced to finding, for example, 95 per cent confidence intervals for their values. Similarly, we can never say with certainty that, for example, $\alpha \neq 0$ in equation [1.4], i.e. that liquid assets influence consumption. We can merely test statistically the hypothesis $\alpha = 0$ and reject it or not at, for example, the 5 per cent level of significance. It is when we reject $\alpha = 0$ that we say 'liquid assets are significant at the 5 per cent level'.

At this point it is worth considering the meaning of the term 'level of significance'. For example, to say that a hypothesis is rejected at 'the 5 per cent level of significance' is an admission that there is a probability of 5 per cent that it has been wrongly rejected. That is, that there is a probability of 5 per cent that the hypothesis was true all along and that the characteristics in the data that led to its rejection occurred simply by chance. Hence, if we reject the hypothesis $\alpha = 0$ in [1.4] at the 5 per cent level of significance, we are saying that we believe liquid

3

assets influence consumption but acknowledge a probability of 5 per cent that the statistical association that led us to this conclusion could have occurred by chance.

The fact that the significance level of a test is an admission of the existence of chance has one important implication. Suppose we were interested in other possible determinants of household consumption. Imagine we tried adding, one at a time, twenty different variables to the right-hand side of [1.4]. Remember that, even if such a variable is of no importance in the determination of consumption, there is a 1 in 20, or 5 per cent, probability that it will appear 'significant at the 5 per cent level' purely by chance. Hence, if we try twenty such variables we must expect one of them to appear significant even if *none* of them are of real importance. The danger now is that we might forget the nineteen 'unsuccessful' variables and focus attention on the single 'significant' one, maintaining that we had uncovered evidence that it is an important determinant of consumption. What we would have done, however, is to have confused hopelessly the business of hypothesis *testing* with that of hypothesis *formulation*. The statistical relationship we have uncovered *may* reflect a genuine causal link but it is also possible that it represents a purely spurious relationship that happens to exist just in the data we have observed. We have *formulated* a hypothesis by 'observing' this data. What we cannot do is to *test* this hypothesis using the *same* body of data and it is silly to claim that we have. A hypothesis formulated from one data set obviously needs to be tested on a *new* data set.

The above procedure is an extreme example of what is commonly referred to as 'data-mining'. Unfortunately, such data-mining, albeit in a moderate form, appears to be a fairly common practice in much empirical economic research. One finds impressive-looking regression equations presented in many published papers. What should be realised is that the presented regressions are almost certainly the 'most successful' of a whole series of 'trial' regressions, the vast majority of which do not appear. The presenter may not have tried the twenty variables of the above example, but he will probably have tried two or three and also experimented with different definitions of the one that worked best.[5] Although it is probably an inevitable consequence of the paucity of economic data, there is therefore a tendency for hypothesis formulation and testing to get mixed up in economic research. Because of this it is probably wise to take many of the regression equations reported in the applied chapters of this book with just a slight pinch of salt and mentally downgrade the significance of variables and the overall performance of presented equations. The 'non-statistically minded' reader may have some difficulty in fully understanding what has just been said but, if this is the case, it would be a good idea if he/she returned to this introduction after reading the theoretical Chapters 2–5.

The technique of multiple regression is described in Chapter 2. Because the existence of the random disturbance in relationships such as [1.4] means that this technique will yield only *estimates* of parameters like A, α and β, we are inevitably concerned with the quality of these estimates. *Estimates* are always obtained by the use of some estimating formula or *estimator* and we would obviously like this estimator to be a 'good' one in some sense. Part of Chapter 2 is therefore concerned with defining the properties that we would like our estimators to have. We then consider the conditions under which the least squares method most commonly used in multiple regression analysis will yield estimators possessing these properties. The necessary conditions make up what is frequently referred to as the *classical multiple regression model*. Unfortunately they turn out to be rather restrictive conditions.

Firstly, it is necessary that disturbances such as ε in equation [1.4] should satisfy a whole series of assumptions many of which are unlikely to be met. Secondly, the manner in which we are normally forced to collect our data turns out to be important. Because we are unable to perform controlled experiments we are unable to fix for ourselves the sample values of explanatory variables such as Y and L in [1.4]. Instead, we have to accept any values thrown up by chance by the economic system we are observing. In the jargon, the explanatory variables are *stochastic* or *random* rather than *non-stochastic* or *non-random*. The consequences of this are often serious, particularly if the relationship we are interested in is but one of a simultaneous system of such relationships. Since we represent most economic systems in this way, this is the most common situation.

The consequences of breakdowns in the assumptions that make up the classical regression model and the alternative procedures that are available are considered in detail in Chapters 3 and 4. Indeed, the analysis of such breakdowns and the devising of alternative estimating procedures make up the main subject matter of theoretical econometrics. It is Chapter 4 that is concerned with problems arising out of the simultaneity of most economic relationships. Chapter 5 lists some extensions of normal regression analysis which we will find are used frequently in the applied chapters in the remainder of the book.

Chapters 6–10 each cover an important area of applied work in econometrics. Empirical exercises are included at the end of each of the applied chapters. These involve the use of actual data on the UK economy for estimating regression equations arising out of the material of the preceding chapter. Working with realistic data is a vital part of any course in econometrics since only by actually trying to estimate economic relationships will a student begin to acquire a 'feel' for the difficulties involved. Any of the various statistical packages, such as TSB/ESB, DEMOS and GENSTAT, currently available in UK universities is suitable for tackling these exercises. There is, in fact, no need for the reader to wait until Chapter 6 before turning to the exercises. Early parts of each exercise can and should be attempted once Chapter 2 has been read and understood.

Finally, in Chapter 11, the structure and uses of the major UK macroeconometric models are discussed. We consider how such models are used in forecasting and as an aid to policy formulation. Successful forecasting and the provision of sensible policy prescriptions are two of the ultimate aims of econometrics.

When reading the applied chapters, the reader may be struck by the fact that there appears to be no coherent pattern in the econometric research work performed in the various areas we cover. Unfortunately much empirical work in economics has suffered from the lack of a coherent and constructive research strategy. Work tends to proceed in virtual isolation, taking only token account of previous research in an area. Equations are estimated in a purely *ad hoc* manner with only the most precursory reference to economic theory. The requirements of a constructive research strategy are well summarised in Davidson, *et al.* (1978). Firstly, any new 'model' should only supplant old 'models' if it can account not only for all previously accepted results but also explain some new phenomena that the old models cannot. Secondly, a new model must have a sound basis in economic theory. Thirdly, any new model must be able to account for *all* the properties of the data under consideration. In particular, it should be able to explain the results obtained by previous researchers using the same data set and also explain why their research methods led to such conclusions.

Such a constructive research strategy is now being followed by workers in a number of fields in economics. A rigorous example of the approach is provided by the paper on the UK consumption function by Davidson, *et al.* referred to above. We shall discuss this paper in Chapter 7 but the approach will also be encountered in the chapters on investment and on the demand for money. A characteristic of the approach is to estimate equations involving not the 'levels' of variables but their rates of change. Many economic time series 'trend' either continuously upward or continuously downward (the price level in the postwar UK is an obvious example). Such trend variables will always be highly correlated and there is an obvious danger that such correlations will be at least partly spurious. Working in terms of the rate of change of variables will frequently remove trend elements (until recently the rate of change in the UK price level showed no definite trend either upwards or downwards). Spurious correlations can thus be avoided although there is a danger that unless equations are properly specified vital information relating to the levels of variables will not be made use of.

Another distinctive characteristic of the approach is to start with a very general formulation and then use the data evidence to simplify the estimating equation along lines consistent with economic theory. This contrasts with the more conventional approach adopted by many investigators where economic theory is used to specify an initial simple form for estimating equations which is then modified according to the characteristics of the data. The problem with the new approach is that such economic theory as exists frequently provides little more information than that certain variables bear some proportionate relationship to one another when in steady state. For example, the equilibrium relationship between consumption and income or capital stock and output can be taken as one of proportionality. This leaves so much scope for data-based simplification of the general equations, by, for example, experimenting with various lag structures, that some economists would regard the approach as verging on the 'data-mining' discussed earlier. However, the data-based approach at the very least provides a standard by which the explanatory power of more conventionally estimated equations can be judged. Possibly a judicious combination of the two approaches will prove the most fruitful in future research efforts.

At this stage the reader may find some difficulty in fully appreciating some of the issues just discussed. However, if this is the case then it should prove helpful to re-read this introduction once the book as a whole has been studied.

Notes

1. Those familiar with Charles' Law will recognise that the actual relationship between V, P and T is $PV/T =$ constant. Hence, since this implies $V = $ (constant) TP^{-1}, experimentation should yield $\alpha = 1$ and $\beta = -1$.
2. This implies that the original equation [1.2] should be rewritten as $C = AL^{\alpha}Y^{\beta}\theta$ where θ is the 'antilog' of ε, i.e. $\theta = e^{\varepsilon}$. θ must be assumed always greater than zero, otherwise consumption would be negative and $\varepsilon = \log \theta$ would not be defined.

3. ε may also reflect the fact that we cannot always measure variables with perfect accuracy. While a relationship such as [1.3] could hold for the true values of C, L and Y it may well not hold exactly for the data we obtain. Possible errors in the measurement of C, L and Y are thus another reason for adding a random disturbance to [1.3].
4. The situation is analogous to that when we attempt to estimate a population mean, μ, by the mean of a random sample, $\bar{x}$. The reader should be familiar with the fact that $\bar{x}$ is subject to sampling variability, i.e. that different random samples will yield different values for $\bar{x}$.
5. For example, the percentage annual rate of price inflation can be calculated in several ways. Similarly, there are alternative definitions for the 'broad money stock'.

2 Multiple regression analysis

In this chapter we shall be concerned with the so-called 'classical linear regression model'. A working knowledge of the two-variable regression model will be assumed and we shall deal mainly with what is known as multiple regression. However, we first revise some crucial aspects of simple two-variable regression analysis.

2.1 Revision of some important concepts in two-variable regression

In simple regression analysis a linear relationship is assumed between a *dependent* variable Y and an *explanatory* variable X

$$Y = \beta_1 + \beta_2 X + \varepsilon \tag{2.1}$$

For example, Y might be the weekly consumption expenditure of a household of given size and composition and X the weekly dispossable income of such a household. β_1 and β_2 are fixed constants and ε is a random *disturbance*. The disturbance reflects, firstly, all factors other than disposable income which influence the consumption expenditure of this type of household, e.g. its tastes, social and educational background, the size of its bank balance, etc. ε may therefore be positive or negative. It might be positive for a household which because of past savings has a large positive bank balance and may be negative for a household which has incurred large debts. Secondly, the disturbance reflects the basic unpredictable or random nature of human behaviour. We do not expect two households with the same disposable income and identical in other respects to, necessarily, make exactly the same consumption expenditure. Neither can we expect a given household to make exactly the same consumption expenditure in two successive weeks even when the conditions under which it operates remain unchanged.

The disturbance ε may be regarded as a random variable with its own probability distribution and it is convenient to assume for the moment that its average or expected value is zero, i.e. $E(\varepsilon) = 0$. Taking expectations over equation [2.1], we then have for a household of given income X

$$E(Y) = \beta_1 + \beta_2 X \tag{2.2}$$

Equation [2.2] is sometimes referred to as the *population regression line* and β_1 and β_2 are population parameters. $E(Y)$ may be regarded as the average or expected consumption expenditure of households with the given disposable income X. The parameter β_1, of course, represents the expected expenditure of a household with zero income while β_2 measures the change in expected expenditure per unit change in disposable income X. The population regression line is represented by the solid line in Fig. 2.1, β_1 and β_2 being the intercept and slope of this line.

Equation [2.2] refers to a population of households and in practice the investigator never discovers the exact position of this line, i.e. he never gets to know the precise values of the parameters β_1 and β_2. The population regression line has to be estimated from sample data.

Suppose a random sample of size n is available.[1] This consists of observations on Y and X for n households of the given type. The observations may refer to a 'cross-section' of households during a given week or alternatively they may be 'time series data' on a single household over n separate weeks. Provided [2.1] holds for the population of households from which the sample is drawn we may write

$$Y_i = \beta_1 + \beta_2 X_i + \varepsilon_i \qquad i = 1, 2, 3, \ldots n \qquad [2.3]$$

where Y_i is the consumption expenditure of the ith household in the sample and X_i is its disposable income.[2] ε_i is the value of the disturbance for the ith household in the sample during the particular week in which it was observed. Notice that the sample provides no information on the sample values of ε. The ε_i's are unknown and, since the exact values for β_1 and β_2 are never discovered, it can be seen from equation [2.3] that they will remain unknown even though the sample provides the values Y_i and X_i.

Equation [2.2], the population regression line, is estimated by a *sample regression line*. The estimation is performed by fitting (using some method which we need not yet specify), a line to a 'scatter diagram' of the sample values of consumption Y on income X. We shall write the sample regression line as

$$\hat{Y} = \hat{\beta}_1 + \hat{\beta}_2 X \qquad [2.4]$$

where $\hat{\beta}_1$ and $\hat{\beta}_2$ are estimates of the parameters β_1 and β_2 and $\hat{Y}$ is known as the fitted or *predicted value of Y*. $\hat{Y}$ is so called because, on substituting the sample values for income X, i.e. the X_i's, into equation [2.4], we obtain a set of predicted consumption expenditures, $\hat{Y}_i$, – one for each household in the sample. That is, we have

$$\hat{Y}_i = \hat{\beta}_1 + \hat{\beta}_2 X_i \qquad i = 1, 2, 3, \ldots, n \qquad [2.5]$$

The sample regression line (with intercept $\hat{\beta}_1$ and slope $\hat{\beta}_2$) is represented by the broken line in Fig. 2.1. Since it is merely an estimate of the population regression line it will not normally coincide with it.

For any given household in the sample, predicted Y, i.e. $\hat{Y}$, will not normally be the same as actual observed Y. This is simply another way of saying that points in the scatter diagram will not normally lie exactly on the sample regression line. The difference between Y and $\hat{Y}$ may be positive or negative, is called a *residual* and is given the symbol e. There will be a residual associated with each household in the sample, i.e. we have

$$e_i = Y_i - \hat{Y}_i \qquad \text{for } i = 1, 2, \ldots, n \qquad [2.6]$$

or using [2.5]

$$Y_i = \hat{\beta}_1 + \hat{\beta}_2 X_i + e_i \qquad \text{for } i = 1, 2, \ldots, n \qquad [2.7]$$

It is crucial to distinguish clearly between the residuals, i.e. the e_i's, and the disturbances, i.e. the ε_i's. The difference is illustrated in Fig. 2.1 for the seventh

2.1 Population and sample regression lines.

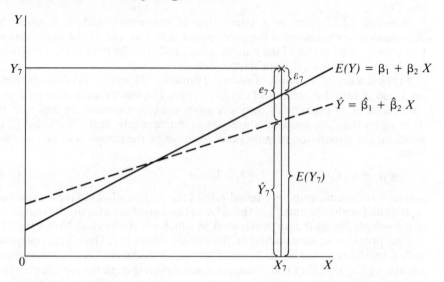

household in the sample. During the week it was observed, this household had consumption Y_7 and income X_7 and would be represented in a scatter diagram by the point (X_7, Y_7) designated by a cross in Fig. 2.1. The disturbance for this household, ε_7, is the difference between its actual consumption expenditure when observed, Y_7, and the average or expected expenditure of such households, which we may write as $E(Y_7)$, when they have an income of X_7. It is therefore, as illustrated in Fig. 2.1, the vertical distance between the designated point and the population regression line. As already mentioned ε_7 is, and remains, unknown. The residual for the seventh household, e_7, is the difference between actual consumption expenditure and the predicted value for such expenditure obtained by using the sample regression line. In Fig. 2.1 it is the vertical distance between the point and the sample regression line. Since the positions of both point and sample regression line are known, *the residual* e_7 *unlike the disturbance* ε_7 *can be calculated*. Since the sample regression line is an estimate of the population regression line, the residual e_7 can be regarded as an estimate of the unknown ε_7.

Summarising we have the following relationships for this seventh household. From the population regression line [2.2] we have the expected expenditure of a household with such an income

$$E(Y_7) = \beta_1 + \beta_2 X_7$$

Actual expenditure will not normally equal expected expenditure but

$$Y_7 = E(Y_7) + \varepsilon_7 = \beta_1 + \beta_2 X_7 + \varepsilon_7$$

From the sample regression line we have the predicted expenditure of a household with income X_7

$$\hat{Y}_7 = \hat{\beta}_1 + \hat{\beta}_2 X_7$$

Actual expenditure will not normally equal predicted expenditure but

$$Y_7 = \hat{Y}_7 + e_7 = \hat{\beta}_1 + \hat{\beta}_2 X_7 + e_7$$

10

Similar distances and residuals exist and similar relationships will of course hold for each of the n households in the sample.

We have deliberately said nothing up to this point about how the population regression line is estimated and the sample regression line obtained. It should be realised that whatever method is used (and there are many), a set of residuals will be generated – one for each household or observation. Different methods will yield different sets of residuals. It is assumed that the reader is aware that the most common method of estimation is the so-called *method of least squares*. That is, that simple regression line is chosen, i.e. those values for $\hat{\beta}_1$ and $\hat{\beta}_2$ are selected, which minimises the sum of the squared residuals i.e. the quantity $\sum_{i=1}^{n} e_i^2$.

There is nothing inherently virtuous about the method of least squares. As we shall see later it will yield 'good' estimates of the parameters only when a relatively large number of rather restrictive assumptions are satisfied. However, it does have the advantage that it is still applicable when the dependent variable is influenced by more than one explanatory variable. Suppose, for example, that for households of the given type it was felt more appropriate to replace the population regression line [2.2] by

$$E(Y) = \beta_1 + \beta_2 X + \beta_3 L \qquad [2.8]$$

where L represents the stock of liquid assets of such households and β_3 is another parameter. Actual consumption of such households is now given by

$$Y = \beta_1 + \beta_2 X + \beta_3 L + \varepsilon \qquad [2.9]$$

where ε is a disturbance of the same nature as that in the previous discussion.[3]

Suppose the investigator is interested in the size of the parameters β_2 and β_3. β_2 measures the change in average or expected consumption expenditure, $E(Y)$, per unit change in disposable income when a household's stock of liquid assets remains constant. β_3 measures the change in $E(Y)$ per unit change in the stock of liquid assets when the household's disposable income remains constant.

In the physical sciences it would perhaps be possible for the investigator to set up a controlled experiment in which a variable such as L is held constant, the variable X is allowed to vary and the resultant values of Y are observed. Since L is held constant, equation [2.8] can be rewritten as

$$E(Y) = \beta_1' + \beta_2 X \qquad [2.10]$$

where $\beta_1' = \beta_1 + \beta_3 \bar{L}$ and $\bar{L}$ is the fixed value of L.

Equation [2.10] is formally equivalent to [2.2] so that we are back in the world of two-variable regression and estimates of the parameter β_2 may be obtained from the scatter diagram of Y on X. Similarly, if it were possible to set up a controlled experiment in which X were held constant, then the parameter β_3 could be estimated by observing the scatter of Y on L.

Most economic relationships involve more than two variables. It is very rarely the case that a population regression equation will contain just one explanatory variable. Unfortunately, however, in economics or econometrics controlled experiments are almost never feasible so that it is not possible in the above situation to hold variables such as X or L constant. In such a situation variations in, for example, the L variable, would make it extremely unlikely that 'good' estimates of the parameter β_2 could be obtained merely by observing the scatter of Y on X. Similarly, 'good' estimates of β_3 could not be obtained from the scatter diagram of Y on L. However, the method of least squares, so frequently used in two-variable regression, is also applicable to the estimation of parameters in equations such as [2.8]. It is to its use in so-called multiple regression that we now turn.

2.2 Least squares estimation with more than one explanatory variable

Assume that a linear relationship exists between a dependent variable Y and k explanatory variables $X_1, X_2, X_3, \ldots, X_k$.

$$Y = \beta_1 X_1 + \beta_2 X_2 + \beta_3 X_3 \ldots \beta_k X_k + \varepsilon \qquad [2.11]$$

where ε is a disturbance of similar nature to that of the previous section and the β_j's $(j = 1, 2, \ldots, k)$ are constants. It is often convenient to have a constant or intercept term in [2.11] and we can achieve this by specifying that the variable X_1 always takes the value unity, so that [2.11] becomes

$$Y = \beta_1 + \beta_2 X_2 + \beta_3 X_3, \ldots, + \beta_k X_k + \varepsilon \qquad [2.11a]$$

an equation with $k - 1$ 'genuine' explanatory variables.[4]

Assuming that $E(\varepsilon) = 0$, then by taking expectations over [2.11a] we have for a given set of values of the explanatory variables

$$E(Y) = \beta_1 + \beta_2 X_2 + \beta_3 X_3, \ldots, + \beta_k X_k \qquad [2.12]$$

Equation [2.12] is known as the *population regression equation* and the β_j's as population regression parameters. For example, β_3 *measures the effect of a change in* X_3 *on* $E(Y)$ *when all the other explanatory variables remain constant.* Specifically it measures the change in $E(Y)$ per unit change in X_3 under these conditions. β_1 is sometimes called the *intercept* and $\beta_2, \beta_3, \ldots, \beta_k$ the regression *slope coefficients*.

The population regression equation is and remains unknown to the investigator. It has to be estimated from sample data. Suppose we have available a sample of n observations, each observation consisting of a value for the dependent variable Y and a set of corresponding values for the $k - 1$ explanatory variables, $X_2, X_3, \ldots, X_k$. Provided [2.11a] holds for the population from which the sample is drawn we may write

$$Y_i = \beta_1 + \beta_2 X_{2i} + \beta_3 X_{3i}, \ldots, + \beta_k X_{ki} + \varepsilon_i \qquad (i = 1, 2, 3, \ldots, n) \qquad [2.13]$$

where Y_i is the value of Y pertaining to the ith sample observation and X_{ji} is the value of the jth explanatory variable pertaining to the ith observation. For example X_{38} is the value taken by the third X variable in the eighth sample observation. ε_i is the unknown disturbance associated with the ith observation.

Suppose (using some as yet unspecified method), the sample data is used to estimate the population regression equation [2.12] by a sample regression equation which we write as

$$\hat{Y} = \hat{\beta}_1 + \hat{\beta}_2 X_2 + \hat{\beta}_3 X_3, \ldots, + \hat{\beta}_k X_k \qquad [2.14]$$

where $\hat{\beta}_1, \hat{\beta}_2, \hat{\beta}_3, \ldots, \hat{\beta}_k$ are estimates of $\beta_1, \beta_2, \beta_3, \ldots, \beta_k$ respectively. $\hat{Y}$ is again known as the predicted value of Y, since on substituting the sample values for the explanatory variables into [2.14] we obtain a set of predicted values for $\hat{Y}$– one for each observation in the sample. We can write these predicted values as

$$\hat{Y}_i = \hat{\beta}_1 + \hat{\beta}_2 X_{2i} + \hat{\beta}_3 X_{3i}, \ldots, + \hat{\beta}_k X_{ki} \qquad (i = 1, 2, 3, \ldots, n) \qquad [2.15]$$

As in two-variable regression there is no reason why the actual sample Y values, the Y_i's should be the same as the predicted values of Y, the $\hat{Y}_i$'s. The difference is again referred to as a residual and given the symbol e. There will be a residual associated with each observation in the sample, i.e. we have

$$e_i = Y_i - \hat{Y}_i$$

or using [2.15]

$$Y_i = \hat{\beta}_1 + \hat{\beta}_2 X_{2i}, \ldots, + \hat{\beta}_k X_{ki} + e_i \qquad (i = 1, 2, 3, \ldots, n) \qquad [2.16]$$

Since the $\hat{\beta}_j$'s, the actual sample values for Y and those for the X_j's are known it is possible to calculate, using [2.16], each of the e_i's. We stress again, however, that the corresponding disturbances, the ε_i's, are and remain unknown. They cannot be obtained from [2.13] because the regression parameters, the β_j's, are unknown.

The set of residuals we obtain will depend on the predicted values of Y and hence on the sample regression equation we use to estimate the population regression equation. Different sample regression equations will result in different sets of residuals. Ideally we would like the residuals to be in some sense 'as small as possible'.

If the method of least squares is adopted we select that sample regression equation, i.e. those values for $\hat{\beta}_1, \hat{\beta}_2, \hat{\beta}_3, \ldots, \hat{\beta}_k$, which minimises the sum of the squared residuals, i.e. *as in two-variable regression we make the quantity* $\sum_{i=1}^{n} e_i^2$ *as small as possible*.

The least squares estimators for the multiple regression case may be derived as follows:

Let $S = \sum_i e_i^2 = \sum_i (Y_i - \hat{\beta}_1 - \hat{\beta}_2 X_{2i} - \hat{\beta}_3 X_{3i}, \ldots, \hat{\beta}_k X_{ki})^2$

Partially differentiating S with respect to each of the $\hat{\beta}_j$'s in turn and equating these partial derivatives to zero we obtain

$$\frac{\partial S}{\partial \beta_1} = -2 \sum_i (Y_i - \hat{\beta}_1 - \hat{\beta}_2 X_{2i} - \hat{\beta}_3 X_{3i}, \ldots, \hat{\beta}_k X_{ki}) = 0 \qquad [2.17]$$

$$\frac{\partial S}{\partial \beta_2} = -2 \sum_i X_{2i} (Y_i - \hat{\beta}_1 - \hat{\beta}_2 X_{2i} - \hat{\beta}_3 X_{3i}, \ldots, \hat{\beta}_k X_{ki}) = 0$$

$$\vdots$$

$$\frac{\partial S}{\partial \beta_k} = -2 \sum_i X_{ki} (Y_i - \hat{\beta}_1 - \hat{\beta}_2 X_{2i} - \hat{\beta}_3 X_{3i}, \ldots, \hat{\beta}_k X_{ki}) = 0$$

Notice, for future reference, that the set of equation [2.17] could be rewritten as

$$\sum_i e_i = 0, \quad \sum_i X_{2i} e_i = 0, \quad \sum_i X_{3i} e_i = 0, \ldots, \sum_i X_{ki} e_i = 0$$

Rearranging [2.17] we obtain the so-called 'least squares normal equations'.

$$\sum_i Y_i = \hat{\beta}_i n + \hat{\beta}_2 \sum_i X_{2i} + \hat{\beta}_3 \sum_i X_{3i}, \ldots, + \hat{\beta}_k \sum_i X_{ki}$$

$$\sum_i X_{2i} Y_i = \hat{\beta}_1 \sum_i X_{2i} + \hat{\beta}_2 \sum_i X_{2i}^2 + \hat{\beta}_3 \sum_i X_{2i} X_{3i}, \ldots, + \hat{\beta}_k \sum_i X_{2i} X_{ki} \qquad [2.18]$$

$$\vdots$$

$$\sum_i X_{ki} Y_i = \hat{\beta}_1 \sum_i X_{ki} + \hat{\beta}_2 \sum_i X_{ki} X_{2i} + \hat{\beta}_3 \sum_i X_{ki} X_{3i}, \ldots, + \hat{\beta}_k \sum_i X_{ki}^2$$

Since the quantities $\sum Y_i, \sum X_{2i}, \sum X_{3i}, \sum X_{2i} Y_i, \sum X_{2i}^2$, etc. may all be obtained from the sample data and n is simply the sample size, [2.18] consists of a set of k linear equations in the k unknown $\hat{\beta}_j$'s. These equations can be solved to yield a unique set of expressions for the $\hat{\beta}_j$'s, provided two conditions are met:
1. The sample size exceeds the number of parameters being estimated, i.e. $n > k$.
2. As far as their sample values are concerned, none of the explanatory variables can be represented as an exact linear function of one or more of the other explanatory variables.

If either of these conditions is not met it is not difficult to show that the k equations in [2.18] are no longer all independent of one another and hence do not yield a unique solution for the $\hat{\beta}_j$'s. By the second condition we mean that relationships such as, for example, $X_{2i} = 3 + 5X_{3i} - 8X_{5i}$ for all i, do not hold amongst the sample values of the explanatory variables. When such a relationship does hold we have a case of what is known as 'perfect multicollinearity'. We shall return to the topic of multicollinearity in the next chapter.

When the above conditions are met, the unique set of expressions for $\hat{\beta}_1, \hat{\beta}_2, \hat{\beta}_3, \ldots, \hat{\beta}_k$ obtained from [2.18] are known as the *ordinary least squares* (*OLS*) *estimators* of the parameters $\beta_1, \beta_2, \beta_3, \ldots, \beta_k$ respectively. They are termed 'ordinary' to distinguish them from the different sets of estimators which may be obtained by more complicated variants of the least squares method.

The solution of equations [2.18] is rarely, except in the two-variable case, attempted 'by hand'. Computer programs for calculating values for the OLS estimators are readily available and the reader is expected to use such programs in the empirical exercises later in the book. It is not, therefore, absolutely necessary for the reader to follow the rest of the material in this section where we shall derive expressions for the OLS estimators.

To obtain the OLS estimators we shall write the normal equations [2.18] in matrix form as

$$\mathbf{X'Y} = (\mathbf{X'X})\hat{\beta} \qquad [2.19]$$

$$\text{where } \mathbf{X} = \begin{bmatrix} 1 & X_{21} & X_{31} & ,\ldots, & X_{k1} \\ 1 & X_{22} & X_{32} & ,\ldots, & X_{k2} \\ 1 & X_{23} & X_{33} & ,\ldots, & X_{k3} \\ \cdot & \cdot & \cdot & & \cdot \\ \cdot & \cdot & \cdot & & \cdot \\ \cdot & \cdot & \cdot & & \cdot \\ 1 & X_{2n} & X_{3n} & & X_{kn} \end{bmatrix} \quad \mathbf{Y} = \begin{bmatrix} Y_1 \\ Y_2 \\ Y_3 \\ \cdot \\ \cdot \\ \cdot \\ Y_n \end{bmatrix} \text{ and } \hat{\beta} = \begin{bmatrix} \hat{\beta}_1 \\ \hat{\beta}_2 \\ \hat{\beta}_3 \\ \cdot \\ \cdot \\ \cdot \\ \hat{\beta}_k \end{bmatrix}$$

X therefore consists of an $n \times k$ matrix of all the sample values for the explanatory variables. Notice that the ith row of **X** consists of those values pertaining to the ith sample observation, while the jth column consists of the sample values for just the jth explanatory variable. Since X_1 is always unity the first column of X consists of a row of 1's. **Y** is an $n \times 1$ column vector containing the sample values for Y and $\hat{\beta}$ is a $k \times 1$ vector containing the least squares estimators.

Premultiplying [2.19] by the inverse of the matrix **X′X**, we obtain

$$\hat{\beta} = (\mathbf{X'X})^{-1}\mathbf{X'Y} \qquad [2.20]$$

Thus the vector of least squares estimators is obtained by multiplying the inverse of the matrix product **X′X** into the matrix product **X′Y**. It is instructive to consider the structure of these matrix products.

$$\mathbf{X'X} = \begin{bmatrix} n & \sum X_{2i} & \sum X_{3i},\ldots, & \sum X_{ki} \\ \sum X_{2i} & \sum X_{2i}^2 & \sum X_{2i}X_{3i},\ldots, & \sum X_{2i}X_{ki} \\ \sum X_{3i} & \sum X_{3i}X_{2i} & \sum X_{3i}^2,\ldots, & \sum X_{3i}X_{ki} \\ \vdots & \vdots & \vdots & \vdots \\ \sum X_{ki} & \sum X_{ki}X_{2i} & \sum X_{ki}X_{3i},\ldots, & \sum X_{ki}^2 \end{bmatrix} \quad \mathbf{X'Y} = \begin{bmatrix} \sum Y_i \\ \sum X_{2i}Y_i \\ \sum X_{3i}Y_i \\ \vdots \\ \sum X_{ki}Y_i \end{bmatrix}$$

Thus **X′X** is a symmetric $k \times k$ matrix containing the sums of squares and cross-products of the sample values of the explanatory variables, while $X'Y$ is a $k \times 1$ vector containing the sums of cross-products of the dependent variable Y with each explanatory variable in turn.[5] It is clear that the nature of these matrix products is such that expressions in terms of simple algebra for the least squares estimators, the $\hat{\beta}_j$'s, will be extremely complicated and 'messy' except in the most simple of cases where there are only one or at most two explanatory variables. This is why the more compact matrix expression [2.20] is usually preferred and why a computer program is generally used for calculating values for the OLS estimators. However, as an example we shall derive the least squares estimators in simple non-matrix terms for the case of one explanatory variable.

In two-variable regression the matrix products become

$$\mathbf{X'X} = \begin{bmatrix} n & \sum X_i \\ \sum X_i & \sum X_i^2 \end{bmatrix} \quad \text{and} \quad \mathbf{X'Y} = \begin{bmatrix} \sum Y_i \\ \sum X_iY_i \end{bmatrix}$$

where we have replaced X_2 by the single explanatory variable X. Therefore, using [2.20]

$$\hat{\beta} = \begin{bmatrix} \hat{\beta}_1 \\ \hat{\beta}_2 \end{bmatrix} = \begin{bmatrix} n & \sum X_i \\ \sum X_i & \sum X_i^2 \end{bmatrix}^{-1} \begin{bmatrix} \sum Y_i \\ \sum X_iY_i \end{bmatrix}$$

$$= \frac{1}{n\sum X_i^2 - (\sum X_i)^2} \begin{bmatrix} \sum X_i^2 \sum Y_i - \sum X_i \sum X_iY_i \\ -\sum X_i \sum Y_i + n\sum X_iY_i \end{bmatrix}$$

Thus we see that $\hat{\beta}_2$, the OLS estimator of the slope of the population regression line [2.2], is given by the expression

$$\hat{\beta}_2 = \frac{n\sum X_iY_i - \sum X_i \sum Y_i}{n\sum X_i^2 - (\sum X_i)^2} = \frac{n\sum x_iy_i}{n\sum x_i^2} = \frac{\sum x_iy_i}{\sum x_i^2}$$

15

where $x_i = X_i - \bar{X}$ and $y_i = Y_i - \bar{Y}$, $\bar{X}$ and $\bar{Y}$ being the sample means of the X_i's and the Y_i's.

The reader should be familiar with this expression for $\hat{\beta}_2$ but will probably be less familiar with the expression that can be obtained above for $\hat{\beta}_1$, the OLS estimator of the intercept of the population regression line. $\hat{\beta}_1$ is, in fact, usually and more conveniently calculated by using the first of the normal equations [2.18] which in the present case reduces to

$$\sum Y_i = \hat{\beta}_1 n + \hat{\beta}_2 \sum X_i$$

Dividing throughout by n and rearranging we have $\hat{\beta}_1 = \bar{Y} - \hat{\beta}_2 \bar{X}$ which may be used to obtain $\hat{\beta}_1$ once $\hat{\beta}_2$ has been calculated.

Multiple versus simple regression coefficients

Consider again the situation represented by equation [2.8] where household consumption, Y, is not only influenced by disposable income, X, but also by its stock of liquid assets, L. Suppose that the investigator estimates two regression equations, one containing the liquid assets variable and the other not

$$\hat{Y} = \hat{\beta}_1' + \hat{\beta}_2' X \qquad\qquad [2.21]$$

$$\hat{Y} = \hat{\beta}_1 + \hat{\beta}_2 X + \hat{\beta}_3 L \qquad\qquad [2.22]$$

One point should be clarified immediately. The OLS estimate $\hat{\beta}_2'$, obtained from [2.21] in the absence of the L variable, will *not* normally be the same as the $\hat{\beta}_2$ obtained from the estimation of an equation such as [2.22] which contains L.[6] In equation [2.21] no attempt is made to allow for the influence of liquid assets on consumption. In equation [2.22] however, the OLS estimate, $\hat{\beta}_2$, represents an attempt to assess the influence of a change in disposable income on consumption under the *ceteris paribus* condition that liquid assets are constant.[7] In the present case, it is likely that X and L will be positively correlated across households – high income households will tend to have large stocks of liquid assets. Thus, in equation [2.21], $\hat{\beta}_2'$ will reflect not only the influence of variations in disposable income but also that of the parallel variations in liquid assets. However, in [2.22], $\hat{\beta}_2$ reflects only the effect of variations in X under the *ceteris paribus* condition that L is constant. Hence, we are likely to find $\hat{\beta}_2' > \hat{\beta}_2$. Such a result is quite usual. The addition of further variables to a regression equation will normally lead to changes in the values of the estimated coefficients attached to the variables already present.[8] For an excellent explanation of why the OLS estimation procedure can be regarded as an attempt to assess the *ceteris paribus* effects of changes in explanatory variables, see Stewart (1984: 88–95).

Sampling variability of the ordinary least squares estimators

Once a set of OLS estimates has been computed from a given sample it must be realised that these estimates are specific to that particular sample. If it were possible to take a second and further samples and to compute OLS estimates for each such sample, there is no reason why any of these sets of estimates should coincide with those obtained from the first sample. Different samples will consist of different sets of observations and hence will yield different sets of estimates, i.e. the OLS estimators are subject to *sampling variability*.

Thus if repeated samples were taken (all of identical size n) we might obtain a wide distribution of values for $\hat{\beta}_1$, for $\hat{\beta}_2$, for $\hat{\beta}_3$, etc. As we shall see, each $\hat{\beta}_j$ is a random variable in its own right with its own sampling distribution. In economics of course normally only one, not many, samples can be taken. However, it is possible, given suitable assumptions, to derive theoretically the form of these sampling distributions and hence obtain expressions for certain parameters, e.g. their mean and variance, relating to them.

Knowledge of the sampling distributions of the $\hat{\beta}_j$'s enables us to make inferences about the corresponding population parameters, i.e. the β_j's. Thus if we know the sampling distribution of $\hat{\beta}_3$, for example, we could not only make a point estimate of β_3 but also: (a) test hypotheses concerning the value of β_3; (b) obtain confidence intervals for β_3. We shall return to these aspects of regression analysis later in the chapter.

At this point we should remember that there is nothing inherent in the method of least squares that ensures that estimators of population regression parameters so obtained are 'good' estimators. A number of assumptions concerning, in particular, the disturbance must be satisfied if this is to be so. However, before examining these assumptions it is necessary to consider in some detail what we might mean by the term 'good estimator'. The next section therefore consists of a digression on the desirable properties of estimators and their sampling distributions.

2.3 Small-sample and large-sample properties of estimators

Consider a random variable Y whose probability distribution has, as one of its parameters, β, which we wish to estimate. In other words, we have a population consisting of a 'very large number' of value for Y, and β is a characteristic of this population, e.g. β might be the population mean or alternatively the population variance.

The parameter β is to be estimated from a random sample consisting of n observations on the variable Y which we write as $Y_1, Y_2, Y_3, \ldots, Y_n$. An estimator of β, for which we use the symbol $\hat{\beta}$, has to be constructed by substituting the sample observations on Y into some expression involving all, or possibly only some, of these sample observations. Thus an estimator of β can be written as[9]

$$\hat{\beta} = \hat{\beta}(Y_1, Y_2, Y_3, \ldots, Y_n) \qquad [2.23]$$

For example, if β is the population mean an estimator which might be employed is the sample mean in which case

$$\hat{\beta} = \frac{Y_1 + Y_2 + Y_3, \ldots, Y_n}{n} \qquad [2.24]$$

The reader should not need reminding that different random samples (of the given size n) will contain different values of the variable Y and hence, using [2.23], will yield different values for $\hat{\beta}$, i.e. different estimates of the parameter β. The estimator $\hat{\beta}$ is a random variable with its own probability distribution (normally called a sampling distribution). The distribution for $\hat{\beta}$ will have a mean, generally written $E(\hat{\beta})$ and a variance generally written

$$\sigma_{\hat{\beta}}^2 = E[\hat{\beta} - E(\hat{\beta})]^2$$

Properties of estimators such as $\hat{\beta}$ are generally classified into so-called *small sample* properties and so-called *large sample* or *asymptotic* properties. If the sampling distribution of an estimator possesses a certain property and possesses the attributes of this property no matter what the size of the samples from which estimates are derived, then that property is known as a small sample property. This is because the attributes of the property are possessed by the estimator *even for small samples*. It is implicitly understood that they are also possessed when the sample size is large. In contrast, if the sampling distribution of an estimator possesses the attributes of a property only when the sample size becomes very large or tends to infinity, then such a property is known as a large sample or asymptotic property. The attributes of such properties do not hold when the sample size is small.

Desirable small sample properties of an estimator

Unbiasedness

An estimator, $\hat{\beta}$, is said to be an *unbiased* estimator of β if and only if

$$E(\hat{\beta}) = \beta \qquad\qquad [2.25]$$

That is, $\hat{\beta}$ is unbiased if the mean of its sampling distribution is equal to β, the parameter being estimated.

A sampling distribution for an unbiased estimator is illustrated in Fig. 2.2. Since the illustrated distribution is symmetric (as is often the case) its mean is at the centre of the distribution and, because of the unbiasedness property, is equal to the parameter being estimated.

In everyday terms unbiasedness simply means that if repeated samples of a given size were taken, the 'average' value of the $\hat{\beta}$'s obtained would equal β. Some of the values for $\hat{\beta}$ obtained would 'underestimate' β and others would 'overestimate' β but there would be no systematic tendency towards error in either direction.

2.2 Sampling distribution for an unbiased estimator.

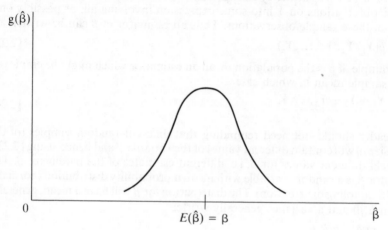

If equation [2.25] does not hold for an estimator then the estimator is said to be *biased* and the quantity $E(\hat{\beta}) - \beta$ is known as the *bias*. If the bias is positive then $\hat{\beta}$ systematically overestimates β. If the bias is negative then $\hat{\beta}$ systematically underestimates β.

Finally, notice that in defining unbiasedness no reference was made to sample size. Thus when [2.25] holds for an estimator it holds regardless of sample size and in particular holds when the sample size is small. Thus unbiasedness is a small-sample property.

Efficiency
Unbiasedness alone is not a particularly reassuring property. If the variance of the sampling distribution of $\hat{\beta}$ were large then, even if $\hat{\beta}$ were unbiased, the values of $\hat{\beta}$ that would be obtained if repeated samples were taken would tend to be widely dispersed about β. Since in practice only one sample is generally taken, it would therefore be quite possible for the specific value of $\hat{\beta}$ obtained from that one sample to be 'unluckily' very different from β, the parameter being estimated. Clearly then, we would like the variance of any unbiased estimator we use to be as small as possible. The smaller is this variance, i.e. the smaller the dispersion of the $\hat{\beta}$'s about β, the lower is the probability of obtaining a specific value for $\hat{\beta}$ which is 'very different' from β.

An estimator, $\hat{\beta}$, is said to be an *efficient* estimator of β if and only if:
(i) it is an unbiased estimator of β, i.e. $E(\hat{\beta}) = \beta$;
(ii) amongst all unbiased estimators it has the minimum variance, i.e. $\text{var}(\hat{\beta}) \leqslant \text{var}(\beta^*)$ where β^* is any other unbiased estimator.[10]

Notice that before an estimator can be efficient it must first be unbiased. For the reason outlined above an efficient estimator is also sometimes called a *best unbiased* estimator. Notice again that no reference to the sample size is involved in the definition of an efficient estimator. Hence efficiency is a small-sample property.

The word 'efficient' is sometimes used in a relative sense. Thus if two estimators are unbiased but one has a smaller variance than the other, then the first is said to be the more efficient. For example, both the sample mean, $\bar{X}$, and the sample median, m, are unbiased estimators of the mean, μ, of a univariate population, but the sample mean is the more efficient estimator since it has the smaller variance. This is illustrated in Fig. 2.3.

Whereas it is often quite simple to determine whether an estimator is unbiased or not it is a more complex matter to determine whether or not it is efficient. To establish efficiency we have to compare the variance of an estimator with the variances of all other unbiased estimators and there may be very many of these. For this reason it is sometimes convenient to restrict attention to a smaller sub-class of unbiased estimators. For example, it is often relatively easy to find the unbiased estimator with the minimum variance if we restrict ourselves to considering only so-called *linear estimators*.

A linear estimator is an estimator which is a linear function of the sample observations. Therefore for $\hat{\beta}$ to be a linear estimator we must have

$$\hat{\beta} = \hat{\beta}(Y_1, Y_2, Y_3, \ldots, Y_n) = a_1 Y_1 + a_2 Y_2 + a_3 Y_3, \ldots, + a_n Y_n \qquad [2.26]$$

where the a's are constants. For example, the sample mean $\bar{Y}$ is a linear estimator

2.3 Sampling distributions for the mean and the median.

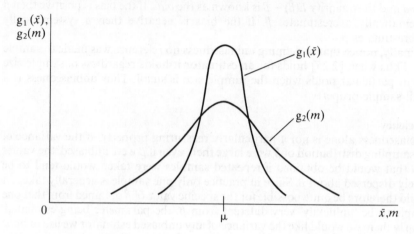

of the population mean since

$$\bar{Y} = \left(\frac{1}{n}\right)\sum_i Y_i = \left(\frac{1}{n}\right)Y_1 + \left(\frac{1}{n}\right)Y_2 + \left(\frac{1}{n}\right)Y_3, \ldots, + \left(\frac{1}{n}\right)Y_n$$

where n is a constant, being the fixed sample size.

Restricting ourselves to linear estimators leads to the definition of a third small sample property.

Best linear unbiasedness

An estimator, $\hat{\beta}$, is said to be a *best linear unbiased estimator* (or BLUE) of β if and only if:
(a) it is a linear estimator, i.e. $\hat{\beta} = \sum_i a_i Y_i$ where the a_i's are constants;
(b) it is unbiased, i.e. $E(\hat{\beta}) = \beta$;
(c) amongst all linear unbiased estimators it has the minimum variance, i.e. $\text{var}(\hat{\beta}) \leqslant \text{var}(\tilde{\beta})$ where $\tilde{\beta}$ is any other linear unbiased estimator.

A BLUE estimator is not generally as 'good' an estimator as an efficient one. Except for the case where the efficient estimator is itself linear (in which case the BLUE and the efficient estimator are identical), there will be non-linear estimators with smaller variances than the BLUE. However, no unbiased estimator by definition can have a variance smaller than that of the efficient estimator. In many cases, however, the problems involved in finding the efficient estimator are such that we have to content ourselves with using (when it can be derived) the BLUE.

Finally, we should note that it must always be good sense when estimating a parameter to make use of all the information available to us. For example, it would be wiser to estimate a population mean by the sample mean rather than the sample median since the median makes use only of the ranking of the sample observations and not their absolute size. For this reason, the sample mean is as we have seen, a more efficient estimator than the sample median. In fact, it can be shown that in general an estimator cannot be *the* efficient estimator unless it makes use of all available information.

Asymptotic distributions and probability limits

Before we move on to discuss some desirable large-sample properties of estimators the reader needs to be familiarised with the concepts of asymptotic distributions and probability limits. Consider the following example.

Suppose we are concerned with estimating the mean, μ, of a non-normal population of values for the random variable Y. We estimate μ by $\bar{Y}$, the mean of a random sample size n, so let us consider the sampling distribution for $\bar{Y}$.

For small values of n, since the population is non-normal, all we can say about the sampling distribution for $\bar{Y}$ is that it has a mean $E\bar{Y} = \mu$ and a variance $\sigma_{\bar{Y}}^2 = \sigma^2/n$ where σ^2 is the population variance. However, as n becomes larger, we know by the central limit theorem that the sampling distribution for $\bar{Y}$ approaches a normal distribution with the above mean and variance

i.e. as $n \to \infty$ $\qquad \bar{Y} \to N(\mu, \sigma^2/n)$ $\qquad\qquad$ [2.27]

The larger n becomes the more closely the distribution for $\bar{Y}$ can be approximated by the above normal distribution. This normal distribution is known as the *asymptotic distribution* of $\bar{Y}$. In general the asymptotic distribution of an estimator, $\hat{\beta}$, is that distribution which the sampling distribution for $\hat{\beta}$ approaches as the sample size tends to infinity.

However, this is not, in the present case, the final form taken by the sampling distribution. Clearly as $n \to \infty$ the variance of $\bar{Y}$, $\sigma_{\bar{Y}}^2 = \sigma^2/n$, tends to zero. Thus as $n \to \infty$ the sampling distribution of $\bar{Y}$ collapses onto a single point equal to μ, the population mean. (When $\bar{Y}$ is distributed with mean μ and zero variance, then $\bar{Y}$ can take only one value – that of μ.) When the sampling distribution of an estimator collapses onto a single point in this manner, that point is known as the *probability limit* of the estimator. Thus the probability limit of $\bar{Y}$ is μ. This is generally written

plim $\bar{Y} = \mu$ $\qquad\qquad\qquad\qquad\qquad\qquad\qquad\qquad\qquad\qquad$ [2.28]

Note that asymptotic distributions are not necessarily normal as in the above example (although in practice they often are). Also sampling distributions do not always collapse onto a single point as above (although they typically do). Furthermore, even if the sampling distribution does so collapse it may not, as in the above case, collapse onto the parameter being estimated.

The asymptotic distribution of an estimator will have a mean and a variance. The mean of the asymptotic distribution is called the *asymptotic mean* of the estimator and the variance of the asymptotic distribution is called the *asymptotic variance*. The asymptotic mean is generally easy to derive. We need merely consider what happens to the mean of the sampling distribution of the estimator as $n \to \infty$. In general, for any estimator $\hat{\beta}$ the asymptotic mean is given by $\underset{n \to \infty}{\text{Limit}} E(\hat{\beta})$. In the above example $E(\bar{Y}) = \mu$ and remains so as $n \to \infty$, so the asymptotic mean of $\bar{Y}$ is equal to μ.

The asymptotic variance is conceptually harder to derive. It is not equal to $\underset{n \to \infty}{\text{Limit}}$ var $\hat{\beta}$. In the above case, for example. $\underset{n \to \infty}{\text{Limit}}$ var $\bar{Y}$ equals $\underset{n \to \infty}{\text{Limit}} \sigma^2/n = 0$, whereas the variance of the asymptotic distribution we know to be σ^2/n. We shall not pursue further the problem of deriving asymptotic variances.

21

Desirable large-sample or asymptotic properties of estimators

Asymptotic unbiasedness

An estimator, $\hat{\beta}$, is said to be an *asymptotically unbiased* estimator of β if and only if

$$E\hat{\beta} \rightarrow \beta \text{ as } n \rightarrow \infty \qquad \text{i.e. Limit}_{n \rightarrow \infty} E(\hat{\beta}) = \beta.$$

Thus asymptotic unbiasedness implies that an estimator becomes unbiased as the sample size becomes very large. Its asymptotic mean is equal to the parameter being estimated. Note that unbiasedness, since that is a property which holds for *any* sample size, implies asymptotic unbiasedness. However, the converse need not be true. If an estimator is asymptotically unbiased (i.e. unbiased for large samples), it does not follow that it is unbiased for small samples. The most common example of an asymptotically unbiased but biased estimator is the sample variance

$$\hat{\sigma}^2 = \sum (Y_i - \bar{Y})^2 / n$$

when used to estimate the variance, σ^2, of a univariate population. It can be shown that

$$E(\hat{\sigma}) = \left(\frac{n-1}{n}\right)\sigma^2 \neq \sigma^2$$

Hence, $\hat{\sigma}^2$ is a biased estimator of σ^2. However, as

$$n \rightarrow \infty \quad \left(\frac{n-1}{n}\right) \rightarrow 1 \quad \text{and} \quad \text{so } E(\hat{\sigma}^2) \rightarrow \sigma^2$$

Hence, $\hat{\sigma}^2$ is an asymptotically unbiased estimator of σ^2.

Consistency

As estimator, $\hat{\beta}$, is said to be a *consistent* estimator of β if and only if

$$\text{plim } \hat{\beta} = \beta.$$

Thus an estimator, $\hat{\beta}$, is consistent, if, as $n \rightarrow \infty$, its sampling distribution collapses onto a single point (i.e. the probability limit of $\hat{\beta}$ exists) and that point coincides with the parameter being estimated. We have already come across one example of a consistent estimator at the beginning of this subsection. Since plim $\bar{Y}$ exists and is equal to μ, the sample mean is said to be a consistent estimator of the population mean. If plim $\hat{\beta} \neq \beta$ then $\hat{\beta}$ is said to be *inconsistent*.

A sufficient condition for an estimator to be consistent is that both its bias (when it is present) and its variance should tend to zero as the sample size n tends to infinity. Sampling distributions for such estimators are illustrated in Fig. 2.4a and 2.4b. Figure 2.4a refers to an estimator which is biased for 'small' samples but for which both bias and variance tend to zero as the sample size increases. In Fig. 2.4b the estimator is unbiased for all sample sizes but the variance again tends to zero as n increases. The sampling distribution for $\bar{Y}$, mentioned above, provides an example of this latter sequence.

Consistent estimators possess some very useful properties which we shall make

2.4a A biased but consistent estimator.

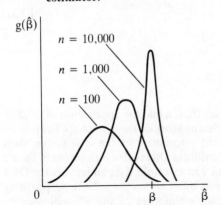

2.4b An unbiased and consistent estimator.

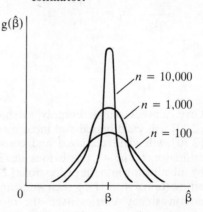

considerable use of in the rest of this book. These properties are listed below but are considered in more detail in the appendix to this chapter.

1. If $\hat{\beta}$ is a consistent estimator of β then $f(\hat{\beta})$ is a consistent estimator of the quantity $f(\beta)$. For example, if β can be consistently estimated by $\hat{\beta}$, then β^2, $\log \beta$, etc. can be consistently estimated by $\hat{\beta}^2$, $\log \hat{\beta}$, etc.

2. If $\hat{\beta}_1$ is a consistent estimator of β_1 and $\hat{\beta}_2$ is a consistent estimator of β_2, then $f_1(\hat{\beta}_1)f_2(\hat{\beta}_2)$ is a consistent estimator of $f_1(\beta_1)f_2(\beta_2)$ where f_1 and f_2 may be any functions of β_1 and β_2 respectively. That is, β_1/β_2, $\beta_1^2 \log \beta_2$, etc. can be consistently estimated by $\hat{\beta}_1/\hat{\beta}_2$, $\hat{\beta}_1^2 \log \hat{\beta}_2$, etc.

These properties are sometimes described by the phrase 'consistency carries over'. However, it must be stressed that the properties of unbiasedness and asymptotic unbiasedness do not 'carry over' in this way. For example, just because $E(\hat{\beta}_1) = \beta_1$ and $E(\hat{\beta}_2) = \beta_2$ it is *not* generally true that $E(\hat{\beta}_1/\hat{\beta}_2) = \beta_1/\beta_2$.

Obtaining consistent or unbiased estimators is rarely simply a matter of estimating the equations 'suggested by theory'. This should become clear after the next few chapters but some inkling of the usefulness of the above properties can be obtained by considering the estimation of the following 'demand equation'

$$q = \alpha_0 + \alpha_1 p + \alpha_2 p^s + \alpha_3 x + \varepsilon \qquad [2.29]$$

where q and p are the demand for and price of some good, p^s is the price of a substitute good and x is some index of consumer income. As we shall discover in Chapter 4, the estimation of [2.29] is much complicated by the possible existence of a supply equation for the good in question. However, in Section 6.3 we shall see that for certain goods whose supply can be considered as 'predetermined' in some manner, it is appropriate to invert [2.29] to obtain

$$p = -\left(\frac{\alpha_0}{\alpha_1}\right) + \left(\frac{1}{\alpha_1}\right)q - \left(\frac{\alpha_2}{\alpha_1}\right)p^s - \left(\frac{\alpha_3}{\alpha_1}\right)x - \left(\frac{\varepsilon}{\alpha_1}\right) \qquad [2.30]$$

and apply the OLS estimating procedure to [2.30] rather than [2.29]. Equation [2.30] can be rewritten as

$$p = A_0 + A_1 q + A_2 p^s + A_3 x + u$$

23

where the α's are related to the A's as follows

$$\alpha_1 = \frac{1}{A_1} \qquad \alpha_0 = -\frac{A_0}{A_1} \qquad \alpha_2 = -\frac{A_2}{A_1} \qquad \alpha_3 = -\frac{A_3}{A_1} \qquad\qquad [2.31]$$

and

$$u = -\frac{\varepsilon}{\alpha_1}$$

Given a predetermined supply, we shall see that, while the application of OLS to [2.29] will yield biased and inconsistent estimators of the α's, its application to [2.30] will yield unbiased and consistent estimators of the A's. Given such estimators of the A's, an obvious idea is to obtain alternative estimators of the α's by substituting into the expressions [2.31]. For example, if $\hat{A}_1$ and $\hat{A}_2$ are the OLS estimators of A_1 and A_2, then we estimate α_2 by $\alpha_2^* = -\hat{A}_2/\hat{A}_1$. Since the property of consistency 'carries over' the resultant estimators of the α's will also be consistent. For example, since $\hat{A}_1$ and $\hat{A}_2$ are consistent estimators of A_1 and A_2, it follows that $\alpha_2^* = -\hat{A}_2/\hat{A}_1$ must be a consistent estimator of $\alpha_2 = -A_2/A_1$. Hence, we have a way of obtaining consistent estimators of the α's. Unfortunately, however, the estimators are not unbiased since this property does not 'carry over'. Just because $\hat{A}_1$ and $\hat{A}_2$ are unbiased estimators of A_1 and A_2 it does not follow that $-\hat{A}_2/\hat{A}_1$ is an unbiased estimator of $-A_2/A_1$. The estimators have desirable large-sample properties only.

Similar use will be made of the properties of consistent estimators in all the applied chapters of this book.

Asymptotic efficiency

An estimator $\hat{\beta}$ is said to be an *asymptotically efficient* estimator of β if and only if:
(i) it is a consistent estimator of β, i.e. plim $\hat{\beta} = \beta$;
(ii) no other consistent estimator of β has a smaller asymptotic variance.[11]

This is the large-sample property that is probably the most difficult to grasp. An asymptotically efficient estimator is best viewed as that estimator, out of the class of all estimators that are consistent, whose sampling distribution collapses 'most quickly' as $n \to \infty$ onto the parameter being estimated. Clearly, if an estimator is consistent the more quickly it collapses as $n \to \infty$ the better. Since the smaller the variance of the asymptotic distribution, the nearer is the distribution to its final collapse for any given very large n, we prefer that consistent estimator that has the smallest asymptotic variance.

Finally, we must remember that when an estimator possesses the attributes of any of the large sample properties just discussed it becomes possessed of them only as the sample size tends to infinity. The same estimator will possess these attributes only approximately for large samples (large is not infinite!) and possibly not at all when the sample size is small.

Maximum likelihood estimation

We conclude this section by attempting to give readers an intuitive grasp of a method of estimation which is frequently used nowadays in econometrics – *maximum likelihood estimation* (MLE). We shall do this by way of a specific example.

Suppose we have a population of values for a variable Y, which is 'binary' in nature. That is, the Y variable can take only the values zero or unity. We shall refer to the case $Y = 0$ as a 'failure' and the case $Y = 1$ as a 'success'. For example, the population might consist of 'items' produced by a machine. A defective item might then be regarded as a failure for which $Y = 0$ and a 'good' item as a success for which $Y = 1$.

Let the proportion of successes in the population, (i.e. the probability that $Y = 1$), be π. Suppose that a random sample size n, represented by $(Y_1, Y_2, Y_3, \ldots, Y_n)$ is to be taken from the population. We do not know beforehand what the Y values in this sample will be, merely that some will be zero and the rest unity. However, if π were known it would be possible to calculate the separate probabilities of drawing each of all possible sets of Y values. For example, if the sample size were $n = 5$, then the probability of drawing the sample $Y_1 = 0$, $Y_2 = 1$, $Y_3 = 1$, $Y_4 = 0$, $Y_5 = 1$ would be

$$(1 - \pi)(\pi)(\pi)(1 - \pi)(\pi)$$

Hence, if we knew that $\pi = 0.3$, for example, then we would calculate the probability of drawing this particular sample as $(0.7)^2(0.3)^3 = 0.01323$.

Similarly, the probability of drawing the sample $Y_1 = 1$, $Y_2 = 1$, $Y_3 = 0$, $Y_4 = 1$, $Y_5 = 1$ would be

$$(\pi)(\pi)(1 - \pi)(\pi)(\pi)$$

which if we knew $\pi = 0.3$ would yield a value $(0.7)(0.3)^4 = 0.00567$. Obviously, the probability of any possible sample outcome can be calculated in this way if π is known.

Now let us look at this situation in reverse. Suppose the proportion of successes in the population, π, is *unknown* but we wish to estimate it from a *single* sample for which the Y values are *known*. We could then use the above procedure to calculate for *alternative possible values of* π the probability of obtaining the known Y values in the sample. The MLE of π is that value for which this probability is the greatest. It is that value of π that would generate the *given* sample most often if very many samples were taken. Colloquially it is that value of π that is 'most likely' to have generated the sample that was, in fact, drawn. For example, suppose again that $n = 5$, and that the sample actually drawn is $Y_1 = 1$, $Y_2 = 0$, $Y_3 = 1$, $Y_4 = 0$, $Y_5 = 1$. Using the above procedure we can calculate, for values of π between 0 and 1, the probability of obtaining this particular sample outcome. Such probabilities, or sample likelihoods as they are called, are tabulated and illustrated in Fig. 2.5.

Both table and graph indicate that the sample likelihood is a maximum when $\pi = 0.6$. Thus 0.6 is the MLE of π – not altogether surprisingly since the sample contained precisely 60 per cent successes.

In practice MLEs are not calculated in the above arithmetical manner. For example, in the above case, the probability obtained for drawing a particular sample will depend on the value given to π and on the Y values in the sample. That is, giving the symbol L to this probability or likelihood, we have for a sample size n

$$L = L(\pi, Y_1, Y_2, Y_3, \ldots, Y_n) \qquad [2.32]$$

In practice the precise algebraic form of [2.32] is derived, expressing the exact manner in which L is dependent on π and the Y values. Equation [2.32] is then

25

2.5 Sample likelihoods for varying values of π.

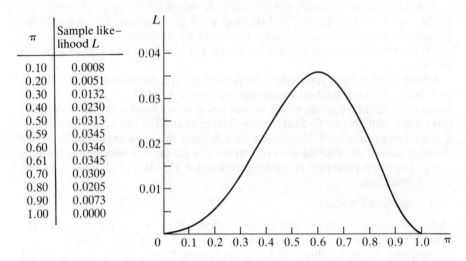

π	Sample like-lihood L
0.10	0.0008
0.20	0.0051
0.30	0.0132
0.40	0.0230
0.50	0.0313
0.59	0.0345
0.60	0.0346
0.61	0.0345
0.70	0.0309
0.80	0.0205
0.90	0.0073
1.00	0.0000

known as the *likelihood function* for the sample values. For the given Y values in the sample, [2.32] is then a function of π alone and the maximum likelihood estimator of π is that value that maximises the likelihood function. This maximisation is usually performed by differentiating L with respect to the relevant parameters treating the given sample values as constants. In the above case differentiation would be with respect to π alone.

Notice that in order to obtain the likelihood function [2.32] and, hence, derive the MLE of π, it was necessary to know the form of the parent population. Such knowledge is always necessary if MLEs are to be obtained and in practice it is frequently assumed that the parent population is normally distributed.

Provided we have some knowledge of the distribution of the disturbances, the maximum likelihood method of estimation can be used to estimate the parameters of regression equations such as [2.12]. In fact, as we shall see in the next section, under certain fairly restrictive conditions the estimators of the β_j's in [2.12] obtained in this way are identical to the OLS estimators. However, in many situations the two types of estimators will differ. The advantage of the maximum likelihood method is that, under quite general conditions, it can be shown to yield estimators that are consistent and asymptotically efficient – i.e. have desirable large sample properties. While such estimators will not generally have any desirable small sample properties, we shall see in the next chapter that in econometrics it is the exception rather than the rule for the OLS estimators to possess *any* desirable properties at all – large or small. Given such circumstances MLEs clearly have a useful role to play in the analysis of economic data. For example, we shall see in Section 4.3 that the method is frequently of value in the estimation of equations that are subject to so-called 'simultaneous equation bias', while in Section 5.1 we shall note its use in the estimation of equations arising out of what is known as the 'adaptive expectations hypothesis'. We shall also encounter the method on a number of occasions in the applied section of this book.

2.4 The classical linear multiple regression model

In this section we list a series of assumptions which taken together comprise the so-called classical linear multiple regression model.

We assume, as in Section 2.2, that a linear relationship exists between the dependent variable Y and the $k-1$ explanatory variables $X_2, X_3, \ldots, X_k$. Thus given a sample of n observations we again have equation [2.13]

$$Y_i = \beta_1 + \beta_2 X_{2i} + \beta_3 X_{3i}, \ldots, + \beta_k X_{ki} + \varepsilon_i \qquad (i = 1, 2, 3, \ldots, n) \qquad [2.13]$$

To complete the specification of the classical multiple regression model we add the following assumptions:

1. Each of the explanatory variables is non-stochastic with values fixed in repeated samples.
2. $E(\varepsilon_i) = 0$ for all i.
3. $\text{Var}(\varepsilon_i) = \sigma^2 = \text{const.}$ for all i.
4. $\text{Cov}(\varepsilon_i, \varepsilon_j) = 0$ for all $i \neq j$.
5. Each ε_i is normally distributed.
6. The number of observations exceeds the number of parameters being estimated, i.e. $n > k$.
7. No exact linear relationship exists between the sample values of any two or more of the explanatory variables.

Provided these assumptions hold, the OLS estimators described in Section 2.2 possess all the desirable large and small sample properties described in the previous section. However, if, as is often the case in econometrics, any of the listed assumptions become invalid, then the OLS estimators lose some or all of these desirable properties. We shall now discuss in turn the meaning of each of these assumptions, beginning with the first.

A stochastic or random variable is a variable the value of which is determined by some chance or random mechanism according to some given probability distribution. To say that an explanatory variable is non-stochastic implies that its values are not randomly determined but are in fact chosen or fixed beforehand by the investigator (usually to suit his own objectives). The first part of assumption 1, then, is simply a way of saying that the n sample values for each of the $k-1$ explanatory variables, i.e. the X_{ji}'s, have been chosen in this way. Notice, however, that no such control is assumed over the values of the dependent variable. From [2.13], the Y_i's in the sample depend not only on the X_{ji}'s but also on the n random disturbances, i.e. the ε_i's. The investigator has no control over the ε_i's and in effect, having chosen the values for the X variables, sits back and observes the values for Y which result from the combined influences of the X's and the disturbance. The Y_i's then, unlike the X_{ji}'s are stochastic or random, deriving their randomness from the random nature of the ε_i's.

The second part of assumption 1 merely establishes the framework within which the sampling distributions of the OLS estimators are to be set. The assumption is that, if repeated samples all size n were drawn, the values taken by the explanatory variables (the X_{ji}'s chosen by the investigator) would be the same for each and every sample, i.e. would be 'fixed in repeated samples'. For the reasons just outlined, however, the values for the dependent variable, the Y_i's, *will* vary from sample to sample and, hence, so will the values obtained for the OLS estimators which depend on both the Y_i's and the X_{ji}'s. Sampling distributions for the OLS estimators will therefore still arise despite the fixed nature of the X_{ji}'s. However, these sampling distributions are those that would be obtained when all samples taken contain identical values for the X-variables.

While the assumption of non-stochastic explanatory variables might be not unreasonable in many situations in the physical sciences where controlled experiments are possible, it is quite clearly a non-starter in most economic-type situations. Controlled experiments are rarely possible in economics and the usual situation is that the dependent and explanatory variables are all stochastic. The explanatory variables take on values determined by some chance mechanism contained in the economic system the investigator is observing. The dependent variable is stochastic because it is determined jointly by the stochastic explanatory variables and the stochastic or random disturbance.

Given the implausibility of assumption 1, the reader may well ask what purpose there is in deriving properties for the OLS estimators which are dependent on such an assumption. However, provided we are prepared to make certain assumptions about the relationship between the explanatory variables and the disturbance, then, as we shall see in the next chapter, it is possible to relax the assumption of non-stochastic explanatory variables without affecting the properties of the OLS estimators. In the meantime, it is convenient for expository purposes to retain the assumption however unreasonable it may seem.

Assumptions 2–5 refer to the probability distributions of the disturbances, i.e. the ε_i's. It is helpful here if we revert for the moment to the case of two-variable regression. In Fig. 2.6 the population regression line $E(Y) = \beta_1 + \beta_2 X$ is shown.

In the two-variable model, given assumption 1, the values for the single explanatory variable X, i.e. $X_1, X_2, \ldots, X_n$, are predetermined constants so that when repeated samples of size n are taken these values remain fixed. Consider, for example, the X value pertaining to the tenth observation in each of these samples, i.e. X_{10}. Whilst X_{10} does not vary from sample to sample, the disturbance associated with this tenth value, i.e. ε_{10}, of course, does vary. Assumption 2 simply specifies that the mean value of this disturbance, taken over very many samples

2.6 The population regression line.

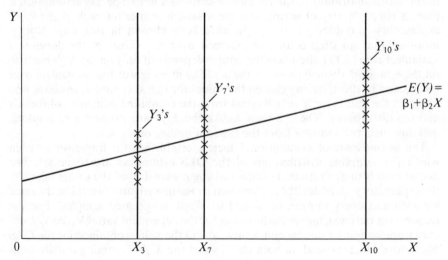

28

all with the same X_{10}, is zero. Similarly, the mean values of the disturbances ε_3, ε_7, etc. associated with the fixed X_3, X_7, etc. are also assumed to be zero. We have, in fact, already made use of this assumption in more general form to move from equation [2.1] to the population regression line [2.2]. The assumption implies that the varying Y_3's, Y_7's and Y_{10}'s, etc. obtained when repeated samples are taken are all 'equally spaced' above and below the population regression line as illustrated in Fig. 2.6 (remember that an ε_{10}, for example, is the distance between a Y_{10} and the population regression line). Notice that we are now treating Y_3, Y_7, Y_{10}, etc. as variables in their own right.

Assumption 3 specifies that the variance of the ε_{10}'s obtained over many samples is the same as the variance of the ε_7's which in turn is the same as the variance of the ε_3's, etc., etc. This implies that the dispersion or 'spread' of the Y_{10}'s about the population regression line is the same as that of the Y_7's and the Y_3's, etc.

When assumption 3 holds the disturbances are said to be *homoscedastic*. This assumption is probably most likely to break down when there is a large variation in the size of the n values of the explanatory variable. For example, returning to the consumption function example of Section 2.1, suppose the n X values referred to the disposable incomes of a cross-section of households, some with incomes close to subsistence level, others with much higher incomes. The consumption expenditures of the low-income households are unlikely to depart far from their mean value $E(Y)$, since such households do not possess the savings to finance high above-average expenditures whereas expenditures far below average would mean consuming below subsistence level. Thus the disturbances for such households are likely to be uniformly small and hence to have a small variance. High-income households, however, are not restricted by such constraints so that the disturbances for these households might have a much larger variance. Thus, in general the variance of the ε_i's tends not to be constant but to vary directly with the size of the explanatory variable.

Assumption 4 specifies that the covariance and, hence, the correlation between any two of the disturbances taken over many samples is zero. Thus in repeated samples there is, for example, no tendency for samples with large positive ε_{10}'s to also have large positive ε_7's. Similarly there is no tendency for samples with large positive ε_{10}'s to also have large negative ε_3's. Both positive and negative correlations are ruled out.

When assumption 4 holds the disturbances are said to be *non-autocorrelated*. This assumption is usually held to break down most frequently with time series data. Consider again the consumption function example but suppose each sample now consists of observations on a single household during n successive weeks. During certain weeks any household is likely to make consumption expenditures above the average for its current level of income because of, for example, illness, visitors or any other abnormal circumstance. It will therefore have positive disturbances during these weeks. However, the abnormal circumstance, if present during one week, will tend to be present in the following week and maybe even in the week after that. Thus if we consider a large number of samples, then those samples which happen to have large ε_3's, for example, will also tend to have large ε_4's and possibly large ε_5's. The assumption of non-autocorrelated disturbances therefore breaks down.

Assumption 5 specifies that, for example, the ε_{10}'s that would be obtained if 'very many' samples were taken, are normally distributed about their zero mean.

29

Similarly, for the ε_7's, the ε_3's, etc. This means that the Y_{10}'s, the Y_7's, the Y_3's, etc. are all normally distributed about the population regression line. More precisely, each Y_i is normally distributed about its mean

$$E(Y_i) = \alpha + \beta X_i$$

The implication of this assumption is that there is only a small probability of obtaining values for a Y_i 'far away' from its mean but a much larger probability of obtaining values 'close' to the mean.

Finally assumptions 6 and 7 are included to ensure that it is possible to solve the normal equations [2.18] for a unique set of OLS estimators.

Properties of the OLS estimators

In this subsection it is implicitly assumed throughout that assumptions 6 and 7 holds so that an unique set of OLS estimators exists.

(a)
If assumption 1 holds then the OLS estimators are *linear estimators*, i.e. they are linear functions of the sample observations. Since the sample values for the explanatory variables are not 'observed' but are fixed constants, the sample observations consist simply of the values for the dependent variable Y, i.e. $Y_1, Y_2, Y_3, \ldots, Y_n$. If we consider [2.20] it is easy to see that the OLS estimators, the elements of the vector $\hat{\boldsymbol{\beta}}$, are indeed linear estimators in the above sense. We can rewrite [2.20] as

$$\hat{\boldsymbol{\beta}} = \mathbf{CY}$$

where $\mathbf{C} = (\mathbf{X'X})^{-1}\mathbf{X'}$
is, given assumption 1, a $k \times n$ matrix of fixed constants.
Thus we have that

$$\hat{\beta}_1 = C_{11}Y_1 + C_{12}Y_2 + C_{13}Y_3 + ,\ldots, + C_{1n}Y_n$$
$$\hat{\beta}_2 = C_{21}Y_1 + C_{22}Y_2 + C_{23}Y_3 + ,\ldots, + C_{2n}Y_n$$
$$\vdots$$
$$\hat{\beta}_k = C_{k1}Y_1 + C_{k2}Y_2 + C_{k3}Y_3 + ,\ldots, + C_{kn}Y_n$$

where C_{ji} is the element in the jth row and ith column of the matrix $\mathbf{C}$ and, also, all such C_{ji}'s are constants.

(b)
If assumptions 1 and 2 hold the OLS estimators have the small sample property of *unbiasedness*, i.e. $E(\hat{\beta}_j) = \beta_j$ for all j, and the large sample property of consistency, i.e. plim $\hat{\beta}_j = \beta_j$ for all j. The property of unbiasedness is most easily derived in the multiple regression case by just noting that the set of equations [2.13] can be rewritten in matrix from as $\mathbf{Y} = \mathbf{X}\boldsymbol{\beta} + \boldsymbol{\varepsilon}$, where we have already defined the matrices $\mathbf{Y}$ and $\mathbf{X}$ and

$$\boldsymbol{\beta} = \begin{bmatrix} \beta_1 \\ \beta_2 \\ \vdots \\ \beta_k \end{bmatrix} \quad \text{and } \boldsymbol{\varepsilon} = \begin{bmatrix} \varepsilon_1 \\ \varepsilon_2 \\ \vdots \\ \varepsilon_n \end{bmatrix}$$

are column vectors containing, respectively, the k population regression parameters and the n sample values for the disturbances. Substituting in [2.20] we have

$$\hat{\beta} = (X'X)^{-1}X'Y = (X'X)^{-1}X'(X\beta + \varepsilon)$$
$$= (X'X)^{-1}X'X\beta + (X'X)^{-1}X'\varepsilon = \beta + C\varepsilon \qquad [2.33]$$

The matrix equation [2.33] represents the set of equations

$$\hat{\beta}_1 = \beta_1 + C_{11}\varepsilon_1 + C_{12}\varepsilon_2 + C_{13}\varepsilon_3, \ldots, + C_{1n}\varepsilon_n$$
$$\hat{\beta}_2 = \beta_2 + C_{21}\varepsilon_1 + C_{22}\varepsilon_2 + C_{23}\varepsilon_3, \ldots, + C_{2n}\varepsilon_n \qquad [2.34]$$
$$\vdots$$
$$\hat{\beta}_k = \beta_k + C_{k1}\varepsilon_1 + C_{k2}\varepsilon_2 + C_{k3}\varepsilon_3, \ldots, + C_{kn}\varepsilon_n$$

where the C_{ji}'s are as defined above. Taking expectations over each equation in [2.34] and remembering that the C_{ji}'s are all constants because of assumption 1 and that, by assumption 2, $E(\varepsilon_i) = 0$ for all i, we easily obtain $E(\hat{\beta}_j) = \beta_j$ for all j.

To prove that, given assumptions 1 and 2, the OLS estimators are also consistent is rather more complicated and interested readers are referred to Johnston (1972: 274–5). We content ourselves here with noting that consistency implies that, as the sample size $n \to \infty$, the sampling distribution for each of the $\hat{\beta}_j$'s will collapse onto the respective β_j being estimated.

(c)
If assumptions 1–4 all hold it can be shown that the OLS estimators are BLUE, i.e. of all linear unbiased estimators they have the smallest variance. The proof of this property is also rather complicated and a matrix proof for the multiple regression case is provided in Johnston (1984:173–4). The variances of the OLS estimators may be found by considering again the inverse of the matrix product $X'X$. Let x^{jj} be the jth diagonal element in $(X'X)^{-1}$. Then it can be shown that

$$\text{var}(\hat{\beta}_j) = \sigma^2 x^{jj} \qquad (j = 1, 2, 3, \ldots, k) \qquad [2.35]$$

where σ^2 is the constant variance of the ε_i's. In fact, for the expression [2.35] to be valid only assumptions 1, 3 and 4 are necessary. The square root of $\text{var}(\hat{\beta}_j)$ is often called the *standard error of* $\hat{\beta}_j$.

As an example, consider again simple two-variable regression. In this case

$$(X'X)^{-1} = \frac{1}{n\sum_i X_i^2 - (\sum X_i)^2} \begin{bmatrix} \sum_i X_i^2 & -\sum_i X_i \\ -\sum_i X_i & n \end{bmatrix}$$

Thus applying [2.35] we have

$$\text{var}(\hat{\beta}_1) = \frac{\sigma^2 \sum X_i^2}{n\sum x_i^2} \quad \text{and} \quad \text{var}(\hat{\beta}_2) = \frac{\sigma^2}{\sum x_i^2}$$

expressions which the reader should be familiar with.

(d)
If assumptions 1–5 all hold then it can be shown that (a) the OLS estimators are

31

efficient and *asymptotically efficient*; (b) the OLS estimators are *maximum likelihood estimators*. Thus, if we add the assumption of normally distributed disturbances to the first four assumptions then, firstly, the OLS estimators have the minimum variance not only of all linear unbiased estimators but of all unbiased estimators. Also since they are now asymptotically efficient, of all consistent estimators, the OLS estimators are the ones that collapse 'most quickly' onto the parameters being estimated as the sample size increases.

Secondly, given assumptions 1–5, the OLS estimators are MLEs. That is, if we apply the maximum likelihood method, the estimators obtained for the β_j's are identical to the OLS estimators. Given assumption 1, we can treat all X-values as constants. Since, by assumption 5, each ε_i is normally distributed then, recalling equation [2.13]

$$Y_i = \beta_1 + \beta_2 X_{2i} + \beta_3 X_{3i}, \ldots, + \beta_k X_{ki} + \varepsilon_i \qquad [2.13]$$

we see that each Y_i also has a normal distribution. This is because, under present assumptions, [2.13] implies that each Y_i is simply the sum of a constant plus a normally distributed ε_i. Since adding a constant to a random variable will merely change the position on the horizontal axis but not the shape or 'spread' of its probability distribution, it follows that the Y_i's are also normally distributed. That is, if repeated samples were taken, each sequence of Y_i's obtained would be normally distributed with a mean of

$$EY_i = \beta_1 + \beta_2 X_{2i} + \beta_3 X_{3i}, \ldots, \beta_k X_{ki} \quad \text{and a variance of} \quad \sigma^2.^{12}$$

Knowing their distribution enables a likelihood function for the Y_i's akin to [2.32] to be formulated.[13] In this case the sample likelihood will depend on the underlying parameters of the regression model, i.e. the β_j's and σ^2, and on the sample values obtained

$$L = L(\beta_1, \beta_2, \beta_3, \ldots, \beta_k, \sigma^2, Y_1, Y_2, Y_3, \ldots, Y_n)$$

The values of σ^2 and the β_j's which maximise L are the MLEs. As already noted, the estimators of the β_j's found in this way are identical to the OLS estimators.[14] The maximum likelihood method, however, also yields an estimator of σ^2, the variance of the ε_i's. In passing, we note that this estimator is, in fact, $\hat{\sigma}^2 = \sum e_i^2/n$ which we shall see in the next subsection is a biased estimator of σ^2. This illustrates the point that MLEs are not necessarily unbiased although they may have this property as, of course, do the estimators of the β_j's in this case.

(e)
If assumptions 1 and 5 hold then the OLS estimators are normally distributed. By assumption 1 they are linear functions of the sample observations. i.e. the Y_i's. But as we have just seen, given assumptions 1 and 5, each Y_i is normally distributed. Since any linear function of normally and independently distributed variables is itself normally distributed, it follows that the sampling distributions for OLS estimators must also be normal.

In fact if assumptions 2–4 also hold then the OLS estimator of the regression parameter β_j, i.e. $\hat{\beta}_j$, is normally distributed with mean $E\hat{\beta}_j = \beta_j$ and variance $\sigma_{\hat{\beta}_j}^2 = \sigma^2 x^{jj}$. That is

$$\hat{\beta}_j \quad \text{is} \quad N(\beta_j, \sigma_{\hat{\beta}_j}^2) \quad \text{for} \quad j = 1, 2, 3, \ldots, k \qquad [2.36]$$

As we have pointed out, whether or not the OLS estimators possess the properties just listed will depend on which, if any, of the assumptions of the classical regression model are valid. We shall examine in detail the consequences of breakdowns in these assumptions in the next chapter.

Making inferences about the regression parameters

If σ^2, the constant variance of the disturbances, were known, then [2.36] could be used as the basis for either computing confidence intervals for any of the parameters or for testing hypotheses concerning their true value. In practice, of course, σ^2 is unknown and therefore has to be estimated. Since we may regard each e_i as an estimate of the corresponding ε_i, an obvious way of estimating the variance of the disturbances is to calculate the variance of the known sample residuals. That is, estimate σ^2 by the quantity

$$\hat{\sigma}^2 = \frac{\sum_i (e_i - \bar{e})^2}{n} = \frac{\sum_i e_i^2}{n}$$

where $\bar{e} = \sum_i e_i/n$, the mean of the sample residuals, is equal to zero from the first equation in [2.17]. However, it can be shown[15] that $\hat{\sigma}^2$ is a biased estimator of σ^2 and that in fact $E\hat{\sigma}^2 = ((n-k)/n)\sigma^2$, i.e. $\hat{\sigma}^2$ tends to underestimate σ^2. An unbiased estimator of σ^2 is given by

$$s^2 = \left(\frac{n}{n-k}\right)\hat{\sigma}^2 = \frac{\sum_i e_i^2}{n-k}$$

since

$$Es^2 = \frac{n}{n-k}E\hat{\sigma}^2 = \sigma^2$$

Once an unbiased estimate of σ^2 has been obtained we may obtain unbiased estimates of the variances of the $\hat{\beta}_j$'s by using $s_{\hat{\beta}_j}^2 = s^2 x^{jj}$. The estimated standard error of $\hat{\beta}_j$ is then $s_{\hat{\beta}_j} = s\sqrt{x^{jj}}$ for all j.

From [2.36] we can see that $(\hat{\beta}_j - \beta_j)/\sigma_{\hat{\beta}_j}$ is a standard normal variable and it follows that, for all j,

$(\hat{\beta}_j - \beta_j)/s_{\hat{\beta}_j}$ has a student's t distribution with $n-k$, d.f.   [2.37]

We can now use [2.37] either:

(a) to construct confidence intervals for any of the β_j. For example, a 95 per cent confidence interval for β_6 is given by

$\hat{\beta}_6 \pm t_{0.025} s_{\hat{\beta}_6}$

(b) to test hypotheses concerning the true values of any of the β_j. For example, if we wished to test the null hypothesis $\beta_4 = 1$ against the alternative hypothesis $\beta_4 \neq 1$, the quantity $(\hat{\beta}_4 - 1)/s_{\hat{\beta}_4}$ may be used as a test statistic since when null is true it has a student's t-distribution.

Notice that the ability to make inferences about the regression parameters, the β_j's, is dependent on the assumption that the disturbances, the ε_i's, are normally distributed. Without this assumption [2.36] and hence [2.37] would not hold.

Presentation of regression results

In presenting OLS regression results it has become customary to write down the estimated sample regression equation with the estimated standard errors of the

OLS estimators placed in parentheses beneath the corresponding OLS estimates. Thus, if we were estimating a simple consumption function with two explanatory variables X_2 (income) and X_3 (liquid assets) we would present

$$Y = 246 + 0.643X_2 + 0.216X_3 \qquad R^2 = 0.992$$
$$ (54.6) \quad (0.053) \qquad (0.092)$$

where in the notation of the previous section

$$\hat{\beta}_1 = 246, \ \hat{\beta}_2 = 0.643, \ \hat{\beta}_3 = 0.216$$
$$s_{\hat{\beta}_1} = 54.6, \ s_{\hat{\beta}_2} = 0.053, \ s_{\hat{\beta}_3} = 0.092$$

and the meaning of R^2 is discussed in the next subsection.

Often in econometrics we are concerned with testing an hypothesis that a given regression parameter is zero. For example, in the above case we might wish to test the hypothesis that β_3, the liquid assets coefficient in the population regression equation, is zero. Such an hypothesis implies that liquid assets have no influence on consumption expenditure. From [2.37] we see that the test statistic for testing such a null hypothesis is of the simple form $\hat{\beta}_3 / s_{\hat{\beta}_3}$, i.e. the ratio of the estimate $\hat{\beta}_3$ to its estimated standard error. Provided this ratio exceeds the relevant critical t-value we would reject the hypothesis that liquid assets have no influence on consumption. When this occurs it has become customary to say that the variable 'liquid assets' is 'statistically significant' in the determination of consumption expenditure.

The ratio of an estimate to its estimated standard error is often called a 't-ratio' and is sometimes presented in parentheses in place of the estimated standard error.

Suppose, as an example, the above regression result was based on a sample size $n = 20$. Then under the null hypothesis $\beta_3 = 0$, the test statistic or t-ratio, has student's t-distribution with $n - k = 17$ degrees of freedom. Using a 0.05 level of significance and a one tail test the relevant critical t-value is $t_{0.05} = 1.74$. The t-ratio from the regression result is $0.216/0.092 = 2.35$. Hence, we would reject the null hypothesis and say that the liquid assets variable is 'significant at the 5 per cent level'.

This is probably a good point for the reader to make a first effort at the empirical exercises in the applied chapters of this book. The early parts of each exercise all involve simple OLS estimation.

Measures of 'goodness of fit'

The method of least squares ensures that the sample regression equation obtained is the equation that best 'fits' the sample observations in the sense that it minimises the sum of the squared residuals. However, the best 'fit' need not necessarily be a particularly good one and the residuals may still be relatively large. (In two-variable regression the sample regression line may not fit closely the points in the scatter diagram.) It is therefore usually desirable to have some measure of the 'goodness of fit' of a sample regression equation estimated by OLS. Such measures are naturally based on the sum of the squared OLS residuals, $\sum_i e_i^2$. One obvious measure is the so called *standard error of the residuals* which is simply the square root of the residual variance, s^2, i.e.

$$s = \sqrt{\left(\sum_i e_i^2 / (n - k) \right)}.$$

The problem with s is that once its value has been obtained we have no standard by which to judge whether its value is 'high' or 'low'. (The lower its value the better the 'fit' but does a value $s = 0.034$, for example, mean the 'fit' is 'good' or bad?) This problem can be overcome to a certain extent by the use of a measure based on the so-called decomposition of the sample variation in the Y variable. Just as in two-variable regression, the sample variation in Y or 'total sum of squares' is given by

$$\sum_i (Y_i - \bar{Y})^2 = \sum_i (\hat{Y}_i + e_i - \bar{Y})^2$$

$$= \sum_i (\hat{Y}_i - \bar{Y})^2 + \sum_i e_i^2 - 2\sum_i (\hat{Y}_i - \bar{Y})e_i$$

In multiple regression

$$\sum_i (\hat{Y}_i - \bar{Y})e_i = \sum_i (\hat{\beta}_1 + \hat{\beta}_2 X_{2i} + \hat{\beta}_3 X_{3i}, \ldots, + \hat{\beta}_k X_{ki})e_i - \bar{Y}\sum_i e_i = 0$$

using the fact that the equations in [2.17] can be written

$$\sum_i e_i = 0, \quad \sum_i X_{2i}e_i = 0, \quad \sum_i X_{3i}e_i = 0, \text{ etc.}$$

We therefore obtain

$$\sum_i (Y_i - \bar{Y})^2 = \sum_i (\hat{Y}_i - \bar{Y})^2 + \sum_i e_i^2 \qquad [2.38]$$

Hence, as in two-variable regression, the total sum of squares (SST) can be decomposed into an 'explained sum of squares' (SSE) and the residual sum of squares (SSR). The explained sum of squares measures the variation in Y which can be attributed to the influence of the X variables.

A frequently used measure of 'goodness of fit' is the *coefficient of multiple determination* defined as

$$R^2 = \frac{SSE}{SST} = 1 - \frac{SSR}{SST} = 1 - \frac{\sum_i e_i^2}{\sum_i (Y_i - \bar{Y})^2} \qquad [2.39]$$

R^2 measures the proportion of the total variation in Y which can be explained by the sample regression equation, i.e. which can be attributed to the influence of the explanatory variables. Since R^2 is a proportion, it must be between zero and unity so that this gives us some standard by which we can judge whether a given value of R^2 is high or low, that is whether the 'fit' is good or bad. However, we are still faced with the problem of deciding how different from zero R^2 must be before we judge a 'fit' to be 'good'.

To provide a statistical answer to this question, notice from the definition of R^2 that it depends both on the Y_i's and the e_i's in the sample on which it is based. Therefore, if repeated samples were taken, R^2 would vary from sample to sample. R^2 is, in fact, a random variable with its own sampling distribution. Now suppose that the population regression equation [2.12] were such that all the β_j's apart from β_1 were zero, i.e. the dependent variable was totally uninfluenced by the explanatory variables. This means that *for the population* the SSE must be zero

35

and, hence, so must what we might call the 'population R^2'. However, since we observed a sample and not the population, even if the β_j's are, in fact, all zero, we are unlikely to obtain OLS estimates which are exactly zero and, hence, unlikely to obtain a zero value either for the sample SSE or for the sample value of R^2.

Now what really concerns us is whether R^2 is sufficiently different from zero (i.e. whether the 'fit' is sufficiently 'good') for us to reject the null hypothesis that the 'population R^2' is zero, i.e. the hypothesis that the explanatory variables do not influence the dependent variable. To decide this we use the fact that under the above null hypothesis the sampling distribution for $\left(\dfrac{n-k}{k-1}\right)\left(\dfrac{R^2}{1-R^2}\right)$ has an F-distribution with $(k-1, n-k)$ degrees of freedom.

Clearly, if $R^2 = 0$ the above test statistic is zero and the larger the sample R^2 the larger the test statistic. If R^2 is sufficiently large for the test statistic to exceed the relevant critical F-value we reject the null hypothesis.

Summarising then, the coefficient of multiple determination, R^2, may be used to test the overall influence of the explanatory variables on the dependent variable – specifically, to test the joint hypothesis that

$$\beta_j = 0 \quad \text{for} \quad j = 2, 3, \ldots, k$$

At this point a note of caution should be introduced over the interpretation of 'high' and 'significant' values of R^2. Goodness of fit does not *necessarily* reflect any *causal* relationship between dependent and explanatory variables. Correlations can be at least partly *spurious*, particularly when the variables involved exhibit consistent trends, either upwards or downwards, over time. For example many macroeconomic variables, such as the general price level or the level of national output in most developed economies, have moved consistently upwards during the greater part of the postwar era. In addition, it is not always realised by beginners in econometrics that it is unnecessary for two variables to be trending in the same direction for a high but possibly spurious correlation to exist between them.

Suppose, for example, a variable is falling consistently over time so that we may approximate its time path by $Y_t = 50 - 0.2t$ where t is time and Y_t is the value of the variable at time t. Further, suppose that another variable, X, totally unrelated to Y, just happens to be trending upwards over time so that we can approximate its path by $X_t = 5 + 0.4t$. It is not difficult to show that the approximate linear relationship $Y_t = 52.5 - 0.5X_t$ will hold between Y and X over time. Clearly, if we used OLS to regress Y on X we would obtain an extremely good fit and 'high' R^2 despite the fact that no causal link existed between the two variables. The *statistically* significant value for R^2 found would simply be a reflection of the trends in the variables.

Since much econometric work is concerned with 'time series' data it is therefore wise not to become too obsessed (as many beginners tend to be) with the value of R^2. R^2's for time series regression equations are typically very high compared with those obtained from 'cross-sectional' data for which the trending problem does not arise. For example, as we shall see in the empirical exercise in the appendix to Chapter 7, it is a simple matter to obtain R^2's as high as 0.98 for consumption functions estimated from time series data.

A popular method of attempting to overcome the problem of spuriously high R^2's is to estimate relationships between the rates of change of variables rather than between their absolute levels. The effect of looking at the rate of change in a variable is typically to remove much of the trend element. For example while output and prices in most postwar economies have trended steadily upwards, this is not generally true of rates of growth in output or of inflation rates. Unfortunately when attention is concentrated on relationships between rates of change there is a real danger that valuable information on the relationship between the levels of the variables will be lost. This point should become clearer when the reader has tackled (in Section 7.6) the approach to the UK consumption function pioneered by Davidson, *et al.* (1978). In addition, while working in terms of rates of change may help overcome spurious correlation problems, it can also introduce fresh problems not present when levels equations are considered. The nature of such problems will become apparent when we consider a controversy over the estimation of UK demand for money equations in Section 10.6.

The coefficient of multiple determination R^2 is sometimes used as an aid in choosing between two alternative specifications of a regression equation. A simple example would be where the first specification involved two explanatory variables only and the second involved three such variables (one or two of which might be those involved in the first specification). It is obviously tempting invariably to choose that specification with the highest R^2.

However, when extra explanatory variables are added to a regression equation, R^2 cannot decrease and will almost certainly increase, regardless of the true importance of these variables in determining the values of the dependent variable. This should be clear from [2.39], since $\sum(Y_i - \bar{Y})^2$ remains unchanged when extra X variables are added and $\sum e_i^2$ cannot increase but will probably decrease. For this reason research workers often prefer to measure 'goodness of fit' by a quantity generally called the 'adjusted R^2', given the symbol $\bar{R}^2$ and defined as

$$\bar{R}^2 = R^2 - \left(\frac{n-1}{n-k}\right)(1 - R^2) \qquad [2.40]$$

The precise theoretical reasons for using the expression [2.40] need not concern us here and the reader need only note that the purpose of $\bar{R}^2$ is to assist 'goodness of fit' comparisons between regression equations which differ with respect to either the number of explanatory variables or the number of observations. Notice in particular that $\bar{R}^2 < R^2$, except in the case where $R^2 = 1$, that for given values of R^2 and n, $\bar{R}^2$ declines as k, the number of parameters being estimated increases, and that unlike R^2, $\bar{R}^2$ can take negative values (it generally does so when R^2 is very close to zero).

For the reasons just outlined it is possible that $\bar{R}^2$ may fall (unlike R^2) when extra variables are added to a regression equation. Thus, in comparing the 'goodness of fit' of different specifications of a regression equation, one is on firmer ground if one considers $\bar{R}^2$ rather than R^2.

Finally, two further warnings are necessary. Firstly, comparisons of R^2 and $\bar{R}^2$ will not be appropriate when comparing equations with different dependent variables. For example, in the empirical exercise in the appendix to Chapter 10, we shall estimate demand for money equations firstly with the nominal money stock and then with the real money stock as the dependent variable. R^2 in two such equations will be measuring different quantities – in one case the proportion of variations in the nominal money stock that can be explained and in the other case the proportion of variations in the real money stock. The R^2's are not comparable and an alternative measure of goodness of fit is needed such as the standard error of the residuals mentioned at the beginning of this section.

Secondly, while comparisons of alternative specifications of a regression equation by means of R^2 and $\bar{R}^2$ are often a necessary part of applied work in econometrics, such procedures can be taken too far. We have already mentioned the tendency for 'beginners' in such work to attach overmuch importance to the value of R^2. This is sometimes reflected by students adopting an 'everything but the kitchen sink' approach, trying variable after variable on the right-hand side of estimating equations, in a desperate attempt to obtain 'highly significant' values for R^2. We have already stressed that high R^2's are not necessarily an indicator of causality, but in addition readers should note that *such a procedure is nothing more than an example of the 'data-mining' warned against in Chapter 1*. High R^2's obtained by such techniques are virtually meaningless.

Further reading

For those who feel the need for a refresher course in basic statistics, Walpole (1982) provides a well-organised treatment of topics including probability, mathematical expectations, sampling distributions and two-variable regression. The two-variable regression model is also well covered in most introductory econometrics texts, e.g. Kmenta (1971), Johnston (1984) Kelejian and Oates (1981), and Stewart and Wallis (1981). A most readable discussion of the properties of estimators is to be found in Kmenta, Chapter 6. The classical multiple regression model is well covered in Kelejian and Oates and in Stewart and Wallis although those with an intense dislike of matrix algebra may prefer Kmenta. A 'fully-fledged' matrix treatment can be found in Johnston (1984). Finally, a more intuitive approach, providing many valuable insights, is provided by Stewart (1984).

APPENDIX
The properties of consistent estimators

We present here some intuitive and highly non-rigorous 'demonstrations' (they cannot be referred to as 'proofs') of the properties of consistent estimators mentioned in Section 2.3.

1.

If $\hat{\beta}$ is a consistent estimator of β then $f(\hat{\beta})$ is a consistent estimator of $f(\beta)$.
Consider the sampling distribution of $\hat{\beta}$. Since $\hat{\beta}$ is a consistent estimator of β, as $n \to \infty$ this sampling distribution 'collapses' onto the point β. In very non-technical terms[16] this means that for very large samples the estimator $\hat{\beta}$ actually equals β the parameter being estimated. Now, if $\hat{\beta} = \beta$ it follows that, again for very large samples, we must have $1/\hat{\beta} = 1/\beta$, $\log \hat{\beta} = \log \beta$, etc. and in general it will be true that $f(\hat{\beta}) = f(\beta)$.

Now consider the sampling distributions of the quantities $1/\hat{\beta}$, $\log \hat{\beta}$, etc. Since for very large samples $1/\hat{\beta} = 1/\beta$, the sampling distribution for $1/\hat{\beta}$ must 'collapse' onto $1/\beta$ as $n \to \infty$. Similarly, the sampling distribution for $\log \hat{\beta}$ must 'collapse' onto $\log \beta$ and in general, as $n \to \infty$, the sampling distribution for any $f(\hat{\beta})$ must 'collapse' onto $f(\beta)$. Thus if $\hat{\beta}$ is a consistent estimator of β, $1/\hat{\beta}$ is a consistent estimator of $1/\beta$, $\log \hat{\beta}$ is a consistent estimator of $\log \beta$ and in general $f(\hat{\beta})$ is a consistent estimator of $f(\beta)$.

Notice that such a property does not generally hold for unbiased estimators. For example, if $\hat{\beta}$ is an unbiased estimator of β it does not follow that $1/\hat{\beta}$ is an unbiased estimator of $1/\beta$. The following simple numerical example should make this clear.

Suppose $\beta = 4$ and the estimator $\hat{\beta}$ can take three possible values, 3, 4 and 5 with the following probabilities

$$P_r(\hat{\beta} = 3) = 0.25, \quad P_r(\hat{\beta} = 4) = 0.5, \quad P_r(\hat{\beta} = 5) = 0.25$$

$\hat{\beta}$ is clearly an unbiased estimator of β since $E(\hat{\beta}) = 4 = \beta$. Consider, however, the quantity $1/\beta = 0.25$ which we estimate by $1/\hat{\beta}$. The estimator $1/\hat{\beta}$ can take any of the values, 1/3, 1/4 and 1/5, with

$$P_r(1/\hat{\beta} = 1/3) = 0.25, \quad P_r(1/\hat{\beta} = 1/4) = 0.5, \quad P_r(1/\hat{\beta} = 1/5) = 0.25$$

$1/\hat{\beta}$ can be seen to be a biased estimator of $1/\beta$ since

$$E(1/\hat{\beta}) = 1/3(0.25) + 1/4(0.5) + 1/5(0.25) = 0.258$$

2.

If $\hat{\beta}_1$ is a consistent estimator of β_1 and $\hat{\beta}_2$ is a consistent estimator of β_2 then $f_1(\hat{\beta}_1)f_2(\hat{\beta}_2)$ is a consistent estimator of $f_1(\beta_1)f_2(\beta_2)$.

Consider the sampling distributions of $\hat{\beta}_1$ and $\hat{\beta}_2$. Since $\hat{\beta}_1$ and $\hat{\beta}_2$ are consistent estimators, as $n \to \infty$ the distribution for $\hat{\beta}_1$ 'collapses' onto β_1 and the distribution for $\hat{\beta}_2$ 'collapses' onto β_2. Non-technically we have that for very large samples $\hat{\beta}_1 = \beta_1$ and $\hat{\beta}_2 = \beta_2$. Therefore, for very large samples, $f_1(\hat{\beta}_1)f_2(\hat{\beta})$ must equal $f_1(\beta_1)f_2(\beta_2)$. For example

$$\hat{\beta}_1^2 \log \hat{\beta}_2 = \beta_1^2 \log \beta_2, \quad (\hat{\beta}_1)^{1/2}(\hat{\beta}_2)^{-1} = (\beta_1)^{1/2}(\beta_2)^{-1}, \text{ etc., etc.}$$

Consider next the sampling distributions for $\hat{\beta}_1^2 \log \hat{\beta}_2, (\hat{\beta}_1)^{1/2}(\hat{\beta}_2)^{-1}$, etc., etc. Since for very large samples, $\hat{\beta}_1^2 \log \hat{\beta}_2 = \beta_1^2 \log \beta_2$ the sampling distribution for $\hat{\beta}_1^2 \log \hat{\beta}_2$ must 'collapse' onto $\beta_1^2 \log \beta_2$ as $n \to \infty$. Similarly, the sampling distribution for $(\hat{\beta}_1)^{1/2}(\hat{\beta}_2)^{-1}$ must 'collapse' onto $(\beta_1)^{1/2}(\beta_2)^{-1}$ and, in general, as $n \to \infty$, the sampling distribution for $f_1(\hat{\beta}_1)f_2(\hat{\beta}_2)$ must 'collapse' onto $f_1(\beta_1)f_2(\beta_2)$. Thus $f_1(\hat{\beta}_1)f_2(\hat{\beta}_2)$ is a consistent estimator of $f_1(\beta_1)f_2(\beta_2)$.

Notice, again, that this second property does not hold in general for unbiased estimators. If $\hat{\beta}_1$ and $\hat{\beta}_2$ are unbiased estimators of β_1 and β_2 respectively it does not follow that $f_1(\hat{\beta}_1)f_2(\hat{\beta}_2)$ is an unbiased estimator of $f_1(\beta_1)f_2(\beta_2)$. Firstly, as we have already noted, the fact that $E\hat{\beta}_1 = \beta_1$ and $E\hat{\beta}_2 = \beta_2$ does not generally mean that $Ef(\hat{\beta}_1) = f(\beta_1)$ and $Ef(\hat{\beta}_2) = f(\beta_2)$. Secondly, even if it did, it would not generally be true that

$$Ef_1(\hat{\beta}_1)f_2(\hat{\beta}_2) = f_1(\beta_1)f_2(\beta_2)$$

This equality would only hold for the special case where the variables $f_1(\hat{\beta}_1)$ and $f_2(\hat{\beta}_2)$ were independent.

Notes

1. For a discussion of such terms as 'random sample' and 'population' see: Kmenta (1971: 3–5).
2. We have used Y and X without subscripts as shorthand for the variables they represent. In two-variable regression analysis, when X and Y appear with subscripts, e.g. X_7 and Y_7, then they should be regarded as actual numbers taken by the variables concerned, e.g. Y_7 is the consumption of the seventh household in the sample. However, since, when repeated samples are taken, Y_7 will vary from sample to sample, it will sometimes be necessary to interpret Y_7 itself as a random variable. Similarly, for all the X_i and Y_i. Whenever this second interpretation is adopted we shall draw attention to it.
3. Although it does not now, of course, include the influence of liquid assets.
4. The reader could regard equation [2.11a] as a generalisation of the simple consumption equation of Section 2.1 but where we no longer restrict ourselves to households of a given size or composition. Thus X_2, X_3, X_4, and X_5 might refer to the income, liquid assets, size and composition, respectively, of households. The disturbance now reflects all *other* influences plus the random responses of households. Notice that in multiple regression when X_2, X_3, etc. appear with a single subscript they are simply a shorthand for the variables, income, liquid assets, etc. that they represent.
5. Remember that the first explanatory variable X_1 always takes the value unity. Hence, for example, the value in the top left-hand corner of $\mathbf{X'X}$ is given by $\sum_{i=1}^{n} 1 = n$.
6. Formulae such as those given by [2.20] into which we may substitute sample values to obtain estimates of population parameters are known as '*estimators*'. However, once the substitution has been performed and a specific value obtained that value is referred to as an '*estimate*' of the parameter.
7. It is actually an attempt to assess the results of a 'laboratory experiment' in which L is held constant and the effect of variations in X and Y examined.
8. The only exception in fact is when an additional variable is completely uncorrelated with the variables already present.
9. The reader may object at this point that the estimators we have derived in the previous two sections were functions of more than one variable (a Y-variable and one or more X-variables). However, this 'difficulty' will resolve itself in due course.
10. Although this definition is common in econometrics, some statisticians define efficiency differently. The mean square error of an estimator is defined as $E(\hat{\beta} - \beta)^2$ and can be shown to be equal to the sum of the variance of $\hat{\beta}$ and the square of its bias. Since both the variance and bias of an estimator are quantities we would like to be 'small', the efficient estimator is sometimes defined as that with the minimum mean square error. What we have defined as the efficient estimator is then referred to simply as the minimum variance or best unbiased estimator.
11. Strictly speaking $\hat{\beta}$ must be consistent in the sense that its bias and variance tend to zero as $n \to \infty$. Very occasionally one does meet other types of consistent estimator.
12. We are now treating each Y_i as a random variable rather than some given number to be substituted into an expression such as [2.20].

13. The reader may find it helps understanding to paraphrase such phrases as 'a likelihood function for the Y_i's' by, for example, 'an expression for the probability of obtaining a given set of Y_i's'. However, such a substitution is not strictly correct for continuous variables since then the probability of obtaining any given Y_i's is zero.
14. See, for example, Stewart and Wallis (1981: 133–6) for a proof of this in the two-variable case.
15. See, for example, Johnston (1984:180–1).
16. The difficulty here is that since $\hat{\beta}$ is a random variable we cannot, strictly speaking, talk about what happens to *the* value of $\hat{\beta}$ as $n \to \infty$ but only about what happens to the distribution of possible values for $\hat{\beta}$. Thus, while we can say that, as $n \to \infty$, the probability of $\hat{\beta}$ differing from β tends to zero, it is not correct to say that as $n \to \infty$ the value of $\hat{\beta}$ tends to β.

3 Breakdowns in classical assumptions

In the previous chapter we listed the series of assumptions which make up the classical linear regression model and described the properties possessed by the OLS estimators when these assumptions hold. In this chapter we shall be concerned with the consequences for OLS estimators of breakdowns in the classical assumptions and with what alternative estimating procedures, if any, should be followed when such breakdowns occur. In addition we shall consider, in the final section of this chapter, the consequences of applying the normal OLS formulae under conditions where the classical assumptions 1–7 (p. 27) all hold but where the population regression equation [2.12] has been incorrectly specified.

3.1 Stochastic explanatory variables

The first assumption of the classical model was that each explanatory variable was non-stochastic or non-random in the sense that its sample values were fixed or chosen by the investigator. Given this assumption it was then possible to envisage a situation where, if many samples were taken, each sample would contain the same fixed X_{ji}'s. This established the framework within which we viewed the sampling distributions for the OLS estimators. Non-randomness is obviously an implausible assumption for virtually all economic data. The investigator is almost always in the position of having to accept whatever data observations are available, rarely being able to fix the values of any of the variables in which he is interested. We must therefore consider the situation where the economic system under observation determines (in equation [2.13]) not only the values of the random disturbances, (and hence the values of the dependent variable, Y), but also the values of the explanatory variables, i.e. the X_{ji}'s.

When the explanatory variables in a regression equation are stochastic, the consequences for the OLS estimators depend on the relationship between the explanatory variables and the disturbance – more precisely on the extent to which the X variables can be regarded as being independent of ε. It will be helpful if, for the moment, we refer back to simple two-variable regression where the underlying population regression line is given by $E(Y) = \beta_1 + \beta_2 X$. This is depicted in Fig. 3.1.

Suppose now that the single explanatory variable X and the disturbance ε are for some reason *positively correlated*. There will then be a tendency for 'high' sample values of X (high X_i's) to coincide with 'high' sample values of the disturbance (high ε_i's). Similarly there will be a tendency for 'low' X_i's to coincide with 'low' ε_i's. Since $E\varepsilon_i = 0$, a 'high' ε_i means a positive ε_i and a 'low' ε_i means a

3.1 Positive correlation between disturbance and explanatory variable.

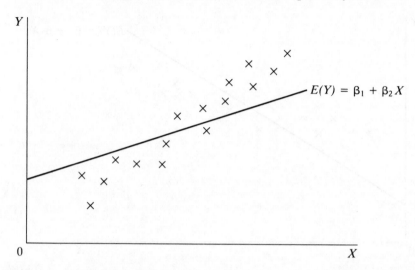

negative ε_i. Remembering that the ε_i's represent the vertical distances of points in a scatter diagram from the population regression line, it should be clear that, under these conditions, any sample of values for Y and X is likely to result in a scatter diagram similar to that illustrated in Fig. 3.1. Points in the scatter will lie above the population regression line for 'high' values of X and below that line for 'low' values of X. The crucial point is that all the investigator ever observes is the scatter of points – he never gets to know the underlying population regression line. It follows that a sample regression line fitted to the scatter of points by the OLS method is likely to have a steeper slope than the unknown population regression line. Thus when X and ε are positively correlated the OLS estimators are likely to overestimate β_2, the slope, and underestimate β_1, the intercept, of the population regression line. Similar but opposite consequences follow from a negative correlation between X and ε. This case is illustrated in Fig. 3.2, where now it can be seen that the OLS estimators are likely to underestimate β_2 and overestimate β_1.

We may summarise the above arguments by saying that when the explanatory variable X and the disturbance ε are correlated, the OLS estimators of β_1 and β_2 are *biased*, the direction of the bias depending on the nature of the correlation. Furthermore, *this bias will persist even for large samples*. Under such conditions a larger sample will simply result in a larger number of points in the scatter, merely confirming the 'false impressions' given by the scatters in Figs 3.1 and 3.2. Hence, since no matter how large the sample size is made the bias in the OLS estimators persists, these estimators must not only lose the small sample property of unbiasedness but also the large sample property of consistency. It should be clear that under such conditions, if the sampling distributions for $\hat{\beta}_1$ and $\hat{\beta}_2$, the OLS estimators, collapse on to a single point as the sample size increases (i.e. if plim $\hat{\beta}_1$ and plim $\hat{\beta}_2$ exist) then these points cannot be equal to the true β_1 and β_2. Thus $\hat{\beta}_1$ and $\hat{\beta}_2$ must be inconsistent estimators of β_1 and β_2.

In multiple regression similar problems arise. It is not difficult to show that in this case the OLS estimators lose their desirable small and large sample

3.2 Negative correlation between disturbance and explanatory variable.

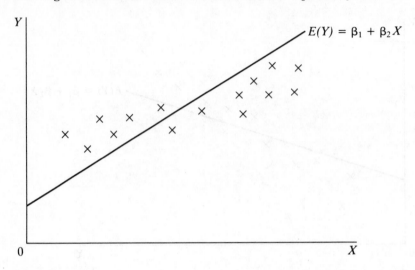

properties whenever one or more of the explanatory variables is correlated with the disturbance. Since many econometric equations are estimated from time series data, with each observation referring to a different month, quarter or year, the sort of correlations we have been discussing above involve a relationship between the value of one of the explanatory variables and the contemporaneous value of the disturbance. For this reason the above is often referred to as the *contemporaneously correlated case.*

If we ask ourselves under what conditions the above small and large sample biases will disappear, it is obvious that the absence of any contemporaneous correlations between the explanatory variables and the disturbance will help. However, the absence of such correlations is, in fact, sufficient only to restore to the OLS estimators the large sample property of consistency. In fact, if the OLS estimators are to retain the property of unbiasedness then it is necessary that each stochastic explanatory variable should be *independent* of the contemporaneous disturbance and *also of all future and past disturbances.* To see this, consider again the equations [2.34] (p. 31). Taking expectations we have

$$E\hat{\beta}_j = \beta_j + EC_{j1}\varepsilon_1 + EC_{j2}\varepsilon_2 + EC_{j3}\varepsilon_3, \dots, + EC_{jn}\varepsilon_n \quad j = 1, 2, 3, \dots, k$$

For the OLS estimators to be unbiased all the $EC_{ji}\varepsilon_i$ terms must disappear. Since $C = (X'X)^{-1}X'$, its elements, the C_{ji}'s are rather complicated non-linear functions of *all* the sample values of the explanatory variables, i.e. the X_{ji}'s. If the C_{ji}'s had been *linear* functions of the X_{ji}'s, then for the $EC_{ji}\varepsilon_i$ terms to disappear all we would have required was an absence of *linear* correlation between X_{ji}'s and ε_i's.[1] However, because the C_{ji}'s are non-linear functions of the X_{ji}'s, unbiasedness also requires the absence of more complicated 'non-linear correlations'. For this we require independence (which implies the absence of both linear and non-linear relationships), between each explanatory variable and all disturbances. If the reader finds this argument difficult to follow, a good intuitive treatment of the problem can be found in Stewart (1976: 51–55). Since for unbiasedness we require not merely non-correlation but independence between each explanatory variable

44

and all disturbances, we shall therefore refer to this situation as the *independence case*.

The intermediate case, where the explanatory variables are merely *contemporaneously uncorrelated* with the disturbance, typically arises when one of the explanatory variables is a lagged value of the dependent variable. Consider for example the following equation

$$Y_t = \beta_1 + \beta_2 X_{2t} + \beta_3 X_{3t} + \beta_4 Y_{t-1} + \varepsilon_t \qquad [3.1]$$

where we have replaced the usual i subscripts by t subscripts to indicate that the equation is to be estimated from time series data. The third explanatory variable is simply the 'previous period's' value of the dependent variable Y. Equations such as [3.1] occur very frequently in econometrics. In particular, as we shall see in Section 5.1, they can arise in two very well-known economic models – the 'partial adjustment' model and the 'adaptive expectations' model. These models will appear regularly in the applied chapters of this book – particularly in those on consumption, investment and the demand for money. However, we defer discussion of them until Chapter 5 and consider here only the econometric implications of lagged dependent variables.

If equation [3.1] is lagged by one period it becomes clear that Y_{t-1}, although it may be uncorrelated with ε_t, will, given the values of the explanatory variables in period $t-1$, depend on ε_{t-1}. Hence, the third explanatory variable in [3.1] is not independent of all *past* values of the disturbance. It follows, from the previous discussion, that the OLS estimators of the parameters of equations such as [3.1] will not be unbiased, although it can be shown that they will retain the large sample property of consistency.

Summarising the above, the breakdown of the assumption of non-stochastic X-variables means that the OLS estimators retain both the properties of unbiasedness and consistency only when each and every explanatory variable is independent of all disturbance values, past, present and future. Indeed, we can see that non-stochastic explanatory variables represent a special case of the general independence case since, if the values of the X variables are fixed by the investigator, then they must necessarily be independent of all disturbance values.

It is assumption 1 that is the most obvious 'non-starter' as far as most econometric investigation is concerned. It will therefore be helpful at this point to consider how the classical assumptions 2–5 concerning the disturbances may be reformulated for the case where we have stochastic rather than non-stochastic explanatory variables. Since the values of the explanatory variables can no longer be treated as fixed constants, we can now, strictly speaking, consider only *conditional* distributions of the ε_i's, i.e. the distributions we would obtain for *given* sets of values for the X variables. It is possible that these distributions could differ, depending on the set of X values under consideration. This implies that, in *two-variable* regression, for example, we must reformulate assumptions 2–5 as:

2′ $E(\varepsilon_i | X_1 X_2 X_3, \ldots, X_n) = 0$ for all i

3′ $\text{Var}(\varepsilon_i | X_1 X_2 X_3, \ldots, X_n) = \sigma^2 = \text{const}$ for all i

4′ $\text{Cov}(\varepsilon_i \varepsilon_j | X_1 X_2 X_3, \ldots, X_n) = 0$ for all $i \neq j$

5′ For given $X_1, X_2, \ldots, X_n$ each ε_i is normally distributed

Consider the disturbances associated with, for example, the fourth and seventh sample observations, i.e. ε_4 and ε_7. Under the present alternative to assumption 1, we must envisage separate distributions for ε_4 and ε_7 for each and every possible set of X values. What assumptions 2′ 3′ and 4′ now state, however, is that, for *each* of these given sets of X values, the expected values of ε_4 and ε_7 are both zero, the variances of ε_4 and ε_7 are both equal to the same constant, σ^2, and the covariance between ε_4 and ε_7 is zero. Finally, assumption 5′ states that, for *each* given set of X values, ε_4 and ε_7 are both normally distributed. Assumptions 2′–5′ have, of course, similar implications for all the ε_i's.

Suppose we are able to assume that the explanatory variable is independent of the disturbance. Since for independent variables marginal (i.e. unconditional) and conditional distributions are identical, the conditional properties of the ε_i's are then identical to the marginal or unconditional properties. Hence assumptions 2′–5′ reduce to assumptions 2–5 so that no reformulation of these assumptions is necessary. If, however, we are unable to make the independence assumption then we must reformulate assumptions 2–5 as 2′–5′.

So far we have only considered the effect of stochastic X-variables on the unbiasedness and consistency properties of the OLS estimators. Clearly, however, if the small sample property of unbiasedness is lost – as it is in the contemporaneously correlated and uncorrelated cases, then the OLS estimators can no longer be efficient. They may still have a small sampling variance, but, from the definitions of Section 2.3, unbiasedness is a necessary prerequisite if an estimator is to be efficient. Similarly, if the large sample property of consistency is also lost – as it is in the contemporaneously correlated case, then so, necessarily, must be the property of asymptotic efficiency.

For the 'independence case', where the properties of unbiasedness and consistency are retained, since the X variables are stochastic, the OLS estimators are no longer *linear* estimators in the sense that they can be expressed in the form $\sum a_i Y_i$ where the a_i are constants. The a_i are functions of the X_{ji}'s – the sample values of the explanatory variables which can no longer be treated as predetermined constants. Hence the OLS estimators cannot, strictly speaking, be regarded as best *linear* unbiased estimators. However, they do retain the property of efficiency under these conditions – i.e. they have the minimum sampling variance of all unbiased estimators whether linear or non-linear. To see this, consider their sampling variances for a *given* set of specified values for the X-variables (i.e. their 'conditional' variances). That is, suppose we consider the population of all observations on Y and the explanatory X variables but concentrate for the moment just on that part of the population that contains the given specified set of X values. An infinite number of samples can be drawn from this 'subpopulation' all yielding different values for the OLS estimators. Since each such sample contains the same set of X values, these values can be treated *as if* they are constants. We know that the OLS estimators are efficient under such assumptions.[2] However, they will be efficient whatever given set of X values we specify, i.e. whatever part of the full population we preselect. Since they are efficient for *any* preselected set of X values they must therefore be efficient in the fullest sense.

From the above discussion of the problems associated with stochastic explanatory variables it is clear that the greatest difficulties arise under the so-called contemporaneously correlated case. Unfortunately this is the case which probably arises most frequently in econometrics. We shall, in the next chapter, examine in detail one factor which almost invariably gives rise to such contemporaneous correlations between explanatory variable and disturbance –

the simultaneity of many economic relationships. Here, however, we turn to another aspect of econometric research which gives rise to the same problems – the question of *errors in the measurement of economic variables.*

Errors of measurement

Many economic data series represent only an approximation to the 'true' underlying values of the variable that the investigator really wishes to measure. Such errors of measurement could arise because totals are estimated only on a sample basis or maybe because data series measure concepts slightly different from those that appear in economic theory. Recall again the case of two-variable regression, where the underlying population regression line is given by $E(Y) = \beta_1 + \beta_2 X$. For a sample size n we have, for the 'true' values of the variables X and Y

$$Y_i = \beta_1 + \beta_2 X_i + \varepsilon_i \qquad i = 1, 2, 3, \ldots, n \qquad [3.2]$$

where the ε_i's are disturbances obeying all the classical assumptions listed in the previous chapter. Suppose, however, that instead of observing the true X_i and Y_i we observe, for each i, X_i^* and Y_i^* where

$$Y_i^* = Y_i + v_i \quad \text{and} \quad X_i^* = X_i + \omega_i \qquad [3.3]$$

and v_i and ω_i represent errors in measuring the ith values of Y and X respectively. We shall assume that each v_i and ω_i has a zero mean and a constant variance, that errors made in observing X and Y at any one point of observation are independent of errors made at any other point, that the two errors are contemporaneously uncorrelated with one another and that they are contemporaneously uncorrelated with the disturbance in equation [3.2]. Such assumptions correspond to many situations that are likely to be found in the real world.

Suppose we attempt to estimate β_1 and β_2 using the observed Y_i^* and X_i^* instead of the true Y_i and X_i. Using [3.3] the regression equation [3.2] can be rewritten as

$$Y_i^* = \beta_1 + \beta_2 X_i^* + (\varepsilon_i + v_i - \beta_2 \omega_i) \qquad i = 1, 2, 3, \ldots, n \qquad [3.4]$$

This is a regression equation in the observable variables with a 'composite' disturbance given by the expression in parentheses. The problem is that this disturbance is dependent on the ω_i's as are, (from [3.3]), the values of the explanatory variable, the X_i^*'s. Thus, in equation [3.4], the explanatory variable and the disturbance are contemporaneously correlated so that application of the OLS method to this equation will lead to biased and inconsistent estimators of β_1 and β_2. The direction of the bias will depend on the nature of the correlation which, in turn, depends on the sign of β_2.[3]

Notice that it is the errors in the measurement of the explanatory X variable that cause the estimation problems. If the explanatory variable is observed without error, i.e. if $\omega_i = 0$ for all i, then [3.4] reduces to

$$Y_i^* = \beta_1 + \beta_2 X_i^* + (\varepsilon_i + v_i) \qquad i = 1, 2, 3, \ldots, n \qquad [3.5]$$

and we now have no contemporaneous correlation between explanatory variable and disturbance. Equation [3.5] in fact has the same statistical properties as the more familiar equation [3.2]. Equation [3.2] is sometimes referred to as an *errors-in-equation model* and equation [3.5] as a *generalised errors-in-equation model*, since [3.5] has a composite disturbance which behaves in an identical manner to the disturbance in equation [3.2].

Finally, consider the case where the disturbance in equation [3.2] is identically zero. This amounts to assuming that the relationship between Y and X is deterministic rather than stochastic. Since randomness is generally believed to be an intrinsic element in any economic relationship, this case is rarely likely to arise in econometrics. However we shall have reason to refer to it when we discuss the empirical version of the so-called permanent income hypothesis in Section 7.4 on the consumption function. The present case is generally known as the *errors in variables model* and here the only reason why points in a sample scatter diagram do not lie exactly on the underlying population regression line, $EY = \beta_1 + \beta_2 X$, is because of errors in measurement.

In the errors in variables model, since $\varepsilon_i = 0$, equation [3.4] reduces to

$$Y_i^* = \beta_1 + \beta_2 X_i^* + (v_i - \beta_2 \omega_i) \qquad i = 1, 2, 3, \ldots, n \qquad [3.6]$$

and we again have a situation where disturbance and explanatory variable are contemporaneously correlated. The application of the OLS method to equation [3.6] thus leads to biased and inconsistent estimators of β_1 and β_2.[4]

Although we have discussed errors of measurement in the context of two-variable regression, the various cases are exactly paralleled in multiple regression. Errors in the measurement of the dependent variable cause no problems. However, errors in the measurement of any of the explanatory variables mean that the OLS estimators lose both the properties of unbiasedness and that of consistency.

Instrumental variables

A method sometimes adopted to overcome the problem of contemporaneous correlation, particularly when it arises as the result of measurement error, is that of *instrumental variable estimation*. To gain an intuitive grasp of this approach, consider the case of two-variable regression where the OLS normal equations [2.18] reduce to

$$\sum Y_i = \hat{\beta}_1 n + \hat{\beta}_2 \sum X_i$$
$$\sum X_i Y_i = \hat{\beta}_1 \sum X_i + \hat{\beta}_2 \sum X_i^2 \qquad [3.7]$$

We can regard the first equation in [3.7] as being obtained by summing [3.2] throughout and ignoring the term $\sum \varepsilon_i$. Similarly, the second equation can be obtained by multiplying [3.2] throughout by X_i and again summing, this time ignoring the term $\sum X_i \varepsilon_i$. Since $E\varepsilon_i = 0$, if the X variable in [3.2] is uncorrelated with the disturbance, then ignoring the $\sum \varepsilon_i$ and $\sum X_i \varepsilon_i$ terms is justifiable provided we are dealing with large samples. For this reason, the OLS estimators obtained by solving the normal equations [3.7] are consistent. However, when correlation exists between X and the disturbance we can no longer ignore the $\sum X_i \varepsilon_i$ term and the OLS estimators become inconsistent.

Suppose, however, we can find a so-called 'instrumental variable' Z which *while correlated with X is uncorrelated with the disturbance*. If in obtaining the second of the above normal equations we multiplied [3.2] throughout by Z_i rather than X_i, then (this time ignoring the term $\sum Z_i \varepsilon_i$) the normal equations would become

$$\sum Y_i = \beta_i^* n + \beta_2^* \sum X_i$$
$$\sum Z_i Y_i = \beta_1^* \sum Z_i + \beta_2^* \sum Z_i X_i \qquad [3.8]$$

Since Z is by assumption uncorrelated with the disturbance we are justified in ignoring the $\sum Z_i \varepsilon_i$ term for large samples. Hence the estimators of β_1 and β_2 obtained by solving [3.8] are consistent unlike the OLS estimators obtained by solving [3.7]. The solution to the equations [3.8] is in fact (letting $z_i = Z_i - \bar{Z}$):

$$\beta_2^* = \frac{\sum z_i y_i}{\sum z_i x_i} \quad \text{and} \quad \beta_1^* = \bar{Y} - \beta_2^* \bar{X} \qquad [3.9]$$

The expressions [3.9] are known as *instrumental variable estimators* of β_1 and β_2. In multiple regression, finding such consistent estimators involves finding 'instruments' for *each* explanatory variable that happens to be correlated with the disturbance. Such instruments must, in each case, be correlated with the relevant explanatory variable but uncorrelated with the disturbance.

In selecting instrumental variables it is intuitively obvious that the correlation between 'instruments' and relevant explanatory variables should be as large as possible. While this is not necessary for consistency, *the larger are such correlations the smaller will be the asymptotic variances of the estimators obtained.* That is, the more rapidly will their sampling distributions collapse on to the parameters being estimated as the sample size increases.

In practice the problem of finding instruments which are sufficiently highly correlated with the explanatory variables and the necessity of checking whether these instruments are indeed uncorrelated with the disturbance somewhat reduces the theoretical attractiveness of the method. However, a favourite procedure is to use either the preceding or subsequent period value of an explanatory variable as its instrument. For example, if equations [3.4] and [3.6] referred to time series data then, replacing i subscripts by t subscripts, either X_{t-1}^* or X_{t+1}^* would be used as the instrumental variable for X_t^*. Since we assume that measurement errors at different observation points are independent of one another, we can regard such instruments as uncorrelated with the composite disturbances in [3.4] or [3.6]. Hence, since both X_{t-1}^* and X_{t+1}^* are likely to be highly correlated with X_t^*, either would be a suitable instrument. Similarly, if [3.4] or [3.6] refer to cross-sectional data then, writing X_{it}^* as the current period value of X_i^*, suitable instruments would be either the values X_{it-1}^* for all i, or the values X_{it+1}^* for all i. Notice, however, that this requires further data for the full cross-section (i.e. for all i) on either the preceding period values of X_i^* or the subsequent period values of X_i^*. Such data may not always be available.

An example of the above procedure is provided in the classic paper by Liviatan (1963) on the consumption function, discussed in the penultimate subsection of Section 7.4. Liviatan had available data on a cross-section of households for *two successive years*. When estimating a cross-sectional consumption function for any one of these years, he was therefore able to use, as alternative instruments for income, both income and consumption in the *other* year.

Despite the difficulties of finding suitable instruments, instrumental variable estimation is virtually the only available method of dealing with a contemporaneous correlation which arises from an errors-in-variables problem. We shall deal in the next chapter with the alternative estimation procedures that can be used when the contemporaneous correlation arises because of simultaneity in economic relationships.

3.2 Breakdowns in assumptions concerning the disturbances

We shall now consider the effects on the OLS estimators of breakdowns in assumptions 2–5 of the classical model. In the present chapter we mainly consider the consequences of single breakdowns in the classical assumptions rather than the simultaneous breakdown of two or more of these assumptions. However, since assumption 1 – that of non-stochastic X variables – is so obviously a non-starter in econometric work, it would be somewhat unreal to consider break-downs in the assumptions concerning the disturbances while still retaining assumption 1 intact. However, as we saw in the previous section, even if assumption 1 is relaxed then, provided we are prepared to assume the explanatory X variables are independent of the disturbances, we do not need to alter our interpretation of assumptions 2–5. Thus the following discussion of the consequences of breakdowns in assumptions concerning the disturbances can be regarded as occurring either in the context of non-stochastic explanatory variables or in the context of stochastic explanatory variables that are independent of the disturbances.

Suppose we wish to estimate a population regression equation, which for given values of two explanatory variables X_2 and X_3 has the form

$$EY = \beta_1 + \beta_2 X_2 + \beta_3 X_3 \qquad\qquad [3.10]$$

If the sample size is n then we have

$$
\begin{aligned}
Y_i &= EY_i + \varepsilon_i \\
&= \beta_1 + \beta_2 X_{2i} + \beta_3 X_{3i} + \varepsilon_i \qquad i = 1, 2, 3, \ldots, n \qquad [3.11]
\end{aligned}
$$

All of what follows in this section can easily be generalised to the case of more than two explanatory variables.

The second assumption in the classical model stated that the means or expected values of the disturbances associated with each sample observation were all zero, i.e. $E\varepsilon_i = 0$ for all i. The breakdown of this assumption always has undesirable consequences for the OLS estimator of the intercept β_1 in equation [3.10]. However, it may not necessarily have such consequences for the OLS estimators of the regression slopes β_2 and β_3. Suppose all the classical assumptions except for assumption 2 hold but, for each sample observation, the associated disturbance now has a non-zero mean or expected value equal to some constant μ. That is, we replace the assumption $E\varepsilon_i = 0$ by $E\varepsilon_i = \mu = $ constant. If we now take expectations over equation [3.11] we obtain, for given values of X_2 and X_3,

$$
\begin{aligned}
EY_i &= \beta_1 + \mu + \beta_2 X_{2i} + \beta_3 X_{3i} \\
&= \beta_1^* + \beta_2 X_{2i} + \beta_3 X_{3i} \qquad i = 1, 2, 3, \ldots, n \qquad [3.12]
\end{aligned}
$$

The form of the relationships [3.12] is identical to those that arise from the population regression line [3.10] when $E\varepsilon_i = 0$, except for the fact that the intercept is now $\beta_1^* = \beta_1 + \mu$ instead of β_1. Thus OLS will yield estimators of the regression slopes β_2 and β_3 possessing all the desirable small and large sample properties. However, since μ is unknown, there is no way in which we can obtain either unbiased or even consistent estimators of the intercept β_1. Clearly, the OLS estimator of β_1^* will be a biased estimator of β_1.

Suppose now that, instead of $E\varepsilon_i = \mu$, we had $E\varepsilon_i = \mu_i \neq$ const, i.e. the expected values of the disturbances were not all equal. This would imply that the mean value of the dependent variable, Y, in equation [3.12] depended on other factors apart from the values of X_2 and X_3. This would suggest that the population regression line [3.10] had been miss-specified in some way – maybe by the omission of one or more further important explanatory variables. However, we will leave problems associated with such mis-specifications until later in the chapter. We merely point out at this stage that in such circumstances the application of OLS to equation [3.12] would be unlikely to provide unbiased or consistent estimators of β_2 and β_3 let alone β_1.

Heteroscedasticity

The third assumption in the classical model stated that all disturbances had a common variance, i.e. var $\varepsilon_i = \sigma^2 =$ const for all i. In the previous chapter we saw that this assumption of *homoscedastic disturbances* was most likely to break down when there was a large variation in the size of the explanatory variables. This typically occurs either with cross-sectional data or when a long span of time series data is available. The disturbances are then said to be *heteroscedastic* and we have the case of heteroscedasticity.

We saw in our discussion of the properties of the OLS estimators that only the classical assumptions 1 and 2 were necessary for these estimators to possess the properties of unbiasedness and consistency. Obviously, then, the breakdown of assumption 3 does not affect these properties. However, the assumption of homoscedasticity was necessary if the OLS estimators were to possess the properties of best-linear unbiasedness and asymptotic efficiency. Thus under heteroscedasticity the OLS estimators *remain unbiased and consistent but are no longer BLUE or asymptotically* efficient.[5] This has two implications. Firstly, the loss of the small sample property of BLUEness means that there must now be some other linear unbiased estimators which have smaller sampling variances than the OLS estimators. Clearly, whatever the size of the sample such estimators are to be preferred. Secondly, the loss of the large sample property of asymptotic efficiency means that there now exist consistent estimators possessing sampling distributions that, as the sample size increases, collapse more quickly on to the regression parameters being estimated than do the OLS estimators. While there is little point in seeking for such estimators if the sample size is small, they are obviously to be preferred when large samples are available.

Unfortunately, heteroscedasticity has consequences which are not limited to the OLS estimators themselves. When the assumption of homoscedasticity fails it can be shown that the usual expressions, $s^2 x^{jj}$, used to estimate the sampling variances of the OLS estimators (see Section 2.4 on making inferences), no longer provide unbiased estimates of the true values of these quantities. This has potentially an even more serious consequence. It means that we can no longer rely on usual inferential procedures – i.e. we can no longer rely on any confidence intervals computed for the regression parameters, the β_j's, and neither can we rely on the usual procedures for testing hypotheses about them. For example, if the expressions $s^2 x^{jj}$ tend to underestimate the true variances of the $\hat{\beta}_j$'s, then confidence intervals are likely to be narrower than they should be, giving a false impression as to the precision of the point estimates obtained. Also we are likely to find ourselves incorrectly regarding explanatory variables as 'statistically significant' when they are not.[6] In fact, it can be shown that precisely this sort of situation arises when the variance of the disturbance tends to increase the further are the sample values of explanatory variables from their mean (see, for example, Kmenta 1971: 256).

The seriousness of the consequences of heteroscedasticity means that an investigator clearly needs to know whether it is present or not. If necessary, he can then follow suitable corrective procedures. There is, in fact, no universally accepted procedure for 'testing' for heteroscedasticity but a number of tests have been proposed. Since heteroscedasticity is a property of the disturbances and in practice these disturbances remain unknown, all such tests proceed by examining the known residuals, i.e. the e_i's obtained in the OLS estimation procedure. These may be treated as estimates of the ε_i's – the unknown disturbances. We saw in Section 2.4 that for many economic relationships the pattern of heteroscedasticity, when present, is such that the variance of *disturbances* increases as the sizes of the explanatory variables increase. The procedure followed is therefore to look for any increase in the variability in the least squares *residuals* as the sizes of the X-variables increase. For example, suppose in a two-variable regression problem we obtained a scatter diagram similar to that shown in Fig. 3.3.

The line shown in Fig. 3.3 is the estimated *sample* regression line so that the residuals, the e_i's, represent the vertical distances of the (known) points in the scatter from this (known) line. Since in this scatter the spread of the residuals about the sample regression clearly seems to increase as X increases, we would conclude that the disturbances associated with the underlying population regression line are likely to be heteroscedastic.

It is, however, possible that scatters such as that in Fig. 3.3 could occur purely

3.3 Residual pattern suggestive of heteroscedasticity.

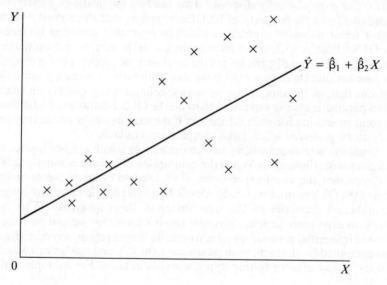

by chance. Remember that the OLS residuals are subject to sampling variability just as are the estimators themselves so that such a scatter could arise even when the unknown disturbances are in fact homoscedastic. Some form of inferential statistical testing procedure is therefore necessary. The two most frequently used are the Spearman Rank Correlation test and the Goldfeld–Quandt test. For a fuller discussion of these tests and others see Johnston (1984:298–302).

The Spearman Rank test involves calculating the coefficient of *rank* correlation between the sample values of the explanatory variable and the *absolute* values of the associated residuals. If the rank correlation is significantly different from zero then we reject the hypothesis of homoscedasticity. Notice that we cannot use the normal correlation coefficient to assess the relationship between residuals and sample X-values. Since a property of the OLS estimation procedure is that $\sum X_i e_i$ and $\sum e_i$ are both zero, it follows that $\sum (X_i - \bar{X})(e_i - \bar{e}) = 0$ so that the sample covariance between residuals and X values is identically zero. Hence, so is the normal correlation coefficient.

The Goldfeld–Quandt test is, strictly speaking, only applicable when heteroscedasticity takes the form $\text{var } \varepsilon_i = \sigma^2 X_i^2$ where $\sigma^2 = \text{const}$ – i.e. when the variance of the disturbances increases with the square of the explanatory variable. The test procedure is to first rank the sample observations according to the size of the explanatory variable and then run separate OLS regressions for the 'high' X values and the 'low' X values.[7] The variances of the residuals are then calculated for each regression. If heteroscedasticity is present the residual variance for the 'high-X' regression is likely to be greater than that for the 'low-X' regression. In fact, the null hypothesis of homoscedasticity is rejected if the ratio of the two variances is sufficiently greater than unity.

Although we have described the above tests in the context of two-variable regression they can also be applied in multiple regression. In the multiple regression case, however, it is necessary to specify which explanatory variable the disturbance variance is related to. The ranking required for either test is then applied merely to this explanatory variable.

Dealing with heteroscedasticity

When heteroscedasticity is believed to be present the standard procedure is to 'transform' the equation being estimated so that its disturbance becomes homoscedastic rather than heteroscedastic and still obeys all the other classical assumptions. Ordinary least squares can then be applied to the transformed equation. In practice this normally means making some assumption about the form of the heteroscedasticity. Suppose, for example, we wish to estimate equation [3.10] and suspect that the heteroscedasticity takes the form $\text{var } \varepsilon_i = \sigma^2 X_{2i}^2$, i.e. variances are proportional to the square of the value of the first explanatory variable. In this case the disturbances can be transformed into the homoscedastic kind by dividing by X_{2i} for all i, since

$$\text{var}(\varepsilon_i / X_{2i}) = (1/X_{2i})^2 \text{ var } \varepsilon_i = \sigma^2$$

However, to preserve the validity of the model this transformation must be applied to all terms in equation [3.11] which then becomes

$$\frac{Y_i}{X_{2i}} = \beta_1 \left(\frac{1}{X_{2i}} \right) + \beta_2 + \beta_3 \left(\frac{X_{3i}}{X_{2i}} \right) + \frac{\varepsilon_i}{X_{2i}} \qquad i = 1, 2, 3, \ldots, n$$

We may rewrite this as

$$Y_i^* = \beta_2 + \beta_1 X_{2i}^* + \beta_3 X_{3i}^* + \varepsilon_i^* \qquad i = 1, 2, 3, \ldots, n \qquad [3.13]$$

where $Y_i^* = Y_i/X_{2i}$, $X_{2i}^* = 1/X_{2i}$, $X_{3i}^* = X_{3i}/X_{2i}$ and $\varepsilon_i^* = \varepsilon_i/X_{2i}$. Equation [3.13] is an equation in values of the 'transformed' variables Y^*, X_2^* and X_3^* and more importantly has a *homoscedastic* disturbance. Hence, we can obtain BLUE estimators of the parameters β_2, β_1 and β_3 (which appear in the original equations [3.10] and [3.11]), by using the OLS method to regress the *transformed* variable Y^* on the two *transformed* explanatory variables X_2^* and X_3^*. Moreover, our estimates of the variances and standard errors of these estimators will no longer be biased as they would be if we applied OLS directly to equation [3.11]. Notice, however, that now it will be the *intercept* in the sample regression equation which yields the estimate of β_2 (the coefficient of X_2 in the original equation) and the *coefficient on X_2^** in the sample regression equation which yields the estimate of β_1 (the intercept in the original equation).

The transformation required to overcome the problem of heteroscedasticity depends on the precise form of the heteroscedasticity present. For example, if it were believed that $\operatorname{var} \varepsilon_i = \sigma^2 X_{3i}$, i.e. the variance of the disturbances was proportional to the size of the explanatory variable X_3, then equation [3.11] has to be divided throughout by $\sqrt{X_{3i}}$ to yield

$$\frac{Y_i}{\sqrt{X_{3i}}} = \beta_1 \left(\frac{1}{\sqrt{X_{3i}}} \right) + \beta_2 \left(\frac{X_{2i}}{\sqrt{X_{3i}}} \right) + \beta_3 \sqrt{X_{3i}} + \frac{\varepsilon_i}{\sqrt{X_{3i}}} \qquad [3.14]$$

The disturbance in equation [3.14] is homoscedastic since

$$\operatorname{var}(\varepsilon_i/\sqrt{(X_3)}) = (1/X_3) \operatorname{var} \varepsilon_i = \sigma^2 = \text{const.}$$

Hence, OLS may be applied to [3.14] to obtain BLUEs of $\beta_1 \beta_2$ and β_3. There is a minor problem here in that [3.14] does not contain an intercept. However, the OLS method can easily be adapted to accommodate this and many computer programs are available that minimise the residual sum of squares subject to the constraint that the regression equation passes through the origin.

It should be clear that the above procedures can be generalised to take account of any form of heteroscedasticity. In general, if $\operatorname{var} \varepsilon_i = \sigma^2 \lambda_i$ where λ_i is *any* function of the sizes of one or more of the explanatory variables, then we can always transform our equation into one containing a homoscedastic disturbance by dividing throughout by $\sqrt{\lambda_i}$. Ordinary least squares can then be applied to the transformed equation. Notice that, although the expressions used to obtain the estimates of β_1, β_2 and β_3 will be the normal OLS estimators when expressed in terms of values of the transformed variables, they will not be the OLS estimators when expressed in terms of the original variables. For this reason they are referred to as *generalised least squares (GLS) estimators*, generalised in this case because, for the special case $\lambda_i = 1$ for all i, they reduce to the OLS estimators.

The reader should have noticed that if the above procedures are to be applied, it is necessary to assume something about the form of the heteroscedasticity before estimation is undertaken. The most common assumption made is that the variance of the disturbances is proportional to the square of the size of one of the explanatory variables. While there is little empirical evidence in favour of such a formulation, its popularity presumably arises from the fact that the transformed equation does contain an intercept. For example, in Chapter 7 on the consumption function, we will find that instead of using consumption, C, or saving, S, investigators sometimes adopt the average propensity to consume, C/Y, or the average propensity to save, S/Y, as the dependent variable. The implicit assumption being made is that the disturbance variance is proportional to the square of income, Y, which is included among the explanatory variables. For similar reasons we shall find, in Chapter 10, demand for money equations not with the money stock, M, as dependent variable but M/Y which is the inverse of the income velocity of circulation.

Another situation where a form of GLS estimator is used occurs when variables refer to the group means of classified data. For example, expenditure surveys are often published with households classified according to income or total expenditure levels and the only published data refer to the mean expenditures of such groups. As we shall see in Chapter 6, when we discuss the estimation of Engel curves from cross-sectional data, regression equations fitted to such group means are likely to be subject to heteroscedastic disturbances and a GLS estimation procedure is necessary.

Autocorrelated disturbances

The fourth assumption in the classical model specifies that the covariance, and hence the correlation, between any two disturbances is zero, i.e.

$$\text{cov}(\varepsilon_i \varepsilon_j) = 0 \qquad \text{for all } i \neq j$$

When this assumption breaks down we have *autocorrelated disturbances*. We suggested in the previous chapter that autocorrelation was most likely to occur with time series data and when this happens it is also referred to as *serial correlation*. The problem with time series data is that all the random and independent factors which the disturbance term is supposed to represent are, if operating in a particular manner during any one period, likely to operate in a similar manner during the next and maybe following periods. The disturbance in any one period tends to 'spill over' into subsequent periods. For example, suppose the dependent variable is the output of a firm and that output is pushed below 'normal' during one month as a result of industrial action. Then, since there is a likelihood that such industrial action or at least its effects may persist into the following month, output is likely to be depressed during this period too. In this example if the disturbance is negative in one month it is likely to be negative in the following month as well. Note, however, that the longer the period of observation the less serious are such effects likely to be. Thus serial correlation is less likely to be a problem with annual data than it is, for example, with monthly data.

The consequences of autocorrelated disturbances are generally similar to those of heteroscedasticity. Assumption 4 in the classical model (like assumption 3) is necessary if the OLS estimators are to be BLUEs and asymptotically efficient estimators. However, it is not necessary for unbiasedness or consistency. Thus under autocorrelation (as under heteroscedasticity) the OLS estimators *remain unbiased and consistent but are no longer BLUE or asymptotically efficient*. The similarity with the consequences of heteroscedasticity extends to the usual OLS expressions for estimated standard errors. These are again biased estimators of the true standard errors so that under autocorrelation *we cannot rely on the normal confidence intervals for regression parameters or on the standard test procedures*.

Most attempts to handle the problem of autocorrelation have proceeded under the assumption that disturbances follow *a first order autoregressive scheme*.[8] This involves replacing all the normal classical assumptions about the generation of the disturbances by the specification

$$\varepsilon_t = \rho\varepsilon_{t-1} + u_t \qquad -1 < \rho < 1 \qquad t = 1, 2, 3, \ldots, n \qquad [3.15]$$

where u is a further 'disturbance' or random variable. Thus the value of the disturbance in the present period t is determined partly by the value of the disturbance in the previous period $t - 1$ and partly by the value of u in the present period. ρ is a parameter in the relationship. Notice that when discussing autocorrelation it is customary to use t subscripts rather than i subscripts, since this problem typically arises with time series data. The random variable, u, is assumed to possess all the properties attributed to ε in the normal classical model.[9] Given these assumptions it is not difficult to show that ε itself will also satisfy assumptions 2, 3 and 5 in the classical model – i.e. $E\varepsilon_t = 0$, var $\varepsilon_t = \sigma^2 =$ const and each ε_t is normally distributed. However, the ε_t's do not satisfy assumption 4. In fact, it can be shown (see, for example Kmenta 1971: 271–2) that

$$\text{cov}(\varepsilon_t\varepsilon_s) = \rho^{t-s}\sigma^2 \neq 0 \qquad \text{for all } t \neq s \qquad [3.16]$$

Thus equation [3.15] represents a specification for the ε_t's that satisfies all the classical assumptions concerning the disturbances except that of non-autocorrelation. Notice two points about equations [3.15] and [3.16]. Firstly, the nature of the autocorrelation present will depend on the sign of the parameter ρ. This parameter is restricted to be within the range plus and minus unity.[10] If ρ is positive then equation [3.15] implies that (since $Eu_t = 0$) a positive disturbance value in one period will *tend* to be followed by a positive disturbance value in the next period. Similarly, negative disturbance values will *tend* to follow negative disturbance values. Thus we can expect sequences of positive disturbance values broken only because of sufficiently negative *actual* values for u, followed by sequences of negative disturbance values broken only by sufficiently positive *actual* values for u. This form of autocorrelation is known as *positive autocorrelation*. It is obviously very much in tune with the economic interpretation of serial correlation given above where disturbing factors tend to 'spill over' from one period to another. If ρ is negative then we have *negative autocorrelation* and there is a tendency for positive disturbance values to follow negative disturbance values and vice versa. It is obviously more difficult to think of economic circumstances which would give rise to this sort of behaviour and for this reason we expect to encounter positive autocorrelation more frequently than negative autocorrelation in most econometric work.

The second point about the first-order autoregressive scheme follows from equation [3.16]. Since $\sigma^2 = $ const and $-1 < \rho < 1$, the covariance and hence the correlation between disturbances associated with any two periods declines as the interval between the two periods, $t - s$, increases. This is also in line with our economic interpretation since it implies that disturbing factors in any period are less likely to spill over into periods in the more distant future than they are into periods in the near future.

When the disturbance in a regression equation follows the first order scheme [3.15] it is possible to say something about the direction of the bias in the OLS expressions for estimated standard errors. If ρ in [3.15] is positive, then if the explanatory variables in the regression equation follow a definite trend over the sample period, it can be shown that the normal OLS expressions for standard errors underestimate the true standard errors of the OLS estimators (see, for example, Kmenta 1971: 282). Since positive rather than negative autocorrelation is to be expected with economic data, and since many economic variables possess a definite trend, either upwards or downwards, we can therefore frequently expect such downward bias. This means that confidence intervals will be narrower than they should be and we will tend to treat explanatory variables as 'statistically significant' when they are not.[11]

Obviously there is no reason to believe that equation [3.15] will always be an adequate representation of serial correlation when it occurs. For example, when using non-seasonally adjusted quarterly data, disturbances in any one quarter are likely to be akin to those in the same quarter in previous years (e.g. fuel and light expenditure is always highest during the winter quarter). Hence a 'fourth order scheme' of the kind

$$\varepsilon_t = \rho \varepsilon_{t-4} + u_t$$

may be more appropriate. Also, more complicated schemes of the kind

$$\varepsilon_t = \rho_1 \varepsilon_{t-1} + \rho_2 \varepsilon_{t-2} + u_t, \text{ etc.}$$

where the disturbance in period t is directly related to more than just the previous period's disturbance, are possible. However, as with heteroscedasticity, some specific alternative to the classical assumption frequently has to be made and, for the reasons outlined at the beginning of this subsection, the first order scheme is often likely to be a good approximation to the actual process generating the disturbances.

Since the values of the disturbances are unknown, tests for autocorrelation, like those for heteroscedasticity, involve treating the known residuals as estimates of the ε_t's. Easily the best-known such test is that devised by Durbin and Watson (1950 and 1951). Consider the expression

$$\frac{\sum_{t=2}^{n}(\varepsilon_t - \varepsilon_{t-1})^2}{\sum_{t=1}^{n}\varepsilon_t^2} \qquad [3.17]$$

Suppose autocorrelation follows the first order scheme [3.15]. For positive autocorrelation ($\rho > 0$), successive disturbance values will tend to have the same sign and the quantities $(\varepsilon_t - \varepsilon_{t-1})^2$ will tend to be small relative to the squares of the actual values of the disturbances. We can therefore expect the value of the expression [3.17] to be low. Indeed, for the extreme case $\rho = 1$, it is possible that $\varepsilon_t = \varepsilon_{t-1}$ for all t so that the minimum possible value of [3.17] is zero. However, for negative autocorrelation, since positive disturbance values now tend to be followed by negative ones and vice versa, the quantities $(\varepsilon_t - \varepsilon_{t-1})^2$ will tend to be large relative to the squares of the ε_t's. Hence, the value of [3.17] now tends to be 'high'. The extreme case here is when $\rho = -1$ when it is possible that $\varepsilon_t = -\varepsilon_{t-1}$ for all t, in which case [3.17] takes its maximum value of 4.

These upper and lower limits for [3.17] suggest that when $\rho = 0$ we should expect the expression [3.17] to take a value in the neighbourhood of 2. Notice, however, that when $\rho = 0$, equation [3.15] reduces to $\varepsilon_t = u_t$ for all t, so that ε takes on all the properties of u – in particular it is no longer autocorrelated. Thus in the absence of autocorrelation we can expect [3.17] to take a value close to 2, when negative autocorrelation is present a value in excess of 2 and maybe as high as 4, and when positive autocorrelation is present a value lower than 2 and maybe close to zero.

Unfortunately, it is not in practice possible to compute the expression [3.17] since, as we have repeatedly stressed, the ε_t's are not observable. The Durbin–Watson statistic is calculated by replacing the ε_t's in [3.17] by the observable residuals, the e_t's. That is, we compute

$$d = \frac{\sum_{t=2}^{n}(e_t - e_{t-1})^2}{\sum_{t=1}^{n} e_t^2} \qquad [3.18]$$

Illustrative calculations by Durbin and Watson show that, assuming equation [3.15] holds, then if $\rho = 0$ the 'd-statistic', like the expression [3.17] ranges around the value 2. However, it must be remembered that both [3.17] and [3.18] are merely sample statistics and are hence subject to sampling variability. Thus, even when no autocorrelation is present and $\rho = 0$, a range of values is possible for d and it is feasible that we obtain an actual value some distance from 2. Such a problem is, of course, quite usual in statistical inference but there is an additional difficulty in this case. Given a null hypothesis of $\rho = 0$, the sampling distribution for the d-statistic depends on the sample size n, the number of explanatory variables k' and also *on the actual sample values of the explanatory variables*. Thus the critical values at which we might, for example, 'reject the null hypothesis of no autocorrelation at the 5 per cent level of significance', depend very much on the sample we have chosen. It is not feasible to tabulate critical values for all possible sets of sample values. What is possible, however, is, for given values of n and k', to find *upper and lower bounds* such that the actual critical values for *any* set of sample values will fall within these known limits. Tables are available which give these upper and lower bounds for various levels of n and k' and for specified levels of significance.

Suppose we wish to test the null hypothesis $\rho = 0$ against the alternative hypothesis of positive autocorrelation. The Durbin–Watson test procedure is illustrated in Fig. 3.4. Under the null hypothesis the actual sampling distribution of d, for the given n and k' and for the given sample X values, is shown by the unbroken curve. It is such that 5 per cent of the area beneath it lies to the left of the point d^*, i.e. $P_r(d < d^*) = 0.05$. If d^* were known, we would reject the null hypothesis at the 5 per cent level of significance if for our sample $d < d^*$. Unfortunately, for the reason given above, d^* is unknown. The broken curves

3.4 The Durbin–Watson test procedure.

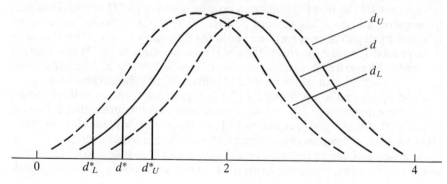

labelled d_L and d_U represent, for given values of n and k', the upper and lower limits to the sampling distribution of d within which the actual sampling distribution must lie *whatever the sample X-values*. The point d_U^* and d_L^* are such that the areas under the respective d_U and d_L curves to the left of these points are in each case 5 per cent of the total area, i.e. $P_r(d_L < d_L^*) = P_r(d_U < d_U^*) = 0.05$. It is the points d_U^* and d_L^*, representing the upper and lower bounds to the unknown d^*, that are tabulated for varying values of n and k'. Clearly, if the sample value of the Durbin–Watson statistic lies to the left of d_L^* it must also lie to the left of d^*, while if it lies to the right of d_U^* it must also lie to the right of d^*. However, there is an 'inconclusive region', since if d lies between d_L^* and d_U^* we cannot know whether it lies to the left or right of d^*. The decision criterion for the Durbin–Watson test is therefore of the following form:

for $d < d_L^*$ reject the null hypothesis of no autocorrelation in favour of positive autocorrelation

for $d > d_U^*$ do not reject null hypothesis, i.e. insufficient evidence to suggest positive autocorrelation

for $d_L^* < d < d_U^*$ test inconclusive

Because of the symmetry of the distributions illustrated in Fig. 3.4 it is also possible to use the tables for d_L^* and d_U^* to test the null hypothesis of no autocorrelation against the alternative hypothesis of negative autocorrelation, i.e. $\rho < 0$. The decision criterion then takes the form:

for $d > 4 - d_L^*$ reject the null hypothesis of no autocorrelation in favour of negative autocorrelation

for $d < 4 - d_U^*$ do not reject null hypothesis, i.e. insufficient evidence to suggest negative autocorrelation

for $4 - d_L^* > d > 4 - d_U^*$ test inconclusive

Note that tables for d_U^* and d_L^* are constructed to facilitate the use of 'one-tail' rather than 'two-tail' tests, i.e. the alternative hypothesis is either $\rho > 0$ or $\rho < 0$ but rarely $\rho \neq 0$. We shall not provide a numerical example of the Durbin–Watson test here but such examples may be found in the empirical exercises in the appendices to Chapters 6–10.

Further tests for autocorrelation

Two important limitations on the use of the Durbin–Watson statistic must be noted. Firstly the test is, strictly speaking, only a test for *first order autocorrelation*. There is no reason why it should successfully detect, for example, fourth order schemes of the type

$\varepsilon_t = \rho\varepsilon_{t-4} + u_t$

It is therefore important that it should not be applied mechanically without an *examination of the individual residuals themselves*. Such a visual examination of the time series of residuals is a valuable source of information in its own right and should be an automatic part of any form of regression analysis. The examination may not only help to identify any form of autocorrelation that may be present but can also sometimes help to reveal the source of the 'autocorrelation'. We shall return to this point in the concluding section of this chapter.

If the presence of higher order autoregressive schemes is suspected then it becomes necessary to examine the *autocorrelations* between a disturbance in period t and the disturbance k periods previous. The autocorrelation of order k is the simple correlation between ε_t and ε_{t-k}, i.e.

$$\rho_{kt} = \frac{E\varepsilon_t\varepsilon_{t-k}}{\sqrt{E\varepsilon_t^2 E\varepsilon_{t-k}^2}} \qquad \text{for all} \quad k \neq 0 \text{ and all } t$$

If we assume homoscedasticity (which implies $E\varepsilon_t^2 = E\varepsilon_{t-k}^2$), and in addition assume that all covariances $E\varepsilon_t\varepsilon_{t-k}$ remain constant over time,[12] then the process generating the disturbances is said to be *stationary* and we can rewrite ρ_{kt} as independent of time

$$\rho_k = \frac{E\varepsilon_t\varepsilon_{t-k}}{E\varepsilon_t^2} \qquad \text{for all} \quad k \neq 0$$

and approximate each such ρ_k by the *sample autocorrelation*

$$r_k = \frac{\sum_{t=k+1}^{n} \varepsilon_t\varepsilon_{t-k}}{\sum_{t=1}^{n} \varepsilon_t^2} \qquad \text{for all} \quad k \neq 0$$

Since the sample ε_t values are unknown we have to examine the *residual autocorrelation*

$$\hat{r}_k = \frac{\sum_{t=k+1}^{n} e_t e_{t-k}}{\sum_{t=1}^{n} e_t^2} \qquad \text{for all} \quad k \neq 0$$

If a value for any $\hat{r}_k$ is obtained which is significantly different from zero, then the null hypothesis $\rho_k = 0$ is rejected and kth order autocorrelation is accepted as present.[13]

It is possible to consider all the r_k simultaneously by computing the portmanteau statistic of Box and Pierce (1970)

$$Q_m = n \sum_{k=1}^{m} \hat{r}_k^2$$

Under the null hypothesis of no autocorrelation (i.e. $\rho_k = 0$ for all k), this statistic has an approximate χ^2 distribution with m degrees of freedom, m being the number of residual autocorrelations we wish to consider. There are, however, several problems with this test. Firstly, it is invalid when lagged dependent variables appear among the explanatory variables (as we shall see, a similar criticism applies to the Durbin–Watson test). Secondly, Q_m only has an approximate χ_m^2 distribution when m is small relative to the sample size n. However, if m is kept small higher orders of autocorrelation are not being tested for and therefore may be missed. Finally, there is some evidence that 'small' values of Q_m do not necessarily mean the absence of autocorrelation so that in such cases it is wise to examine each $\hat{r}_k$ individually.

A second limitation of the Durbin–Watson test is that it is invalid, even as a test for first order autocorrelation, if applied to a regression equation which includes a lagged dependent variable among its explanatory variables. Suppose, for example, that ε_t in equation [3.1] follows the first order autoregressive scheme given by [3.15]. Equation [3.1] can now be rewritten in the form

$$Y_t = \beta_1 + \beta_2 X_{2t} + \beta_3 X_{3t} + \beta_4 Y_{t-1} + \rho\varepsilon_{t-1} + u_t \qquad [3.1A]$$

Lagging [3.1] by one period we see that ε_{t-1} and Y_{t-1} are correlated. Hence, considering [3.1A], some part of the effect of ε_{t-1} on Y_t will be attributed to the effect of Y_{t-1} (thus causing the bias in the OLS estimator of β_4) and less will appear in the residuals. The residuals will therefore mainly reflect the influence of the u_t in equation [3.1A]. Hence, since u is non-autocorrelated by assumption, we will tend to underestimate the extent of serial correlation in equation [3.1] when we examine the OLS residuals. For this reason the Durbin–Watson statistic is biased towards 2 under such circumstances, i.e. it is no longer a reliable guide to the presence of serial correlation.

Durbin (1970) has developed an alternative test procedure for the case where a lagged dependent variable appears among the explanatory variables. He shows that in the absence of serial correlation the statistic

$$h = (1 - 0.5d)\sqrt{\frac{n}{1 - ns_{\hat{\beta}_i}^2}}$$

where d is the normal Durbin–Watson statistic and $s_{\hat{\beta}_i}^2$ is the estimated variance of the OLS estimator of the coefficient on Y_{t-1}, is normally distributed for large samples. It may therefore be used to test the null hypothesis $\rho = 0$ in these circumstances.[14] Again, we do not provide a numerical example here but leave illustrations of the h-test to the exercises provided later in the book.

It is important to have a valid test for autocorrelation in the presence of a lagged dependent variable because of the serious consequences for the OLS estimation procedure when autocorrelation is present under such circumstances. We have already seen that the application of OLS to equations such as [3.1] leads to biased (but consistent) estimators because of the relationship between Y_{t-1} and ε_{t-1}. If, in addition, ε_t in equation [3.1] follows, for example, the first order scheme [3.15], then ε_t also becomes dependent on ε_{t-1}. Hence, ε_t and Y_{t-1} will be related and we have a case of contemporaneous correlation between the disturbance and one of the explanatory variables. Under such conditions we know that OLS estimators are not merely biased but inconsistent as well. Notice that, although the presence of a first order scheme alone leads to neither bias nor inconsistency and the presence of a lagged dependent variable alone leads to bias but not inconsistency, *the combination of autocorrelation and a lagged dependent variable results in the OLS estimators being both biased and inconsistent.*

We have already observed that equations such as [3.1] arise frequently when use is made of the so-called 'partial adjustment' and 'adaptive expectations' models. Unfortunately, these models also tend to yield estimating equations with autocorrelated disturbance terms. Thus the combination of lagged dependent variable and autocorrelated disturbance is by no means uncommon in econometrics. For example, we shall see the partial adjustment model generating such an awkward combination in Sections 6.5 and 9.2 and the adaptive expectations model yielding it in Sections 7.4 and 10.2.

Dealing with a first order scheme
When autocorrelation is believed to be present, the alternative estimation procedure is akin to that for heteroscedasticity in that the idea is to transform the regression equation so as to remove the autocorrelation from the disturbances. Suppose, again, that we wish to estimate equation [3.10] but that on this occasion the disturbances follow the first order autoregressive scheme given by equation [3.15]. Multiplying equation [3.11] throughout by ρ, replacing the i subscripts by

t subscripts and lagging the equation by one period yields

$$\rho Y_{t-1} = \rho\beta_1 + \rho\beta_2 X_{2t-1} + \rho\beta_3 X_{3t-1} + \rho\varepsilon_{t-1} \qquad [3.19]$$

Subtracting [3.19] from [3.11] then yields

$$Y_t - \rho Y_{t-1} = \beta_1(1-\rho) + \beta_2(X_{2t} - \rho X_{2t-1}) + \beta_3(X_{3t} - \rho X_{3t-1}) + \varepsilon_t - \rho\varepsilon_{t-1}$$
$$[3.20]$$

We may rewrite this as

$$Y_t^* = \beta_1(1-\rho) + \beta_2 X_{2t}^* + \beta_3 X_{3t}^* + u_t \qquad [3.21]$$

using equation [3.15] and where $Y_t^* = Y_t - \rho Y_{t-1}$, $X_{2t}^* = X_{2t} - \rho X_{2t-1}$ and $X_{3t}^* = X_{3t} - \rho X_{3t-1}$. Equation [3.21] is an equation in values of the transformed variables Y^*, X_2^* and X_3^*. It contains a disturbance u that, by assumption, has all the normal classical properties *including that of non-autocorrelation*. We can therefore safely apply OLS to [3.21] in the knowledge that the estimators obtained together with the usual formulae for their estimated standard errors will have all the desirable properties.[15] These estimators are another example of Generalised Least Squares estimators since again they are only OLS estimators when expressed in terms of the transformed variables.

There is one rather severe snag in the above procedure. It requires a knowledge of ρ, the 'autoregressive parameter' in equation [3.15]. This is required, firstly to construct the transformed variables Y^*, X_2^* and X_3^*, and secondly to 'unscramble' an estimate of β_1, the intercept in the original equation, from the estimate obtained for $\beta_1(1-\rho)$ when OLS is applied to the transformed equation [3.21]. Unfortunately, of course, ρ is generally unknown and has to be estimated.

The most common method of estimating ρ is to take equation [3.15], replace the disturbance values, ε_t, by the OLS residuals, e_t, obtained from the straightforward regression of Y on X_2 and X_3, and use OLS to regress e_t on e_{t-1}. The OLS estimator $\hat{\rho}$ obtained in this way is known as the *Cochrane–Orcutt coefficient*.[16]

The transformed variables Y^*, X_2^* and X_3^* can now be constructed using the estimated $\hat{\rho}$ instead of the true ρ and OLS can then be applied to the transformed equation [3.21]. This procedure is usually referred to as the Cochrane–Orcutt two-stage procedure.

A problem with the above method is that the properties of the final estimators of the β_j's will depend very much on the estimated $\hat{\rho}$. Under autocorrelation, there are more efficient estimators of the β_j's than the OLS estimators. There are therefore better ways of estimating the disturbances than using the OLS residuals and hence more efficient methods of estimating ρ than from these residuals. For this reason the so-called *Cochrane–Orcutt iterative procedure* is sometimes used (Cochrane and Orcutt 1949). This involves treating the above $\hat{\rho}$ as merely a 'first round' estimate of ρ. The regression coefficients obtained by the application of OLS to equation [3.21], when Y^*, X_2^* and X_3^* are constructed using $\hat{\rho}$, are then regarded as merely 'first round' estimates, $\hat{\beta}_1, \hat{\beta}_2$ and $\hat{\beta}_3$. A 'second round' estimate of ρ is then obtained by applying OLS to residuals calculated as $Y_t - \hat{\beta}_1 - \hat{\beta}_2 X_{2t} - \hat{\beta}_3 X_{3t}$. This second-round estimate of ρ can then be used to reconstruct the variables Y^*, X_2^* and X_3^* and hence to obtain second-round estimates of β_1, β_2 and β_3 by applying OLS to [3.21] using these reconstructed variables. This procedure may be continued to yield 'third round' and 'fourth round' estimates, etc. until the estimates 'converge', i.e. until successive estimates of the β_j's and ρ are approximately the same. The estimators obtained by this procedure have been shown to be maximum-likelihood estimators and to be consistent and asymptotically equivalent to best linear unbiased estimators. For examples of equations estimated either by the full iterative Cochrane–Orcutt procedure or simply the two-stage method see equation [10.37] (p. 314) and those in Table 10.1 of this book. A full numerical example of the iterative procedure is provided in the empirical exercise in the appendix to Chapter 8.

An alternative method of dealing with a first order scheme is that of Hildreth and Lu (1960). A grid or range of values for ρ (e.g. 0.1, 0.2, 0.3, ..., 1.0), is selected and separate series for the variables Y^*, X_2^* and X_3^* constructed using *each* value of ρ on the grid. Ordinary least squares is then used to estimate a version of [3.21] for each value of ρ and the estimated equation giving the lowest residual sum of squares selected. The value of ρ giving the best equation is taken as the estimate, $\hat{\rho}$, and the coefficients of the best equation provide estimates of β_1, β_2 and β_3. The estimators obtained by this procedure are asymptotically equivalent to MLEs. We shall come across an example of the use of the Hildreth–Lu procedure when discussing the paper on fixed investment by Bischoff (1969) in Section 9.4.

Finally, note that both the Cochrane–Orcutt and Hildreth–Lu procedures can be adapted to handle autoregressive schemes other than those of the first order.

Non-normally distributed disturbances

Assumption 5 in the classical model stated that each disturbance was normally distributed. Since only assumptions 1–4 were necessary for the OLS estimators to possess the properties of BLUEness and consistency, the breakdown of assumption 5 is not too serious as far as the properties of these estimators are concerned. They do, however, lose the property of efficiency. That is, if assumption 5 does not hold, there will be other *non-linear* unbiased estimators of the regression equation parameters which have smaller sampling variances. Also, the OLS estimators will no longer be maximum-likelihood estimators and while remaining consistent they will no longer be asymptotically efficient.

The major importance of assumption 5 in the classical model was that it ensured that the OLS estimators were normally distributed. This enabled us, by switching to the t-distribution to allow for the fact that σ^2 is unknown and has to be estimated, to compute confidence intervals for, and test hypotheses about, the population regression parameters. Thus, if the disturbances are non-normally distributed, then the hypothesis-testing procedures described in Section 2.4 are no longer strictly valid.

It can, however, be shown that, as the sample size n approaches infinity, the sampling distributions of the OLS estimators approach the normal distribution regardless of the form of the distribution of the disturbances. That is, the larger the sample size the more closely can the distributions of the OLS estimators be approximated by normal distributions. It follows that for 'large' samples ($n > 50$ to be on the safe side) we can still rely on our standard testing procedures and confidence intervals even when assumption 5 breaks down. The real problem, of course, arises with 'small' samples. Although there is no real justification for doing so, most investigators in this case carry on regardless, applying the standard test procedures in the hope that either assumption 5 is valid or that any departures from normality are not sufficiently severe to invalidate results.

In principle, it is possible to test for non-normality in the disturbances. The residuals are again treated as estimates of the disturbance values and various 'goodness of fit' tests can be performed to check whether the distribution of residuals is approximately normal. Such tests, however, are rarely performed in practice.

3.3 Factors resulting in a lack of precision in the OLS estimators

Assumption 6 in the classical model requires that the number of observations, n, should exceed the number of parameters being estimated, k. If this assumption does not hold then the OLS estimating method breaks down. In the case of two-variable regression (i.e. $k = 2$) the reason for this breakdown is intuitively clear. If $n = 1$ then we have only one point in the two-dimensional scatter diagram through which an infinite number of sample regression lines may pass. With two points in the scatter there will be a single sample regression line passing through both points with, hence, a zero residual sum of squares. The OLS estimator of σ^2 now yields $\sum e_i^2/(n-2) = 0/0$ which is indeterminate so that in this case no inferences about the population parameters are possible. Analogous situations arise in multiple regression.

Even when $n > k$, but the number of 'degrees of freedom', $n - k$, is not large, difficulties arise because the OLS estimators will lack 'precision', i.e. confidence intervals for population parameters will be wide. For example, with two explanatory variables the sampling variances of the OLS estimators $\hat{\beta}_2$ and $\hat{\beta}_3$ can be shown to be (see, for example, Kmenta 1971: 388)

$$\sigma_{\hat{\beta}_2}^2 = \frac{\sigma^2}{\sum x_2^2(1-r^2)} \quad \text{and} \quad \sigma_{\hat{\beta}_3}^2 = \frac{\sigma^2}{\sum x_3^2(1-r^2)} \qquad [3.22]$$

where r is the simple correlation between X_2 and X_3. Since the smaller is n, the smaller are the quantities $\sum x_2^2$ and $\sum x_3^2$ likely to be, one consequence of a 'lack of sufficient degrees of freedom' is that the standard errors of the OLS estimators tend to be large. Moreover, confidence intervals for β_2 and β_3 depend not only on the standard errors but also on the relevant critical values from the student's t-distribution.[17] The lower is $n - k$, the larger are these t-values and this is an additional factor leading to wide confidence intervals under these circumstances. A further consequence of high standard errors and high critical t-values is that, since we test hypotheses of the kind $\beta_j = 0$ by comparing the test statistic $\hat{\beta}_j/s_{\hat{\beta}_j}$ with the relevant t-value, we are rarely going to be in a position to reject such hypotheses. Hence, explanatory variables are rarely going to appear as 'significant'.

At this point it is worth pointing out that the quantities

$$\sum x_2^2 = \sum (X_2 - \bar{X}_2)^2 \quad \text{and} \quad \sum x_3^2 = \sum (X_3 - \bar{X}_3)^2$$

may be small even when the sample size n is large. This will occur when there is *little variation in the sample values of X_2 and/or X_3*. Again this will result in a reduction in the precision of the OLS estimators, this time reflecting the fact that if an X variable shows little variation we can hardly expect to assess accurately its effect on the dependent Y variable.

We shall encounter both the problem of insufficient degrees of freedom and that of a lack of variation in explanatory variables when we consider the estimation of the demand equation for a single good in Sections 6.1 and 6.3. In theory, the demand for a good depends not only on its own price but on the price of *all* other goods. However, the 'degrees of freedom problem' precludes the inclusion of all such prices in a demand equation. In practice, investigators are usually restricted to including only a general price index or the price of a close substitute, in addition to income and 'own-price' variables. Theory also tells us that demand depends not on absolute but on relative prices. However, since prices tend to move together over time, price ratios or relative prices show little variation. For this reason we shall see that demand equations estimated with income and relative price ratios as the explanatory variables tend to provide useful information about the influence of consumers' income on demand, but much less information about the effect of relative price changes.

Multicollinearity

The final assumption in the classical model states that no exact linear relationship exists between the sample values of any two or more of the explanatory variables. When this assumption fails the OLS estimating procedure itself breaks down. To obtain an intuitive idea of why this is so suppose, again, that we are attempting to estimate the population regression equation [3.10]. Suppose, also, that our sample data is such that $X_{2i} = 2 + 3X_{3i}$ in equation [3.11] i.e. the sample values of X_2 are exactly linearly related to the sample values of X_3.

Suppose that a sample regression equation that 'minimises' the residual sum of squares, $\sum e_i^2 = \sum (Y_i - \hat{Y}_i)^2$, is given by

$$\hat{Y} = 10 + 20X_2 + 5X_3 \qquad [3.23]$$

It may appear at first sight that the numbers 10, 20 and 5 in equation [3.23] must represent the OLS estimates of β_1, β_2 and β_3 in equation [3.10]. However, since for all sample observations we have $X_2 = 2 + 3X_3$, we can rewrite equation [3.23] as

$$\hat{Y} = 10 + 10X_2 + 10(2 + 3X_3) + 5X_3$$

or

$$\hat{Y} = 30 + 10X_2 + 35X_3 \qquad [3.24]$$

Since $X_2 = 2 + 3X_3$, the predicted values of Y_i, i.e. the $\hat{Y}_i$'s, obtained from equation [3.24] by substituting the sample values of X_2 and X_3, must be identical to the $\hat{Y}_i$'s obtained using equation [3.23]. Since the sample values of Y, the Y_i's, also remain unchanged (we are still referring to the same sample), it follows that the residual sum of squares, $\sum e_i^2$, obtained from the sample regression equations [3.24] and [3.23] will be the same. Hence, if [3.23] 'minimises' $\sum e_i^2$ then so, too, must [3.24]. Clearly, we need not stop here. It is possible to construct under these circumstances any number of sample regression lines all yielding the same 'minimum' $\sum e_i^2$. One further example would be

$$\hat{Y} = 10 + 40X_2 - 20(2 + 3X_3) + 5X_3$$

or

$$\hat{Y} = -30 + 40X_2 - 55X_3 \qquad [3.25]$$

What this means is that there are an infinite number of sets of values for the estimators of β_1, β_2 and β_3 in equation [3.10], all yielding the same 'minimum' $\sum e_i^2$.[18] Obviously then, there are no unique OLS estimates so that the OLS estimating procedure breaks down.

When an *exact* linear relationship exists between explanatory variables as above, the situation is often referred to as one of *complete multicollinearity*. Complete multicollinearity means that we are in a situation of 'complete uncertainty' concerning the unknown parameters β_1, β_2 and β_3 in the population regression equation. We can have no idea whether to estimate β_1, β_2 and β_3 by, for example, the 10, 20 and 5 appearing in [3.23], the 30, 10 and 35 in [3.24] or the -30, 40 and -55 in [3.25], etc., etc.

Complete multicollinearity very rarely occurs in practice. However, a situation which does frequently arise, particularly for time series data where the variables may be subject to strong trend elements,[19] is one in which two or more of the explanatory variables are approximately linearly related. This situation also causes estimation difficulties and the closer the approximation to a linear relationship the more severe these difficulties tend to become.

Considering again the estimation of equation [3.10], suppose that the relationship $X_2 = 2 + 3X_3$ holds merely approximately rather than exactly for all sample observations. In such a situation there *will* be unique estimates of β_1, β_2 and β_3, i.e. a unique sample regression equation, which minimises $\sum e_i^2$. The OLS method therefore no longer breaks down completely. The problem now is that there will be many other sets of estimates for β_1, β_2 and β_3, i.e. many other sample regression lines, all with residual sums of squares not equal to but 'very close' to the minimum $\sum e_i^2$ yielded by the OLS sample regression line. Under these circumstances we will lack confidence and be uncertain about the precision of the actual OLS estimates since there are so many other sets of estimates which appear 'almost as good'. The higher the 'degree' of multicollinearity in the sample data the greater, other things being equal, will be the degree of our uncertainty about the true values of β_1, β_2 and β_3.

In statistical terms the precision of an estimate is reflected in the size of its standard error (from which confidence intervals are constructed). High collinearity between X_2 and X_3, when it leads to considerable uncertainty about the true values of β_1, β_2 and β_3, is therefore reflected in *large standard errors and sampling variances* for the OLS estimators of these parameters. As an example, suppose we were attempting to assess the influence on consumer expenditure, C, of two explanatory variables – personal disposable income, Y, and the net liquid asset holdings of consumers, L. The following OLS regression equations are obtained from postwar time series data:

$$\hat{C} = 153 + 0.93Y \qquad\qquad R^2 = 0.93 \qquad\qquad\qquad\qquad [3.26]$$
$$\phantom{\hat{C} = }(16) \quad (0.06)$$

$$\hat{C} = 246 + 0.64L \qquad\qquad R^2 = 0.81 \qquad\qquad\qquad\qquad [3.27]$$
$$\phantom{\hat{C} = }(28) \quad (0.05)$$

$$\hat{C} = 84 + 0.78Y + 0.43L \qquad R^2 = 0.95 \qquad\qquad\qquad\qquad [3.28]$$
$$\phantom{\hat{C} = }(61) \quad (0.53) \quad\ (0.37)$$

Equations [3.26] and [3.27] illustrate that the variables Y and L, when included alone as explanatory variables, can explain 93 per cent and 81 per cent respectively of variations in C and in each case appear highly significant.

However, when both variables are included together as explanatory variables, there is a distinct 'mushrooming' of the standard errors attached to each coefficient in equation [3.28]. As a result, although Y and L can jointly explain 95 per cent of the variation in C, neither of their coefficients appears significantly different from zero in the multiple regression equation. Equation [3.28], in fact, suggests high collinearity between Y and L during the sample period – not surprisingly since both disposable income and net liquid assets will have exhibited strong upward trends during the postwar era. Our uncertainty as to the true importance of each explanatory variable (caused by the multicollinearity problem) is reflected in the size of the standard errors in equation [3.28].[20] These would result in any confidence intervals for parameters of the underlying population regression line being very wide indeed.

We shall encounter examples of multicollinearity problems in each of the applied chapters of this book. For example in Chapter 6 we shall find that in the demand equation for any good the two most important explanatory variables – income and own-price are, typically, highly correlated over time. Similarly in Chapter 8, when estimating production functions we shall find that capital and labour inputs tend to be highly correlated in both cross-sectional and time series data. Here the multicollinearity problem is accentuated if, in attempting to allow for technical progress over time, time itself is included as an additional explanatory variable. In Chapter 10 we shall see that the uncertainty resulting from multicollinearity has prevented any firm conclusion being reached as to what is the most appropriate 'scale' variable in demand for money functions. All three possible scale variables – income, permanent income and non-human wealth tend to move together over time. Similarly, the high correlation between different interest rate variables has made it impossible to decide which such variable is best included in demand for money functions as a proxy for the opportunity cost of holding money.

When considering the consequences of multicollinearity it must be remembered that (except in the case of complete multicollinearity when the OLS estimating procedure breaks down) multicollinearity itself does not involve the violation of any of the assumptions of the classical regression model. The OLS estimators will still possess *all* the desirable properties of BLUEness, etc. Also, the usual formulae will still provide us with unbiased estimators of the standard errors of the OLS estimators. Provided all the classical assumptions hold, the OLS estimation procedure is still 'the best available' – the problem is that when multicollinearity is severe the best available is not very good. It is not that we cannot trust our usual hypothesis-testing procedures – unlike under autocorrelation or heteroscedasticity these are still valid. Unfortunately when multicollinearity is present they may not tell us very much.

We have already noted that one consequence of multicollinearity is the likelihood of large standard errors on the regression coefficients leading to *imprecision in our estimates of population regression line parameters* (the β_j's). A further consequence of large sampling variances for the OLS estimators is that *specific estimates of the β_j's may have large errors*. The fact that the OLS estimators remain unbiased or even BLUE simply means that, if we were to take many samples, the estimates obtained would be 'on average' equal to the parameters being estimated. Since in practice we take but a single sample, unbiasedness is of cold comfort if the 'spread' of estimates obtained over many samples is very wide – as it may be when multicollinearity is severe. It may well be the case that, for the single sample we take, estimates obtained will be a considerable distance away from the true values of the parameters we are estimating. Such 'instability' in the OLS estimates also tends to manifest itself in drastic changes in the values of the OLS estimators when merely a few extra observations are added to the available sample. This is yet another illustration of the basic uncertainty that exists about the true values of the β_j parameters when serious multicollinearity is present.

A further typical consequence of collinear explanatory variables is that *it may become impossible to disentangle their individual influences on the dependent variable.* This is well illustrated by equations [3.26–3.28]. The first two of these equations, taken separately, suggest that either disposable income or liquid assets could be regarded as an important determinant of consumer expenditure. However, despite the fact that taken together in equation [3.28] Y and L can explain 95 per cent of the variation in C, it is not possible to deduce which is the more important. This, of course, is because of the large standard errors in [3.28]. These make it impossible on the basis of [3.28] to reject either the hypothesis that disposable income has no influence on consumer expenditure or the hypothesis that liquid assets have no influence. This difficulty arises because of the common upward trend in the three variables C, Y and L. The upward trend in consumers' expenditure could be attributed either to the upward trend in disposable income or to the upward trend in liquid asset holdings. However, on the basis of sample information alone we cannot tell which of the upward trends in Y and L is the determining factor.

When faced with a regression equation such as [3.28] there is a strong temptation to drop the 'least significant variable', in this case L. It is particularly tempting to do this if, as in [3.26] and [3.28], it leads to little deterioration in the goodness of fit of the equation. The danger now is that we may be omitting an explanatory variable which is an important determinant of the dependent variable but whose importance has been obscured by the multicollinearity that is present. As we shall see in the next section, such 'specification errors' have serious consequences for our estimates of the coefficients attached to other variable(s) in the equation.

The possibility that variables may be incorrectly dropped from an estimating equation becomes even more likely when the investigator is faced with equations containing more than two explanatory variables. Remember that assumption 7 of the classical model states that there should be no linear relationship between the sample values of any two *or more* of the explanatory X variables. For example, with four explanatory variables X_2, X_3, X_4 and X_5, exact linear relationships of the form

$$X_2 = 5 + 4X_3 + 7X_5 \quad \text{or} \quad X_3 = 3X_2 + X_4 - 5X_5$$

will lead to a complete breakdown in the OLS estimation method just as surely as more simple relationships such as $X_2 = 2 + 3X_3$. Similarly, when such relationships hold only approximately, the consequences are likely to be very similar to those of an approximate relationship $X_2 \approx 2 + 3X_3$. There will be uncertainty about the true values of underlying parameters, manifesting itself in high standard errors for the OLS estimators. Unfortunately, while linear relationships between just two explanatory variables are not difficult to detect, more complicated relationships such as those above may be easily 'missed' by the investigator.

In our discussion of autocorrelation and heteroscedasticity we spent consider-able time on test procedures for determining whether these were present in the population of disturbances under study. If they were present alternative estimating procedures were necessary. The situation is somewhat different in the case of multicollinearity. Firstly, when testing for autocorrelation or heterosced-asticity we were able to formulate hypotheses concerning population parameters (e.g. the autoregressive parameter ρ). Such standard inferential procedures are not possible for multicollinearity. This is because multicollinearity is an attribute of the sample observations rather than of the population from which the observations have been drawn.[21] Secondly, for heteroscedasticity or autocor-relation a clear distinction can be drawn between cases where they are present (e.g. $\rho \neq 0$) and corrective procedures are necessary, and cases where they are not present (e.g. $\rho = 0$). No such clear distinction exists in the case of multicollinearity. Suppose we rule out the theoretically possible but in practice highly unlikely cases of complete multicollinearity and 'total absence' of multicollinearity (where each and every explanatory variable is completely uncorrelated with all other explanatory variables).[22] What we are then concerned with is the 'degree' of multicollinearity or the 'extent' to which linear relationships appear among the explanatory variables. The closer the approximation to a linear relationship the higher the degree of multicollinearity. The problem, however, is that a given degree of multicollinearity does not always have the same consequences.

Consider again the case where we are attempting to estimate the population regression equation [3.10]. In such a case, we see from equation [3.22] that the variances of the OLS estimators of β_2 and β_3 will be estimated as

$$s_{\hat{\beta}_2}^2 = \frac{s^2}{\sum x_2^2(1 - r^2)} \quad \text{and} \quad s_{\hat{\beta}_3}^2 = \frac{s^2}{\sum x_3^2(1 - r^2)} \qquad [3.29]$$

where s^2 is the residual variance. r is again the simple correlation between the sample values of X_2 and X_3 by which we may measure the degree of multicollinearity. Clearly, as r increases the estimated variances (which are unbiased estimators of the true variances), and hence the standard errors of $\hat{\beta}_2$ and $\hat{\beta}_3$ will increase in size. As $r \to 1$ and we approach the case of complete multicollinearity the rate of increase will become rapid. However, for a given degree of multicollinearity (i.e. a given r), the size of the standard errors also depends on the residual variance s^2 (measuring the 'overall fit' of the equation) and on $\sum x_2^2$ and $\sum x_3^2$ which measure the variability in the sample values of X_2 and X_3. Thus it is possible to obtain relatively 'low' standard errors and well-determined regression coefficients even when multicollinearity as measured by r is 'high', provided the overall fit of the equation is good and/or there is a sufficiently wide variation in the sample values of X_2 and X_3.

The upshot of the above is that, when we have an estimated equation with relatively well-determined coefficients and low standard errors, we need not be particularly concerned by the extent of multicollinearity among the explanatory variables. Remember that the OLS estimators retain all their desirable properties regardless of any multicollinearity present. Also, in contrast to the situation under heteroscedasticity or autocorrelation, the estimated standard errors remain unbiased estimates of the true standard errors. Hence, if the estimated standard errors are small the extent of multicollinearity (unlike, for example, the possible presence of serial correlation) is of no real consequence.

It is when the estimated standard errors are large that we begin to suspect that the presence of multicollinearity may be having a detrimental effect on the precision of our estimating procedure. For example, high standard errors combined with a very good 'overall fit' (as measured, for example, by R^2) is a virtually certain indicator of multicollinearity. Verification of its presence, however, may not necessarily be an easy matter. Approximate linear relationships between any *two* variables can be picked up by the examination of the simple 'zero order' correlations between each pair of explanatory variables. However, these will not indicate the presence of more complex relationships involving more than two explanatory variables. To cover such cases Farrar and Glauber (1967) have suggested that a more reliable guide is to compute the coefficient of multiple determination, R^2, between each X variable and the $k - 1$ remaining X variables. If any of these R^2's is close to unity then the extent of multicollinearity must be severe.

At this point a strong warning must be given against the temptation invariably to attribute large standard errors and insignificant regression coefficients to the presence of multicollinearity. It is obvious that large standard errors can occur in an equation such as [3.28] even in the absence of any severe multicollinearity if neither of the explanatory variables is an important determinant of the dependent variable. This situation will be signalled by a low coefficient of multiple determination R^2 and a high residual variance for the estimated equation. Hence, it is easy to spot in practice. The most dangerous temptation arises when high standard errors occur on some or all of the explanatory variables in an equation with a good overall fit and when some degree of multicollinearity is clearly present. It is very tempting under these circumstances to blame any insignificance in the regression coefficients on the multicollinearity that is present. However, *there can be no guarantee that in the absence of multicollinearity these coefficients would have appeared significant.* High standard errors *may* simply reflect multicollinearity but can also arise because the relevant variable is genuinely unimportant. Of course, since the overall fit is a good one, we must expect some of the explanatory variables to become significant in the absence of multicollinearity. But there can be no guarantee that they all will. For example, in equation [3.28] Y and L between them explain 95 per cent of the variation in C, so one at least of these variables appears to be important. Hence, in the absence of multicollinearity at least one of the two variables Y and L is likely to appear highly significant. However, it is by no means necessarily the case that both will.

Summarising the last few paragraphs, if the coefficients of a regression equation are well determined with low standard errors we need not be over-concerned with any multicollinearity that is present. When standard errors are high, multicollinearity may well be present (particularly when R^2 is high) but we should be wary of regarding all such high standard errors as simply the consequence of multicollinearity. Multicollinearity does, frequently, result in high standard errors but it is not the only such cause.

When it is apparent that multicollinearity is handicapping the precise estimation of population regression parameters, there is very little that can be done apart from the seeking of *new* information. Additional sample observations, for which the approximate linear relationships present in the original data no longer hold, will obviously help resolve the problem. While extra observations with this property are likely to be difficult to obtain, increasing the sample size, even if it leaves the extent of the multicollinearity unchanged, may of itself be of assistance. For example, consider the case of two explanatory variables. The expressions [3.29] indicate that even if r remains unchanged, since an increased sample size leads to larger values of $\sum x_1^2$ and $\sum x_2^2$, it must also result in smaller standard errors provided the overall fit of the equation does not worsen.

Extra information may also take the form of 'extraneous' estimates of some of the regression parameters. Suppose, again, that we are attempting to estimate the population regression line [3.10] under conditions where the sample values of X_2 and X_3 are highly correlated. If an extraneous estimate of, for example, the parameter β_2 is already available from some source other than the available sample, the multicollinearity problem can be circumvented. If β_2^* is the extraneous estimate, then we can use the sample data to form the variable $Y - \beta_2^* X_2$ and estimate the regression equation

$$Y - \widehat{\beta_2^* X_2} = \hat{\beta}_1 + \hat{\beta}_3 X_3 \qquad [3.30]$$

$\hat{\beta}_1$ and $\hat{\beta}_3$ provide the estimates of β_1 and β_3. This approach has been much used in demand equations when estimation is handicapped by the high time series correlation between the explanatory variables income and prices. Extraneous estimates of the coefficient on the income variable are obtained from cross-sectional data. We shall discuss this approach more fully in Section 6.3.

3.4 Specification errors

So far in this chapter we have considered the consequences of breakdowns in the classical assumptions under the 'maintained hypothesis' that the population regression equation [2.12] (p. 12) has been correctly specified. However, [2.12] is as much a part of the classical regression model as are the assumptions 1–7, so we conclude by considering the effect on the OLS estimators of an incorrectly specified population regression equation. There are basically two ways in which equation [2.12] could be mis-specified. Firstly, we might include too many or too few explanatory variables. Secondly, we might assume that the population regression equation is of linear form (as implied by [2.12]) when it is not. We consider first cases where the number of explanatory variables has been incorrectly specified.

The case where we include explanatory variables in [2.12] when they do not, in fact, have any influence on the dependent Y variable is relatively easily disposed of. Such a mis-specification simply implies that some of the β_j parameters in equation [2.12] take the value zero. Provided assumptions 1–7 hold the OLS estimators of all the β_j's will still be unbiased and consistent although, of course, for those variables incorrectly included in the population regression equation we will have 'unbiased estimators of zero'. The OLS estimators of the non-zero β_j's, however, are unlikely to remain BLUE or efficient. Suppose an 'irrelevant' explanatory variable is correlated with any of the other explanatory variables. It follows from our discussion of multicollinearity that this will lead to an unnecessary increase in the sampling variances and standard errors of all explanatory variables, including the 'relevant' ones.[23] Only when the irrelevant variables are completely uncorrelated with the other variables will the OLS estimators of the non-zero β_j remain efficient.

The omission of a 'relevant' explanatory variable has even more serious consequences. The disturbance in the classical regression model is supposed to encapsulate the influence on the dependent Y variable of all factors other than those represented by the explanatory X-variables. It is therefore possible to regard an omitted relevant explanatory variable as being represented by the disturbance. However, if the omitted variable is correlated with any of the other explanatory variables then *we will have a case of contemporaneous correlation between these variables and the disturbance.* We know from Section 3.1 that under these circumstances the OLS estimators become *biased and inconsistent.* The direction of the biases involved will depend: (a) on the directions of the correlations between the omitted and the remaining explanatory variables, and (b) on the signs of the β_j's associated with the omitted variables.

For example, consider again the case where the population relationships are given by [3.10] and [3.11] but where we apply OLS to

$$Y_i = \beta_1 + \beta_2 X_{2i} + \varepsilon_i^* \qquad\qquad [3.31]$$

where in fact $\varepsilon_i^* = \beta_3 X_{3i} + \varepsilon_i$. If $\beta_3 > 0$, then if the correlation between the X_{2i}'s and the X_{3i}'s, r, is positive, this will lead to positive correlation between the ε_i^*'s and the X_{2i}'s. We then have a situation equivalent to that illustrated in Fig. 3.1 with OLS tending to overestimate β_2 and underestimate β_1. However, if $\beta_3 > 0$ and $r < 0$, then the correlation between the ε_i^*'s and the X_{2i}'s will be negative and the situation will be as in Fig. 3.2. On the other hand, if $\beta_3 < 0$, then the directions of the correlations between the ε_i^*'s and the X_{2i}'s will be reversed.

As can be imagined the problem of possible omitted variables is a frequent one in econometrics. We quote but two examples here. In Section 6.4 we shall be concerned about a wide range of omitted variables when considering the estimation of income elasticities of demand from cross-sectional data. In Section 8.5 we meet a similar problem when estimating one of the parameters of the CES production function via the marginal productivity equation for labour.

In practice, the fact that an important explanatory variable has been omitted from a regression equation can sometimes be picked up by an examination of the residuals and their behaviour over time. In Fig. 3.5a and 3.5b time is measured on the horizontal axis with positive residuals plotted above and negative residuals below this axis. In Fig. 3.5a the residuals exhibit a strong positive time trend suggesting the omission of an explanatory variable itself containing a strong trend element. The residual plot in Fig. 3.5b again suggests an important variable has been omitted – this time one exhibiting a definite cyclical pattern.

Both of the above patterns of residuals would be reflected in a low value for the Durbin–Watson statistic so that this situation well illustrates the need for a visual examination of the residuals. Without such an examination, there would be a strong temptation to treat incorrectly the problem as one arising solely because of serial correlation in the disturbances. As we shall see in later chapters, low Durbin–Watson statistics frequently arise in practice because of '*dynamic mis-specifications*' of the population regression line where the omitted explanatory variables consist of lagged values of the dependent variable.

The second most common form of specification error is where the population regression equation is of non-linear form. Economic relationships are frequently of a non-linear kind so the standard equation [2.12] (p. 12) is often likely to be inappropriate. When it is suspected that the population regression equation is non-linear there are a number of simple non-linear functions by

3.5a A positive time trend in the residuals.   **3.5b A cyclical pattern in the residuals.**

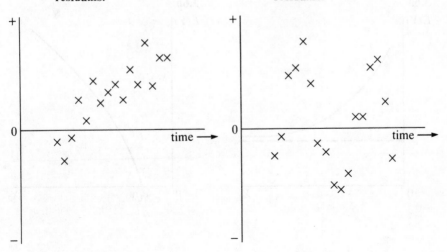

which we may attempt to approximate it. For example, in two-variable regression instead of $EY = \beta_1 + \beta_2 X_2$ we might specify

$$E(Y) = \beta_1 + \beta_2\left(\frac{1}{X_2}\right) \qquad\qquad [3.32]$$

or

$$E(Y) = \beta_1 + \beta_2 \log X_2 \qquad\qquad [3.33]$$

or

$$E(Y) = \beta_1 X_2^{\beta_2} \qquad\qquad [3.34]$$

These functions are illustrated for positive β_1 and β_2 in Fig. 3.6a, 3.6b and 3.6c respectively. It is left to the reader to determine the shape of these functions for negative values of their parameters.

Population regression equations such as [3.32] and [3.33] would be estimated by using as explanatory variables the 'transformed' variables, $1/X_2$ and $\log X_2$ and applying OLS in the usual manner. The straightforward estimation of [3.34], however, requires the additional assumption that the disturbance is 'multiplicative' in form. That is, it enters the population relationship in the form

$$Y = (EY)(\varepsilon) = \beta_1 X_2^{\beta_2}\varepsilon \qquad\qquad [3.35]$$

rather than as $Y = EY + \varepsilon = \beta_1 X_2^{\beta_2} + \varepsilon \qquad\qquad [3.35A]$

Multiplicative disturbances may or may not be a reasonable assumption but, provided [3.35] is valid, we obtain by taking logarithms

$$\log Y = \log \beta_1 + \beta_2 \log X_2 + \log \varepsilon \qquad\qquad [3.36]$$

Equation [3.36] is linear in the logarithms of the variables. Hence, provided the

3.6 Non-linear relationships between EY and X.

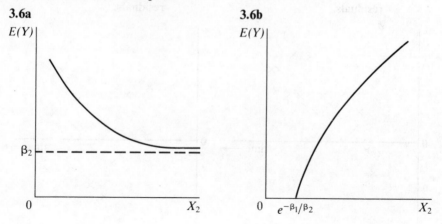

3.6a

3.6b

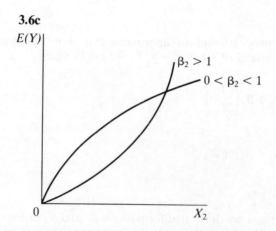

3.6c

transformed disturbance 'log ε' obeys the usual classical assumptions, we may safely apply OLS and regress the transformed variable 'log Y' on the transformed variable 'log X_2'. The only minor complication is that the intercept in this regression yields an estimate of log β_1 rather than β_1. Note, however, that [3.35A] cannot be transformed into a linear equation in this way so that the assumption of multiplicative disturbances is crucial for straightforward estimation by OLS.

Equations such as [3.32–3.34] can easily be generalised for the multiple regression case. A favourite form is the generalisation of [3.34]

$$EY = \beta_1 X_2^{\beta_2} X_3^{\beta_2}, \ldots, X_k^{\beta_k} \qquad [3.37]$$

Like [3.34] this equation is linear in the logarithms. Also its parameters, the β_j's $(j = 2, 3, \ldots, k)$, can be interpreted as the elasticities of the dependent Y variable with respect to each of the explanatory variables. This property makes

[3.37] an obvious choice of estimating equation when such elasticities are of particular interest. For example, it is frequently used in the estimation of demand equations for a single good and for demand for money equations. Since the Cobb–Douglas production function is linear in the logarithms we shall also encounter equations such as [3.37] in Chapter 8.

When an attempt is made to estimate a non-linear population regression equation by a linear sample regression equation we cannot expect the OLS estimators to be unbiased or consistent. It is possible using Taylor's theorem[24] to approximate any of equations [3.32–3.34] by an equation of the form

$$EY = \beta_1 + \beta_2 X_2 + \beta_3 X_2^2 + \beta_4 X_2^3 \ldots \tag{3.38}$$

where the β_j's in equation [3.38] depend on the mean of X_2. Attempting to estimate non-linear population regression equations by linear estimating equations can therefore be seen to be analogous to omitting relevant explanatory variables. Moreover, the omitted variables (in this case X_2^2, X_2^3, X_2^4, etc. etc.) are clearly correlated with X_2 and in this situation we already know that the OLS estimators lose the properties of unbiasedness and consistency.

An incorrectly specified form for the population regression equation is best spotted by an examination of the residuals. For example, if we attempted to estimate a population relationship such as [3.33] (as illustrated in Fig. 3.6b), by a linear regression line then we are likely to observe a residual pattern as in Fig. 3.7.

In Fig. 3.7, a sequence of negative residuals is followed by a positive sequence and then another negative sequence. This suggests an incorrectly specified regression equation. If such sequences occur over time they will be picked up by, for example, the Durbin–Watson statistic. Again, without a close visual examination of the residuals, the temptation will be to regard the problem as one arising solely out of serial correlation rather than resulting from a mis-specification.

3.7 Residual pattern suggestive of a mis-specification.

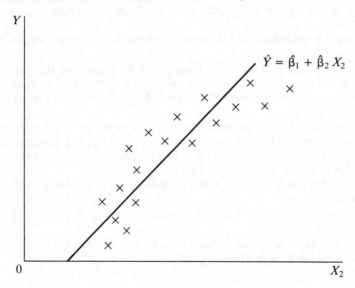

Further reading

Breakdowns in the classical assumptions are covered in all the introductory textbooks mentioned in Further Reading at the end of Chapter 2. Non-matrix treatment is given by Kmenta (1971) and Kelejian and Oates (1981). The problems of errors in measurement and instrumental variables are well covered in Kmenta and at a more advanced level in Johnston (1984). Autocorrelation and heteroscedasticity are thoroughly covered in Stewart and Wallis (1981) and in Kmenta, while a formal matrix–algebra treatment of generalised least squares can be found in Johnston. Valuable intuitive insights into these problems are provided by Stewart (1984). Multicollinearity and specification errors are most clearly treated in Kmenta.

Notes

1. Remember that if X, Y, $Z = X + Y$ and u are random variables, then if u is uncorrelated with both X and Y, $EZu = E(X + Y)u = EXEu + EYEu = 0$ provided $Eu = 0$. Notice that contemporaneous non-correlation alone between X_{ji}'s and ε_i's is insufficient for unbiasedness since each C_{ji} depends on all X_{ji}'s.
2. We are of course assuming at the moment that all other assumptions of the classical model hold.
3. In fact, the covariance between explanatory variable and disturbance in [3.4] is given by $-\beta_2\sigma_\omega^2$ where σ_ω^2 is the variance of ω. Thus, if β_2 is positive, the contemporaneous correlation will be negative and we have a situation similar to Fig. 3.2, with OLS tending to underestimate β_2 and overestimate β_1.
4. The covariance between explanatory variable and disturbance is again $-\beta_2\sigma_\omega^2$ so that, for positive β_2, OLS again tends to underestimate β_2 and overestimate β_1.
5. Also, if they are no longer BLUE then, of course, they can no longer be efficient.
6. Since we test null hypotheses of the form $\beta_j = 0$ by examining the t-ratios $\hat\beta_j/s\sqrt{x^{jj}}$ then, if $s\sqrt{x^{jj}}$ tends to underestimate the true standard error of β_j, we may find ourselves rejecting null at a given level of significance when we should not do so.
7. A number of central observations, C, are, in fact, omitted before the separate regressions are run. The ratio of residual variances then has an F distribution with degrees of freedom dependent on C and on the sample size. There are various rules of thumb for deciding on C.
8. Autocorrelated disturbances are sometimes referred to as autoregressive disturbances.
9. That is, $Eu_t = 0$, var $u_t = $ const for all t, $\text{cov}(u_t u_s) = 0$ for all $t \neq s$ and u_t is normally distributed.
10. A value of ρ outside these limits would imply ε values of ever-increasing absolute size which is economically unrealistic.
11. See note 6.

12. That is, for each k, $E\varepsilon_t\varepsilon_{t-k} = $ const for all t. Hence, for example, the covariance between ε_3 and ε_7 is the same as the between ε_4 and ε_8 which is also the same as that between ε_7 and ε_{11}.

13. Since, when $\rho_k = 0$, r_k can be shown to be asymptotically normally distributed with mean $-1/n$ and variance $1/n$, in practice for large values of n and k $\hat{r}_k$ is regarded as significantly different from zero at the 5 per cent level if $\hat{r}_k > 2/\sqrt{n}$ or $< -2/\sqrt{n}$.

14. An extension of the h-test is possible to test for higher order auto-correlation in the presence of lagged dependent variables. For a simple statement of this extended test (known as the Lagrange multiplier test) see Stewart and Wallis 1981: 230–1.

15. Since by carrying out the transformation we have 'lost an observation' this is not strictly correct and the application of OLS to [3.21] will not yield *best* linear unbiased estimators.

16. The intercept term has to be suppressed in this regression. The resulting OLS estimator is $\hat{\rho} = \dfrac{\sum e_t e_{t-1}}{\sum e_t^2}$.

17. Remember that, for example, 95 per cent confidence intervals for β_2 are given by $\hat{\beta}_2 \pm t_{0.025} s_{\hat{\beta}_2}$ where $s_{\hat{\beta}_2}$ is the estimate of $\hat{\sigma}_{\beta_2}$.

18. There are, in fact, an infinite number of sample regression equations all equally successful in explaining sample variations in Y.

19. Students sometimes fail to realise that it is not necessary for variables to have a common upward or downward trend for them to be highly correlated. For example, if X_2 is 'upward trending' and can be approximately represented by $X_2 = 3 + 0.02t$ where t is time, while X_3 is 'downward trending' and can be approximated by $20 - 0.03t$, then the linear relationship $X_3 = 24.5 - 1.5X_2$ will approximately hold between the two variables.

20. The effect of high multicollinearity on standard errors can also be seen by considering the equations [3.22]. The higher is r, the correlation between X_2 and X_3, the larger are the sampling variances $\sigma_{\hat{\beta}_2}^2$ and $\sigma_{\hat{\beta}_3}^2$.

21. If an exact or approximate linear relationship between explanatory variables exists in the *population* then this means that we have ignored an important feature of reality and the model needs to be respecified to take account of such a relationship.

22. Just as in practice a perfect correlation between the sample values of explanatory variables (i.e. an exact linear relationship) is highly unlikely, so is a zero correlation between sample values.

23. For example, with one explanatory variable, X_2, we have var $\hat{\beta}_2 = \sigma^2/\sum x_2^2$. If a second irrelevant explanatory variable, X_3, is added to the regression equation then from [3.22] var $\hat{\beta}_2 = \sigma^2/\sum x_2^2(1 - r^2)$. The ratio of these two variances is $1/(1 + r^2)$. Thus, if the correlation r between X_3 and X_2 exceeds zero, the inclusion of X_3 will increase the variance of β_2.

24. See, for example, Glaister 1972: 125.

4 Simultaneous equation systems

In this chapter we shall be concerned with the problems arising when attempts are made to estimate systems of simultaneous equations. It will be assumed that the reader is familiar with such distinctions as those between exogenous and endogenous variables and between the structural and reduced forms of a model.

In the previous two chapters we concentrated attention on the estimation of single equations in which it was assumed that the only endogenous variable was the dependent variable and that the explanatory variables were truly exogenous. It was implicitly assumed that the only relationship between the variables in an equation was that described by the equation itself. However, economic models typically involve a set of relationships designed to explain the behaviour of the endogenous variables in the model. This gives rise to the possibility that additional relationships between the dependent and explanatory variables in any single equation may exist and that the explanatory variables may themselves be endogenous. For example, in the simple consumption function introduced at the beginning of Chapter 2 causation was assumed to be from the income variable to the consumption expenditure variable. However, if we were estimating such a function for the aggregate economy, we would be unable to ignore the fact that consumption expenditure was an important determinant of national income. There would therefore be a reverse causation present from the consumption variable to the income variable. An additional relationship between income and consumption would exist, apart from the consumption function, and these two relationships together could be regarded as jointly determining the endogenous variables, income and consumption.

The question we now attempt to answer concerns the extent to which the existence of a set of simultaneous relationships, in which a given equation is embedded, affects the manner in which we should attempt to estimate that equation. In the next section we discuss the separate but related problems of identification and simultaneous equation bias. In Section 4.2 we examine some of the methods used to estimate simultaneous equation systems.

4.1 The problems of identification and simultaneous equation bias

Imagine that we wished to estimate the 'demand curve' for some typical non-durable household commodity and to this end collected time series data on the price, P, of the commodity and on the quantity bought and sold, Q. If we now proceeded, somewhat naively, to regress (by OLS) quantity Q on price P, we would probably soon realise that our simple regression equation bore little relation to the demand curve we were trying to estimate.

Firstly, the demand curve of the elementary economics textbook is drawn up under what is usually referred to as the *ceteris paribus* assumption. That is, the demand curve sketches the relationship between price and demand that would hold if all other variables influencing demand were held constant. Just conceivably we might have been fortunate enough to have collected our data on P and Q at a time when all such variables did, in fact, remain unchanged. However, even if this were the case, we might eventually begin to wonder, that if this were the best method of estimating the demand curve for the commodity, how we would have proceeded if we had wished to estimate its supply curve instead. The supply curve, after all, also sketches out a relationship between P and Q given the *ceteris paribus* assumption.

At this stage we would probably pause and do some serious rethinking. Suppose, on reflection, we decided that the market we were observing could be described by the following two-equation model

$$Q = a_0 + a_1 P + a_2 P^s + a_3 Y + u \qquad \text{demand equation} \quad [4.1]$$

$$Q = b_0 + b_1 P + b_2 P^s + v \qquad \text{supply equation} \quad [4.2]$$

where the a's and the b's are unknown parameters, Y is the income of purchasers of the commodity, P^s is the price of a close substitute and u and v are disturbances.

Equations [4.1] and [4.2] represent the *structural equations* of the model, P and Q are the *endogenous* variables, while P^s and Y are assumed to be *exogenous* variables. Notice that for simplicity we assume that the market always clears, i.e. that quantity demanded is always equal to quantity supplied, both being represented by the symbol Q.

Suppose, for the sake of argument, that during the time we observed Q and P the exogenous variables P^s and Y actually did remain constant. The structural equations could then be written as

$$Q = a_0' + a_1 P + u \qquad \text{demand equation} \quad [4.1A]$$

$$Q = b_0' + b_1 P + v \qquad \text{supply equation} \quad [4.2A]$$

where $a_0' = a_2 P^s + a_3 Y$ and $b_0' = b_0 + b_2 P^s$ are constants.

Suppose, further, that the disturbances u and v were always identically zero. All we could ever observe under these conditions would be a single pair of values for P and Q, those at the intersection point of the curves $Q = a_0' + a_1 P$ and $Q = b_0' + b_1 P$. No 'scatter' of points would be generated since throughout our time series we would continue to observe this single point. Even if the disturbances u and v were non-zero and varied from period to period, during each such period we would still be observing merely the intersection point of two curves. Any scatter of points obtained over different periods would merely be a series of such intersection points generated by the continually shifting demand and supply curves. This is illustrated in Fig. 4.1 where D_1 and S_1 are the demand and supply curves, respectively, for period 1 and D_2 and S_2 are those for period 2, and so on.

If we attempted to fit a line to such a scatter of points, by OLS or any other means, we would obviously be estimating neither demand curve nor supply curve but rather what is sometimes called a 'mongrel' equation containing elements of both. This is the simplest case of the so-called *identification problem*. Identification of either curve can only be achieved provided it remains stationary over time while the other curve shifts. For example, in Fig. 4.2 the supply curve S remains stationary while the demand curve shifts and the intersection points obtained

4.1 Shifting demand and supply curves.

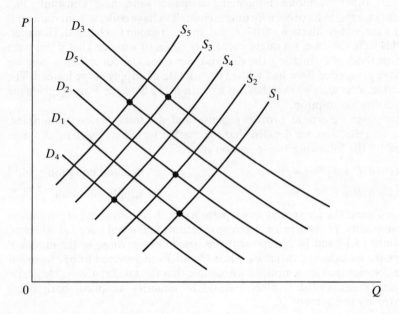

4.2 Shifting demand and stationary supply curve.

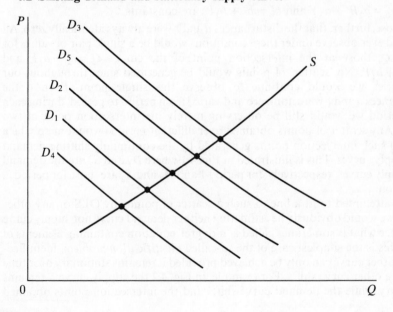

trace out the supply curve. Such shifts in the demand curve might occur for two possible reasons. Firstly, the demand disturbance, u, might vary sharply from period to period while the supply disturbance, v, remained very close to zero. Secondly, if the income variable in the demand equation [4.1] were to fluctuate sharply instead of remaining constant as so far assumed, this would also cause the demand curve to shift while leaving the supply curve unaffected. Notice, however, that fluctuations in the variable P^s, which appears in both equations [4.1] and [4.2], would not be an aid to identification since this would cause shifts in both curves.

Suppose we now move a little closer to reality. Assume that only income of the two exogenous variables in [4.1] and [4.2] remains constant over time and that P^s, the price of the close substitute, varies as do P and Q. We now have

$$Q = a_0'' + a_1 P + a_2 P^s + u \qquad\qquad \text{demand equation} \quad [4.1B]$$

$$Q = b_0 + b_1 P + b_2 P^s + v \qquad\qquad \text{supply equation} \quad [4.2B]$$

where $a_0'' = a_0 + a_3 Y$.

If we attempted to use multiple regression techniques to estimate [4.1B] or [4.2B] we would again face an identification problem since we cannot distinguish statistically between one equation and the other. Again, we would obtain a 'mongrel' equation containing elements of both [4.1B] and [4.2B]. In the multivariate case it is easier to illustrate this algebraically. Suppose λ and μ are *any* two constants. Then multiplying [4.1B] by λ and [4.2B] by μ and adding we have, eventually

$$Q = \frac{\lambda a_0'' + \mu b_0}{\lambda + \mu} + \left[\frac{\lambda a_1 + \mu b_1}{\lambda + \mu} \right] P + \left[\frac{\lambda a_2 + \mu b_2}{\lambda + \mu} \right] P^s + \frac{\lambda u + \mu v}{\lambda + \mu} \qquad [4.3]$$

If equations [4.1B] and [4.2B] are valid, then equation [4.3] must be equally valid. Moreover, [4.3] is statistically of identical form to [4.1B] and [4.2B]. Also, since λ and μ may take any values we like, the model under the present assumptions generates an infinite number of such equations all of identical statistical form.[1] Clearly, if we attempt to estimate (using OLS or any other method) an equation in which Q is a linear function of P and P^s, we can have no idea which of this infinite number of equations we have estimated. This is the identification problem expressed in algebraic form.

We are now in a position to define more precisely the term 'identified equation'.

An equation is identified provided it is not possible to derive, by taking linear combinations of equations in the model, another equation of exactly the same form as the equation being considered.

Clearly in the present case neither supply nor demand equation is identified since, by taking a linear combination of [4.1B] and [4.2B], we obtained [4.3].

At this point it should be stressed that if an equation is unidentified then there is *no manner in which unbiased or even consistent estimators of its parameters may be obtained.* For example, even if we believed we had found an estimation method that somehow yielded 'unbiased' estimators, the question then arises – unbiased estimators of what? In the present example, do we have unbiased estimators for the demand equation, the supply equation or some version of equation [4.3]? We can have no idea which equation we are, in fact, estimating.

Let us now return to the original version of the model given by equations [4.1] and [4.2] in which both exogenous variables P^s and Y vary over time. If we take a linear combination of [4.1] and [4.2] in the same manner as we derived [4.3], the 'mongrel' equation now becomes

$$Q = \frac{\lambda a_0 + \mu b_0}{\lambda + \mu} + \left[\frac{\lambda a_1 + \mu b_1}{\lambda + \mu}\right]P + \left[\frac{\lambda a_2 + \mu b_2}{\lambda + \mu}\right]P^s + \left[\frac{\lambda a_3}{\lambda + \mu}\right]Y + \frac{\lambda u + \mu v}{\lambda + \mu}$$

[4.4]

There is clearly no way in which [4.4] can be confused with [4.2]. It contains the variable Y, whereas the supply equation does not. Thus, the supply equation is now identified since it is not possible to obtain an equation of similar form by taking linear combinations of equations [4.1] and [4.2]. However, the demand equation remains unidentified since it can obviously be confused with [4.4].

Observe that the supply equation becomes identified because of the appearance of the income variable Y *in the demand equation* – but not in the supply equation. However, it is instructive to regard this as a restriction on the form of the supply equation which we can regard as having the most general form

$$Q = b_0 + b_1 P + b_2 P^s + b_3 Y + v$$

Notice for future reference that the fact that Y does not appear in the supply equation can now be regarded as the imposition of the restriction $b_3 = 0$ on the form of this equation.

It must be stressed that, despite the fact that under the present assumptions the supply equation is identified, *the OLS method of estimation will still yield biased and inconsistent estimators of its parameters*. This can be best understood by considering the *reduced form* of equations [4.1] and [4.2]. Expressing the endogenous variables as functions of the exogenous variables and the disturbances we obtain the reduced form equations[2]

$$Q = \frac{a_0 b_1 - a_1 b_0}{b_1 - a_1} + \left[\frac{a_2 b_1 - a_1 b_2}{b_1 - a_1}\right]P^s + \left[\frac{a_3 b_1}{b_1 - a_1}\right]Y + \frac{b_1 u - a_1 v}{b_1 - a_1}$$ [4.5]

$$P = \frac{a_0 - b_0}{b_1 - a_1} + \left[\frac{a_2 - b_2}{b_1 - a_1}\right]P^s + \left[\frac{a_3}{b_1 - a_1}\right]Y + \frac{u - v}{b_1 - a_1}$$ [4.6]

From equation [4.6] it can be seen that the endogenous variable, P, is influenced by both disturbances u and v. However, it is the contemporaneous correlation between P and the disturbance v that is crucial because P is an endogenous variable on the right-hand side of the supply equation. The fact that it is correlated with the disturbance in that equation means, as we saw in Section 3.1, that OLS will yield biased and inconsistent estimators of the supply equation parameters. This is the problem of *simultaneous equation bias*. It arises because of the simultaneous nature of equations [4.1] and [4.2]. Both these equations involve relationships between the endogenous variables Q and P and, given the values of the exogenous variables P^s and Y, they jointly determine the values of Q and P. The structural equations of simultaneous systems typically include endogenous variables on their right-hand sides and, as in the present case, these variables will typically be correlated with the corresponding disturbances. We stress again that this is a separate problem from that of identification. Even if an equation is identified, its estimation may, and probably will, involve the problem of simultaneous equation bias.

Moving from reduced form to structural form

The reduced-form equations [4.5] and [4.6] enable us to illustrate another aspect of the identification problem. These equations may be written as

$$Q = A_0 + A_1 P^s + A_2 Y + U \qquad \text{[4.5A]}$$

$$P = B_0 + B_1 P^s + B_2 Y + V \qquad \text{[4.6A]}$$

where

$$A_0 = \frac{a_0 b_1 - a_1 b_0}{b_1 - a_1}, \quad A_1 = \frac{a_2 b_1 - a_1 b_2}{b_1 - a_1}, \quad A_2 = \frac{a_3 b_1}{b_1 - a_1}$$

$$B_0 = \frac{a_0 - b_0}{b_1 - a_1}, \quad B_1 = \frac{a_2 - b_2}{b_1 - a_1}, \quad B_2 = \frac{a_3}{b_1 - a_1} \qquad \text{[4.7]}$$

$$U = \frac{b_1 u - a_1 v}{b_1 - a_1}, \quad V = \frac{u - v}{b_1 - a_1}$$

The A's and the B's are known as the *reduced-form parameters* and U and V as reduced-form disturbances. Suppose the reduced-form parameters were known.[3] The interesting question now arises of whether, given such knowledge of the reduced-form parameters, it is possible to derive values for the structural parameters, i.e. the a's and the b's. In other words, can the system of equations [4.7] be solved for the structural parameters. This question is more easily tackled if we rearrange the system [4.7] into the two subsystems

$$\begin{array}{ll} A_0 - a_1 B_0 = a_0 & A_0 - b_1 B_0 = b_0 \\ A_1 - a_1 B_1 = a_2 \qquad \text{[4.8]} & A_1 - b_1 B_1 = b_2 \qquad \text{[4.9]} \\ A_2 - a_1 B_2 = a_3 & A_2 - b_1 B_2 = 0 \end{array}$$

The splitting of a system of equations such as [4.7] into two subsystems like [4.8] and [4.9] requires a knack which is not easily acquired. Indeed, such a split is not always possible. The reader is not expected to acquire this knack but merely to observe that solving the subsystems [4.8] and [4.9] will yield identical expressions for the a's and the b's to those obtained by solving the combined system [4.7]. The advantage of the split is that subsystem [4.8] involves the demand equation parameters (i.e. the a's) only, while subsystem [4.9] involves the supply equation parameters (i.e. the b's) only.

Consider subsystem [4.9] first. Since the A's and B's are known, this consists of three linear equations in the three unknowns b_0, b_1 and b_2. It may therefore be uniquely solved for these unknowns, the solution, in fact, being

$$b_1 = A_2/B_2, \quad b_2 = A_1 - [A_2/B_2] B_1 \quad \text{and} \quad b_0 = A_0 - [A_2/B_2] B_0 \qquad \text{[4.10]}$$

Thus, given knowledge of the reduced-form parameters, it *is* possible to derive the parameters of the identified supply equation.

Now consider subsystem [4.8]. This consists of *three* linear equations in the *four* unknowns a_0, a_1, a_2 and a_3 and hence will have more than one solution.[4] In fact, if α is any number, then *any* set of values for the a's of the following form will satisfy subsystem [4.8]

$$a_1 = \alpha, \quad a_2 = A_1 - \alpha B_1, \quad a_3 = A_2 - \alpha B_2 \quad \text{and} \quad a_0 = A_0 - \alpha B_0$$

Thus, even given knowledge of the reduced-form parameters, it is *not* possible to derive unique values for the parameters of the unidentified demand equation. In fact, any demand equation of the form

$$Q = (A_0 - \alpha B_0) + \alpha P + (A_1 - \alpha B_1)P^s + (A_2 - \alpha B_2)Y + u$$

when combined with the unique supply equation [4.2], (with the b's given by [4.10]), will have a reduced form identical to [4.5A] and [4.6A].

It will probably we helpful if at this point we introduce some numbers into the above equations. Suppose that the reduced-form parameters in [4.5A] and [4.6A] were known to have the following values

$A_0 = 0.3$	$A_1 = 0.2$	$A_2 = 0.1$
$B_0 = 0.2$	$B_1 = 0.1$	$B_2 = 0.3$

We could then derive unique values for the supply equation parameters using [4.10]. That is, $b_1 = 0.333$, $b_2 = 0.167$ and $b_0 = 0.233$. The supply equation implied by the above reduced-form parameters is therefore

$$Q = 0.233 + 0.333P + 0.167P^s + v \qquad [4.11]$$

Subsystem [4.8], however, becomes

$$0.3 - 0.2a_1 = a_0,$$
$$0.2 - 0.1a_1 = a_2$$
$$0.1 - 0.3a_1 = a_3$$

There are an infinite number of sets of values for the a's which will satisfy this subsystem. We can assign any value α to a_1 and then use the equations to obtain a_0, a_2 and a_3. The resultant set of a's will represent a solution. For example, if we let $a_1 = -0.2$ then $a_0 = 0.34$, $a_2 = 0.22$, and $a_3 = 0.16$. It is easily verified that these values satisfy the subsystem. The demand equation implied is

$$Q = 0.34 - 0.2P + 0.22P^s + 0.16Y + u$$

However, we can also set a_1 equal to, for example, -0.4. This would yield a solution $a_1 = -0.4$, $a_0 = 0.38$, $a_2 = 0.24$, $a_3 = 0.22$, and a demand equation

$$Q = 0.38 - 0.4P + 0.24P^s + 0.22Y + u$$

The reader should verify that either of these demand equations when combined with the supply equation [4.11] will yield reduced-form equations with values for the A's and B's as above. Similarly, by selecting different values for α we can generate an infinite number of such demand equations, all of which when combined with supply equation [4.11] yield this same reduced form. Hence, while such a reduced form implies an unique supply equation, it is consistent with an infinite number of possible demand equations.

It is no accident that, whereas we were able to obtain unique values for the parameters of the supply equation, which we know under the present assumptions to be identified, we were unable to do so for the unidentified demand equation. In general, while it is possible to move from the reduced-form parameters to the structural parameters of an identified equation, *it is impossible to do so when an equation is unidentified.*

To re-enforce this point, suppose the income variable, Y, had not been present in the demand equation. That is, $a_3 = 0$ and demand equation [4.1] reduces to

[4.1B]. We already know that under these assumptions not only the demand equation but also the supply equation is unidentified. In terms of the reduced-form equations, [4.5A] and [4.6A], the absence of the Y variable implies $A_2 = B_2 = 0$. The two subsystems [4.8] and [4.9] now reduce to

$$\begin{aligned} A_0 - a_1 B_0 &= a_0 \\ A_1 - a_1 B_1 &= a_2 \end{aligned} \quad \text{and} \quad \begin{aligned} A_0 - b_1 B_0 &= b_0 \\ A_1 - b_1 B_1 &= b_2 \end{aligned}$$

Both the subsystems now consist of *two* linear equations in *three* unknowns. Hence, we can solve neither for the a's nor the b's. This reflects the fact that when $a_3 = 0$ neither demand equation nor supply equation is identified.

Identification by the use of linear restrictions

Consider again the more general case where the demand and supply equations are given by [4.1] and [4.2] respectively. We have already seen that the supply equation may be regarded as being identified by the placing of a restriction on the values of its parameters. Specifically, this restriction was the simple one that $b_3 = 0$ in the equation

$$Q = b_0 + b_1 P + b_2 P^s + b_3 Y + v$$

Identification can sometimes be achieved by specifying more complicated linear restrictions on the values of structural parameters. For example, suppose all the variables in the present model had been defined in logarithmic form so that all the structural parameters could be interpreted as elasticities. Consumer theory suggests that in the demand equation the sum of such elasticities should be zero,[5] i.e. $a_1 + a_2 + a_3 = 0$. The true form of [4.1] then becomes

$$Q = a_0 + a_1 P + a_2 P^s - (a_1 + a_2)Y + u \qquad [4.1C]$$

The 'mongrel' equation that can be formed by taking linear combinations of [4.1C] and [4.2] is

$$Q = \frac{\lambda a_0 + \mu b_0}{\lambda + \mu} + \left[\frac{\lambda a_1 + \mu b_1}{\lambda + \mu}\right]P + \left[\frac{\lambda a_2 + \mu b_2}{\lambda + \mu}\right]P^s - \left[\frac{\lambda a_1 + \lambda a_2}{\lambda + \mu}\right]Y + \frac{\lambda u + \mu v}{\lambda + \mu}$$

This equation is no longer of the same form as the demand equation since it will not generally have the property that the sum of the coefficients on the variables P, P^s and Y equals zero. This property only holds when $\lambda = 1$ and $\mu = 0$, in which case the mongrel equation reduces to the demand equation. Thus the imposition of the linear restriction $a_1 + a_2 + a_3 = 0$ on the parameters of the demand equation serves to identify it.

The imposition of the above linear restriction also makes it possible to derive unique values for the structural parameters of the demand equation once the reduced-form parameters are known. Previously, this was not possible because we were unable to obtain a unique solution to subsystem [4.8]. However, we may now add the restriction $a_1 + a_2 + a_3 = 0$ to [4.8], making a new subsystem containing in all four equations in the four unknowns a_0, a_1, a_2, a_3. These may now be uniquely solved for the demand equation parameters. For example, in our previous numerical example the expanded subsystem [4.8] becomes

$$0.3 - 0.2a_1 = a_0$$
$$0.2 - 0.1a_1 = a_2$$
$$0.1 - 0.3a_1 = a_3$$
$$a_1 + a_2 + a_3 = 0$$

which now has the unique solution $a_0 = 0.4$, $a_1 = -0.5$, $a_2 = 0.25$, and $a_3 = 0.25$, implying the demand equation

$$Q = 0.4 - 0.5P + 0.25P^s + 0.25Y + u$$

We shall encounter the problems of identification and simultaneous equation bias many times in this book. They are not merely something to do with demand and supply curves! They will arise whenever we have a system of simultaneous economic relationships. For example, in Chapter 7 the simplest consumption function model we consider is the two-equation system

$$C = \alpha + \beta Y + w$$
$$Y = C + Z$$
[4.12]

where C, Y and Z are consumption, income and non-consumption expenditure respectively. C and Y are endogenous to the system and Z is exogenous. The first equation is a simple Keynesian consumption function containing a disturbance w, and the second is an equilibrium condition. The second equation does not require estimating because we know that the coefficients on the C and Z variables are both unity. We therefore consider the problem of estimating the first equation. The absence of Z from the consumption function clearly identifies it. Any mongrel equation formed from the two equations must obviously contain Z. We need therefore only be concerned with the problem of simultaneous equation bias. The reduced-form of the model is

$$C = \frac{\alpha}{1 - \beta} + \left[\frac{\beta}{1 - \beta}\right]Z + \frac{w}{1 - \beta}$$

$$Y = \frac{\alpha}{1 - \beta} + \left[\frac{1}{1 - \beta}\right]Z + \frac{w}{1 - \beta}$$

We see from the second reduced-form equation that Y is correlated with w, i.e. the explanatory variable in the consumption function is correlated with the disturbance in that equation. Hence, OLS will yield *biased and inconsistent* estimators of the consumption function parameters *despite the fact that they are identified*. Some other method of estimation is therefore necessary. The direction of the OLS bias can easily be determined. The parameter β represents the MPC and hence may be expected to lie between zero and unity. We can therefore see from the reduced form that Y will be positively correlated with w. This means we will have a situation similar to that illustrated in Fig. 3.1 (p. 43) with the OLS estimators overestimating the MPC, β, and underestimating the intercept in the consumption function, α.

We shall come across simultaneous equation systems in all the applied chapters of this book. For example, in Section 8.3 we shall see that production functions have to be viewed as but one equation in at least a three-equation system. These other relationships, normally involving the equating of marginal products to factor prices, have to be allowed for in the estimation of the production function. Similarly, in Section 10.2, when estimating demand for money equations, we shall see that account must be taken of the possible existence of supply of money equations.

The general case

Economic models frequently consist of considerably more than the two relationships of the simple models we have so far been considering. When there are many equations in a model, deciding whether a particular equation is identified or not obviously becomes a more complicated affair. Fortunately 'general' conditions have been derived for such cases. The most frequently used of these is the so-called *order-condition for identification* which we state but do not derive:

A necessary (but not sufficient) condition for an equation in a model to be identified is that the total number of restrictions on its (structural) parameters should be at least as great as the number of equations in the model less one. That is we must have $R \geqslant G - 1$ where R is the number of restrictions and G is the number of equations in the model.

This condition is 'necessary but not sufficient' because, although it must hold if an equation is to be identified, the mere fact that it does hold is not sufficient to guarantee identification. The restrictions referred to may be either of the more general kind of the last subsection, or the simple 'excluded variable' type used to identify the supply equation in our example.

A sufficient condition for identification known as the *rank-condition* also exists. However, it would be difficult to state or prove this condition given the level of mathematics used in this book. Equations which satisfy the rank condition necessarily satisfy the order condition but the reverse is not true. Fortunately, this latter possibility is relatively rare and in most cases the order condition alone may be used to determine the identification status of an equation. For example, in our original two-equation demand-and-supply model given by equations [4.1] and [4.2], $G - 1$ is obviously equal to 1. The demand equation has no restrictions on its parameters so that R is zero and equation [4.1] is unidentified. The supply equation, however, has one restriction – the absence of Y, so that $R = 1$ for this equation and hence it is identified.

At this point it should be noted that the general condition just introduced applies only to simultaneous systems that are linear in the endogenous variables. This was true of both the systems we have so far examined. However, many economic systems are non-linear in the endogenous variables. For example, suppose we replaced the system given by [4.1] and [4.2] by

$$Q = a_0 + a_1 P + a_2 P^s + a_3 Y + u \qquad \text{demand equation}$$
$$Q = b_0 + b_1 \sqrt{(P)} + b_2 P^s + v \qquad \text{supply equation}$$

The endogenous own-price variable, P, now appears non-linearly in the supply equation. Other less-contrived examples are not difficult to think of. For example, many models contain the money wage rate, w, and the general price level, p, as endogenous variables. If such a model also seeks to explain the real wage rate, w/p, then clearly the endogenous w/p is a non-linear function of the endogenous w and p. A similar problem would arise if a model contained as endogenous variables price, p, quantity sold, q, and total revenue $R = pq$.

The rules for linear systems cannot be applied to non-linear systems. For example, for the linear system given by equations [4.1] and [4.2], we have seen that the demand equation is unidentified. However, the replacement of [4.2] by the above non-linear supply curve does, in fact, serve to identify the demand equation. We shall not pursue the question of identification in non-linear systems here, but the interested reader is referred to Kelejian and Oates (1981: Ch. 8) for an understandable introduction.

Identification by the use of restrictions on the disturbances

The order condition for identification in linear systems just discussed applies only when the sole means of identification is via linear restrictions on structural parameters. However, identification may also sometimes be achieved by specifying restrictions on the disturbances in the model. We have, in fact, already come across one such example. In the first case we considered, where the demand and supply equations were given by [4.1A] and [4.2A] respectively, we saw that the supply equation would become identified if it were possible to specify that the demand disturbance, u, varied more widely than the supply disturbance, v. Specifically the restrictions

$$\operatorname{var} v = 0 \quad \text{and} \quad \operatorname{var} u > 0$$

would serve to identify the supply equation.

These restrictions would also have served to identify the supply equation in the second case considered, where the demand and supply equations were given by [4.1B] and [4.2B] respectively. In this case the mongrel equation [4.3] could not be distinguished from either the demand or supply equations. However, it contained a disturbance term which we may write as

$$\varepsilon = \left[\frac{\lambda}{\lambda + \mu}\right] u + \left[\frac{\mu}{\lambda + \mu}\right] v \qquad \text{[4.13]}$$

If the above restrictions on u and v hold then, whereas the supply equation now contains a disturbance with zero variance, the mongrel equation contains a disturbance with a non-zero variance given by

$$\operatorname{var} \varepsilon = \left[\frac{\lambda}{\lambda + \mu}\right]^2 \operatorname{var} u$$

The supply equation is therefore no longer of the same form as the mongrel equation and is hence identified. The demand equation, however, still contains a disturbance with non-zero variance and therefore remains unidentified.

Finally, identification may also be achieved if it is possible to specify restrictions on the relationships between disturbances in different equations. Suppose in the model represented by [4.1B] and [4.2B] we specify that $\operatorname{cov}(u, v) = 0$, i.e. that there is no contemporaneous correlation between demand disturbance, u, and supply disturbance, v. The demand equation [4.1B] now contains a disturbance, u, which is uncorrelated with v. However, the mongrel equation [4.3] contains a disturbance, given by [4.13], which is quite clearly correlated with v. It is therefore possible to distinguish between the demand equation and the mongrel equation and so the demand equation becomes identified.

Similarly, the supply equation [4.2B] now contains a disturbance, v, which is uncorrelated with u. It also becomes identified since it cannot now be confused with the mongrel equation which contains a disturbance which we see from [4.13] is correlated with u. Thus the restriction $\text{cov}(u,v) = 0$, if it could be imposed, would serve to identify both demand and supply equations.

4.2 The estimation of simultaneous relationships

In the previous section we have seen, firstly, that if any single equation in a set of simultaneous equations is unidentified then it is impossible to obtain unbiased or even consistent estimates of its parameters. Secondly, even if such an equation were identified, the OLS estimators of its parameters will normally be subject to simultaneous equation bias. In this section we shall be concerned mainly with the various methods that have been devised for combating this bias. However, we begin by considering one rather special type of simultaneous system in which the OLS method of estimation is not, in fact, subject to it.

Recursive systems

Consider the following three-equation system in its structural form

$$
\begin{aligned}
Y_1 &= a_0 + a_1 X_1 + a_2 X_2 + \varepsilon_1 \\
Y_2 &= b_0 + b_1 X_1 + b_2 X_2 + b_1' Y_1 + \varepsilon_2 \\
Y_3 &= c_0 + c_1 X_1 + c_2 X_2 + c_1' Y_1 + c_2' Y_2 + \varepsilon_3
\end{aligned}
\qquad [4.14]
$$

The Y variables are endogenous, the X variables are exogenous, $\varepsilon_1, \varepsilon_2$ and ε_3 are disturbances and the a's, b's and c's are structural parameters. Since the X variables are by definition determined outside the above model, we may assume that they are independent of the disturbances.

Considering only restrictions on the structural parameters and using the criteria developed in the previous section, the reader should be able to deduce that only the first of the equations in the above system is identified. Suppose, however, we add the restrictions that the three disturbances are contemporaneously uncorrelated with one another, i.e.

$$\text{cov}(\varepsilon_1, \varepsilon_2) = \text{cov}(\varepsilon_1, \varepsilon_3) = \text{cov}(\varepsilon_2, \varepsilon_3) = 0$$

Then, just as in the demand/supply model of the previous section, this serves to identify all the equations in the model.

In the first structural equation none of the explanatory variables are endogenous so that the problem of simultaneous equation bias does not arise. This equation is identified and the X variables are by assumption uncorrelated with ε_1. The OLS method of estimation may therefore be applied to the first structural equation to obtain unbiased and consistent estimators of its parameters. The problem of estimating the remaining two equations in the model is best illustrated by considering the reduced form, which in this case is particularly easy to derive.

The first reduced-form equation is identical to the first structural equation. The second reduced-form equation may be obtained by substituting the first reduced-form equation into the second structural equation. Finally, the third reduced-form equation may be obtained by substituting the first two reduced-form equations into the third structural equation. The reduced form obtained in this way has the following form

$$Y_1 = A_0 + A_1 X_1 + A_2 X_2 + \varepsilon_1$$
$$Y_2 = B_0 + B_1 X_1 + B_2 X_2 + b'_1 \varepsilon_1 + \varepsilon_2 \qquad\qquad [4.15]$$
$$Y_3 = C_0 + C_1 X_1 + C_2 X_2 + (c'_1 + b'_1 c'_2)\varepsilon_1 + c'_2 \varepsilon_2 + \varepsilon_3$$

where the A's, B's and C's are functions of the a's, b's and c's but the precise form of these functions need not concern us.

What is significant about the reduced-form equations [4.15] is what they tell us about the relationships between the endogenous variables in the model and the disturbances. Firstly, Y_1 is uninfluenced by either ε_2 or ε_3. In particular, Y_1 is independent of ε_2, the disturbance in the second equation, and is the only endogenous variable among the explanatory variables in that equation. This means that the OLS estimators of the parameters of this equation will not be subject to simultaneous equation bias. Secondly, Y_2 is uninfluenced by ε_3. Thus, both endogenous variables on the right-hand side of the third structural equation are independent of the disturbance in that equation. Hence, we may also apply OLS to the estimation of the third equation without worrying about the problem of bias.

The lack of dependence between the endogenous explanatory variables and the corresponding disturbances stems from the rather special shape of the structural form [4.14]. Notice that the first structural equation contains no endogenous explanatory variables, the second equation contains just the first endogenous variable on the right-hand side, while only the third equation contains both the first and second endogenous variables on the right-hand side. This structure, plus the assumption of contemporaneous non-correlation between the disturbances, means that the values of the endogenous variables are determined *recursively*. That is, firstly Y_1 is determined by the exogenous variables and ε_1. Secondly, once Y_1 is determined, the value of Y_2 is determined by Y_1, the exogenous variables and ε_2. Finally, and only after Y_1 and Y_2 are determined, Y_3 is determined by Y_1 and Y_2, the exogenous variables and ε_3. Thus the endogenous variables are determined recursively rather than simultaneously and, indeed, it could be argued that [4.14] is not a simultaneous system at all.

Summarising, the specification that the disturbances are uncorrelated across equations ensures that each equation in [4.14] is identified. The independence between right-hand side endogenous variables and the corresponding disturbances ensures the absence of simultaneous equation bias. Hence, since the X variables are independent of the disturbances by definition, the application of OLS to each equation of the model in turn will yield unbiased and consistent estimates of all the structural parameters.

When a model such as [4.14] is characterised, firstly by disturbances which are uncorrelated across equations, and secondly by the special structural form described above, it is known as a *recursive system*. These are the only types of simultaneous systems for which the OLS method of estimation will provide unbiased and consistent estimators.

In certain situations the X variables in a recursive model may not be all truly exogenous. Typically, some of them may be *lagged endogenous variables*. The expression '*predetermined variables*' is sometimes used to cover both exogenous and lagged endogenous variables. When any of the predetermined variables on the right-hand side of a structural equation in a recursive system are lagged endogenous, then OLS will yield consistent but not unbiased estimators. This follows from the discussion of stochastic explanatory variables in Section 3.1.

For examples of simple recursive systems, see Wold's (1958) reformulation of the Suits (1955) water-melon market model in Section 6.3 and models IIA and IIB in the subsection on simultaneity in Section 10.2.

Indirect least squares

When a model is non-recursive, the simplest method of estimating its structural parameters is (if applicable) the method known as *Indirect Least Squares* (ILS). Consider again the two-equation model represented by equations [4.1] and [4.2]. In the absence of any restrictions on the disturbances, the demand equation [4.1] is unidentified. However, the supply equation [4.2] is not and may be estimated by ILS. The method involves applying the OLS technique to the reduced-form equations of the model – in this case equations [4.5A] and [4.6A]. These equations contain, on the right-hand side, only exogenous variables which may be assumed to be independent of the reduced-form disturbances. Ordinary least squares may therefore be used to obtain unbiased and consistent estimates of the reduced-form parameters.[6] That is, we compute the sample regression equations

$$\hat{Q} = \hat{A}_0 + \hat{A}_1 P^s + \hat{A}_2 Y$$
$$\hat{P} = \hat{B}_0 + \hat{B}_1 P^s + \hat{B}_2 Y \qquad\qquad [4.16]$$

where the $\hat{A}$'s and $\hat{B}$'s are the OLS estimates of the A's and the B's.

We have already seen that, if the reduced-form parameters were known, then by solving subsystem [4.9] it is possible to derive the values of the structural parameters of the identified supply equation. These values are given by [4.10]. This suggests that we use the *estimated* reduced-form parameters to obtain *estimates* of the structural parameters of the supply equation. The form of the estimators is given by [4.10]. We have

$$b_1^* = \hat{A}_2/\hat{B}_2, \quad b_2^* = \hat{A}_1 - [\hat{A}_2/\hat{B}_2]\hat{B}_1 \quad \text{and} \quad b_0^* = \hat{A}_0 - [\hat{A}_2/\hat{B}_2]\hat{B}_0$$

The estimators b_0^*, b_1^* and b_2^* of the structural parameters b_0, b_1 and b_2 are known as the *ILS estimators*. Since the A's and B's are consistent estimators of the reduced-form parameters, the b^*'s are consistent estimators of the structural parameters of the supply equation. However, the b^*'s are not unbiased despite the fact that the A's and B's have this property. This is because, as we have seen in Section 2.3, while the property of consistency 'carries over' that of unbiasedness does not. Thus the ILS estimators have desirable *large sample* properties only.

Notice that the ILS method will not yield estimates of the structural parameters of the demand equation. This is obvious from the fact that the subsystem [4.8] does not have a unique solution, and reflects the unidentified status of the demand equation under the present assumptions.

As a further example of the ILS method of estimation, consider the simple consumption model [4.12]. The reduced form of this model, given below [4.12] can be written as

$$C = A_0 + A_1 Z + W \qquad [4.17]$$
$$Y = B_0 + B_1 Z + W$$

where

$$A_0 = B_0 = \frac{\alpha}{(1 - \beta)}, \quad A_1 = \frac{\beta}{(1 - \beta)}, \quad B_1 = \frac{1}{(1 - \beta)} \quad \text{and} \quad W = \frac{w}{(1 - \beta)}$$

To obtain ILS estimators of α and β in the consumption function we therefore apply OLS to the reduced-form equations [4.17] to obtain estimators, $\hat{A}$'s and $\hat{B}$'s, of the reduced-form parameters. The required ILS estimators are then given by

$$\beta^* = \hat{A}_1/\hat{B}_1 \quad \text{and} \quad \alpha^* = \hat{A}_0/\hat{B}_1 = \hat{B}_0/\hat{B}_1$$

Although the OLS estimators of the A's and B's above will be unbiased and consistent, the ILS estimators of α and β will again only retain the property of consistency.

It may seem that we obtain two separate estimators of α by the above procedure, $\hat{A}_0/\hat{B}_1$ and $\hat{B}_0/\hat{B}_1$. However, because the data used will satisfy the identity $Y = C + Z$, not only are A_0 and B_0 equal but so will be their OLS estimates, $\hat{A}_0$ and $\hat{B}_0$.[7] A model of this type is in fact estimated in the empirical exercise at the end of Chapter 7.

The method of ILS appears to be a fairly straightforward method of overcoming the problem of simultaneous equation bias when estimating identified equations. Unfortunately, in practice, the method frequently breaks down and for this reason we shall encounter relatively few examples of it in this book. Consider again the two-equation model given by [4.1] and [4.2] but suppose that a third exogenous variable, Z, appears in the demand equation. For example, Z might be an index of tastes. The model now becomes

$$Q = a_0 + a_1 P + a_2 P^s + a_3 Y + a_4 Z + u \qquad \text{demand equation} \quad [4.18]$$

$$Q = b_0 + b_1 P + b_2 P^s + v \qquad \text{supply equation} \quad [4.19]$$

The identification status of the equations appears to be unchanged but as we shall see it has now become impossible to estimate the supply equation by ILS. The reduced form now becomes

$$Q = A_0 + A_1 P^s + A_2 Y + A_3 Z + U$$
$$P = B_0 + B_1 P^s + B_2 Y + B_3 Z + V \qquad [4.20]$$

where

$$A_3 = \frac{a_4 b_1}{b_1 - a_1} \quad \text{and} \quad B_3 = \frac{a_4}{b_1 - a_1} \qquad [4.21]$$

The expressions for the remaining reduced-form parameters and the disturbances remain as in [4.7].

If the reduced-form parameters were known, then to derive the structural parameters we would now have to solve the subsystems

$$A_0 - a_1 B_0 = a_0$$
$$A_1 - a_1 B_1 = a_2$$
$$A_2 - a_1 B_2 = a_3 \qquad [4.22]$$
$$A_3 - a_1 B_3 = a_4$$

$$A_0 - b_1 B_0 = b_0$$
$$A_1 - b_1 B_1 = b_2$$
$$A_2 - b_1 B_2 = 0 \qquad [4.23]$$
$$A_3 - b_1 B_3 = 0$$

Subsystem [4.22] consists of four linear equations in the five unknown a's and hence has many solutions. This reflects the fact that the demand equation remains unidentified. Subsystem [4.23] now consists of four linear equations in three unknown b's. Apparently we have 'too many' equations and normally such a system would involve inconsistencies and have no solution. This appears to be the case here since the third and fourth equations yield seemingly contradictory values for b_1, i.e. $b_1 = A_2/B_2$ and $b_1 = A_3/B_3$. However, the two ratios A_2/B_2 and A_3/B_3 are, in fact, identical and both equal to b_1. This can be seen by considering [4.7] and [4.21]. Subsystem [4.23] therefore involves no inconsistencies and still yields the unique solution

$$b_1 = A_2/B_2, \quad b_2 = A_1 - [A_2/B_2]B_1 \quad \text{and} \quad b_0 = A_0 - [A_2/B_2]B_0 \qquad [4.24]$$

Alternatively we could replace A_2/B_2 by A_3/B_3 in tne above solution without affecting the value of the b's. Clearly, the supply equation remains identified. The difficulty in estimating its parameters arises *because we do not know the exact values of the reduced-form parameters but only have estimates of them.* Just because the 'true' ratios A_2/B_2 and A_3/B_3 are identical does not mean that the two estimated ratios $\hat{A}_2/\hat{B}_2$ and $\hat{A}_3/\hat{B}_3$ will be. Generally, the $\hat{A}$'s and $\hat{B}$'s will differ from the A's and B's so that we must expect the ratios $\hat{A}_2/\hat{B}_2$ and $\hat{A}_3/\hat{B}_3$ to differ.[8] This means that the ILS method of estimation yields, in this case, two estimates of the parameter b_1, namely, $\hat{A}_2/\hat{B}_2$ and $\hat{A}_3/\hat{B}_3$. Similarly, as can be seen from [4.24], it also yields two estimates for each of b_2 and b_0 – one involving the ratio $\hat{A}_2/\hat{B}_2$ and the other $\hat{A}_3/\hat{B}_3$. Since there is no obvious way in which we can choose between the two sets of estimates, the ILS method, in effect, breaks down.

When ILS breaks down in this manner the equation concerned and its parameters are said to be *overidentified* and an alternative method of estimation must be used. Overidentification can only occur when an equation is identified in the sense of Section 4.1 and hence only when the order condition stated there is satisfied. Recall that for a structural equation to be identified we must have $R \geqslant G - 1$, where R is the number of restrictions on its parameters and G is the total number of equations in the model. Overidentification can be detected by considering how this condition is satisfied. *Overidentification occurs whenever the order condition is satisfied as an inequality,* i.e. when $R > G - 1$ as it is for the supply equation [4.19]. When the order condition is satisfied as an equality, i.e. when $R = G - 1$, the equation concerned and its parameters are said to be *exactly identified* and the problems associated with overidentification do not arise.

Two-stage least squares

The method of estimation that has been most frequently used in overcoming the problems of overidentification is that of *two-stage least squares* (TSLS). We shall illustrate this method by describing how it would be used to estimate the supply equation in the two-equation model given by [4.18] and [4.19].

When estimating the supply equation [4.19], simultaneous equation bias arises because of the appearance of the endogenous variable, P, as an explanatory variable in this equation. The basic idea of TSLS is that we 'purge' such variables of their troublesome correlation with the disturbance in the equation concerned. The *first stage* of the TSLS procedure for estimating an overidentified equation is therefore as follows. We take all endogenous explanatory variables in the equation and use OLS to regress *each* in turn on *all* the predetermined variables in the model. In the present example this involves regressing P on the exogenous variables P^s, Y and Z. We then have, for each observation in the available sample

$$P_i = \hat{B}_0 + \hat{B}_1 P_i^s + \hat{B}_2 Y_i + \hat{B}_3 Z_i + E_i \qquad [4.25]$$

where the $\hat{B}$'s are estimated OLS regression coefficients and the E_i's are the residuals from the OLS regression performed.

Now since $P_i = \hat{P}_i + E_i$, where the $\hat{P}_i$'s are the predicted values of P obtained from [4.25], we can write the supply equation which we wish to estimate as

$$Q = b_0 + b_1 P + b_2 P^s + v$$
$$= b_0 + b_1 (\hat{P} + E) + b_2 P^s + v$$

or

$$Q = b_0 + b_1 \hat{P} + b_2 P^s + b_1 E + v \qquad [4.26]$$

Equation [4.26] differs from the original supply equation [4.19] in that it has $\hat{P}$ as an 'explanatory' variable rather than P and $b_1 E + v$ as a 'disturbance' rather than v. It is possible to show that both $\hat{P}$ and P^s, the right-hand side variables in [4.26], are for large samples uncorrelated with the 'disturbance' $b_1 E + v$. Hence, for large samples, the problem of simultaneous equation bias is circumvented and the OLS estimation procedure when applied to [4.26] will provide estimators with the usual desirable large sample properties. In particular, they will be consistent but not, of course, unbiased.

The *second stage* of the TSLS procedure is therefore to replace any endogenous variables on the right-hand side of the equation being estimated by their predicted values obtained from the OLS regressions performed in the first stage. This effectively purges them of their correlation with the disturbance in the equation. Ordinary least squares may then be applied to the reconstituted structural equation to obtain consistent estimates of its parameters.

There is no reason why the TSLS procedure should not be used to estimate the parameters of an exactly identified equation. However, if this were done it can be shown that the estimates obtained would be identical to those obtained by the ILS method described in the previous subsection. Since TSLS is a more cumbersome procedure than ILS, it is therefore not usually adopted to estimate exactly identified equations.

If an attempt were made to estimate the parameters of an unidentified equation by TSLS then, not surprisingly, the procedure breaks down. We can illustrate this by considering the unidentified demand equation of the two-equation model [4.18] and [4.19]. The TSLS procedure would involve replacing the endogenous variable P in equation [4.18] by values of $\hat{P}$ obtained from equation [4.25]. However, $\hat{P}$ is an exact linear function of the variables P^s, Y and Z which all appear in the demand equation [4.18]. Thus, the second stage of the TSLS procedure would involve attempting to regress by OLS the variable Q on a set of explanatory variables which are exactly multicollinear. As we know from Section 3.3, OLS breaks down in these circumstances.

Finally, notice that TSLS is a method which can be used to estimate a single equation in a system. This contrasts with certain 'complete system' methods of estimation in which all the equations in a model have to be estimated simultaneously.

The application of TSLS to a single equation in a system of simultaneous relationships does not require complete knowledge of the structure of every relationship in the system. The only knowledge required is the precise specification of the single equation being estimated and a list of all the exogenous variables which influence the system. For example, in estimating the supply equation in the above model, no reference was made to the specification of the demand equation but we did require the knowledge that the three exogenous variables influencing the system were Y, P^s and Z.

We conclude this subsection with a further example of TSLS in action. Suppose we wish to estimate the following 'wage price model'

$$W = a_0 + a_1 P + a_2 U + a_3 S + u \qquad [4.27]$$

$$P = b_0 + b_1 W + b_2 X + b_3 M + v \qquad [4.28]$$

In this two-equation model the rate of wage inflation, W, and the rate of price inflation, P, are endogenous. There are four exogenous variables: U, the level of unemployment; S an index of strike activity; X the rate of increase in labour productivity, and M the rate of increase in import prices. Both equations are overidentified (verify this) and if the reduced form is derived it will be seen that P in the wage equation is correlated with u, and W in the price equation is correlated with v. Ordinary least squares will therefore yield biased and inconsistent estimates of the parameters of both equations.

To obtain TSLS estimates of all the parameters in the model, the first stage is to take the right-hand side endogenous variables, P and W, and use OLS to regress each in turn on all four exogenous variables, U, S, X and M. Estimates of the wage equation parameters are then obtained by replacing P in that equation by the predicted values, $\hat{P}$, obtained from the first stage and applying OLS to the resultant equation. Similarly, the TSLS estimates of the price equation parameters are obtained by replacing W in that equation by the $\hat{W}$ values obtained in the first stage.

For an example of equations estimated by TSLS see those estimated by Zellner, Huang and Chau (1965) in Section 7.5 on the role of liquid assets in the consumption function. For a numerical example of the technique see the exercise at the end of Chapter 7.

4.3 Maximum likelihood estimation of overidentified equations

The method of maximum likelihood estimation described in Section 2.3 can also be used to estimate the parameters of overidentified structural equations. The method may be used either to estimate a single equation in a set of simultaneous relationships or to estimate all such relationships at the same time. When attention is concentrated on a single equation the method adopted is known as *limited information maximum likelihood* (LIML) and we consider this procedure first. We shall illustrate its use in estimating the overidentified supply equation of the simple market model given by equations [4.18] and [4.19]. Suppose we have a sample, size n, from which we wish to obtain our estimates, i.e. we have

$$\left. \begin{array}{l} Q_i = a_0 + a_1 P_i + a_2 P_i^s + a_3 Y_i + a_4 Z_i + u_i \\ Q_i = b_0 + b_1 P_i + b_2 P_i^s + v_i \end{array} \right\} \qquad i = 1, 2, 3, \ldots, n$$

From the reduced form of this model given by equations [4.20] we also have

$$\left. \begin{array}{l} Q_i = A_0 + A_1 P_i^s + A_2 Y_i + A_3 Z_i + U_i \\ P_i = B_0 + B_1 P_i^s + B_2 Y_i + B_3 Z_i + V_i \end{array} \right\} \qquad (i = 1, 2, 3, \ldots, n)$$

The values of the reduced-form disturbances are given by

$$U_i = \frac{b_1 u_i - a_1 v_i}{b_1 - a_1} \quad \text{and} \quad V_i = \frac{u_i - v_i}{b_1 - a_1} \left. \right\} \qquad (i = 1, 2, 3, \ldots, n)$$

They are linear combinations of the structural form disturbances, the u_i's and the v_i's. Hence, provided the u_i's and the v_i's are all normally distributed with zero means, they will themselves be normally distributed with zero means and constant variances which we shall label σ_U^2 and σ_V^2 respectively. σ_U^2 and σ_V^2 will be dependent on the constant variances of the u_i's and the v_i's. Hence, for given values of the exogenous variables, if repeated samples were taken, then each sequence of Q_i's obtained would be normally distributed with a mean

$$E(Q_i) = A_0 + A_1 P_i^s + A_2 Y_i + A_3 Z_i$$

and a variance of σ_U^2.[9] Similarly, each sequence of P_i's obtained would be distributed normally with a mean

$$E(P_i) = B_0 + B_1 P_i^s + B_2 Y_i + B_3 Z_i$$

and a variance of σ_V^2. Knowing their distributions enables a likelihood function for the Q_i's and P_i's, similar to [2.32] (p. 25), to be formed.[10] In this case, the sample likelihood depends on

1. The sample values of Q_i and P_i obtained, i.e. $Q_1, Q_2, \ldots, Q_n$ and $P_1, P_2, \ldots, P_n$.
2. The reduced-form parameters, since A_0, A_1, A_2 and A_3 determine $E(Q_i)$ and B_0, B_1, B_2 and B_3 determine $E(P_i)$.
3. The two variances σ_U^2 and σ_V^2.
4. The covariance ρ_{UV} between the U_i's and the V_i's. This quantity appears because the U_i's and the V_i's are both dependent on the u_i's and the v_i's and hence are not independent of one another. It follows that P_i and Q_i are not independent and that the sample likelihood also depends on ρ_{UV}.

Thus, again denoting the sample likelihood by L, we have in this case

$$L = L(Q_1, Q_2, \ldots, Q_n, P_1, P_2, \ldots, P_n, A_0, A_1, A_2, A_3, B_0, B_1, B_2, B_3, \sigma_U^2, \sigma_V^2, \rho_{UV})$$
$$[4.29]$$

We could now, for the given sample Q_i's and P_i's, maximise L as it stands to yield MLEs of the reduced-form parameters and also of σ_U^2, σ_V^2 and ρ_{UV}. The problem with this procedure is that since the supply equation is overidentified, we would not be able to obtain unique estimators of its parameters from the MLEs of the reduced-form parameters. The likelihood function L is therefore maximised *subject to the restriction that the estimators of the reduced-form parameters obtained are such that they do yield unique values for the structural parameters we wish to estimate.* In the present case this would involve maximising L subject to the constraint $A_2/B_2 = A_3/B_3$. This ensures that the subsystem [4.23], with the A's and B's replaced by their MLEs, will yield unique estimators of the b's, i.e. of the supply equation parameters. The estimators of the reduced-form parameters obtained in this way are known as *constrained* as opposed to *unconstrained* MLEs. These constrained estimators are consistent and hence, as the property of consistency 'carries over', the estimators of the supply equation parameters eventually obtained will also be consistent.

For an example of equations estimated by the LIML technique see the second and third equations of Suit's (1959) model of the US water-melon market described in Section 6.3.

As with the method of TSLS, the LIML method can be applied to a single equation. It requires knowledge only of the structure of that equation and a list of the exogenous variables in the model. Hence, the prefix 'limited information'. However, an estimation method which estimates all equations in a model simultaneously, and hence requires knowledge of the structure of every equation in the model, is that known as *full information maximum likelihood* (FIML). We shall illustrate this method by again considering our simple two-equation market model. However, we introduce an extra variable, C, which might be an index of production costs, into the supply equation. Thus, for a sample of size n we have

$$\left.\begin{array}{l} Q_i = a_0 + a_1 P_i + a_2 P_i^s + a_3 Y_i + a_4 Z_i + u_i \\ Q_i = b_0 + b_1 P_i + b_2 P_i^s + b_3 C_i + v_i \end{array}\right\} \quad (i = 1, 2, 3, \ldots, n)$$

The appearance of the variable C in the supply equation means that both equations are now identified – the demand equation exactly identified and the supply equation overidentified.

The FIML method estimates *all* structural parameters in the model directly without, as in the case of LIML, first estimating any reduced-form parameters. If the u_i and the v_i are normally and independently distributed with zero means and constant variances, σ_u^2 and σ_v^2 respectively, it is possible to obtain for given σ_u^2 and σ_v^2 the likelihood function for the u_i's and the v_i's. It is then possible to find, given the values of the exogenous variables, the likelihood function for the endogenous Q_i's and P_i's. This second step is somewhat complicated because, given values for the exogenous variables, the Q_i's and P_i's are jointly determined by the u_i's and v_i's. Thus, given values for the exogenous variables, the values of the Q_i's and P_i's will depend on all the structural parameters and on the values of the u_i's and v_i's. Hence, this second likelihood function when formed will depend on the values for the Q_i's and P_i's, on all the structural parameters and on the two variances σ_u^2 and σ_v^2. Thus we may write in this case

$$L = L(Q_1, Q_2, \ldots, Q_n, P_1, P_2, \ldots, P_n, a_0, a_1, a_2, a_3, a_4, b_0, b_1, b_2, b_3, \sigma_u^2, \sigma_v^2)$$

[4.30]

For given sample values of the Q_i's and P_i's, the likelihood function [4.30] may now be maximised to yield the so-called full information MLEs of the structural parameters. These estimators are consistent and asymptotically efficient but will be generally biased for small samples. For an example of a system estimated by FIML see the estimates of the parameters of the Klein model I macroeconomic model presented in Table 11.1, (p. 338).

4.4 The choice of estimation technique

In deciding which technique should be employed for the estimation of equations in a non-recursive simultaneous system the first consideration is the identification status of the relevant equations. If an equation is unidentified *none of the techniques outlined in the previous two sections will provide consistent estimates of its parameters.* However, even if all the structural equations in a model are unidentified, it is still possible to obtain consistent and sometimes unbiased estimates of the parameters of the reduced-form of the model. This may well be a valuable exercise if the purpose of the model is simply the prediction or forecasting of values of the endogenous variables for given values of the predetermined variables. Such forecasting is most simply performed using the reduced-form and knowledge of the structural parameters is not required. The testing of most of the propositions of economic theory, however, requires the estimation of structural parameters and *this will only be possible when the relevant equation is identified.* Remember that the techniques described in this chapter are for overcoming the problem of simultaneous equation bias not that of non-identification.

If an equation is exactly identified, then all the estimating procedures described previously, with the exception of OLS, can be shown to provide identical estimates of its parameters. Since OLS provides inconsistent estimates, this method may be ruled out and a choice made between the remaining methods. Since they all yield identical estimates, the method adopted is generally either ILS or TSLS, since these methods are both the simplest and the cheapest in terms of computing time. When an equation is overidentified the ILS procedure breaks down and the remaining procedures no longer provide identical estimates of its structural parameters. The problem of choosing between the various estimators in this case will be discussed below.

The case of exact identification is rare in practice. Most applied econometricians assume that the equations they are trying to estimate are overidentified. However, one must beware that the apparent identified status of an equation is not spurious and simply the result of the convenient but unjustified exclusion of certain variables from the equation. An extreme view is, for example, taken by Liu (1960) who argues that, in the real world, relationships typically include many more variables than are normally included in estimated equations. Hence, underidentification is the normal state of affairs and under such conditions the only sensible procedure would be the estimation of reduced-form equations with many predetermined variables.

When an equation is overidentified, provided the available sample is a 'large' one, choice between estimation methods can fairly safely be made by balancing computing time and cost against the asymptotic efficiency of the various consistent estimators available. It is a general rule that the more relevant information used in an estimation procedure, the smaller the asymptotic variances of the estimators obtained, i.e. the more asymptotically efficient are these estimators. Thus, TSLS and LIML, which make use of the same information about the economic model concerned, provided estimators with the same asymptotic variance. Since both provide consistent estimators they are asymptotically equally efficient. However, TSLS involves less computing time and therefore has generally been preferred to LIML.

Complete system estimation methods such as FIML and a method we have not discussed – three-stage least squares, make use of more information concerning the complete system and hence are asymptotically more efficient than TSLS and LIML. Three-stage least squares, however, requires considerably more computational effort than TSLS and the maximisation of the likelihood function in FIML involves the solution of a system of non-linear equations in the estimators required. This could not be attempted without a complicated computer package.

It must also be remembered that the above ranking of the various estimators by their asymptotic properties depends very much on the economic model under consideration being correctly specified. That is, the relevant equations must contain the correct variables and be of the right functional form while the disturbances must have all the properties they are assumed to have. Complete system estimation methods – i.e. FIML and three-stage least squares, since they involve making assumptions about all equations in the model, are the most sensitive to various specification errors. This is another justification for the popularity of TSLS.

In many situations, unfortunately, we will not have available the 'large' samples assumed in the preceding two paragraphs. When only 'small' samples are available the above ranking in terms of asymptotic properties is of little use. For example, all the estimators discussed are biased for small samples. Unfortunately, little is known about the small-sample properties of estimators usually adopted for simultaneous systems. However, such evidence that exists suggests that the large-sample superiority of the consistent estimators persists even for small samples. In the absence of specification errors complete system methods still appear best, although it is these methods that again seem most sensitive to such errors.

 ## Further reading

For an understandable treatment, at a relatively simple mathematical level, of the order and rank conditions for identification, see Stewart and Wallis (1981). A rigorous matrix development of these conditions is contained in Johnston (1984). Kelejian and Oates (1981) consider the identification problem in non-linear simultaneous equation systems. The first section of Chapter 11 in Johnston (1984) is a good non-matrix introducion to the estimation of simultaneous systems. Two-stage least squares is thoroughly treated in Kelejian and Oates (1981). Non-matrix treatments of the limited and full information maximum likelihood methods of estimation are rare but standard matrix treatments of these methods plus that of three-stage least squares can be found in Kmenta (1971), with examples, and in Johnston.

 ## Notes

1. That is, all such equations can be written in the form $Q = \text{constant} + \text{constant}(P) + \text{constant}(P^s) + \text{disturbance}$. The disturbance in [4.3] is the quantity $(\lambda u + \mu v)/(\lambda + \mu)$, which is a linear combination of u and v.

2. These are most easily derived by equating the right-hand sides of [4.1] and [4.2] and solving for P to yield [4.6]. Substitution for P in either [4.1] or [4.2] then yields [4.5].

3. The reduced-form parameters are not, of course, normally known but as we shall see in the next section it is generally possible to obtain consistent and often unbiased estimates of them.

4. It is assumed that the reader is familiar with the fact that a system of linear equations will normally have one and only one solution when the number of equations equals the number of unknowns. If the number of equations exceeds the number of unknowns then normally there will be no solution, while if the number of unknowns exceeds the number of equations there will be an infinite number of solutions. See, for example, Hadley (1965: Ch. 5).

5. This is equivalent to saying that an equiproportionate change in money income and all prices leaves demand unchanged.

6. If the predetermined variables in a model include any lagged endogenous variables, then these will appear among the explanatory variables in the reduced form. The OLS estimators of reduced-form parameters will then still be consistent but no longer unbiased. This follows from the discussion in Section 3.1.

7. To see this, apply the two-variables OLS formulae to show that $\hat{B}_1 - \hat{A}_1 = 1$. This means that $\bar{Y} = \bar{C} + (\hat{B}_1 - \hat{A}_1)\bar{Z}$. Now use the OLS formulae to show that $\hat{A}_0 = \hat{B}_0$.

8. Unlike in the previous consumption function example, there are no identities in the data to ensure they will be the same.

9. For example, if we treat the exogenous variables as non-stochastic, we have $Q_i = \text{const} + U_i$ so that $\text{var } Q_i = \sigma_U^2$.

10. As before, the reader may find it helps understanding to paraphrase the term 'likelihood function' by, for example, 'expression for the joint probability of obtaining a given set of P_i's and Q_i's'.

5 Some further useful techniques

5.1 Distributed lag models

It is often the case in economics that the current value of a dependent variable, Y, depends not only on the current value of some explanatory variable, X, but also on past or 'lagged' values of that variable. For example, in a simple consumption function, consumption may depend not only on current income but, for reasons of habit or inertia, also on past levels of income. We may therefore often need to write

$$Y_t = \alpha + \beta_0 X_t + \beta_1 X_{t-1} + \beta_2 X_{t-2}, \ldots + \beta_m X_{t-m} + \varepsilon_t \qquad [5.1]$$

Equation [5.1] is known as a *distributed lag formulation* because the effect of the X-variable is distributed over a number of periods.

Assuming non-stochastic X and that ε obeys all the usual assumptions, OLS will yield BLUE and consistent estimators of the parameters of equation [5.1]. Unfortunately, if the maximum lag length m (and hence the number of parameters to be estimated) is large relative to the sample size we run into the 'degrees of freedom problems' mentioned in Section 3.3. Even if the sample size is relatively large, we may still experience difficulties in obtaining precise well-determined estimates of the β_j's because the various 'lagged' values of X are likely to be multicollinear. This could be particularly serious if we hoped to determine the length of the lag, i.e. the value of m, by examining the statistical significance of the coefficients on the lagged variables.

Because of these difficulties it is rare for a distributed lag model to be estimated in as general a form as [5.1]. Rather, some *a priori* restriction is frequently placed on the form of the β_j's so as to reduce the number of independent parameters that have to be estimated.

Geometric lag distributions

One of the simplest restrictions that can be placed on the β_j's is that they should decline in a geometric progression

$$Y_t = \alpha + \beta_0(X_t + \theta X_{t-1} + \theta^2 X_{t-2}, \ldots,) + \varepsilon_t \quad 1 < \theta < 0 \qquad [5.2]$$

In this case the influence of X extends indefinitely into the past but successive lagged values of X have a declining effect on Y since θ lies between 0 and 1. The estimation of [5.2] can now be simplified by applying the *Koyck transformation*. Multiplying [5.2] by θ and lagging by one period yields

$$\theta Y_{t-1} = \theta\alpha + \beta_0(\theta X_{t-1} + \theta^2 X_{t-2} + \theta^3 X_{t-3}, \ldots,) + \theta\varepsilon_{t-1} \qquad [5.3]$$

Subtracting [5.3] from [5.2] then yields

$$Y_t - \theta Y_{t-1} = \alpha - \theta\alpha + \beta_0 X_t + \varepsilon_t - \theta\varepsilon_{t-1}$$

or

$$Y_t = \alpha(1-\theta) + \beta_0 X_t + \theta Y_{t-1} + v_t \quad \text{where} \quad v_t = \varepsilon_t - \theta\varepsilon_{t-1} \qquad [5.4]$$

Compared with [5.1], there are only three parameters to be estimated in [5.4] and the number of explanatory variables has been reduced to two thus alleviating any multicollinearity problem. Hence if, for example, we estimate an equation

$$\hat{Y}_t = 64 + 0.3 X_t + 0.6 Y_{t-1} \qquad [5.5]$$

we would estimate $\hat{\beta}_0 = 0.3$, $\hat{\theta} = 0.6$ and $\hat{\alpha} = 64/(1-\hat{\theta}) = 160$. Estimates of the coefficients in the original equation [5.2] can then by obtained using $\hat{\beta}_0$ and $\hat{\theta}$. That is

$$\hat{Y}_t = 160 + 0.3 X_t + 0.18 X_{t-1} + 0.108 X_{t-2}, \ldots \qquad [5.6]$$

There is, however, one major problem in estimating equation [5.4]. It is that the disturbance term

$$v_t = \varepsilon_t - \theta\varepsilon_{t-1}$$

is very likely to be autocorrelated. Since

$$v_{t-1} = \varepsilon_{t-1} - \theta\varepsilon_{t-2}$$

we can see that both v_t and v_{t-1} have a term in common, i.e. ε_{t-1}, and hence will not normally be independent. In fact, only when ε_t in equation [5.2] follows a first-order autoregressive scheme with parameter $\rho = \theta$, will v_t in equation [5.4] be non-autocorrelated. Then we have (see Section 3.2)

$$\varepsilon_t = \theta\varepsilon_{t-1} + u_t$$

so that $v_t = u_t$ which is non-autocorrelated by assumption. Since there is no obvious reason why the values of θ and ρ should coincide we can normally rule this case out and expect v_t to be autocorrelated. Unfortunately, we know from Section 3.2 that the combination of autocorrelated disturbance term and lagged dependent variable results in a case of contemporaneous correlation between disturbance and lagged variable. Hence, application of OLS to equation [5.4] will lead to biased and inconsistent estimates of its parameters. A disturbance of the form

$$v_t = \varepsilon_t - \theta\varepsilon_{t-1}$$

is sometimes referred to as a *first-order moving average* disturbance.

If consistent estimates of α, β_0 and θ are to be obtained from the estimation of [5.4] then the simplest method is that of instrumental variables. We saw in Section 3.1 that this is one possible method of dealing with a problem of contemporaneous correlation between disturbance and explanatory variable. The obvious procedure here is to use X_t as its own instrument and to use X_{t-1} as the instrument for Y_{t-1}. X_t is by assumption uncorrelated with ε_t and perfectly correlated with itself, while X_{t-1} is also uncorrelated with ε_t but likely to be highly correlated with Y_{t-1}. X_t and X_{t-1} are therefore suitable instruments. Unfortunately, however, X_t and X_{t-1} are likely to be highly correlated themselves so these estimators, although consistent, may be very inefficient.

Another possibility is to use a version of the GLS procedure, described in Section 3.2 as a possible solution to heteroscedasticity and the first order autoregressive scheme. The idea is to transform equation [5.4] in such a way that the disturbance obeys all the classical assumptions. Such a transformation can be found but its application requires prior knowledge of θ. The required estimate of θ can be obtained using the instrumental variable method just described. Alternatively, it is possible to estimate α, β_0 and θ simultaneously using the maximum likelihood methods described in Section 4.3.[1]

Adaptive expectations and partial adjustment models

There are two very well-known economic models which lead to a distributed lag formulation virtually identical to equation [5.2]. Consider first a situation where Y_t depends not on the actual value of X but on its expected or 'permanent' value X^*

$$Y_t = \alpha + \beta X_t^* + \varepsilon_t \qquad [5.7]$$

The most common interpretation of X_t^* is that it represents permanent income in the Friedman sense. We shall encounter such an interpretation both in Chapter 7 on the consumption function and in Chapter 10 on the demand for money. Since X_t^* is unobservable we need to specify how it is determined. Consider the following scheme for determining X_t^*

$$X_t^* - X_{t-1}^* = \lambda(X_t - X_{t-1}^*) \qquad 0 \leqslant \lambda \leqslant 1 \qquad [5.8A]$$

or

$$X_t^* = \lambda X_t + (1 - \lambda) X_{t-1}^* \qquad [5.8B]$$

Equation [5.8] is an example of what is known as an *adaptive expectations hypothesis* and λ in this context is known as an *adjustment coefficient*. From [5.8A] we see that if actual 'income' in period t, X_t, exceeds expected 'income' in the previous period, X_{t-1}^*, ideas about expected 'income' are revised upwards so that expected 'income' in period t, X_t^*, exceeds that of the previous period. The extent of the adjustment depends on the size of λ which lies between zero and unity. For the extreme case, $\lambda = 1$, adjustment is complete because then $X_t^* = X_t$ so that actual and expected 'income' are identical. For the other extreme, $\lambda = 0$, no adjustment at all takes place and expected 'income' remains unchanged being uninfluenced by actual 'income' whatever its magnitude. In general, the larger is λ the greater the extent of the adjustment.

Notice that successive substitution is [5.8B] for X_{t-1}^*, X_{t-2}^*, etc. leads to

$$\begin{aligned} X_t^* &= \lambda X_t + (1 - \lambda)\lambda X_{t-1} + (1 - \lambda)^2 X_{t-2}^* \\ &= \lambda X_t + (1 - \lambda)\lambda X_{t-1} + (1 - \lambda)^2 \lambda X_{t-2} + (1 - \lambda)^3 X_{t-3}^* \\ &= \lambda X_t + (1 - \lambda)\lambda X_{t-1} + (1 - \lambda)^2 \lambda X_{t-2} + (1 - \lambda)^3 \lambda X_{t-3} + (1 - \lambda)^4 \lambda X_{t-4} \cdots \end{aligned}$$
$$[5.9]$$

Thus, in determining expected 'income' most weight is given to current 'income', X_t, and successively declining weights to past levels of 'income', X_{t-1}, $X_{t-2}, X_{t-3}, \ldots$

Substitution of [5.9] into [5.7] then yields

$$Y_t = \alpha + \beta \lambda [X_t + (1 - \lambda)X_{t-1} + (1 - \lambda)^2 X_{t-2}, \ldots] + \varepsilon_t \qquad [5.10]$$

Equation [5.10] is identical to the geometric lag equation [5.2] except that $\beta_0 = \beta\lambda$ and $\theta = 1 - \lambda$. By applying the Koyck transformation as before, i.e. lagging [5.10] by one period, multiplying throughout by $1 - \lambda$ and subtracting the result from [5.10], we obtain

$$Y_t = \alpha\lambda + \beta\lambda X_t + (1 - \lambda)Y_{t-1} + \varepsilon_t - (1 - \lambda)\varepsilon_{t-1} \qquad [5.11]$$

which is identical to [5.4] except that again, of course, $\beta_0 = \beta\lambda$ and $\theta = 1 - \lambda$. Therefore if we were to accept the underlying adaptive expectations hypothesis, our estimated equation [5.5] would suggest $1 - \hat{\lambda} = 0.6$ so that $\hat{\lambda} = 0.4$, $\hat{\beta} = 0.3/\hat{\lambda} = 0.75$ and $\hat{\alpha} = 64/\hat{\lambda} = 160$. Thus we would estimate the behavioural relationship [5.7] as

$$\hat{Y}_t = 160 + 0.75 X_t^* \qquad [5.12]$$

and the adjustment coefficient in the adaptive expectations equation [5.8A] as 0.4. This value of 0.4 would imply that 40 per cent of any difference between actual and expected 'income' is reflected in the revised estimate of expected 'income'.

In estimating the adaptive expectations model we must, of course, remember that the disturbance in [5.11] like that in [5.4] is almost certain to be autocorrelated. Thus, the presence of Y_{t-1} in equation [5.11] means that the straightforward application of OLS will again yield biased and inconsistent estimators. Hence, it is necessary to employ one of the alternative methods of estimation mentioned above for the general geometric lag.

The second model that leads to the geometric lag equation [5.2] is the *partial adjustment model*. Suppose the desired level of Y at time t, Y_t^*, depends on some explanatory variable, X, plus a disturbance obeying the usual assumptions

$$Y_t^* = \alpha + \beta X_t + \varepsilon_t \qquad [5.13]$$

For example, the desired level of a firm's capital stock may depend on its output, or a household's optimal level of consumption expenditure may depend on its income. However, time may be necessary before actual Y can be adjusted to its optimal or desired level so that Y and Y^* are not normally the same. That is, the adjustment of actual Y to a change in X does not occur instantaneously. Such lagged adjustment might be the result of inertia or the persistence of habit in a household or technological delays in the construction of a firm's capital equipment (see Sections 7.2 and 9.1 respectively). Suppose that the relationship between actual and desired Y is as follows

$$Y_t - Y_{t-1} = \mu(Y_t^* - Y_{t-1}) \qquad 0 \leqslant \mu \leqslant 1 \qquad [5.14A]$$

or

$$Y_t = \mu Y_t^* + (1 - \mu)Y_{t-1} \qquad [5.14B]$$

That is, if desired Y in period t exceeds actual Y in the previous period, then actual Y in period t is increased above its level of the previous period but not by the full extent of the difference between Y_t^* and Y_{t-1}. The adjustment in Y is only partial and the extent of the movement in actual Y towards its desired level depends on the size of μ. At one extreme μ is unity and adjustment is complete since then $Y_t = Y_t^*$. At the other extreme $\mu = 0$ so that $Y_t = Y_{t-1}$ and no adjustment at all takes place. In general, the extent of the adjustment and hence the speed with which Y adjusts to X over time will depend on the size of μ. The larger μ the more rapid the adjustment. μ is again known as an adjustment coefficient but notice that its interpretation is totally different to that of λ in equation [5.8A].

Substitution of [5.13] into [5.14] now yields

$$Y_t = \alpha\mu + \beta\mu X_t + (1 - \mu)Y_{t-1} + \mu\varepsilon_t \qquad [5.15]$$

Apart from the disturbance, [5.15] is of identical form to equation [5.11] with μ now replacing λ. Notice, however, that in this case the disturbance is not autocorrelated (provided ε_t in equation [5.13] is non-autocorrelated). Hence *the application of* OLS *to equation* [5.15] *will yield consistent estimators* although the presence of Y_{t-1} means they will not be unbiased. The estimation of a partial adjustment model therefore presents fewer problems than that of an adaptive expectations model.

Finally, notice that successive substitution for Y_{t-1}, Y_{t-2}, etc. in [5.15] leads to

$$Y_t = \alpha + \beta\mu[X_t + (1 - \mu)X_{t-1} + (1 - \mu)^2 X_{t-2}, \ldots] + \xi_t \qquad [5.16]$$

where

$$\xi_t = \mu\varepsilon_t + \mu(1 - \mu)\varepsilon_{t-1} + \mu(1 - \mu)^2\varepsilon_{t-2}, \ldots$$

Equation [5.16] is identical to equation [5.2] with $\beta_0 = \beta\mu$ and $\theta = 1 - \mu$ so that the partial adjustment model, like the adaptive expectations model, also implies a geometric lag.

Suppose, again, that we had obtained an estimated equation such as [5.5]. We have already seen that we could interpret such an equation in terms of an adaptive expectations model with adjustment parameter $\lambda = 0.4$. However, we could equally well interpret [5.5] in terms of equation [5.15] and conclude that it arose out of a partial adjustment process in which μ in equation [5.14A] was 0.4. The point is that, without prior knowledge of which model is appropriate, we cannot know whether the importance of the lagged dependent variable, Y_{t-1}, in equation [5.5] arises because of an adaptive expectations mechanism or because of lagged adjustment of actual Y to its desired level. This is a consequence of the fact that both equations [5.7] and [5.13] involve unobservable variables− expected X in equation [5.7] and desired Y in equation [5.13]. In transforming these equations into relationships between the observable actual X and Y variables we lose the ability to discriminate between the two competing models.

It follows that the importance of lagged dependent variables could arise because of either 'expectational lags' or 'adjustment lags' or possibly both. This suggests that in any attempt to discover the relative importance of the two types of lag we should combine them into a single model in which desired Y depends on expected X. That is

$$Y_t^* = \alpha + \beta X_t^* + \varepsilon_t \qquad [5.17]$$

where X^* is determined by the adaptive expectations mechanism [5.8A] and Y adjusts to Y^* through the partial adjustment mechanism [5.14A]. The estimated sizes of λ and μ would then help us decide on the relative importance of expectational and adjustment-type lags. However, we shall delay considering such a model in detail until we study the problems of estimating demand for money equations in Section 10.2.

However it arises, one of the problems with the geometric distributed lag formulation [5.2] is that it may not be appropriate for the weights in the lag structure to decline immediately as we move from the present value of the explanatory variable further into the past. Sometimes it may be the case that a

5.1 An inverted V-type lag distribution.

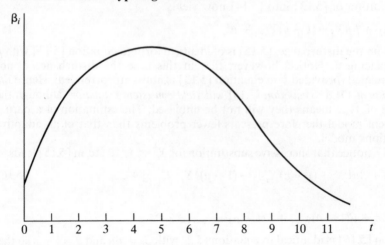

change in the X variable has little effect on the Y variable for the first few periods. The β's in equation [5.1] might follow an 'inverted V' distribution as illustrated in Fig. 5.1, firstly rising to a peak but declining thereafter. As we shall see in Chapter 9, for example, such a distribution could describe the adjustment of a firm's capital stock to a sustained increase in its output. Capacity constraints in the capital goods industry and the long and variable gestation period for many capital goods means that the effect of an output change does not make its maximum impact until some periods later. However, before considering how the geometric lag can be generalised to yield such an inverted V-shape we require some knowledge of lag operators.

Lag operators

The lag operator L is defined by

$$LX_t = X_{t-1} \qquad [5.20]$$

The lag operator may be applied more than once so that

$$L(LX_t) = L^2X_t = X_{t-2}, \quad L(L^2X_t) = L^3X_t = X_{t-3}, \text{ etc., etc.} \qquad [5.21]$$

It may also be handled algebraically like an ordinary variable. For example

$$L^4L^6X_t = L^{10}X_t = X_{t-10} \qquad [5.22]$$

Similarly

$$L^5(3X_t + 7X_{t-1} + 5Y_t) = 3X_{t-5} + 7X_{t-6} + 5Y_{t-5} \qquad [5.23]$$

We can therefore write the distributed lag equation [5.1], generalised to the case $m = \infty$, as

$$Y_t = \alpha + \beta_0 X_t + \beta_1 LX_t + \beta_2 L^2 X_t + \beta_3 L^3 X_t + ,..., + \varepsilon_t$$
$$= \alpha + \beta(L)X_t + \varepsilon_t \qquad [5.24]$$

where $\beta(L)$ is a polynomial in L. That is

$$\beta(L) = \beta_0 + \beta_1 L + \beta_2 L^2 + \beta_3 L^3, \ldots \qquad [5.25]$$

It is also possible to divide by L and to divide by functions of L. For example $(1/L)X_t$ simply means that variable which yields X_t when the lag operator is applied. Hence

$$\left(\frac{1}{L}\right)X_t = X_{t+1} \qquad [5.26]$$

Similarly, $(1/\beta(L))Y_t$ means that variable which yields Y_t when $\beta(L)$ is applied. For example, if

$$Y_t = 3X_t + 4X_{t-1} + 2X_{t-2}$$
$$= (3 + 4L + 2L^2)X_t$$

then

$$\left(\frac{1}{3 + 4L + 2L^2}\right)Y_t = X_t \qquad [5.27]$$

It is instructive to handle the geometric lag structure and the Koyck transformation using the lag operator notation. We may write [5.2] as

$$Y_t = \alpha + \beta_0(1 + \theta L + \theta^2 L^2 + \theta^3 L^3, \ldots,)X_t + \varepsilon_t$$
$$= \alpha + \left(\frac{\beta_0}{1 - \theta L}\right)X_t + \varepsilon_t \qquad [5.28]$$

using the expression for the sum to infinity of a convergent geometric series. Hence, multiplying throughout by $1 - \theta L$,

$$(1 - \theta L)Y_t = (1 - \theta L)\alpha + \beta_0 X_t + (1 - \theta L)\varepsilon_t$$

or

$$Y_t = \alpha(1 - \theta) + \beta_0 X_t + \theta Y_{t-1} + \varepsilon_t - \theta \varepsilon_{t-1} \qquad [5.29]$$

which is identical to equation [5.4][2]

Rational lags

A technique which, as we shall see in Section 9.3, has been used frequently in econometric studies of investment is to approximate the general *infinite* distributed lag, $\beta(L)$, in equation [5.25] by the ratio of two finite polynomials. That is

$$\beta(L) = \frac{\gamma(L)}{w(L)} = \frac{\gamma_0 + \gamma_1 L + \gamma_2 L^2, \ldots, \gamma_k L^k}{1 + w_1 L + w_2 L^2, \ldots, w_l L^l} \qquad [5.30]$$

Any lag function of the form [5.25] can be approximated by this so-called *rational lag function* provided l and k are chosen appropriately. In fact, l and k have to be chosen prior to the estimating process. For example, if $l = 2$ and $k = 2$ then [5.24] becomes

$$Y_t = \alpha + \left(\frac{\gamma_0 + \gamma_1 L + \gamma_2 L^2}{1 + w_1 L + w_2 L^2}\right)X_t + \varepsilon_t \qquad [5.31]$$

Multiplying throughout by $w(L) = 1 + w_1 L + w_2 L^2$, we obtain

$$(1 + w_1 L + w_2 L^2) Y_t = (1 + w_1 L + w_2 L^2)\alpha + (\gamma_0 + \gamma_1 L + \gamma_2 L^2) X_t$$
$$+ (1 + w_1 L + w_2 L^2)\varepsilon_t \qquad [5.32]$$

so that the equation actually estimated is

$$Y_t = \alpha(1 + w_1 + w_2) + \gamma_0 X_t + \gamma_1 X_{t-1} + \gamma_2 X_{t-2}$$
$$- w_1 Y_{t-1} - w_2 Y_{t-2} + u_t \qquad [5.33]$$

where

$$u_t = \varepsilon_t + w_1 \varepsilon_{t-1} + w_2 \varepsilon_{t-2}$$

Notice, however, that the disturbance, u_t, in equation [5.33] is of second-order moving average form and will be autocorrelated if ε_t obeys the classical assumptions. Hence, since the equation contains two lagged values of the dependent variable, OLS will yield biased and inconsistent estimators of its parameters.

As can be seen from [5.28], the geometric lag is a special case of [5.30] with $\gamma(L) = \beta_0$ and $w(L) = 1 - \theta L$, i.e. $k = 0$ and $l = 1$.

Given estimates of all the parameters in equations such as [5.33], it is possible to deduce all the implied values for the β's in equation [5.24] and hence the precise manner in which Y reacts over time to a change in X. For example, if we obtain

$$Y_t = 5.1 + 0.4X_t + 0.8X_{t-1} + 1.1X_{t-2} + 1.1Y_{t-1} - 0.4Y_{t-2} \qquad [5.34]$$

then this implies

$$\gamma(L) = 0.4 + 0.8L + 1.1L^2$$
$$w(L) = 1 - 1.1L + 0.4L^2$$

From [5.30] we have

$$\beta(L)w(L) = \gamma(L)$$

or

$$(\beta_0 + \beta_1 L + \beta_2 L^2 + \beta_3 L^3, \ldots,)(1 - 1.1L + 0.4L^2) = 0.4 + 0.8L + 1.1L^2 \quad [5.35]$$

By comparing coefficients of the various powers of L in equation [5.35] we obtain

$$\beta_0(1) = 0.4$$
$$\beta_0(-1.1) + \beta_1(1) = 0.8$$
$$\beta_0(0.4) + \beta_1(-1.1) + \beta_2(1) = 1.1$$
$$\beta_0(0) + \beta_1(0.4) + \beta_2(-1.1) + \beta_3(1) = 0$$
$$\beta_0(0) + \beta_1(0) + \beta_2(0.4) + \beta_3(-1.1) + \beta_4(1) = 0$$

etc., etc.

These equations may now be solved recursively for the β's yielding $\beta_0 = 0.4$, $\beta_1 = 1.24$, $\beta_2 = 2.30$, $\beta_3 = 2.04$, $\beta_4 = 1.32$, etc., etc.

Hence, since $1 + w_1 + w_2 = 0.3$ so that $\alpha = 17$, the estimated version of [5.24] is

$$Y_t = 17 + 0.4X_t + 1.24X_{t-1} + 2.30X_{t-2} + 2.04X_{t-3} + 1.32X_{t-4}, \ldots, \qquad [5.36]$$

Thus in this case we happen to obtain a typical inverted V lag distribution. Since *any* distributed lag function $\beta(L)$ can be approximated by the ratio of two finite polynomials, $\gamma(L)$ and $w(L)$, provided l and k are sufficiently large, the usefulness of the technique for estimating inverted V-type distributions is clear.

Consider again the general distributed lag equations [5.1] and [5.24]. The *long-run multiplier effect* of a change in X is the change in the *equilibrium* value of Y resulting from a unit sustained change in X. This is given by the sum of the β coefficients. However, it can be calculated directly from equations such as [5.33] by using [5.30]. Since

$$\beta_1 + \beta_2 + \beta_3 \ldots = \beta(1) = \frac{\gamma(1)}{w(1)} = \frac{\gamma_1 + \gamma_2 + \gamma_3, \ldots, \gamma_k}{1 + w_2 + w_3, \ldots, w_l}$$

the required multiplier can be obtained by taking the ratio of the γ coefficients to the w coefficients in the estimated equation. For example, for [5.34] we have

$$\sum \beta_j = \frac{\sum \gamma_j}{\sum w_j} = \frac{0.4 + 0.8 + 1.1}{1 - 1.1 + 0.4} = 7.67$$

Alternatively, of course, using [5.36]

$$\sum \beta_j = 0.4 + 1.24 + 2.30 + 2.04 + 1.32 \ldots = 7.67$$

Polynomial or Almon lags

The lag structures considered so far involve infinite lags. An alternative is to assume that the influence of a change in X on the Y variable is complete after a finite number of periods, i.e. there is a finite maximum lag. Such an assumption is built into the technique developed by Almon (1965). Consider again the general distributed lag equation [5.1] which assumes a maximum lag of m periods.

$$Y_t = \alpha + \beta_0 X_t + \beta_1 X_{t-1} + \beta_2 X_{t-2}, \ldots, \beta_m X_{t-m} + \varepsilon_t \qquad [5.37]$$

The Almon technique, unlike, for example, the Koyck approach, does not assume a rigid relationship between the β's. All that is assumed is that the relationship between the β's can be approximated by some polynomial. For example, if the β's describe some form of inverted V distribution with $m = 8$ as in Fig. 5.2, then a curve drawn through the points in this figure may be approximated by a second-order polynomial, i.e.

$$\beta_i = a_0 + a_1 i + a_2 i^2 \qquad [5.38]$$

The general rule is that the degree of the polynomial should be at least one more than the number of turning points in the curve. Notice that if it is possible to approximate all the β's in [5.37] by equation [5.38], then we must have

$$\beta_0 = a_0$$
$$\beta_1 = a_0 + a_1 + a_2$$
$$\beta_2 = a_0 + 2a_1 + 4a_2^2 \qquad [5.38A]$$
$$\vdots$$
$$\beta_m = a_0 + ma_1 + m^2 a_2$$

so that equation [5.37] becomes

$$Y_t = \alpha + a_0 X_t + (a_0 + a_1 + a_2) X_{t-1}$$
$$+ (a_0 + 2a_1 + 4a_2^2) X_{t-2}, \ldots, (a_0 + ma_1 + m^2 a_2) X_{t-m} + \varepsilon_t \qquad [5.39]$$

5.2 Points that can be approximated by a second-order polynomial.

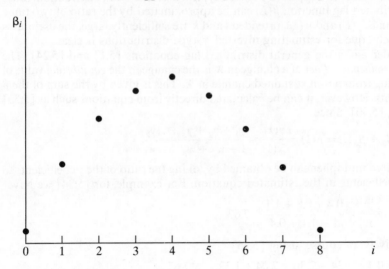

We can rearrange [5.39] to give

$$Y_t = \alpha + a_0 \sum_{i=0}^{m} X_{t-i} + a_1 \sum_{i=0}^{m} i X_{t-i} + a_2 \sum_{i=0}^{m} i^2 X_{t-i} + \varepsilon_t \qquad [5.40]$$

It is now possible to define three new variables

$$Z_{0t} = \sum_{i=0}^{m} X_{t-i}, \quad Z_{1t} = \sum_{i=0}^{m} i X_{t-i}, \quad Z_{2t} = \sum_{i=0}^{m} i^2 X_{t-i}$$

so that [5.40] can be rewritten as

$$Y_t = \alpha + a_0 Z_{0t} + a_1 Z_{1t} + a_2 Z_{2t} + \varepsilon_t \qquad [5.41]$$

The parameters in [5.41] may now be estimated by normal OLS methods provided we can specify an appropriate value for m, the maximum lag length. For example, if $m = 6$, the Z variables would be constructed from the original X variable as

$$Z_{0t} = X_t + X_{t-1} + X_{t-2} + X_{t-3} + X_{t-4} + X_{t-5} + X_{t-6}$$
$$Z_{1t} = X_{t-1} + 2X_{t-2} + 3X_{t-3} + 4X_{t-4} + 5X_{t-5} + 6X_{t-6} \qquad [5.42]$$
$$Z_{2t} = X_{t-1} + 4X_{t-2} + 9X_{t-3} + 16X_{t-4} + 25X_{t-5} + 36X_{t-6}$$

Once estimates of a_0, a_1 and a_2 are obtained, estimates of the parameters $\beta_0, \beta_1, \beta_2, \ldots, \beta_m$ in the original equation [5.37] may be computed using [5.38A]. Moreover, it can be shown that, provided the maximum lag length, m, exceeds the order of the polynomial used (in the above case the order is 2), the estimators of the β's obtained using the Almon technique are more efficient (i.e. have smaller variances) than those obtained by the direct application of OLS to [5.37].

Notice that the polynomial [5.38] is used only to determine the parameters for values of i from zero to m. Outside this range the lag coefficients are specified to be zero. An additional possibility is to 'tie down' the lag distribution by imposing the 'end-point restrictions' that $\beta_0 = \beta_m = 0$. This has the effect of reducing the number of 'a parameters' to be estimated by two. In the above example with $m = 6$

the end-point restrictions would imply, using [5.38A], that

$$0 = a_0$$
$$0 = a_0 + 6a_1 + 36a_2$$

This, in turn, implies that $a_0 = 0$ and $a_1 = -6a_2$. Imposing these restrictions on [5.41] yields

$$Y_t = \alpha + a_2(Z_{2t} - 6Z_{1t}) + \varepsilon_t$$

or

$$Y_t = \alpha + a_2 W_t + \varepsilon_t \qquad\qquad [5.43]$$

where

$$W_t = Z_{2t} - 6Z_{1t} = -5X_{t-1} - 8X_{t-2} - 9X_{t-3} - 8X_{t-4} - 5X_{t-5}$$

The coefficient a_2 may now be estimated from [5.43], regressing Y_t on W_t. Since $a_0 = 0$ and $a_1 = -6a_2$, equations [5.38A] may then be used to estimate the unknown remaining β's.

Early users of the Almon lag technique typically made use of end-point restrictions either for *a priori* reasons or simply because of the reduction in the number of parameters involved. Unfortunately, the use of such restrictions will lead to biased estimates of the remaining non-zero β parameters unless the polynomial equation [5.38] does indeed yield values of zero for $i = 0$ and $i = m$. Nowadays, therefore, the tendency is to refrain from the use of end-point restrictions. Rather, if restrictions such as $\beta_m = 0$ are required then the maximum lag length is reduced to $m - 1$ and X_{t-m} omitted from equation [5.37].

The advantages of the Almon technique are the variety of the lag distributions that can be generated and the fact that, unlike the rational lag procedure, it does not involve transformations which lead to a violation of the classical assumptions. If the disturbance term in equation [5.37] obeys these assumptions then so does that in equations [5.41] and [5.43]. The disadvantages of the technique are that in practice we will not know the maximum lag length or the order of the most appropriate polynomial before estimation. In practice, the degree of the polynomial has to be high enough for the lag distributions obtainable to accommodate any likely pattern for the β's. However, it must be kept lower than m if the technique is to fulfil its purpose, which is to reduce the number of parameters that have to be estimated. The maximum lag length is best found by varying m so as to maximise, for example, the $\bar{R}^2$ statistic. Unfortunately, since the X variables are likely to be highly multicollinear, variations in $\bar{R}^2$ are likely to be small. However, by combining goodness-of-fit criteria with *a priori* criteria concerning the pattern of the β's (e.g. that they should all be non-zero) it is often possible to arrive at some 'best' value for m. For an example of the Almon lag procedure see equation [9.30] (p. 265), estimated by Almon herself in Chapter 9. For a numerical example of the technique see the empirical exercise in the appendix to that chapter.

5.2 Dummy variables

Up to this point we have assumed that the variables we deal with can be measured in quantitative terms. Not infrequently, however, we may encounter certain very relevant variables that are of a qualitative nature without any obvious scale of measurement. For example, we might believe that an important determinant of expenditure on fixed investment by firms was the operation or otherwise of a government system of investment incentives. Similarly, the existence or not of an 'incomes policy' might be thought to have a significant effect on the rate of wage inflation. One way of assessing the influence of such factors would, of course, be to estimate two separate regression equations, one using data from a period when the qualitative variable was 'operational' and another using data from a period when it was not. However, an alternative procedure is available which involves the estimation of only one equation.

To take yet another example, suppose we wished to estimate a demand equation for 'meat' and that our sample period included a sequence of years when purchases of certain types of meat were subject to rationing or some other form of control. We do not have data on different kinds of meat but must estimate an equation referring to all kinds – both controlled and uncontrolled. Abstracting from price effects we might hypothesise a simple linear equation

$$Q_t = a_1 + a_2 Y_t + \varepsilon_t \qquad [5.44]$$

where Q is 'demand for meat' measured in £m's of expenditure at constant prices and Y is an index of the real income of consumers.

Suppose we believed that controls did not influence the parameter a_2 in equation [5.44], i.e. had no influence on the marginal propensity to consume meat, but simply affected the intercept term, a_1. Given such an assumption, we can specify an estimating equation that is valid both for years during which controls were operative and for years when they were not

$$Q_t = a_1 + a_2 Y_t + b_1 D_t + \varepsilon_t \qquad [5.45]$$

where $b_1 < 0$ and

$D_t = 1$ for 'controlled years' $\qquad D_t = 0$ for 'uncontrolled years'.

Equation [5.45], combined with the definition of D, implies that during years when the purchase of meat was not controlled and $D_t = 0$, the demand equation was given by equation [5.44]. However, during other years when $D_t = 1$, we have

$$Q_t = (a_1 + b_1) + a_2 Y_t + \varepsilon_t \qquad [5.46]$$

To estimate an equation such as [5.45] simply involves constructing a 'dummy' variable D, taking the value unity whenever controls were operative and zero when they were not, and applying normal multiple regression techniques treating this variable just like any other. For example, suppose we estimated

$$\hat{Q}_t = 24 + 0.2 Y_t - 5 D_t \qquad [5.47]$$

This would simply imply

$$\hat{Q}_t = 24 + 0.2 Y_t \quad \text{for uncontrolled years} \qquad [5.48]$$

and

$$\hat{Q}_t = 19 + 0.2 Y_t \quad \text{for controlled years} \qquad [5.49]$$

Equations [5.48] and [5.49] are illustrated in Fig. 5.3. We see that, given our present model, the operation of controls on meat purchases results in a parallel downward shift in the demand function. This implies that introducing controls leads to a decrease in meat purchases of £5 m no matter what the level of income.

5.3 A parallel downward shift in the demand function.

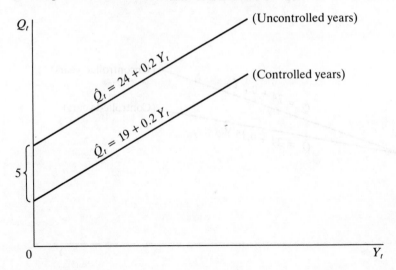

To test whether this estimate of £5m is significantly different from zero in the statistical sense we need simply examine the t-ratio on the coefficient D_t in equation [5.47].

It may justifiably be argued that the imposition of controls on certain types of meat purchase might be just as likely to affect the marginal propensity to consume meat, a_2, as it would the intercept in [5.44]. However, this situation may also be handled by specifying

$$Q_t = a_1 + a_2 Y_t + b_2 Y_t D_t + \varepsilon_t \qquad [5.50]$$

where b_2 is presumed to be negative and D_t is defined as before. This implies the equations

$$Q_t = a_1 + a_2 Y_t + \varepsilon_t \quad \text{for uncontrolled years} \qquad [5.51]$$

and

$$Q_t = a_1 + (a_2 + b_2) Y_t + \varepsilon_t \quad \text{for controlled years} \qquad [5.52]$$

Thus it is now the MPC that is smaller during years when controls operate. Equation [5.50] would be estimated simply by including the 'multiplicative' dummy variable $Y_t D_t$ in the estimating equation instead of the 'intercept' dummy D_t. $Y_t D_t$ would take the value zero when controls were not operative but take a value equal to Y_t in years when they were. Suppose, for example, we estimated

$$\hat{Q}_t = 24 + 0.2 Y_t - 0.05 Y_t D_t \qquad [5.53]$$

This would imply the demand functions illustrated in Fig. 5.4. Now the slope rather than the intercept of the demand function varies according to whether controls are operative.

The dummy variable technique can easily be generalised to the case where we have more than one 'genuine' explanatory variable. For example, a more plausible specification for the demand equation for meat might be

$$Q_t = a_1 + a_2 Y_t + a_3 P_t + a_4 F_t + \varepsilon_t \qquad [5.54]$$

5.4 A change in the slope of the demand function.

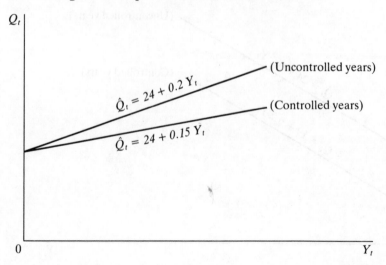

where P_t and F_t are indices of the price of meat and the prices of 'non-meat' foods. If we wished the intercept in [5.54] to change with the imposition of controls we could specify

$$Q_t = a_1 + a_2 Y_t + a_3 P_t + a_4 F_t + b_1 D_t + \varepsilon_t \qquad [5.55]$$

However, if we wished to consider the effect of controls on the parameters a_2, a_3 and a_4 we could specify

$$Q_t = a_1 + a_2 Y_t + b_2 Y_t D_t + a_3 P_t + b_3 P_t D_t + a_4 F_t + b_4 F_t D_t + \varepsilon_t \qquad [5.56]$$

and examine the significance of the estimates of b_2, b_3 and b_4.[3]

Dummy variables represent a most useful extension to regression analysis since they enable us to allow for variables which cannot be measured in quantitative units. Their values need not be restricted to zero or unity. For example, in Chapter 7, we shall see that a number of recent papers on the UK consumption function seek to allow for a rescheduling of expenditures in anticipation of rises in indirect taxation. An intercept dummy is defined to take the value +1 in the quarter prior to the tax change, −1 in the quarter after the tax change but zero in all other quarters. Thus, the net effect of the dummy is zero but it influences the timing of expenditures. We shall encounter intercept-type dummies in all the applied chapters of this book. The use of multiplicative dummies to allow for changes in the slope coefficients of regression equations is more rare.

Seasonal dummies

It is sometimes necessary to introduce more than one dummy variable into a regression equation. The most frequent reason for doing so is to allow for seasonal variations. For example, if we thought that the intercept term in our demand for meat equation [5.44] varied from quarter to quarter (more meat might be purchased in the winter quarter) we could specify

$$Q_t = a_1 + a_2 Y_t + b_1 D_{1t} + b_2 D_{2t} + b_3 D_{3t} + \varepsilon_t \qquad [5.57]$$

where $D_{1t} = 1$ for winter quarter $D_{1t} = 0$ otherwise
$\quad\quad\quad D_{2t} = 1$ for spring quarter $D_{2t} = 0$ otherwise
$\quad\quad\quad D_{3t} = 1$ for summer quarter $D_{3t} = 0$ otherwise
This would imply the following demand equations

$$Q_t = a_1 + b_1 + a_2 Y_t + \varepsilon_t \qquad \text{(winter quarter)}$$
$$Q_t = a_1 + b_2 + a_2 Y_t + \varepsilon_t \qquad \text{(spring quarter)}$$
$$Q_t = a_1 + b_3 + a_2 Y_t + \varepsilon_t \qquad \text{(summer quarter)}$$
$$Q_t = a_1 + a_2 Y_t + \varepsilon_t \qquad \text{(autumn quarter)}$$

The significance of seasonal effects could then be determined by examining the t-ratios on the estimates of b_1, b_2 and b_3 in equation [5.57].

Notice that the seasonal effects are represented by three, not four dummy variables. *We do not need to include a fourth dummy to allow for the autumn quarter.* In fact, if we attempted to introduce another dummy:

$$D_{4t} = 1 \text{ for autumn quarter} \qquad D_{4t} = 0 \text{ otherwise}$$

we would find our estimating procedures breaking down. This is because we would then have an exact linear relationship of the form

$$D_{1t} + D_{2t} + D_{3t} + D_{4t} = 1$$

between the dummy variables, holding during all quarters. This would be a case of complete multicollinearity in which case, as we know from Section 3.3, all estimating procedures break down.

If it were thought that seasonal variations affected the marginal propensities to consume in [5.57] rather than the intercept, then this could be allowed for by introducing the winter, spring and summer dummies multiplicatively

$$Q_t = a_1 + b_1 Y_t D_{1t} + b_2 Y_t D_{2t} + b_3 Y_t D_{3t} + a_2 Y_t + \varepsilon_t \qquad [5.58]$$

Such an equation implies marginal propensities to consume of

$$a_2 + b_1, \quad a_2 + b_2, \quad a_2 + b_3 \quad \text{and} \quad a_2$$

during winter, spring, summer and autumn quarters respectively.

The use of seasonal dummies is easily extended to equations such as [5.54] which contain more than one 'genuine' explanatory variable.

5.3   Testing for parameter stability

There are often occasions in applied econometric work when we may wish to know whether an economic relationship has changed. For example, we might wish to test whether the parameters of a 'prewar' consumption function differed from those of the postwar function. In recent years tests for parameter stability have been used most frequently in studies of the demand for money. The stability of demand for money functions has, of course, important implications for monetary policy.

The most well-known tests of parameter stability are probably those due to Chow (1960b). To illustrate the idea behind these tests, suppose we suspect a sudden change or shift in the parameters of a demand for money function in the middle of our sample period. The first of the Chow tests proceeds as follows. Ordinary least squares regressions are run for the two subperiods (i.e. for the periods before and after the suspected shift in the function) and also for the 'pooled' or full period. Suppose that the residual sums of squares for these regressions are $\sum e_1^2$, $\sum e_2^2$ and $\sum e_p^2$ respectively. Now consider the quantity

$$\frac{\sum e_p^2 - (\sum e_1^2 + \sum e_2^2)}{\sum e_1^2 + \sum e_2^2} \tag{5.59}$$

[5.59] measures the proportionate increase in the sum of squared residuals that results from fitting a single regression to the full period rather than permitting the 'greater freedom' of fitting separate equations for each subperiod. Given the null hypothesis of parameter stability (i.e. no sudden shift in the function) we should expect this quantity to be 'small'. However, if a shift has occurred we must expect it to be 'larger'. The two cases are illustrated in Fig. 5.5 and 5.6 where we abstract from any variables other than the demand for money and the rate of interest.

In both cases, points in the scatter referring to one subperiod are shown by crosses and to the other subperiod by dots. Figure 5.5 illustrates the scatter we might obtain when the function shifts. The two solid lines show the fitted OLS equations for the two subperiods. Clearly, if we were to restrict ourselves to fitting a *single* equation to all points (i.e. the dotted single line) there will be a large increase in the absolute size of residuals and, hence, in the sum of squared residuals for the whole period. Figure 5.6 illustrates a scatter we might obtain in the case of parameter stability. Now, replacing the two separate lines by a single line fitted to all points would lead to very little increase in the size of residuals.

The problem, of course, is to determine how large the quantity [5.59] should be before we can safely reject the hypothesis of parameter stability. Luckily, it is not difficult to show that, under the null hypothesis of parameter stability, the quantity

$$\left\{ \frac{\sum e_p^2 - (\sum e_1^2 + \sum e_2^2)}{\sum e_1^2 + \sum e_1^2} \right\} \left\{ \frac{n_1 + n_2 - 2k}{k} \right\} \tag{5.60}$$

where n_1 and n_2 are the sizes of the two subsamples and k is the number of

5.5 A change in parameter values.   **5.6 No change in parameter values.**

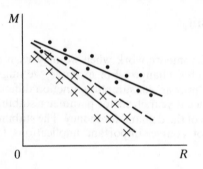 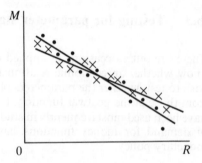

parameters being estimated, has an F distribution with

$$(k, n_1 + n_2 - 2k)$$

degrees of freedom. Hence, it may be used as a test statistic and compared with the relevant critical F value.

The second of the two Chow tests covers the situation where the size of the second sample n_2 is less than k. It is then not possible to run an OLS regression for this second subsample. Consider, however, the quantity

$$\frac{\sum e_p^2 - \sum e_1^2}{\sum e_1^2} \qquad [5.61]$$

Equation [5.61] represents the proportionate increase in the sum of squared residuals that results from fitting an OLS regression to the pooled $n_1 + n_2$ observations rather than just to the first n_1 observations. The greater is this quantity, the more inclined we will be to reject the null hypothesis of parameter stability. In fact, given the hypothesis of parameter stability, the quantity

$$\left\{ \frac{\sum e_p^2 - \sum e_1^2}{\sum e_1^2} \right\} \left\{ \frac{n_1 - k}{n_2} \right\} \qquad [5.62]$$

has an F distribution with $(n_2, n_1 - k)$ degrees of freedom and may therefore be used as a test statistic in this situation.

Notice that the Chow tests test simply for some unspecified change in parameter values. This might be a change in the intercept, in one of the slope parameters or both. If we wanted to focus attention on shifts in any particular parameter we could resort to the dummy variable techniques of the previous section. For empirical examples of the Chow tests see the empirical exercise at the end of Chapter 10.

5.4   Restrictions on the parameters of regression equations

In applied econometric work we may often believe that the parameters of a population regression equation should satisfy certain restrictions. One of the simplest examples of such a restriction is when we *suspect or require the intercept to be zero*. For example, we shall see in Sections 7.4 and 7.5 that all the main theories of the consumption function can lead to time series estimating equations that do not contain an intercept. Also, we have already encountered the problem of suppressing the intercept when considering the estimation of the parameter ρ in the first-order autoregressive scheme discussed in Section 3.2.

Consider the case of a single explanatory variable where, in the absence of an intercept, the population regression line becomes

$$EY = \beta_2 X_2 \qquad [5.63]$$

If we believe that the population regression line has no intercept, then obviously it makes sense to estimate it by a sample regression line, $\hat{Y} = \hat{\beta}_2 X_2$, without an intercept. Applying the OLS principle, this means minimising a sum of squared residuals given by

$$S = \sum e_i^2 = \sum (Y_i - \hat{Y}_i)^2 = \sum (Y_i - \hat{\beta}_2 X_{2i})^2 \qquad [5.64]$$

In effect we are choosing, out of all sample regression lines *that pass through the origin*, that which best fits the sample observations.

Differentiating [5.64] with respect to $\hat{\beta}_2$, the only coefficient we have to estimate, and equating to zero yields

$$\frac{dS}{d\hat{\beta}} = -2\sum X_{2i}(Y_i - \hat{\beta}_2 X_{2i}) = 0 \qquad [5.65]$$

Solving [5.65] we obtain the OLS estimator of $\hat{\beta}_2$ as

$$\hat{\beta}_2 = \frac{\sum X_{2i} Y_i}{\sum X_{2i}^2} \qquad [5.66]$$

Notice that [5.66] has the same form as the normal OLS estimator of β_2 in two-variable regression, $\hat{\beta}_2 = \sum x_{2i} y_i / \sum x_{2i}^2$. The difference is that when the intercept is suppressed the deviations of Y and X_2 from their sample means are replaced by the actual values of Y and X_2. That is, $y_i = Y_i - \bar{Y}$ is replaced by Y_i and $x_{2i} = X_{2i} - \bar{X}$ is replaced by X_{2i}. A similar result, in fact, holds in multiple regression. With intercept suppressed, it can be shown that equation [2.20] (p. 15) will still yield the OLS estimators of the slope coefficients provided we replace actual values of variables by deviations and redefine $\mathbf{X}$ as an $n \times (k-1)$ matrix in which the column of ones in the original $\mathbf{X}$ matrix has been suppressed.

If, instead of simply accepting that the intercept be suppressed, we wished to test the validity of its suppression, the obvious procedure is to estimate the equation in the normal manner with intercept included. We can then test the hypothesis that β_1, the intercept in the population regression line, is zero by performing the normal t-test on our estimated intercept.

Linear restrictions

Normally, economic theory provides information, not about the precise value of individual regression parameters, but about relationships between them. It may suggest that the β_j's in a population regression equation such as [2.12] (p. 12) obey some *linear restriction*. For example, in Section 6.1 we note that consumer theory suggests that all price and income elasticities in a demand equation should sum to zero. Hence, if we estimate a demand equation using the logarithmic form [3.37] then, since the β_j's now represent elasticities, theory implies the *linear restriction* $\sum \beta_j = 0$. Similarly, in Chapter 8 we shall encounter the Cobb–Douglas production function. This can be written in the form

$$Q = BK^{\beta_2} L^{\beta_3} u \qquad [5.67]$$

where Q is output, K and L are capital and labour inputs and u is a multiplicative disturbance of the kind discussed in Section 3.4. Taking logarithms yields

$$Y = \beta_1 + \beta_2 X_2 + \beta_3 X_3 + \varepsilon \qquad [5.68]$$

where $Y = \log Q, X_2 = \log K, X_3 = \log L, \beta_1 = \log B$ and $\varepsilon = \log u$. As is demonstrated in Section 8.1, constant returns to scale in such a production function means that its parameters obey the *linear restriction*

$$\beta_2 + \beta_3 = 1.$$

Consider a situation where we wish to estimate an equation such as [5.68] and

118

where we believe that the restriction

$$\beta_2 + \beta_3 = 1$$

is valid. That is, we believe a population relationship exists of the form

$$Y = \beta_1 + \beta_2 X_2 + (1 - \beta_2)X_3 + \varepsilon \qquad [5.69]$$

If we now attempt to estimate [5.69] by the normal OLS procedure, regressing Y on X_2 and X_3, we would obtain a sample regression equation

$$\hat{Y} = \hat{\beta}_1 + \hat{\beta}_2 X_2 + \hat{\beta}_3 X_3 \qquad [5.70]$$

We could now attempt to obtain estimates of the parameters β_1 and β_2 by comparing the coefficients in [5.69] and [5.70]. However, it should be immediately clear that we have a problem since we would have *three* known coefficients, $\hat{\beta}_1$, $\hat{\beta}_2$ and $\hat{\beta}_3$ from which we would have to obtain estimates of *two* parameters, β_1 and β_2. Unless the estimates $\hat{\beta}_2$ and $\hat{\beta}_3$ obey the restriction $\beta_2 + \hat{\beta}_3 = 1$, we will obtain two estimates of β_2, one equal to $\hat{\beta}_2$ and that other equal to $1 - \hat{\beta}_3$. Since, even if the *true* coefficients of X_2 and X_3 in [5.69] sum to unity, it is unlikely that their *estimates* $\hat{\beta}_2$ and $\hat{\beta}_3$ will do so, this will be the most common outcome. In fact, we have a case of *overidentification*, akin to that described in Section 4.2 in the context of moving from reduced-form parameters to structural parameters. If we are to obtain a unique estimate of β_2 some modification of the estimating procedure is necessary.

The OLS estimators $\hat{\beta}_1$, $\hat{\beta}_2$ and $\hat{\beta}_3$ in [5.70] are obtained by minimising the sum of squared residuals

$$\sum e_i^2 = \sum (Y_i - \hat{Y}_i)^2 = \sum (Y_i - \hat{\beta}_1 - \hat{\beta}_2 X_{2i} - \hat{\beta}_3 X_{3i})^2 \qquad [5.71]$$

If we are to obtain a unique estimate of β_2 then [5.71] has to be minimised *subject to the restriction that* $\hat{\beta}_2 + \hat{\beta}_3 = 1$. This can be achieved either using the Lagrangian multiplier method or, alternatively, substituting the constraint into [5.71] and then minimising in the usual way. The latter method is the more instructive since on substitution of $\hat{\beta}_2 + \hat{\beta}_3 = 1$ into [5.71], we then have to minimise

$$\sum e_i^2 = \sum \{Y_i - \hat{\beta}_1 - \hat{\beta}_2 X_{2i} - (1 - \hat{\beta}_2)X_{3i}\}^2$$
$$= \sum \{(Y_i - X_{3i}) - \hat{\beta}_1 - \hat{\beta}_2 (X_{2i} - X_{3i})\}^2 \qquad [5.72]$$

However, choosing $\hat{\beta}_1$ and $\hat{\beta}_2$ so as to minimise [5.73] is exactly the same as choosing them so as to minimise the residual sum of squares when estimating a relationship of the kind

$$(Y - X_3) = \beta_1 + \beta_2 (X_2 - X_3) + \varepsilon \qquad [5.73]$$

Thus the simplest way of obtaining estimates that yield a unique value for β_2 is to construct new variables $Y^* = Y - X_3$ and $X_2^* = X_2 - X_3$ and then use OLS to compute

$$\hat{Y}^* = \hat{\beta}_1 + \hat{\beta}_2 X_2^*$$

which is equivalent to

$$\hat{Y} = \hat{\beta}_1 + \hat{\beta}_2 X_2 + (1 - \hat{\beta}_2)X_3 \qquad [5.74]$$

The above method of estimation is known as *restricted least squares*. Notice that *the form of the equation eventually estimated, [5.73], is obtained simply by manipulating* [5.69]. Provided the classical assumptions hold when applied to [5.73], the restricted least squares estimators will possess all the usual desirable small and large sample properties.

The restricted least squares method may always be used to solve over-identification problems arising from the existence of one or more linear restrictions on regression parameters. For example, suppose we believed the underlying population relationship was

$$Y = \beta_1 + \beta_2 X_2 + \beta_2 X_3 + \beta_4 X_4 + (1 - \beta_4)X_5 + \varepsilon \qquad [5.75]$$

We require therefore to compute a sample regression equation

$$\hat{Y} = \hat{\beta}_1 + \hat{\beta}_2 X_2 + \hat{\beta}_3 X_3 + \hat{\beta}_4 X_4 + \hat{\beta}_5 X_5 \qquad [5.76]$$

subject to the two linear restrictions $\hat{\beta}_2 = \hat{\beta}_3$ and $\hat{\beta}_4 + \hat{\beta}_5 = 1$. The simplest way to do this is to note that [5.75] can be rearranged as

$$Y - X_5 = \beta_1 + \beta_2(X_2 + X_3) + \beta_4(X_4 - X_5) + \varepsilon \qquad [5.77]$$

Thus, we use our data to construct new variables

$$Y^* = Y - X_5, \quad X_2^* = X_2 + X_3 \quad \text{and} \quad X_4^* = X_4 - X_5.$$

and compute the sample regression equation

$$\hat{Y}^* = \hat{\beta}_1 + \hat{\beta}_2 X_2^* + \hat{\beta}_4 X_4^*$$

which is equivalent to

$$\hat{Y} = \hat{\beta}_1 + \hat{\beta}_2 X_2 + \hat{\beta}_2 X_3 + \hat{\beta}_4 X_4 + (1 - \hat{\beta}_4)X_5 \qquad [5.78]$$

The restricted least squares estimates of β_1, β_2 and β_3 are then the $\hat{\beta}_1, \hat{\beta}_2$ and $\hat{\beta}_3$ in [5.78].

Testing linear restrictions

It is rarely the case that we are prepared to accept without question an *a priori* restriction suggested by economic theory. Rather, the purpose of estimating 'restricted equations' such as [5.73] and [5.77] is normally to *test* the restrictions implied by them. Consider our first example, where the unrestricted sample regression equation was given by [5.70] and the restricted version, incorporating $\hat{\beta}_2 + \hat{\beta}_3 = 1$, by [5.74]. Since both these equations are estimated by OLS, it is possible in each case to split the total sum of squares in the dependent Y variable, SST, into an explained sum of squares and a residual sum of squares, as indicated by equation [2.38] (p. 35). That is

$$\text{SST} = \text{SSE}_U + \text{SSR}_U \qquad \text{for the unrestricted equation}$$
$$\text{SST} = \text{SSE}_R + \text{SSR}_R \qquad \text{for the restricted equation}$$

where in each case SSE represents that part of SST that can be explained by the explanatory X variables and SSR is the residual sum of squares, $\sum e_i^2$.

It should be intuitively clear that the residual sum of squares for an unrestricted equation such as [5.70] is likely to be smaller than for the corresponding restricted equation [5.74]. In [5.70] we consider all possible values for $\hat{\beta}_1, \hat{\beta}_2$ and $\hat{\beta}_3$ as we seek to minimise the residual sum of squares. However, in [5.74] we are permitted to consider only values for $\hat{\beta}_2$ and $\hat{\beta}_3$ which obey the restriction $\hat{\beta}_2 + \hat{\beta}_3 = 1$. To put it another way, we are likely to be able to explain more of the total variation in Y when we do not restrict our search than when we do restrict it. We can therefore expect

$$\text{SSR}_R > \text{SSR}_U \quad \text{and} \quad \text{SSE}_R < \text{SSE}_U \qquad\qquad [5.79]$$

However, the extent of the differences expressed in [5.79] will depend very much on whether or not the restriction imposed in [5.74] is valid, i.e. on whether the true underlying values of β_2 and β_3 obey the restriction $\beta_2 + \beta_3 = 1$. If the restriction is valid, then the unrestricted estimates of β_2 and β_3 are unlikely to differ much from the restricted estimates. Hence, we would be able to explain as much of SST with the restricted estimates as we could with the unrestricted ones. Therefore, there would be little difference between the residual sum of squares for the restricted equation, SSR_R, and that for the unrestricted equation, SSR_U. If, however, the restriction is not valid and $\beta_2 + \beta_3 \neq 1$, then we can expect the unrestricted estimates to sum to something different from unity and, hence, to differ from the restricted estimates which, of course, still satisfy $\hat{\beta}_2 + \hat{\beta}_3 = 1$. Thus, if the restriction is not valid we can expect a major difference between the restricted residual sum of squares SSR_R and its unrestricted equivalent SSR_U.

The above argument suggests that we should reject the null hypothesis $\beta_2 + \beta_3 = 1$ (i.e. that the restriction is valid) if the quantity $\text{SSR}_R - \text{SSR}_U$ is 'sufficiently large'. However, as it stands $\text{SSR}_R - \text{SSR}_U$ depends on the units of measurement we are working in. To obtain an expression independent of measurement units we can use instead $(\text{SSR}_R - \text{SSR}_U)/\text{SSR}_U$, but this, of course, still leaves the question of how large this ratio has to be before we reject the restriction. Fortunately, it is not difficult to show that, given the null hypothesis $\beta_2 + \beta_3 = 1$, the quantity

$$\frac{\text{SSR}_R - \text{SSR}_U}{\text{SSR}_U/(n-k)} \text{ has an } F \text{ distribution with } (1, n-k) \text{ degrees of freedom} \quad [5.80]$$

We can therefore use [5.80] as a test statistic and reject the null hypothesis if it exceeds the relevant critical F value.

Test statistics such as [5.80] are available for testing any linear restriction or restrictions. In the general case where we wish to test simultaneously the validity of h restrictions, then the test statistic

$$\frac{(\text{SSR}_R - \text{SSR}_U)/h}{\text{SSR}_U/(n-k)} \text{ has an } F \text{ distribution with } (h, n-k) \text{ degrees of freedom} \quad [5.81]$$

For example, if we wished to test the restrictions implied by equation [5.75], i.e. that $\beta_2 = \beta_3$ and $\beta_4 + \beta_5 = 1$, then h would equal 2 and SSR_R would be the residual sum of squares associated with [5.78], while SSR_U would be that associated with the unrestricted equation [5.76]. The $n - k$ in the denominator of [5.81] refers to the degrees of freedom associated with the unrestricted equation [5.76], n being the sample size and k the number of *unrestricted* parameters.

When employing the above test the reader should always keep in mind the basic idea of the test. We reject a restriction or restrictions if the proportionate increase in the sum of squared residuals resulting from their imposition (i.e. $(\text{SSR}_R - \text{SSR}_U)/\text{SSR}_U$) is sufficiently large. Numerical examples of this test can be found in the appendices to Chapters 6 and 8.

A useful special case of the above test occurs where the restrictions specify simply that some or all of the parameters in the population regression equation are zero. For example, given a population relationship

$$Y = \beta_1 + \beta_2 X_2 + \beta_3 X_3 + \beta_4 X_4 + \beta_5 X_5 + \varepsilon \qquad [5.82]$$

we might wish to test the joint hypothesis $\beta_3 = \beta_4 = \beta_5 = 0$. For example, the sample values of X_3, X_4 and X_5 might be highly correlated so that, even if none of these variables appeared statistically significant on the usual t-tests we might suspect that this was simply the result of the multicollinearity. We would then be testing whether the *combined* influence of X_3, X_4 and X_5 on Y was significant. If we reject the restrictions $\beta_3 = \beta_4 = \beta_5 = 0$ we are saying that their combined influence is significant and that the multicollinearity is obscuring the true influence of at least one of the variables X_3, X_4 and X_5. In this case we would estimate

$$\hat{Y} = \hat{\beta}_1 + \hat{\beta}_2 X_2 + \hat{\beta}_3 X_3 + \hat{\beta}_4 X_4 + \hat{\beta}_5 X_5 \qquad \text{unrestricted equation} \quad [5.83]$$
$$\hat{Y} = \hat{\beta}_1 + \hat{\beta}_2 X_2 \qquad \text{restricted equation} \qquad [5.84]$$

The number of restrictions used in the test statistic [5.81] will in this case be $h = 3$, the number of variables whose combined influence we are testing for.

A final special case arises when we test the hypothesis that *all* the slope parameters in the population regression equation are zero. In equation [5.82] this would imply

$$\beta_2 = \beta_3 = \beta_4 = \beta_5 = 0$$

We would now be testing for the existence of any relationship at all between the explanatory X variables and Y. We might wish to do this if all the X variables were highly correlated with one another. In this case, since the restricted equation would contain *no* explanatory variables, the restricted *explained* sum of squares must be zero so that SSR_R must now equal the total sum of squares SST. The test statistic [5.81] therefore now becomes

$$\frac{(\text{SST} - \text{SSR}_U)/(k-1)}{\text{SSR}_U/(n-k)} = \frac{\text{SSE}_U/(k-1)}{\text{SSR}_U/(n-k)} \qquad [5.85]$$

It is left for the reader to deduce that the test statistic [5.85] is, in fact, identical to that given in terms of R^2, the coefficient of multiple determination, at the conclusion of Chapter 2.

Non-linear restrictions

Economic models are just as likely to suggest non-linear restrictions on the coefficients of estimating equations as they are to suggest linear restrictions. We shall encounter such non-linear restrictions in, for example, equation [6.26] (p. 141) which refers to the demand for a durable good. Similar equations to [6.26] are also derived in Section 9.1 on theories of investment behaviour. Other examples of non-linear restrictions occur in Zellner, Huang and Chau's (1965) study of the consumption function discussed in Section 7.5 and in Feige's (1967) model of the demand for money, presented as equation [10, 20] (p. 300) and also discussed at the beginning of Section 10.5.

To illustrate the problems arising from non-linear resctictions, consider the

estimation of a population relationship

$$Y = \beta_1 + \beta_2 X_2 + \beta_3 X_3 + \beta_2 \beta_3 X_4 + \varepsilon \qquad [5.86]$$

In [5.86] we have the non-linear restriction that the coefficient on X_4, β_4 equals $\beta_2\beta_3$. Clearly, if we estimate [5.86] by a sample regression equation of the form

$$\hat{Y} = \hat{\beta}_1 + \hat{\beta}_2 X_2 + \hat{\beta}_3 X_3 + \hat{\beta}_4 X_4 \qquad [5.87]$$

then we have an overidentification problem. Three parameters β_1, β_2 and β_3 have to be obtained from four estimated coefficients $\hat{\beta}_1, \hat{\beta}_2, \hat{\beta}_3$ and $\hat{\beta}_4$. There is no reason why the estimate of β_2 obtained from $\hat{\beta}_2$ should coincide with that obtained by taking the ratio $\hat{\beta}_4/\hat{\beta}_3$.

The difficulty, now, is that because of the non-linearity of the constraint, it is not possible to manipulate [5.86] in the way we were able to manipulate [5.69] and [5.75] to obtain [5.73] and [5.77] respectively. We can no longer incorporate the constraint into our underlying relationship so as to provide an estimating equation of convenient form that can be tackled by OLS. There is no alternative in this case than to attempt to minimise the residual sum of squares

$$\sum e_i^2 = \sum (Y_i - \hat{Y}_i)^2 = \sum (Y_i - \hat{\beta}_1 - \hat{\beta}_2 X_{2i} - \hat{\beta}_3 X_{3i} - \hat{\beta}_4 X_{4i})^2 \qquad [5.88]$$

subject to the restriction $\hat{\beta}_4 = \hat{\beta}_2\hat{\beta}_3$. The problem is that the 'normal equations' obtained from this minimisation are, not surprisingly, non-linear and do not lead to convenient expressions for the $\hat{\beta}$'s that can be written-down in algebraic form. They have to be solved by purely numerical techniques. For example, in the present case this might involve selecting a value for, say, $\hat{\beta}_2$ and then finding the values for $\hat{\beta}_1, \hat{\beta}_3$ and $\hat{\beta}_4$ that minimise [5.88] given this value of $\hat{\beta}_2$. For example, if we set $\hat{\beta}_2 = 2$, then the constraint becomes $\hat{\beta}_4 = 2\hat{\beta}_3$ and [5.88] may be written as

$$\begin{aligned}\sum e_i^2 &= \sum \{Y_i - \hat{\beta}_1 - 2X_{2i} - \hat{\beta}_3 X_{3i} - 2\hat{\beta}_3 X_{4i}\}^2 \\ &= \sum \{(Y_i - 2X_{2i}) - \hat{\beta}_1 - \hat{\beta}_3(X_{3i} + 2X_{4i})\}^2 \end{aligned} \qquad [5.89]$$

Since for the given $\hat{\beta}_2$ the restriction becomes linear, the minimisation of [5.89] is straightforward, following the lines already described for linear restrictions. The minimisation, however, has to be performed for the whole range of possible values for $\hat{\beta}_2$ until the overall minimum value of $\sum e_i^2$ is found. The set of values $\hat{\beta}_1, \hat{\beta}_2, \hat{\beta}_3$ and $\hat{\beta}_4$ yielding this minimum are known as the *non-linear least squares estimators*.

The problem with non-linear least squares is that, since we can no longer express the estimating equation in a convenient linear form, it is difficult to deduce the properties of the estimators obtained. However, it can be shown that, provided the regression disturbances are normally distributed, non-linear least squares estimators are MLEs and are, hence, consistent and asymptotically efficient.

Further reading

The early development of the geometric lag was by Koyck (1954). An excellent survey is that of Griliches (1967). A good and understandable introduction to MLE of distributed lag models is contained in Kmenta (1971). Johnston (1984) also contains a section on the estimation of such models. The use of dummy variables as dependent variables and as the only explanatory variables in a regression equation is covered in Stewart and Wallis (1981) and extensively dealt with in Kmenta (1971). Estimation subject to non-linear restrictions is a difficult topic not dealt with in many introductory texts but, again, Kmenta contains an understandable introduction.

Notes

1. See, for example, Klein (1958) and Zellner and Geisel (1970).
2. Since α is a constant $L^2\alpha = L\alpha = \alpha$.
3. It is, of course, possible to include both the multiplicative dummies and the intercept dummy in the estimating equation at the same time. However, this can be shown to be exactly equivalent to estimating two separate equations – one for controlled years and one for uncontrolled years.

6 Demand analysis

One of the first relationships encountered by the reader of any elementary economics textbook is that between the demand for a commodity and its price. It is therefore natural that we should begin the applied part of this text by considering the problems involved in estimating such a demand relationship. Indeed, the estimation of demand equations provides one of the earliest examples of the application of econometric techniques and dates back to the work of Moore in 1914. The importance of such empirical work should be obvious. At the micro-level any firm or industry benefits from accurate forecasts of the future level of demand for its products. Also, at the macro-level, forecasts of aggregate consumption expenditure may be insufficiently revealing since identical levels of such expenditure may have different impacts on the economy depending on their composition. Before examining any particular demand studies we consider some general problems.

6.1 Specification of the demand equation

Traditional consumer theory suggests that the demand of a utility-maximising consumer for any commodity depends on the prices of all commodities available to the consumer and on his total expenditure. Thus

$$q_i = q_i(p_1, p_2, \ldots, p_i, \ldots, p_n, x) \qquad i = 1, 2, 3, \ldots, n \qquad [6.1]$$

where q_i and p_i are the quantity demanded and price of the ith commodity, there are n commodities in all, and $x = \sum_i p_i q_i$ is total expenditure which for the moment we shall take as given.

Unfortunately, consumer theory has nothing to say about the precise functional form of equation [6.1] which is dependent on the consumer's (unspecified) preferences. Moreover, there can be little satisfaction in knowing that in theory all prices should be included in a demand equation since in practice sample sizes are often relatively small. We are therefore likely to be confronted with the 'degree of freedom' problem described in Section 3.3. Our estimates will lack precision unless we restrict ourselves to a limited number of explanatory variables. Theory does, however, provide us with some limited information about demand equations. For example, an equiproportionate change in all prices and total expenditure should leave demand unchanged, i.e. theory implies that [6.1] is homogeneous of degree zero in the p_i's and x. Furthermore, the Slutsky equation implies that own-price substitution effects are negative (see for example Henderson and Quandt 1980: 25–8). This is the well-known law of demand and for consistency with theory the own-price and income derivatives of a demand equation should therefore always obey the restriction $\partial q_i/\partial p_i + q_i(\partial q_i/\partial x) < 0$.

By and large, however, theory is of little help in the specification of a demand equation and for this reason empirical versions of equation [6.1] are typically of an *ad hoc* nature. Functional forms are chosen for their ease of estimation and explanatory price variables normally restricted to own-price, the prices of close substitutes and complements and maybe the general price level. Common specifications are therefore

$$q_i = \alpha_0 + \alpha_1 p_i + \alpha_2 p_s + \alpha_3 \Pi + \alpha_4 x + \alpha_5 t + \varepsilon_i \qquad [6.2]$$

$$q_i = A p_i^{\alpha_1} p_s^{\alpha_2} \Pi^{\alpha_3} x^{\alpha_4} e^{\alpha_5 t} \varepsilon_i \qquad [6.3]$$

where p_s is the price of a close substitute, Π is the general price level, t is a time trend and ε a disturbance. The time trend is frequently included as an additional variable in an attempt to capture the influence of changing tastes. Specification [6.2] has the advantage of being linear. Specification [6.3] is linear in the logarithms and has the additional property that the α parameters can be interpreted as elasticities which are the quantities frequently of most interest in demand studies.

One point concerning specifications [6.2] and [6.3] needs further explanation. Consumers in general will be intertemporal utility-maximisers so that current demand for any commodity depends on all current and future prices and on 'total lifetime resources' rather than merely on current prices and total current expenditure. However, provided we can regard the consumer as adopting a 'two-stage' approach to his intertemporal problem – firstly deciding on his total current expenditure, x, and, once x is determined, only then deciding its allocation between commodities on the basis of their current prices – it is possible to justify the above specification. Many demand studies, however, replace the total expenditure variable in [6.2] and [6.3] by a measure of the consumer's disposable income, only part of which is devoted to current expenditure. This procedure is much harder to justify theoretically and, indeed, most economists would consider the replacement of total lifetime resources by current income as a serious mis-specification. The distinction between the two is, as we shall see in the next chapter, the basis of the life cycle and permanent income hypotheses concerning aggregate consumption expenditure.

The homogeneity restriction may either be imposed prior to estimation or equations [6.2] and [6.3] can be estimated as they stand. Imposing homogeneity implies specifying that demand is a function of *relative* prices and *real* total expenditure so that [6.2] and [6.3] become

$$q_i = \alpha_0 + \alpha_1 \left(\frac{p_i}{\Pi} \right) + \alpha_2 \left(\frac{p_s}{\Pi} \right) + \alpha_4 \left(\frac{x}{\Pi} \right) + \alpha_5 t + \varepsilon_i \qquad [6.4]$$

$$q_i = A \left(\frac{p_i}{\Pi} \right)^{\alpha_1} \left(\frac{p_s}{\Pi} \right)^{\alpha_2} \left(\frac{x}{\Pi} \right)^{\alpha_4} e^{\alpha_5 t} \varepsilon_i \qquad [6.5]$$

Comparing [6.3] and [6.5] we see that, for the logarithmic specification, imposing homogeneity is equivalent to imposing the linear restriction

$$\alpha_1 + \alpha_2 + \alpha_3 + \alpha_4 = 0$$

on [6.3]. Hence, if both [6.3] and [6.5] are estimated, then it is possible to test for homogeneity by applying the F-test described in Section 5.4. If the residual sum of

126

squares in an estimated version of [6.5] is sufficiently larger than that in [6.3], then the null hypothesis of homogeneity is rejected.

Most studies of the demand for a single good have, in fact, been concerned more with estimation than with the testing of economic theory. Working in terms of relative prices and real income reduces the multicollinearity between price and total expenditure variables that is frequently present in time series data. However, although homogeneity is typically imposed, little use has been made in estimation of the negativity restriction on the own-price substitution effect implied by the Slutsky equation. This is because of the difficulties of imposing an inequality-type restriction as opposed to the equality implied by homogeneity.

6.2 The aggregation problem

There are two broad sources of data normally available for the estimation of demand equations – time series data and cross-sectional data. Time series data normally refers to the purchases of large, sometimes economy-wide, groups of households over timespans of anything up to 100 years. Cross-sectional data comes from the so-called 'budget surveys' of the patterns of expenditure among individual households. The latter type of data is of particular use for focusing on the response of demands to changes in income or total expenditure. This is because of the typically large variation in income levels in a cross-section and because, since the surveys are normally completed within a brief time interval, it is legitimate to treat all households as facing almost identical prices.

Consumer theory refers to the *individual* consumer's demand for *individual* goods. However, available data tends to be aggregate in two senses. It typically refers not to individual goods but to broad classifications, e.g. 'food', 'clothing', etc. and almost always refers to large groups of, rather than individual, consumers. This is equally as true of much published cross-sectional data as it is of time series data. Budget surveys tend to provide information on broad categories of expenditure of all households within quite widely defined income classes.[1] Unfortunately, the fact that theory suggests a relationship between demand, total expenditure and prices for the individual consumer by no means guarantees that an identical or even similar relationship will hold at the aggregate level. The derivation of conditions under which 'micro-relationships' can be 'added together' to provide a 'macro-relationship' of the same form is known as *the aggregation problem*. Although we first approach this problem in the context of demand analysis, it should be clear that similar problems are likely to arise in the estimation of any aggregate or macro-relationship.

We shall pay particular attention here to the problem of *aggregating over consumers*. Although the theoretical conditions under which it is permissible to treat broad commodity groupings as a single good are quite restrictive, it appears that as long as goods are classified according to the different needs they satisfy (e.g. into 'clothing', 'entertainment' etc.) the errors involved are not large even when these conditions are not exactly met.

Suppose that household j's demand for a good is given by

$$q_j = \alpha_{0j} + \alpha_{1j}p + \alpha_{2j}p^s + \alpha_{3j}x_j + \varepsilon_j \qquad [6.6]$$

where p and p^s are own price and the price of a substitute good and x_j is household j's total expenditure. If necessary, the price and expenditure variables can be regarded as having been deflated by some general price index, and other variables could be added to [6.6] without affecting what follows. Notice, however, that only x_j of the explanatory variables has been subscripted so that we are assuming that all households face identical prices although their total expenditures will differ. ε_j is a disturbance relating to the jth household, obeying all the classical assumptions listed in Section 2.4.

Given [6.6] for each individual household, we seek conditions under which a macro- or aggregate relationship will exist of the form

$$\bar{q} = \alpha_0 + \alpha_1 p + \alpha_2 p^s + \alpha_3 \bar{x} + \varepsilon \qquad [6.7]$$

where $\bar{q}$ and $\bar{x}$ are the arithmetic means of the demands and total expenditures of all households,[2] the α_i are constants and ε is a 'macro-disturbance' with the same properties as each ε_j.

If there are N households in all then, from [6.6]

$$\bar{q} = \frac{\sum q_j}{N} = \frac{\sum \alpha_{0j}}{N} + \left(\frac{\sum \alpha_{ij}}{N} \right) p + \left(\frac{\sum \alpha_{2j}}{N} \right) p^s + \left(\frac{\sum x_j \alpha_{3j}}{\sum x_j} \right) \bar{x} + \frac{\sum \varepsilon_j}{N} \qquad [6.8]$$

where the summations are over all households. Aggregation, therefore, leads to an equation similar to the required [6.7] with the macro-parameters α_0, α_1 and α_2 equal to the arithmetic means of the corresponding micro-parameters, i.e. $\alpha_0 = \sum \alpha_{0j}/N$, etc. However, α_3 is equal to a *weighted* mean of the micro α_{3j}'s. That is, $\alpha_3 = \sum w_j \alpha_{3j}$ where each $w_j = x_j / \sum x_j$. The weights, the w_j's are equal to the proportion of aggregate total expenditure made by each household. The aggregate disturbance ε is simply the arithmetic mean of the ε_j and hence has the same properties as each individual ε_j.[3]

The problem with equations [6.7] and [6.8] is that α_3 remains constant over time only if the weights, the w_j's, remain constant. This will only occur if the distribution of total expenditures across households remains unchanged over time. If this distribution changes, then α_3 varies and can no longer be regarded as a 'parameter' so that [6.7] is no longer a macro-equivalent of [6.6]. Only if all households have *identical marginal propensities to spend*, i.e. if $\alpha_{3j} = k = $ constant for all j, will α_3 and, hence, aggregate demand be independent of the distribution of total expenditures. In such a case

$$\alpha_3 = \frac{\sum x_j k}{\sum x_j} = \frac{k \sum x_j}{\sum x_j} = k = \text{constant}$$

Equal marginal propensities to spend is a very restrictive condition for 'exact aggregation'. However, less restrictive conditions are necessary if we adopt the so-called *convergence approach*. When aggregating over many households, provided that the x_j and the α_{3j} are distributed independently of one another (e.g. households do not tend to have *both* large total expenditures x_j *and* large marginal propensities α_{3j}) then the expenditure-weighted mean of the α_{3j} will be approximately equal to their arithmetic mean no matter what the distribution of expenditures.[4] Thus, we will have a close approximation to exact aggregation. The crucial requirement, however, is the independence of the x_j's and the α_{3j}'s. A positive correlation (as is likely in the case of 'luxury' goods) or a negative

128

correlation (as is likely in the case of necessities) will lead to the expenditure-weighted mean overestimating or underestimating, respectively, the true arithmetic mean of the α_{3j}'s. Unfortunately, since all commodities are either luxuries or necessities, even this less restrictive condition for aggregation is unlikely to hold in practice. Thus, in many cases a macro-equation like [6.7] with constant α's will only exist when the distribution of total expenditures remains unchanged.

We have so far only considered the aggregation problem in the context of linear demand equations. Suppose, however, that household j's demand equation is given by, for example,

$$q_j = A_0 p^{\alpha_1} p_s^{\alpha_2} x_j^{\alpha_3} \qquad [6.9]$$

Notice that the α's and A are not subscripted in [6.9] so we have simplified somewhat by assuming that these parameters are the same for all households. Equation [6.9] is linear in the logarithms

$$\log q_j = \alpha_0 + \alpha_1 \log p + \alpha_2 \log p_s + \alpha_3 \log x_j \qquad \alpha_0 = \log A \qquad [6.10]$$

so that an analysis similar to that for [6.6] is possible. Summing over all households and dividing by N yields

$$\frac{\sum \log q_j}{N} = \alpha_0 + \alpha_1 \log p + \alpha_2 \log p_s + \alpha_3 \left(\frac{\sum \log x_j}{N} \right)$$

since $\sum \alpha_0 = n\alpha_0$, etc. Thus, a macro-relationship of the same form as [6.10] can be derived provided we define the macro-variables $\bar{q}$ and $\bar{x}$ such that $\log \bar{q} = (\sum \log q_j)/N$ and $\log \bar{x} = (\sum \log x_j)/N$. However, this is equivalent to defining $\bar{q}$ and $\bar{x}$ as the *geometric* rather than the arithmetic means of the corresponding micro-variables.[5] Unfortunately, it is not possible to calculate geometric means from normal aggregate data although, occasionally, use can be made of known relationships between arithmetic and geometric means.

If a demand equation cannot, like [6.9], be transformed into a linear relationship then aggregation problems become even more complex and for this reason are frequently ignored by investigators. Hicks (1956: 55) provides an intuitive argument in support of this.

'*To assume that the representative consumer acts like the ideal consumer is a hypothesis worth testing; to assume that an actual person, the Mr Brown or Mr Jones who lives round the corner does in fact act in such a way does not deserve a moment's consideration.*'

Thus, consumer theory can only be expected to apply to the representative consumer who may not, in fact, exist but who can be interpreted as a statistical average. So, to determine the demand equation for the representative consumer, we must consider the arithmetic averages of demands and total expenditures – the approach adopted in most studies.

6.3 Estimation from time series data

Early time series studies such as those of Schultz (1938) concentrated mainly on staple agricultural products, since the only available data at that time related to such homogeneous commodities. Studies for more heterogeneous manufactured goods were not possible until price indices and total expenditure series for such goods became generally available.

We have already considered in the previous chapter the problems of identification and simultaneity that may arise in the estimation of demand equations from time series data. We will merely stress one point here. In practice, it may seem a simple matter to find variables appearing in the supply equation and not the demand equation and vice versa which apparently serve to identify both equations. However, what really matters is *the extent to which these variables vary* during the sample period. If demand determining factors vary more over time than the supply determining factors then, no matter how many variables can justifiably be included in the supply equation, their lack of variation will mean that it is the supply rather than the demand equation which is 'traced out' by the data. Luckily, as we have noted, most early demand studies dealt with agricultural goods where, because of weather conditions, crop failures, etc. supply conditions were, in fact, extremely variable. For this reason it is probable that early demand studies did, indeed, deal with demand rather than supply relationships, although they paid little formal attention to identification problems. With manufactured commodities there is no reason why supply conditions should be more variable than demand conditions, so in such cases the identification problem requires more careful attention.

We saw in the last chapter that, because of the problem of simultaneity, the OLS estimation method will normally yield biased and inconsistent estimators for the demand equation parameters even when that equation is identified. There are, however, two not uncommon situations where the application of OLS is quite appropriate. The first such exception is when *own-price is a predetermined variable*. For example, this is the case for many public utilities such as gas and electricity where price tends to be set independently of market conditions by public regulation or government dictat. Since own-price is no longer endogenous, its presence on the right-hand side of the demand equation no longer gives rise to OLS bias. A well-known example that makes use of such conditions is the study by Fisher and Kaysen (1962) of the demand for electricity in the US.

The second case where OLS may be more safely applied is where *supply itself is predetermined* and we can replace the supply equation by the simple statement

$$\bar{q} = \bar{q}_0 = \text{predetermined}$$

This might well be a valid specification for a perishable agricultural commodity. The supply of such commodities is subject to exogenous weather variations and is virtually totally inelastic with respect to current price because of time lags involved in planting and harvesting. Adding a demand equation such as [6.7] to the above supply statement and making the market clearing assumption (justified here by the perishable nature of the good) results in a model in which the only endogenous variable is own price, p. An obvious procedure is then to rewrite the demand equation [6.7] with the endogenous own-price as the dependent variable

$$p = -\frac{\alpha_0}{\alpha_1} + \left(\frac{1}{\alpha_1}\right)\bar{q}_0 - \left(\frac{\alpha_2}{\alpha_1}\right)p_s - \left(\frac{\alpha_3}{\alpha_1}\right)\bar{x} - \frac{\varepsilon}{\alpha_1} \qquad [6.7A]$$

Since all the explanatory variables in [6.7A] are either exogenous like p^s and $\bar{x}$ or predetermined like $\bar{q}_0$, they can be considered as independent of the disturbance, $-\varepsilon/\alpha_1$. Hence, the application of OLS to [6.10] will yield unbiased

130

and consistent estimators of its parameters. From these estimators it is then possible to obtain estimators of the α parameters in the original demand equation [6.7]. However, recalling Section 2.3 and the appendix to Chapter 2, note that the α estimators will not be unbiased but merely consistent, since only the property of consistency 'carries over'. For example, although we can obtain an unbiased estimator of $1/\alpha_1$ by applying OLS to [6.7A], its reciprocal will not be an unbiased estimator of α_1. A well-known early example of the above procedure is that of Fox (1958) who, using US data for 1922–41, estimated demand elasticities for various food products.

Ordinary least squares, however, can only be used in the estimation of demand equations in such special cases as the above and normally resort has to be made to simultaneous equation estimating techniques. A well-known study which makes use of such techniques is that by Suits (1955) of the US water-melon market. This provides an excellent illustration of the problems of constructing empirical simultaneous equation models.

Suits's model contains three equations: a crop-supply schedule, a harvest-supply schedule and a demand schedule. The crop-supply schedule is similar to that of Fox above in that decisions to plant are determined by last year's conditions and other predetermined factors. His crop-supply equation estimated by OLS is

$$Q = 769 + 34J - 155K + \underset{(0.156)}{0.587}P_{-1} - \underset{(0.095)}{0.320}C_{-1} - \underset{(0.238)}{0.141}T_{-1} \qquad [6.11]$$

Q is the total number of water-melons *available* for harvest, P_{-1} is the previous year's farm price of water-melons. C_{-1} and T_{-1} are the previous-year prices of cotton and other vegetables respectively and represent the opportunity cost of planting water-melons since these crops compete with water-melons for farm space. J and K are dummy variables representing government policy and the influence of the Second World War. The equation is estimated from US annual data for 1919–51 with the variables measured in logarithmic terms so that the 0.587 coefficient on P_{-1} is the own-price elasticity of crop supply. Since all the explanatory variables are predetermined, simultaneity problems do not arise in the estimation of this equation so the OLS method is, in fact, used.

However, decisions to harvest as distinct from decisions to plant are influenced by *current* prices. The model therefore contains a separate harvest supply equation which relates the number of water-melons actually *harvested*, X, to the current farm price of water-melons and the farm wage rate W. However, since X cannot exceed Q, this relationship only holds when $X < Q$ and has to be estimated ignoring all years when no unharvested crop is reported (i.e. when $X = Q$). Since data on X is only available in the later part of the period, the harvest supply equation has to be estimated using 1930–51 data, and to conserve degrees of freedom the price and wage variables are entered in ratio form

$$X = -118.04 + \underset{(0.110)}{0.237}(P/W) + \underset{(0.114)}{1.205}Q \qquad [6.12]$$

Since the variables are in logarithmic form, coefficients again represent elasticities and we can write $0.237(P/W)$ as $0.237P - 0.237W$. Thus, the own-price elasticity of harvested supply is much smaller than that of crop supply. Also the elasticity of harvested supply with respect to crop supply is not significantly different from unity. This implies that, given P/W, a percentage change in crop supply leads to a roughly equal percentage change in harvested supply.

Finally, Suits's demand equation relates the farm price of water-melons to per capita disposable income Y/N, per capita market supply X/N and an index F of the cost of shipping water-melons from farm to market

$$P = -140.16 + 1.530(Y/N) - 1.110(X/N) - 0.682F \qquad [6.13]$$
$$ (0.088) (0.246) (0.183)$$

The F variable is included since it is the market price of water-melons, that is determined by market forces, whereas the farm price P is less than the market price by a factor dependent on shipping costs. Equation [6.13] is also estimated in logarithmic form so that, rearranging to get X/N on the left-hand side, this equation yields estimates of -0.9 for the own-price elasticity of demand and 1.38 for the income elasticity. This equation also has to be estimated using the shorter 1930–51 period.

The endogenous variables in the above three-equation model are Q, P and X. All other variables are treated as exogenous or predetermined. Y and W are exogenous because the water-melon market represents a very small part of the US economy and also has little influence via the demand for farm labour on W. Notice, however, that equations [6.12] and [6.13] both contain endogenous variables on the right-hand side. Hence, OLS estimates of these equations would be subject to simultaneous equation bias and Suits's estimates, quoted above, were obtained by the LIML method described in Section 4.3.

An interesting reformulation of the Suits model is that of Wold (1958) who models the water-melon market as a recursive system similar to those described in Section 4.2. The endogenous variables are again Q, P and X and they are determined recursively in that order. First, Q is determined by a crop-supply equation identical to that specified by Suits. Next P is determined by real income per capita and by the difference between demand and supply

$$P = \alpha_0 + \alpha_1 \left[\left(\frac{X^*}{N} \right)_{-1} - \frac{Q}{N} \right] + \alpha_2 \left(\frac{Y}{N} \right) \qquad [6.14]$$

Consumer demand, X^*, is given by the harvest X when part of the crop is left unharvested but is unknown for those years when the full crop is harvested. Since it is expected demand that influences the pricing decisions of merchants, last year's per capita demand $(X^*/N)_{-1}$ appears as a proxy for expected per capita demand in equation [6.14]. Real income per capita appears, since as real income increases there is more room for margins between price and production cost.

Given Q and P, per capita demand is then determined by price and real income per capita

$$\frac{X^*}{N} = \beta_0 + \beta_1 P + \beta_2 \left(\frac{Y}{N} \right) \qquad [6.15]$$

The recursive nature of Wold's system means that, provided the disturbances are not correlated across equations (otherwise an identification problem would arise) it can be estimated consistently simply by applying OLS to each equation in turn. However, l'Esperance (1964) has subjected both Suits's original model and Wold's reformulated system to forecasting tests using post-1951 data. Suits's simultaneous system performed better than Wold's recursive system, hence suggesting that it was a better representation of the water-melon market.

Multicollinearity and extraneous estimators

Perhaps the greatest obstacle to obtaining precise estimates of both total expenditure and price elasticities from time series data alone is the multicollinearity frequently found between the expenditure and price variables. For postwar data particularly this collinearity is the result of the strong upward trends exhibited by both types of variable. Its consequence, as we have seen in Section 3.3, is to increase the standard errors associated with estimated coefficients, thus implying a lack of precision in these estimates. It is possible to reduce the multicollinearity that is present by 'imposing homogeneity' and using as explanatory variables *real* total expenditure and *relative* prices. However, since there is typically far greater variation in the real expenditure variable than in relative price variables, this procedure tends to yield fairly well-defined estimates of real expenditure elasticities but rather imprecise estimates of relative price elasticities. We are thus faced with another factor listed in Section 3.3 as leading to lack of precision in the OLS estimators – insufficient variation in the values of explanatory variables. In addition, any multicollinearity remaining after the switch to real expenditure and relative prices may prevent use being made of any limited variation in relative prices that exists.

As we have already mentioned in Section 3.3, investigators have tended to get round the multicollinearity problem by obtaining an extraneous estimator of the real expenditure elasticity from cross-sectional data. Cross-sectional data is often ideal for this purpose, firstly because it is generally reasonable to assume an absence of price variation over the cross-section and, secondly, because many cross-sections contain wide variations in the real-expenditure variable. Provided the extraneous estimator is unbiased then time series estimators of price elasticities obtained by estimating equations such as [3.30] (p. 71) will also be unbiased. Moreover, as originally demonstrated by Durbin (1953), the sampling variability of the price-elasticity estimators obtained in this way will almost certainly be far less than that obtained in the normal time series regression of quantity demanded on both expenditure and price variables. In other words, the use of an extraneously estimated total expenditure elasticity results in far greater precision in the estimation of price elasticities.

Even if an unbiased estimate of the total expenditure elasticity can be obtained from cross-sectional data (and we shall consider the problems of obtaining such an estimate in the next section) serious interpretational difficulties may have to be considered before the estimate can be slotted into a time series equation. It is by no means obvious that the elasticity of total expenditure obtained from a cross-section of individual households *at a given point in time* is conceptually the same as that relevant to the behaviour of an aggregate of households or even an individual household *over a period of time*. Imagine two households of widely differing total expenditures in a cross-section. Suppose the circumstances of the 'poorer' household were changed suddenly in such a manner as to enable it to make, if it wishes, the same total expenditure as the other 'wealthier' household. In the *short run*, before the first household has adjusted to its new circumstances, habit may leave the pattern and maybe even the level of its total expenditure unchanged. However, in the *long* run the composition and level of its expenditures are likely to match those of the wealthy household. If it is reasonable to assume that most houses in a cross-section are well adjusted to their financial circumstances, we can therefore expect cross-sectional data to yield estimates of *long-run* total expenditure elasticities. However, when we consider the behaviour of one or more households over time, it may well be that the data does not conform to traditional static consumer theory. Time series data consists usually of annual or quarterly observations. However, because of habit or inertia, complete adjustments to changes in prices or total expenditure may take longer than one quarter and even longer than one year. For this reason it is often argued that it is predominantly *short run* elasticities that tend to be estimated from time series data.

The above arguments do not mean that it is impossible to make use of extraneous estimates but that such estimates should be used with caution. When dealing with time series data, allowances must be made for lags in the process of adjustment to changes in total expenditure and prices if the two elasticity concepts are to be comparable. As we shall see, such allowances are particularly important in the cases of durable and 'habit-forming' goods and for this reason we shall later devote a separate section to this problem.

6.4   The estimation of Engel curves

Cross-sectional relationships between expenditure on a specific good and the level of income or total expenditure are traditionally referred to as 'Engel curves'. This is in honour of E. Engel who, as the result of cross-sectional studies performed in the mid-nineteenth century, proposed his well-known 'law' that the income elasticity of the demand for food is always less than unity. We have already noted the great advantage of cross-sectional studies – that, apart from minor variations due to geographical and social factors, all prices facing households in the cross-section can be treated as constant. This, of course, enables investigators to concentrate on the relationship between household demands for particular commodities and household income or total expenditure.

The major problem in obtaining adequate cross-sectional estimates of total expenditure elasticities is that expenditure on any good will vary from household to household for reasons other than variations in household resources. The most important of these 'nuisance' variables are probably the size and composition of households, although such factors as age, social class, education, etc. will also be of relevance. While aggregate values of such variables will change only slowly over time and hence can be ignored in time series studies, it is clear that considerable variation is to be expected over a typical cross-section. Our analysis of Section 3.4 suggests that, unless these nuisance variables happen to be completely uncorrelated with total expenditure over the cross-section, biased estimates of total expenditure elasticities are likely to be obtained if they are omitted from the estimating equation. There is therefore a danger of possibly serious specification error. Unfortunately it is obviously likely that household size will be positively correlated with total expenditure. Hence, as our analysis in Section 3.4 indicates, OLS estimators of total expenditure elasticities will be upward-biased if this variable is omitted. Similarly, correlations between any other nuisance variables and total expenditure will also lead to OLS bias.

Most attention has, in fact, been given to household size and composition variables. Other nuisance variables are normally dealt with either by using dummy variables to allow for, for example, differences in social class, or by dealing only with subsamples within the total cross-section. An obvious way of allowing for household size, S, is to include such a variable in the estimating equation. This, however, is likely to lead to problems of multicollinearity (S will usually be correlated with total expenditure). It also raises the question of how S is to be measured. Obviously, a household consisting of one adult and three children should not be regarded as the same 'size' as one consisting of four adults. Early investigators made much use of what are known as *equivalent adult scales*. These defined the size of a household as $S = \sum \lambda_j n_j$ where n_j was the number of individuals of the 'jth type' in the household and λ_j was the 'weight' attached to the jth type. λ_j was conventionally set equal to unity for an adult male and weights for other individuals were determined according to their nutritional requirements relative to adult males. For example, the so-called 'Amsterdam scale' assigned a weight of 0.9 to an adult female. There are two major problems with such scales. Firstly, they are obviously inappropriate for non-food commodities and, secondly, they have a 'normative' aspect. Nutritional experts may believe that an adult female requires 0.9 times the food of an adult male but there can be no guarantee that households will plan their budgets on the basis of such an assumption.

An approach pioneered by Prais and Houthakker (1955) and Barten (1964) which attempts to deal with many of the above problems is to allow the *data* to determine the λ_j and to work in terms of expenditures 'per equivalent adult household'. Specific weights, in fact, have to be estimated for each commodity and general weights estimated to compute the household 'size' used to deflate consumer expenditure. However, there are problems. It is obviously desirable that the functional forms of Engel curves should be such that the sum of expenditures on all goods should equal a household's total expenditure. Unfortunately, if the Engel curves satisfy such an 'adding-up criterion', it can be shown (see, for example, Muellbauer (1974) and (1980)) that the specific weights are unidentified. The problem is that for n goods we have to estimate n specific weights from n Engel curves. However, if the Engel curves satisfy the adding-up criterion they can provide only $n - 1$ independent pieces of information – one too few to identify the specific weights. In fact, the ratios of the specific weights can then be estimated, but not their absolute sizes.

A further problem with cross-sectional data is that expenditure surveys often divide households into wide classifications based on income or total expenditure levels. Published data therefore tends to refer to the 'group means' of such classes, i.e. instead of having data on each household in a class, the only information we have refers to the mean expenditures of all households in the class. Equations must then be estimated using such group means as the basic observations and this causes problems.

Abstracting from problems of size and composition, suppose household j has the following Engel curve for a particular commodity

$$p_j q_j = \alpha + \beta x_j + \varepsilon_j$$

135

where ε_j is a disturbance obeying all the usual classical assumptions. In particular, var $\varepsilon_j = \sigma^2 = \text{constant}$ for all j.

If there are n households within a particular class, the mean expenditure on the commodity for the whole class will be

$$\overline{pq} = \alpha + \beta\bar{x} + \bar{\varepsilon} \qquad [6.16]$$

where $\bar{x}$ is mean total expenditure for the class and $\bar{\varepsilon} = (1/n)\sum \varepsilon_j$. It is group means such as $\overline{qp}$ and $\bar{x}$ which form the basic observations when estimating Engel curves from classified data. However, the variance of the disturbance in [6.16] is σ^2/n. Hence, if classes vary in size, so will the variance of the disturbance associated with them. Thus, an estimating equation based on [6.16] will have a *heteroscedastic disturbance* and the consequences described in Section 3.2 will follow.

The solution to the problem is to adopt the GLS procedure also described in [3.2]. In this case, since var $\bar{\varepsilon} = \sigma^2/n$, we divide [6.16] throughout by $1/\sqrt{n}$ to obtain

$$(\sqrt{n})(\overline{qp}) = \alpha(\sqrt{n}) + \beta(\sqrt{n})(\bar{x}) + u$$

where $u = \bar{\varepsilon}(\sqrt{n})$. Since var $u = n$ var $\bar{\varepsilon} = \sigma^2$, this equation has a homoscedastic disturbance. Hence, OLS may be used to regress the variable $(\sqrt{n})(\overline{qp})$ on $(\sqrt{n})$ and $(\sqrt{n})(\bar{x})$ to obtain estimates of α and β. Notice that the intercept has to be suppressed in the manner of Section 5.4 for this regression.

Much experimentation has been engaged-in to determine the most appropriate *functional form* for Engel curves. Many goods, while luxuries at sufficiently low levels of income and total expenditure, become necessities as total expenditure increases. Hence, *a priori* considerations suggest that total expenditure elasticities will decline as total expenditure x rises. Values in excess of unity are possible for low values of x while at very high values of x, if 'saturation' sets in, elasticities could fall to zero. The full shape of an Engel curve may therefore look something like the 'sigmoid'-shaped curve illustrated in Fig. 6.1a, with an elasticity of unity reached at the point Q. However, functional forms which yield this sigmoid shape are rather complex and in practice simpler, typically two-parameter, curves have commonly been fitted to cross-sectional data. Since variations in total expendi-

6.1a A sigmoid-shaped Engel curve. **6.1b Logarithmic and semi-logarithmic Engel curves.**

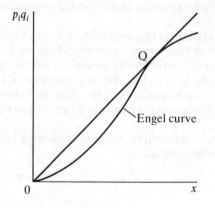

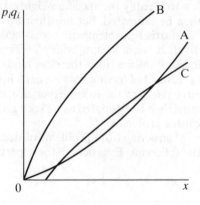

ture are never large enough to reveal the full shape of an Engel curve, functional forms which approximate either the lower or the upper portion of the curve can be expected to fit such data reasonably well. A popular curve which can be used to approximate the lower part of the Engel curve, before the elasticity shows any definite tendency to fall, is the constant-elasticity or logarithmic curve. For commodity i

$$p_i q_i = A_i x^{\beta_i} \tag{6.17}$$

Such curves are illustrated in Fig. 6.1b. Curve A has an elasticity, β_i, in excess of unity and curve B an elasticity between zero and unity.

For cases where the elasticity is likely to decline as total expenditure rises, the 'semi-log' curve may be most appropriate.

$$p_i q_i = \alpha_i + \beta_i \log x \tag{6.18}$$

This is illustrated by curve C in Fig. 6.1b and has an elasticity equal to $\beta_i / p_i q_i$. This curve has the additional advantage of intersecting the total expenditure axis at the point where $\log x = -\alpha_i / \beta_i$ and hence is useful in cases where a commodity is not purchased below a certain level of total expenditure.

Engel curves are typically estimated with expenditure rather than quantity as the dependent variable. However, since it is possible to treat price p_i as a constant over the cross-section, equations such as [6.17] and [6.18] can be converted into demand equations of the same functional form by the simple process of dividing throughout by p_i. The use of expenditure rather than quantity can cause confusion, however, when there is considerable variation in the quality of a good. For example, expenditure on coffee can be on good-quality 'genuine' coffee or on a poorer-quality 'instant' brand. Rises in total expenditure over the cross-section may coincide with a switching from the purchase of instant to the purchase of genuine coffee. If this occurs, then since instant coffee is the lower-priced, increases in expenditure on coffee will tend to exceed increases in the quantity (e.g. number of jars) purchased. There is therefore a danger that the 'true' total expenditure elasticity will be overestimated if expenditure is used as the dependent variable. Ideally, in such cases elasticities should be estimated only for homogeneous categories of commodities (e.g. both genuine *and* instant coffee), but data limitations frequently prevent this.

The explanatory variable used is normally total expenditure rather than income since answers to questions concerning a household's income are notoriously unreliable. We have seen that there are sound theoretical reasons for preferring total expenditure to income, but this choice sometimes causes problems when cross-sectionally estimated elasticities are used as extraneous estimates in time series equations. Investigators have tended to use income as the 'resource variable' in time series studies. To obtain extraneous estimates of income elasticities it is then necessary to multiply the extraneous total expenditure elasticity by some arbitrary estimate of the elasticity of total expenditure with respect to income.

Probably the most well-known work on Engel curves is the study of UK cross-sectional data by Prais and Houthakker (1955). They experimented with five functional forms but eventually rejected all but the logarithmic and semi-log forms [6.17] and [6.18]. The semi-log form proved especially suitable for food items which tend to become necessities at fairly low levels of total expenditure. However, estimates of total expenditure elasticities tended to be very similar no

6.1 Food elasticities obtained using log and semi-log functions

Food	Farinaceous	Dairy	Vegetables	Fruit	Meat	Fish
Logarithmic	0.35	0.48	0.58	1.03	0.62	0.76
Semi-log	0.36	0.53	0.62	1.20	0.69	0.84

Source: Prais and Houthakker (1955)

matter what non-linear functional form was fitted. Some examples of the elasticities found are given in Table 6.1. For the semi-log function (where the elasticity varies along the curve) the value given is that at the point of mean expenditure. The ranking by size of the elasticities is about what one would expect on *a priori* considerations.

Engel curves such as those fitted by Prais and Houthakker are sometimes criticised for not satisfying the so-called 'adding-up' criterion mentioned earlier (p. 135). That is, if all Engel curves had either of these forms then the sum of all expenditures would not equal total expenditure, i.e. $\sum p_i q_i \neq x$. One of the few functional forms for Engel curves that satisfy this criterion is the linear form $p_i q_i = \alpha_i + \beta_i x$ which will do so provided $\sum \alpha_i = 0$ and $\sum \beta_i = 1$. In fact, it can be shown that this is the only functional form for which the OLS estimation method will yield estimated Engel curves which automatically satisfy the adding-up criterion. One of the earliest of modern studies using budget survey data, that of Allen and Bowley (1935), did, in fact, employ linear Engel curves. Unfortunately, linear Engel curves almost always provide inferior fits to the non-linear specifications and recent studies have been more concerned with finding adequate representations of the data than with satisfying the adding-up criterion.

6.5 The demand for durable goods

Static consumer theory yields equilibrium values for quantities demanded for given configurations of prices and total expenditure. It also implies an instantaneous adjustment to new equilibrium values in response to any external change. Consumers, however, are likely to react only gradually to a change in prices or total expenditure and this will give rise to 'lags' in their adjustment to a new equilibrium. A major reason for such lags is that many goods are *durable goods*.

Since a durable good lasts for more than one 'period' this means that past purchases of such a good influence a consumer's present behaviour. Similarly, present purchases will influence his future behaviour. If a consumer purchases a new hi-fi set during one week and the following week the price of such sets declines then static theory would suggest an increase in his purchases of hi-fi sets. However, a far more likely response is that the consumer will delay purchasing another hi-fi set for some considerable time, thus holding expenditure *below its new 'equilibrium' level*.

The above example well illustrates a number of crucial points concerning durable goods. Firstly, a durable good is a discrete indivisible quantity (unlike many non-durables which can be approximately regarded as almost infinitely divisible). Thus a consumer cannot purchase one-fiftieth of a hi-fi set. Secondly, we have to distinguish between *purchases* of a durable good and the consumption of the services which it yields. The flow of purchases adds to the *stock* of durable goods held by consumers while the consumption of services leads to depreciation, depletion or physical deterioration in the stock. Thirdly, a distinction can be made between purchases which represent a *replacement demand*, matching some depletion in the stock, and purchases representing a 'new demand' which results in a net increase in the stock.

The fact that adjustment to equilibrium levels of demand may not be instantaneous is the basis of the so-called *stock adjustment models* of the demand for durable goods. Ignoring any aggregation problems, suppose that the equilibrium or desired stock of the durable good, S_t^*, is a linear function of real total expenditure, x_t, and the relative price of the good, p_t. That is

$$S_t^* = \alpha_0 + \alpha_1 p_t + \alpha_2 x_t + \varepsilon_t \qquad\qquad [6.19]$$

where ε_t is a disturbance.[6]

Actual stock, S_t, however, does not normally equal desired stock, but is determined by a partial adjustment model of the kind described in Section 5.1

$$S_t - S_{t-1} = \lambda(S_t^* - S_{t-1}) \qquad 0 < \lambda < 1 \qquad\qquad [6.20]$$

That is, the adjustment in actual stock equals only a fraction λ of the difference between desired and actual stock. In general, the longer the time period involved the greater will be the extent of the adjustment and the larger the adjustment coefficient λ.

Stocks of the durable good are normally assumed to depreciate at a constant rate, δ, per period and can therefore be related to quantities purchased of the good by the equation

$$S_t = (1 - \delta)S_{t-1} + q_t \qquad\qquad [6.21]$$

where q_t represents purchases per period. Using equations [6.19], [6.20] and [6.21], an equation for q_t can be derived which does not involve the unobservable desired stock variable and which hence may, hopefully, be estimated.

$$q_t = S_t - S_{t-1} + \delta S_{t-1} \qquad\qquad [6.22]$$
$$\quad\, = \lambda(S_t^* - S_{t-1}) + \delta S_{t-1}$$

or

$$q_t = \lambda\alpha_0 + \lambda\alpha_1 p_t + \lambda\alpha_2 x_t + (\delta - \lambda)S_{t-1} + \lambda\varepsilon_t \qquad\qquad [6.23]$$

Purchases are therefore dependent not only on relative price and total expenditure, but also on the stock carried over from the previous period. Thus, as we have noted, past purchases influence present decisions. Notice that since δ can be interpreted as the proportion of beginning-period stock which becomes unusable during the period, equation [6.22] divides total purchases into net additions to stock and 'replacement' purchases. In the aggregate context, however, a 'replacement purchase' does not necessarily imply that a *given* consumer has replaced, for example, his hi-fi set with a new one. The first δS_{t-1} of total purchases are regarded as replacements whoever does the purchasing and if, in fact, total purchases are less than δS_{t-1}, then net additions to stock, $S_t - S_{t-1}$, will be negative.

The major problem in estimating [6.23] is that of finding data on S_t, the actual stock of the durable good. The stock will consist of goods of different ages or 'vintages' and, hence, an index number problem is involved. In an early study of the demand for automobiles in the US, Chow (1957; 1960) actually constructs a series for S_t taking a weighted sum of registrations at the end of each year with weights proportional to the prices of automobiles of different brands and ages. Measuring q_t as annual purchases of new cars per capita and p_t as the ratio of a car price index to a general price index, he estimated from US annual data for 1921–53

$$q_t = 0.08 - 0.020 p_t + 0.012 x_t - 0.23 S_{t-1} \qquad R^2 = 0.858 \qquad [6.24]$$
$$ (0.003) \quad\;\; (0.001) \quad\;\; (0.047)$$

A disposable income variable was used for x_t rather than total expenditure. Notice that the parameters in [6.23] are unidentified since there are only four coefficients from which $\alpha_0, \alpha_1, \alpha_2, \lambda$ and δ have to be estimated. However, Chow obtains an extraneous estimate of the depreciation parameter $\delta = 0.25$ by comparing the prices of cars of different ages. Comparison of equation [6.24] with [6.23] then yields the parameter values

$$\lambda = 0.48, \quad \alpha_0 = 0.17, \quad \alpha_1 = -0.042 \quad \text{and} \quad \alpha_2 = 0.025$$

The value for the adjustment parameter λ suggests, from [6.20], that just under half of any difference between actual and desired stocks are made up during the year. Long-run elasticities of demand (i.e. those holding when actual stocks are completely adjusted to desired levels and $S_t = S_t^*$) can be evaluated at the point of sample means using the above values, and Chow obtains values of -0.63 for the long-run price elasticity and 1.7 for the long-run income elasticity. Because of the value obtained for λ these are approximately twice as large as the short-run elasticities obtainable from equations [6.23] and [6.24].

Frequently data on stocks of durables are unobtainable, partly because of 'vintage' effects and the problem of obtaining an adequate external estimate of the depreciation parameter δ. An alternative approach, first adopted by Stone and Rowe (1957) for UK consumer durables, is as follows. Alternative series for S_t are constructed using equation [6.21], taking an arbitrary starting value, S_0, for S_{t-1}, and using actual data on purchases combined with various assumed values for δ. Thus, series are constructed as

$$S_t = q_t + (1-\delta) q_{t-1} + (1-\delta)^2 q_{t-2} + \ldots, + (1-\delta)^{t-1} q_1 + (1-\delta)^t S_0$$
$$[6.25]$$

for different values of δ. When [6.25] is substituted into [6.23], the arbitrary S_0 is absorbed into the constant term and a value of δ is eventually selected which gives the best-fitting version of equation [6.23]. Thus δ is, in fact, estimated from the data as are λ and the α's. A method of estimation first suggested by Nerlove (1958) involves transforming equation [6.23] so as to eliminate the stock variable altogether. Lagging [6.23] by one period and multiplying throughout by $1-\delta$ yields

$$(1-\delta) q_{t-1} = (1-\delta)\lambda\alpha_0 + (1-\delta)\lambda\alpha_1 p_{t-1} + (1-\delta)\lambda\alpha_2 x_{t-1}$$
$$+ (1-\delta)(\delta-\lambda)S_{t-2} + (1-\delta)\lambda\varepsilon_{t-1}$$

Substracting this equation from [6.23] we have

$$q_t - (1 - \delta)q_{t-1} = \delta\lambda\alpha_0 + \lambda\alpha_1 p_t - (1 - \delta)\lambda\alpha_1 p_{t-1} + \lambda\alpha_2 x_t - (1 - \delta)\lambda\alpha_2 x_{t-1}$$
$$+ (\delta - \lambda)[S_{t-1} - (1 - \delta)S_{t-2}] + \lambda\varepsilon_t - (1 - \delta)\lambda\varepsilon_{t-1}$$

Moreover, since from equation [6.21] we have

$$S_{t-1} - (1 - \delta)S_{t-2} = q_{t-1}$$

we eventually obtain

$$q_1 = \delta\lambda\alpha_0 + \lambda\alpha_1 p_t - (1 - \delta)\lambda\alpha_1 p_{t-1} + \lambda\alpha_2 x_t - (1 - \delta)\lambda\alpha_2 x_{t-1}$$
$$+ (1 - \lambda)q_{t-1} + \lambda\varepsilon_t - (1 - \delta)\lambda\varepsilon_{t-1} \qquad [6.26]$$

Equation [6.26] expresses purchases as a function of price, total expenditure and lagged values of price, total expenditure and purchases. Despite the absence of the stock variable, however, equation [6.26] presents a number of estimation problems. Firstly, the equation is 'overidentified' in the sense that it involves six coefficients from which we must obtain values for five parameters. For example, the ratio of the coefficients on p_t and p_{t-1} will provide one estimate of δ but the ratio of the coefficients on the expenditure variables will provide a second, almost certainly different, estimate. This means that either extraneous estimates of δ must be used or a non-linear estimating procedure of the kind described at the end of Section 5.4 must be adopted which minimises the sum of squared residuals subject to constraints which ensure unique values for each estimated parameter.

Secondly, if the disturbance ε_t in equation [6.19] is non-autocorrelated, then the composite disturbance in equation [6.26], i.e.

$$u_t = \lambda\varepsilon_t - (1 - \delta)\lambda\varepsilon_{t-1}$$

will be autocorrelated since both u_t and u_{t-1} will be dependent on ε_{t-1}. This autocorrelation, when combined with the appearance of the lagged dependent variable q_{t-1} among the explanatory variables, means, as we saw in Section 3.2, that normal OLS procedures will yield biased and inconsistent estimators of the parameters of [6.26]. Maximum likelihood procedures which explicitly take account of the autocorrelation are therefore necessary if consistent estimators are to be obtained.

Despite these estimation difficulties, the stock adjustment model has proved a popular vehicle for explaining the importance of lagged variables in demand equations for durable goods. However, other dynamic models can also give rise to estimating equations similar to [6.26] and it may in practice prove difficult to discriminate between competing models. For example, we turn next to a generalisation of the stock adjustment model first suggested by Houthakker and Taylor (1970).

The state adjustment model

We have already noted in our discussion of time series data that, because of habit and inertia, lagged adjustment to equilibrium values may be a characteristic of the demand for non-durable as well as durable goods. Houthakker and Taylor (1970) propose the following equation for *both* durable and non-durable goods

$$q_t = \beta_0 + \beta_1 p_t + \beta_2 x_t + \gamma S_{t-1} + \varepsilon_t \qquad [6.27]$$

S_t is now a 'state variable', to be interpreted in the case of durables simply as the beginning period stock of the good, but in the case of non-durables representing a psychological 'stock of habits' since in this case tastes and hence purchases are assumed to be influenced by past consumption. For durables [6.27] is identical to the stock adjustment equation [6.23] with $\gamma = \delta - \lambda$, while for non-durables it is simply assumed that $\gamma > 0$. Stocks of habit are determined by an equation identical to [6.21] except that δ is now interpreted as the rate (assumed constant) at which habits decay. Note that further purchases increase the stock of habits.[7] Also, [6.25] in the present context implies that habits depend on past purchases and an 'original' stock of habits S_0, but since $0 < \delta < 1$, recent past purchases are the most important in determining S_t.

Equations [6.27] and [6.21] can be manipulated in the same way as [6.19] and [6.21] to yield

$$q_t = \delta\beta_0 + \beta_1 p_t - (1 - \delta)\beta_1 p_{t-1} + \beta_2 x_t - (1 - \delta)\beta_2 x_{t-1}$$
$$+ (1 + \gamma - \delta)q_{t-1} + \varepsilon_t - (1 - \delta)\varepsilon_{t-1} \qquad [6.28]$$

Thus the stock variable is again eliminated, [6.28] being an identical estimating equation to [6.26] although it is given a different interpretation for habit-forming goods.

The advantage of the Houthakker–Taylor model is that it can be applied to any good – durable, habit-forming or *both*. The sign of γ in [6.27] depends on the properties of the relevant good. If $\gamma < 0$, then 'inventory effects' are held to outweigh 'habit-forming' effects while, if $\gamma > 0$, habit-forming effects pre-dominate.[8] More importantly however, the sign of γ determines the relationship between short- and long-run elasticities. The long-run relationship between purchases, prices and total expenditure can be obtained by setting

$$q_t = q_{t-1}, \quad p_t = p_{t-1} \quad \text{and} \quad x_t = x_{t-1}$$

in equation [6.28]. This yields

$$q_t = \frac{\delta\beta_0}{\delta - \gamma} + \frac{\delta\beta_1}{\delta - \gamma} p_t + \frac{\delta\beta_2}{\delta - \gamma} x_t \qquad [6.29]$$

The long-run effect of changes in p_t or x_t is therefore $\delta/(\delta - \gamma)$ times the short-run effect. Hence, if $\gamma < 0$, then short-run effects are greater than long-run effects, whereas if $\gamma > 0$ then (provided $\gamma < \delta$ as invariably found by Houthakker and Taylor) long-run effects are the more important. Any difference between short- and long-run elasticities has important implications for the effect of, for example, changes in indirect taxation on purchases and the marked differences found by Houthakker and Taylor were put forward as a clear justification for their model.

Houthakker and Taylor investigate eighty-one forms of consumer expenditure using annual US data over the period 1929–64. For sixty-five of their eighty-one categories the state adjustment model performs best and in forty-six of these cases the γ coefficient turns out to be positive, implying larger elasticities in the long run than in the short run.[9] These goods represented 61 per cent of total US consumer expenditure.

As an example, consider the following equation for 'clothing, including luggage' estimated by OLS. (Note, however, that the Durbin–Watson statistic is an invalid test for autocorrelation because of the presence of q_{t-1} among the explanatory variables. Autocorrelation is to be expected given the moving average disturbance in [6.28] and its presence together with q_{t-1} would make OLS inconsistent.)

$$q_t = 17.595 + 0.0763\Delta x_t + 0.0173x_{t-1} + 0.6243q_{t-1} \quad R^2 = 0.904 \quad \text{d.w.} = 2.03$$
$$\quad\;\; (8.905) \quad (0.0242) \qquad (0.0074) \qquad (0.1479)$$

Price variables turned out to be incorrectly signed for this category and were dropped from the equation. Since the terms in Δx_t and x_{t-1} can be rewritten as $0.0763x_t - 0.0590x_{t-1}$, the above equation implies the following values for the parameters in equation [6.28]

$$\beta_1 = 0, \quad \beta_2 = 0.0763, \quad \delta = 0.227 \quad \text{and} \quad \gamma = -0.149$$

Notice, firstly, that since $\gamma < 0$, inventory effects outweigh habit-forming effects for this category of good. The depreciation parameter is 0.227 although we cannot say to what extent this represents depreciation in stocks of goods or stocks of habit. β_2 measures the short-run effect of a total expenditure change and is positive as expected. The long run effect is given by

$$\frac{\delta\beta_2}{(\delta - \gamma)} = 0.046$$

Thus, because $\gamma < 0$, the long-run effect of a total expenditure change is less than the short-run effect.

The model is also estimated for eleven much broader categories of expenditure. For example, for 'automobiles and parts', the short-run income elasticity is 5.06 falling to 1.07 in the long run. This reflects the high durability of automobiles ($\gamma < 0$) since, although initially purchases respond sharply to a change in income, such purchases raise future stocks of automobiles and this has the effect of reducing future purchases. On the other hand, 'food and beverages' have a short-run income elasticity of 0.72 rising to 0.85 in the long run. Here habit influences outweigh any inventory effects that may be present ($\gamma > 0$) and initial purchases increase the 'stock' of habits which reinforces future demand.

The adjustment models outlined in this section are obviously a definite improvement on models in which all adjustments to equilibrium values are assumed to occur instantaneously. They do, however, fail to make allowance for a number of factors which may be of particular importance in the demand for durable goods. For example, no account is taken of expectations about the future price of durable goods, although such expectations might well affect demand, particularly as far as the timing of replacement demand is concerned. Indeed, replacement demand in these models is virtually defined to be a constant proportion of beginning-period stock, whereas in practice economic conditions could result in either an advancement or a delay in replacement purchases. Such 'discretionary' replacement is, in fact, a feature of the more recent models of Smith (1975) and Westin (1975).

Another problem with adjustment models is that it is not clear how borrowing constraints such as government credit restrictions should be introduced into the analysis. One possibility is to add government policy variables to equation [6.19] and this is a method occasionally followed. However, such constraints are just as likely to affect the speed at which adjustment takes place. This confusion is partly the result of the *ad hoc* nature of the models – insufficient attention is paid to the reasons why adjustment is not instantaneous. The way forward may well involve the development of models in which partial adjustment arises *as a result* of utility-maximising behaviour, i.e. as a natural choice of the rational consumer.

6.6 Estimating complete systems of demand equations

During the past quarter-century a second approach to the estimation of demand equations has developed, involving the estimation of complete systems of equations encompassing all current spending made by consumers. Traditional consumer theory leads to the system of n demand equations given by equation [6.1]. We have seen that, when attention is confined to just one of these equations, investigators are inevitably forced by degrees of freedom problems to adopt an *ad hoc* approach of dubious theoretical validity involving the suppression of most explanatory price variables. However, if the full system of demand equations [6.1] is considered, the degrees of freedom problem can be reduced and the number of independent parameters limited not by *ad hoc* methods but by making use of the series of restrictions on the parameters of equation [6.1] which are implied by consumer theory.

These restrictions arise partly because of the existence of the consumer's budget constraint and partly because of the assumption of utility maximisation.[10] The budget constraint is

$$p_1 q_1 + p_2 q_2 + p_3 q_3 + \cdots + p_n q_n = x$$

Partially differentiating the budget constraint with respect to x yields

$$p_1 \frac{\partial q_1}{\partial x} + p_2 \frac{\partial q_2}{\partial x} + p_3 \frac{\partial q_3}{\partial x} + \cdots + p_n \frac{\partial q_n}{\partial x} = 1 \qquad [6.30]$$

Partially differentiating with respect to $p_1, p_2, \ldots, p_n$ in turn yields the set of restrictions

$$p_1 \frac{\partial q_1}{\partial p_j} + p_2 \frac{\partial q_2}{\partial p_j} + p_3 \frac{\partial q_3}{\partial p_j} + \cdots + p_n \frac{\partial q_n}{\partial p_j} = -q_j \qquad j = 1, 2, 3, \ldots, n \qquad [6.31]$$

Equations [6.30] and [6.31] are sometimes referred to as the *aggregation* restrictions. *Homogeneity* has already been mentioned in the single equation context but applies, of course, to all n equations in [6.1]. Since homogeneity implies that the sum of all price elasticities plus the total expenditure elasticity equals zero, we can express these n restrictions as

$$\frac{p_1 \partial q_i}{q_i \partial p_1} + \frac{p_2 \partial q_i}{q_i \partial p_2} + \frac{p_3 \partial q_i}{q_i \partial p_3} + \cdots + \frac{p_n \partial q_i}{q_i \partial p_n} + \frac{x \partial q_i}{q_i \partial x} = 0 \qquad i = 1, 2, 3, \ldots, n$$

or, multiplying throughout by q_i

$$p_1 \frac{\partial q_i}{\partial p_1} + p_2 \frac{\partial q_i}{\partial p_2} + p_3 \frac{\partial q_i}{\partial p_3} + \cdots + p_n \frac{\partial q_i}{\partial p_n} = -x \frac{\partial q_i}{\partial x} \qquad i = 1, 2, 3, \ldots, n \qquad [6.32]$$

We have already come across the Slutsky equation or 'law of demand' in the single equation context and it applies to all n equations in the system

144

$$\frac{\partial q_i}{\partial p_i} + q_i \frac{\partial q_i}{\partial x} < 0 \qquad i = 1, 2, 3, \ldots, n \qquad\qquad [6.33]$$

The n equations [6.33] are known as the *negativity* restrictions and in fact follow from the assumption of utility maximisation. However, utility maximisation also implies $n(n-1)/2$ so-called *symmetry* restrictions involving more than just one equation

$$\frac{\partial q_i}{\partial p_j} + q_j \frac{\partial q_i}{\partial x} = \frac{\partial q_j}{\partial p_i} + q_i \frac{\partial q_j}{\partial x} \qquad \text{for all} \quad i \neq j \qquad\qquad [6.34]$$

In the single-equation context the imposition of homogeneity reduced the number of independent parameters to be estimated by one. Similarly, imposition of any of the 'equality-type' restrictions [6.30–6.32] and [6.34] has the same effect on the number of independent parameters to be estimated in the system [6.1] whatever functional form is chosen. However, not all the restrictions listed above are independent of one another, since it can be shown that the aggregation and symmetry restrictions taken together imply homogeneity. There are therefore

$$\tfrac{1}{2}n(n+1) + 1$$

independent equality-type restrictions in all. Notice, however, that the aggregation and symmetry restrictions are *cross-equation* restrictions, involving the parameters of *all* equations in [6.1]. Their imposition, therefore, requires the simultaneous estimation of all demand equations in the system.

In an n equation demand system there will, in the absence of restrictions, be n^2 price parameters and n total expenditure parameters to be estimated. Hence, ignoring the negativity restrictions (which, being inequalities, are more difficult to impose) the imposition of the theoretical restrictions reduces the total number of independent parameters to

$$n^2 + n - \tfrac{1}{2}n(n+1) - 1 = \tfrac{1}{2}n(n+1) - 1 \qquad\qquad [6.35]$$

Thus, in, for example, a twelve-equation system the number of parameters to be estimated falls from 156 to 77. In practice, limited sample sizes mean that this is still likely to be too many, so at first sight it may seem that the full system approach falls foul of degrees of freedom difficulties just as does the concentration on a single equation. Econometricians, however, have been reluctant to abandon this approach, firstly because of its sounder theoretical foundation, and secondly because the imposition of the theoretical restrictions should, provided they are valid, enable more precise estimates of demand equation parameters to be obtained. The most efficient estimators, i.e. those with the smallest sampling variances, are those that make use of all available valid information. Since many of the theoretical restrictions are cross-equation in nature, they cannot be imposed on each equation in isolation so that efficient estimation implies the estimation of the full system.

The way out of the 'degrees of freedom deadlock' has been to impose further restrictions on demand equations which are derived by making special assumptions about the consumer's utility function. In this way it is possible to reduce dramatically the number of independent parameters that have to be estimated. The most popular of these special assumptions is that known as *additivity* or 'want independence'. A consumer's preferences are said to be want-independent if they can be represented by a utility function which is additive in the sense that the marginal utility of any one good is independent of the quantities consumed of all other goods.[11] Advocates of the additivity assumption argue that it is acceptable provided 'goods' are defined in a sufficiently broad manner. For example, the marginal utility of 'entertainment' is unlikely to be much affected by the quantity of 'clothing' consumed. However, additivity is a somewhat extreme assumption, for it can be shown that it implies that goods cannot be inferior and neither can they be complements in the modern Hicksian sense. Its major advantage is that, *provided* it is a valid assumption, it reduces the number of independent parameters in a demand system from the $\frac{1}{2}n(n+1) - 1$ of equation [6.35] to as few as n. Many economists, however, would regard so few independent responses as, in itself, unrealistic. Fortunately there are a number of assumptions, less restrictive than additivity, which increase the number of independent responses beyond n but still keep them well below that of equation [6.35].

In estimating demand systems two approaches are possible. Firstly, the precise form of the utility function can be specified. Hence, a system of demand equations can be derived which are guaranteed to satisfy at least the general restrictions [6.30–6.34] implied by consumer theory. The advantage of such an approach is the increase in degrees of freedom available; the disadvantages that it cannot be used to *test* the restrictions of the theory and a loss in generality resulting from whatever precise form is given to the utility function. The second approach is to begin with a set of demand equations which are capable of satisfying theoretical restrictions but do not necessarily do so. With this approach it is possible to test theoretical restrictions, but the obvious disadvantage here is that since re-strictions are not imposed we come up against the degrees of freedom problem. Furthermore, although properties of the utility function are not *explicitly* specified in this approach, there is a real danger that in deciding on particular functional forms for the demand equation we may be *implicitly* imposing restrictions on the underlying utility function which, for all we know, are totally unacceptable. In the next section we shall concentrate on two well-known demand systems, one representing the first of the above approaches and the other the second. We also consider, more briefly, some other complete system models of demand.

The linear expenditure system

The linear expenditure system (LES), first extensively used by Stone (1954), does have an explicitly specified utility function

$$U = \beta_1 \log(q_1 - \gamma_1) + \beta_2 \log(q_2 - \gamma_2) + \cdots + \beta_n \log(q_n - \gamma_n) \qquad [6.36]$$

where the β's and γ's are parameters and, if the logarithms are to be defined, it is necessary that $q_i > \gamma_i$ for all i. Maximisation of [6.36] subject to the usual budget constraint

$$p_i q_i = x$$

leads, after some manipulation, to the system of demand equations

$$p_i q_i = p_i \gamma_i + \beta_i [x - \sum_j p_j \gamma_j] \qquad i = 1, 2, 3, \ldots, n \qquad [6.37]$$

with $0 < \beta_i < 1$ for all i. The great advantage of this system is that it expresses q_i as a *linear* function of x/p_i (a measure of real total expenditure) and of relative prices

p_j/p_i and this makes for ease of estimation. In fact, it can be shown that [6.37] is *the only linear demand equation which satisfies all the theoretical restrictions.*

An appealing way of interpreting equation [6.37] is to regard expenditure p_iq_i on good i as made up of two parts. One part, $p_i\gamma_i$, is the minimum possible expenditure on good i so that γ_i is to be interpreted as the 'subsistence level' of consumption for good i. Hence, a portion of total expenditure, $\sum p_i\gamma_i$, is committed to unavoidable subsistence purchases. The remainder of total expenditure, $x - \sum p_i\gamma_i$, is sometimes referred to as 'supernumerary expenditure' and is spent on all goods in constant proportions. Thus the second part of expenditure on good i is always some constant fraction, β_i, of supernumerary expenditure.

While ease of estimation is the obvious attraction of the LES, it should be clear from equation [6.36] that the underlying utility function is an additive one so that the system suffers from the limitations of additive systems mentioned above. Notwithstanding this, the LES has proved a popular method of estimating the magnitude of consumer responses to expenditure and price changes. Estimated systems have then been used for forecasting purposes. Stone and his associates (1964) used a system based on data going back to the beginning of the century to forecast UK demand up until 1970. Other well-known estimated LES's are those of Pollock and Wales (1969) for the US, Goldberger and Gamaletsos (1970) for thirteen OEC countries and, more recently, Deaton (1975) who estimated a thirty-seven-equation system for the UK.

The Rotterdam model

The Rotterdam model exemplifies the second of the two approaches to the estimation of demand systems and has, until recently, proved the most popular method of attempting to 'test' the restrictions implied by consumer theory. The Rotterdam model, first developed by Theil (1965) and Barten (1966), employs as dependent variables, not quantities demanded, q_i, but variables of the form

$$w_i\left(\frac{dq_i}{q_i}\right) = w_i d \log q_i,$$

where

$$w_i = \left(\frac{p_iq_i}{x}\right)$$

is the proportion of total expenditure allocated to good i. This may seem a strange choice unless it is remembered that consumer theory is concerned with the allocation of total expenditure between various goods. It therefore makes sense to consider the 'budget shares', w_i, rather than the q_i. Furthermore, a budget share w_i changes as total expenditure, x, and price, p_i, change both directly because it depends on x and p_i and indirectly because the consumer adjusts q_i the quantity demanded. That is,

$$dw_i = \frac{\partial w}{\partial q_i} dq_i + \frac{\partial w}{\partial p_i} dp_i + \frac{\partial q_i}{\partial x} dx$$

$$= \frac{p_i}{x} dq_i + \frac{q_i}{x} dp_i - \frac{p_iq_i}{x^2} dx = w_i \frac{dq_i}{q_i} + w_i \frac{dp_i}{p_i} - w_i \frac{dx}{x}$$

or

$$dw_i = w_i d \log q_i + w_i d \log p_i - w_i d \log x \qquad [6.38]$$

Since changes in total expenditure and prices are taken as given by the consumer, only that part of dw_i represented by the first term on the right-hand side of [6.38] can be thought of as being endogenously determined. This makes $w_i d \log q_i$ a very appropriate choice as the dependent variable in a demand equation.

Demand equations with such a dependent variable can be obtained by taking the total differential of equation [6.1] and multiplying throughout by w_i/q_i. This eventually yields

$$w_i d \log q_i = \sum_j \Pi_{ij} d \log p_j + \mu_i \sum_j w_j d \log q_j \qquad i = 1, 2, 3, \dots, n \qquad [6.39]$$

where $\mu_i = p_i(\partial q_i/\partial x)$ is the marginal propensity to consume good i and Π_{ij} is the product of w_i and the 'income-compensated' elasticity of demand for good i with respect to the price of good j. Changes in expenditure are reflected in equation [6.39] by the $\sum w_j d \log q_j$ term which is a measure of real income. Notice that [6.39] as it stands is completely general, since it is derived from [6.1] without specifying any particular form for the demand equations. It is hence implied by *any* underlying utility function. The equations [6.39] represent a 'differential demand equation system' since they determine changes in demand rather than the demands themselves.

The μ_i and the Π_{ij} in equations [6.39] will normally be dependent on total expenditure, x, and on all prices. The Rotterdam model however, 'parameterises' the μ_i and the Π_{ij}, treating them as constants and ignoring their dependence on x and on prices. This may seem a somewhat drastic procedure but if estimation is to proceed at all then some quantities have to be parameterised.[12] The great advantage of treating the μ_i and Π_{ij} as constants is that it enables the theoretical restrictions [6.30–6.34] to be rewritten as equations which are *unchanged for all values of total expenditure and prices.* When the restrictions are formulated in terms of first derivatives, then, as an examination of [6.30–6.34] indicates, their precise form will depend on levels of x and prices. However, in terms of the μ_i and Π_{ij} they become

$$\text{Aggregation} \begin{cases} \mu_1 + \mu_2 + \mu_3 + \cdots \mu_n = 1 & [6.30A] \\ \Pi_{1j} + \Pi_{2j} + \Pi_{3j} + \cdots \Pi_{nj} = 0 & j = 1, 2, 3, \dots, n & [6.31A] \end{cases}$$

$$\text{Homogeneity} \quad \Pi_{i1} + \Pi_{i2} + \Pi_{i3} + \cdots \Pi_{in} = 0 \qquad i = 1, 2, 3, \dots, n \qquad [6.32A]$$

$$\text{Negativity} \quad \Pi_{ii} < 0 \qquad i = 1, 2, 3, \dots, n \qquad [6.33A]$$

$$\text{Symmetry} \quad \Pi_{ij} = \Pi_{ji} \qquad \text{for all} \quad i \neq j \qquad [6.34A]$$

Notice that the 'strongest' of the restrictions, i.e. [6.30–6.32] and [6.34] are now of especially simple linear form and moreover retain exactly this form *for every observation in a sample* and this makes their imposition a relatively simple matter. By contrast, if the derivatives in [6.30–6.34] are parameterised then the restrictions to be imposed would vary in form from observation to observation.

It may now seem that the Rotterdam model presents a perfect method of either testing the restrictions of consumer theory or of enforcing them and reaping the benefits of more efficient estimation. However, the parameterisation of the μ_i and the Π_{ij} has implications which were not foreseen by the originators of the system. As first shown by D. McFadden in an unpublished paper, differential demand equations in which the μ_i and Π_{ij} are constants can only arise when the demands themselves are determined by a system of the following kind

$$q_i = \mu_i \left(\frac{x}{p_i} \right) \qquad i = 1, 2, 3, \ldots, n$$

This demand system implies that expenditure on any good, $p_i q_i$, is a constant proportion, μ_i, of total expenditure, x, no matter what the structure of relative prices. A moment's reflection should convince the reader that 'expenditure proportionality' is a clearly implausible description of consumer behaviour. In addition, the above demand system can easily be shown to arise from the maximisation of the additive utility function $U = \sum \mu_i \log q_i$ and, hence, *must necessarily satisfy all the theoretical restrictions.*

These unexpected implications may seem to damage severely any claim the Rotterdam model has to be a completely general demand system. Moreover, if the Rotterdam model automatically satisfies the theoretical restrictions it can hardly be used to test them! However, empirical versions of the Rotterdam model, in which variables of the kind $w_i(\log q_{it} - \log q_{it-1})$ are used to approximate the log differentials of equation [6.39], certainly do not suggest expenditure proportionality. Moreover, Rotterdam theorists claim that their system can be regarded as a first-order approximation to any arbitrary demand system (see, for example, Theil 1975). However, McFadden's result well illustrates the unforeseen dangers of arbitrary parameterisation in this area of empirical research.

Typically, maximum likelihood methods have been used to estimate Rotterdam systems. Well-known studies are those of Barten (1969) using Dutch data for 1921–63 and Deaton (1974) for UK data from 1900–70. The most interesting feature of this work is that the theoretical restriction of homogeneity, and also possibly that of symmetry, *appears to be rejected by the data.* Equiproportionate changes in total expenditure and prices do *not* appear to leave quantities demanded unchanged. This apparent rejection of theory could be attributed to the fact that the Rotterdam model is at best an approximation. However, as we shall see in a moment, other investigators using different demand systems, involving different approximations, have come up with similar results. Although research in this field is bedevilled by the need to find parameterisations which have no undesirable implications, and there is always the possibility that non-homogeneity may be a consequence of the model used rather than a property of the data, this unanimity is impressive.

Other models of demand

It is often useful in applied demand analysis to work not in terms of the normal 'direct' utility function but from the so-called *indirect utility function*. For example, in the simple two-good case if a consumer is assumed to maximise a utility function

$$U = U(q_1, q_2) \qquad [6.40]$$

149

subject to the budget constraint

$$p_1 q_1 + p_2 q_2 = x \qquad [6.41]$$

then we obtain the two demand equations

$$q_1 = q_1(p_1, p_2, x) \qquad [6.42]$$
$$q_2 = q_2(p_1, p_2, x)$$

Substituting these expressions for q_1 and q_2 back into [6.40] we obtain the maximum utility obtainable for any given combination of p_1, p_2 and x. This yields the indirect utility function

$$U^* = U^*[q_1(p_1, p_2, x), \quad q_2(p_1, p_2, x)] \qquad [6.43]$$

Alternatively, we may *start* with the indirect utility function [6.43]. If we specify a precise functional form for [6.43] then functional forms for the demand equations [6.42] can easily be obtained by using *Roy's Identity* which states that[13]

$$q_i = -\frac{\partial U^*}{\partial p_i} \bigg/ \frac{\partial U^*}{\partial x} \qquad [6.44]$$

Houthakker (1960) suggested that, in the general case, [6.43] should be specified as

$$U^* = \alpha_1 \left(\frac{p_1}{x}\right)^{\beta_1} + \alpha_2 \left(\frac{p_2}{x}\right)^{\beta_2} + \ldots, + \alpha_n \left(\frac{p_n}{x}\right)^{\beta_n} \qquad [6.45]$$

This specification implies that the indirect utility function is homogeneous of degree zero in prices and total expenditure. This is a necessary requirement of theory since in [6.43] each q_i is homogeneous of degree zero in prices and x. Applying Roy's Identity to [6.45] and taking logarithms, now yields a system of demand equations known as the *indirect addilog model*.

$$\log q_i = \log \alpha_i \beta_i + (\beta_i + 1) \log\left(\frac{x}{p_i}\right) + \log\left\{ \sum_k \alpha_k \beta_k \left(\frac{x}{p_k}\right)^{\beta_k} \right\}$$

$$i = 1, 2, 3, \ldots, n \qquad [6.46]$$

The indirect addilog model is akin to the LES in that, since it is derived using the assumption of utility maximisation, its equations must necessarily satisfy all the restrictions of consumer theory. However, the non-linearity of [6.46] makes estimation more complicated than for the LES. Moreover, when direct comparisons of the two models have been made, the indirect addilog model appears to fit data worse than the LES.

Of demand systems not necessarily satisfying the theoretical restrictions and which hence may be used for testing them, the simplest used in applied work has been the *double logarithmic system*

$$q_i = A p_1^{\alpha_{1i}} p_2^{\alpha_{2i}} p_3^{\alpha_{3i}} \ldots p_n^{\alpha_{ni}} x^{\beta_i} \qquad [6.47]$$

The parameters in this system are, of course, elasticities. Unfortunately, when the theoretical restrictions are expressed in terms of elasticities then, just as was the case when they were expressed in terms of first derivatives, they do not remain unchanged for all configurations of total expenditure and prices. The model cannot therefore satisfy fully these restrictions. Investigators generally test the restrictions at one particular combination of expenditure and prices. If the restrictions are satisfied for this combination of expenditure and prices it is assumed that they will be satisfied approximately for other combinations.

Results with this model have been very similar to those for the Rotterdam model. For example, (Byron (1970a and 1970b) and Lluch (1971)) both found the homogeneity and symmetry restrictions to be rejected. However, like the Rotterdam model, the double-log model is at best an approximation and in this case the approximation has yielded some strange results. Byron found that despite the fact that his (Dutch) data satisfied the aggregation restrictions in that it obeyed the budget constraint for all observations, his tests rejected one of the aggregation restrictions. Such a result has to reflect the model used rather than any deficiency in consumer theory. This result highlights the necessity, noted at the end of our discussion of the Rotterdam model, of where possible making a clear distinction between findings which genuinely represent properties of the data under analysis and those which are simply a reflection of the model in use.

The desire actually to test the restrictions of consumer theory has more recently led to attempts to approximate either the direct or the indirect utility function by some so-called 'flexible functional form' that contains sufficient parameters to be regarded as an adequate approximation to whatever the 'true' underlying utility function happens to be. The best-known approach along these lines is that of Christensen, Jorgenson and Lau (1975). In the first of their two specifications, *the direct translog model*, they approximate the negative of the logarithm of the *direct* utility function by a function which is quadratic in the logarithms of the quantities consumed

$$-\log U = \alpha_0 + \sum_i \alpha_i \log q_i + \sum_i \sum_j \beta_{ij} \log q_i \log q_j \qquad [6.48]$$

Maximisation of such a utility function subject to the usual budget constraint leads to a system of equations expressing the budget shares, w_i, of the n goods as functions of the logarithms of the quantities consumed.

In their second specification, *the indirect translog model*, Christensen, Jorgenson and Lau approximate the logarithm of the *indirect utility* function by a function quadratic in the logarithms of the ratios of prices to total expenditure

$$\log U^* = \alpha_0 + \sum_i \alpha_i \log\left(\frac{p_i}{x}\right) + \sum_i \sum_j \beta_{ij} \log\left(\frac{p_i}{x}\right) \log\left(\frac{p_j}{x}\right) \qquad [6.49]$$

Using Roy's Identity [6.44], a system of budget share equations is again obtained, this time expressing the w_i as functions of the logarithms of the price-expenditure ratios.

The authors argue that since [6.48] and [6.49] can be regarded as second-order Taylor approximations to *any* direct or indirect utility function, data should conform to the demand systems they have derived (together with the restrictions implied) if consumer theory is to be regarded as valid. They use maximum likelihood methods to estimate their system for US annual data for 1929–72 using three commodity groupings – non-durable consumption goods, services from durable consumption goods and other services. They conclude that their results imply a rejection of the theory of demand. However, [6.48] and [6.49] are merely approximations (whether good or bad) to the true utility functions, so that a rejection of consumer theory on the basis of the translog models is no more final than a rejection on the basis of the Rotterdam or double log models. What is more convincing, of course, is that *all* three models, each using different approximations, come up with exactly the same result – that the restrictions implied by consumer theory do not hold.

6.7 More recent developments and some conclusions

Much recent work in the analysis of consumer demand makes use of the concept of *duality*. The consumer's problem is normally expressed as that of choosing quantities consumed so as to maximise utility subject to the budget constraint that total expenditure should not exceed a given level x. However, it may be reformulated as that of choosing quantities so as to minimise the total expenditure necessary to achieve a given utility level U.

Just as we obtained the indirect utility function of the previous section by substituting for quantities demanded into the direct utility function, so we can obtain the consumer's so-called *cost-function* by substituting the solutions to the expenditure-minimising problem into the expression for total expenditure. In the two-good case, the consumer minimises

$$x = p_1 q_1 + p_2 q_2$$

subject to the constraint that he attains a given utility U^* where

$$U^* = U^*(q_1, q_2) \tag{6.50}$$

This yields cost-minimising values of q_1 and q_2 which depend on U^* and the given prices, p_1 and p_2

$$q_1 = f_1(p_1, p_2, U^*): \quad q_2 = f_2(p_1, p_2, U^*) \tag{6.51}$$

The equations [6.51] are normally referred to as *Hicksian compensated demand functions*. Substituting back into equation [6.50] for q_1 and q_2 yields the consumer's *cost function*

$$x^* = x(p_1, p_2, U^*) \tag{6.52}$$

The cost function yields the minimum expenditure necessary to obtain the utility level U^* at given prices, p_1 and p_2. It is directly analogous to a firm's cost function which gives the minimum cost of producing a given output at given factor prices. It is homogeneous of degree unity in prices because if, for example, prices double then the cost of obtaining a given utility level must also double.

The usefulness of the cost function is that differentiating with respect to p_1 and p_2 leads back to the equations [6.51].[14] The normal demand equations [6.42] can then be obtained by substituting for U^* in [6.51] using the indirect utility function [6.43] which expresses U^* as a function of p_1, p_2 and x. Thus, *any* function which is homogeneous of degree unity can be used to generate a system of demand equations which satisfy the theoretical restrictions. For example, Deaton and Muellbauer (1980) adopt the following form for the cost function

[6.52] in the n good case

$$\log x^* = \alpha_0 + \sum_i \alpha_i \log p_i + \sum_i \sum_j \gamma_{ij} \log p_i \log p_j + U^* \beta_0 p_1^{\beta_1} p_2^{\beta_2} p_3^{\beta_3} \ldots p_n^{\beta_n} \qquad [6.53]$$

This yields a system of budget share-type demand equations which Deaton and Muellbauer term the *Almost ideal demand system* (AIDS). This system has a number of advantages. Firstly, the cost equation [6.53] contains sufficient parameters to be regarded as a close approximation to any cost function and hence any underlying preference ordering. The AIDS is therefore as general as the translog model, and, for reasons we shall not go into, far easier to estimate.

Secondly, the budget share equations generated contain sufficient parameters to be regarded as a first-order approximation to any demand system whether that system is consistent with demand theory or not. The AIDS is therefore also as general as the Rotterdam model. However, it does not have the restrictive implications of the Rotterdam model mentioned in the last section. Moreover, it can be shown that for the AIDS, just as for the Rotterdam model, the general restrictions of demand theory are unchanged for all configurations of total expenditure and prices. This makes the AIDS a suitable vehicle for testing these restrictions.

Deaton and Muellbauer estimate their system using British data for 1954–74 involving eight non-durable commodity groups. They find that in four of these groups – food, clothing, housing and transport – the homogeneity restriction is rejected. The cross-equation symmetry restrictions are also rejected and, moreover, unlike in some previous studies (e.g. Deaton 1974) symmetry is rejected whether or not the maintained hypothesis includes homogeneity. Thus, yet again, we appear to arrive at the conclusion that available data is inconsistent with consumer theory. Of course, the AIDS involves approximations, but we can now list four models – Rotterdam, log-linear, translog and AIDS – all making use of different approximations but all producing the same result – an apparant rejection of consumer theory.

It would be premature to reject consumer theory on the basis of these findings, however. In estimating demand systems questions of simultanity and identification are frequently ignored, possibly because estimation problems are complex enough as it is. Similarly, aggregation problems are rarely considered. Moreover, the complete system studies performed to date have more fundamental weaknesses.

Firstly, consumption decisions involve intertemporal choices. As indicated earlier, most demand studies begin by assuming that total *current* expenditure is given. A consumer is regarded as firstly deciding what part of his 'total lifetime resources' is to be allocated to current expenditure, and only then to decide on the allocation of total current expenditure between various goods and services. However, the conditions under which such 'two-stage budgeting' will be consistent with lifetime utility maximisation are rather restrictive. If such conditions do not hold even approximately then attention has to be given to the intertemporal aspects of demand.

Secondly, even the consumer's total lifetime resources cannot be regarded as given exogeneously. A consumer can, to some extent, decide for himself how many hours work he will put in during his life. For given present and future wage rates, the consumer therefore has some control over his lifetime resources. Neo-classical consumer theory allowed for this by including 'leisure', defined as the difference between hours worked and maximum time available for work, in the consumer's utility function. The budget constraint was then reformulated with the wage *rates* taken as given rather than total resources. However, there are obvious difficulties with this approach. Workers' choice of hours is often limited by the job specification – a more plausible choice is between working or not working. Furthermore, if wage rates are dependent on labour supply then the budget constraint will no longer be linear and such non-linearities will be accentuated by complex tax and social security systems.

Finally, perhaps the greatest weakness of complete system studies to date is their failure, in most cases, to make any allowance for dynamic factors. We have seen, in the single-equation context, the importance of allowing for a lagged adjustment to equilibrium values – whether this be because of habit effects or because of the durable nature of many goods. Yet in many systems the influence of habit is ignored and durable goods are treated no differently from non-durables. It is in the building of dynamic full-system models, on the problem of intertemporal choices, and on integrating labour supply decisions with expenditure decisions that much future work is likely to concentrate.

APPENDIX
Empirical exercise

As our first empirical exercise we shall estimate some simple demand equations for certain categories of non-durable consumers' expenditure. Firstly, we will estimate demand equations for food using annual data for 1956–80. All data is taken from the *Economic Trends Annual Supplement* (*ETAS*) 1983. We define variables as follows.

Quantity demand Q_t = expenditure on food in constant 1975 prices
Income Y_t = total personal disposable income in current prices
Price of food P_t = implied deflator of expenditure on food
General price index Π_t = implied deflator of total consumers' expenditure.

Q_t is taken from page 26 of the above publication and Y_t from page 19. We use constant price data for Q_t because this is the nearest approximation to 'quantity' we have. P_t can be obtained by dividing figures for food expenditure in current prices (ETAS 1983: 23) by the corresponding constant prices figures. We can do this because constant price figures always equal current price figures divided by the relevant price index. Similarly, Π_t can be obtained by taking the ratio of total consumers' expenditure in current prices (ETAS 1983: 23) to that in constant prices (ETAS 1983: 26). Observe that all four variables share a strong upward trend throughout the sample period.

The reader should attempt to duplicate all the regression results that follow using whatever OLS computer program is available to him. Examples of suitable programs were given in Chapter 1. Your program will probably contain transformation routines that will enable you to form the variables P_t and Π_t without the necessity of computing them by hand.

Firstly, regressing quantity on food price alone yields

$$\hat{Q}_t = 10{,}919 + 977.7\,P_t \qquad\qquad R^2 = 0.435 \quad d = 0.11 \qquad\qquad\qquad [\text{A6.1}]$$
$$\phantom{\hat{Q}_t = }(191.6)\quad(232.4)$$

This is, not surprisingly, unsatisfactory – the coefficient of P_t although 'significant' has an incorrect positive sign attached to it and the Durbin–Watson statistic is extremely low. The reason for this is not difficult to find. We have omitted several potentially important explanatory variables from the equation – income and the prices of other goods are obvious candidates. In the absence of such variables, all we can expect to observe is a positive relationship between Q_t and P_t which reflects no more than the common upward trend in these variables during our sample period.

Now let us introduce Y_t and Π_t as additional explanatory variables – the latter to represent 'all other prices' which consumer theory tells us should also influence the demand for food

$$\hat{Q}_t = 11{,}272 - 15{,}872\,P_t + 0.00838\,Y_t + 15{,}806\,\Pi_t \quad R^2 = 0.658$$
$$\phantom{\hat{Q}_t = }(528.9)\quad(5{,}645)\qquad(0.0356)\qquad(7{,}767)\qquad d = 0.56 \qquad [\text{A6.2}]$$

Although the Durbin–Watson statistic is still very low, both price variables are significant at the 5 per cent level and P_t now has the correct sign. The t-ratios on P_t and Π_t are 2.81 and 2.04 respectively whereas, with $n - k = 25 - 4 = 21$ d.f., critical t-values are $t_{0.05} = 1.72$ and $t_{0.01} = 2.52$. The sign to be expected on Π_t depends on the balance of income and substitution effects. As all other prices rise, with the price of food and money income remaining constant, there will be a substitution effect increasing demand for food as its relative price falls but an income effect reducing demand as real income falls. The net effect will depend on the balance of these two factors. The positive sign on Π_t suggests that the substitution effect predominates. Do you think this reasonable?

The smallness in *absolute* terms of the coefficient on Y_t compared with those on P_t and Π_t simply reflects the units of measurement used. Y_t is measured in millions of pounds whereas the price variables are in index number form. However, the Y_t coefficient is not only small but statistically insignificantly different from zero, with a t-ratio of only 0.24. This is unexpected but could be partly the result of multicollinearity between the three explanatory variables. The t-ratios on the other variables are also relatively low considering that R^2 indicates that nearly 66

A6.1 Residuals from equation [A6.2]

Year	Residual	Year	Residual	Year	Residual
1956	−693	1965	50	1974	345
1957	−601	1966	229	1975	135
1958	−568	1967	263	1976	147
1959	−353	1968	218	1977	184
1960	−232	1969	202	1978	366
1961	−133	1970	184	1979	137
1962	−55	1971	271	1980	−1027
1963	45	1972	134	1981	
1964	149	1973	601	1982	

per cent of the variation in Q_t can be explained by P_t, Y_t and Π_t. In fact, the simple correlations between Y_t and P_t and between Y_t and Π_t are as high as 0.995 and 0.998 respectively. The reader should see what happens if either P_t or Π_t is omitted from [A6.2].

It is tempting to regard the low Durbin–Watson statistic as reflecting an autocorrelated disturbance term. The residuals from [A6.2] are shown in Table A6.1 and we can clearly observe sequences of negative and then positive residuals suggestive of positive autocorrelation. But as we observed in Section 3.4 such a pattern of residuals can also result from a mis-specification of the equation. So, before we go rushing off into a Cochrane–Orcutt routine, let us try re-estimating the equation in natural logarithms. (Your program should have a transformation routine that will do this for you)

$$\log \hat{Q}_t = 6.778 - 0.610 \log P_t + 0.234 \log Y_t + 0.358 \log \Pi_t$$
$$\quad\quad (0.351) \quad (0.095) \quad\quad\quad (0.031) \quad\quad\quad (0.129)$$
$$R^2 = 0.982 \quad d = 1.72 \quad [A6.3]$$

The overall fit of the equation appears to have improved dramatically and the Durbin–Watson statistic rises sharply.[15] In fact, there is no evidence of autocorrelation in [A6.3]. The upper and lower critical values for d are in this case $d_L = 1.12$ and $d_U = 1.66$, if we use a 5 per cent level of significance. A low d-statistic does not always reflect autocorrelation! However, do not be too impressed by the high R^2. An R^2 of 0.98–0.99 is not particularly difficult to achieve with time series data such as this, with all four variables Q_t, P_t, Y_t and Π_t 'trending' so steadily upwards. What is more interesting is that the income variable in [A6.3] is now highly significant. Its t-ratio is 7.55 compared with 6.42 and 2.78 for P_t and Π_t. This is despite the fact that the simple correlations between $\log Y_t$ and $\log P_t$ and between $\log Y_t$ and $\log \Pi_t$ are still as high as 0.986 and 0.992 respectively. As we noted in Section 3.3, severe multicollinearity does not always result in insignificant coefficients provided the overall fit is good. Notice also that the absolute magnitudes of the slope coefficients are now similar – in a log formulation they represent elasticities, which are independent of units of measurement. Do you think the sizes of these elasticities reasonable for an expenditure category such as food?

We noted in the first section of this chapter that consumer theory suggests the elasticities in an equation such as [A6.3] should sum to zero. In fact, they sum to 0.018. This is not zero but is the difference statistically significant? To find this out we can apply the F-test for a linear restriction described in Section 5.4. Enforcing the restriction implies estimating an equation in which Q depends on *real* income Y/Π and the *relative* price of food P/Π.

$$\log \hat{Q}_t = 7.405 - 0.726 \log(P_t/\Pi_t) + 0.178 \log(Y_t/\Pi_t)$$
$$\quad\quad (0.135) \quad (0.077) \quad\quad\quad\quad (0.012)$$
$$R^2 = 0.979 \quad d = 1.84 \quad [A6.4]$$

The residual sum of squares for the unrestricted equation [A6.3] is $SSR_U = 1.409 \times 10^{-3}$ while that for the restricted equation [A6.4] is $SSR_R = 1.655 \times 10^{-3}$. The test statistic [5.81] in this case is therefore

$$\frac{(SSR_R - SSR_U)/1}{SSR_U/(n-k)} = \frac{1.655 - 1.409}{1.409/(25-4)} = 3.67$$

With (1, 21) d.f. the critical values for F are $F_{0.05} = 4.32$ and $F_{0.01} = 8.02$. Therefore we do not reject the restriction. The data appears to confirm what economic theory predicts!

Notice, finally, that the t-values of P_t/Π_t and Y_t/Π_t in [A6.4] are 9.43 and 14.83 respectively, considerably higher than those in [A6.3] despite the fact that R^2 is a little lower. This reflects a reduction in multicollinearity as we replace P_t, Y_t and Π_t by P_t/Π_t and Y_t/Π_t. The simple correlation between P_t/Π_t and Y_t/Π_t is only 0.720.

For a second demand equation illustration we use quarterly seasonally *unadjusted* data on the expenditure category 'drink and tobacco' for 1956–65. The equivalent version of [A6.3] for this data is

$$\log \hat{Q}_t = -13.87 + 0.623 \log P_t + 2.04 \log Y_t - 4.51 \log \Pi_t$$
$$\quad\quad\quad (3.31) \quad (0.456) \quad\quad\quad (0.304) \quad\quad\quad\quad (1.04)$$
$$R^2 = 0.733 \quad d = 1.66$$

However, with seasonally unadjusted data it obviously makes sense to include the seasonal dummy variables, described in Section 5.2, in our equation

$$\log \hat{Q}_t = 0.230 - 0.201 \, D1 - 0.092 \, D2 - 0.043 \, D3 - 0.429 \log P_t$$
$$\quad\quad\quad (1.14) \quad (0.010) \quad\quad (0.008) \quad\quad (0.008) \quad\quad (0.134)$$
$$\quad\quad + 0.747 \, Y_t - 0.358 \log \Pi_t$$
$$\quad\quad\quad (0.105) \quad\quad (0.349) \quad\quad\quad R^2 = 0.982 \quad d = 2.12 \quad\quad\quad [A6.5]$$

In [A6.5], D1 is the 'first quarter' dummy, taking the value unity in the first quarter and zero in all other quarters, D2 is the 'second quarter' dummy and D3 is the 'third quarter' dummy. No 'fourth quarter' dummy is included, (why?). All three dummies are significant with t-ratios of 20.1, 11.5 and 5.4 respectively (with $n - k = 40 - 7 = 33$ d.f., $t_{0.05} = 1.68$).

The intercepts for the different quarters implied by [A6.5] are 0.029 for the first quarter, 0.138 for the second quarter, 0.187 for the third quarter and 0.230 for the fourth quarter. Consumption of drink and tobacco obviously builds up to a peak in the festive season!

The coefficients on P_t and Y_t in [A6.5] have the correct sign and are both significant with t-ratios of 3.20 and 7.11 respectively. However, that on the general price index is not statistically significantly different from zero – its t-ratio is only 1.03. The negative sign attached to the Π_t variable suggests that, if anything, the income effect of rises in other prices outweighs the substitution effect. The coefficients on P_t, Y_t and Π_t are again elasticities, since [A6.5] is in log form, so economic theory suggests they should sum to zero. In fact, they sum to -0.040. It is left to the reader to impose the restriction that the elasticities sum to zero and to carry out the F-test of Section 5.4.

The reader should now estimate some demand equations for himself/herself. Use the annual data on pages 23 and 26 of *ETAS* 1983 to estimate demand equations for 'drink and tobacco', 'fuel and light', 'clothing and footwear' 'durable household goods' and 'cars and motor-cycles'. You will have more trouble obtaining satisfactory values for Durbin–Watson statistics than we did with food. A number of these categories refer to durable goods and others are 'habit-forming'. Reading Section 6.5 may give you some ideas for finding a more adequate dynamic specification for your equations. Remember, though, that the

Durbin–Watson test is invalid when the explanatory variables include a lagged dependent variable.

You can also estimate quarterly demand equations both for 1956–65 and for any later periods of your choice. This would give you an opportunity to perform the first of the Chow tests described in Section 5.3, and see whether the parameters of your demand equations change over time. The comments of the previous paragraph also apply to quarterly demand equations, of course. In addition, remember that if you are attempting to allow for 'habit', etc. then demand *four* quarters earlier may be as important in determining current demand as is demand *one* quarter earlier. Inebriation on one New Year's Eve may lead to a greater desire for inebriation on the next!

Finally, notice that we have used disposable income rather than total expenditure in all our estimated equations. While this is a procedure frequently followed in the time series estimation of demand equations, we know from our discussion in Section 6.1 that there are strong theoretical reasons for preferring total expenditure. You can therefore re-estimate your equations, replacing income by total expenditure, and see whether results are more in accordance with the predictions of theory.

Notes

1. This has become less of a problem. Now that full details of family expenditure surveys in the US and the UK are available on microfilm, researchers need no longer rely on standard published sources.
2. Working in terms of simple arithmetic means implies that we are ignoring for the moment the fact that households are likely to vary in their size and composition.
3. ε will, in fact, be non-autocorrelated and normally distributed with zero mean and, provided all the ε_j can be treated as independent variables, variance equal to $\sigma^2/n = $ constant where $\sigma^2 = \mathrm{var}\,\varepsilon_j$
4. We can write the relevant term in [6.8] as

$$\left(\frac{\sum x_j \alpha_{3j}}{\sum x_j}\right)\bar{x} = \frac{\sum x_j \alpha_{3j}}{N}$$

If x_j and α_{3j} are independently distributed, then

$$Ex_j\alpha_{3j} = Ex_j E\alpha_{3j}$$

Thus, for large N

$$\frac{\sum x_j \alpha_{3j}}{N} \simeq \left(\frac{\sum x_j}{N}\right)\left(\frac{\sum \alpha_{3j}}{N}\right) = \left(\frac{\sum \alpha_{3j}}{N}\right)\bar{x}$$

Thus the coefficient of $\bar{x}$ in [6.8] becomes approximately equal to $\sum \alpha_{3j}/N$.
5. The geometric mean of a set of n numbers, $x_1, x_2, x_3, \ldots, x_n$ is defined as

$$\tilde{x} = (x_1 x_2 x_3 \ldots x_n)^{1/n}$$

i.e. the nth root of the product of the n numbers. Hence, the log of such a mean is

$$\log \tilde{x} = \frac{1}{n}\log(x_1 x_2 \ldots x_n) = \frac{1}{n}\sum \log x_j$$

6. Consumer theory would suggest that the desired flow of *services* from the good depends (given homogeneity) on real total expenditure and relative prices. However, if we assume that services yielded are proportional to stock held and represent all relative prices by p_t, the ratio of own price to a general index of prices, an equation such as [6.19] can be obtained.

7. The unit of measurement for S_t is chosen so as to make the coefficient of q_t in equation [6.21] equal to unity.

8. Unfortunately this flexibility means that it is often possible to rationalise away unlikely values for underlying parameters. For example, in the stock adjustment model an unacceptably high value for the depreciation parameter δ or a value for the adjustment parameter λ which is in excess of unity can both be explained away by claiming that habit effects are present.

9. The authors, in fact, originally formulate their model in continuous terms and derive a discrete approximation for estimating purposes. They use an estimation method which allows for any autocorrelation that may be present. For details of this method, referred to as 'three pass least squares' readers should consult Houthakker and Taylor (1970).

10. In the empirical literature on demand systems the restrictions that follow are normally derived in matrix terms. However, for a traditional but rather more tedious derivation, see, for example, Henderson and Quandt (1980: 18–33).

11. An additive utility function has to take the form

$$U = f_1(q_1) + f_2(q_2), + \cdots +, f_n(q_n)$$

if it is to possess this property. Hence the name 'additive'.

12. In a demand system which is linear in the logarithms, for example, it is the elasticities which are parameterised and whose dependence on x and all prices is ignored.

13. See, for example, Phlips (1974: 29).

14. This property is often referred to as *Shephard's Lemma* – see, for example, Diewart (1974).

15. The R^2's, in equations [A6.2] and [A6.3] are, however, not strictly comparable. Whereas in [A6.2] R^2 measures the proportion of variations in Q that can be explained by variations in P, Y and π, in [A6.3] it refers to the proportion of variations in $\log Q$ that can be explained by $\log P$, $\log Y$ and $\log \pi$.

Consumption functions

In the previous chapter we considered, firstly, the estimation of demand equations for individual commodities and, secondly, the estimation of the sets of demand equations which arise when an individual consumer allocates a given total expenditure amongst the many commodities available to him. In this chapter we concentrate on the factors which determine the way a consumer divides his total disposable income between total consumption and saving. We shall be concerned, however, with consumption as theoretically defined – i.e. with the sum of consumer expenditures on *non-durable* goods and services plus the value of the flow of services obtained by consumers from durable goods. While total consumer expenditure might be a more relevant aggregate from the economic policy point of view, we dealt with expenditure on consumer durables in the last chapter. Furthermore, non-durable consumption represents a large proportion (between 85 and 90 per cent in the UK for example) of total spending in any economy so that its determination is of considerable importance in its own right.

We begin by considering some of the early empirical work on the consumption function.

7.1 The absolute income hypothesis

The term 'consumption function' originates in Keynes's *General Theory of Employment, Interest and Money* where Keynes put forward his 'fundamental psychological law' that consumption increases as income increases but that the increase in consumption is less than the increase in income. The Keynesian consumption function may be summarised by the following four propositions advanced by Keynes with varying emphasis.

1. Current real consumption is a 'fairly stable' function of current real income, i.e. $C = f(Y)$ where C and Y are the real consumption and real income respectively of an individual consumer.
2. The marginal propensity to consume lies between zero and unity, i.e.
$$0 = \frac{\partial C}{\partial Y} < 1$$
3. The MPC is less than the average propensity to consume (APC), i.e.
$$\frac{\partial C}{\partial Y} < \frac{C}{Y}$$
4. As real income rises the MPC falls.

The expression 'fairly stable' indicates that, while other factors such as interest rates and windfall changes in capital values might also affect real consumption, it was real income that was the dominant force in the Keynesian scheme of things.

A consumption function with the above properties is shown in Fig. 7.1. Note that property (3) above implies that the function must have an intercept.

Keynes laid far greater emphasis on the first two of the above propositions and these are all that are necessary for most of the analysis in the *General Theory*. These two propositions together comprise what is normally referred to as the *absolute income hypothesis* (AIH) although nowadays other variables tend to be added to ensure that the function fits available data.[1]

Keynes's ideas concerning the consumption function led quite naturally to a series of attempts to test the validity of the above propositions. However, the estimation of consumption functions involves a number of preliminary data problems, although scant attention was paid to them in early empirical work.

There is little difficulty as far as income data is concerned. The variable referred to by Keynes can be fairly closely identified with real personal disposable income, i.e. income in constant price terms net of taxes on income and insurance contributions, etc. Unfortunately, deciding on the relevant consumption variable is not so easy. Theoretically, consumption may be regarded as the sum of expenditures on 'non-durable' consumer goods and the value of the flow of services on 'durable' consumer goods. However, in practice there are obvious difficulties in drawing a precise line between those goods which are durable and those which are non-durable. For example, clothing is usually classed as a non-durable but clearly possesses many of the attributes of a durable good. Hopefully, acceptance of the standard data classifications for such items does not seriously affect empirical results. A more serious difficulty is the flow of services from what are obviously durable goods. The value of this flow is an important element in consumption and should also be included in a consumer's income. Unfortunately, data concerning it is very rarely available. The majority of empirical studies have therefore defined consumption as either consumption

7.1 A 'Keynesian' consumption function.

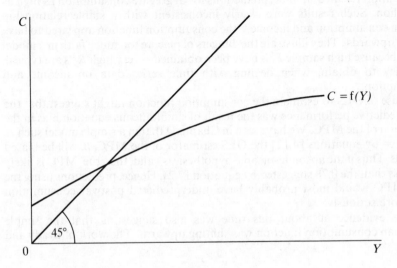

expenditure on non-durables or the sum of expenditures on durables and non-durables.[2]

A further problem arises when attempts are made to estimate consumption functions from aggregate time series data. The Keynesian consumption function is formulated in terms of the individual consumer, so in using economy-wide data we face an aggregation problem similar in nature to that for demand equations discussed in Section 6.2. For example, suppose the ith individual's consumption function in real terms is given by

$$C_i = \alpha_i + \beta_i Y_i + \varepsilon_i \qquad \qquad [7.1]$$

For meaningful aggregation we must assume either that the parameter β_i is constant for all individuals or, appealing to the 'convergence approach', that it is distributed across individuals in a manner which is independent of income. In either case the aggregate function obtained expresses *per capita real consumption* as a function of *per capita real income*.

Early empirical studies of the consumption function involved either cross-sectional data, i.e. budget survey data for individual households in a given year, or aggregate time series data for the relatively short time span of the 1930s. First impressions appeared to confirm the propositions listed above. In particular, real consumption did, indeed, appear to be a stable function of real income and the function did possess an intercept.

Doubts were first cast on the simple Keynesian consumption function in the early postwar years. It was found that functions fitted to prewar US data, when used for forecasting purposes, seriously underpredicted postwar consumption expenditure in the US. Such underpredictions were well illustrated by Davis (1952). Using annual US data in per capita constant price terms, he fitted by OLS a simple consumption function and obtained for 1929–40

$$C = 11.45 + 0.78 Y_t \qquad R^2 = 0.986 \qquad \qquad [7.2]$$
$$(0.02)$$

However, despite the extremely good 'fit' for 1929–40, forecasts for 1946–50 using this equation resulted in underpredictions for aggregate consumption as high as $12 billion. Such results were clearly inconsistent with a stable relationship between consumption and income – the consumption function appeared to have shifted 'upwards'. They illustrate the dangers of placing too much faith in a model simply because high sample R^2's have been obtained – very high R^2's are typical, and easy to obtain, when dealing with time series data on income and consumption.

The use of OLS to estimate the consumption function might suggest that the poor predictive performance was the result of simultaneous equation bias in the estimation of the MPC. We have seen in Chapter 4 that in a simple model such as that given by equations [4.12] the OLS estimator of the MPC, β, will be biased upwards. Thus if the absolute-income hypothesis is valid, the 'true' MPC is likely to be less than the 0.78 suggested by equation [7.2]. Hence, predictions using the 'true' MPC would most probably have underpredicted postwar consumption even more seriously.

Other evidence at about this time was also suggesting that the simple Keynesian consumption function was shifting upwards. The work of Brady and

7.2 Long- and short-run consumption functions.

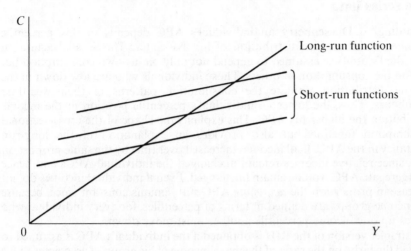

Friedman (1947) suggested that, while cross-sectional budget studies for any given year tended to confirm the shape illustrated in Fig. 7.1, the evidence from successive budget studies taken over a period of years was that although the MPC remained relatively constant the intercept was shifting upwards.

The most important findings, however, were those of Kuznets (1942). Examining US data over the period 1879–1938, he found that over long periods the APC, measured as the ratio of consumption to national income, had remained relatively constant at about 0.9. The long-run constancy of the APC was later confirmed by Goldsmith (1955) using data for personal income rather than national income.

By the late 1940s a clear contradiction appeared to have arisen. Long-run time series data suggested a consumption function with a constant APC, i.e. a linear function with no intercept. However, cross-sectional budget studies consistently suggested a function of typical Keynesian shape, and similar functions tended to be estimated from short-run (ten to twenty years) time series data. These differences could be reconciled empirically by postulating a 'short-run' consumption function of Keynesian shape which shifted upwards over time, as illustrated in Fig. 7.2. However, economic reasons for the upward movement were unclear. Most of the theoretical and empirical work concerning the consumption function performed during the next twenty years was aimed directly or indirectly at reconciling these apparant contradictions.

7.2 The relative income hypothesis

The first serious attempt at explaining both time series and cross-sectional data was provided by the so-called *relative income hypothesis* (RIH) developed independently by Duesenberry (1949) and Modigliani (1949).

Reconciliation of cross-sectional data with long-run time series data

According to Duesenberry an individual's APC depends on his percentile position in the income distribution of his associates. This is so because an individual's utility is assumed to depend not only on his own consumption but also on the consumption of others. Those individuals who are low down in the income distribution emulate the consumption patterns of their wealthier neighbours. Thus, the lower an individual's percentile position in the income distribution the higher his APC. This explains the shape of the cross-sectional consumption function but also provides an explanation of the long-run constancy in the APC. If all incomes increased over time by the same proportion then, since relative incomes remain unchanged the individual APCs and hence the aggregate APC would remain unchanged. Even if individual incomes do not increase in proportion the *aggregate* APC still remains constant since, because the income groups are defined in terms of percentiles, for every individual who moves up one income percentile another must move down.

A simpler version of the RIH is obtained if the individual's APC is assumed to depend (linearly) on the ratio of the mean income of his group of associates to his own income. Suppose that C_{it} and Y_{it} are the consumption and income of individual i at time t and we have

$$\frac{C_{it}}{Y_{it}} = \alpha_0 + \alpha_1 \left(\frac{\bar{Y}_t}{Y_{it}} \right) \qquad \alpha_0 > 0, \quad \alpha_1 > 0 \qquad\qquad [7.3]$$

where

$$\bar{Y}_t = \frac{\sum Y_{it}}{n}$$

is the mean income of the group. Thus, for given t, as individual income falls, the APC rises because of the 'emulation effect'. The above equation may be written as

$$C_{it} = \alpha_0 Y_{it} + \alpha_1 \bar{Y}_t \qquad\qquad [7.4]$$

For cross-sectional data in a given year, i.e. for given t, [7.4] may be written

$$C_i = \alpha_1 \bar{Y} + \alpha_0 Y_i \qquad\qquad [7.5]$$

Since $\bar{Y}$ is a constant, the cross-sectional consumption function is of the typically Keynesian form usually obtained from this type of data with an intercept of $\alpha_1 \bar{Y}$ and MPC $= \alpha_0$.

For time series data we may aggregate [7.4] over all n individuals in the group

$$\sum_i C_{it} = \alpha_0 \sum_i Y_{it} + n\alpha_1 \bar{Y}_t \qquad\qquad [7.6]$$

Hence per capita consumption is given by

$$\bar{C}_t = \frac{\sum C_{it}}{n} = \alpha_0 \left(\frac{\sum Y_{it}}{n} \right) + \alpha_1 \bar{Y}_t = (\alpha_0 + \alpha_1) \bar{Y}_t \qquad\qquad [7.7]$$

Thus the long-run time series consumption function implied by the RIH has a constant APC $= \alpha_0 + \alpha_1$ and hence no intercept. Note also that the time series

MPC is also equal to $\alpha_0 + \alpha_1$ and thus is greater than the cross-section MPC which is α_0. This also squares with empirical findings.

Reconciliation of short-run and long-run time series data

Duesenberry (1949) and Modigliani (1949) argued that habit and the desire to maintain living standards meant that an individual's consumption depended not only on the size of his income relative to that of his associates but also on its size relative to its previous highest or peak value. Thus during times of recession individuals would offset temporary reductions in income by consuming a larger proportion of their incomes. The APC of a group of consumers therefore depends on the size of its current income relative to its previous peak income. That is

$$\frac{C_t}{Y_t} = \beta_0 + \beta_1 \left(\frac{Y_0}{Y_t} \right) \qquad \beta_0 > 0, \quad \beta_1 > 0 \qquad [7.8]$$

where Y_0 is the previous peak income of the group. This equation may be written as

$$C_t = \beta_0 Y_t + \beta_1 Y_0 \qquad [7.9]$$

Suppose income grows steadily at a constant geometric rate, g. Then, previous peak income $Y_0 = Y_{t-1}$ and moreover $Y_t = (1 + g)Y_{t-1}$. Equation [7.9] then becomes

$$C_t = \left[\beta_0 + \frac{\beta_1}{1 + g} \right] Y_t \qquad [7.10]$$

If we consider long periods of time (e.g. 1880–1950), income may be regarded as having grown at a constant rate with only minor cyclical fluctuations. Hence, [7.10] implies that *long-run* time series data will yield a consumption function without an intercept and with a constant APC equal to $\beta_0 + \beta_1/(1 + g)$

If, however, there were to be a short-run cyclical fall in income then $Y_t < Y_0$ and Y_0 remains constant until income rises to this level again. Equation [7.9] may now be written as

$$C_t = \beta'_1 + \beta_0 Y_t \qquad [7.11]$$

an equation with an intercept $\beta'_1 = \beta_1 Y_0 = \text{const}$ and an MPC of β_0. Thus, the 'short-run' time series consumption function implied by the relative income argument is Keynesian in shape with an MPC which is lower than the long-run MPC, $\beta_0 + \beta_1/(1 + g)$, obtained from equation [7.10].

This reconciliation of long- and short-run time series findings is perhaps best illustrated by considering Fig. 7.3. Suppose the initial level of income is Y^* and that income grows steadily over time until it reaches the level Y_0. Points are therefore traced out along the long-run function given by equation [7.10]. However, if income starts to decline cyclically once it reaches Y_0, consumption falls back along the flatter short-run consumption function $C_t = \beta_1 Y_0 + \beta_0 Y_t$ which has an intercept. Consumption remains on this curve until income re-attains the level Y_0. Once income grows beyond Y_0, however, further points are traced out on the long-run consumption function. Suppose the next cyclical income peak is Y'_0. When income falls back below this level, consumption falls

7.3 The 'ratchet' effect.

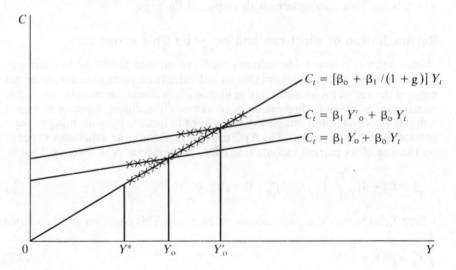

back along the new short-run function $C_t = \beta_1 Y'_0 + \beta_0 Y_t$.

But this function has a larger intercept than the previous short-run function because $Y'_0 > Y_0$. There is therefore a 'ratchet effect' with the short-run consumption function periodically shifting upwards.

One further interesting point arises from the above explanation of time series data. Equation [7.10] implies that the greater the long-run rate of growth in real income the lower is the APC, i.e. the larger the proportion of income that is saved. This was in accordance with observations on saving ratios for different countries over periods of time. Countries with the highest income-growth rates do tend to have the highest average propensities to save (APS).

As an illustration of a time series equation estimated with the RIH in mind, consider the equation estimated from annual US data by Modigliani (1949)

$$\frac{S_t}{Y_t} = 0.096 + 0.125\left[\frac{Y_t - Y_0}{Y_t}\right] \tag{7.12}$$

Note first that Modigliani adopts the APS rather than saving *per se* as his dependent variable. When fitting consumption functions to long-run time series data it is almost certain that the income variable will show considerable growth during the sample period. If, as is possible, the disturbance term in the underlying consumption function has a variance which is related to the size of the income variable, then if the estimating equation is formulated with income as one of the explanatory variables we are likely to encounter the problem of heteroscedasticity. However, as we saw in Section 3.2, a typical response to such a problem is to attempt to transform the estimating equation into one with a constant variance by dividing throughout by the 'offending' variable. For this reason some researchers (like Modigliani) prefer to work with consumption and saving ratios rather than the consumption and saving variables themselves.

It is easy to convert equation [7.12] into a form identical to [7.9]. Multiplying throughout by Y_t and noting that $S_t = Y_t - C_t$ we obtain

$$C_t = 0.777 Y_t + 0.125 Y_0 \tag{7.13}$$

Hence Modigliani's equation implied a short-run MPC of $\beta_0 = 0.777$ and, assuming a long-run rate of growth in real income of $g = 0.03$, a long-run MPC of $\beta_0 + \beta_1/(1 + g) = 0.898$. Notice that both short-run and long-run consumption functions are deduced from the *single* estimated equation [7.12] or its equivalent [7.13], which is fitted to all the available data. Hence, it is not the case that the short-run function is obtained from a data span of, for example, 15–20 years, and the long-run function from maybe 100 years. No matter what the length of the sample period, the same RIH estimating equation is fitted.

The relative income explanation of time series data can be slightly reformulated if current consumption is made a function not of previous peak income but of previous peak consumption. That is, equation [7.9] can be replaced by

$$C_t = \beta_0 Y_t + \beta_1 C_0 \tag{7.14}$$

where C_0 is previous peak consumption. This leads to long- and short-run consumption functions essentially similar to those illustrated in Fig. 7.3.

Brown (1952) generalised this alternative approach with his 'habit persistence' model. He argued that the influence of past consumption is continuous and not limited to situations where current consumption levels are below their previous peak. Thus consumption in any one period is always influenced by consumption in the previous period and we may write

$$C_t = \beta_0 Y_t + \beta_1 C_{t-1} \tag{7.15}$$

If consumption grows over time, the 'short-run' relationship between C_t and Y_t therefore moves continuously upwards. In fact, if consumption grows at a long-run rate g, then since $C_t = (1 + g)C_{t-1}$ a long-run consumption function, again with a constant APC, is obtained. That is

$$C_t = \left(\frac{\beta_0}{1 - (\beta_1/1 + g)} \right) Y_t \tag{7.16}$$

7.3 The life-cycle hypothesis

Duesenberry's explanation of the pattern of income-consumption data, with its assumption that an individual's utility depends not only on the goods he consumes but also on the consumption of others, involves a microeconomic theory totally different from the traditional Hicksian demand analysis. Other attempts at reconciling the apparently conflicting evidence have been based on a more orthodox micro-foundation.

Consider, for example, the special case of a consumer faced with the problem of maximising utility over just two periods. That is, he must allocate his resources between consumption in the first period, C_1, and that in the second period, C_2. The consumer's preferences may be summarised by the system of indifference curves shown in Fig. 7.4 which are concave for the usual reasons. Suppose the consumer's total receipts or income in the first period is Y_1 and in the second period Y_2, and let r be the interest rate. The maximum the consumer can spend on

7.4 Utility maximisation over two periods.

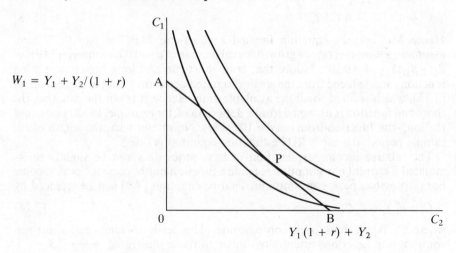

$$W_1 = Y_1 + Y_2/(1 + r)$$

consumption during the first period is $Y_1 + Y_2/(1 + r)$ – his income during the first period plus the maximum loan he can repay with his income of the second period. If he consumed this quantity in the first period, he would have nothing to spend in the second period so this possibility is represented by the point A in Fig. 7.4. Alternatively, if the consumer spent nothing in the first period his maximum consumption level in the second period would be $Y_1(1 + r) + Y_2$ – his first-period income, plus interest earned on it, plus his second-period income. This possibility is represented by the point B. The line AB represents the consumer's budget constraint, i.e. it defines all possible combinations of C_1 and C_2 that may be chosen by the consumer, assuming he wishes to have no resources remaining at the end of the second period.

The consumer's optimal combination of C_1 and C_2 is where the budget line is tangential to an indifference curve, i.e. the point P in Fig. 7.4. What is interesting about P is that, given the set of indifference curves, its position and hence first-period consumption, C_1, depends on income in *both* periods and on the interest rate. *There is no way in which we can derive the AIH from a traditional microeconomic analysis.* Specifically, the position of point P depends on the height and slope of the budget constraint. The height of the line AB clearly depends on the quantity $Y_1 + Y_2/(1 + r)$ which is normally referred to as the consumer's total wealth, W_1, in the first period. The slope of the line is given by $- 1/(1 + r)$ and is hence dependent on the interest rate. Thus, optimal consumption in either period is a function of W_1 and r.

Algebraically, the consumer maximises a utility function $U = U(C_1, C_2)$ subject to the condition that C_1 and C_2 satisfy the budget constraint[3]

$$Y_1 + \frac{Y_2}{1+r} = C_1 + \frac{C_2}{1+r}.$$

The solution to this constrained optimisation problem is given by $C_1 = f_1(W_1, r)$ and $C_2 = f_2(W_1, r)$. The precise shape of the functions f_1 and f_2 will depend on the consumer's indifference map, but it is clear from Fig. 7.4 that the greater W_1, i.e.

168

the greater OA, the larger will be C_1 and C_2. Also, as the rate of interest rises with W_1 constant, the budget line becomes less steep and we have a pure substitution effect with first-period consumption falling while second-period consumption rises. Thus, as r rises the consumer substitutes future consumption for present consumption.

An interesting and not too implausible special case arises if we assume that the consumer's utility function is *homothetic*. Graphically, this means that the slopes of the indifference curves are the same along any straight line drawn through the origin.[4] Thus, for a given rate of interest, as W_1 increases and the budget line is shifted outwards parallel to itself, the optimal ratio C_1/C_2 remains unchanged regardless of the magnitude of W_1. The ratio C_1/C_2 will, however, depend on the tastes of the consumer, as represented by the precise form of his indifference map, and on the rate of interest. The constancy of the optimal ratio C_1/C_2 when combined with the above budget constraint means that C_1 and C_2 are, in fact, constant proportions of W_1. That is, $C_1 = \gamma_1 W_1$ and $C_2 = \gamma_2 W_2$ where the γ's are again dependent on consumer preferences and the rate of interest.[5]

Consider finally the situation where the consumer exhibits an absence of 'time preference proper' and where the rate of interest is zero. The absence of such time preference implies that each indifference curve is symmetrical about a line through the origin at an angle of 45° to each axis. This is illustrated in Fig. 7.5 and means that the consumer is indifferent between, for example, $C_1 = 100$, $C_2 = 30$ and $C_1 = 30$, $C_2 = 100$. A zero interest rate implies that the budget constraint has a slope of -1 and hence its point of tangency with any indifference curve is always on the 45° line. Thus, $C_1 = C_2$, i.e. under these very special conditions the consumer plans to consume at exactly the same rate in each period. In Fig. 7.5

$$C_1 = OX \text{ and } C_2 = OY$$

We shall refer back to this particular case later.

The above analysis was not new and indeed the early part of it was identical to that of Fisher (1907). It was adopted and generalised by Modigliani and Brumberg (1954) in their *life-cycle hypothesis* (LCH). Modigliani and Brumberg assumed that a household plans its lifetime consumption pattern so as to

7.5 Absence of 'time preference proper'.

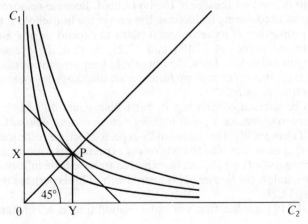

maximise the total utility it obtains from consumption during its lifetime. In the empirical version of their hypothesis it is assumed that households do not plan to leave assets to their heirs so that a household of age T maximises a utility function of the form

$$U = U(C_T, C_{T-1}, C_{T+2}, \ldots, C_L) \tag{7.17}$$

where C_i ($i = T, T+1, T+2, \ldots, L$) is planned consumption at age i and L is the household's expected age at 'death'. Since the household plans to exactly exhaust its resources during its lifetime, [7.17] is maximised subject to the lifetime budget constraint

$$A_{T-1} + Y_T + \sum_{i=T+1}^{N} \frac{Y_i^e}{(1+r)^{i-T}} = \sum_{i=T}^{L} \frac{C_i}{(1+r)^{i-T}} \tag{7.18}$$

A_{T-1} is non-human wealth (i.e. physical and financial assets) carried over from the households $(T-1)$th year, Y_T is the household's earned or non-property income at age T, Y_i^e is its expected non-property income at age i and N is the household's age at retirement. Note that it is non-property income that enters the budget constraint. For the reader who is uncertain why this should be so, the constraint is derived for the three-period case in Appendix B to this chapter.

Modigliani and Brumberg now adopt the simplifying assumption that the utility function [7.17] is homothetic. As we might expect from our simple two-period example this implies that planned current consumption is given by

$$C_T = \gamma_T W_T \tag{7.19}$$

where W_T is the household's total expected lifetime resources at age T. That is, it is the sum of all terms on the left-hand side of the budget constraint [7.18]

$$W_T = A_{T-1} + Y_T + \sum_{i=T+1}^{N} \frac{Y_i^e}{(1+r)^{i-T}} \tag{7.20}$$

Similarly planned consumption in future years is given by

$$C_i = \gamma_i W_T \qquad i = T+1, T+2, \ldots, L \tag{7.21}$$

The γ_i's in equations [7.19] and [7.21] will be dependent on the rate of interest and on the household's tastes and preferences as in the simple two-period case. However, they will also depend on the age of the household. Because resources are to be completely exhausted during its lifetime, the nearer the household is to 'death' the larger the proportion of its resources it plans to expend during any given year. The important aspect of [7.19] and [7.21] is that the γ_i's are independent of the magnitude of W_T. Thus, the household keeps the ratios of its planned consumption expenditures in any two future years unchanged no matter what the size of its lifetime resources.[6]

Two points need to be stressed concerning, in particular, equation [7.19].

Firstly, *a change in current income* Y_T *will influence current consumption* C_T *only to the extent that it changes* W_T, the household's expected lifetime resources. Normally, changes in Y_T, unless they lead to revisions in expectations concerning future income, i.e. to changes in the Y_i^e's, can be expected to have little influence on current consumption unless the household is near 'death'. This is perhaps the main conclusion of the LCH.

Secondly, equation [7.19] implies that current consumption is a constant proportion of total lifetime resources. This is the famous 'proportionality postulate'. It follows from the assumption made above of a homothetic utility function. However, the implications of the LCH remain largely unchanged if this convenient assumption is dropped. We can see from the simple two-period case discussed earlier that current consumption would remain a function of total lifetime resources, although the relationship would no longer be one of strict proportionality. Thus a change in current income would still only influence current consumption via its normally small effect on total lifetime resources. The proportionality postulate is not therefore a necessarily vital part of the LCH.

To sample the true flavour of the LCH it is instructive to consider, as we did for the two-period case, a situation where there is an absence of 'time preference proper' and where the interest rate is zero. The household then plans to consume its wealth at a constant rate throughout its lifetime. Since the income of a typical household varies throughout its lifespan, it is interesting to compare the time profiles of expected income and planned consumption for a household of 'average' size under the above assumptions. Such a household might expect its real income to rise steadily until somewhere near its anticipated retirement age and to decline thereafter. Such a profile is illustrated in Fig. 7.6 for the case where consumption proceeds at a constant rate.

It is apparent from Fig. 7.6 that even in the absence of time preference and with a zero rate of interest a household will still borrow and save. A major motive for saving in the life-cycle model is therefore the desire to flatten out the lifetime stream of consumption expenditures. Without dis-saving during the later part of its life and saving in the middle section the household would be forced to spend its whole income (no more and no less) during each of its future years.

The above analysis has important implications for the aggregate saving ratio in an economy. Recall that the time series version of the RIH provided a reason why there should be a positive relationship between the rate of growth in real income and the APS. The LCH provides a possibly more fundamental reason. Consider first a static, no-growth economy with a constant population and age distribution

7.6 Time profile of average household.

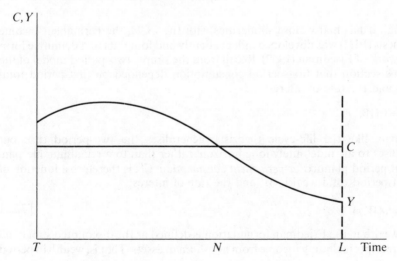

and an absence of technical change. Such an economy in cross-section could be likened to a series of households at different points in their life-span. Aggregate saving would therefore be zero since, provided there was no saving for heirs, the saving of the working population would just be counterbalanced by the dis-saving of the retired. If the economy were growing because of an increase in population, then clearly the greater number of younger households would mean that saving would exceed dis-saving and the aggregate saving ratio would be positive. However, even with a constant population, if technical change results in rising income and output per head, then those currently in employment will have higher incomes and expected incomes than did currently retired consumers when they were earning. Those currently employed plan to consume more per head in retirement than do the currently retired. Thus, saving will again exceed dis-saving and, moreover, the greater the rate of growth in real income per head the greater will be the aggregate saving ratio. This relationship was, in fact, first put forward by Harrod (1948) but was further developed by Modigliani (1966).

Ando and Modigliani (1963) adopted equation [7.19] for estimation from aggregate time series data. Problems in estimating the expected non-property income of consumers meant that their final equation simply involved regressing aggregate consumption, C_t, on aggregate current non-property income, Y_t, and the aggregate net wealth of consumers, A_{t-1}. Their most important finding was that, for annual US data for 1929–59, A_{t-1} was a significant determinant of C_t. The MPC out of net worth was estimated to be in the region 0.07–0.10. If the aggregate consumption function is, in fact, of the form

$$C_t = \alpha A_{t-1} + \beta Y_t$$

then this provides another explanation of the upward shifts in the short-run consumption function. If A_{t-1} is omitted from the regression of C_t on Y_t, then the estimated short-run consumption function will have a positive intercept and shift upwards over time as positive saving increases A_{t-1}.

7.4 The permanent income hypothesis

Although it has many close similarities with the LCH, the permanent income hypothesis (PIH) was developed independently and found its first definitive form in the work of Friedman (1957). Recall from the simple two-period model of the previous section that first-period consumption depended on first-period total wealth and the rate of interest, i.e.

$$C_1 = f_1(W_1, r).$$

Friedman, like the life-cycle theorists, generalises the two-period case but generalises to an 'indefinitely long horizon' rather than to a remaining lifespan. Present period planned or *permanent consumption*, C^P, is therefore a function of present period total wealth, W, and the rate of interest

$$C^P = q(W, r) \tag{7.22}$$

Total wealth in the Friedman formulation is defined as the discounted sum of *all* future receipts including income from non-human assets. That is, wealth in period

t is given by

$$W_t = Y_t + \frac{Y_{t+1}}{1+r} + \frac{Y_{t+2}}{(1+r)^2} + \frac{Y_{t+3}}{(1+r)^3} \cdots \cdots \qquad [7.23]$$

where Y_t is total expected receipts in period t. Note that in a perfectly competitive world with complete certainty the Modigliani–Brumberg and the Friedman measures of wealth would be identical. In such a world the value of non-human assets would be exactly equal to the discounted sum of future income from them.

Friedman now makes use of the simplifying assumption that the consumer's utility function is homothetic and equation [7.22] becomes

$$C^P = qW \qquad [7.24]$$

where the factor of proportionality, q, is dependent on the consumer's tastes and on the rate of interest.

Friedman next introduces the concept of *permanent income*, Y^P. This is defined, theoretically, as the maximum amount a consumer could consume while maintaining his wealth intact. It is, in fact, the rate of return on wealth, i.e. $Y^P = rW$. To see this, consider again the two-period model of the previous section. Initial wealth is W_1. If the individual consumed nothing during the first period, his wealth would have grown to $W_1(1+r)$ by the start of the second period. However, if he consumed a quantity rW_1 in the first period his wealth at the start of the second period would be W_1, i.e. he would have maintained his wealth intact. This argument extends, of course, to the multiperiod case.

We can now rewrite equation [7.24] as

$$C^P = q\left(\frac{Y^P}{r}\right) = kY^P \qquad [7.25]$$

where $q = rk$

Note that consumption is now related to a flow concept (permanent income) rather than a stock concept (wealth). Friedman, in fact, has annuitised W since permanent income can be regarded as that level of income which, if received in perpetuity, would have a discounted present value equal to W. This can be seen by solving the following equation for Y^P

$$W = \frac{Y^P}{1+r} + \frac{Y^P}{(1+r)^2} + \frac{Y^P}{(1+r)^3} \cdots \cdots \qquad [7.26]$$

The right-hand side is a convergent geometric series with common ratio $1/(1+r)$. Summing this to infinity yields Y^P/r so that we obtain $Y^P = rW$ as before.

The replacement of a stock concept (W) by the flow concept (Y^P) does, however, raise one awkward inconsistency. If an individual consumes an amount exactly equal to his permanent income, then by definition his wealth remains unchanged. However, equation [7.25] implies that a consumer will normally consume less than his permanent income (empirical estimates of k tend to be in the range 0.8–0.9) and, hence, that wealth will be perpetually increasing. While the annuitisation of wealth and the switch to an implied infinite life span can be justified by maintaining that a household attaches as much importance to consumption by its heirs as to its own consumption, it is difficult to see why it should plan for an ever-increasing level of wealth.

The quantity k in equation [7.25] depends on the tastes of the household and

173

on the rate of interest. However, under conditions of uncertainty Friedman introduces an additional motive for saving – the need to accumulate a reserve of wealth for emergencies. Since human wealth makes a less satisfactory reserve than non-human wealth, the proportion of permanent income consumed, k, is made to depend, also, on the proportion of total wealth which is held as non-human wealth. For a given rate of interest this ratio is directly proportional to the ratio of non-human wealth to permanent income for which Friedman uses the symbol w. Thus we have

$$C^P = k(r, w, u)Y^P \qquad [7.27]$$

where u is a portmanteau variable reflecting the consumer's tastes.

Notice the basic similarities between the PIH and the LCH. In Friedman's model an increase in current income influences current consumption only to the extent that it changes W and, hence, permanent income. Moreover, although equation [7.25] implies a proportionate relationship between C^P and Y^P, the 'proportionality postulate' is again not vital to the model. Even if the homotheticity assumption is dropped, C^P remains a function of W and hence, of permanent income rather than current income.

There are, however, clear if relatively minor, differences between the models. The annuitisation of total wealth means that the stock of non-human assets does not appear explicitly in Friedman's consumption function. However, Friedman does distinguish between the different influences of human and non-human wealth on consumption. The factor of proportionality, k, i.e. the APC out of permanent income, is dependent on the ratio of the two. In the Modigliani–Brumberg formulation, as can be seen from equations [7.20] and [7.19], the effect on planned consumption of an extra £1 of resources is identical whether that £1 is an addition to non-human assets or an addition to the present value of future income. Finally, in the life-cycle model the household merely looks ahead to the end of its life. Friedman's annuitisation of total wealth suggests that his household has an infinite life or at any rate attaches as much importance to the consumption of its heirs as it does to its own consumption.

Permanent income and measured income

When we attempt to relate the PIH to actual data we face obvious problems. Current or 'measured' income is clearly different from the theoretical concept of permanent income and even if we had adequate 'flow of services' data on current or 'measured' consumption this would still differ from planned or permanent consumption. Friedman regards measured income, Y, as being made up of two components – a permanent component, Y^P, and a *transitory* component, Y^t. Measured consumption, C, is similarly divided into *permanent consumption, C^P*, and *transitory consumption, C^t*. Thus we have

$$Y = Y^P + Y^t \quad \text{and} \quad C = C^P + C^t \qquad [7.28]$$

The empirical definition of Y^P is that it is the normal or expected or unfortuitous income of the consumer. This roughly corresponds to the theoretical definition but is purposely left vague by Friedman since '*the precise line to be drawn between permanent and transitory components is best left to the data themselves, to be whatever seems to correspond to consumer behaviour*' (Friedman 1957: 23). In other words, since, theoretically, planned or permanent consumption depends on permanent income, then, empirically, permanent income must be whatever quantity that in practice the consumer regards as determining his planned consumption. The transitory component of income is to be regarded as that which arises from accidental or chance occurrences, while permanent and transitory consumption may be interpreted as planned and 'unplanned' consumption respectively.

To give his model operational content, i.e. to make it capable of being contradicted by observed data, Friedman makes the following assumptions:

Y^P is uncorrelated with Y^t and C^P is uncorrelated with C^t [7.29]

Y^t is uncorrelated which C^t [7.30]

The lack of correlation assumed between permanent and transitory components is uncontroversial and indeed virtually follows from the definition of a transitory component. However, a zero correlation between transitory income and transitory consumption implies that any unforeseen increment in income does not result in unplanned consumption. This is obviously more open to debate. Friedman justifies it, firstly, by pointing out that actual, as opposed to planned, saving is commonly regarded as a residual, i.e. even if income is other than as expected the consumer tends to stick to his consumption plan but to adjust his asset holdings. Also, when it is remembered that consumption theoretically includes only the flow of services from durable goods rather than actual expenditure on such goods, the assumption begins to look more reasonable. If a receipt of transitory income is spent on the purchase of durable goods then this expenditure may be largely classified as saving. Some empirical support for this second justification is provided by Darby (1972; 1974) whose work is discussed on p. 182 below.

Friedman's model as specified above is formally almost exactly equivalent to the 'errors in variables' model described in Section 3.1. The 'true' variables are C^P and Y^P and are linked by the underlying deterministic relationship $C^P = kY^P$. However, C^P and Y^P are observed with measurement errors C^t and Y^t respectively, so that we, in fact, observe C and Y. Moreover, as in Section 3.1, the errors of measurement are uncorrelated with each other and are also uncorrelated with the true values of the variables concerned. The only minor difference from the model of Section 3.1 is that the basic relationship $C^P = kY^P$ does not contain an intercept. Substituting for C^P and Y^P in $C^P = kY^P$ we obtain

$$C = kY + (C^t - kY^t)$$ [7.31]

If [7.31] is regarded as a relationship expressing measured consumption, C, as a function of measured income, Y, then it contains a 'disturbance', $C^t - kY^t$, which is negatively correlated with the explanatory variable which is $Y = Y^P + Y^t$. Thus, if we regress measured C on measured Y, then, as the model of Section 3.1 suggests, the OLS estimator of the slope coefficient (in this case k) will be downward-biased. Similarly, the OLS estimator of the intercept (in this case zero) will be upward-biased. Moreover, these biases will persist however large is the sample. Friedman, in fact, shows that for the OLS regression $\hat{C} = \hat{\alpha} + \hat{\beta}Y$, for large samples

$$\hat{\beta} = kP_y \qquad \text{where } P_y = \frac{\text{var } Y^P}{\text{var } Y^t + \text{var } Y^P} = \frac{\text{var } Y^P}{\text{var } Y} \leqslant 1$$ [7.32]

175

Also, provided the mean transitory components of income and consumption are zero then

$$\hat{\alpha} = k(1 - P_y)\bar{Y}^P \qquad [7.33]$$

where $\bar{Y}^P$ is the mean value of permanent income. P_y is *the proportion of the variation in measured income which results from variations in the permanent component of income.* Thus, if $P_y < 1$, i.e. if variations in Y are in any part due to a transitory component, then $\hat{\alpha} > 0$ and $\hat{\beta} < k$. That is, we will observe a consumption function with an intercept and with a shallower slope than the underlying function $C^P = kY^P$.

It is now possible to use the PIH to reconcile, firstly, the findings from short-run and long-run aggregate time series data.

Figure 7.7a illustrates the time path of aggregate income for a typical Western economy since, say, the turn of the century. The dotted line indicates the secular trend rate of growth in income whereas actual income exhibits cyclical fluctuations about this trend. The trend line may be interpreted as reflecting the growth in permanent income. Had actual income followed the trend line this would have implied that *aggregate* transitory income was always zero (although it may have been positive or negative for *individual* households). Hence, all the variation in aggregate income would be due to variations in the permanent component. Hence, $P_y = 1$ and the observed consumption function would have the form $C = kY$. Even if income follows the cyclical pattern of Fig. 7.7a over the long term the variations in income are still dominated by variations in the permanent component so that P_y is still close to unity. Thus we still observe a function of roughly the form $C = kY$.

Suppose, however, we consider, for example, merely a ten-year period. Such a period is illustrated in Fig. 7.7b which is actually a 'blown-up' version of the boxed area in Fig. 7.7a. For this period the secular trend no longer dominates the path of actual income so that transitory movements account for a considerable

7.7a The relationship between measured and permanent income in the long run.

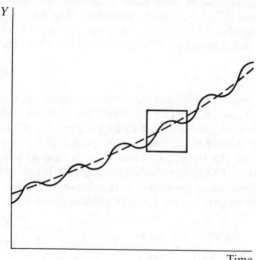

Time

7.7b The relationship between measured and permanent income in the short run.

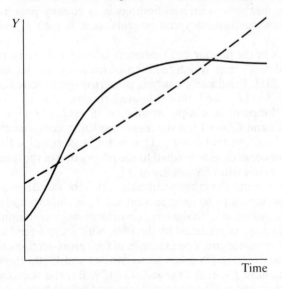

part of the total variation in income. Thus, $P_y < 1$ and hence $\hat{\alpha} > 0$ and $\hat{\beta} < k$, and we observe for this period a flatter consumption function with an intercept. The PIH is therefore able to explain why long-run time series data yield a function of proportionate form while short-run data yield one of typical Keynesian form.

For cross-sectional data the PIH again predicts a consumption function with an intercept. Since we are now dealing with individual households, transitory components are certainly not zero and will make an important contribution to the cross-sectional variation in income. Thus, $P_y < 1$ and again we have $\hat{\alpha} > 0$ and $\hat{\beta} < k$. We shall not reproduce here the famous diagram on page 34 of Friedman (1957) which illustrates the cross-sectional case, since this may be found in many standard macroeconomic texts.

Tests of the permanent income hypothesis using cross-sectional data

Friedman (1957) presents a series of often quite ingenious tests of his hypothesis, the majority of these tests being based on cross-sectional data. His book is deservedly recognised as a classic in its procedure of formulating an hypothesis on the basis of existing data, and generating predictions from that hypothesis which can be tested against further data. However, many of his predictions can also be derived, even if sometimes with a little more difficulty, from the RIH. Also, as Mayer (1972) in particular has stressed, very few of his tests are direct tests of the more controversial aspects of the PIH, namely the proportionality postulate and the zero correlation between the transitory components of income and consumption. The majority of Friedman's results are equally consistent with a model in which C^P depends on Y^P but not in a proportionate manner, and in which the correlation between transitory components is much smaller than that between the permanent components but is nevertheless non-zero. However, as we

177

have already noted, proportionality is not a vital part of the PIH. Also, the reconciliation of time series and cross-sectional findings is as equally possible with a 'low' correlation between transitory components as it is with a zero correlation.

To give readers some idea of the flavour of Friedman's book, we describe in this subsection one of Friedman's tests which tends to provide support for his hypothesis but not for the RIH. Friedman's analysis is carried out in terms of both the estimated MPC, $\hat{\beta} = kP_y$, and the estimated income elasticity of consumption measured at the point of sample means, i.e. $\hat{E} = (dC/dY)(\bar{Y}/\bar{C})$. Since $\hat{E} = \hat{\beta}(\bar{Y}/\bar{C}) = kP_y(\bar{Y}/\bar{C})$ and $C^p = kY^p$, if the mean transitory components are zero then $\bar{Y} = \bar{Y}^p$ and $\bar{C} = \bar{C}^P$ so that $\hat{E} = P_y$. That is, for large samples, the estimated income elasticity of consumption is equal to the proportion of the total variations in income which result from variations in Y^P.

In a series of tests, Friedman compares cross-sections in which the variations in transitory incomes can be presumed to be unimportant, i.e. P_y is close to unity, with cross-sections where variations in Y^t make large contributions to variations in Y, i.e. P_y is much less than unity. As predicted by the PIH, both $\hat{\beta}$ and $\hat{E}$ tend to be larger for the first type of cross-section. For example, of four cross-sections of urban and non-farm households in the US taken between 1941 and 1950,[7] three 'non-wartime' cross-sections have $\hat{\beta}$'s in the range 0.73–0.79. But the wartime cross-section, 1944, for which transitory income variations are likely to have been most important, had a $\hat{\beta}$ as low as 0.57. However, since $\hat{\beta} = kP_y$, this lower value for $\hat{\beta}$ could be the result of a lower k, i.e. a lower APC, resulting from higher precautionary savings during unsettled wartime conditions. Thus a more impressive comparison is between the respective income elasticities of consumption, since $\hat{E}$ is not dependent on k. For the non-wartime years the $\hat{E}$'s range from 0.80 to 0.87 whereas for 1944 $\hat{E} = 0.70$. Such findings provide impressive support for PIH yet it is hard to explain them on the basis of either the AIH or the RIH.

We do not have the space here to do justice to Friedman's book but the reader is encouraged to examine it for himself. Especially striking are the tests concerning 'year on year income changes' (pp. 101–102) and 'income correlations' (pp. 104–105).

Time series estimation under the permanent income hypothesis

A major problem that arises when attempts are made to estimate equations concerning the PIH is that normal data refers to measured income, Y_t, rather than permanent income Y_t^p. Friedman suggests that, for aggregate time series data, permanent income in period t may be estimated by

$$Y_t^p = \lambda Y_t + \lambda(1 - \lambda)Y_{t-1} + \lambda(1 - \lambda)^2 Y_{t-2}\dots \qquad 0 < \lambda < 1 \qquad [7.34]$$

That is, he adopts what is known as a *distributed lag* formulation with geometrically declining weights.[8] The argument is that consumers will give most weight to their current income in assessing their permanent income and successively declining weights to whatever income has been in the past. This formulation clearly stresses the 'expected' nature of permanent income. Also, as reference to Section 5.1 should make clear, equation [7.34] implies that permanent income is determined by what we referred to as an *adaptive expectations hypothesis.* In this case, that is

$$Y_t^p - Y_{t-1}^p = \lambda(Y_t - Y_{t-1}^p) \qquad 0 < \lambda < 1 \tag{7.35}$$

Thus, differences between permanent and measured income lead to an adjustment in the perceived level of permanent income. The extent of the adjustment depends on the size of λ which we can therefore expect to be larger for annual data than, for example, for quarterly data.

Friedman's time series work was, however, based on versions of equation [7.34]. He computed various time series for Y_t^p using a different value for λ in each case, truncating [7.34] after sixteen terms. Using annual real per capita US data for 1905–51 he then ran regressions of the form[9]

$$\hat{C}_t = \hat{\alpha} + \hat{\beta} Y_t^p \tag{7.36}$$

for each Y_t^p series and chose that value of λ which provided the closest fit. The highest R^2 was obtained for $\lambda = 0.33$. For this equation the intercept term was insignificant with· a very low t-ratio and the estimate of k was $\hat{\beta} = 0.88$. This supported the hypothesis that the relationship between C^p and Y^p was one of proportionality. Also the value obtained for $\hat{\beta}$ was close to the observed APC for the period.

Perhaps of greatest interest in these results was the relatively low weight attached to current income in the determination of permanent income. In fact, a value for λ of 0.33 suggests that incomes of three or more years previous are assigned as much as 30 per cent of the total weight used to assess permanent income. These results, if correct, suggest that the AIH (where $\lambda = 1$ and all the weight is assigned to current income so that Y^p and Y are identical) is a serious mis-specification of the true consumption function.

Since, from the basic relationship $C^p = kY^p$ and equation [7.34], the MPC current measured income is $k\lambda$, the practical importance of a low λ is that it implies a low MPC. Hence, the various Keynesian multipliers will have low 'impact' values and this has obvious policy implications. For example, the short-run or impact effect of an exogenous change in non-consumption expenditure will be much smaller than the long-run effect. However, Friedman's time series conclusions are not universally accepted. For example, Wright (1969), reworking Friedman's data, with only a minor modification for wartime years, obtained a value for λ as high as 0.8. Similarly, Zellner, Huang and Chau (1965) and especially Zellner and Geisel (1970) also present results that imply, for annual data, a value of λ closer to unity. A value of λ near unity would imply that the distinction between permanent and measured income is by no means clear-cut so that the AIH becomes a much less serious mis-specification. In contrast however, Darby (1974) argues that estimates of λ are commonly biased upwards because expenditures on durable goods are frequently included in the definition of consumption. When allowance is made for this, Darby obtains a value for λ as low as 0.1 for annual data. There is clearly, then, considerable disagreement about the size of this coefficient.

Friedman's estimating procedure can, of course, be simplified by application of the Koyck transformation. Adding a disturbance term ε_t to the basic relationship $C_t^p = kY_t^p$, and applying the same procedure as in Section 5.1 yields in this case

$$C_t^p = k\lambda Y_t + (1 - \lambda)C_{t-1}^p + \varepsilon_t - (1 - \lambda)\varepsilon_{t-1} \tag{7.37}$$

Equation [7.37] no longer includes the unobservable permanent income variable but still involves present period and lagged permanent consumption. However, on substituting

$$C_t^p = C_t - C_t^t$$

the equation becomes

$$C_t = k\lambda Y_t + (1 - \lambda)C_{t-1} + C_t^t - (1 - \lambda)C_{t-1}^t + \varepsilon_t - (1 - \lambda)\varepsilon_{t-1} \qquad [7.38]$$

Equation [7.38] can be regarded as expressing measured consumption, C_t, as a function of measured income Y_t, C_{t-1} and a composite disturbance given by u_t where

$$u_t = C_t^t - (1 - \lambda)C_{t-1}^t + \varepsilon_t - (1 - \lambda)\varepsilon_{t-1} \qquad [7.39]$$

For example, Evans (1969) estimated, using US annual data for 1929–62, the equation

$$C_t = 0.280 Y_t + 0.676 C_{t-1}$$
$$\quad (0.041) \quad\ (0.052) \qquad\qquad\qquad\qquad [7.40]$$

Such estimates imply a value of

$$\lambda = 1 - 0.676 = 0.324$$

and a value for

$$k = \frac{0.280}{\lambda} = 0.86.$$

Both these estimates are obviously very close to those obtained by Friedman.

However, as we already know from our discussion in Section 5.1, there are severe problems when OLS is applied to equations such as [7.38]. The combination of autocorrelated disturbance term and lagged dependent variable means the OLS estimators will be both biased and inconsistent. The Friedman approach at least yields MLEs of k and λ.

Notwithstanding the technical difficulties of estimating equation [7.38], there is a more fundamental problem. Notice first that, disregarding the disturbance, this equation has exactly the same specification as that for equation [7.15], i.e. for Brown's habit-persistence model. That is, C_t is dependent on Y_t and C_{t-1}. Indeed, consider the following model where *optimal* or *desired* consumption, C_t^*, depends on measured income and a disturbance

$$C_t^* = kY_t + \varepsilon_t \qquad [7.41]$$

Suppose, also, that *actual* consumption is determined by a *partial adjustment* process as described in Section 5.1. That is

$$C_t - C_{t-1} = \lambda(C_t^* - C_{t-1}) \qquad\qquad 0 < \lambda < 1 \qquad [7.42]$$

Thus differences between desired and actual consumption are not immediately eliminated because of 'habit persistence'. The speed with which they are eliminated depends on the size of λ which now, of course, has a totally different interpretation to that in equation [7.35]. Substituting for C_t^* in [7.42] yields

$$C_t = k\lambda Y_t + (1 - \lambda)C_{t-1} + \lambda\varepsilon_t \qquad [7.43]$$

180

Equation [7.43], apart from the specification of the disturbance, has exactly the same form as equation [7.38], the estimating equation obtained from the PIH.

It can be seen that, since both hypotheses are formulated initially in terms of 'unobservable' variables such as permanent income and optimal consumption, it becomes extremely difficult to discriminate, from time series data, between the PIH and the habit-persistence version of the RIH. When expressed in terms of 'measurable' variables both yield, apart from the disturbance specification, identical estimating equations, the only difference being the interpretation one places on the coefficients. That interpretation depends crucially on which of the underlying hypotheses is valid – the PIH or the habit-persistence version of the RIH.

Further tests of the permanent income hypothesis

Friedman (1957) suggests a number of additional tests of the PIH and these have been followed-up by various researchers. One such test concerns the lack of correlation between the transitory components of income and consumption and concentrates on the effect on consumption of 'windfall gains', i.e. receipts or payments to consumers which were totally unexpected, are not expected to recur and do not recur.

One point concerning the relationship between consumption and transitory income should be clarified at the outset. If a consumer receives £1 of transitory income the PIH *does not* imply that he does not increase his consumption. It is true that there is no increase in *transitory* consumption and hence the £1 of transitory income is saved. But this £1 is added to the consumer's total wealth and since permanent income, Y^p, is the rate of return on this wealth there is a rise in Y^p of £1 times the rate of return on wealth. Hence, since $C^p = kY^p$, *permanent consumption* rises by £k times the rate of return. Thus the MPC transitory income is not zero but kr where r is the rate of return. This is, however, still less than the MPC permanent income which is, of course, k.

Friedman treats the λ he estimates from his time series analysis as an estimate of r. To see why, consider equation [7.34]. An increase in transitory income during period t, i.e. Y_t^t, must increase Y_t by the same amount. Hence, permanent income Y_t^p must rise by λ times the increase in Y_t^t. However, since the extra transitory income is initially saved and added to the consumer's total wealth, the increase in permanent income must also equal r times the increase in Y_t^t. Hence, $\lambda = r$. Friedman estimates λ and hence r as 0.33 so that, whereas the MPC permanent income is $k = 0.9$, he maintains that the MPC transitory income should be $kr = 0.3$ and not zero.

A rate of return on wealth of 33 per cent may seem remarkably high. However, we must remember that we are concerned here with a consumer's total wealth including his human capacities such as his earning power. Since there is no free market in human capacities (except in a slave society) a consumer's estimate of r must be essentially subjective rather than objectively based on existing markets. Friedman (1963: footnote 14) argues that 33 per cent is not an unduly high value for this subjective rate of return and, moreover, as already noted, the work of Darby (1974) suggests a value of λ as low as 0.1.

The first major study of windfall gains was that of Bodkin (1959). Bodkin considered the behaviour of a group of war veterans who received an unexpected National Service Life Insurance Dividend in 1950. Such a dividend can be considered as transitory income and Bodkin therefore regressed the consumption of the war veterans on their regular income, Y, and on the windfall, D. He obtained

$$C = 959.3 + 0.56Y + 0.72D \qquad R^2 = 0.60$$
$$\quad (56.6) \quad (0.01) \quad (0.11)$$

Thus the MPC transitory income appeared much higher than the 0.3 predicted by Friedman and even higher than the MPC measured income – a result that seemed to refute the PIH. Friedman, however, responded by pointing out that the windfall or dividend might, in this case, be acting as a proxy or substitute variable for permanent income. Since the size of the windfall depended on the length of time an insurance policy had been in force, its size was likely to be correlated with the war veteran's age. Since permanent income tends to depend on age, this meant that the size of the windfall was likely to be linked to the size of permanent income. Hence the high MPC windfalls.

Subsequently Bird and Bodkin (1965), taking account of Friedman's criticism, reworked the data, including in their regressions additional variables which were themselves proxies for permanent income. They eventually concluded that their results were inconclusive, being consistent with both the AIH and a 'loose' version of the PIH where the correlation between transitory components is low but not zero.

Another well-known study of windfalls is that of Kreinin (1961). These windfalls were German war reparations paid to Israeli citizens during 1957–58. Kreinin found that the MPC out of these windfalls was low (0.167 and statistically insignificant) while the MPC for other more regular income was much higher (0.857 with an estimated standard error of 0.105). However, even the PIH does not suggest that the MPC windfalls is zero so that Kreinin's results are not in complete conformity with it.

It is also possible to use time series data to assess the influence of transitory income on consumption. Given a permanent income series obtained from equations such as [7.34], the definition $Y = Y^p + Y^t$ can always be used to construct a series for transitory income. This suggests estimating equations of the form

$$C_t = k_1 + k_2 Y_t^p + k_3 Y_t^t + \varepsilon_t \qquad [7.44]$$

and testing whether k_3, the coefficient on transitory income, is significantly different either from zero or from that on Y_t^p.

Darby (1972; 1974) estimates such equations using both annual and quarterly US data, and the coefficient on Y_t^t is, indeed, always smaller than that on Y_t^p. Of additional interest is that Darby uses three alternative definitions of consumption: C_1 = expenditure on non-durables, $C_2 = C_1$ + expenditure on clothing and shoes, and $C_3 = C_2$ + expenditure on consumer durables. The narrower the definition of consumption, the smaller is the coefficient on transitory income. This is as predicted by the PIH because spending on durables is more correctly regarded as saving. Hence, its exclusion from the consumption variable should reduce that variable's dependence on transitory income.

Finally, in this subsection, we consider a quite ingenious early test performed by Liviatan (1963). We have already noted that the PIH is formally equivalent to an 'errors in variables' model and that OLS bias is caused by the correlation between explanatory variable and disturbance in equation [7.31] which we reproduce here

$$C = kY + (C^t - kY^t) \qquad\qquad [7.31]$$

As we saw in Section 3.1 the normal response to an 'errors in variables' problem is the method of instrumental variables. In this case, to obtain consistent estimates, we require an instrumental variable which is highly correlated with the explanatory variable, Y, but uncorrelated with the disturbance, $C^t - kY^t$.

When data for a cross-section of households is available for two successive years and when equation [7.31] is estimated for *one* of these years, then obvious alternative instruments for Y are income or consumption *in the other year*. These are the instruments used by Liviatan in his study of the 1958–59 Israel Reinterview Savings Survey.

Liviatan first estimates [7.31] (with an intercept) for 1958 and 1959 using income 'in the other year' as the obvious instrument. He thus obtains estimates of the true MPC permanent income, k, and also of the elasticity of consumption out of permanent income $E = k(\bar{Y}/\bar{C})$. According to the PIH, E should be unity if the proportionality postulate is valid. For both 1958 and 1959 Liviatan's estimates of E are clearly less than unity. This apparently contradicts the proportionality postulate since the sample is large and, provided the instrumental variable employed is uncorrelated with the disturbance, the estimator used is unbiased for such samples.

However, as Friedman promptly pointed out, transitory incomes in successive years are likely to be positively correlated (unforeseen happenings may spread over more than one year). Hence, since the disturbance in [7.31] is negatively related to transitory income in the one year, and since other-year income (the instrument) is positively related to transitory income in the other year, we should expect a negative correlation between instrument and disturbance. This means Liviatan's estimators of k and, hence, E would be downward-biased and this could explain why the estimates of E are less than unity.

Liviatan, however, also uses as an instrument 'other year' consumption. Now transitory consumption expenditures in successive years are also likely to be positively correlated. But the disturbance in [7.31] is positively related to transitory consumption in the one year and the instrument, other-year consumption, is positively related to transitory consumption in the other year. Thus, in this case instrument and disturbance are likely to be *positively* correlated. Hence, if other-year consumption is used as the instrument for Y, the estimators of k and E can be expected to be, if anything, *upward-biased* for large samples. Therefore the estimates of k and E so obtained can be regarded as 'upper bounds' on the true values, so that if the estimate of E is still less than unity then this constitutes very strong evidence against the proportionality postulate.

Liviatan's 1958 and 1959 estimates of E, obtained by this method, are still significantly less than unity. To quote Friedman's final comment, *'if these results should be confirmed for other bodies of data, they would constitute relevant and significant evidence that the elasticity of permanent components is less than unity'* (Friedman 1963: p. 63).

Alternative specifications of the disturbance in time series data

In estimating consumption functions from time series data, we have seen in equations [7.38] and [7.43] that both the PIH and the habit-persistence version of the RIH lead to identical estimating equations apart from the specification of the disturbance. Zellner and Geisel (1970) consider the effect on the estimates obtained of making different assumptions concerning this specification. If we assume that, in the aggregate, transitory consumption is always zero (i.e. 'on average' consumers tend to carry out their consumption plans) then equation [7.38] may be written as

$$C_t = k\lambda Y_t + (1 - \lambda)C_{t-1} + \varepsilon_t - (1 - \lambda)\varepsilon_{t-1} \qquad [7.45]$$

Zellner and Geisel, using a slightly different notation, make four alternative assumptions about the specification of the disturbance in equation [7.45].

1. $\varepsilon_t - (1 - \lambda)\varepsilon_{t-1} = v_t$
2. $\varepsilon_t = v_t$
3. $\varepsilon_t = \rho\varepsilon_{t-1} + v_t$
4. $\varepsilon_t - (1 - \lambda)\varepsilon_{t-1} = \gamma[\varepsilon_{t-1} - (1 - \lambda)\varepsilon_{t-2}] + v_t$

where v_t in each case is normally distributed with zero mean and constant variance and is non-autocorrelated.

The first assumption implies that the disturbance in [7.45] obeys all the classical assumptions. This is the only assumption under which OLS would yield consistent estimators. These estimators would not, however, be unbiased because of the appearance of lagged consumption among the explanatory variables. Assumptions (2) and (3) imply, respectively, that the disturbance in the basic PIH relationship

$$C_t^p = kY_t^p + \varepsilon_t$$

firstly, obeys all the classical assumptions and, secondly, follows a first-order autoregressive process. Finally, assumption (4) implies that the disturbance in equation [7.45] itself follows a first-order autoregressive process. Each of the last three assumptions means that the disturbance in [7.45] is autocorrelated in some manner and also correlated with the explanatory variable C_{t-1}. Thus, under

7.1 The effect of alternative specifications of the disturbance

Assumption	$1 - \lambda$	k	$k\lambda$	ρ	γ
1.	0.66	0.89	0.31		
	(0.11)	(0.03)	(0.09)		
2.	0.45	0.94	0.52		
	(0.03)	(0.16)	(n.c)		
3.	0.66	0.94	0.32	0.69	
	(0.09)	(0.46)	(n.c)	(0.02)	
4.	0.77	0.96	0.22		− 0.13
	(0.09)	(0.01)	(n.c)		(0.14)

Note: Figures in parentheses are estimated standard errors
Source: Zellner and Geisel (1970)

these assumptions the OLS estimators would not even be consistent and all standard statistical tests would be invalid.

Zellner and Geisel obtain maximum likelihood (and hence consistent) estimators for each of the four assumptions, using US quarterly data. Their results are reproduced in Table 7.1.

As far as the parameters of equation [7.45] are concerned, the estimate of k, the long-run APC, is relatively insensitive to the assumption made about the disturbance. However, the estimates of $1 - \lambda$ and hence $k\lambda$, the short-run MPC, vary far more. This result suggests that estimates of consumption function parameters may depend very much on the assumptions made about the disturbance term. A correct specification of the disturbance may therefore be crucial if adequate estimates are to be obtained.

7.5 The role of liquid assets and other wealth-type variables

The idea that variables relating to the consumer's stock of non-human wealth should be included in the consumption function can be traced right back to Keynes's *General Theory*. Also, as we have seen, such a variable is assigned an important role in time series estimating equations based on the LCH. Frequently, however, a lack of adequate data on total non-human wealth has meant that researchers have had to rely either on the liquid asset component of such wealth or to construct their own series from past data on saving. For example, Townend (1976), using quarterly postwar UK data found that a liquid assets variable was a significant determinant of non-durable consumption. Stone (e.g. 1964; 1973) constructs wealth data for the UK using the relationship

$$W_t = W_0 + \sum_{i=1}^{t} S_i$$

where W_0 refers to wealth in some 'bench-mark' year for which data is available and S_i is saving in year i. Although data constructed in this way will not reflect changes in wealth arising from 'revaluations' (i.e. capital gains), Stone interprets his variable as 'permanent wealth' and invariably found it to be significant in his consumer expenditure equations.

A well-known US time series study of the influence of liquid assets is that of Zellner, Huang and Chau (1965). Basically, they suggest a consumption function of the following form

$$C_t = kY_t^p + \alpha(L_{t-1} - L_t^d) + u_t \qquad [7.46]$$

where L_{t-1} stands for liquid asset holdings at the beginning of the current period and L_t^d is the desired level of such assets during the current period. If $\alpha > 0$, an asset adjustment process therefore leads to a reduction in consumption when the desired asset stock exceeds the actual asset stock and an increase in consumption if L_t^d is less than L_{t-1}. Y_t^p is permanent income and u_t is a disturbance. Y_t^p is assumed to be determined by an adaptive expectations process identical to equation [7.35] and the desired stock of liquid assets is assumed to be proportional to permanent income i.e. $L_t^d = \eta Y_t^p$.

Substituting for L_t^d in equation [7.46] yields

$$C_t = \alpha L_{t-1} + (k - \eta\alpha)Y_t^p + u_t \qquad [7.47]$$

Applying the Koyck transformation to equation [7.47] then gives

$$C_t - (1 - \lambda)C_{t-1} = \alpha L_{t-1} - (1 - \lambda)\alpha L_{t-2} + (k - \eta\alpha)[Y_t^p - (1 - \lambda)Y_{t-1}^p]$$
$$+ u_t - (1 - \lambda)u_{t-1}$$

Using equation [7.35], the following equation in terms of 'observable' variables is obtained

$$C_t = (1 - \lambda)C_{t-1} + \alpha L_{t-1} - (1 - \lambda)\alpha L_{t-2} + \lambda(k - \eta\alpha)Y_t + u_t - (1 - \lambda)u_{t-1}$$
$$[7.48]$$

There are, however, a number of problems in actually estimating equation [7.48]. Firstly, the composite disturbance term is almost certain to be autocorrelated. Secondly, of the four parameters to be estimated, two, λ and α, are overidentified and two, k and η, are underidentified. To see this suppose we have an estimated version of equation [7.48]

$$C_t = \hat{\beta}_1 + \hat{\beta}_2 C_{t-1} + \hat{\beta}_3 L_{t-1} + \hat{\beta}_4 L_{t-2} + \hat{\beta}_5 Y_t \qquad [7.49]$$

Given the $\hat{\beta}$'s, to obtain estimates of λ, α, k and η we need to solve the equations

$$\hat{\beta}_2 = 1 - \lambda$$
$$\hat{\beta}_3 = \alpha \qquad [7.50A] \qquad \hat{\beta}_5 = \lambda(k - \eta\alpha) \qquad [7.50B]$$
$$\hat{\beta}_4 = -\alpha(1 - \lambda)$$

The subsystem [7.50A] yields two alternative values for λ and α and so these parameters are overidentified. However, even if we had unique values for λ and α, there is no way in which we could obtain values for k and η from equation [7.50B]. Thus k and η are underidentified.

Using quarterly US data for 1947–61 in real per capita terms, the authors first estimate [7.48] ignoring the autocorrelation and identification problems. They use OLS and also TSLS to overcome any problems of simultaneity. When TSLS is used the regression coefficient on L_{t-2} is roughly equal to minus the product of those on C_{t-1} and L_{t-1}.

That is,

$$\hat{\beta}_4 = -\hat{\beta}_2\hat{\beta}_3$$

This is exactly as suggested by equation [7.48]. Zellner, Huang and Chau therefore re-estimate [7.49] subject to the restriction that $\hat{\beta}_4 = -\hat{\beta}_2\hat{\beta}_3$, using the non-linear least squares estimating technique described in Section 5.4. This deals with the overidentification problem, but, of course, k and η remain underidentified.

To deal with the autocorrelation problem the authors approximate the composite disturbance in [7.48] by a first-order autoregressive scheme. When these refinements to the estimation process are made, the TSLS estimates of λ, α and the quantity $m = k - \eta\alpha$ are, respectively[10]

$$\hat{\lambda} = 0.127 \qquad \hat{\alpha} = 0.697 \qquad \hat{m} = 0.405$$
$$(0.041) \qquad (0.153) \qquad (0.120)$$

This estimate of λ derived from quarterly data suggests an adaptive expectations process somewhat more rapid than that estimated by Friedman when using annual data. If η is given the value of 0.764, which is the sample average ratio of liquid assets to income, then the estimates of m and α imply a value for $k = 0.937$ which appears reasonable. More important, however, is that the estimate of α is clearly significantly different from zero. This supports the hypothesis that an imbalance in liquid asset holdings has an effect on consumption expenditure.

The Ball–Drake wealth model

In the past two decades there have been many time series studies of the relationship between aggregate consumption and the stock (liquid or otherwise) of consumers' wealth. However, very few of these studies pay much attention to the precise type of consumer behaviour which might cause wealth variables to be important. An exception is the model developed by Ball and Drake (1964). Similar ideas had been put forward by Spiro (1962) and were further developed by Clower and Johnson (1968).

In the Ball–Drake model individuals are assumed to be short-sighted in the face of uncertainty and their basic motive for saving is a broad precautionary one. The arguments in the consumer's utility function are current real consumption and current real non-human wealth. That is

$$U_t = U(C_t, W_t) \qquad\qquad [7.51]$$

where W_t is wealth at the end of the (short) period over which utility is maximised and C_t is consumption during that period. Thus, the consumer does not ignore the future but safeguards against its uncertainties by accumulating wealth. The more wealth he accumulates the more secure he feels and, given his rate of consumption, the more utility he derives. The future is therefore allowed-for without making the possibly unrealistic assumption of a rigorous intertemporal utility maximisation required by the LCH and the PIH.

The utility function is maximised subject to the budget constraint

$$W_{t-1} + Y_t = C_t + W_t \qquad\qquad [7.52]$$

where W_{t-1} is real wealth at the beginning of the period and Y_t is real income during the period. W_{t-1} and Y_t are taken as given during the maximising process. If [7.51] is assumed to be homothetic then the optimal relationship between C_t and W_t is one of proportionality, i.e. $W_t = hC_t$. Substituting in [7.52] then yields the consumption function

$$C_t = \frac{1}{1+h} Y_t + \frac{1}{1+h} W_{t-1} \qquad\qquad [7.53A]$$

or

$$C_t = \frac{1}{1+h} Y_t + \frac{h}{1+h} C_{t-1} \qquad\qquad [7.53B]$$

Aggregating over all consumers, it can be seen that the wealth hypothesis has led to an identical estimating equation for time series data to that obtained both from the PIH and the habit-persistence version of the RIH. C_t is again dependent on Y_t and C_{t-1}. However, in this case an extra prediction is derived – the coefficients in [7.53B] should sum to unity if the wealth hypothesis is valid.

Implications of the wealth hypothesis

Suppose the consumer's income grows at a constant rate, g, so that

$$Y_t = (1 + g) Y_{t-1}.$$

From [7.53B] we then have

$$\frac{C_t}{Y_t} = \frac{1}{1+h} + \frac{h}{1+h}\left(\frac{C_{t-1}}{Y_t}\right) = \frac{1}{1+h} + \frac{h}{(1+h)(1+g)}\left(\frac{C_{t-1}}{Y_{t-1}}\right)$$

or, letting $\bar{C}_t$ represent the APC in period t,

$$\bar{C}_t = \frac{1}{1+h} + \frac{h}{(1+h)(1+g)}\bar{C}_{t-1} \qquad [7.54]$$

The 'equilibrium' average propensity to consume $\overline{\text{APC}}$ can now be obtained by setting

$$\bar{C}_t = \bar{C}_{t-1} = \overline{\text{APC}}$$

in equation [7.54] in which case

$$\overline{\text{APC}} = \frac{1}{1 + h - (h/(1 + g))} \qquad [7.55]$$

Thus, the higher the rate of growth in income, the lower is the equilibrium APC and the higher the equilibrium APS. In fact, if a consumer's income remains constant, i.e. if $g = 0$, then saving will eventually fall to zero. In effect, the consumer eventually acquires a stock of wealth, sufficiently large relative to his income, to preclude the need for further precautionary saving.

Aggregating again over all consumers, it can now be seen that the wealth hypothesis provides yet another explanation of why economies with high growth rates tend to have large saving ratios. Also, the long-run constancy in the APC can be explained by the stability of long-run growth rates in real income, while cyclical fluctuations in the APC can be attributed to cyclical fluctuations in the growth rate. Finally, the findings from cross-sectional data can also be explained. High-income consumers tend to be those who have recently experienced a high-income growth rate while low-income consumers will have experienced only low rates of income growth. Thus high-income consumers will tend to have smaller APCs than low-income consumers.

Empirical testing of the wealth hypothesis

Although equation [7.53B] contains identical variables to the estimating equations arising out of the PIH and the RIH, the wealth hypothesis does generate further testable predictions by which it is possible in principle to discriminate between it and rival hypotheses. We have already noted the prediction that estimates of the coefficients in [7.53B] should sum to unity. In addition, since the coefficients in equation [7.53B] are both functions of h, the optimal ratio between wealth and consumption, they may also be estimated in a completely different manner by examining the actual ratio between personal wealth and consumption during the sample period. If the wealth hypothesis is valid such estimates should coincide, at least roughly, with those obtained by regression analysis.

Since it was first formulated the wealth hypothesis has come under consider-able empirical attack because of the apparent non-fulfilment of its predictions. For example, although Ball and Drake maintained that equations estimated from both UK and US data yielded coefficients summing to unity, this was disputed by Evans (1967b). Further evidence on this has been provided by, for example, Mayer (1972). Using *cross-sectional* data for samples of both Swiss and German households, Mayer found that the sum of the coefficients on Y_t and C_{t-1} was consistently less than unity. As far as time series data are concerned researchers have also, generally, found this sum to be significantly less than unity.

It is also true that estimates of the coefficients of equation [7.53B] obtained from the calculation of wealth-consumption ratios do not appear to coincide with regression estimates. This point was forcefully made by Evans in the reference given above. For the US, wealth-consumption ratios are about $h = 5.0$–6.0 for annual data. This implies from [7.53B] a short-run MPC of about 0.14–0.17. However, Evans estimated a number of US consumption functions with different specifications and invariably found a short-run MPC much higher than this.

Before assessing the strength of these empirical criticisms of the wealth hypothesis, it is necessary to consider the conceptual difficulties implicit in the original Ball–Drake model. Firstly, the model makes no allowance for possible differences between planned and actual magnitudes. It could be argued that equation [7.51] should refer to planned or expected utility and that C_t and W_t should be interpreted as planned consumption and, more importantly, planned end-period wealth. The optimal relationship $W_t = hC_t$ would then refer to planned but not necessarily to actual magnitudes.

Secondly, the budget constraint [7.52] makes no allowance for capital gains. If C_t and W_t are interpreted as planned quantities then the budget constraint should really be

$$W_{t-1} + Y_t + G_t = C_t + W_t \qquad [7.56]$$

G_t is the consumer's expected capital gain on the known beginning-period asset stock, W_{t-1}, and Y_t is now expected income during the period. Now, even if G_t is, in fact, zero, it has to be assumed that *all* the consumer's plans and expectations are realised (e.g. *actual* capital gains must also be zero) if the optimal relationship $W_t = hC_t$ is to hold for actual as well as planned magnitudes. This seems rather a large assumption to make for the uncertain world which the wealth hypothesis was formulated to deal with. However, if the optimal relationship does not hold for actual C_t and W_t, then it is no longer possible to make the substitution (in terms of actual magnitudes) $W_{t-1} = hC_{t-1}$, in equation [7.53A] to obtain a valid equation [7.53B]. Hence, provided wealth data is available, it would seem better to base tests of the wealth hypothesis on [7.53A] rather than [7.53B].

These conceptual difficulties do not represent a fundamental criticism of the Ball–Drake hypothesis. The idea of including *current* consumption only, together with *current* wealth in the utility function, remains an attractive one and the model could be adapted to allow for the above difficulties. Moreover, since the empirical criticisms discussed earlier are all based on the (probably invalid) equation [7.53B] they do not constitute evidence against the basic *idea* of the wealth hypothesis.

Ball and Drake's estimation of equation [7.53B] rather than [7.53A] reflected the fact that, at least for the UK at that time, there was a lack of adequate time series data on consumer net worth. Recent improvements in the availability of such data (see, for example, Central Statistical Office 1978) now make it possible to pay direct attention to equation [7.53A]. However, problems arise in the estimation of [7.53A] that are not immediately obvious.

If the wealth hypothesis is a valid description of consumer behaviour then the lag on the wealth variable in equation [7.53A] must be regarded as being equal to the length of the 'planning interval' over which the consumer seeks to maximise utility. Just because data is annual, for example, does not mean that the length of the lag should be set equal to exactly one year, so that the estimation of [7.53A] is not such a simple matter as it might initially seem. Furthermore, there is no reason to suppose that once a consumer has formulated one plan over a given planning period, he should wait until the end of that planning period before formulating a new plan. The wealth hypothesis was designed to apply to an uncertain world in which plans and expectations are almost never realised, and the non-realisation of expectations may lead to a very rapid revision of consumer plans. Thomas (1981) attempts to deal with such problems, developing a model based on equation [7.53A] which distinguishes between three separate intervals: an 'observation interval' depending on the nature of the data (e.g. with annual data it is one year etc.), a 'planning interval' as described above, and a 'review interval' representing the time between the successive revision of plans.

Similar comments, of course, apply to equation [7.53B] and in particular to the lag on the consumption variable on the right-hand side of that equation. Yet whenever [7.53B] has been estimated as a 'test' of the wealth hypothesis, this lag is invariably set equal to one year for annual data and one quarter for quarterly data. This, then, is a further reason to treat with scepticism the 'failure' of the wealth hypothesis to pass such tests.

The role of capital gains

The stock of consumer's wealth changes not merely because of saving decisions but also because of market revaluations of assets already in the stock, i.e. 'capital gains'. Capital gains have been referred to above on a number of occasions but we have yet to consider the exact manner in which they might influence a consumer's behaviour. Since capital gains are an 'accrual', akin to income, it is conceivable that they have a direct effect on consumption similar to that of income as well as an indirect effect via changes in consumer wealth. If so, the measured income concept appearing in consumption functions might be more appropriately defined to include at least some component of capital gains.

Bhatia (1972) uses annual US data for 1948–64 to test both for a direct 'income-type' effect and an indirect effect via wealth. He maintained that regression results suggested that capital gains do affect consumption via wealth, but that there was no direct effect via income. On the other hand, Feldstein and Fane (1973), using annual UK data for 1948–69, and Feldstein (1973) using annual US data for 1929–66 present evidence of a direct effect for capital gains over and above any effect via wealth. However, capital gains which result from companies retaining part of their profits are found to have a much greater effect on consumption than gains arising simply from market revaluations. This is to be expected if consumers regard the retaining of earnings by companies in which they have shares as providing a more permanent type of capital gain than those arising out of revaluations.

Bhatia (1979) maintains that these findings, at least as far as the US is concerned, are the result of the method used by Feldstein to calculate capital gains. Feldstein subtracts personal saving from changes in household wealth – an unreliable method because of deficiencies in data on net wealth and saving. Using alternative estimates of capital gains, based on changes in asset-price indices, Bhatia finds no evidence for a direct capital gains effect and again claims detection of a significant indirect effect via wealth. The precise role of capital gains and the most appropriate definition of income therefore remains unclear.[11]

7.6 Recent work on the consumption function

In recent years much attention has been paid to the possible influences of the price level and the rate of inflation on consumer expenditure. In the models of the previous sections it was implicitly assumed that any changes in the price level could be ignored. For example, suppose we added a price variable to a simple LCH estimating equation and obtained

$$C_t = \alpha + \beta Y_t + \gamma W_t + \delta P_t + \varepsilon_t \qquad [7.57]$$

where C_t, Y_t and W_t are real per capita consumption, income and wealth respectively and P_t is an index of consumer prices which has also been used to deflate the other variables. Economic theory suggests that the price coefficient, δ, in equation [7.57] should be zero. A rise in the price level, with real income and real wealth remaining constant, must imply an equiproportionate rise in money income and in money wealth and hence should lead to no change in consumption expenditure. If δ was positive in equation [7.57] then this would imply that consumers were exhibiting the phenomenon commonly known as 'money illusion'. A positive δ means that a rise in P_t, with Y_t and W_t constant, results in a rise in consumption. Consumers must therefore be treating the equiproportionate rise in money income and money wealth as if it were a rise in real income and real wealth and 'not noticing' the rise in prices.

Branson and Klevorick (1969) estimated a consumption function basically similar to [7.57] although it contained fairly complex lags on the income and price variables. Using quarterly US data for 1955–65, they found their equivalent of δ to be significantly greater than zero and concluded that a significant degree of money illusion existed in the US consumption function.

Juster and Wachtel (1972) have considered the effects of high rates of price *change* on the consumption function. They found that high inflation rates tended to *reduce* US consumption expenditure. They argued that this was because high inflation rates are historically associated with variable inflation rates. Hence, if consumers do not expect a similar variability in money income, future real income will be subject to greater uncertainty during times of high inflation and this will lead to greater precautionary savings.

Deaton (1978) also considers inflation rates but argues that it is *accelerating* inflation that reduces consumer expenditure. For example, suppose that past inflation has been of 5 per cent per annum, that consumers expect this inflation rate to continue but that the inflation rate has, in fact, accelerated to 10 per cent. A consumer, purchasing a specific good, will find its price higher than expected but, because his expectations are still based on the past inflation rate, he will not realise that the prices of all goods have risen to the same extent. An absolute rise in the price of all goods is therefore confused with a relative price rise for the good that the consumer is considering buying. The consumer may therefore decide to revise, temporarily, his expenditure plans and refrain from buying the good. Since all consumers are in the same position (although not all buying the same good) the aggregate APS declines whenever inflation accelerates, i.e. whenever the actual exceeds the expected inflation rate.

The underlying consumption function in Deaton's model is of the Friedman type and the model is estimated using quarterly US data for 1954–74 and quarterly UK data for 1955–74. The expected inflation rate is, in fact, assumed to be constant so that changes in the APS are made to depend on the actual rate of inflation. Deaton does, indeed, find that, for both countries, changes in the APS are positively related to the inflation rate.

Deaton's results for the US are consistent with those of Juster and Wachtel but it is difficult to reconcile them with those of Branson and Klevorick. If the rate of *change* in the APS rises as the rate of price *change* rises, then consumption *levels* must fall as the price *level* rises. This implies a negative δ in equation [7.57] in contrast to the positive value found by Branson and Klevorick. For the UK, similar results concerning the inflation rate were obtained by Townend (1976), although their consumption function also included a liquid assets variable.

The possibility that there may be a link between the rate of inflation and the level of consumer expenditure provides one feasible explanation of a striking feature of recent behaviour. Many Western economies have experienced a sharp increase in their saving/income ratios during the 1970s.

For example, in the UK the APS (defined as personal saving as a proportion of personal disposable income) had risen from approximately 8 per cent during the 1960s to nearly 16 per cent at the end of the 1970s. It is obviously tempting to attribute this phenomenon to the accelerating inflation rates recently experienced by many Western economies. However, an equally plausible explanation is provided by the wealth hypothesis of the previous section. Rapid inflation seriously erodes the real value of that part of a consumer's wealth that he holds in assets such as bank deposits that are fixed in money terms. Also, since stock market prices have generally failed to keep pace with inflation during the 1970s and 1980s the non-money fixed assets in a consumer's portfolio are also likely to have declined in real value. Such a decline in real wealth may have reduced the level of consumer expenditure occurring at a given level of real income.

A data-based approach

The conflict between competing explanations of rising APS is well illustrated by considering the recent studies of Davidson, Hendry, Sbra and Yeo (1978) – (henceforth DHSY) – and Hendry and Ungern–Sternberg (1980). The DHSY paper is a thorough study of postwar UK quarterly data, concentrating mainly on the dynamic properties and lag structure of the relationship between disposable income and non-durable consumption rather than the economic behaviour underlying it. DHSY are perplexed that previous investigators of this relationship had come to widely different conclusions regarding, for example, lag structures and short-run marginal propensities to consume. To highlight the issues involved they concentrate on three previous studies – those of Hendry (1974), Ball, *et al.* (1975) and Wall, *et al.* (1975). They aim not only to resolve the conflicts in the three studies but also to discover why the research methods of the three papers led to such different conclusions. The work by DHSY is the first important example of the 'data-based' approach to applied econometric work described in Chapter 1.

DHSY find that, even when a common sample period of identical non-seasonally adjusted data is used, with identical functional forms and data transformations, the three models still seem to lead to different conclusions. Remaining possible reasons for this are the varying lag structures employed in the three studies and the different estimating methods and test statistics used.

The above standardisation by sample period, etc. enables DHSY to 'nest' the three competing hypotheses as special cases of a general hypothesis or estimating equation. This enables them to test, on purely statistical grounds, which provides the best description of the UK relationship between income and consumption. On the basis of standard statistical criteria such as goodness of fit, the best of the three models appears to be that of Wall, *et al.* which is of the form

$$\Delta C_t = \alpha_0 + \alpha_1 \Delta Y_t + \alpha_2 \Delta Y_{t-1} \qquad \alpha_0 > 0 \qquad [7.58]$$

where ΔC_t and ΔY_t are the quarterly changes in consumption and income.

Unfortunately, the statistically preferred equation [7.58] has some rather strange economic properties. For example, it implies that even if the level of income were to remain constant indefinitely, in which case

$$\Delta Y_t = \Delta Y_{t-1} = 0$$

consumption would continue to rise without limit since under such conditions $\Delta C_t = \alpha_0 > 0$. In other words, equation [7.58] has no static equilibrium solution. Also, the equation implies that the adjustment of consumption to any change in income is complete after just two quarters and, moreover, is apparently independent of any disequilibrium in the previous *levels* of the variables C_t and Y_t. Normally, when consumption is, for example, 'well above' its equilibrium level relative to income, the increase in C_t accompanying an increase in Y_t can be expected to be much smaller than would have been the case if C_t and Y_t had previously been well adjusted to each other.

With the aim of resolving this conflict between economic and statistical criteria, DHSY present a model of their own. The 'steady state' or 'equilibrium' relationship between income and consumption is assumed to have the following form

$$C_t^* = KY_t^* \qquad [7.59]$$

where C_t^* and Y_t^* represent 'equilibrium' values. For example [7.59] might represent an underlying relationship between permanent income and permanent consumption. Alternatively, it could be interpreted as equation [7.41] in which case C_t^* represents 'optimal' consumption and Y_t^* is merely measured income. Taking natural logarithms of [7.59] yields

$$c_t^* = k + y_t^* \qquad [7.60]$$

where lower-case letters denote logarithms.

However, consumption and income are not usually equal to their equilibrium values and we normally observe a 'disequilibrium relationship' involving lagged values of c_t and y_t. DHSY represent this disequilibrium relationship by

$$c_t = k^* + \beta_1 y_t + \beta_2 y_{t-1} + \alpha c_{t-1} \qquad [7.61]$$

193

The equilibrium or steady state solution to [7.61] can be obtained, for a zero growth rate, by setting

$$c_t = c_{t-1} = c_t^*$$

and

$$y_t = y_{t-1} = y_t^*$$

and is given by

$$c_t^* = \frac{k^*}{1-\alpha} + \left(\frac{\beta_1 + \beta_2}{1-\alpha}\right)y_t^* \qquad [7.62]$$

For equation [7.62] to be consistent with the actual equilibrium solution [7.60] we therefore require $k^* = k(1-\alpha)$ and $\beta_1 + \beta_2 + \alpha = 1$. If these restrictions are imposed on the disequilibrium relationship [7.61], that equation becomes

$$c_t = k(1-\alpha) + \beta_1 y_t + \beta_2 y_{t-1} + (1 - \beta_1 - \beta_2)c_{t-1} \qquad [7.63]$$

or

$$c_t - c_{t-1} = \beta_1(y_t - y_{t-1}) + \gamma(k + y_{t-1} - c_{t-1}) \qquad [7.64]$$

where

$$\gamma = 1 - \alpha = \beta_1 + \beta_2$$

Equation [7.64] is a relationship which in equilibrium reduces to [7.60]. Notice, however, that the last term in this equation

$$k + y_{t-1} - c_{t-1}$$

represents the *extent of disequilibrium between the levels of consumption and income in the previous period*. Equation [7.64] therefore relates changes in consumption not merely to changes in income, as does Wall, *et al.*'s equation [7.58], but also includes a disequilibrium term. That is, if previous levels of c_t and y_t satisfy the equilibrium relationship [7.60], then

$$c_{t-1} = k + y_{t-1}$$

and the change in consumption depends only on the change in income. Otherwise, it depends also on the extent to which previous levels of c_t and y_t depart from their equilibrium relationship.

DHSY show that k in equation [7.60] depends on the growth rates of income and consumption. Such growth rates remained relatively constant during Wall, *et al.*'s sample period so that $k \simeq$ constant and hence

$$y_{t-1} - c_{t-1} \simeq \text{const.}$$

DHSY are therefore able to account for the good statistical performance of the Wall, *et al.* equation by pointing to the high collinearity between the constant term in that equation and the disequilibrium term $k + y_{t-1} - c_{t-1}$.

The constant term was able, in fact, to undertake the role of the required but absent disequilibrium term.

Since DHSY use non-seasonally adjusted data, it makes more sense to relate c_t to c_{t-4}, i.e. consumption in the same quarter last year, than to c_{t-1}

consumption in the last quarter. Hence, the appropriate lag length in equation [7.64] is four quarters rather than one quarter and for estimating purposes the equation can be rewritten as

$$c_t - c_{t-4} = \gamma k + \beta_1(y_t - y_{t-4}) - \gamma(c_{t-4} - y_{t-4}) \qquad [7.65]$$

DHSY in fact, estimate a slightly generalised version of [7.65] with the constant term suppressed

$$c_t - c_{t-4} = \underset{(0.04)}{0.49}(y_t - y_{t-4}) - \underset{(0.05)}{0.17}\Delta_1(y_t - y_{t-4}) - \underset{(0.01)}{0.06}(c_{t-4} - y_{t-4}) + \underset{(0.004)}{0.01}D_t$$

$$R^2 = 0.71 \quad s = 0.0067 \quad d = 1.6 \quad z = 23$$

$$[7.66]$$

where $\Delta_1(y_t - y_{t-4})$ is the quarterly change in $y_t - y_{t-4}$ and D_t is a dummy variable introduced to account for advance warning of purchase tax increases in the second quarter of 1968. s is the standard error of the residuals and z is the Box–Pierce portmanteau autocorrelation statistic described in Section 3.2.

DHSY interpret [7.66] in terms of a simple 'feed-back' model whereby consumers plan to spend in any quarter what they spent in the same quarter of the previous year, (i.e. $c_t = c_{t-4}$), but where this quantity is modified by, firstly, a proportion of the annual change in income that has occurred $(0.49[y_t - y_{t-4}])$, secondly, whether that change is itself increasing or decreasing $(-0.17\Delta_1[y_t - y_{t-4}])$, and finally a feedback from the previous C/Y ratio $(-0.06[c_{t-4} - y_{t-4}])$ which ensures coherence with the long-run target outcome $C_t = KY_t$.

Equation [7.66] was estimated for 1958–70. Although data for 1971–75 was available it is used merely for 'post sample' predictions. Unfortunately, [7.66] consistently overpredicts consumption during the period. To get round this problem DHSY are forced to invoke the Deaton hypothesis described above and to add price variables to the equation. Their final preferred equation is

$$c_t - c_{t-4} = \underset{(0.04)}{0.47}(y_t - y_{t-4}) - \underset{(0.05)}{0.21}\Delta_1(y_t - y_{t-4}) - \underset{(0.02)}{0.10}(c_{t-4} - y_{t-4})$$

$$+ \underset{(0.003)}{0.01}D_t - \underset{(0.07)}{0.13}(p_t - p_{t-4}) - \underset{(0.15)}{0.28}\Delta_1(p_t - p_{t-4}) \qquad [7.67]$$

$$R^2 = 0.77 \quad s = 0.0061 \quad d = 1.8 \quad z = 19$$

where p_t is the log of the implied consumption deflator (i.e. an index of consumer prices). Equation [7.67] satisfactorily predicts consumption during 1971–75 so DHSY are eventually able to resolve their forecasting problem.

There are, however, some slightly worrying aspects concerning the DHSY, study. Firstly, while their basic equation [7.66] is rigorously derived by the addition of disequilibrium effects to underlying theory, the inflation effects are rather awkwardly tagged-on at the end in an *ad hoc* attempt to resolve the forecasting problem. Secondly, it appears that when data for 1958–70 only was available, DHSY felt no need to consider inflation effects. Only when 1971–75 data became available and the forecasting problem emerged were they led to introduce price variables into their equation. However, proper assessment of the forecasting ability of any equation must necessarily wait until it can be tested against data that was not made use of in its formulation.

Finally, it is possible to show that the importance of the variables $p_t - p_{t-4}$ and $c_{t-4} - y_{t-4}$ in equation [7.67] can be explained in terms of a wealth effect. Intuitively, it can be seen that $c_{t-4} - y_{t-4}$ can be regarded as reflecting changes in wealth that arise from saving, while $p_t - p_{t-4}$ could represent reductions in the real value of money fixed assets resulting from a rise in prices. Indeed, Bean (1978) demonstrates that the size of the coefficients in [7.67] is perfectly consistent with such an interpretation. The UK Treasury model now incorporates a consumption equation of the DSHY kind but in fact interprets it in terms of wealth effects rather than Deaton-type inflation effects.

The paper by Hendry and Ungern–Sternberg (1980), henceforth HUS, goes some way to resolving the above issues. They begin by noting that equations such as [7.64] have a major flaw as a complete account of the dynamic behaviour of flow variables. Since c_t and y_t are rarely equal this means that some latent asset stock must be changing and changes in this stock may itself affect the change in c_t. This, of course, is merely another way of saying that wealth effects may be an influence on consumption.

Wealth or 'cumulative saving' effects are introduced into the model by assuming that consumers seek to maintain constant ratios not only between consumption and income but also between the latent asset stock and income. Thus as well as [7.59] and [7.60] we have another 'equilibrium relationship'

$$A_t^* = BY_t^* \quad \text{or} \quad a_t^* = b + y_t^* \qquad [7.68]$$

where A_t is the latent asset stock or wealth variable and lower-case letters again represent natural logarithms.

In disequilibrium 'costs' or 'losses' are incurred if c_t or a_t differ from their equilibrium values. The consumer is assumed to minimise a quadratic function of these losses subject to a budget constraint. This eventually leads to an equation of the form

$$c_t - c_{t-1} = \theta_0 + \theta_1(y_t - y_{t-1}) - \theta_2(c_{t-1} - y_{t-1}) + \theta_3(a_{t-1} - y_{t-1}) \qquad [7.69]$$

Notice that [7.69] can be regarded as a generalisation of [7.64] since it includes two disequilibrium-type variables:

$$c_{t-1} - y_{t-1}$$

and

$$a_{t-1} - y_{t-1},$$

the latter reflecting the extent of previous period disequilibrium between the asset stock and income.[12]

Another important aspect of the HUS work is their redefinition of the personal disposable income variable, Y. The normal definition includes interest receipts which, since the personal sector is a substantial net creditor, comprise a not insubstantial proportion of Y. During times of high inflation nominal interest rates rise, thus increasing the interest component of Y. However, such increases are offset by inflation-induced capital losses on monetary assets and such losses are not reflected in Y. Since it seems illogical to include only one but not both of these inflation-induced effects, HUS redefine Y to reflect capital losses on monetary assets. A new income variable $Y^\dagger$ is defined as

$$Y^\dagger = Y - h\dot{p}L \qquad [7.70]$$

In equation [7.70], L is the real stock of liquid assets, used to proxy the stock of monetary assets and $\dot{p}$ is the inflation rate. Thus, $\dot{p}L$ is the capital loss on liquid assets. The parameter, h, is introduced to account for possible scale effects arising from wrongly chosen measures for p and L. When disposable income is redefined in this way the apparent fall in the APC during the 1970s becomes much less marked.

HUS begin their empirical work by re-estimating DHSY's equation [7.67] for the period 1962–72 and testing its predictions for 1973–77. The predictions are much less impressive than over the DHSY period and re-estimation over HUS's full sample period confirmed an apparent change in parameter values particularly for the $\Delta_1(p_t - p_{t-4})$ price variable. HUS therefore seek to improve on the DSHY specification by:

1. Including a liquid assets variable as a proxy for a_{t-1} in the manner suggested by equation [7.69].
2. Redefining income as Y^+ defined in equation [7.70]. h was determined by a 'grid search'. That is, regressions were run for alternative values of h (in steps of 0.1). The minimum residual sum of squares lay in the interval $0.4 < h < 0.6$ so that a value $h = 0.5$ was selected for most of the analysis.
3. Introducing seasonal dummy variables into the equation since the strong seasonal behaviour of C/Y suggested a steady state solution of the form $c_t = k_i + y_t$ (where k_i varies seasonally) rather than $c_t = k + y_t$.

HUS's preferred equation is of the form

$$c_t - c_{t-4} = \alpha_1 A y_t^+ + \alpha_2(c_{t-4} - y_{t-4}^+) + \alpha_3(\bar{l} - \bar{y}^+)_{t-1} + \alpha_4\Delta_1 l_{t-1}$$
$$+ \text{constant} + \text{dummy variables} \qquad [7.71]$$

where l_t is the logarithm of the liquid asset variable. It is based on a quarterly version of equation [7.69] with some generalisations –

$$A y_t^+ = 3\Delta_4 y_t^+ + 2\Delta_4 y_{t-1}^+ + \Delta_4 y_{t-2}^+$$

is a simple Almon polynomial used to capture the distributed lag on $\Delta_4 y_t^+$, and

$$(\bar{l} - \bar{y})_{t-1} = \log\left(\frac{L_{t-1} + L_{t-2} + L_{t-3} + L_{t-4}}{Y_{t-1}^+ + Y_{t-2}^+ + Y_{t-3}^+ + Y_{t-4}^+}\right) = \log\left(\frac{\bar{L}}{\bar{Y}^+}\right)_{t-1}$$

Equation [7.71] proves superior to the original DHSY specification and also passes the second of the Chow tests for parameter stability described in Section 5.4. *Both* disequilibrium variables are significant and the coefficient on $c_{t-4} - y_{t-4}^+$ is nearly twice as large as in the original DHSY specification. The steady state solution to the model is

$$C/Y^+ = K_i\left(\frac{L}{Y^+}\right)^{0.44} \qquad \text{where} \quad Y^+ = Y - \tfrac{1}{2}\dot{p}L$$

and where K_i varies seasonally and also depends on the growth rate.

The significance of the HUS work is that it suggests that inflation rates do not influence the conventionally measured APC directly in the Deaton manner but rather do so via wealth effects and through a mismeasurement of real income. In particular, the importance of a real balance or wealth effect is strongly supported. Such results were confirmed not only for the UK but also for the West German economy by Ungern–Sternberg (1981) in a separate paper.

7.7 Conclusions

There are a number of alternative hypotheses concerning the consumption function. To a greater or lesser extent they are all intuitively appealing on *a priori* grounds but, given all the empirical evidence that has been accumulated during the last thirty years, most economists would probably support some version of the PIH or LCH as being the most likely explanation of observed consumer behaviour. It is certainly generally accepted that consumption cannot be explained by current income alone, as suggested by the original AIH, and that past income levels, for whatever reason, are also relevant.

It must be realised, however, that the competing hypotheses are not necessarily mutually exclusive. The importance of past income levels found in time series studies may well be the result of both permanent income effects *and* relative income effects. Also, although the 'shallowness' of the cross-sectional consumption function may chiefly be the result of the effects suggested by Friedman, the underlying function could still have an intercept because of relative income effects.

Again, there is nothing irreconcilable about the wealth hypothesis and the LCH. It is possible to envisage a general model in which a consumer maximises utility over an interval of given length and in which utility depends on consumption during the interval and on end-interval wealth. One special case of this model would be the LCH, where the maximisation interval is the remaining life-span of the household and where end-interval wealth receives little or no weight in the utility function. Another special case would be the wealth hypothesis in which the maximisation period is very short and in which wealth figures prominently in the utility function.

One issue on which there is still not complete agreement is whether non-human wealth should be included explicitly in the consumption function, as in the LCH and the wealth hypothesis, or should be included in total wealth and annuitised as in the PIH. If non-human wealth appears explicitly in consumption functions and is positively related to consumer expenditure, then this provides one possible explanation for the recent increases in the APS. We may be experiencing a classic 'real balance effect' in which rapidly rising prices reduce the level of real consumer wealth. Thus the inflation effects noted by Deaton and others may be the result, not of increased uncertainty or consumer confusion over prices, but simply of an attempt by consumers to restore their real asset position. The most recent empirical work suggests that this may well be the case.

APPENDIX A
Empirical exercise

We shall begin by estimating from annual time series data for 1956–81 the very simple specification for the consumption function implied by the AIH. All data is again taken from *ETAS* 1983. You should again try and duplicate all the regression results quoted below. Initially we define real income and consumption variables as

Consumption C_t = consumer's expenditure in constant 1975 prices

Income Y_t = gross domestic product at factor cost in constant 1975 prices

C_t is taken from page 18 and Y_t from page 12 of *ETAS* 1983. Using OLS to regress C_t on Y_t yields

$$\hat{C} = 3383 + 0.649Y_t \qquad R^2 = 0.979 \quad d = 0.65$$
$$\quad (1682) \quad (0.020)$$

[A7.1]

Equation [A7.1] represents a typical 'Keynesian' consumption function. The income variable is highly significant with a t-ratio of 32.5 and the intercept term is also significant at the 5 per cent level with a t-ratio of 2.0. With $n - k = 26 - 2 = 24$ d.f., critical t-values are $t_{0.05} = 1.71$ and $t_{0.01} = 2.49$. The equation, of course, implies an MPC of 0.649 always less than the APC because of the positive intercept. The high R^2 is unsurprising since both variables exhibit a strong upward trend virtually throughout the sample period. The very low Durbin–Watson statistic is an obvious cause of concern but probably reflects not autocorrelation but some serious mis-specification in the equation. In fact, as we shall see in a moment, we have adopted a rather implausible and over-simple specification even for the AIH. However, for the moment we will stick to the above specification for illustrative purposes.

We have seen, in both Chapters 4 and 7, that the OLS estimators of the MPC are biased upwards because of simultaneous equation bias. Let us therefore add to our underlying consumption function the identity

$$Y_t = C_t + Z_t$$

so that we have the two-equation model given by equations [4.12]. Z_t is 'non-consumption expenditure' which we treat as exogenous. Z_t can be constructed from C_t and Y_t using the identity

$$Z_t = Y_t - C_t$$

This can be done using a transformation within your program. As we saw in Chapter 4, the consumption function in [4.12] is exactly identified and hence we can estimate it by *indirect least squares* (ILS). Using OLS to regress C_t and Y_t in turn on the exogenous Z_t yields the estimated versions of the reduced-form equations [4.17]

$$\hat{C}_t = 14{,}667 + 1.657Z_t \qquad R^2 = 0.839 \quad d = 0.59$$
$$\quad (3{,}828) \quad (0.148)$$

[A7.2]

$$\hat{C}_t = 14{,}667 + 2.657Z_t \qquad R^2 = 0.931 \quad d = 0.59$$
$$\quad (3{,}828) \quad (0.148)$$

[A7.3]

We can now use the above estimates of the reduced-form parameters to obtain ILS estimates of the consumption function parameters. Using the expressions below [4.17] we obtain

$$\beta^* = \frac{1.657}{2.657} = 0.624 \qquad \alpha^* = \frac{14{,}667}{2.657} = 5{,}520$$

Notice that we do obtain unique values for β^* and α^*. The intercept terms [A7.2] and [A7.3] are identical. As pointed out in Chapter 4 this is a consequence of your data satisfying the identity

$$Y_t = C_t + Z_t.$$

The ILS method of estimation therefore yields the consumption function

$$\hat{C}_t = 5{,}520 + 0.624 Y_t \qquad\qquad\qquad\qquad\qquad\qquad\text{[A7.4]}$$

Notice that [A7.4] has a larger intercept and smaller MPC than those in the OLS version [A7.1]. This is consistent with the tendency for OLS to underestimate the intercept and overestimate the MPC. It also confirms, as far as it goes, the suggestion made at the end of Chapter 4 that the large-sample advantages of consistent estimators appear to persist even for smaller samples.

In practice, we would place little reliance on the estimated consumption function [A7.4], obtained as it was from such a simply specified model. One obvious improvement in the specification of the AIH is to redefine our income variable as

Y_t^d = Real personal disposable income in constant 1975 prices

Data on this respecified income variable is taken from page 18 of *ETAS* 1983. It clearly makes sense to relate consumption to income net of taxation, national insurance contributions, etc. Re-estimation of [A7.1] by OLS now yields

$$\hat{C}_t = 8654 + 0.763 Y_t^d \qquad R^2 = 0.994 \quad d = 0.86 \qquad\qquad\text{[A7.5]}$$
$$\phantom{\hat{C}_t = }(795) \ \ (0.012)$$

Y_t^d, in fact, works rather better than Y_t. R^2 is even higher and the t-ratio on the income variable rises to 63.6. The d-statistic is improved but remains low (with a 5 per cent significance level, upper and lower critical values for d are

$$d_U = 1.46$$

and

$$d_L = 1.30).$$

However, we must beware of attributing this to some simple autoregressive scheme. The AIH is an especially simple specification of consumer behaviour and as we have already stressed, low d-statistics are as likely to reflect a mis-specification of the estimating equation as they are an autocorrelated disturbance term.

The estimates in [A7.5] are again, of course, subject to simultaneous equation bias. However, our distinction between Y_t and Y_t^d means we now have a slightly more complicated simultaneous system to deal with. Suppose we specify the three-equation system

$$C_t = \alpha + \beta Y_t^d + \varepsilon_t, \qquad Y_t = Y_t^d + T_t, \qquad Y_t = C_t + Z_t \qquad\text{[A7.6]}$$

Z_t and Y_t are as defined previously and 'net taxes', T_t, is simply the difference between 'total income', Y_t, and disposable income, Y_t^d. The endogenous variables in this three-equation system are C_t, Y_t and Y_t^d, whereas T_t and non-consumption expenditure Z_t will be treated as exogenous.

You should be able to deduce without difficulty that the consumption function in [A7.6] is overidentified. We can therefore no longer estimate it by ILS but will use the two-stage least squares (TSLS) estimating procedure described at the end of Section 4.2. In the present case this involves firstly, regressing Y_t^d on both the exogenous variables Z_t and T_t. Secondly, the actual Y_t^d values are replaced by the predicted values, $\hat{Y}_t^d$, obtained from the first stage and the consumption function re-estimated. Your program may enable you to do this 'in one go', otherwise you will have to perform two OLS regressions. Either way, TSLS yields

$$\hat{C}_t = 9{,}078 + 0.756Y_t^d \qquad\qquad R^2 = 0.994 \quad d = 0.83 \qquad\qquad \text{[A7.7]}$$
$$\phantom{\hat{C}_t = }(811) \quad (0.013)$$

Notice that the tendency for OLS to underpredict intercept and overpredict MPC is again confirmed, although the differences between [A7.7] and [A7.5] are not as marked as those between [A7.4] and [A7.1].

We shall now attempt to compare the performances of two competing hypotheses concerning consumption – the AIH and the RIH. We shall do this using seasonally adjusted quarterly data for 1966–75. We will again use Y_t^d as our income variable – data can be found on pages 21–22 of *ETAS* 1983. However, we shall redefine our consumption variable as

C_t^N = consumer expenditure on 'non-durables' in constant 1975 prices
 = C_t *minus* expenditure on durable household goods, cars and motor-cycles in constant 1975 prices

The data needed to construct C_t^N can be found on pages 29–30 of *ETAS* 1983. We used total consumption expenditure, C_t, in our previous models because we could hardly treat spending on durable goods as 'exogenous'.

Using OLS to regress C_t^N on Y_t^d alone yields

$$\hat{C}_t^N = 4{,}257 + 0.575Y_t^d \qquad\qquad R^2 = 0.967 \quad d = 1.37 \qquad\qquad \text{[A7.8]}$$
$$\phantom{\hat{C}_t^N = }(287) \quad (0.017)$$

Again we obtain a typical 'Keynesian' consumption function with a highly significant intercept term. However, the d-statistic is somewhat low. For $n = 40$ with one explanatory variable, the critical d-values are $d_U = 1.54$ and $d_L = 1.40$ using a 5 per cent significance level.

To test one version of the RIH we construct the variable Y_0^d – previous peak disposable income. This has to be constructed from the Y_t^d data series and is best done by hand. The first eight observations on Y_0^d are (in £ millions) 14,466, 15,083, 15,083, 15,083, 15,083, 15,083, 15,083, 15,114. Remember that when income rises previous peak income is simply the previous quarter's income. Inclusion of Y_0^d in the estimating equation yields

$$\hat{C}_t^N = 4{,}247 + 0.519Y_t^d + 0.057Y_0^d \qquad\qquad R^2 = 0.967 \quad d = 1.19 \qquad\qquad \text{[A7.9]}$$
$$\phantom{\hat{C}_t^N = }(288) \quad (0.066) \quad\;\; (0.064)$$

The coefficient on Y_0^d is statistically insignificant with t-ratio of only 0.89 and there is some deterioration in the d-statistic compared with [A7.8]. You should now see whether better results are obtained using the alternative RIH variable – previous peak consumption.

The most general version of the RIH – the Brown 'habit-persistence, model –

suggests the inclusion of lagged consumption, C_{t-1}^N, in the estimating equation. This results in

$$\hat{C}_t^N = 1{,}888 + 0.234 Y_t^d + 0.585 C_{t-1}^N \qquad\qquad R^2 = 0.981 \quad d = 2.09 \qquad [A7.10]$$
$$\phantom{\hat{C}_t^N = } (488) \quad (0.064) \quad\;\; (0.108)$$

There is a rise in R^2 compared with [A7.8] and the lagged consumption variable is significant with a t-ratio of 5.42. However, the appearance of a lagged dependent variable in the equation makes the Durban–Watson test for autocorrelation invalid so we will compute the Durban h-statistic described in Section 3.2. In this case

$$h = (1 - 0.5d)\sqrt{\frac{n}{(1 - ns_\beta^2)}} = -0.045\sqrt{\frac{40}{(1 - 40(0.108)^2)}} = -0.39$$

Since under the null hypothesis of no autocorrelation h has a standard normal distribution, we find no evidence of autocorrelation (at the 5 per cent level of significance we would reject the hypothesis of no autocorrelation if h lay outside the range 0 ± 1.96).

Equation [A7.10] yields an estimated *short-run* MPC of 0.234. You should now use [A7.10] to obtain an estimate of the *long-run* MPC. Refer to the last part of section 7.2. You will need to estimate the long-run growth rate in consumption. The significant intercept in [A7.10] implies that the long-run consumption function also contains an intercept. Obtain an estimate of this long-run intercept.

We must beware of regarding the significance of C_{t-1}^N in [A7.10] as evidence in favour of the RIH. As equations [7.38] and [7.43] indicate, both the habit persistence and the permanent income models imply an equation of the form [A7.10], so the importance of C_{t-1}^N could equally well be interpreted as evidence in favour of the PIH. When you tackle the empirical exercise in the appendix to Chapter 10 you will have to construct permanent income variables for alternative values of λ using a variant of equation [7.35]. You can then refer back to the present exercise and try replacing measured income in equation [A7.8] by your permanent income variables. If the value of λ yielding the best-performing equation is less than unity then this will suggest that the PIH is more successful than the AIH in explaining variations in consumption.

We have pointed out on a number of occasions, both in this exercise and the last, that it is not difficult to achieve a 'high R^2' when variables in a regression equation exhibit a consistent trend throughout the sample period. The time-honoured manner of eliminating the trend from variables and reducing the possibility of 'spurious' correlations is to 'first-difference' all variables, i.e. in the present case, work in terms of the *changes* in income and consumption rather than in their *levels*. Clearly, if

$$C^N = \alpha + \beta Y^d$$

then

$$\Delta C^N = \beta \Delta Y^d$$

and we can attempt the estimation of β by regressing ΔC^N on ΔY^d. Notice, however, that we would not expect to find a significant intercept term in the 'differenced' equation even when $\alpha \neq 0$. For comparison with many of the equations in Section 7.6 we shall work this time with seasonally *unadjusted* quarterly data for 1966–75.[13] With seasonal dummies D1, D2, and D3 included for the first, second and third quarters, the equivalent of [A7.8] is

$$\hat{C}_t^N = 4{,}980 + 0.573\,Y_t^d - 1{,}308\text{D1}_t - 854\text{D2}_t - 534\text{D3}_t$$
$$\quad\;\;(332)\quad(0.019)\qquad(88)\qquad\quad(87)\qquad\quad(87)$$
$$R^2 = 0.973 \quad d = 1.92 \qquad [A7.11]$$

Apart from the seasonally varying intercept, [A7.11] is, in fact, very similar to [A7.8]. The d-statistic is higher but remember that, strictly speaking, it tests only for *first-order* autoregressive schemes. With seasonally unadjusted quarterly data a *fourth-order* scheme might be more likely. (How would you test for this?) The data required for [A7.11] is taken from pages 19–20 and 27–8 of *ETAS* 1983.

When calculating changes in C_t^N and Y_t^d with this type of data it makes sense to compare the current values of variables not with their values one quarter previous but with their values four quarters previous. For example, it is of more interest to compare fourth-quarter (i.e. festive!) consumption in 1973 with fourth-quarter consumption in 1972 rather than with third-quarter consumption in 1973.

We therefore define our 'differenced' variables as

$$C_t^N - C_{t-4}^N$$

and

$$Y_t^d - Y_{t-4}^d$$

Regressing the change in consumption on the change in income and the seasonal dummies yields

$$C_t^N - C_{t-4}^N = 138 + 0.391(Y_t^d - Y_{t-4}^d) - 49\text{D1}_t - 38\text{D2}_t - 56\text{D3}_t$$
$$\qquad\quad(54)\quad(0.043)\qquad\qquad(74)\qquad(73)\qquad(73)$$
$$R^2 = 0.708 \quad d = 1.69 \qquad [A7.12]$$

To compute the above regression for the full 1966–75 period your computer will require values of C_t^N and Y_t^d for each quarter in 1965. It requires them to compute

$$C_t^N - C_{t-4}^N$$

and

$$Y_t^d - Y_{t-4}^d$$

for the 1966 quarters. Notice that R^2 has fallen compared with [A7.11]. But now the statistical significance of the income variable cannot be attributed to common trends in income and consumption. If you examine the

$$C_t^N - C_{t-4}^N$$

and

$$Y_t^d - Y_{t-4}^d$$

series you will find no definite trends either upwards or downwards. Notice also that although the seasonal dummies are not significant in [A7.12] the intercept is.

If [A7.12] results from 'differencing' an underlying relationship of the kind

$$C_t^N = \alpha + \beta Y_t^d$$

can you work out what this significant intercept term implies for such a relationship?

In the paper by DHSY (1978) discussed in Section 7.6, the point was made very strongly that changes in consumption depend not only on *changes* in income but also on the extent of disequilibrium between the *levels* of income and consumption in previous periods. Since we have specified a linear, rather than a log-linear, relationship, the extent of disequilibrium is measured by

$$C_t^N - \alpha - \beta Y_t^d$$

so we have to represent it by including C_{t-4}^N and Y_{t-4}^d separately in our equation rather than include a composite

$$c_{t-4} - y_{t-4}$$

variable as in the DHSY equations. Including such variables yields (to save space the results for the dummy variables are not quoted this time)

$$C_t^N - C_{t-4}^N = 2{,}062 + 0.421(Y_t^d - Y_{t-4}^d) - 0.310 C_{t-4}^N + 0.153 Y_{t-4}^d$$
$$\phantom{C_t^N - C_{t-4}^N =} (577) \quad (0.042) \qquad\qquad (0.126) \qquad\quad (0.079)$$
$$R^2 = 0.790 \quad d = 2.10 \qquad \text{[A7.13]}$$

R^2 rises quite sharply compared with [A7.12] and C_{t-4}^N and Y_{t-4}^d have t-ratios of 2.46 and 1.94 respectively (critical values for t in this case are $t_{0.05} = 1.66$ and $t_{0.01} = 2.38$). We can also conjecture that the t-ratios might have been higher but for the not unsurprisingly high collinearity between C_{t-4}^N and Y_{t-4}^d. Equation [A7.13], then, provides support for DHSY's contention that 'disequilibrium effects' should always be included in first-differenced consumption functions.

You should now re-estimate [A7.13] in logarithmic terms so that you can compare your results with some of the DHSY equations presented in Section 7.6. You can also try adding variables such as

$$\Delta_1(y_t^d - y_{t-4}^d)$$

and price variables

$$p_t - p_{t-4}$$

and

$$\Delta_1(p_t - p_{t-4})$$

For the price level you can use data on the retail price index (all items) from pages 116–17 of *ETAS* 1983. You can then try re-estimating your equations for an extended sample period of 1966–81 and testing for parameter stability using the second of the Chow tests described in Section 5.3. Finally, if you want to try adding wealth variables to any of your equations, whether in levels or differences, you can start by using the series on liquid assets of the personal sector (Table 9.4 in recent editions of the Central Statistical Office publication *Financial Statistics*).

APPENDIX B

We derive here the lifetime budget equation [7.18] for a three-period case. Suppose we have a household in its tenth year ($T = 10$) that intends to retire at the end of its eleventh year ($N = 11$) and expects to die(!) at the end of its twelfth year ($L = 12$). The lifetime budget constraint therefore becomes

$$A_9 + Y_{10} + \frac{Y_{11}^e}{1 + r} = C_{10} + \frac{C_{11}}{1 + r} + \frac{C_{12}}{(1 + r)^2} \qquad [B7.1]$$

To derive [B7.1] we make the simplifying assumption that interest on non-human wealth is always paid at the beginning of the year. The household's budget constraint for its *tenth year* is then given by

$$A_9(1 + r) + Y_{10} = C_{10} + A_{10} \qquad [B7.2]$$

where Y_{10} *represents earned or non-property income only*, since unearned income is already included in the constraint as $A_9 r$. Similarly, the household's budget constraints for its *eleventh and twelfth years* are given by

$$A_{10}(1 + r) + Y_{11}^e = C_{11} + A_{11} \qquad [B7.3]$$

and

$$A_{11}(1 + r) = C_{12} \qquad [B7.4]$$

where Y_{11}^e is expected earned income in the eleventh year

$$Y_{12}^e = 0$$

since the household has now retired and

$$A_{12} = 0$$

because household plans to have no resources left at death.

From [B7.4] we have

$$A_{11} = \frac{C_{12}}{1 + r}$$

Substituting for A_{11} in [B7.3] yields

$$A_{10} = \frac{C_{11}}{1 + r} + \frac{C_{12}}{(1 + r)^2} - \frac{Y_{11}^e}{1 + r}$$

Substituting for A_{10} in [B7.2] yields

$$A_9(1 + r) + Y_{10} = C_{10} + \frac{C_{11}}{1 + r} + \frac{C_{12}}{(1 + r)^2} - \frac{Y_{11}^e}{1 + r}$$

which on rearrangement yields the three-year budget constraint [B7.1] provided we interpret A_9 in equation [B7.1] as *including* interest received during the household's tenth year.[14] Thus, by combining the budget constraints for each separate year, we eventually obtain the lifetime budget constraint.

Notes

1. For example, a liquid assets variable is often included as an additional explanatory variable in postwar UK consumption functions.
2. For the US economy a data series does, in fact, exist for depreciation on consumer durables.
3. To see that this is the budget constraint equation, substitute the intercept and slope of the line AB into the general equation for a straight line $C_1 = (\text{intercept}) + (\text{slope}) C_2$.
4. The marginal rate of substitution of C_1 for C_2 thus depends only on the ratio C_1/C_2 and not on the absolute magnitudes of C_1 and C_2.
5. If the optimal ratio $C_1/C_2 = k$ then, since

$$W_1 = C_1 + \frac{C_2}{(1+r)},$$

we have

$$\gamma_1 = \frac{k(1+r)}{k+kr+1} \quad \text{and} \quad \gamma_2 = \frac{1+r}{k+kr+1}$$

6. '*If the individual receives an additional dollar's worth of resources he will allocate it to consumption at different times in the same proportion in which he had allocated his total resources prior to the addition*' (Ando and Modigliani 1963: 56).
7. See: Friedman (1957: 44–5).
8. Readers actually consulting the relevant section (Friedman 1957: 142–52) may become somewhat confused at this point. Friedman originally formulates Y_t^p as a *continuous* function of past and present income with exponentially declining weights and also builds-in a factor reflecting secular long-run growth in Y_t^p. However, since his data is in annual form he has to use a discrete approximation of his continuous function when actually estimating his consumption function. This discrete approximation involves the geometrically declining weights of [7.34]. However, the λ of equation [7.34] is equal to $1 - e^{-\beta}$ in the continuous formulation where β is the weight attached to the current *instantaneous* rate of flow of income as opposed to λ which is the weight attached to the current year's income in the discrete approximation. Friedman estimates β as 0.4 which yields $\lambda = 1 - e^{-0.4} = 0.33$. However, Friedman and others sometimes refer to the 0.4 as the weight attached to current income and this can cause confusion.
9. Strictly speaking, if $C_t^p = \alpha + \beta Y_t^p$ then $C_t = \alpha + \beta Y_t^p + C_t^t$ but transitory consumption C_t^t can be regarded simply as a disturbance.
10. Zellner, Huang and Chau use a slightly different notation. Their λ, is in fact, $1 - \lambda$ in the notation of this chapter.
11. Feldstein's findings, if substantiated, have important implications for corporate taxation policy. Traditionally, the disposable income variable used in consumption functions includes the dividend component but not the retained-earnings component of profits. A switch from dividends to retained earnings (induced by a higher tax rate on dividends) therefore leads to a rise in company saving that is not fully matched by a fall in personal saving so that

total private saving rises. However, if income is more correctly defined to include retained earnings then any switch from dividends to retained earnings leaves consumption and, hence, total private saving, unchanged.

12. Note that [7.69] may be rewritten as

$$c_t - c_{t-1} = \theta_0 - k\theta_2 + b\theta_3 + \theta_1(y_t - y_{t-1}) + \theta_2(k + y_{t-1} - c_{t-1})$$
$$- \theta_3(b + y_{t-1} - a_{t-1})$$

13. We used seasonally adjusted data to test the RIH so that we might construct a meaningful series for Y_0^d.

14. A more consistent formulation of [B7.1] would be

$$A_9 + \frac{Y_{10}}{1+r} + \frac{Y_{11}^e}{(1+r)^2} = \frac{C_{10}}{1+r} + \frac{C_{11}}{(1+r)^2} + \frac{C_{12}}{(1+r)^3}$$

8 Production functions

The concept of a production function plays an important role in both micro- and macroeconomics. At the macro-level it has been combined with marginal productivity theory to explain the prices of the various factors of production and the extent to which these factors are utilised. It is therefore important in theories of economic growth and in theories of distribution. At the micro-level it is of interest because of its usefulness in the analysis of such problems as the degree to which substitution between the various factors of production is possible and the extent to which firms experience decreasing or increasing returns to scale as output expands. At both the macro- and micro-levels the production function has been used as a tool for assessing what proportion of any increase in output over time can be attributed to, firstly, increases in the inputs of factors of production; secondly, to the existence of increasing returns to scale; and thirdly, to what is commonly referred to as 'technical progress'.

We begin this chapter with a brief review of the neo-classical production function and its role in the theory of the firm and then introduce two examples of this type of production function which have been much used in empirical work.

8.1 The neo-classical production function

The production function in the traditional theory of the firm expresses output Q as a function of, typically, two inputs: capital, K, and labour, L

$$Q = Q(K, L) \tag{8.1}$$

The variables Q, K and L are flow variables so that [8.1] expresses a flow of output as a function of the flows of services provided by the two factor inputs. Thus K represents the flow of services provided by the existing capital stock rather than the capital stock itself. K therefore depends not only on the size of the capital stock but also on the extent of its utilisation. All the variables are assumed to be continuously variable and infinitely divisible. Moreover, the inputs are assumed to be continuously substitutable at all levels of production.[1] An important point to be noted at the outset is that, for given levels of K and L, equation [8.1] defines the maximum possible level of output Q. Thus the *technical* problem of how to achieve the greatest output from given inputs is assumed to be solved and we are not concerned with it. However, because of factor substitutability, a given output can be produced by many alternative combinations of inputs. The problem of deciding which input combination provides the given output at minimum cost is an economic problem which we *are* concerned with. Equation [8.1] is not then confined to least-cost combinations of capital and labour.

8.1 Diminishing marginal productivity of labour.

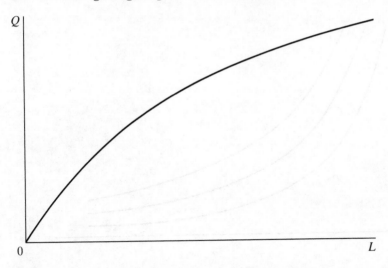

The production function is assumed to be such that the marginal products of capital, $\partial Q/\partial K$, and labour $\partial Q/\partial L$, are both always positive but 'diminishing'. Thus, for example, *if capital inputs remain constant*, the relationship between output and labour input is as shown in Fig. 8.1. This illustrates the so-called 'law of diminishing marginal productivity'. Similarly, if labour inputs are fixed, then as capital inputs increase the marginal product of capital declines.

Diminishing marginal productivity must not be confused with 'decreasing returns to scale'. The returns to scale implied by a production function depend on the response of output to an equiproportionate change in *both inputs*. If equation [8.1] is homogeneous of degree n, then depending on whether n is less than, equal to, or greater than, unity, equiproportionate increases in inputs will lead to less than proportionate, equiproportionate, or more than proportionate increases in output. That is, we have decreasing, constant, or increasing returns to scale respectively. In terms of equation [8.1]

$$Q(\lambda K, \lambda L) = \lambda^n Q(K, L)$$

where λ is the given equiproportionate change in factor inputs. Thus for $n > 1$ a production function may exhibit both diminishing marginal productivity and increasing returns to scale. It must be remembered, however, that all production functions are not homogeneous and that some, while exhibiting increasing returns to scale at, for example, low levels of K and L, may show decreasing returns to scale at higher input and output levels.

The fact that K and L are assumed to be continuously substitutable means that there are an infinite number of possible combinations of factor inputs (implying a wide variety of alternative techniques) which may be used to produce a given output. Such possible combinations trace out a constant-product curve or isoquant similar to those shown in Fig. 8.2. The higher the given level of output the further from the origin is the corresponding isoquant. The slope of an isoquant yields the rate at which one factor can be substituted for another without altering the level of output. The absolute value of this slope is known as

8.2 Isoquants convex to the origin.

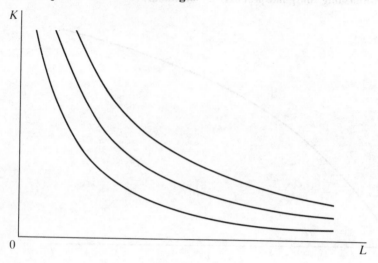

the marginal rate of substitution (MRS)

$$\text{MRS} = -\frac{dK}{dL} \qquad\qquad [8.2]$$

Also, taking the total derivative of [8.1] we have

$$dQ = \frac{\partial Q}{\partial K}dK + \frac{\partial Q}{\partial L}dL = 0$$

since output is assumed constant along the isoquant. Thus,

$$\text{MRS} = -\frac{dK}{dL} = \frac{\partial Q}{\partial L}\bigg/\frac{\partial Q}{\partial K} \qquad\qquad [8.3]$$

The MRS is therefore equal to the ratio of the two marginal products. The MRS is assumed to decrease as more and more labour is substituted for capital. That is, the greater the ratio of labour inputs to capital inputs the greater the quantity of labour needed to replace one unit of capital without reducing output. This means that isoquants are convex to the origin. The more convex the isoquants, the more limited are substitution possibilities generally.

The MRS is obviously a useful measure of the extent to which it is possible to substitute one factor for another in the production of a given output. However, it is measured in terms of units of capital divided by units of labour (e.g. one machine hour per ten man-hours) and hence its size is dependent on the units in which labour and capital are measured. An alternative measure which sums up the substitution possibilities of a production function and is independent of units of measurement is the elasticity of substitution, defined as

$$\sigma = \frac{d(K/L)}{K/L}\bigg/\frac{d(\text{MRS})}{\text{MRS}} \qquad\qquad [8.4]$$

It is therefore the proportionate change in the capital/labour ratio occurring, as we move along an isoquant, divided by the accompanying proportionate change in the MRS. Thus, if the isoquants are relatively flat (i.e. substitution is relatively easy), then movements along an isoquant (i.e. changes in the K/L ratio) are accompanied by little change in the MRS and hence the elasticity of substitution is high. However, if the isoquants have a pronounced curvature, implying that substitution possibilities are more limited, then σ will be low. The meaning of this concept will become clearer once factor prices are introduced into the analysis.

Nothing yet has been said about what determines the proportions in which factor inputs are combined. This is an economic as opposed to technical problem and, at the micro-level, the production function is usually set in a model of firm behaviour in which the firm maximises profits, π, where

$$\pi = pQ - mK - wL \qquad [8.5]$$

and p, m and w are the prices of output, capital and labour flows respectively. Assuming perfect competition in the product and factor markets, the firm is a price-taker and p, m and w may be treated as given. The firm then maximises [8.5] subject to the constraints that inputs and outputs should satisfy the production function [8.1]. Forming the Lagrangean

$$H = pQ - mK - wL - \lambda[Q - Q(K, L)]$$

the first-order conditions for a maximum are

$$\frac{\partial H}{\partial Q} = p - \lambda = 0, \quad \frac{\partial H}{\partial K} = -m + \lambda \frac{\partial Q}{\partial K} = 0, \quad \frac{\partial H}{\partial L} = -w + \lambda \frac{\partial Q}{\partial L} = 0$$

Eliminating the Lagrangean multiplier, λ, we thus obtain the so-called *marginal productivity conditions*

$$\frac{\partial Q}{\partial K} = \frac{m}{p} \quad \text{and} \quad \frac{\partial Q}{\partial L} = \frac{w}{p} \qquad [8.6]$$

Thus each factor is utilised up to the point where its marginal product equals its real price (in terms of output produced). Provided the required second-order conditions are satisfied, solving [8.6] together with [8.1] yields the profit-maximising values of Q, K and L.[2]

In this context the production function must be seen as merely one relationship in a three-equation system (comprised of [8.1] and [8.6]) which *jointly determines the values of the endogenous variables* Q, K *and* L and in which the exogenous variables are m/p and w/p. Thus, given the above simple economic model, we see that the factor inputs, K and L, cannot be regarded as exogenous variables determining Q as the original single equation [8.1] might superficially suggest.

An alternative economic model which has important empirical applications is that in which output Q is assumed to be predetermined. The firm's aim is then to minimise costs subject to the constraint on its level of output. Retaining the assumption that the firm is a price-taker, costs

$$C = mK + wL \qquad [8.7]$$

are therefore minimised subject to the output constraint

$$Q^0 = Q(K, L) \qquad [8.8]$$

where Q^0 is the predetermined level of output. Forming the Lagrangean

$$H = mK + wL - \lambda[Q^0 - Q(K, L)]$$

the first-order conditions for a minimum are

$$\frac{\partial H}{\partial K} = m + \lambda\frac{\partial Q}{\partial K} = 0, \qquad \frac{\partial H}{\partial L} = w + \lambda\frac{\partial Q}{\partial L} = 0$$

which together yield the cost-minimising condition

$$\text{MRS} = \frac{\partial Q}{\partial L}\bigg/\frac{\partial Q}{\partial K} = \frac{w}{m} \qquad\qquad [8.9]$$

Thus factor inputs should be combined in such a way that the MRS equals the factor price ratio. Solving equations [8.8] and [8.9] then yields the cost-minimising levels of K and L. Notice that we now have a *two*-equation system which jointly determines the endogenous variables K and L and in which the exogenous variables are now Q, w and m.

The introduction of the factor prices m and w into the analysis yields further insight into the concept of the elasticity of substitution. Notice from [8.6] that the profit-maximisation model as well as the cost-minimisation model also implies that factors will be combined so as to equate the MRS with the ratio of factor prices. Indeed, even if the assumption that the firm is a price-taker in the product market is dropped, profit maximisation still implies equation [8.9]. This means that we can rewrite equation [8.4], our definition of the elasticity of substitution as

$$\sigma = \frac{d(K/L)}{K/L}\bigg/\frac{d(w/m)}{w/m} \qquad\qquad [8.10]$$

Thus σ is given by the proportionate change in the capital/labour ratio divided by the proportionate change in the factor price ratio. When the price of labour rises relative to that of capital, firms will attempt to substitute capital for labour and increase the K/L ratio. When such substitution is possible only to a limited extent, a given proportionate change in w/m will lead to only small changes in K/L and the elasticity of substitution will be small. However, when considerable substitution is possible, σ will be large.

The Cobb–Douglas production function

The production function that has been most frequently employed in empirical work is the Cobb–Douglas production function. Douglas, working in the late 1920s, observed that the share of total US national output going to labour had remained approximately constant over time. That is, in aggregate terms

$$wL = \beta pQ \qquad\qquad [8.11]$$

where β is a constant between zero and unity.

As we shall see presently, the underlying production function which gives rise to the empirical observation [8.11] is

$$Q = AK^\alpha L^\beta \qquad\qquad [8.12]$$

The Cobb–Douglas production function [8.12] has a number of convenient properties. The parameters, α and β, measure the *elasticities* (assumed constant and between zero and unity) of output with respect to capital and labour respectively. The parameter, A, may be regarded as an *efficiency* parameter, since for fixed inputs K and L, the larger is A, the greater is the maximum output Q obtainable from such inputs.

The marginal products of capital and labour are given by

$$\frac{\partial Q}{\partial K} = \alpha A K^{\alpha-1} L^{\beta} = \alpha \frac{Q}{K}, \quad \frac{\partial Q}{\partial L} = \beta A K^{\alpha} L^{\beta-1} = \beta \frac{Q}{L}$$

Both 'diminish' as the relevant factor input increases since both $(\alpha - 1)$ and $(\beta - 1)$ are negative quantities. Assuming the firm is a price-taker and a profit-maximiser, equations [8.6] imply that the marginal productivity conditions for this production function are

$$\alpha \frac{Q}{K} = \frac{m}{p}, \quad \beta \frac{Q}{L} = \frac{w}{p} \qquad [8.13]$$

Notice that the equations [8.13] can be rewritten as $\alpha = mK/pQ$ and $\beta = wL/pQ$. Thus, if the marginal productivity conditions hold, the exponents α and β in the Cobb–Douglas function are equal to the respective shares of capital and labour in the value of total output.[3] It is, in fact, the second of the equations [8.13] which leads to Douglas's empirically observed equation [8.11].

For the Cobb–Douglas case, the three-equation simultaneous system determining the endogenous Q, K and L in the profit-maximising model is given by equations [8.12] and [8.13]. For the two-equation cost-minimising model with predetermined output, the cost-minimising condition is given by

$$\text{MRS} = \frac{\partial Q}{\partial L} \bigg/ \frac{\partial Q}{\partial K} = \frac{\beta K}{\alpha L} = \frac{w}{m} \qquad [8.14]$$

and this together with equation [8.12] yields the simultaneous system in the two endogenous variables K and L, with Q, m and w being in this case exogenous.

Note that for both models the optimising conditions imply that

$$\frac{K}{L} = \left(\frac{\alpha}{\beta}\right)\left(\frac{w}{m}\right) \qquad [8.15]$$

Thus, for a given factor price ratio, the greater is α/β the greater is the optimal capital/labour ratio. Thus the size of the exponent α, relative to that of β, determines the 'capital-intensity' of the productive processes represented by a Cobb–Douglas function.

The Cobb–Douglas function is homogeneous of degree $\alpha + \beta$ since

$$Q(\lambda K, \lambda L) = A(\lambda K)^{\alpha}(\lambda L)^{\beta} = \lambda^{\alpha+\beta} A K^{\alpha} L^{\beta} = \lambda^{\alpha+\beta} Q(K, L) \qquad [8.16]$$

Thus if $\alpha + \beta > 1$ we have increasing returns to scale, if $\alpha + \beta = 1$ we have constant returns to scale and if $\alpha + \beta < 1$ we have decreasing returns. Note, however, that the returns to scale property is the same at all levels of output. For example, the Cobb–Douglas function cannot exhibit increasing returns at low Q and decreasing returns for high Q.

The Cobb–Douglas function is also restricted in that it implies an elasticity of substitution which is constant and always equal to unity. This is probably best understood if we accept either the profit-maximisation or cost-minimisation models, although it is a property of the Cobb–Douglas function itself and is not dependent on market conditions or firm behaviour. It then follows from equation [8.14] that, since α/β is constant, a 1 per cent increase in the ratio of factor prices, w/m, must lead to a 1 per cent increase in the capital labour ratio, K/L. From the alternative definition of σ given by equation [8.10] we see that this implies an elasticity of substitution equal to unity for the Cobb–Douglas function.

One awkward problem with the profit-maximising model, introduced above, concerns the question of whether a three-equation system such as that formed by equations [8.12] and [8.13] yields a single determinate solution corresponding to a point of maximum profit. This will depend on whether the second-order conditions as well as the first-order conditions for a maximum are met. Wallis (1979), for example, shows that in the Cobb–Douglas case the condition is that $\alpha + \beta < 1$, i.e. that there should be decreasing returns to scale.[4]

Suppose the second-order conditions for a maximum are *not* met and we have $\alpha + \beta \geqslant 1$, i.e. constant or increasing returns to scale. If, for example, $\alpha + \beta = 1$ then three outcomes are possible. If product and factor prices are such that there is some given combination of inputs which yield a positive profit, then profit can always be increased by expanding the scale of output and there is no finite maximum level of profits. If prices are such that any given input combination yields a negative profit then any scale of output will yield a negative profit and the firm cannot stay in business. Finally, if profits are zero for any given output combination, then they are zero at all levels of output and the size of the firm is indeterminate. Similar strange results occur if $\alpha + \beta > 1$, i.e. if there are increasing returns to scale.

In practice we cannot just rule out the possibility of constant or increasing returns to scale – certainly not without estimating α and β first. Obviously, there are no *a priori* reasons why firms should not operate under conditions of non-decreasing returns to scale. When they do so it is obvious that in practice the value of Q *is* determined in some manner or other – firms *do* have a definite size, whether it be large or small. The answer to this apparently baffling problem is to relax the assumptions of perfect competition where all prices are given and Q, K and L can be varied at will. However, this involves making prices endogenous to the system and, hence, necessitates the addition of extra equations to the model, namely, demand for product and supply of factor relationships.

The constant elasticity of substitution production function

As already noted, the Cobb–Douglas production function has an elasticity of substitution, σ, which is always equal to unity. This is a particularly restrictive property. One of the purposes of production function analysis is to examine the extent to which factor substitution is possible and such substitution may obviously vary between firms and industries. For example, if we wished to compare the substitution possibilities in two different industries, the estimation of Cobb–Douglas functions for each industry could tell us nothing of value. An improvement would be some form of production function in which σ, although still, maybe, a constant, could take alternative values other than unity. *The constant elasticity of substitution* (CES) production function has such a form.

The CES function was first introduced by Arrow, Chenery, Minhas and Solow (SMAC) in 1961, who estimated cross-sectional equations of the form

$$\frac{Q}{L} = \frac{1}{\beta}\left(\frac{w}{p}\right)^{\chi}$$ [8.17]

Notice, from [8.11] or [8.13] that a Cobb–Douglas function, given profit-maximisation under perfect competition, implies that χ in equation [8.17] should be unity. SMAC however, obtained estimated values for χ which were consistently less than unity and deduced, assuming profit-maximisation, perfect competition and constant returns to scale, that the production function giving rise to [8.17] must have the form

$$Q = \gamma[\delta K^{-\theta} + (1 - \delta)L^{-\theta}]^{-1/\theta}$$ [8.18]

where γ, δ and θ are parameters to be interpreted shortly. Equation [8.18] specifies the CES production function.

The parameter γ is to be interpreted as an *efficiency parameter* akin to the A in the Cobb–Douglas function, since for given δ and θ, the larger is γ the greater is the maximum output Q obtainable from given inputs K and L.

The marginal products of capital and labour are given by

$$\frac{\partial Q}{\partial K} = \frac{\delta\gamma}{K^{1+\theta}}[\delta K^{-\theta} + (1 - \delta)L^{-\theta}]^{-(1+\theta)/\theta} = \frac{\delta}{\gamma^{\theta}}\left(\frac{Q}{K}\right)^{1+\theta}$$

$$\frac{\partial Q}{\partial L} = \frac{(1-\delta)\gamma}{L^{1+\theta}}[\delta K^{-\theta} + (1 - \delta)L^{-\theta}]^{-(1+\theta)/\theta} = \frac{(1-\delta)}{\gamma^{\theta}}\left(\frac{Q}{L}\right)^{1+\theta}$$ [8.19]

Assuming profit maximisation under perfect competition the marginal productivity equations corresponding to [8.6] are

$$\frac{\delta}{\gamma^{\theta}}\left(\frac{Q}{K}\right)^{1+\theta} = \frac{m}{p}, \quad \frac{(1-\delta)}{\gamma^{\theta}}\left(\frac{Q}{L}\right)^{1+\theta} = \frac{w}{p}$$ [8.20]

The second of these conditions leads to SMAC's estimating equation [8.17] with $\chi = 1/1 + \theta$ and $1/\beta = (\gamma^{\theta}/1 - \delta)^{1/1+\theta}$. For the CES function the three-equation simultaneous system determining the endogenous variables Q, K and L in the profit-maximising model is given by [8.18] and [8.20].

The MRS is

$$\left(\frac{1-\delta}{\delta}\right)\left(\frac{K}{L}\right)^{1+\theta}$$

so that for the cost minimisation model with predetermined output, the two-equation system determining the endogenous K and L is given by [8.18] together with

$$\left(\frac{1-\delta}{\delta}\right)\left(\frac{K}{L}\right)^{1+\theta} = \frac{w}{m}$$ [8.21]

Equation [8.21] also holds for the profit-maximisation model since it may be derived from [8.20]. It is instructive to rewrite [8.21] as

$$\frac{K}{L} = \left(\frac{\delta}{1-\delta}\right)^{1/1+\theta}\left(\frac{w}{m}\right)^{1/1+\theta}$$

Since the quantity $(\delta/1 - \delta)^{1/1+\theta}$ is a constant, it follows that a 1 per cent rise in the factor price ratio w/m leads to a $(1/1 + \theta)$ per cent rise in the capital-labour ratio.

From equation [8.10] this implies that the CES function has an elasticity of substitution $\sigma = 1/1 + \theta$.[5] Because of its relationship with σ, θ is known as the *substitution parameter*

$$\theta = \frac{1}{\sigma} - 1 \tag{8.22}$$

Possible values for θ range from $\theta = \infty$ (when $\sigma = 0$ and substitution is impossible) to $\theta = -1$ (when $\sigma = \infty$, the isoquants are straight lines and substitution possibilities are greatest). When $\theta = 0$, $\sigma = 1$ as for the Cobb–Douglas function, and it can be shown that for this value of θ the CES function, in fact, reduces to the Cobb–Douglas function.[6] The fact that σ can take different values means that the CES function, unlike the Cobb–Douglas function, is a suitable tool for investigating the varying substitution possibilities between, for example, different industries.

Equation [8.21] may also be rewritten as

$$\frac{wL}{mK} = \frac{(1-\delta)}{\delta}\left(\frac{K}{L}\right)^{\theta} \tag{8.23}$$

so that, for a given capital/labour ratio and a given value of θ, we see that as δ rises the ratio of labour's share in total output to capital's share declines. For this reason δ is known as the *distribution parameter*. In contrast, for the Cobb–Douglas function the ratio of factor shares is a constant.

The CES function [8.18] implies constant returns to scale and may be generalised to

$$Q = \gamma[\delta K^{-\theta} + (1-\delta)L^{-\theta}]^{-v/\theta} \tag{8.24}$$

The function [8.24] is homogeneous of degree v since

$$Q(\lambda K, \lambda L) = \gamma[\delta(\lambda K)^{-\theta} + (1-\delta)(\lambda L)^{-\theta}]^{-v/\theta}$$
$$= \lambda^{v}\gamma[\delta K^{-\theta} + (1-\delta)L^{-\theta}]^{-v/\theta} = \lambda^{v}Q$$

Hence, v is a returns-to-scale parameter since for $v > 1$, $v = 1$ and $v < 1$ we have increasing returns, constant returns and decreasing returns to scale respectively. The parameters γ, θ and δ in equation [8.24] have exactly the same interpretation as those in [8.18].

8.2 Matching the models to the real world – some conceptual problems

It takes little thought to realise that, regardless of the precise form adopted for the production function, the simple economic models of the firm described in the previous section are a far cry from the firms of a modern industrial economy. A firm typically produces more than one output and employs more than two separate factors of production. Raw material and intermediate-good inputs are frequently as important as capital and labour inputs and, furthermore, no inputs can be treated as completely homogeneous in quality. There are many different types of labour inputs – skilled and unskilled is an obvious and often too simple classification – whereas capital equipment clearly varies even more considerably both in its form and up-to-dateness.

However, even if data on all such variables was accessible and sufficient observations were available, potential multicollinearity problems are so severe that some form of aggregation is inevitably necessary. A frequent first step is to work in terms of the real output actually originating in the firm, i.e. in terms of 'value added'. Value added is defined in this context as

$$V = \bar{Q} - \bar{M} \qquad [8.25]$$

where

$$\bar{Q} = \sum_{i=1}^{n} p_i Q_i \quad \text{and} \quad \bar{M} = \sum_{i=1}^{s} v_i M_i \qquad [8.26]$$

p_i and v_i are the prices, in some base year, of the ith output Q_i and ith intermediate input M_i respectively. Base year prices are used because we wish $\bar{Q}$, a weighted measure of total output, and $\bar{M}$, a weighted measure of total intermediate input, to be in 'real' or 'constant price' terms. Value added, V, is then expressed as a function of single indices $\bar{K}$ and $\bar{L}$ of capital and labour, which may themselves simply be weighted averages of the individual capital and labour inputs

$$V = V(\bar{L}, \bar{K}) \qquad [8.27]$$

Equation [8.27] is clearly akin to the production functions of the theoretical models in the previous section. Unfortunately, the conditions under which this vast simplification is legitimate are very restrictive. They have been derived by Green (1964) and we shall not discuss them here except to say that they are rather unlikely to be met in practice. However, one implication of adopting a value-added formulation is relatively clear. Equation [8.27] implies that

$$\bar{Q} = \bar{M} + V(\bar{K}, \bar{L}) \qquad [8.28]$$

Such a formulation implies that the 'marginal product' of intermediate-good inputs is constant and equal to unity. It is not at all clear that such a rigid and fixed relationship between output and, for example, raw material inputs is likely to provide an adequate approximation of reality.

When dealing with the individual firm, aggregation need not necessarily be as complete as that above. It is often still possible to retain maybe two or three separate types of input for both capital and labour. However, some degree of aggregation is always necessary and this invariably causes theoretical problems.

Aggregate production functions

In practice, production functions are not only estimated for individual firms but often for entire industries or industrial sectors and even for the economy as a whole. Just as it is possible to aggregate individual demand curves to obtain a market demand curve, so it may seem possible to aggregate micro-production functions to obtain an 'aggregate production function'. However, there are serious conceptual problems involved with the idea of a macro-production function. We consider, first, the problems which arise when aggregation is performed over firms all within the same industry.

Firstly, there are the more-or-less standard aggregation problems that we have already met in demand analysis. Suppose the individual firms have production functions of Cobb–Douglas type. Since we are dealing with a single industry, the range of available productive techniques is likely to be similar for each firm. Hence, it may not be unreasonable to assume that the exponents α and β in the Cobb–Douglas function are the same for all firms and this simplifies the aggregation problems involved. However, since the Cobb–Douglas function is merely linear in the logarithms this means, as we saw in Section 6.2, that sensible aggregation now requires macro-variables to be defined as the geometric rather than the arithmetic means of the corresponding micro-variables.

Secondly, there are less obvious but more deep-seated difficulties. Since the production function is only one of a system of three simultaneous equations, the marginal productivity conditions need to be aggregated too. Even if such aggregation is possible, there is no guarantee that the macro-marginal productivity conditions obtained by differentiating the macro-production function will be of the same form as those obtained by aggregating the micro-marginal productivity conditions.

There are also problems created by the possible presence of external economies of scale. For example, if each individual firm were operating under constant returns to scale but the inputs and outputs of all firms expand, external economies would mean that aggregate output expands at a proportionately greater rate than do aggregate inputs. Hence, the aggregate production function would exhibit increasing returns to scale although the micro-functions did not. The whole is greater than the sum of its parts.

Aggregation is also frequently performed over firms or industries with widely different types of output and this creates even greater problems. Available techniques of production are now likely to vary considerably from industry to industry and it is no longer remotely realistic to suggest that, for example, the exponents α and β in a Cobb–Douglas function are the same in all industries. The capital intensity of the productive process will vary. The convergency approach to aggregation, outlined in Section 6.2, indicates that, under these conditions, sensible aggregation requires the parameters α and β to be distributed independently, across firms, of the input variables K and L. However, given competitive markets it is easy to see that this condition is unlikely to be met. From equation [8.15] we see that, since the factor price ratio w/m can be considered to be constant across industries under competitive conditions, high values of K are likely to be associated with high values of α. Similarly, high values of L are associated with high values of β. In economic terms capital inputs are greatest in capital-intensive industries and labour inputs greatest in labour-intensive industries.

All this might not matter too much if the correlations between K and α and between L and β remained similar over time, i.e. if both labour-intensive and capital-intensive industries always expanded at the same rate. A fixed relationship between aggregate output and aggregate inputs could then exist, although it would not be possible to interpret the aggregate α and β as simple means of the corresponding micro-parameters. However, different industries generally expand at different rates. When this is the case, the expansion of aggregate outputs will depend on how the increased inputs are distributed across industries. For example, increases in aggregate output will be greater if the extra labour inputs go to labour-intensive industries rather than capital-intensive industries. However, which industries new factor inputs will flow to depends on factor prices, which in the *non-competitive* conditions generally prevailing are likely to vary from industry to industry. Hence, in general, the increase in aggregate output will depend on these relative prices. Thus, aggregate output is not only dependent on aggregate inputs but also on relative factor prices and hence on market conditions. The idea of the production function as a purely *technical* relationship, independent of economic decision-making, has been lost.

It should be clear from the above discussion that the very concept of an aggregate production function is a nebulous one. The question naturally arises of whether there is any point in trying to estimate such a 'hazy' relationship. However, it is an attractive proposition to attempt to find some simple relationship which sums up the whole technology under which an economy operates. Although such an estimated relationship cannot be a 'pure' technical one it may still prove a useful statistical description of the relationships between aggregate Q, K and L. The attractiveness of the production function approach has meant that investigators have not been deterred by the conceptual problems involved.

Measuring the inputs and outputs – aggregation in practice

Whether one is dealing with a single firm, an industry or the entire manufacturing sector, the measurement of either inputs or outputs almost invariably involves the aggregation of heterogeneous quantities and should therefore involve the construction of index numbers or weighted averages.

The most easily measured of the variables involved is probably the flow of labour inputs which can generally be measured in terms of man-hours. However, there are many types of labour input – male and female, skilled and unskilled, etc. – and ideally some weighted measure of total labour input should be derived. Appropriate weights would be base-period hourly wage rates for the different types of labour, provided that these wage rates adequately measure the relative usefulness of the various labour flows in the productive process. Base-year wage rates need to be used since we wish to measure labour input in physical or 'constant price' terms and abstract from any changes in the value of labour inputs which arise simply because of changes in its price. However, difficulties will still arise if the quality of the various labour inputs changes much over time and there is the obvious problem of which year should be selected as the base year. In practice, the procedure just described is often approximated by aggregating the money values of inputs in current price terms and deflating by any available index of labour input prices. However, unweighted measures of labour flows are also frequently used, e.g. total man-hours, and on occasion even stock measures such as the total number of employees.

As we have seen, even for the individual firm, total output is generally heterogeneous, so that its measurement also involves problems of aggregation. When different output flows have to be aggregated, market prices are generally used as weights on the assumption that these best represent the relative values of different outputs to society. Market prices in some base year should be used since again we wish our aggregate measure to be in real or constant-price terms. However, as with labour inputs, changes in quality cause obvious problems. Again, in practice, the procedure frequently used is to measure total output in current prices and then to deflate by the most appropriate available index of output prices.

When dealing with an individual firm either net output (i.e. value-added) or gross output data may be available. If the value-added formulation is adopted the normal procedure is to aggregate gross output in current prices and deflate by an appropriate index, aggregate intermediate-good inputs in current prices and deflate by an appropriate index, and then to subtract the latter measure from the former. If a gross output measure is used then the aggregate measure of intermediate-good inputs becomes an additional argument on the right-hand side of the production function. When production functions are estimated for an industry or industrial sector, indices of industrial production are generally used as measures of output. These are value-added measures so that in such cases it is not necessary to construct indices for intermediate-good inputs.

The greatest difficulties arise in the measurement of capital inputs. The index number problems caused by variations in quality are far more serious than in the case of outputs and labour inputs because of the existence of technical progress and innovation over time. Old machines become obsolete and provide inferior services to new up-to-date machines. Furthermore, while we require a measure of the flow of capital services, existing data is almost invariably concerned with the stock of capital equipment. If such data is used, variations in the utilisation of the capital stock become important because if utilisation varies then a given capital stock will provide varying rates of flow of capital services. In practice, the money value of capital stock measured in terms of its replacement cost in some base year is generally used as the capital input variable. Such figures may be either in gross terms or net of depreciation estimates. Attempts are sometimes made to adjust such figures for varying utilisation by using the available data on the percentage of the labour force that is unemployed or 'unutilised'. However, this implies making the assumption that the percentage utilisation of capital is identical to the percentage employment of labour.

Occasionally, use is made of the assumption that all revenue accrues to either labour or capital in an attempt to estimate capital inputs. Given knowledge of Q, p, L, w and m, the accounting identity, $pQ = wL + mK$, which this assumption implies, may be used to estimate K. Notice, however, that in the context of the models of the previous section, this method implies that 'profits' are always zero. Furthermore, as we shall see in the next section, there are serious difficulties in the interpretation of estimated production functions when this accounting identity holds.

Estimation of K via the above accounting identity requires data on the price of capital, m. We shall also see in the following sections that data on factor prices is frequently necessary if consistent estimators of the production function parameters are to be obtained. Since the input variables are flow variables, m is the rental price of capital, i.e. it is the price of hiring capital for a given period of time. However, since under perfect competition a firm will be indifferent between hiring or purchasing and then selling a machine, m is usually calculated as the total cost of actually owning fixed capital.[7] These costs involve the opportunity cost of having funds tied up in fixed capital, depreciation costs, and any capital losses/gains resulting from changes in the price of capital goods. If r is the rate of interest, δ the depreciation rate and q the price of capital goods, then the sum of opportunity costs and depreciation costs will be $q(r + \delta)$. It is measures such as this, sometimes adjusted for capital losses/gains, that are normally used as estimates of m, the rental price of capital. Measures of wage costs per unit of time are, of course, more readily available.

8.3 Estimating the micro-production function

In this section we consider some of the problems that arise when attempts are made to estimate a micro-production function from data on individual firms. Discussion is, for the moment, restricted to the Cobb–Douglas function, since all the major problems can be adequately discussed in this context. We consider, first, cross-sectional data and then time series data and in each case describe some of the efforts that have been made to overcome the various problems.

Estimation from cross-sectional data

Suppose we have data on a cross-section of firms all within the same industry, so that all firms are producing essentially similar outputs. Suppose each firm has a Cobb–Douglas production function [8.12]. Since we are dealing with a single industry, it is not unreasonable to assume that the parameters α and β are the same for all firms because feasible production techniques are unlikely to vary to any great extent. Equation [8.12] is deterministic and we therefore need to introduce a disturbance term to account for random or unexplained variations in output. This is most easily done if a disturbance, ε, is introduced in multiplicative form. That is, for the ith firm, we have

$$Q_i = AK_i^\alpha L_i^\beta \varepsilon_i \qquad [8.29]$$

This formulation is convenient since [8.29] is then linear in the logarithms and this facilitates estimation

$$\log Q_i = \log A + \alpha \log K_i + \beta \log L_i + \log \varepsilon_i \qquad [8.30]$$

The disturbance in equation [8.30] may be assumed to have a mean of zero, in which case ε_i in [8.29] has a mean of unity. Also ε_i must always be positive, otherwise [8.29] could yield negative outputs and furthermore $\log \varepsilon_i$ would not be defined.

It is possible in this case to give a meaningful interpretation to the disturbance. It measures the *technical efficiency* of the ith firm's entrepreneur since, the larger is ε_i, the greater the maximum output this firm can achieve from a given quantity of inputs. Equation [8.29] could be written as $Q_i = A_i K_i^\alpha L_i^\beta$ where $A_i = A\varepsilon_i$ so that the introduction of ε_i can be regarded as making the efficiency parameter, A, in equation [8.12] vary from firm to firm.

The multiplicative introduction of ε_i is convenient for another reason. It means that the marginal products of capital and labour for the ith firm can still be written as $\alpha(Q_i/K_i)$ and $\beta(Q_i/L_i)$ which do not depend on the disturbance in the production function.[8] Thus if all firms are profit-maximisers and price-takers, the marginal productivity conditions for the ith firm are, from [8.13]

$$\alpha\left(\frac{Q_i}{K_i}\right) = \frac{m_i}{p_i}, \quad \beta\left(\frac{Q_i}{L_i}\right) = \frac{w_i}{p_i} \qquad [8.31]$$

Random disturbances u_i and v_i may also be introduced multiplicatively into the marginal productivity equations

$$\alpha\left(\frac{Q_i}{K_i}\right) = \left(\frac{m_i}{p_i}\right)u_i, \quad \beta\left(\frac{Q_i}{L_i}\right) = \left(\frac{w_i}{p_i}\right)v_i \qquad [8.32]$$

221

If u_i and v_i are assumed to be always positive and each to have a mean of unity, then departures of u_i and v_i from their mean values imply that the firm's entrepreneur is failing to maximise profits. These disturbances are therefore measures of the firm's *economic efficiency*, i.e. its ability correctly to combine its factor inputs. Taking logarithms we have, from [8.32]

$$\log Q_i = -\log \alpha + \log \left(\frac{m_i}{p_i} \right) + \log K_i + \log u_i \qquad [8.33]$$

$$\log Q_i = -\log \beta + \log \left(\frac{w_i}{p_i} \right) + \log L_i + \log v_i \qquad [8.34]$$

Equations [8.33] and [8.34] are, of course, as convenient for estimation purposes as is equation [8.30]. These equations taken together represent, for each firm, the three-equation simultaneous system in the endogenous Q_i, K_i and L_i with all prices being exogenous. Hence, if we wish to attempt estimation of the production function we must immediately consider the problems both of identification and of simultaneous equation bias. Although the system is non-linear, it is linear in the logarithms so we may apply the normal rules for linear systems.

At first glance there may seem to be no identification problem, since the other equations in the system both contain the variables $\log (m_i/p_i)$ and $\log (w_i/p_i)$ which do not appear in the production function. Recalling the arguments in Section 4.1, it appears impossible to obtain, by taking linear combinations of the equations in the system, an equation of similar form to the production function equation [8.30]. However, we are considering a cross-section of firms, in the same industry at the same point in time and under such conditions it is very likely that each firm will be faced with similar or identical prices. That is, p_i, m_i and w_i are the same for all firms and do not vary through the cross-section. Indeed, the marginal productivity conditions [8.32] imply perfect competition, and at a given moment under perfect competition all firms must be facing the same prices. This means that in the present case [8.33] and [8.34] may be written as

$$\log Q_i = \alpha^* + \log K_i + \log u_i \qquad [8.35]$$
$$\log Q_i = \beta^* + \log L_i + \log v_i \qquad [8.36]$$

where α^* and β^* are constants.

It should now be clear that we *do* have an identification problem, since the production function equation [8.30] could be confused, for example, with a linear combination of the marginal productivity equations [8.35] and [8.36]. To obtain an intuitive grasp of the problem suppose that ε_i, u_i and v_i are unity for all firms, i.e. the disturbances in equations [8.30], [8.35] and [8.36] are always zero. The three-equation system would now be identical for all firms (e.g. they would all have the same production function), and hence all would be producing the same levels of output with identical levels of inputs. In effect, they would all be at the same point on the same isoquant and we cannot hope to estimate a production function from knowledge of just a single point. If, more realistically, the disturbances ε_i, u_i and v_i vary randomly about unity, then all we observe are random departures from this single point.

It is instructive to consider the case where, of the three disturbances, only ε_i varies about unity. That is, the disturbance in the production function equation

[8.30] varies about zero but those in the marginal productivity equations [8.35] and [8.36] are identically zero. Under these conditions the shifting production function 'traces out' the marginal productivity conditions. Any attempt to relate output, Q, to K and L will only yield an estimate of some linear combination of equations [8.35] and [8.36] such as

$$\log Q_i = \frac{\lambda \alpha^* + \mu \beta^*}{\lambda + \mu} + \left(\frac{\lambda}{\lambda + \mu}\right) \log K_i + \left(\frac{\mu}{\lambda + \mu}\right) \log L_i \qquad [8.37]$$

where λ and μ are any two constants. Notice that the coefficients of $\log K_i$ and $\log L_i$ in any such linear combination will invariably sum to unity. Hence attempts to estimate a production function equation like [8.30] will, under these conditions, be *likely to lead to the conclusion that there are constant returns to scale regardless of the true values of α and β.* Economically this is the result of the fact that, since the marginal productivity conditions are satisfied exactly and are identical for all firms, Q, K and L vary across the cross-section in direct proportion to each other. Thus, equiproportionate changes in inputs appear to cause equiproportionate changes in output. Each firm has an identical factor input ratio and firms vary in size only because of varying technical efficiency. That is, a varying ε_i means that different firms obtain different quantities of output from given inputs. This special case well illustrates the dangers of the 'unthinking' estimation of production functions from cross-sectional data.

Although when prices do not vary over the cross-section the production function is unidentified, it should be noted at this point that the marginal productivity equations [8.35] and [8.36] *are* identified. A variable in the model is missing from each of these equations – the labour variable, L, in the case of equation [8.35] and the capital variable, K, in the case of equation [8.36]. Moreover, the coefficient of $\log K_i$ in [8.35] is unity as is that of $\log L_i$ in [8.36]. Neither of these equations can therefore be confused with linear combinations of other equations in the model.

There is a further problem, very much akin to the above, concerning the production function. Suppose the data used in estimation obeys the accounting identity

$$p_i Q_i = m_i K_i + w_i L_i \qquad [8.38]$$

This may artificially be so if, as we saw in the previous section to be sometimes the case, the capital variable K is calculated by using such an identity. Equation [8.38] may be rewritten as

$$Q_i = \left(\frac{m_i}{p_i}\right) K_i + \left(\frac{w_i}{p_i}\right) L_i \qquad [8.39]$$

Since p_i, m_i and w_i are constant over the cross-section, the identity [8.39] expresses Q_i simply as a function of K_i and L_i, just as does the production function [8.29]. Hence, in attempting to estimate [8.29] we may in fact be confusing it with [8.39]. A 'good fit' may merely mean that we have rediscovered the identity that was artificially enforced on the data.

How might these problems be overcome? One obvious possibility is to obtain data in which the prices p_i, m_i and w_i do, in fact, vary over the cross-section. If this were so, the marginal productivity equations [8.33] and [8.34] would contain variables, namely m_i/p_i and w_i/p_i, that do not appear in the production function.

Hence, there would be no question of confusing the production function with the marginal productivity equations and neither could it be confused with any accounting identity.

Prices would vary over the cross-section if the assumption that firms are price-takers no longer held, i.e. if market conditions were imperfectly competitive. Adopting such a model would, however, involve the treating of all prices as endogenous and hence require the introduction of additional demand for output and supply of input equations. An alternative is to use an 'inter-state' cross-section where each observation comes from a similar industry but from a different country or national economy. Since there is no reason why p_i, m_i and w_i should be identical in different countries, this would overcome the identification problem.

One further possible way by which the production function might be identified concerns the disturbances. As we saw in Section 4.1, if the disturbances in the equations of a simultaneous model are uncorrelated then all equations in the model are identified. The problem here is that ε_i, the disturbance in the production function, represents technical efficiency, while the marginal productivity disturbances u_i and v_i represent economic efficiency. Since the technically efficient firm is also likely to be economically efficient, ε_i is likely to be correlated with u_i and v_i so that this route to identification is unlikely to be feasible.

Even if prices vary over the cross-section and we are confident that the production function is identified, the problem of simultaneous equation bias must still be considered. The production function equation is, as we have already noted, only one equation in the simultaneous system consisting of [8.30], [8.33] and [8.34] which jointly determine Q, K and L. The reduced form of this system is

$$\log Q_i = \text{const} - h\alpha \log\left(\frac{m_i}{p_i}\right) - h\beta \log\left(\frac{w_i}{p_i}\right) + h\alpha \log u_i$$
$$+ h\beta \log v_i + h \log \varepsilon_i \qquad [8.40]$$

$$\log K_i = \text{const} - h(1 - \beta)\log\left(\frac{m_i}{p_i}\right) - h\beta \log\left(\frac{w_i}{p_i}\right) - h(1 - \beta)\log u_i$$
$$+ h\beta \log v_i + h \log \varepsilon_i \qquad [8.41]$$

$$\log L_i = \text{const} - h\alpha \log\left(\frac{m_i}{p_i}\right) - h(1 - \alpha)\log\left(\frac{w_i}{p_i}\right) + h\alpha \log u_i$$
$$- h(1 - \alpha)\log v_i + h \log \varepsilon_i \qquad [8.42]$$

where the constants are functions of A, α and β and need not concern us and $h = (1 - \alpha - \beta)^{-1}$. We see from equations [8.41] and [8.42], that $\log K_i$ and $\log L_i$, the explanatory variables in the production function equation [8.30], are correlated with ε_i, the disturbance in that equation. This is the source of the simultaneous equation bias. Thus the OLS estimators of the parameters of equation [8.30] will be biased and inconsistent *even if that equation is identified*.

Provided prices vary over the cross-section this problem can be tackled by using normal simultaneous equation estimating methods. The production function is exactly identified since the number of variables omitted from it $- \log(m_i/p_i)$ and $\log(w_i/p_i)$, is one less than the total number of equations in the system. It may therefore be estimated by, for example, both ILS and TSLS.

However, if prices are constant over the cross-section then not only is the production function unidentified but there are effectively no exogenous variables in the model. This means that the methods of ILS and TSLS cannot even be used to estimate the identified marginal productivity equations.

However, even with constant prices there is one method, pioneered by Klein (1953), by which the parameters α and β may be consistently estimated. This makes use of the identified marginal productivity equations [8.33] and [8.34]. For example, equation [8.34] may be rewritten as

$$\log \beta = \log L_i - \log Q_i + \log\left(\frac{w_i}{p_i}\right) + \log v_i$$

$$= \log\left(\frac{w_i L_i}{p_i Q_i}\right) + \log v_i \qquad [8.43]$$

This suggests that, given n observations in the cross-section, we should estimate $\log \beta$ by

$$\widehat{\log \beta} = \frac{1}{n}\sum_{i=1}^{n} \log\left(\frac{w_i L_i}{p_i Q_i}\right) \qquad [8.44]$$

Provided $\log v_i$ has a mean of zero, $\widehat{\log \beta}$ is easily shown to be an unbiased and consistent estimator of $\log \beta$. For example, using [8.43]

$$E\widehat{\log \beta} = \frac{1}{n}\sum_{i=1}^{n} E \log\left(\frac{w_i L_i}{p_i Q_i}\right)$$

$$= \frac{1}{n}\sum_{i=1}^{n} E(\log \beta - \log v_i) = \log \beta \qquad [8.45]$$

Given that [8.44] provides an estimator of $\log \beta$, an estimator of β is given by the sample geometric mean of labour's share in total output. Similarly, an estimator of α is provided by the geometric mean of capital's share. That is

$$\hat{\beta} = \sqrt[n]{\prod_{i=1}^{n}\left(\frac{w_i L_i}{p_i Q_i}\right)} \qquad \hat{\alpha} = \sqrt[n]{\prod_{i=1}^{n}\left(\frac{m_i K_i}{p_i Q_i}\right)} \qquad [8.46]$$

For obvious reasons this method is known as *the method of factor shares*. It provides consistent but not unbiased estimates of α and β. This is because, although $\widehat{\log \beta}$, for example, is an unbiased estimator of $\log \beta$, the property of unbiasedness, unlike that of consistency, does not 'carry over'.

Note that the method of factor shares enables us to estimate two of the parameters of the production function, α and β, via the identified marginal productivity equations. The validity of the method, however, requires the assumption that marginal products are indeed equated to factor prices and all that this implies about market conditions.

Nerlove's study of electricity supply
Nerlove's (1963) cross-sectional study of the US electricity supply industry provides a classic example of how the problems of identification and simultaneous equation bias may sometimes be overcome. Conditions in this privately owned but publicly regulated industry are such that power must be supplied on

225

demand. Output Q can therefore be regarded as a predetermined variable. Since prices are set by a public commission total revenue is also predetermined, so that the problem of firms within the industry may be regarded as that of minimising total cost. The two-equation model of Section 8.1 therefore becomes relevant, although Nerlove uses a slightly generalised version of this model in which there are three factor inputs – labour, capital and fuel. His production function is of Cobb–Douglas form:

$$Q = A x_1^{\alpha_1} x_2^{\alpha_2} x_3^{\alpha_3} \varepsilon \qquad [8.47]$$

where x_1, x_2 and x_3 are the inputs of labour, capital and fuel respectively and ε is a 'technical efficiency'-type disturbance.

Although the factor markets cannot all be regarded as perfectly competitive it is possible to treat each firm as a price-taker. The capital market is highly competitive while wages and fuel prices are set by long-term contracts so that firms are price-takers in the short run in the labour and fuel markets. Total costs are therefore given by

$$C = p_1 x_1 + p_2 x_2 + p_3 x_3 \qquad [8.48]$$

where p_1, p_2 and p_3, the prices of labour, capital and fuel may be regarded as given. Minimising [8.48] subject to the constraint [8.47] on output, means that firms must equate ratios of marginal products to ratios of factor prices. That is

$$\frac{\partial Q}{\partial x_1} \bigg/ \frac{\partial Q}{\partial x_2} = \frac{\alpha_1 x_2}{\alpha_2 x_1} = \frac{p_1}{p_2}, \quad \frac{\partial Q}{\partial x_1} \bigg/ \frac{\partial Q}{\partial x_3} = \frac{\alpha_1 x_3}{\alpha_3 x_1} = \frac{p_1}{p_3} \qquad [8.49]$$

Equations [8.47] and [8.49] form a three-equation system in which the endogenous variables are the three factor inputs x_1, x_2 and x_3. The exogenous variables are output, Q, and the factor prices. If prices did not vary over the cross-section, the production function [8.47] would not be identified. However, because of the manner in which labour and fuel prices are determined, there is sufficient variation in these variables to remove this problem. There remains the problem of simultaneous equation bias which Nerlove circumvents by estimating via the reduced form.

The reduced form of the system consists of three equations expressing each of the endogenous variables, x_1, x_2 and x_3, as functions of the exogenous variables and the disturbance ε.[9] Note that Nerlove does not introduce disturbances into the marginal productivity equations [8.49]. These are assumed to be satisfied exactly.

Nerlove, however, does not estimate each reduced-form equation separately. Since his data concerns total costs, he estimates a linear combination of the reduced-form equations, which is, in fact, the total cost function. That is, he substitutes the reduced-form expressions for x_1, x_2 and x_3 into [8.48] and obtains

$$C = k Q^{1/r} p_1^{\alpha_1/r} p_2^{\alpha_2/r} p_3^{\alpha_3/r} \varepsilon^{-1/r} \qquad [8.50]$$

where

$$r = \alpha_1 + \alpha_2 + \alpha_3$$

is a returns-to-scale parameter and the constant

$$k = r(A \alpha_1^{\alpha_1} \alpha_2^{\alpha_2} \alpha_3^{\alpha_3})$$

The cost function [8.50] expresses the endogenous total costs as a function of the

226

exogenous Q and the exogenous factor prices. It may be expressed in logarithmic form as

$$\log C = \log k + \left(\frac{1}{r}\right)\log Q + \left(\frac{\alpha_1}{r}\right)\log p_1 + \left(\frac{\alpha_2}{r}\right)\log p_2$$
$$+ \left(\frac{\alpha_3}{r}\right)\log p_3 - \left(\frac{1}{r}\right)\log \varepsilon \qquad [8.51]$$

Provided $-(1/r)\log\varepsilon$ obeys all the classical assumptions (it may be assumed independent of the explanatory variables, since these are all exogenous), then the application of OLS to [8.51] will yield unbiased and consistent estimates of its coefficients. There is a problem, however. The *five* coefficients of [8.51] which are to be estimated are functions of only *four* production function parameters, α_1, α_2, α_3 and r. Thus, the α's and r are overidentified. This problem can be overcome by using the fact that, since $\alpha_1 + \alpha_2 + \alpha_3 = r$, the coefficients on $\log p_1$, $\log p_2$ and $\log p_3$ in equation [8.51] must sum to unity. The equation can therefore be rewritten as

$$\log C - \log p_3 = \log k + \left(\frac{1}{r}\right)\log Q + \left(\frac{\alpha_1}{r}\right)(\log p_1 - \log p_3)$$
$$+ \left(\frac{\alpha_2}{r}\right)(\log p_2 - \log p_3) - \left(\frac{1}{r}\right)\log \varepsilon \qquad [8.51A]$$

Nerlove applies OLS to [8.51A], (i.e. he regresses $\log C - \log p_3$ on $\log Q$, $\log p_1 - \log p_3$ and $\log p_2 - \log p_3$) and obtains

$$\log C - \log p_3 = \text{const} + \underset{(0.175)}{0.721} \log Q + \underset{(0.198)}{0.562}(\log p_1 - \log p_3)$$
$$\underset{(0.192)}{- 0.003}(\log p_2 - \log p_3) \qquad R^2 = 0.92$$

This yields a value $r = 1/0.721 = 1.39$, suggesting *increasing returns* to scale. Notice that the coefficient on $\log p_2 - \log p_3$ has an incorrect sign – Nerlove attributes this to deficiencies in his data series for the price of capital. The coefficient on $\log p_1 - \log p_3$ yields an estimate of the elasticity of output with respect to labour input of $\alpha_1 = 1.39 \times 0.562 = 0.78$.[10]

An examination of the OLS residuals suggests problems, however. When firms are ordered by the size of their output it is found that long runs of positive residuals at low levels of output are followed by long runs of negative residuals at higher levels of output. A possible explanation of this is provided by the fact that, as noted in Section 8.1, the Cobb–Douglas function is restricted in that the returns to scale implied are the same at all levels of output. If, in fact, there were increasing returns to scale at lower levels of output but decreasing returns at higher levels, the true total-cost curve would look like the heavy line in Fig. 8.3. However, by adapting the cost curve [8.51] an attempt is being made to represent the true curve by one similar to the dotted line in Fig. 8.3. This could explain the pattern of residuals observed.

To investigate this possibility, Nerlove divides his sample into five groups of

8.3 True and estimated cost curves.

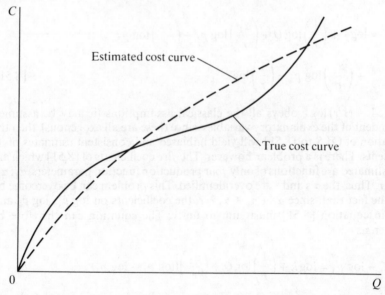

twenty-nine firms each, ordered by the size of their outputs, and runs separate OLS regressions for each such group. In this way five separate segments of the true cost curve are estimated and their returns to scale properties analysed. Not unexpectedly, returns to scale are much greater at low levels of output. For the twenty-nine smallest firms $\hat{r} > 2.5$, but $\hat{r}$ declines as output rises, being less than unity (although not significantly so) for the largest group of firms. Nerlove therefore concludes that, while there are definite increasing returns to scale at the firm level, their extent decreases as output rises.

Estimation from time series data

Time series studies of the production function at the level of the individual firm are relatively rare – mainly because investigators have been more concerned with the 'representative firm' or the industry as a whole. However, it is worth examining the problems of estimating micro-functions from time series data because, in doing so, we can abstract from some of the more difficult conceptual problems that arise when aggregates of firms or industries are considered.

The problems with cross-sectional data that arose because of the constancy of product and factor prices disappear to some extent in time series. Prices facing the individual firm are likely to vary over time so that the possibility of confusing the production function with either the marginal productivity equations or any accounting identity is less. However, notice that in equations [8.33] and [8.34], it is the price ratios m_i/p_i and w_i/p_i which appear in the marginal productivity equations. Thus, identification problems will still arise if product and factor prices show any marked tendency to change at similar rates over time, since this would still leave the price *ratios* constant. The problem of simultaneous equation bias is, of course, present with time series data as with cross-sectional data.

There is, however, a more serious problem with time series data – that of technical progress or innovation over time. In a cross-section, taken at a given point in time, the technology available to each firm can be regarded as given, but this is clearly not the case when we consider a single firm over a period of time. The firm's production function will shift as new and more efficient techniques of production come into existence and are put into practice. A major problem with time series data is therefore that of distinguishing between increases in output resulting from movements along the production function (i.e. from increased inputs), and increases in output which occur because of shifts in the production function resulting from technical progress.

Consider equation [8.29], the production function for the ith firm in a cross-section. The disturbance, ε_i, in this equation represented the technical efficiency of the ith firm. While ε_i could be regarded as a 'random' factor in a cross-section, varying from firm to firm with a mean of unity, when we consider a *single* firm over time it obviously cannot be given this interpretation. A firm which is technically efficient in one year is likely to remain so in the next. Recall that equation [8.29] could be rewritten as

$$Q_i = A_i K_i^\alpha L_i^\beta$$

so that variations in ε_i represented variations in the maximum output that could be obtained from given inputs. When we consider the ith firm only, such maximum output is likely to increase over time because of technical progress. This suggests that one way of handling technical progress is to make the efficiency parameter in a Cobb–Douglas function vary over time and write the individual firm's production function as

$$Q_t = A(t)K_t^\alpha L_t^\beta \varepsilon_t \qquad [8.52]$$

Q_t, K_t and L_t are the output and factor inputs during period t, $A(t)$ is some function of t and ε_t is now a genuinely random disturbance reflecting such factors as strikes, weather conditions, etc.

Before an equation such as [8.52] can be estimated from time series data, some form has to be given to the function $A(t)$. The form most frequently used in practice has been

$$A(t) = Ae^{gt}$$

where A and g are constants, so that [8.52] becomes

$$Q_t = Ae^{gt}K_t^\alpha L_t^\beta \varepsilon_t \qquad [8.53]$$

The interpretation of A and g is straightforward. A is simply the value of $A(t)$ at time $t = 0$. Partially differentiating [8.53] with respect to t yields

$$\frac{\partial Q_t}{\partial t} = gQ_t$$

Hence

$$\frac{\partial Q_t}{\partial t} \bigg/ Q_t = g.$$

Thus g measures the proportionate change in output per time period when input levels are held constant. It is therefore the proportionate change in output that occurs because of technical progress. Equation [8.53] is convenient from the estimating point of view since, taking logarithms, we have

$$\log Q_t = \log A + gt + \alpha \log K_t + \beta \log L_t + \log \varepsilon_t \qquad [8.54]$$

Thus the estimation of [8.53] simply requires the inclusion of a time trend in the usual Cobb–Douglas estimating equation.

The limitations of the above representation of technical progress should be made clear. Obviously the constancy of g and its implication that technical progress occurs at a constant rate may not be realistic. However, there are more serious difficulties. Firstly, the above type of technical progress is that generally known as *neutral* technical progress. That is, it has no effect on the MRS of capital for labour[11] and hence for a given ratio of factor prices does not influence the proportions in which capital and labour inputs are combined.[12] Thus, such technical progress does not affect the capital or labour intensity of the productive process. Unfortunately, it is not difficult to think of technical innovations which have been either labour-saving or capital-saving, so that the assumption of neutral technical progress is obviously restrictive. If non-neutral technical change is to be introduced into [8.53] then it is necessary to permit the ratio α/β to vary over time.

A possibly even more serious limitation of equations like [8.52] is that they represent technical progress that is firstly 'exogenous' and secondly 'disembodied'. Technical progress in this case is exogenous because it has been superimposed on the system, (A is simply assumed to grow over time for no stated reason). In practice, techniques become more efficient because of, for example, 'learning by doing' (Arrow 1962), or by the occurrence of research and development expenditure generated by pressures endogenous to the system.

Disembodied technical progress is a form of exogenous technical progress which has been likened to 'manna from heaven', since when it occurs it transforms all existing factors of production no matter how long these factors have been in existence. This is clearly unrealistic, certainly as far as capital inputs are concerned. The occurrence of some new invention does not normally mean that all existing capital machinery, no matter of what age, can now be fully adopted to take advantage of the new technique. Rather, a firm, if it wishes to make full use of new innovations must normally purchase new machinery which 'embodies' the new technique. It is easy to see that equation [8.52] represents technical progress of the disembodied type. As we have noted, [8.52] implies that for given input levels the maximum output obtainable increases over time. However, [8.52] also implies that the given input levels could consist of exactly the same units of capital and labour. These units must therefore be the recipients of disembodied 'manna from heaven' if the maximum output they can produce is to continually increase.

Notwithstanding the limited nature of the representation of technical progress in [8.52], this is the formulation that has most frequently been employed in empirical work. Only recently have attempts to introduce non-neutral or embodied technical change into econometric-type models become more common.

There is one additional difficulty which may arise with either cross-sectional or time series data. This concerns the likelihood of a high degree of multicollinearity amongst the explanatory input variables in the production function. In a cross-section, it is obvious that large firms will tend to have high levels of both capital and labour inputs and small firms low levels of such inputs. Thus, capital inputs may well be highly correlated with labour inputs. For time series data on an individual firm, capital and labour inputs are again likely to be highly collinear. Moreover, in this case the problem is accentuated if a time trend is included to represent the influence of technical progress. Since the capital and labour input variables are also likely to be trend variables in time series, the problem of multicollinearity may now become really severe.

As we saw in Section 3.3, the consequence of such high multicollinearity is likely to be a lack of precision in the estimation of the production function parameters. This lack of precision would be reflected in high standard errors for the estimators of these parameters. The extent to which multicollinearity has this effect will depend on the overall ability of the explanatory variables to explain variations in the dependent output variable. As we noted in Section 3.3, if the overall 'fit' is good, then the estimates of parameters of the production function may still be well determined even when the input variables are highly correlated. However, when the effects of multicollinearity are severe, there is little that can be done apart from obtaining additional information to break the 'deadlock'. One possibility, which in some cases may be acceptable, is to impose before estimation the restriction that there are constant returns to scale, i.e. that

$$\alpha + \beta = 1$$

Equation [8.29] is then replaced by

$$Q_i = A K_i^\alpha L_i^{1-\alpha} \varepsilon_i = A \left(\frac{K_i}{L_i} \right)^\alpha L_i \varepsilon_i$$

or

$$\frac{Q_i}{L_i} = A \left(\frac{K_i}{L_i} \right)^\alpha \varepsilon_i \qquad\qquad [8.29A]$$

Hence, estimates of A and α may be obtained by regressing $\log(Q_i/L_i)$ on $\log(K_i/L_i)$ and since we now have only one explanatory variable, the problem of multicollinearity has been circumvented.

8.4   Estimating aggregate production functions

As we have already observed, production functions are not only estimated for individual firms but also for entire industries and sometimes for large industrial sectors. We begin this section by considering the problems involved in estimating 'industrial production functions' and then move on to cases where the aggregation process has been carried even further. In each case we discuss the problems in the context of the Cobb–Douglas function.

Industrial production functions

We consider cross-sectional data first. In such studies *each* observation consists of measurements of aggregate inputs and output for an entire industry. A series of observations on the relevant industries is obtained by considering *inter-state* cross-sections. That is, if we were attempting to estimate the production function for the steel industry, one observation might consist of aggregate inputs and output for the US steel industry, another of inputs and output for the UK steel industry, etc., etc.

There are obvious problems with this approach. We have already drawn attention to the conceptual difficulties involved in attempting to aggregate the individual production functions of firms even when they are all within the same industry. Also, the classification of the relevant industry may vary from country to country – what constitutes 'the steel industry' in the UK may differ slightly from what is classified as 'the steel industry' in the US. A more serious problem concerns variations in the 'state of technology' from country to country. Whereas for a cross-section of firms within a single industry it may be not unreasonable to regard the technological knowledge available as varying little from firm to firm, this may not be plausible for an inter-state cross-section. To some extent such variations can be allowed for if we adopt, for example, equation [8.29] as our industrial production function and interpret the disturbance, ε_i, as reflecting differences in technical 'know-how' between countries. However, this implies that technology varies neutrally between countries[13] and there is no real reason why this should be so. If non-neutral technical change is to be introduced then this implies that the ratio of α to β in equation [8.29] should be permitted to vary across countries.

One important advantage of inter-state cross-sections is that product and factor prices do vary from country to country. Thus, considering the three-equation simultaneous model given by equations [8.30], [8.33] and [8.34], where the ith observation now refers to the ith country, we no longer have any problem in identifying the production function. Problems of simultaneous equation bias and multicollinearity of course, remain.

The first major use of an inter-state cross-section was by Arrow, *et al.* (1961) but, since this involved the CES production function, discussion of it is deferred until the next section. Another well-known study is that of Hildebrand and Liu (1965). Although their cross-section is not truly interstate in the above sense – each observation relates to a particular state within the US – factors such as transport costs and labour immobility meant that there was sufficient variation in product and factor prices over the cross-section to remove any problems of identification.

Hildebrand and Liu adopt a production function of basically Cobb–Douglas form but with one major modification. The exponents α and β are permitted to vary over the cross-section and to depend on the quality of the capital and labour inputs. Thus technical differences between firms are allowed to be non-neutral, yet the basic simplicity of the Cobb–Douglas function is retained. The function estimated is of the kind

$$Q_i = A K_i^{\alpha(\log R_i)} L_i^{\beta(\log S_i)} \varepsilon_i \qquad [8.55]$$

where R_i and S_i are measures of the quality of capital and labour respectively. One measure of R_i is inversely related to the 'average age' of the capital equipment in use, while S_i is based on the extent of the education of the labour force employed. The logarithmic transformation of [8.55] is

$$\log Q_i = \log A + \alpha \log R_i \log K_i + \beta \log S_i \log L_i + \log \varepsilon_i \qquad [8.56]$$

Equation [8.56] could be estimated by OLS if $\log Q_i$ were regressed on the variables ($\log R_i \log K_i$) and ($\log S_i \log L_i$). However, there are obvious problems of simultaneity so other equations are introduced into the model. Unusual features of the full model are, firstly, that the assumption of perfect competition is dropped. Product price is allowed to vary with output and a demand for product equation is introduced. Secondly, although capital stock is treated as predetermined, a marginal productivity-of-labour equation is introduced which contains an adjustment mechanism. This allows for the fact that firms cannot instantaneously adjust their labour inputs in response to changes in either productive techniques or market conditions. A new equilibrium position can only be achieved gradually over time.

Hildebrand and Liu estimate their production function for fifteen different industries using both OLS and TSLS. Their data was a 1957 cross-section of US states, with variables expressed in 'per-establishment' form. Their main conclusion is that there are generally increasing returns to scale at the industry level. Equiproportionate changes in capital and labour inputs lead to more than proportionate changes in output in twelve of the fifteen industries even if the quality indices for capital and labour are held constant. If the increasing capital inputs are accompanied by an increase in capital quality (as is likely with new investment) the increasing returns are even more marked and occur in all industries. The influence of technical change is therefore of great importance. Notice, that since the assumption of perfect competition has been relaxed, the conflict between profit maximisation and non-decreasing returns to scale discussed in Section 8.1 no longer arises. Another interesting conclusion is that firms adjust labour inputs very slowly in response to changing conditions. As a result the authors maintain that US industry in general was seriously overemploying labour in the late 1950s.

An exceptional feature of the Hildebrand-Liu study is that, as noted above, the assumption of perfect competition in the product market is dropped. The introduction of a demand for product equation makes it possible to allow for a two-way relationship between output and the price of output. The possibility of such a two-way relationship also occurs at the firm level in the estimation of micro-production functions. While it is not unreasonable to regard the individual firm as a price-taker in the factor markets, it may be less valid to assume that the firm can increase output without influencing product price.

When product price can no longer be regarded as exogenous, estimation methods which treat it as such will be subject to simultaneous equation bias. They allow only for the influence of product price on output but ignore the 'feedback' effect whereby any change in the firm's output has an effect on product price.

The problem of the endogeneity or otherwise of product price has generally been dodged at the firm level simply by assuming that firms are price-takers in the product market. For this reason we did not discuss it in Section 8.3. However, once aggregation is taken beyond the firm level, the problem can no longer be ignored with any safety. Clearly, the feedback effect whereby output influences product price becomes much stronger when we consider the output of firms in aggregate rather than that of an individual firm. Furthermore, once we have aggregated to industry level it is no longer reasonable to regard factor prices as exogenous either. Each individual firm may be a price-taker in the factor markets and hence be able to vary its inputs without influencing their prices. However, variations in aggregate inputs for the entire industry are unlikely to leave factor prices unchanged. If simultaneity problems similar to those discussed above are to be allowed for, then the assumption of infinite elasticities of supply for the factor inputs must be relaxed. Additional supply of factor equations must be introduced into the model making factor prices as well as product price endogenous variables. Obviously, the greater the extent of the aggregation involved, the greater the need to consider the possible endogeneity of the price variables. Unfortunately, the estimators of aggregate production functions have generally been content to ignore such problems.

When attempts are made to estimate industrial production functions from time series data, we meet again all the problems discussed in the previous section concerning the estimation of micro-production functions from such data. In addition, of course, there is now the problem of aggregation over firms and such awkward difficulties as the existence of external economies of scale. These were discussed in Section 8.2.

Technical progress over time is again a problem as it was in the estimation of micro-functions. However, there is now the additional difficulty that different firms within an industry may experience different rates of technical progress. That is, even if each firm has a production function like [8.53], g may vary from firm to firm. If g varies in this manner, then for sensible aggregation we require either that all firms grow at a constant rate over time, or that the input variables K and L should be distributed across firms independently of g. Unfortunately, neither of these conditions is likely to hold. Firms with the highest rate of technical progress are likely to be the most competitive and, hence, will tend to grow at the fastest rate and will also employ the largest inputs of capital and labour. This means that if an aggregate version of equation [8.53] is estimated from time series data then the estimate of g will represent more than just the 'average rate of technical progress'. It will also reflect increases in output resulting from a redistribution of inputs from the less efficient firms to the more efficient ones. It could be said to measure 'economic progress' as well as 'technical progress'.

Production functions for industrial sectors

Much of the empirical work on production functions has been concerned, not with the individual firm or even the industry, but with aggregates such as the entire manufacturing sector or even the whole of private industry. We have already discussed the aggregation problems involved in even the concept of such truly aggregate functions. In this subsection, discussion will be mainly limited to considering the extent to which empirical studies can be regarded as having provided estimates of such functions, nebulous in concept though they may be.

Cross-section studies of the aggregate production function use as observations aggregate data for different industries within the same economy. That is, one observation may consist of aggregate inputs and output for the textile industry, another of inputs and output for the iron and steel industry, etc., etc. The 'production function' estimated in this manner is then interpreted as being that for the industrial or manufacturing sector as a whole. However, one cannot help feeling that a scatter of points obtained in this way must represent not a single sectoral production function but a set of observations, each representing a point on an entirely different production function – one for each industry in the cross-section. This is particularly so if, as in many studies, no attempt is made to allow for the fact that productive techniques, e.g. the degree of capital intensity, are almost certain to vary between industries – far more so, for example, than they do within a cross-section of firms within the same industry.

Results obtained from inter-industry cross-sections are also likely to depend on the manner in which industries have been classified. Walters (1970) provides a neat example of this fact. Suppose the estimated production function suggested increasing returns to scale in the sense that 'larger' industries, while using more inputs than 'smaller' industries, succeeded in producing a more than proportionately higher output. This finding would be entirely the result of the manner in which industries had been classified. If, for example, a finer classification had been used for the 'larger' industries, splitting them up into smaller entities, the results obtained might be entirely reversed with what are now the 'smaller' industries appearing the more productive. A better way of determining the 'size' of an industry is to examine the average size of firms within each classification.

Time series studies of aggregate production functions use as observations aggregate data on, for example, the entire manufacturing sector, gathered over a period of time. The early studies of this nature were mainly carried out by Douglas using a Cobb–Douglas function and were summarised in his 1948 article. No allowance was made for technical progress in these studies, possible identification problems were not considered and the method of estimation was invariably OLS. Despite all this and the conceptual problems involved in the very idea of an aggregate production function, the results appeared uniformly good. A selection is presented in Table 8.1.

On the basis of his results, Douglas concluded that the Cobb–Douglas function represented a fairly general 'law of production' with constant returns to scale, and that the shares of output going to capital and labour were indeed equal to the α and β exponents in the Cobb–Douglas function. This latter finding was interpreted as strong support for the marginal productivity theory of distribution. Given all the problems that were not allowed for, it seems astonishing that these early results should have turned out so well. However, one clue as to why this could have been so is provided by the fact that the relative prices m/p and w/p remained relatively constant over the periods considered. As we saw in the previous section, the production function is unidentified under such conditions and if in addition the data used happens to satisfy an accounting identity such as [8.38], then a good 'fit' may simply be a reflection of this identity.

8.1 Results obtained using the Cobb–Douglas production function

Sample period	α	β	$\alpha + \beta$	Labour share
US 1899–1922	0.30 (0.05)	0.63 (0.15)	0.93	0.61
Victoria 1907–29	0.23 (0.17)	0.84 (0.34)	1.07	n.a.
New South Wales 1901–27	0.20 (0.08)	0.78 (0.12)	0.98	n.a.
New Zealand 1915–35	0.42 (0.11)	0.49 (0.03)	0.91	0.52

Source: Douglas (1948)

Solow's study of US technical progress

The problem of technical progress bedevils the estimation of production functions from aggregate time series data just as it does with industry or firm data. Moreover, the problem of varying rates of technical progress mentioned in the context of industrial time series estimation is now more acute. Variations in g are likely to be even wider between industries than they are between firms within a single industry. An early, if relatively extreme, example of how technical progress might be handled and shifts in the aggregate production function separated from movements along it is provided by Solow (1957).

Solow does not specify the precise form of the production function but assumes that technical progress is both neutral and disembodied so that

$$Q_t = A(t)F(K_t, L_t) \qquad [8.57]$$

Constant returns to scale are assumed so that [8.57] may be written as

$$\frac{Q_t}{L_t} = A(t)F\left(\frac{K_t}{L_t}, 1\right) = A(t)f\left(\frac{K_t}{L_t}\right)$$

or

$$q_t = A(t)f(k_t) \qquad [8.58]$$

where q_t and k_t are output per head and capital per head respectively. Changes in output per head over time are therefore the result of either neutral technical progress or of increases in capital per head. Formally, by total differentiation of [8.58] with respect to time, we have, letting

$$\dot{q} = \frac{dq}{dt}, \quad \dot{k} = \frac{dk}{dt} \quad \text{and} \quad \dot{A} = \frac{dA}{dt},$$

$$\dot{q} = \dot{A}f(k_t) + \frac{\partial q_t}{\partial k_t}\dot{k} \qquad [8.59]$$

Dividing [8.59] by q_t leads to an expression for the proportionate rate of change in output per head

$$\frac{\dot{q}}{q_t} = \frac{\dot{A}}{A(t)} + \frac{\partial q_t}{\partial k_t} \cdot \frac{\dot{k}}{q_t} \qquad [8.60]$$

Solow assumes that factors are paid their marginal products so that

$$\frac{\partial q_t}{\partial k_t} = \frac{\partial Q_t}{\partial K_t} = \frac{m_t}{p_t}$$

Equation [8.60] can now be written as

$$\frac{\dot{q}}{q_t} = \frac{\dot{A}}{A(t)} + \left(\frac{m_t K_t}{p_t Q_t}\right)\frac{\dot{k}}{k_t} \qquad [8.61]$$

Using the relationship [8.61], US annual data on output per man-hour, capital per man-hour and on mK/pQ, the share of capital in total output, Solow is able to estimate, for each year of the period 1909–49, the quantity $\dot{A}/A(t)$. This is an index of technical change, measuring the proportionate change in output per man-hour that would have occurred if capital per man-hour had remained constant. Over

236

the entire sample period the average rate of technical progress is estimated to be 1.5 per cent per annum. Of the total rise in output per man-hour during the forty-year period, Solow estimated that 90 per cent was the result of technical progress (i.e. of shifts in the production function), and only the remaining 10 per cent the result of increases in capital per man-hour (movements along the production function).

As Solow himself acknowledged there are obvious objections to such calculations. Technical progress when defined in this way is simply a name for any increase in output per head which is not the result of increased capital per head. These increases are the result not only of the disembodied neutral technical progress assumed above, but also of increasing returns to scale (both internal and external to the firm) as output expands, redistributive effects as factor inputs switch to more efficient industries, and embodied types of technical change caused by improvements in the quality of capital and in the education of the labour force.

8.5   Estimating the constant elasticity of substitution production function

Estimation of the CES production functions [8.18] and [8.24] is subject to all the problems of identification and simultaneity discussed in the context of the Cobb–Douglas function. We shall not repeat this discussion, but concentrate in this section on the additional difficulties that arise when attempts are made to estimate the CES function.

Such problems arise because, unlike the Cobb–Douglas function, the CES function cannot be linearised by a simple logarithmic transformation. Most investigators have approached its estimation via the marginal productivity conditions [8.20] or [8.21]. The first empirical study of the function was by SMAC (1961) who developed the constant returns to scale formulation [8.18]. As noted in Section 8.1 they began their investigation by estimating [8.17] which may be derived from the second of the marginal productivity equations [8.20] in the form

$$\frac{Q}{L} = \left(\frac{\gamma^\theta}{1-\delta}\right)^{1/1+\theta}\left(\frac{w}{p}\right)^{1/1+\theta} \tag{8.64}$$

Remembering that the elasticity of substitution $\sigma = 1/1 + \theta$, the logarithmic transformation of [8.64] is

$$\log\left(\frac{Q}{L}\right) = \sigma \log\left(\frac{\gamma^\theta}{1-\delta}\right) + \sigma \log\left(\frac{w}{p}\right) \tag{8.65}$$

The coefficient of $\log(w/p)$ in the regression of $\log(Q/L)$ on $\log(w/p)$ therefore yields an estimate of σ. SMAC estimated [8.65] by OLS using an interstate cross-section. Estimates of σ were obtained for twenty-four separate industries using up to nineteen observations (countries) in each case. The values obtained for σ ranged from 0.721 to 1.011. Ten were significantly less than unity at the 5 per cent level and a further four at the 10 per cent level. Hence, SMAC were able to claim that the elasticity of substitution was typically less than unity and that their function was to be preferred to a Cobb–Douglas specification.

Doubts were first cast on the SMAC conclusions by Fuchs (1963) who noted a wide variation in the average wage over the nineteen countries in the cross-section. Fuchs therefore split the SMAC sample into more and less well-developed countries and found, when estimating [8.65], that there were significant differences in the intercept term between the two groups but no significant differences as far as the slope coefficient, σ, was concerned. Fuchs therefore estimated the equation

$$\log\left(\frac{Q}{L}\right) = \beta_0 + \beta_0'D + \sigma\log\left(\frac{w}{p}\right) \tag{8.66}$$

where D is a dummy variable of the kind described in Section 5.2, taking the value unity for more developed and zero for less well-developed countries. Estimates of [8.66] for the twenty-four industries yielded estimates of σ which were now evenly spread about unity with only two of them significantly different from unity at the 5 per cent level of significance. There were problems, however, with the estimate of β_0' which typically turned out to be about -0.2. This implied that the intercept term was smaller for more developed countries. This is contrary to what is to be expected from consideration of the intercept term in [8.65]. More developed countries may be expected to be more efficient (i.e. have a higher γ) and to have more capital-intensive techniques (i.e. have a higher δ). This suggests that the intercept term should have been larger for the more developed countries and Fuchs had difficulty explaining this contradiction.

In their 1961 article, SMAC also make use of the marginal productivity of labour equation to estimate a time series equation for aggregate non-form US data. Equation [8.64] may be rearranged as

$$\frac{wL}{pQ} = (1 - \delta)^\sigma \gamma^{\sigma - 1}\left(\frac{w}{p}\right)^{1 - \sigma} \tag{8.67}$$

Assuming neutral technical progress at a constant rate g, so that the efficiency parameter may be written as $\gamma = \gamma_0 e^{gt}$, a logarithmic transformation of [8.67] yields

$$\log\left(\frac{wL}{pQ}\right) = \sigma\log(1 - \delta) + (\sigma - 1)\log\gamma_0 + (1 - \sigma)\log\left(\frac{w}{p}\right) + (\sigma - 1)gt$$

$$= (\text{const}) + (1 - \sigma)\log\left(\frac{w}{p}\right) + (\sigma - 1)gt \tag{8.68}$$

SMAC estimated [8.68] using Solow's 1909–49 data. This yielded estimates $\hat{\sigma} = 0.595$ and $\hat{g} = 0.018$ with an R^2 of 0.74. The low value obtained for $\hat{\sigma}$ was regarded as evidence against the hypothesis $\sigma = 1$ as was the relatively high R^2 since a Cobb–Douglas function implies $wL/pQ = \text{const}$. The value for g implies an annual rate of growth due to technical progress of 1.8 per cent, which was fairly close to Solow's estimate.

Estimating σ via the marginal productivity equation has the attraction that data is not required on either capital inputs or their price. However, this method does not provide estimates of the other parameters, γ and δ, in the SMAC version of the CES function. Moreover, its validity depends on the assumption that firms are price-takers so that the marginal product of labour is equated to the real wage rate. That is, an economic assumption has to be added to the technical

238

production function relationship. In addition, equation [8.64] is derived under the assumption that there are constant returns to scale. If this assumption is relaxed and the marginal productivity equations derived from the more general equation [8.24], then it is not difficult to show that the estimating equation [8.65] should include $\log Q$ as an additional explanatory variable. In fact,

$$\log\left(\frac{Q}{L}\right) = \sigma \log\left(\frac{\gamma^{\theta/v}}{v(1-\delta)}\right) + \sigma \log\left(\frac{w}{p}\right) + \frac{(1-\sigma)(1-v)}{v}\log Q$$

If $v \neq 1$, so that the above equation holds, then our analysis of specification error in Section 3.4 indicates that the regression of $\log(Q/L)$ on $\log(w/p)$ alone will yield a biased estimator of σ. Only if $\sigma = 1$, in which case $\log Q$ disappears from the equation, or if $\log(w/p)$ and $\log Q$ are uncorrelated, will this bias disappear.

A further problem concerns the exogeneity or otherwise of the real wage rate in equations [8.64] and [8.65]. Exogeneity may be a reasonable assumption at the firm level. But at any higher level of aggregation the adjustment of output and inputs is likely to have a 'feedback effect', via the labour market, on the real wage rate which will lead to simultaneous equation bias. Maddala and Kadane (1966), in fact, reversed the relationship between Q/L and w/p in equation [8.65], effectively treating w/p as the endogenous variable, and regressed $\log(w/p)$ on $\log(Q/L)$. Using the same cross-sectional data as SMAC they obtained very different results with only three of the twenty-four industries having a σ significantly different from unity.

The estimation of the other parameters of the CES function requires data on capital inputs and their price. Given such data, one method of proceeding is via equation [8.21] which equates the marginal rate of substitution to the ratio of factor prices. The logarithmic transformation of [8.21] can be rewritten as

$$\log\left(\frac{K}{L}\right) = \sigma \log\left(\frac{\delta}{1-\delta}\right) + \sigma \log\left(\frac{w}{m}\right) \qquad [8.69]$$

Provided the factor prices can be taken as exogenous, the application of OLS to [8.69] will yield consistent estimators of $\theta = (1/\sigma) - 1$ and of δ from the constant term.[14] Given such estimates, the CES function may then be written as

$$Q = \gamma Z^v \quad \text{where} \quad Z = (\delta K^{-\theta} + (1-\delta)L^{-\theta})^{-1/\theta} \qquad [8.70]$$

A set of observations for Z can then be constructed using the estimates of θ and δ and the available data on K and L. Estimates of γ and v may then be obtained by estimating the equation $\log Q = \log \gamma + v \log Z$.

After the initial investigation by SMAC a series of empirical studies of the CES function were carried out, mainly using US data – both cross-sectional and time series. Dhrymes (1965), for example, used a US interstate cross-section to estimate the elasticity of substitution for seventeen industries both by means of equation [8.65] and using a similar equation derived from the marginal productivity equation for capital

$$\log\left(\frac{Q}{K}\right) = \sigma \log\left(\frac{\gamma^{\theta}}{\delta}\right) + \sigma \log\left(\frac{m}{p}\right) \qquad [8.71]$$

The estimates of σ obtained from [8.65] and [8.71] should be similar. However, those obtained by Dhrymes using [8.65] – the SMAC method – were generally significantly less than unity, while those obtained using [8.71] were in all cases much higher. Dhrymes suggested that it was the SMAC estimator that was at fault, being downward biased because of the assumption of perfect competition in the labour market. If the labour market is imperfectly competitive then the marginal productivity of labour estimating equation [8.65] is no longer valid and should be replaced by

$$\log\left(\frac{Q}{L}\right) = \sigma \log\left(\frac{\gamma^{\theta}}{1-\delta}\right) + \sigma \log\left(\frac{w}{p}\right) + \sigma \log \phi$$

where $\phi = 1 + 1/\eta$ and η is the elasticity of supply of labour.[15] Hence if ϕ and w/p are positively correlated then, since $\sigma > 0$, the standard specification error analysis of Section 3.4 indicates that the normal estimator of σ will be downward biased.

Nerlove (1967), in surveying the results of CES studies, concluded that even slight variations in the period or concepts used tended to result in drastically different estimates of the elasticity of substitution. This is partly because, given the relatively small number of observations available, estimators of σ inevitably lack precision and are subject to considerable sampling variability. However, it is probably true that, despite the early conclusions of SMAC, investigations in general have failed to refute the Cobb–Douglas assumption of a unitary elasticity of substitution.

All the above procedures for estimating the parameters of the CES function involve the use in some form or other of the marginal productivity equations. Hence, behavioural and economic assumptions about how a firm or industry operates have to be made before the estimation can proceed. Kmenta (1967) suggested a more direct approach, considering the more general equation [8.24], the logarithmic transformation of which is

$$\log Q = \log \gamma - \left(\frac{v}{\theta}\right)\log\left[\delta K^{-\theta} + (1-\delta)L^{-\theta}\right] \qquad [8.72]$$

By taking a Taylor series expansion about $\theta = 0$, Kmenta obtains a linear approximation of [8.72]

$$\log Q = \log \gamma + v\delta \log K + v(1-\delta)\log L - \tfrac{1}{2}v\theta\delta(1-\delta)[\log(K/L)]^2 \qquad [8.73]$$

Provided θ is near zero (i.e. provided the elasticity of substitution σ is near unity) [8.73] provides a close and convenient approximation to [8.72]. Hence, estimates of γ, v, δ and θ may be obtained directly by regressing $\log Q$ on $\log K$, $\log L$ and $(\log K/L)^2$. However, there are difficulties if the estimate of θ turns out to be much different from zero (i.e. if σ is much different from unity) because, if this is the case [8.73] no longer closely approximates the CES function.

The equivalent to [8.73] for the Cobb–Douglas function is simply its logarithmic transformation

$$\log Q = \log A + \alpha \log K + \beta \log L \qquad [8.74]$$

If $\theta = 0$ and $\sigma = 1$ as it is for the Cobb–Douglas function then [8.73] reduces to the same form as [8.74]. Hence, when [8.73] is estimated, the significance of the coefficient on $(\log K/L)^2$ provides a test of whether the function is Cobb–Douglas or not. If it is Cobb–Douglas, the coefficient on $(\log K/L)^2$ should not be significant. However, if this estimated coefficient is significantly different from

240

zero (i.e. $\theta \neq 0$), although this means that the Cobb–Douglas form should be rejected, it does not necessarily imply that the function is CES. As already noted, the approximation [8.73] may not then be valid.

There is also a further problem in that the coefficient of $(\log K/L)^2$ is likely, in any case, to be small for typical values of v, θ and δ. For example, suppose $v = 1$, $\delta = 0.5$ and $\theta = 0.5$ (implying $\sigma = 0.67$). The coefficient then has a true value of -0.0625. Given the high degree of multicollinearity probable between the variables $\log K$, $\log L$ and $(\log K/L)^2$, the standard error on the estimate of this coefficient is likely to be large so that the estimate will rarely appear significantly different from zero. In other words, the 'power' of the test is small.

An example of the use of this test and of the Kmenta approximation is provided by Griliches and Ringstad (1971) using cross-sectional interfirm data for different Norwegian industries. They rearrange [8.73] as

$$\log\left(\frac{Q}{L}\right) = \log\gamma + (v-1)\log L + (v\delta)\log\left(\frac{K}{L}\right)$$
$$- \tfrac{1}{2}v\theta\delta(1-\delta)\left[\log\left(\frac{K}{L}\right)\right]^2 \qquad\qquad [8.75]$$

and, with 185 observations on the industry 'suits, coats and dresses', for example, estimate

$$\log\left(\frac{Q}{L}\right) = 1.431 + \underset{(0.025)}{0.142}\log L + \underset{(0.055)}{0.183}\log\left(\frac{K}{L}\right) + \underset{(0.044)}{0.008}\left[\log\left(\frac{K}{L}\right)\right]^2$$

Hence, we have $(\hat{v} - 1) = 0.142$, $(\hat{v}\hat{\delta}) = 0.183$ and $-0.5\hat{v}\hat{\theta}\hat{\delta}(1 - \hat{\delta}) = 0.008$. This implies $\hat{v} = 1.142$, i.e. slightly increasing returns to scale, $\hat{\delta} = 0.160$, i.e. a relatively labour-intensive production function, and $\hat{\theta} = -0.104$, i.e. an elasticity of substitution $\sigma = 1.12$. The closeness of $\hat{\theta}$ to zero suggests the Kmenta approximation to the CES function is valid. However, the coefficient on $(\log K/L)^2$ is not significantly different from zero so the Cobb–Douglas form cannot be rejected. Note, though, that as expected this coefficient is very small so that its insignificance may be due to collinearity among the explanatory variables.

8.6 Further developments

Once the assumption of a unitary elasticity of substitution, σ, implicit in the Cobb–Douglas function, had been superseded by the merely constant σ of the more general CES function, it was clear that the next stage would be the development of variable elasticity of substitution (VES) production functions. Reasons why the elasticity of substitution should vary are not hard to find. For example, σ might be expected to vary with the capital/labour ratio K/L. The greater is this ratio, i.e. the greater the capital intensity of production, the harder it is likely to be to substitute further capital for labour and the lower σ is likely to be. Alternatively, even with a constant K/L ratio, the elasticity of substitution may simply change over time if technical progress affects the ease with which factors may be substituted for each other.

241

Variable elasticity of substitution production functions were indeed developed. Early notable examples were those of Revankar (1971), who developed a model in which σ was a linear function of the capital/labour ratio, and Sato and Hoffman (1968) who presented a series of forms – one similar to Revankar's and another in which σ varied over time. However, a general form for VES functions was finally presented by Christensen, Jorgenson and Lau (1973). The problem had always been that of finding a functional form that not only allowed for a variable elasticity of substitution but was easily estimatable and could be considered a sufficiently close approximation to whatever the underlying productive process actually was. The 'transcendental logarithmic' or *translog production function* of Christensen, Jorgenson and Lau approximates the logarithm of output by a quadratic in the logarithms of the inputs

$$\log Q = \beta_0 + \beta_K \log K + \beta_L \log L + \beta_{KK}(\log K)^2$$
$$+ \beta_{LL}(\log L)^2 + \beta_{LK} \log K \log L \qquad [8.76]$$

The big advantage of [8.76] is the ease with which it may be estimated. Also, since it can be regarded as a second-order Taylor approximation to *any* production function, VES or otnerwise, it can be used to *test* whether the elasticity of substitution is, in fact, constant or not. If we set $\beta_{KK} = \beta_{LL} = -\frac{1}{2}\beta_{LK}$ in [8.76] then the equation becomes

$$\log Q = \beta_0 + \beta_K \log K + \beta_L \log L - \frac{1}{2}\beta_{LK}(\log K - \log L)^2 \qquad [8.77]$$

which is of the same form as [8.73], Kmenta's Taylor approximation to the CES function. Hence, if [8.76] is estimated, the hypothesis of a CES may be tested by checking whether the estimated coefficients of [8.76] obey the restrictions

$$\beta_{KK} = \beta_{LL} = -\frac{1}{2}\beta_{LK}$$

Griliches and Ringstad (1971), in fact, performed such a test for Norwegian manufacturing industry and found a variable elasticity of substitution (i.e. the restrictions did not hold).

The production function [8.76] also has the interesting property that the nature of the returns to scale implied is not the same for all values of the inputs. Griliches and Ringstad, in fact, found increasing returns to scale when firms were small but something very close to constant returns to scale for larger firms. The property of non-varying returns to scale is, of course, one of the limitations of the more restrictive Cobb–Douglas and CES functions.

As we noted at the beginning of Section 8.1, the production function of theory is a technical relationship defining the *maximum* output obtainable from given inputs. However, the statistical model, first introduced as equations [8.29] and [8.30], incorporates a disturbance term which is permitted to take positive or negative values. This implies that empirical studies provide estimates of production functions that yield the *average* output obtainable from given inputs rather than the maximum output. To estimate the production function of theory we need to estimate α and β, in, for example, a Cobb–Douglas function, such that

$$\log Q_i \leqslant \log Q_i^* \qquad [8.78]$$

where

$$\log Q_i^* = \log A + \alpha \log K_i + \beta \log L_i$$

for all observations in the sample. Equation [8.78] implies that actual output, Q_i, is always less than, or equal to, but never greater than, maximum output Q_i^*. One possibility is to choose α and β so as to minimise

$$\sum(\log Q_i - \log A - \alpha \log K_i - \beta \log L_i)^2$$

subject to the set of constraints given by [8.78].

Production functions estimated in this way are referred to as *frontier production functions* and, more recently, attempts have been made to estimate such functions. For example, Schmidt (1976) presents a statistical model for which the above procedure yields MLEs of α and β.

Another area of more recent development is the estimation of empirical versions of so-called *vintage* models of production. In a vintage model the neo-classical assumption of a homogeneous capital stock is relaxed and all items of capital equipment are distinguished by their vintage, i.e. the date of their construction. Machines of a later vintage are more efficient than those constructed earlier but their efficiency is determined by the state of technical knowledge *at the moment of their construction.* They do *not* benefit from any improvements in technology occurring after that date. Old machines cannot be redesigned to accommodate new technology. Vintage models represent a major step towards reality in that new technology now has to be 'embodied' in new kinds of equipment so that the rate of technical progress becomes dependent on the rate of investment in new machines. Thus a 'transmission mechanism' – the investment process – is provided whereby new ideas eventually influence the level of output. Recall that the major deficiencies of the disembodied technical progress described earlier were, firstly, that increases in efficiency were simply superimposed on the system, occurring for no clearly defined reason, and, secondly, that such improvements always affected all machines equally no matter what their age. Clearly, vintage models involve a considerable relaxation of these assumptions.

The first rigorous attempt to formulate a model of embodied technical progress was that of Solow (1960). In the Solow model technical progress proceeds at a constant rate, g, but affects only newly produced capital goods. Separate production functions exist for machines of different vintages. Thus, if Q_v is the output produced by machines of vintage v (i.e. constructed in year v), K_v is the number of machines of that vintage, and L_v is the labour employed on such machines, then (assuming a basic Cobb–Douglas form) the production function for machines of vintage v is

$$Q_v = Ae^{gv}K_v^\alpha L_v^\beta \qquad [8.79]$$

where g is the rate of technical progress. Capital stock of vintage v, K_v, is dependent on investment in machines in the year v and the rate (assumed constant) at which such machines depreciate. Total output is the sum of all outputs obtained from machines of all vintages and Solow was able to derive an aggregate production function in which the normal capital stock variable was replaced by an index of 'effective capital stock'. This index was a weighted sum of all machines with weights declining with age.

One way in which vintage models can be developed further is to relax the neo-classical assumption that capital equipment is 'malleable' and, hence, can be automatically transformed so as to be capable of operation by any number of workers. Capital stock is not generally like 'putty' and cannot be moulded to accommodate any capital/labour ratio. A machine built to be operated by two workers cannot instantaneously be transformed so that it is capable of operation by twenty workers. Models which still retain the assumption of malleability, both at the time of a machine's construction and *throughout the remainder of its life*, are commonly known as 'putty–putty' models. While Solow's original model was of this kind, most empirical models abandon such assumptions. An alternative and probably more realistic assumption is that while machines can be *designed* to accommodate any required capital/labour ratio, once they are constructed the capital/labour ratio can no longer be varied and substitution between capital and labour becomes impossible. Such 'putty–clay' models have in fact been estimated by, for example, King (1972), Ando, *et al.* (1974), Mizon (1974) and Malcomson and Prior (1979). However, because data on the output from each vintage of machine are not generally available, the estimation of such models is a complicated affair, requiring assumptions about the optimal service life of machines. We shall not attempt, therefore, to describe these models in detail here.

A vast number of production studies have been undertaken and published during the postwar era. Unfortunately, such have been the data and specification problems met with, that it is doubtful whether we are much nearer answering many of the questions posed at the beginning of this chapter. The general magnitude of elasticities of substitution, the extent of economies of scale and the quantitative importance of technical progress are not much clearer today than when Douglas undertook his pioneering studies. The principal finding of Nerlove's 1967 survey of CES functions, that even the slightest variation in the period or methods used tends to produce drastically different estimates, is probably as true today as it was a decade and a half ago. It is to be hoped that some of the later developments described above, on which future work is likely to be concentrated, will shed more light on matters.

APPENDIX
Empirical exercise

In this exercise we shall concentrate on estimating production functions from annual data for 1961–81 for the industry grouping referred to as Bricks, Pottery, Glass and Cement in the UK Standard Industrial Classification. We begin by defining the variables

Output Q = Index of production at constant factor cost
Capital K = Gross capital stock at 1975 replacement cost
Labour L = Employees in employment (average of monthly figures)

Q is taken from Table 2.4 in the *National Income and Expenditure* 1982 *Blue Book* (*BB* 1982). You will have more difficulty in constructing the series for K and L. Data on K for 1971–81 can be found in Table 11.8 of *BB* 1982 and data for 1968–70 in the 1979 and 1980 editions. However, the only pre-1968 data you will find *is at* 1970 *rather than* 1975 *replacement cost*. Fortunately, in *BB* 1973 you will also find data for 1968–71 at 1970 replacement cost. You will find that the 1975 cost figures for 1968–71 are almost exactly 2.0 times the 1970 cost figures. To obtain a consistent series at 1975 cost for the whole period the best you can do is to multiply the 1970 replacement cost figures for 1961–67 by the constant factor of 2.0. You will then have 'estimates' of gross capital stock at 1975 cost for 1961–67.

You will have even greater difficulty in constructing a consistent series for L. To begin with, to obtain annual data you will have to taken an average of monthly figures which can be found in Table 12 in the data section of the *Department of Employment Monthly Gazette* (Table 103 in earlier editions). Unfortunately, there have been a whole series of changes in the way data on L has been collected. The major change was in 1971 (you will discover what happened as you construct the series) but there were a number of minor changes too. To construct a consistent series you will therefore have to adopt similar procedures to those used in the construction of the K series. Remember to use *the latest available figures* (footnotes to the table will indicate whether data is provisional or in its final revised form). You should eventually obtain (in thousands) a series for 1961–81 something like 327.8, 331.5, 321.6, 334.3, 336.6, 330.1, 320.8, 322.4, 321.1, 313.4, 301.7, 295.9, 299.2, 293.3, 272.3, 259.3, 258.6, 259.8, 257.9, 242.5, 216.2. Don't be concerned if you fail to get *exactly* these figures.

Collecting data is not normally as easy as it was in our first two empirical exercises (Chapters 6 and 7). Usually *considerable time and tedious effort is necessary if consistent data series are to be obtained*. If this effort is not made, results will be meaningless. There is a very true saying about the feeding of data into multiple regression programs – 'rubbish in, rubbish out!'

Observe that there are two measures of capital stock referred to in *BB* 1982 – net capital stock (see Table 11.7) and gross capital stock (see Tables 11.8, 11.9 and 11.10). To understand the difference between the two measures you should read the article in *Economic Trends* for October 1975. On reading this you may feel that net capital stock would be the more appropriate measure to include in a production function. However, this is not the case and you should satisfy yourself that gross capital is preferable by next reading the article in *Economic Trends* for October 1976.

We now use the above data series to estimate the simple Cobb–Douglas production function $Q = AK^{\alpha}L^{\beta}$. Since the function is linear in the logarithms, we estimate in natural logarithms (you should again try to duplicate all results quoted)

$$\widehat{\log} Q = -2.22 + 0.812 \log K + 1.017 \log L \quad R^2 = 0.859 \quad d = 1.18 \quad [A8.1]$$
$$(1.07) \quad (0.085) \qquad (0.173)$$

Our estimates of the elasticities of output with respect to K and L are therefore $\alpha = 0.812$ and $\beta = 1.017$, both statistically highly different from zero with t-ratios of 9.55 and 5.88 respectively. The negative constant term refers to the natural logarithm of A, and taking antilogs we obtain $A = 0.109$. R^2 is relatively high but the value for the Durbin–Watson statistic suggests we have a problem (with $k' = 2$ explanatory variables and $n = 21$, $d_L = 1.13$ and $d_U = 1.54$ at the 5 per cent significance level, so we are very near the lower limit).

One problem with [A8.1] is that we have defined our input variables in stock terms whereas ideally we need measures of input flows (see equation [8.1]). For the labour variable it will help if we make use of data on average weekly hours worked, given in Table 5.4 (Table 122 of earlier editions) of the data section of the *Department of Employment Gazette*. We therefore obtain a consistent series (watch out for the change in classification in 1969) for the average hours of adult male manual workers and construct a new input variable, $H =$ hours worked, by taking the product of L and average hours worked. Since L refers to all employees, male and female, H has, in fact, been incorrectly constructed.

245

Remember, however, that α and β are elasticities and, hence, independent of the units in which we measure the input variables. H should provide a better measure of variations in labour input than does the raw L variable and the fact that the scale of H is incorrect does not matter. Replacing $\log L$ in [A8.1] by $\log H$ yields

$$\widehat{\log Q} = -\ 5.04 + 0.887 \log K + 0.893 \log H \quad R^2 = 0.878 \quad d = 1.10 \quad [A8.2]$$
$$\phantom{\widehat{\log Q} = -\ } (1.40) \quad (0.087) (0.137)$$

There is indeed an improvement in R^2 but the Durbin–Watson statistic is even lower. While we have entered the labour variable in flow form, we clearly still have a problem with the capital variable. Utilisation of capital stock will have varied during our sample period and is likely to have been particularly low during the recent 'recession years' 1980–81. One rough-and-ready way of attempting to deal with this is to calculate the proportion of the Bricks, Pottery, Glass, and Cement labour force that is actually in employment and apply these proportions to the capital stock figures for each year. This involves assuming that capital stock utilisation is very closely related to labour force utilisation. You will have to do some digging in the *Employment Gazette* for the necessary data, but if you redefine K in this way you will find some further improvement in R^2. However, the improvement is very slight and you will find little change in the d-statistic.

Another deficiency of [A8.2] is that we have made no allowance for technical progress. We can introduce disembodied neutral technical progress by including a time trend in our equation (see equation [8.53]). This simply involves introducing a variable t which takes the value 1 in 1961, 2 in 1962, 3 in 1963, etc., etc.

$$\log Q = -\ 8.57 + 0.0272t + 0.460 \log K + 1.285 \log H \qquad [A8.3]$$
$$ (2.99) \quad (0.0204) \quad (0.333) (0.324)$$
$$R^2 = 0.889 \quad d = 0.92$$

R^2 again rises but there is a further deterioration in the d-statistic. Notice that despite the rise in R^2 both the coefficients on t and $\log K$ are statistically insignificantly different from zero with t-ratios of only 1.33 and 1.38 respectively. However, this is a clear case of multicollinearity – the simple correlation between $\log K$ and t is as high as 0.980.

The coefficient on t suggests an increase in output due to technical progress of about 2.7 per cent per annum which is not unreasonable. However, our estimate of β, the elasticity of output with respect to labour inputs, exceeds unity. What does this imply about the production function and why is it contrary to our *a priori* expectations?

The sum of the output elasticities in [A8.3] is 1.745 which strongly suggests increasing returns to scale. We can, however, test the hypothesis

$$\alpha + \beta = 1$$

by applying the F-test described in Section 5.4. Imposing the restriction implies estimating equation [8.29A] with time trend added.

$$\widehat{\log}\left(\frac{Q}{H}\right) = -\ 5.04 + 0.0358t + 0.0439 \log\left(\frac{K}{H}\right)$$
$$\phantom{\widehat{\log}\left(\frac{Q}{H}\right) = -\ } (3.57) \quad (0.0258) \quad (0.0394)$$
$$R^2 = 0.947 \quad d = 0.45 \qquad\qquad [A8.4]$$

The residual sum of squares for [A8.4] is $SSR_R = 0.06385$ compared with

$SSR_U = 0.03735$

for [A8.3]. Using [5.81] this yields an F-value of 12.04. Since, with $(1,17)$ d.f., critical F-values are

$F_{0.05} = 4.45$

and

$F_{0.01} = 8.40$

we reject the hypothesis of constant returns to scale in favour of increasing returns. Notice, in passing, that despite the high R^2 in [A8.4], neither explanatory variables are significant. This is again a clear-cut case of multicollinearity – the simple correlation between K/L and t is 0.996.

Any conclusions derived from equations estimated thus far must be regarded with a healthy dose of scepticism because of the very low values obtained for the d-statistic. Although such values are as likely to be the result of deficiencies in our capital stock variable and other mis-specifications as they are of an autocorrelated disturbance, we shall take this opportunity to illustrate the Cochrane–Orcutt iterative procedure for dealing with a first-order autoregressive scheme described in Section 3.2. First, however, we shall retest the hypothesis of constant returns to scale in a rather different manner.

The function

$$Q = Ae^{gt}K^{\alpha}H^{\beta}$$

can be rewritten as

$$Q = Ae^{gt}\left(\frac{K}{H}\right)^{\alpha}H^{\alpha+\beta}$$

Hence, an alternative way of testing the hypothesis $\alpha + \beta = 1$ is to estimate this reformulated function and to apply a standard t-test to see whether the coefficient on H is significantly different from unity

$$\log Q = -8.57 + 0.0272t + 0.460\log\left(\frac{K}{H}\right) + 1.746\log H$$

$$\quad\quad (2.99)\quad (0.0204)\quad (0.333)\quad\quad\quad\quad (0.215)$$

$$R^2 = 0.889 \quad d = 0.92 \quad\quad\quad [A8.5]$$

Notice that R^2 and d in [A8.5] are identical to their values in [A8.3] – not surprisingly, since we are really estimating the same equation. However, we can now retest the null hypothesis $\alpha + \beta = 1$, by using the test statistic $(\widehat{\alpha + \beta} - 1)/s_{\widehat{\alpha+\beta}}$ which, given null, has a student's t-distribution with $n - 4 = 17$ d.f. For [A8.5], $\widehat{\alpha + \beta} = 1.746$ and $s_{\widehat{\alpha+\beta}} = 0.215$, so the value of the test statistic is 3.47. This compares with critical t-values of $t_{0.025} = 2.11$ and $t_{0.005} = 2.898$, so we again reject the hypothesis of constant returns to scale.[16]

We shall now apply the Cochrane–Orcutt procedure to equation [A8.5]. The 'first round' estimate of the Cochrane–Orcutt coefficient, obtained from the residuals of [A8.5] is $\hat{\rho} = 0.5088$. The iterative procedure leads to the sequence of values for $\hat{\rho}$ of 0.5088, 0.5771, 0.6471, 0.7166, 0.7694, 0.7998, 0.8176,.... The sequence eventually converges on the value $\hat{\rho} = 0.8824$. The estimates of the

247

production function parameters corresponding to this final $\hat{\rho}$ imply

$$\log Q = -6.43 + 0.0325t - 0.237 \log\left(\frac{K}{H}\right) + 0.918 \log H \qquad [\text{A8.6}]$$
$$(2.60)\quad (0.0192)\quad (0.332)\phantom{\log\left(\frac{K}{H}\right)}\quad (0.385)$$

The estimates of the production function parameters in [A8.6] are somewhat different from the OLS estimates of [A8.5]. However, this is not too surprising since the only property the two types of estimator have in common is the large-sample one of consistency, whereas our sample size is only 21. Provided the low d-statistic in [A8.5] was indeed the result of an autocorrelated disturbance, we can hopefully place more reliance on the estimated standard errors in [A8.6] than we could on those of earlier equations. Let us therefore retest the hypothesis of constant returns to scale using [A8.6] (it was to enable this retest to be performed that the Cochrane–Orcutt procedure was applied to [A8.5] rather than [A8.3]). We now have $\widehat{\alpha + \beta} = 0.918$ and $s_{\widehat{\alpha+\beta}} = 0.385$ so that the value of the test statistic $(\widehat{\alpha + \beta} - 1)/s_{\widehat{\alpha+\beta}}$ is -0.21 for [A8.6]. We no longer therefore reject the hypothesis of constant returns and indeed the coefficient on $\log H$ in [A8.6] suggests decreasing rather than increasing returns to scale.

Our attempt to allow for the low d-statistic in [A8.5] has therefore led us to a different conclusion regarding returns to scale. Unfortunately [A8.6] has some rather peculiar properties. The point estimates of α and β are now -0.237 and 1.155 respectively. Thus, we now not only have an output-labour elasticity in excess of unity but a negative elasticity of output with respect to capital. The mechanical application of 'standard' econometric techniques does not always yield sensible results!

At this point we should perhaps reflect that it might have been better to attempt to improve the specification of [A8.5] before adopting the Cochrane–Orcutt procedure. (The production function might not even be Cobb–Douglas.) Indeed, having worked through the empirical exercises presented so far you may begin to wonder whether there are any circumstances at all in which the application of Cochrane–Orcutt is appropriate! The answer, probably, is that the above procedure should be regarded as something of a last resort, to be embarked upon only when all attempts to find a specification for the production function that does not result in suggestions of autocorrelation have failed.

You should now attempt the estimation of Cobb–Douglas production functions for other industry groupings within the Standard Industrial Classification. Your choice will be largely determined by the capital stock data contained in Table 11.8 of BB 1982 – one obvious possibility is to estimate functions for 'total manufacturing'. You can also estimate the Kmenta approximation to the CES function (equation [8.73]) and even the more general VES form [8.76]. However, do not expect your results always to conform to a priori expectations. The main lesson of this empirical exercise is that it is the exception rather than the rule for multiple regression techniques, to yield parameter estimates that all have the expected signs and magnitudes. Data series rarely reflect precisely what we would like them to, estimating equations are very easily mis-specified and models are often invalid or at least incomplete – we have paid no attention to simultaneity problems in this exercise, yet we know that a production function should be regarded as but one equation in a simultaneous system. Much of applied econometric work consists, not of the mechanical

application of standard techniques, but of the search for appropriate specifications and the construction, wherever possible, of adequate data series.

Notes

1. We are therefore not concerned with the so-called 'fixed coefficient' models of
the productive process and will not consider either, for example, input–output or linear-programming models.
2. Notice that if the production function is homogeneous of degree unity, i.e. if
there are constant returns to scale, then by Euler's theorem we have

$$Q = L(\partial Q/\partial L) + K(\partial Q/\partial K)$$

Hence, if equations [8.6] hold we have

$$pQ = wL + mK$$

in which case $\pi = 0$ and the total payments to labour and capital just
'exhaust' the value of total output.
3. Only in the case of constant returns to scale, of course, will these shares
exactly equal the value of total output.
4. The requirement of decreasing returns to scale is, in fact, perfectly general and
does not depend on the production function having the Cobb–Douglas form.
5. Notice that this implies that the χ parameter in equation [8.17] should also
be interpreted as the elasticity of substitution.
6. See, for example, Heathfield (1971: 53–4).
7. For a more lengthy discussion, see Section 9.1 on Jorgenson's neo-classical
investment model.
8. For [8.29]

$$\frac{\partial Q_i}{\partial K_i} = A\alpha K_i^{\alpha-1} L_i^\beta \varepsilon_i = \alpha \frac{Q_i}{K_i}$$

However, if [8.29] were replaced by

$$Q_i = A K_i^\alpha L_i^\beta + \varepsilon_i$$

then we would have

$$\frac{\partial Q_i}{\partial K_i} = A\alpha K_i^{\alpha-1} L_i^\beta = \frac{\alpha(Q_i - \varepsilon_i)}{K_i}$$

9. For example, the reduced-form equation for labour inputs is

$$x_1 = \left(\frac{Q}{A}\right)^{1/r} \left(\frac{\alpha_2 p_2 \alpha_3 p_3}{\alpha_1 p_1}\right)^{\alpha_1/r} \varepsilon^{-1/r} \quad \text{where } r = \alpha_1 + \alpha_2 + \alpha_3$$

10. Since the price of capital varies little over the cross-section, Nerlove in a
second model treats it as a constant. This reduces the number of explanatory
variables in [8.51] to four again, resolving the identification problem, and
results in a virtually identical estimate of r.

11. For [8.53] we still have $\partial Q_t/\partial K_t = \alpha(Q_t/K_t)$ and $\partial Q_t/\partial L_t = \beta(Q_t/L_t)$ so that

$$\text{MRS} = \left(\frac{\beta}{\alpha}\right)\left(\frac{K_t}{L_t}\right)$$

Since for any K/L ratio the MRS remains constant, we have what is known as Hicks neutral technical progress. It is also Harrod neutral, since for any Q/K ratio, the marginal product of capital is left unchanged. For an excellent introduction to the various kinds of technical progress see Jones (1975: Chs 7 and 8).

12. This form of technical progress means that the isoquants are all shifted towards the origin, but their slopes at the point where they meet *any* ray from the origin (i.e. for any K/L ratio) remain unchanged.

13. In the sense that it leaves both the MRS between capital and labour unchanged for any K/L ratio and the marginal product of capital unchanged for any Q/K ratio.

14. The OLS estimators of the constant term and of σ are unbiased as well as consistent. However, the resultant estimators of θ and δ are merely consistent because the property of unbiasedness, unlike that of consistency, does not 'carry over'.

15. If the assumption of perfect competition in the labour market is relaxed, the marginal productivity of labour equation becomes $\partial Q/\partial L = (1 - \delta)/\gamma^\theta \times (Q/L)^{1+\theta} = \varphi(\omega/p)$.

16. The two tests are, in fact, related and will always give the same result. Notice that the critical F-values for [A8.4] are the squares of the critical t-values for [A8.5], i.e. $F_{0.05} = t_{0.025}^2$ and $F_{0.01} = t_{0.005}^2$. A similar relationship holds for the values of the two test statistics since $(3.47)^2 = 12.04$.

9 Fixed capital investment

We shall be concerned in this chapter with only one of the components of total investment – expenditure on fixed plant and equipment, and do not explicitly consider the determinants of other components such as residential construction and inventory investment.

Investment involves the production of capital goods which are not consumed within the current period and may themselves be used for the production of goods in future periods. Gross fixed investment expenditure is therefore not only an important determinant of short-run fluctuations in the level of economic activity, but is of obvious importance for the long-run growth in capacity of an economy. The fact that capital goods last for more than one period also has implications for the behaviour of firms – the future values of economic variables become as relevant as their current values.

Fixed investment is a flow which adds to the stock of fixed capital. However, the stock of capital itself depreciates with use and has to be replaced. Thus, the change in capital stock equals *net* investment which in turn equals gross investment minus physical depreciation. It is not possible to derive automatically the demand for investment goods from the demand for capital stock. A 'shortage' of capital stock could be made up either very slowly or very quickly, leading to either a low level of investment spread over a long period or a high level of investment over a much shorter period. Most theories of investment behaviour therefore contain two equally important elements:

1. A theory about what determines the optimal stock of capital, K^*.
2. Assumptions about how the actual capital stock, K, adjusts to the optimal stock.

In addition, some assumption has to be made concerning the determinants of *replacement* investment, i.e. goods produced to make good depreciation in the capital stock. It is generally assumed that some constant proportion of the initial stock wears out in each 'period' and is automatically replaced.

9.1 Theories of investment behaviour

Accelerator models

The *naive accelerator* model was first suggested by Clark (1917) as a possible explanation of the volatility of investment expenditure and is based on the assumption of a fixed capital/output ratio. Desired capital stock is assumed to bear some constant relationship to output, i.e.

$$K^* = vQ$$

where Q = output

If the further assumption is made that capital stock is always optimally adjusted in each period, so that $K_t = K_t^*$, then we obtain for net investment

$$I_t = K_t - K_{t-1} = v(Q_t - Q_{t-1}) \qquad [9.1]$$

The deficiencies of the naive accelerator model are well known. The instantaneous adjustment of K to K^* implies, firstly, an infinitely elastic supply of capital goods and, secondly, that the firm always seeks to maintain its constant capital/output ratio. A symmetrical reaction for both increases and decreases in output is assumed, whereas in practice decreases in capital stock are likely to be limited to the rate of physical depreciation. It is therefore not surprising that simple regression estimates of equation [9.1] generally yield very poor fits with estimates of v normally much smaller than suggested by observed capital/output ratios.

The *flexible accelerator*, first developed by Koyck (1954), meets the first of the above deficiencies of the 'naive' accelerator. An instantaneous adjustment of capital stock to its optimal value is no longer assumed. Instead, we have a *partial adjustment* process of the kind described in Section 5.1. In this case

$$K_t - K_{t-1} = \lambda(K_t^* - K_{t-1}) \qquad 0 < \lambda < 1 \qquad [9.2]$$

so that net investment $I_t = K_t - K_{t-1}$ is only some proportion, λ, of that necessary to achieve the optimal capital stock K_t^*. A constant capital/output ratio is still assumed to determine K_t^*

$$K_t^* = vQ_t \qquad [9.3]$$

so that substitution into [9.2] yields

$$K_t - K_{t-1} = v\lambda Q_t - \lambda K_{t-1} \qquad [9.4]$$

or

$$K_t = v\lambda Q_t + (1 - \lambda)K_{t-1} \qquad [9.4A]$$

As usual [9.4] can be represented as a distributed lag formulation with geometrically declining weights. By successive substitution

$$K_t = v[\lambda Q_t + \lambda(1 - \lambda)Q_{t-1} + \lambda(1 - \lambda)^2 Q_{t-2} \ldots] \qquad [9.5]$$

or

$$K_t - K_{t-1} = v[\lambda(Q_t - Q_{t-1}) + \lambda(1 - \lambda)(Q_{t-1} - Q_{t-2}) + \lambda(1 - \lambda)^2(Q_{t-2} - Q_{t-3})\ldots] \qquad [9.5A]$$

Thus capital stock at time t is dependent not only on current output but also on past levels of output. Such lagged effects might be the result of decision-making delays while a firm waits to make sure a rise in output is permanent before attempting to increase its capital stock, administrative delays caused maybe by the time needed to raise finance for new investment, or delivery delays depending on the elasticity of supply in the capital-goods industries. Also, rapid adjustment of K to K^* may involve high 'costs of adjustment' which can be avoided partially if the adjustment is spread over time.

Equation [9.4] above determines changes in capital stock or net investment. Gross investment equals net investment plus any depreciation in the capital stock. In the flexible accelerator model such depreciation is normally assumed to be proportional to the existing capital stock

$$D_t = \delta K_{t-1} \qquad\qquad\qquad [9.6]$$

Hence gross investment GI_t is given by

$$GI_t = K_t - K_{t-1} + \delta K_{t-1} \qquad\qquad\qquad [9.7]$$

in which case using [9.4]

$$GI_t = v\lambda Q_t + (\delta - \lambda)K_{t-1} \qquad\qquad\qquad [9.8]$$

If v and λ are to be estimated from a simple regression of GI_t on Q_t and K_{t-1}, then some prior knowledge of the depreciation parameter, δ, is necessary. It is possible to obtain an extraneous estimate of δ given data on capital stock and gross investment (see later). Alternatively, a Koyck transformation may be applied to [9.8]

$$
\begin{aligned}
GI_t - (1-\delta)GI_{t-1} &= v\lambda Q_t - (1-\delta)v\lambda Q_{t-1} + (\delta - \lambda)K_{t-1} \\
&\quad - (1-\delta)(\delta - \lambda)K_{t-2} \\
&= v\lambda Q_t - (1-\delta)v\lambda Q_{t-1} + (\delta - \lambda)GI_{t-1}
\end{aligned}
$$

since

$$GI_{t-1} = K_{t-1} - (1-\delta)K_{t-2}$$

from [9.7]. Finally, we have

$$GI_t = v\lambda Q_t - (1-\delta)v\lambda Q_{t-1} + (1-\lambda)GI_{t-1} \qquad\qquad\qquad [9.9]$$

All the parameters v, λ and δ may now be obtained directly by the estimation of [9.9]. This equation has the further advantage that its estimation does not require data on the capital stock.[1] An estimated version of this kind of equation is described at the beginning of Section 9.3.

A major criticism of the flexible accelerator model is that the optimal capital stock is determined via a constant capital/output ratio. This would follow only if we assume either a 'fixed coefficients'-type of production function with no possibility of factor substitution, or, alternatively, that the production function exhibits constant returns to scale and that relative factor prices remain unchanged so that there is no cause for a cost-minimising firm to vary its factor proportions. In either case the optimal capital stock is independent of relative prices. As we shall see later, a major advance of Jorgenson's neo-classical model of investment behaviour was that it established a link between the optimal capital stock and relative factor prices.

Financial factors influencing investment behaviour

Neither the naive nor flexible accelerator as described above pays any attention to financial factors. However, since capital equipment lasts longer than one period its purchase necessarily has implications for the future as well as the present. It is normal to regard investment projects as yielding a stream of returns over time. Of relevance to the firm is therefore the present value of this stream, (discounted by the rate of return on alternative uses of funds), and the relationship between this present value and the price of capital goods. Decisions to invest therefore depend on the stream of returns (itself dependent on product market conditions, factor costs and rates of taxation), interest rates and the price of capital goods. Such analysis is, of course, the basis for the derivation of the Keynesian marginal efficiency of capital and marginal efficiency of investment schedules.

Although Keynesian tradition was to regard interest rate effects on investment as swamped by uncertainty over future cash streams, the interest elasticity or otherwise of investment has to be a matter of empirical enquiry. The problem is that of integrating interest rate effects into the accelerator-type models. It is obviously not very satisfactory simply to add interest rate variables, in a purely *ad hoc* manner, to estimating equations derived from the accelerator models. However, it was not until Jorgenson presented his neo-classical theory of investment that a possible way of combining output effects with interest rate and other cost of capital effects became available.

It is not only the cost of funds but also the availability of funds that can be regarded as influencing investment behaviour. Optimal capital stock can be made to depend not on the level of output, as in accelerator models, but on the level of profits or expected profits. Adding a capital stock adjustment process then yields equations identical to [9.3], except that the profits variable replaces the output variable. An early example of this type of model was that of Grunfeld (1960). In this model desired capital stock is assumed to be a linear function of expected profits as proxied by the market value of the firm, V_t

$$K_t^* = \alpha + \beta V_t \tag{9.10}$$

The addition of a capital stock adjustment process

$$GI_t = \lambda(K_t^* - K_{t-1}) + \delta K_{t-1} \tag{9.11}$$

then yields

$$GI_t = \lambda\alpha + \lambda\beta V_t + (\delta - \lambda)K_{t-1} \tag{9.12}$$

It has long been argued (e.g. Meyer and Kuh 1957; Duesenberry 1958) that imperfections in the capital market plus the risks associated with increasing the ratio of debt to earnings lead to strong preferences for the internal financing of investment. This, then, is a further reason why K^* should depend on the level of profits. However, in this type of model, since it is liquidity considerations which are the main influence on investment, desired capital stock may alternatively be made explicitly dependent on liquidity-type variables such as retained earnings.

Where financial variables replace output in the stock-adjustment model, this implies that changes in these variables influence the long-run level of capital stock and, hence, the total net investment that occurs before equilibrium is restored. An alternative approach is to make the *speed of adjustment* of actual to desired stock but not the *long-run level* of stock dependent on financial factors. A major criticism of the flexible accelerator model is that the path by which K adjusts to K^* is superimposed on the model with no rigorous theoretical justification. Eisner and Strotz (1963), however, develop a model in which the firm actually *chooses* its adjustment path taking into account the adjustment costs of all possible paths. The more rapidly the firm adjusts K to K^* the larger are its marginal costs of adjustment, firstly because of rising short-run costs in the capital goods industry, and secondly because of internally rising reorganisational costs as new equipment is integrated into the existing capital stock. The firm chooses its investment path so as to maximise net present value (taking adjustment costs into consideration). If it is assumed that total revenue and adjustment costs are both quadratic functions of K, and that output prices stay constant in all future periods, then the model implies a flexible accelerator relationship identical to equation [9.2]. However, λ is now no longer constant but depends on the rate of interest (assumed constant) at which the firm can borrow or lend without limit. The higher this rate of interest the smaller is λ and hence the slower is the speed of adjustment. Notice, however, that the long-run level of capital stock is independent of the rate of interest.

Gould (1968), however, shows that Eisner and Strotz's justification of the flexible accelerator model is crucially dependent on their assumption that prices are expected to remain, and do remain, constant in all future periods. Once prices are allowed to vary, the rate of investment becomes dependent on the time path of prices even if the long-run optimal level of capital stock is unchanged. Thus if, for example, a rise in output prices is expected for some interval beginning say six months in the future, the firm will increase its level of investment immediately. This is because the rise in output price increases the marginal present value of the firm resulting from extra investment while leaving marginal adjustment costs unchanged. Under these conditions it is no longer possible rigorously to derive the flexible accelerator model.

Coen (1968) also developed a model with varying speeds of adjustment. However, in this case adjustment speed depends not on the rate of interest as in the Eisner–Strotz model but on the firm's liquidity. The adjustment parameter, λ, of the flexible accelerator model increases as the firm's cash flow (or level of internal funds) increases.

Whether optimal capital stock is dependent on output-type variables or financial factors has important implications for policy. If profits are important then company taxation becomes an important policy instrument. However, if output is the key factor then purchase taxes and other methods of influencing demand are likely to be more effective ways of influencing investment. Unfortunately, since profits and output are likely to move together over time, problems of multicollinearity are always likely to make discrimination between the two types of variables difficult.

Jorgenson's neo-classical model

Jorgenson's main contention was that the possibility of substitution between labour and capital inputs had been ignored in most investment studies, e.g. both naive and flexible accelerator models assumed a fixed capital/output ratio. Jorgenson introduces a neo-classical production function into his model, thus recognising the possibility of capital-labour substitution and giving a role to relative factor prices as well as to output levels in the determination of investment behaviour.

In the Jorgenson model the firm maximises present value (i.e. the discounted sum of future expected revenues minus expenditure on capital and labour inputs) subject to the neo-classical production function. A series of powerful and rather restrictive assumptions are then made which we may list as follows:
1. No costs are incurred in adjusting capital stock to its optimal level. In particular, the price of capital goods is unaffected by the speed with which a

firm adjusts. Such assumptions are in direct contrast to those of, for example, the Eisner–Strotz model referred to above.

2. There is perfect competition in all markets. This applies not only to the product and labour markets but also to the markets for new and *second-hand capital goods*. Perfect competition in the market for second-hand capital goods means that a firm can 'hire and fire' machines at will just as, under perfect competition, they can their labour force. The *financial* capital market is also assumed perfect so that the firm can borrow and lend without limit at a given rate of interest. Since all capital markets are perfect, the firm is indifferent between renting capital goods and borrowing the funds to buy them. This is because, under these conditions, the price of capital goods always equals the discounted value of the stream of rental charges that are incurred when one is hired.

3. There is no uncertainty and, hence, no discrepancy between the actual and expected values of variables. In particular, the firm faces known and exogenously determined present and future prices for both its inputs and its outputs.

4. The production function has the usual neo-classical properties.[2]

Capital is homogeneous and *malleable* in the sense that a given quantity of capital can, at any point in its life, be combined with varying quantities of labour in response to changes in relative factor prices.[3] Capital stock is always fully utilised and flows of capital services are proportional to the capital stock.

To obtain an intuitive understanding of the 'equilibrium conditions' in the Jorgenson model, suppose that assumptions (1), (2), (3) and (4) above hold. However, suppose for the moment that instead of maximising present value the firm simply maximises its current instantaneous flow of net revenue, R_t. Assume, also, that the firm hires its capital equipment just as it does its labour. It therefore maximises

$$R_t = p_t Q_t - w_t L_t - m_t K_t \qquad [9.13]$$

where Q_t, L_t and K_t are current flows of output, labour and capital inputs respectively, p_t is the price of output, w_t is the wage rate and m_t is the rental price of capital. R_t is maximised subject to the neo-classical production function

$$Q_t = F(K_t, L_t) \qquad [9.14]$$

The usual Lagrangian multiplier technique then yields the familiar conditions for optimality

$$\frac{\partial Q_t}{\partial K_t} = \frac{m_t}{p_t}; \qquad \frac{\partial Q_t}{\partial L_t} = \frac{w_t}{p_t} \qquad [9.15]$$

That is, the marginal products of capital and labour must equal the real rental price of capital and the real wage rate respectively. These conditions clearly must hold for the case where a firm hires or rents both factors of production. However, a firm may also purchase and sell capital stock. Since, given assumption (2) above, it is indifferent between renting and owning, the total cost of owning one unit of capital stock must be the same as the cost of renting it. The total cost of owning capital stock is composed of three elements. Firstly, there is the opportunity cost of having funds tied up in fixed capital. If the price of capital goods is q_t and the rate of interest r_t then this opportunity cost equals $r_t q_t$. Secondly, capital goods depreciate over time. Assuming a constant depreciation rate, δ, this depreciation cost equals δq_t. Finally, capital goods may change in price so the firm may incur a capital gain or loss on them equal to their change in price, $\dot{q}_t$. Jorgenson refers to the total cost of owning capital stock as the 'user cost' of capital, c_t

$$c_t = r_t q_t + \delta q_t - \dot{q}_t \qquad [9.16]$$

c_t is the implicit or 'shadow price' of capital and must under present assumptions equal m_t, the rental price of capital. Thus the equilibrium conditions [9.15] can also be written

$$\frac{\partial Q_t}{\partial K_t} = \frac{c_t}{p_t}; \qquad \frac{\partial Q_t}{\partial L_t} = \frac{w_t}{p_t} \qquad [9.17]$$

For example, if [9.14] has the Cobb–Douglas form $Q_t = A K_t^\alpha L_t^\beta$ then the equilibrium conditions become,[4]

$$\alpha \left(\frac{Q_t}{K_t} \right) = \frac{c_t}{p_t}; \qquad \beta \left(\frac{Q_t}{L_t} \right) = \frac{w_t}{p_t} \qquad [9.17A]$$

The equilibrium conditions together with the production function form a three-equation simultaneous system which determines optimal values for the three endogenous variables K_t, L_t and Q_t in terms of the exogenous relative factor prices c_t/p_t and w_t/p_t. For example, in the Cobb–Douglas case the equation for optimal capital stock is,[5]

$$K_t^* = B \left(\frac{c_t}{p_t} \right)^{-h(1-\beta)} \left(\frac{w_t}{p_t} \right)^{-h\beta}$$

where B is a function of A, α and β and $h = (1 - \alpha - \beta)^{-1}$. Since assumption (1) above implies that actual capital stock, K, is always adjusted instantaneously to its optimal level, the above equation also determines K. Thus, in the Jorgenson framework changes in capital stock and hence net investment are determined by changes in the relative factor prices c_t/p_t and w_t/p_t.

The above analysis assumes that the firm maximises instantaneous net revenue. When the firm maximises present value instead, the production function [9.14] becomes binding at all present and future moments of time. Since, to determine present value, it is necessary that the firm choose values of Q_t, L_t and K_t at all moments of time t, the maximisation of present value involves the selection of *time paths* for all the endogenous variables in the model. The solution of such a problem involves the use of a relatively advanced mathematical technique known as the 'calculus of variations'. However, it turns out that the resultant equilibrium conditions *are identical to those derived above for the case of instantaneous net revenue maximisation.*

These so-called 'myopic' decision criteria are rather surprising and need some explanation. They imply that even when the firm maximises present value it does not require information about the future time paths of prices. Optimal levels of Q_t, K_t and L_t depend only on current values and the firm behaves exactly as it would if it were an instantaneous net-revenue maximiser. The reasons for this lie in Jorgenson's restrictive assumptions. The absence of adjustment costs means that there is no reason for the firm to slow down adjustment and, hence, balance reduced adjustment costs against any profit foregone as a result of acquiring new

257

capital goods less quickly. Adjustment is always instantaneous and this is one reason why only current prices are relevant. Also, since a perfect market for second-hand capital goods means that a firm can buy and sell capital goods at will, the firm need not be concerned about being left with unwanted capital stock in the event of, for example, a fall in the demand for its product. There is no 'locking in' effect because capital goods can always be easily disposed of. Furthermore, since capital is homogeneous and perfectly malleable, the firm need not be concerned about changing techniques of production – factor proportions can be changed at will and a unit of capital today is a perfect substitute for a unit of capital tomorrow. For these reasons there is no reason why a high current rate of net revenue should be at the expense of future net revenues and, hence, maximising present value is no different to maximising instantaneous net revenue. The firm solves what is essentially a static problem taking into account only current prices and need not concern itself with intertemporal trade-offs.

The significance of Jorgenson's investment model was its attempt to create a rigorous microeconomic theory of investment based on the optimising behaviour of firms. It attempted to combine the capital-labour substitution possibilities inherent in the neo-classical theory of the firm with the concept of present value maximisation. Present value maximisation is introduced into investment theory because capital equipment, once purchased, normally has to be utilised beyond the current period. That is, there is a 'locking in' effect which makes it necessary for firms to pay attention to the possibility that current profits might be at the expense of future profits. Unfortunately, Jorgenson's assumptions eliminate the 'locking in' effect and as a result it is difficult to see why firms in his model should be concerned with present value maximisation at all.

A further major criticism of the Jorgenson model is that, because of the assumption of no adjustment costs, *it has nothing to say about investment as it is usually understood*. Investment is generally regarded as being the result of the adjustment of actual capital stock to its desired level. As noted at the beginning of this chapter, models of investment need to contain not merely a theory about the determination of optimal capital stock but an explanation of the adjustment process. In the Jorgenson model, however, the adjustment problem is assumed away – adjustment is instantaneous and investment occurs only because of *changes in the desired* (*and hence actual*) *capital stock*, brought about, as we have seen, by changes in relative factor prices. We shall see, later, that in his empirical work, Jorgenson is forced to allow for non-instantaneous adjustment by superimposing a very *ad hoc* lag structure onto his theoretical model.

Taxation and user cost
As we have noted, an important feature of the Jorgenson model is its attempt to relate investment to relative prices. The establishment of such a link makes possible, not only the study of the effect of interest rate changes and other components of user cost on investment, but also that of varying tax parameters. Suppose a firm's 'taxable income' is regarded as its total revenue minus spending on labour inputs (spending on current account) minus some proportion, v_t, of its capital (spending on capital account). That is, its spending on labour and a given percentage of its capital costs are 'allowed' against tax.[6] If the tax rate is u_t the firm therefore pays tax at an instantaneous rate equal to

$$T_t = u_t[p_tQ_t - w_tL_t - v_tc_tK_t] \qquad [9.18]$$

If the firm were to maximise its instantaneous net revenue after tax it would maximise

$$R_t - T_t = (1 - u_t)p_tQ_t - (1 - u_t)w_tL_t - (1 - u_tv_t)c_tK_t$$

subject to the production function. Hence the optimality conditions become

$$\frac{\partial Q}{\partial K_t} = \frac{(1 - u_tv_t)c_t}{(1 - u_t)p_t}; \qquad \frac{\partial Q_t}{\partial L_t} = \frac{w_t}{p_t}$$

Under the Jorgenson assumptions these optimality conditions will also hold for the firm that maximises present value. Using [9.16], the quantity

$$c'_t = \frac{(1 - u_tv_t)c_t}{1 - u_t} = \frac{(1 - u_tv_t)q_t\delta}{1 - u_t} + \frac{(1 - u_tv_t)q_tr_t}{1 - u_t} - \frac{(1 - u_tv_t)\dot{q}_t}{1 - u_t} \qquad [9.19]$$

is referred to as the 'after tax' user cost of capital. The actual expression for c'_t will depend on the precise tax regime under which a firm operates. Different proportions of the various components of capital cost may be allowed against tax. For example, if

v_t = proportion of depreciation costs 'allowable'

y_t = proportion of interest payments 'allowable' and

x_t = proportion of capital gains taxable

then the after-tax user cost becomes

$$c'_t = \frac{(1 - u_tv_t)q_t\delta}{1 - u_t} + \frac{(1 - u_ty_t)q_tr_t}{1 - u_t} - \frac{(1 - u_tx_t)\dot{q}_t}{1 - u_t} \qquad [9.20]$$

Since in the Jorgenson model, investment is dependent on user cost it can be seen to be dependent not only on r_t, q_t and δ but also on the tax parameters u_t, v_t, y_t and x_t. However, the quantitative importance of these parameters and of the relative price ratio in general is a matter of empirical investigation.

9.2   Data and estimation problems

The theoretical models of the previous chapter apply to the individual firm whereas the majority of empirical studies of investment refer to industry data or to even wider aggregates such as the whole of the manufacturing sector. It is clear that we face all the aggregation problems discussed in Chapters 6 and 8 with, even for linear estimating equations such as [9.9], sensible aggregation normally requiring independence across firms between the size of parameters and the values of the variables to which they are attached. In addition, the conceptual problems associated with the 'aggregate production function' discussed in Chapter 8 obviously carry over into aggregate investment models which make use of this concept.

However, even if an attempt is made to estimate investment equations for an individual firm, difficulties are likely to be encountered in obtaining required data series. Output, investment and capital stock are all heterogeneous quantities so that their measurement involves index number problems. We have discussed such measurement problems in Chapter 8 and merely note here that the severest problems lie with the capital stock and investment data because of the question of aggregating over different vintages.[7] Normally, such quantities are measured in money terms and deflated by the most appropriate price index that happens to be available. An additional problem with the investment data is that investment takes time. Progress payments on large 'lumpy' items of equipment are included in figures for investment expenditure although they do not represent immediate additions to a firm's capital stock.

The main problem with the output variable is that it is desired, rather than actual, output that is relevant to the investment decision. Actual output may not equal desired output because it may be constrained by the availability of capital stock. However, in practice either current values or some weighted average of past and current values are used. Use is also sometimes made of sales figures in place of output data. Uncertainty over the appropriate way of handling inventory investment means that it is unclear whether the use of sales or output is the more suitable.

As with production function studies, problems arise over the utilisation of capital stock. Capital services input is usually assumed to be proportional to capital stock. However, if K is capital stock and S the per-period flow of services per unit of stock, then the flow of services per period is KS. If S is assumed constant but really varies then, e.g. in the Jorgenson model, price ratios will be mis-specified if the user cost of capital ignores the influence of variations in S on depreciation costs.

In calculating the cost of capital services in neo-classical-type models, current values of the component variables in equations [9.16] and [9.20] will only serve if we are prepared to accept the Jorgenson assumptions and ignore any 'locking in' effects. Otherwise the costs relevant to an investment decision are those expected over the lifetime of the project. However, the precise lifetime is normally uncertain, depending on cost and market considerations as much as the physical lifetime of the project. Even if the lifetime were known there would be the problem of specifying some expectation-generating mechanism. In general, the best that can be done is to replace current values by some combination of current and lagged values.

An index of investment good prices is generally used for q_t in equations [9.16] and [9.20] while r_t is either represented by the long-term bond rate or a weighted average of this rate and the dividend/price ratio for equities. The depreciation parameter, δ, is generally assumed constant and estimated using investment data together with an initial and a terminal value for capital stock. For example, if quarterly investment data is available and capital stock data known for two moments fifty quarters apart then

$$K_t = K_{t-50}(1 - \delta)^{50} + \sum_{i=0}^{49} GI_{t-1}(1 - \delta)^i \qquad [9.21]$$

and δ may be estimated using this relationship.

A major problem in the estimation of investment equations is the specification of the appropriate lag structure. When any of the factors influencing desired capital stock change, a firm is unlikely to attempt or be able to adjust its actual capital stock immediately. There are various reasons for possible delay – both subjective and technical. A firm may wish to be sure that any increase in sales is permanent before placing orders for new capital stock. Once the decision has been made finance has to be raised and orders placed. Frequently, if the capital goods are of a particular specification, stocks are unlikely to be available and immediate delivery will not be possible. Production of capital goods will take time, the gestation period depending on the amount of spare capacity in the capital good industries. Clearly, lag structures will be complicated and may vary between individual firms. This means even greater complexity is to be expected if we deal with the investment behaviour of aggregates of firms. Moreover, the lag structure may vary over time, particularly if there is any variation in the degree of capacity utilisation in capital goods industries or in the availability of finance to firms wishing to expand.

Clearly, we must expect investment to depend not only on current but also on past values of its determining variables. Unfortunately, problems of multicollinearity place severe limits on the number of lagged values of, for example, output that can be included in estimating equations. Hence, in general, some *a priori* restrictions have to be placed on the lag structure to reduce the number of parameters that need to be estimated. The simplest example of this procedure is the 'geometric lag' described in Section 5.1 and used in the flexible accelerator model of the previous section. As seen from [9.5] this implies a geometric lag structure for the relationship between capital stock and output. A major disadvantage of this specification is that it implies maximum impact in the *current period* whereas the discussion above suggests that there may be a delay of several periods before any impact on investment is felt at all. It is possible to reformulate the flexible accelerator so that changes in capital stock in equation [9.2] depend on past rather than current deficiencies in actual capital stock.[8] Although this delays the initial impact of changes in output it still implies that the initial impact is the greatest and that successive lagged values of output are of progressively lesser importance. It is more likely, particularly for aggregates of firms, that the weights in the lag distribution will firstly increase as we move back through previous periods, then reach a peak and finally decline. A likely lag pattern is shown by the solid line in Fig. 9.1.

The increasing weights from the second to the fifth quarter, reflect the fact that while no firms react to a stimulus after one quarter, some react after two quarters, and some after three quarters, etc., etc. Evans (1969), however, suggested that the peak of the subjective or decision-making lag might occur earlier than the 'construction' lag so that the overall lag distribution would have two peaks taking the shape of an 'inverted W' as shown in the dotted line in Fig. 9.1.

As we shall see, all the lag distributions described in Section 5.1 have at various times been used in attempts to capture adequately the dynamic structure of investment equations. However, although *a priori* restrictions on the lag structure can greatly reduce the number of independent parameters that have to be estimated, the transformations involved are likely to lead to autocorrelation problems. For example, if a disturbance term is added to the geometric distributed lag formulation of [9.5] then application of the Koyck transformation results in a 'moving average' disturbance in equations [9.4] and [9.8].[9] If the original disturbance is independent, the disturbances in [9.4] and [9.8] will be autocorrelated and this, combined with the presence of the lagged variable, K_{t-1}, means that OLS will provide biased and inconsistent estimates. Similarly, we shall see in the next section that Jorgenson's use of rational lag distributions in his

9.1 Possible lag distributions for capital stock adjustments.

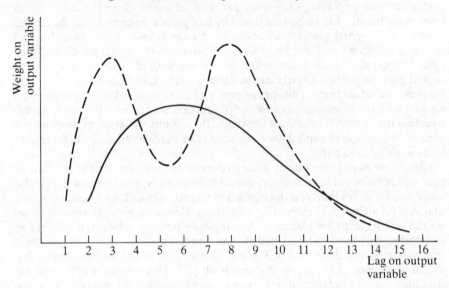

empirical work leads to estimating equations with higher-order moving average disturbance terms.

9.3   Empirical studies of investment behaviour

Accelerator models

There have been relatively few successful attempts to estimate flexible accelerator models that employ the simple geometric lag structure of Section 9.1. Consider, for example, an equation estimated by Hines and Catephores (1970). In this case equation [9.3] is replaced by

$$K_t^* = vQ_{t-n}$$

where Q_{t-n} represents the latest information on the level of output. Equation [9.9] then becomes

$$GI_t = v\lambda Q_{t-n} - (1-\delta)v\lambda Q_{t-n-1} + (1-\lambda)GI_{t-1}$$
$$= v\lambda \Delta Q_{t-n} + \delta v\lambda Q_{t-n-1} + (1-\lambda)GI_{t-1} \qquad [9.22]$$

Hines and Catephores estimate [9.22] from UK quarterly data for 1956–67. GI_t is gross fixed capital formation in manufacturing industry and Q_t an index of manufacturing output. Ordinary least squares yields for the case $n = 3$

$$GI_t = 5.2 + 2.281\Delta Q_{t-3} + 0.393Q_{t-4} + 0.810GI_{t-1} \qquad \bar{R}^2 = 0.902 \qquad [9.23]$$
$$\quad\;\; (0.998) \qquad\quad (0.235) \qquad\quad (0.094)$$

Although the fit of the equation is good, this is mainly the result of the lagged dependent variable on the right-hand side. The implied values for the underlying parameters are $\lambda = 0.19$, $v = 12$ and $\delta = 0.17$. While the value for the adjustment parameter, λ, is feasible, if a little large for quarterly data, the depreciation parameter implies that as much as 17 per cent of capital stock wears out every quarter. No comment on the value of the capital output ratio, v, is possible because output is measured in index number terms. Equation [9.23] is fairly typical of attempts to estimate standard flexible accelerator models. Estimates of underlying parameters are frequently implausible, probably because the simple geometric lag structure used is insufficiently complex to represent investment behaviour in the real world. Hines and Catephores, in fact, widen the determinants of desired capital stock to include financial variables as well as output. Their preferred equation is

$$GI_t = 15.61 + 1.696\Delta Q_{t-3} + 1.230 Q_{t-4} - 28.822 R_{t-6}$$
$$ (0.734) \phantom{\Delta Q_{t-3} + } (0.282) \phantom{Q_{t-4} - } (6.193)$$
$$- 13.559 R_{t-7} + 0.691 GI_{t-1}$$
$$ (2.877) \phantom{R_{t-7} + } (0.084)$$

$$\bar{R}^2 = 0.944 \quad [9.23A]$$

where R_t is the yield on $2\frac{1}{2}$ per cent consols – an unusual choice since firms do not borrow at this rate. However, the shape of the lag distributions are not very plausible – geometric for both output and the rate of interest with the rate of interest effect starting at its peak after six quarters.[10] Attempts to fit an alternative lag structure building up to a peak, by letting desired capital stock depend on expected output (determined by an adaptive expectations process), proved unsuccessful.

Problems of multicollinearity and lack of degress of freedom generally make necessary the use of some *a priori* restrictions on lag structure. An exception is provided by Eisner (1960) who made use of a wealth of cross-sectional data to estimate lag responses freely. The data referred to over 200 firms for 11 consecutive years 1945–55. Equation [9.5A] was replaced by the free form

$$K_t - K_{t-1} = \beta_1(Q_t - Q_{t-1}) + \beta_2(Q_{t-1} - Q_{t-2}) + \beta_3(Q_{t-2} - Q_{t-3})\dots$$

or

$$GI_t = R_t + \beta_1(Q_t - Q_{t-1}) + \beta_2(Q_{t-1} - Q_{t-2}) + \beta_3(Q_{t-2} - Q_{t-3})\dots \quad [9.24]$$

where R_t is replacement expenditure in your t.

To avoid problems of heteroscedasticity (the firms vary widely in size) Eisner deflates by capital stock in base year 1953. Thus [9.24] becomes

$$\frac{GI_t}{K_{53}} = \frac{R_t}{K_{53}} + b_1\left(\frac{Q_t - Q_{t-1}}{Q_{53}}\right) + b_2\left(\frac{Q_{t-1} - Q_{t-2}}{Q_{53}}\right) + b_3\left(\frac{Q_{t-2} - Q_{t-3}}{Q_{53}}\right)\dots$$
$$[9.25]$$

where $b_i = \beta_i(Q_{53}/K_{53})$.

The deflation procedure means that [9.25] effectively expresses the proportionate change in capital stock as a function of current and lagged proportionate changes in output. Thus, under strict accelerator assumptions the b_i should sum to unity.[11] Equation [9.25] is estimated by OLS from the cross-section with net sales used as the output variable and depreciation charges used to proxy R_t. The accelerator coefficients are significantly positive for at least four sales-change lags. However, the *ad hoc* addition of profits variables to [9.25] proves unsuccessful. The accelerator mechanism proves non-linear, being most

263

important in the faster-growing firms. This is as expected since such firms are unlikely to have experienced falling sales or great excess capacity. However, the b_i sum to 0.5 rather than unity, suggesting that only half of proportionate sales changes are reflected in investment. One possible reason for this is that firms may only react to changes in sales which they regard as 'permanent' rather than 'transitory'. In later work, Eisner (1967) develops this idea in his 'permanent income theory of investment'. For example, firms are likely to regard increases in sales for the industry as a whole as more permanent than they would increases merely in their own sales. Thus regressions for firms within industries are likely to yield lower accelerator coefficients than regressions for firms across industries. Similarly, a cross-section of industries should yield coefficients that are higher than both the previous sets. Eisner produces results that suggest that this is indeed the case.

Greenberg (1964) uses a similar data-set to Eisner but adopts the standard flexible accelerator framework [9.2] with one important generalisation. The adjustment parameter, λ, is made a function of financial factors

$$I_t = e^{\alpha + \beta F_t}[K_t^* - K_{t-1}]$$ [9.26]

where F_t represents a financial variable. The equation is transformed into natural log form.

$$\log I_t = \alpha + \beta F_t + \log K_t^* \left(1 - \frac{K_{t-1}}{K_t^*}\right)$$

$$= \alpha + \beta F_t + \log K_t^* + \log \left(1 - \frac{K_{t-1}}{K_t^*}\right)$$

or

$$\log I_t = \alpha + \beta F_t + a_1 \log K_t^* + a_2 \left(\frac{K_{t-1}}{K_t^*}\right)$$ [9.27]

since K_{t-1}/K_t^* is close to unity and where a_1 and a_2 should be unity on a strict accelerator interpretation. Data on the desired and actual capital stock are not available so data on desired and actual capacity utilisation are used instead. This accelerator formulation works well and although profits prove insignificant as the financial variable, both an index of equity prices and an index of new capital goods prices appear to influence the adjustment process. The implication is that the ability to obtain funds has an influence on the speed with which capital stock is adjusted to its optimal level although such factors do not affect the optimal level itself. The failure of the profits variable to reflect such influence may be because, in this case, the available profits data includes both retained earnings and distributed profits.

More complicated lag structures

The fact that the simple geometric lag generally provides an inadequate description of investment behaviour has led to numerous attempts to approximate the time profiles of Fig. 9.1 by alternative lag structures. The problem, as already noted, is that the general lack of degrees of freedom severely restricts the number of parameters that can freely be estimated. This is especially the case with time series data. One of the earliest attempts to tackle this problem was provided by de Leeuw (1962) who fitted an 'inverted V' distribution. That is, the weights increase linearly from zero for the current values of explanatory variables to a peak of $n/2$ for a lag of $n/2$ periods (n is assumed to be even) and then decline linearly until they become zero for a lag of n periods. For example, if the lags in $Y_t = \sum_{t=0}^{n} \beta_i X_{t-i}$ are to be given an inverted-V shape, then if $n = 6$ we have

$$Y_t = a[X_{t-1} + 2X_{t-2} + 3X_{t-3} + 2X_{t-4} + X_{t-5}] \qquad [9.28]$$

The expression in brackets can be constructed as a 'new variable' and the only parameter to be estimated is a. Notice, however, that the maximum lag length is now *assumed* to be $n - 1 = 5$ periods before estimation. Different values of n are tried and the value chosen that yields the maximum R^2. De Leeuw found that the inverted-V worked better than either geometric or rectangular lags and that not only changes in output-induced capital stock requirements influenced investment but also changes in the flow of retained earnings and changes in the industrial bond yield.

The polynomial lags discussed in Chapter 5 provide a generalisation of de Leeuw's approach. This type of lag structure was, in fact, first used (Almon 1965) specifically to try and capture the lagged response of investment to its determinants. Almon uses quarterly survey data for 1953–61 on 1,000 of the largest US manufacturing firms. Her study is of additional interest because it makes use of data on a stage prior to actual construction, i.e. the finance allocation or 'appropriation' stage. That is, factors such as output changes are held to determine the quantity of funds to be *allocated* to new capital equipment. The timing of the actual *spending* of these funds is then determined by institutional and technical factors. Thus if data on appropriations are available, it is possible to bypass the economic question of what variables are important in determining such appropriations and concentrate directly on the manner in which appropriations are converted into spending over time. That is, attention is focused on the distributed lag between appropriations and expenditure. Such an approach requires the assumption that *all* expenditures result from previous appropriations. Also, unless all appropriations are eventually spent, allowance must be made for cancellations.

Almon estimates equations of the form

$$E_t = \text{seasonal dummies} + \sum_{i=0}^{n-1} \beta_i A_{t-i} + \text{constant} \qquad [9.29]$$

where E_t and A_t are expenditures and appropriations in quarter t. The β_i are assumed determined by a fourth degree polynomial with β_{-1} and β_n 'tied down' to zero. Almon experiments with total lag lengths of $n = 6$ to $n = 12$. The criteria for deciding the optimal lag length are $\bar{R}^2$ and a requirement of close similarity of weights between the optimal lag and lags of slightly longer lengths. Negative weights are also regarded as implausible. For total manufacturing, Almon obtained an optimal lag length $n = 8$

$$E_t = \text{dummies} - 113D_t + 0.068A_t + 0.122A_{t-1} + 0.156A_{t-2} + 0.168A_{t-3}$$
$$\phantom{E_t = \text{dummies}} (48) \quad\;\; (0.023) \quad\; (0.017) \qquad (0.013) \qquad (0.021)$$
$$\phantom{E_t = \text{dummies}} + 0.157A_{t-4} + 0.127A_{t-5} + 0.084A_{t-6} + 0.037A_{t-7}$$
$$\phantom{E_t = \text{dummies}} (0.022) \qquad (0.014) \qquad (0.017) \qquad (0.022) \qquad [9.30]$$
$$R^2 = 0.92 \quad d = 1.4$$

265

D_t is a dummy variable introduced to allow for a supply constraint on expenditure resulting from heavy demand plus a steel strike in 1956. It takes the value -1 for 1955(iv)–1956(iv) and $+1$ for the period 1957(i)–1958(i) when a 'catching up' process appeared to be occurring. The sum of the weights in equation [9.30] is 0.919, whereas a value of unity would be expected if all appropriations were converted into expenditure. The difference is the result of cancellations. The lag structure is roughly similar to that illustrated in Fig. 9.1 with appropriations having little immediate effect on expenditure, a maximum impact after two, three and four quarters and then tailing-off. Similar-shaped lag distributions were obtained for fifteen industries within the total manufacturing sector with lag lengths ranging from $n = 8$ to as high as $n = 30$.

Jorgenson's empirical studies

The model used by Jorgenson for his empirical work differs from the theoretical model described earlier in a number of significant ways. For empirical implementation it is obviously necessary to give a definite form to the production function and Jorgenson adopts the simple Cobb–Douglas formulation $Q_t = AK_t^\alpha L_t^\beta$ so that the equilibrium conditions [9.17] become

$$\alpha \frac{Q_t}{K_t} = \frac{c_t}{p_t} \qquad \beta \frac{Q_t}{L_t} = \frac{w_t}{p_t} \qquad [9.31]$$

However, only the first of these conditions is now used to derive an equation for the optimal capital stock

$$K_t^* = \alpha \frac{p_t}{c_t} Q_t \qquad [9.32]$$

with Q_t treated as an exogenous variable together with p_t and c_t. However, this differs from the theoretical model in which, as we saw earlier, Q_t, K_t and L_t are all jointly determined endogenous variables. Jorgenson justifies this apparent inconsistency by suggesting an iterative decision-making process for the firm. Since instantaneous adjustment is not possible, K_t will normally differ from K_t^*. The argument is that, for given K_t, levels of output and labour input are determined by the production function and the marginal product of labour equation, i.e. the firm optimises taking its actual capital stock as given.[12] Then, once output is decided upon, the marginal product of capital equation is used to determine K_t^*, the desired capital stock, using equation [9.32]. Thus optimal capital stock now depends on *both* output and the relative price ratio.

Jorgenson also has to relax the assumption of instantaneous adjustment for his empirical work. Although instantaneous adjustment is *attempted*, it is thwarted by *unanticipated* delivery delays. In each period the firm is assumed to place orders for capital stock, IN_t, sufficient to achieve the optimal stock, K_t^*, for that period once they are delivered. Since in the previous period the firm placed sufficient orders to achieve the optimal stock, K_{t-1}^*, it follows that

$$IN_t = K_t^* - K_{t-1}^* = \Delta K_t^* \qquad [9.33]$$

If μ_j is the proportion of all orders which take j periods to be delivered, then current *net* investment *expenditure* will be a distributed lag function of current

266

and past orders and hence of changes in the desired capital stock

$$I_t = \mu_0 IN_t + \mu_1 IN_{t-1} + \mu_2 IN_{t-2} \cdots$$

$$= \sum_{j=0}^{\infty} \mu_j IN_{t-j}$$

$$= \sum_{j=0}^{\infty} \mu_j \Delta K^*_{t-j} \qquad [9.34]$$

Notice that $\sum \mu_j = 1$ provided no orders are ever cancelled. The μ_j are assumed constant which implies no change in the pattern of delivery delays no matter what the size of the orders placed. Also, if ΔK^*_t were negative, while the firm could start selling capital equipment it is more likely to start cancelling orders. Thus the lag structure in [9.34] can only be applicable for $\Delta K^*_t > 0$. Notice also that the firm is assumed always to behave as if delivery lags are non-existent despite the fact that they continually recur.

Equation [9.34] determines net investment. Replacement investment is assumed to be proportional to the beginning of period stock so that gross investment is given by

$$GI_t = \delta K_{t-1} + \mu_0 \Delta K^*_t + \mu_1 \Delta K^*_{t-1} + \mu_2 \Delta K^*_{t-2} \cdots$$

or using equation [9.32]

$$GI_t - \delta K_{t-1} = \mu_0 \alpha \Delta \left(\frac{pQ}{c} \right)_t + \mu_1 \alpha \Delta \left(\frac{pQ}{c} \right)_{t-1} + \mu_2 \alpha \Delta \left(\frac{pQ}{c} \right)_{t-2} \cdots \qquad [9.35]$$

Jorgenson approximates the infinite lag in equation [9.35] by the rational lag function described in Section 5.1

$$GI_t - \delta K_{t-1} = \mu(L) \alpha \Delta \left(\frac{pQ}{c} \right)_t \qquad [9.36]$$

where

$$\mu(L) = \frac{\gamma(L)}{w(L)} = \frac{\gamma_0 + \gamma_1 L + \gamma_2 L^2 \cdots \gamma_k L^k}{1 + w_1 L + w_2 L^2} \qquad [9.37]$$

Notice that he assumes $l = 2$ in $w(L)$ so that his investment function becomes

$$GI_t - \delta K_{t-1} = \alpha \sum_{j=0}^{k} \gamma_j L^j \Delta \left(\frac{pQ}{c} \right)_{t-j} - w_1 (GI_{t-1} - \delta K_{t-2}) - w_2 (GI_{t-2} - \delta K_{t-3}) \qquad [9.38]$$

Jorgenson decides on the value of k, i.e. the order of the polynomial $\gamma(L)$, and on the number of non-zero γ_j's by choosing that lag structure which yields the lowest estimated standard error for the regression subject to certain *a priori* restrictions. Thus, in his earliest work (1963) only γ_2 is specified as non-zero but in later work, e.g. Jorgenson and Stephenson (1967), $k = 7$ but only four consecutive γ_j's are permitted to be non-zero with the first restricted to being non-negative (this is necessary if the μ_j are to be non-negative). Jorgenson does not have quarterly data on capital stock, but given quarterly data on gross investment, plus the assumption that depreciation is a constant proportion of capital stock, it is possible, using equation [9.21] together with initial and terminal 'benchmark' values of capital stock, to estimate δ and hence the quarterly capital stock figures. This generally gives values in the range $\delta = 0.02$ to $\delta = 0.03$, i.e. a depreciation rate of 2–3 per cent per quarter.

As an example of Jorgenson's results consider the following equation based on quarterly US data covering 1949–60, for electrical machinery and equipment industries

$$GI_t = 0.00150\Delta\left(\frac{pQ}{c}\right)_{t-3} + 0.00133\Delta\left(\frac{pQ}{c}\right)_{t-4} + 0.00254\Delta\left(\frac{pQ}{c}\right)_{t-5}$$
$$ (0.00049) (0.00068) (0.00066)$$

$$+ 0.00091\Delta\left(\frac{pQ}{c}\right)_{t-6} + 0.94305(GI_{t-1} - \delta K_{t-2})$$
$$ (0.00067) (0.15902)$$

$$- 0.17353(GI_{t-2} - \delta K_{t-3}) + 0.02591 K_{t-1}$$
$$ (0.14352) (0.00310)$$

$$R^2 = 0.94 \quad \text{d.w.} = 1.956 \quad [9.39]$$

Gross investment in current prices was obtained from investment survey data and deflated by a price index for investment goods to yield GI_t. The value of output, $(pQ)_t$, was taken to be gross value added for the industry. In calculating user cost c'_t, Jorgenson assumes that firms treat all capital gains and losses as transitory so that we have from [9.20]

$$c'_t = q_t\left[\frac{(1 - u_t v_t)}{(1 - u_t)}\delta + \frac{(1 - u_t y_t)}{(1 - u_t)}r_t\right] \qquad\qquad [9.40]$$

r_t is defined as the ratio of corporate profits after tax plus net monetary interest divided by the market value of firms in the industry. u_t, the income tax rate, is the ratio of corporate tax payments to pretax corporate profits. y_t, the proportion of capital costs allowable against tax, is calculated as the ratio of net monetary interest to the total capital cost. v_t, the proportion of replacement cost allowable, is the ratio of depreciation allowance to total replacement costs. The composite variable c'_t is then calculated for each quarter using the constant value of δ obtained as described above.

The overall fit of the above equation is good and the coefficients relatively well determined. However, the lagged dependent variables on the right-hand side make the Durbin–Watson statistic unreliable. We shall return to the problem of autocorrelation later.

Notice that in equation [9.39] Jorgenson has taken the δK_{t-1} of equation [9.38] over to the right-hand side. This enables him, by including K_{t-1} as an additional explanatory variable in the estimating equation, to obtain an alternative regression estimate of the depreciation parameter δ which provides a check on the estimate obtained in the calculation of K. The regression estimate is always insignificantly different from the capital stock estimate. However, it can be shown that such tests have very low power for discriminating between alternative values of δ because the assumed value of δ is built into the capital stock series used in the regression analysis.

It is also possible to obtain an estimate of α, the elasticity of output with respect to capital input in the Cobb–Douglas production function, from equations such as [9.38]. Since, provided no orders are cancelled

$$\sum \mu_j = 1$$

we have, using [9.37]

$$\sum \mu_j = \mu(1) = \frac{\gamma(1)}{w(1)} = \frac{\sum \gamma_j}{(1 + w_1 + w_2)} = 1$$

We can now obtain an estimate of α by summing the coefficients of the $\Delta(pQ/c)$ variables in [9.38] and dividing by $1 + w_1 + w_2$. For equation [9.39] this yields

$$\hat{\alpha} = \frac{0.00150 + 0.00133 + 0.00254 + 0.00091}{1 - 0.94305 + 0.17353} = 0.02724$$

This value is clearly very low and, indeed, similar small estimates of α are obtained in all Jorgenson's investment work. Jorgenson and Stephenson suggest these low values can be attributed to a downward bias resulting from measurement error in the measurement of desired capital stock and suggest that production function parameters should not be estimated in this way until the accuracy of measurement of desired capital stock can be improved.

Jorgenson's equations can also be used to investigate the effects over time of changes in the desired capital stock. We can rewrite [9.35] as

$$GI_t - \delta K_{t-1} = \mu(L)\Delta K_t^* = \frac{\gamma(L)}{w(L)} \Delta K_t^* \qquad [9.41]$$

Since

$$\gamma(L) = \mu(L)w(L)$$

we therefore have

$$\gamma_3 L^3 + \gamma_4 L^4 + \gamma_5 L^5 + \gamma_6 L^6 = (1 + w_1 L + w_2 L^2)(\mu_0 + \mu_1 L + \mu_2 L^2 + \mu_3 L^3 \ldots) \qquad [9.42]$$

for equations like [9.39]

By comparing coefficients of the various powers of L in equation [9.42] the following equations are obtained

$$\mu_0 = \mu_1 = \mu_2 = 0$$
$$\mu_3 = \gamma_3$$
$$\mu_4 = \gamma_4 - \mu_3 w_1$$
$$\mu_5 = \gamma_5 - \mu_4 w_1 - \mu_3 w_2$$
$$\mu_6 = \gamma_6 - \mu_5 w_1 - \mu_4 w_2$$

Given estimates of the γ_j's and the w_j's it is possible to solve the above equations recursively for the μ_j's. Estimates of the γ_j's are obtained by dividing the estimated coefficients on the $\Delta(pQ/c)$ variables by the estimate $\hat{\alpha}$. For equation [9.39] the time profile of the response of net investment to a change in desired capital stock is shown in Fig. 9.2. The first non-zero μ value is μ_3 which means that a change in K^* does not affect net investment until three quarters later. Its impact is greatest after five and six quarters, falling off gradually thereafter.

Jorgenson and his associates presented, during the late 1960s, a whole series of

9.2 Lag distribution implied by equation [9.39].

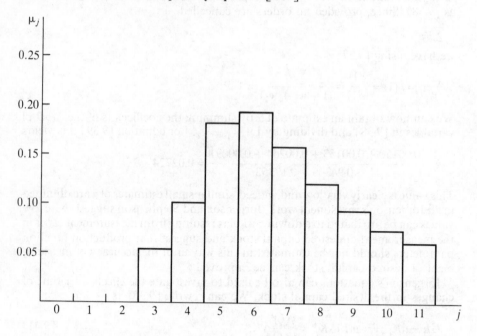

tests of their neo-classical investment model, using data for total manufacturing in the US and also sub-categories and sub-industries within this total. Some of these studies break down the investment process into stages (e.g. Jorgenson 1965), considering firstly how changes in the determinants of K^* affect investment appropriations and, secondly, how appropriations are converted into investment expenditure. Others (e.g. Jorgenson 1963; Jorgenson and Stephenson 1967) look directly at the relationship between changes in K^* and expenditure. The aim of all these studies is to investigate both the determinants of investment expenditure – in particular the long-run relative responses to changes in output and changes in relative prices, and also the time path of these responses. Time paths are invariably similar to Fig. 9.2 with a delay of several quarters before the initial impact of changes in the determinants of K^* are felt. Jorgenson and his colleagues also maintained that their work substantiated their theoretical claim that investment depends on changes in relative prices as well as output changes. Notice, however, that, *whereas Jorgenson's theoretical model refers to the individual firm, the empirical studies are based on aggregate data* sometimes referring to the total manufacturing sector. While some of Jorgenson's theoretical assumptions (e.g. capital malleability) are restrictive enough when applied at firm level they become even more highly implausible when applied to large aggregates of firms. Jorgenson's aggregate investment function is simply a 'blown up' version of his micro-function.

In several papers the ability of the Jorgenson model to explain investment is contrasted with other models. For example, Jorgenson and Siebert (1968) compare five investment models using annual time series data for 1949–63 on fifteen large US firms. In two neo-classical models, desired capital stock is given by $K_t^* = \alpha(pQ/c)_t$, in one case user cost being computed as in equation [9.20], while in the other capital gains are treated as transitory and are omitted. The other models are an 'accelerator model' in which $K_t^* = \alpha Q_t$, an 'expected profits' model with $K_t^* = \alpha V_t$ and a 'liquidity model' in which $K_t^* = \alpha L_t$. Q_t is measured as the value of output deflated by the wholesale price index for the firm's industry, V_t is the market value of the firm deflated by the GNP deflator and L_t is *retained* profits plus depreciation allowances deflated by the price of capital goods. Each of the five models is estimated in the form

$$GI_t - \delta K_{t-1} = \mu(L)\Delta K_t^* \qquad [9.43]$$

and the estimated versions are compared with a naive model in which

$$GI_t = \beta_0 + \beta_1 GI_{t-1} + \beta_2 GI_{t-2} + \beta_3 GI_{t-3} \qquad [9.44]$$

All six models are judged by the goodness of fit of the estimated equations, the statistical significance of the parameter α (without which any of the theoretical models would reduce to a regression of $GI_t - \delta K_{t-1}$ on its lagged values), and on the extent to which they are able to predict peaks and troughs in investment expenditure. The naive model performed worst followed by the liquidity model. The expected profits and accelerator model performed equally well but both were inferior to the neo-classical models. The superiority of formulations using $K_t^* = \alpha(pQ/c)_t$ over equations using $K_t^* = \alpha Q_t$ was held to confirm the important role of the relative price ratio.

If it can be established that p_t/c_t is a significant determinant of investment expenditure then it becomes possible to assess the long-run influences of each of the components making up c_t by using equation [9.40]. If desired capital stock increases, then once actual stock has increased to its new desired level, the long-run increase in investment expenditure will only be that sufficient continually to replace the extra capital stock. The long-run increase in GI_t will therefore be $\delta\Delta K_t^*$ where δ is the depreciation parameter. The long-run response to, for example, a change in the price of capital goods, is therefore $\delta(\partial K_t^*/\partial q_t)$. Since, using [9.32] and [9.40] and assuming zero capital gains.

$$\frac{\partial K_t^*}{\partial c_t} = -\alpha\left(\frac{p_t Q_t}{c_t^2}\right) \quad \text{and} \quad \frac{\partial c_t}{c q_t} = \left(\frac{1 - u_t v_t}{1 - u_t}\right)\delta + \left(\frac{1 - u_t y_t}{1 - u_t}\right)r_t$$

we have

$$\frac{\partial K_t^*}{\partial q_t} = \frac{\partial K_t^*}{\partial c_t}\frac{\partial c_t}{\partial q_t} = -\alpha\frac{p_t Q_t}{c_t^2}\left[\left(\frac{1 - u_t v_t}{1 - u_t}\right)\delta + \left(\frac{1 - u_t y_t}{1 - u_t}\right)r_t\right] \qquad [9.45]$$

Given the regression estimate of α and taking either end-period or average values for p_t, Q_t, c_t and the tax parameters, it is therefore possible to estimate the long-run response to a change in q_t. For example, Jorgenson (1963) provides long-run response values both for market variables (r_t, q_t and p_t) and for the tax parameters (u_t, v_t and y_t). A more detailed analysis of tax effects is presented by Hall and Jorgenson (1967). It is also possible to obtain long-run elasticities of investment expenditure with respect to its determinants but such attempts reveal a basic limitation of Jorgenson's model. It is easy to show, using equation [9.45], that the elasticity of K_t^* with respect to q_t is invariably -1. Similarly, as can be seen from the equilibrium relationship

$$K_t^* = \alpha\left(\frac{p_t Q_t}{c_t}\right)$$

elasticities with respect to output and the relative price ratio are both unity. These unitary elasticities are, in fact, built into the Jorgenson model and stem directly from the assumption of a Cobb–Douglas production function. It is to attempts at generalising Jorgenson's model and relaxing these restrictions that we now turn.

9.4 Criticism of Jorgenson's empirical work

A major claim of the Jorgenson studies was that they established an empirical link between investment expenditure and relative prices. However, as can be seen from equation [9.32] which arises from the Cobb–Douglas specification adopted for the production function, the long-run relative price and output elasticities are, in fact, *constrained* to equal unity and the quantity $(pQ/c)_t$ enters estimating equations as a single variable. The apparent importance of the relative price ratio $(p/c)_t$, arising from the statistical significance of the $(pQ/c)_t$ variables, could have risen solely because of the importance of the output variable Q_t. Furthermore, the use of the composite variable means that the lagged response patterns of investment with respect to output and relative price changes are constrained to be identical, whereas in practice, for reasons outlined below, it is possible that investment may respond more rapidly to output changes than to relative price changes.

These questions were first investigated by Eisner and Nadiri (1968) who relaxed the assumption of unitary relative price and output elasticities by adopting a CES instead of a Cobb–Douglas production function. This leads via the marginal productivity equation for capital to the following equation for desired capital stock

$$K^* = A\left(\frac{p}{c}\right)^\sigma Q\sigma + \frac{1-\sigma}{v} = A\left(\frac{p}{c}\right)^{E_P} Q^{E_Q} \qquad [9.46]$$

The elasticities of desired capital stock with respect to relative prices and output now differ. That with respect to relative prices, E_P, now equals σ, the elasticity of substitution, whereas that with respect to output, E_Q, equals $\sigma + (1 - \sigma)/v$ where v is the returns to scale parameter. Only if $v = 1$, and there are constant returns to scale, will E_Q now equal unity.[13]

Unlike Jorgenson, Eisner and Nadiri use a logarithmic regression equation to facilitate the estimation of elasticities. The Jorgenson relationship $GI_t - \delta K_{t-1} = \Delta K_t = \mu(L)\Delta K_t^*$ is replaced by

$$\Delta \log K_t = \mu(L)\Delta \log K_t^* \qquad [9.47]$$

Since, from [9.46], $\Delta \log K^* = E_P\Delta \log (p/c) + E_Q\Delta \log Q$, generalising, to permit different lagged response patterns to p/c and Q, leads to the estimating equation

$$\Delta \log K_t = \sum_{i=m}^{n} \left[\gamma_{pi} \Delta \log \left(\frac{p}{c}\right)_{t-i} + \gamma_{qi} \Delta \log Q_{t-i} \right] - \sum_{j=1}^{s} w_j \Delta \log K_{t-j} \qquad [9.48]$$

where

$$E_P = \frac{\sum \gamma_{pi}}{1 + \sum w_j} \quad \text{and} \quad E_Q = \frac{\sum \gamma_{qi}}{1 + \sum w_j}$$

It is now possible to test Jorgenson's maintained hypothesis that

$$E_P = E_Q = 1$$

Eisner and Nadiri use Jorgenson and Stephenson's data for total US manufacturing and experiment with the length of the lags, varying m, n and s. They found that, regardless of the lag structures used, the relative price elasticity was clearly less than unity while output elasticities were much higher and frequently in the neighbourhood of unity. It also appeared that the Jorgenson–Stephenson constraint that the first few γ coefficients should be zero was rejected by the data. Better fits were obtained when the γ_i were allowed to run from 1 to 7. Eisner and Nadiri concluded that the high output elasticity suggested the operation of a 'potent' flexible accelerator. Note that if

$$E_P = 0 \quad \text{and} \quad E_Q = 1$$

then [9.46] reduces to the accelerator model. The role of relative prices, the critical element of the neo-classical model, was not confirmed and Jorgenson's results were held to stem from the assumptions built into his model.

Jorgenson paid virtually no attention to stochastic specification in his empirical studies. A disturbance term was simply added to [9.38] and that equation estimated by OLS. However, if a disturbance, u_t, is added to the original investment equation [9.36], then transforming to obtain [9.38] results in a 'moving average disturbance' of the form

$$w(L)u_t = u_t + w_1 u_{t-1} + w_2 u_{t-2}$$

If the original disturbance is independent, then that in equation [9.38] will be autocorrelated and this combined with the presence of lagged dependent variables means that OLS estimators will be biased and inconsistent.

Bischoff (1969) considers an alternative stochastic specification. Consider a levels version of Eisner and Nadiri's equation [9.48]

$$\log K_t = k + \sum_{i=m}^{n} \left[\gamma_{pi} \log \left(\frac{p}{c}\right)_{t-i} + \gamma_{qi} \log Q_{t-i} \right] - \sum_{j=1}^{s} w_j \log K_{t-j} + v_t \qquad [9.49]$$

where the disturbance v_t follows the first-order scheme

$$v_t = \rho v_{t-1} + \varepsilon_t$$

If $\rho = 0$ then OLS estimators of [9.49] would be consistent while if $\rho = 1$ then OLS can be applied to [9.48]. However, if neither of these two special cases hold then [9.49] needs to be transformed in the usual way for dealing with first-order schemes

$$\log K_t - \rho \log K_{t-1} = k(1-\rho) + \sum_{i=m}^{n} \gamma_{pi} \left[\log\left(\frac{p}{c}\right)_{t-i} - \rho \log\left(\frac{p}{c}\right)_{t-i-1} \right]$$

$$+ \sum_{i=m}^{n} \gamma_{qi} \left[\log Q_{t-i} - \rho \log Q_{t-i-1} \right]$$

$$- \sum_{j=1}^{s} w_j [\log K_{t-j} - \rho \log K_{t-j-1}] + \varepsilon_t \qquad [9.50]$$

Using identical data to Eisner and Nadiri, an approximate MLE of ρ is obtained using the Hildreth–Lu method described in Section 3.2. That is, a grid of values for ρ is used and that value selected that minimises the residual sum of squares in [9.50]. This yields a point estimate $\rho = 0.2$ which is not, however, significantly different from 0 or 1. Bischoff therefore tests the hypotheses

$$E_P = 1 \quad \text{and} \quad E_Q = 1$$

under alternative maintained hypotheses about ρ. Only when ρ is set equal to 1 (and hence an equation in differences estimated), are the Eisner and Nadiri results confirmed. For $0 < \rho < 1$, it is not possible to reject the Jorgenson assumptions of unitary elasticities. Bischoff concludes, therefore, that Eisner and Nadiri's result is purely a consequence of their stochastic specification. However, it must be noted that Bischoff takes the process only one step further. A first-order scheme only is allowed for in [9.49], whereas if the disturbance in the original investment equation is independent, higher-order schemes should be expected.

Despite the non-rejection of the Jorgenson maintained hypothesis, point estimates of elasticities are, in fact, rather less than unity, non-rejection being the result of large standard errors. Because of this imprecision in the point estimates, Bischoff considers additional data on investment in equipment in the US private sector as a whole. For this data the hypothesis $\rho = 1$ is rejected but $\rho = 0$ is not. A levels form of the investment equation is therefore used to estimate E_P and E_Q. The hypothesis

$$E_P = 0$$

is invariably rejected while the joint hypothesis

$$E_P = E_Q = 1$$

is not rejected provided different distributed lags are permitted for the influence of relative prices and output. Again, it appears that stochastic specification has a crucial effect on the results.

The question of whether investment responds in the same manner to changes in relative prices as it does to changes in output had been the object of an earlier study of Bischoff (eventually published in revised form 1971). Along with the neo-classical model involving relative prices, it may be appropriate to introduce a 'putty–clay' hypothesis whereby capital, although capable of being moulded into any shape before installation (putty) is no longer malleable once it is installed (clay).[14] Under such conditions, while a fall in the price of capital may lead to a change in the capital/labour ratio and the use of more expensive capital equipment, this can only be brought about as the older capital equipment is

274

replaced or as total capacity is expanded. The existing capital stock is not malleable and cannot be adapted to the new desired capital/labour ratio. When output increases, however, new capital equipment is required immediately and its installation need not await the wearing out of existing equipment. The putty–clay hypothesis therefore implies that the response of investment to a change in output will be more rapid than the response to a change in relative factor prices. The studies of Bischoff suggested that this was indeed the case and that the hypothesis that both variables act with the same lag distribution should be rejected.

Simultaneity problems

A further serious criticism of empirical versions of the neo-classical model should be noted. As we have seen, most such empirical work is based on the addition of distributed lag functions either to [9.32] or first differenced versions of that equation. However, the model of the firm on which the neo-classical approach rests is that presented as equations [8.1] and [8.6]. Output, Q_t, is an endogenous variable so that its appearance on the right-hand side of equation [9.32] is likely to lead to simultaneity problems and OLS bias. Jorgenson ignores such problems, preferring to resort to the iterative arguments outlined below equation [9.32]. However, a more satisfactory econometric procedure would be to treat Q_t as endogenous and estimate the reduced-form equations which express Q_t, K_t and L_t in terms of real factor prices. Such a reduced-form equation for K_t is given below equation [9.17A].

An alternative approach, econometrically satisfactory provided output can be treated as predetermined, is to adopt the cost-minimisation model of the firm presented as equations [8.8] and [8.9]. The reduced-form equations are then factor demand functions expressing the endogenous K_t and L_t as functions of output and relative factor prices. Notice, however, that the equation obtained for desired capital stock by this approach is not generally the same as Jorgenson's. Solving equations [8.12] and [8.14] for K and L leads to

$$K^* = \left(\frac{Q}{A}\right)^{1/(\alpha+\beta)} \left(\frac{\alpha w}{\beta c}\right)^{\beta/(\alpha+\beta)} \qquad [9.51]$$

Thus the output elasticity is no longer unity (unless there are constant returns to scale), the price ratio w/c rather than p/c appears as an explanatory variable and the user cost elasticity is no longer -1.

The cost-minimisation model, of course, leads not only to an equation for optimal capital stock but also an equation for optimal labour inputs. Just as actual capital stock will not normally be at its optimal level so labour inputs will seldom be at their desired level. This suggests an interesting generalisation of the capital stock adjustment models in which the adjustment of *both* capital stock and labour inputs depends on the difference between the actual and optimal values of both factor inputs. That is

$$
\begin{aligned}
K_t - K_{t-1} &= \lambda_{11}(K_t^* - K_{t-1}) + \lambda_{12}(L_t^* - L_{t-1}) \\
L_t - L_{t-1} &= \lambda_{21}(K_t^* - K_{t-1}) + \lambda_{22}(L_t^* - L_{t-1})
\end{aligned}
\qquad [9.52]
$$

where the λ_{ij}'s are adjustment parameters. Such an approach is the basis of the inter-related factor demand model of Nadiri and Rosen (1969).

9.5 Some UK studies using the neo-classical approach

United Kingdom data has been less extensively investigated in the neo-classical context. However, Boatwright and Eaton (1972) adopt the neo-classical approach in an attempt to assess the influence of various governmental incentive schemes aimed at stimulating investment expenditure in plant and machinery in UK manufacturing industry. The major difference from Jorgenson's work is that, like Eisner and Nadiri and Bischoff, they relax the assumption of unitary elasticity of the desired capital stock with respect to relative prices. Using quarterly data for 1959(ii)–1970(iv), a variety of lag distributions are experimented with, and it appears that the relative price elasticity, and hence the elasticity of substitution, is indeed less than unity and somewhere in the range 0.4–0.7. The implied lag structures suggest a peak reaction of investment to a change in desired capital stock after nine or ten quarters. However, identical lagged responses to both output and relative price changes are assumed.

Feldstein and Flemming (1971) use a generalisation of the neo-classical model to assess the influence of investment allowances and tax incentives on fixed investment in the UK. The Jorgenson model is generalised in several ways. Firstly, the Cobb–Douglas technology is abandoned and an attempt is made to relax the assumption of capital malleability. Without malleability and a perfect capital market, decisions are no longer myopic and future values of output and the components of user cost become relevant. To allow for this, all the variables influencing desired capital stock are given a short distributed lag so that the data used reflects recent growth rates in the variables as well as current values.[15]

The user cost of capital [9.20] is rewritten as (assuming zero capital gains)

$$c' = \frac{q(r + \delta)(1 - A)}{1 - u} \qquad [9.53]$$

where A is the discounted value of tax savings due to investment allowances which follow one dollar of investment.[16] However, the possibility that firms may place different weights on the various components of c' is considered, as is the availability of internally generated funds. Thus equation [9.32] for desired capital stock becomes

$$K_t^* = \alpha \left(\frac{p}{c'}\right)_t^{+\sigma} Q_t \qquad [9.54]$$

where

$$\left(\frac{c'}{p}\right)^\dagger = \left(\frac{q}{p}\right)^{\beta_1} (r + \delta)^{\beta_2} (1 - u)^{-\beta_3} (1 - A)^{\beta_4} \theta^{\beta_5} \qquad [9.55]$$

θ in equation [9.55] is a differential tax parameter reflecting the extent to which dividends are taxed more heavily than retained earnings.[17] It reflects the availability of internally generated funds and a negative value for β_5 would imply support for the proposition, mentioned in Section 9.1, that the firm treats retained earnings as a less expensive source of funds than borrowing. This formulation means that availability of funds affects the long-term level of investment and not merely the speed of response as suggested by, for example, the Coen version of the flexible accelerator. It is also a more general approach than

276

that of models in which a simple capital stock adjustment process is combined with the assumption that desired capital stock depends on liquidity.

Feldstein and Flemming estimate their model from UK quarterly data for 1954(ii)–1967(iv). The data includes manufacturing, construction, distribution and other services. Capital stock figures are calculated in the usual manner, thus providing an estimate of the depreciation parameter. Indices of industrial production were used to construct the output variable Q_t. r_t is calculated as a weighted combination of equity and debenture yields. The relative price variable, $(p/q)_t$, is the ratio of a price index for total output to a price index for fixed assets. The tax rate, u_t, reflects income tax, profits tax and corporation tax.

Pascal lag distributions are used in estimation but the precise order of the lag structure has little effect on the estimated long-run elasticities. The various components of the relative price ratio given in equation [9.55] do, indeed, have different elasticities. When all the elasticities are constrained to be equal, investment is much less well explained and σ in equation [9.54] appears to be in the range 0.38–0.49 – similar to values obtained for US data. However, freely estimated elasticities are as high as -1.3 for the allowance variable $1 - A_t$. The tax parameter, θ, is also significant with the expected negative sign, but when freely estimated the other components of the relative price ratio have implausible elasticities often with the wrong sign. Feldstein and Flemming conclude that, because of uncertainty, short-run variations in these components contribute too little information to have an economic impact. However, the significance of the allowance and tax variables is held to confirm their important influence on investment. Constraining all elasticities to be equal as in the standard neo-classical model is therefore misleading, resulting in an understatement of the effects of investment allowances, the ignoring of the effect of retained earnings and an overstatement of the effects of the other components of user cost.

Simulations performed by Feldstein and Flemming using their investment equation show the quantitative importance of allowances and the method of taxation. It is estimated that increases in depreciation allowances accounted for 45 per cent of net capital accumulation after 1954 while, until the differential between tax rates on distributed and retained earnings was ended in 1958, it raised annual investment by some 15 per cent.

A data-based approach

In a recent paper, Bean (1981) applies to investment behaviour the data-based type of analysis first used by Davidson, *et al.* (1978) in their study of UK consumption and mentioned in Chapter 1. The procedure is to begin by estimating from quarterly data a very general form of investment equation which (in logarithmic form) is

$$\log GI_t = \alpha + \sum_{i=1}^{10} \beta_i \log GI_{t-i} + \sum_{i=1}^{10} \gamma_i \log Q_{t-i} + mt + \varepsilon_t \qquad [9.56]$$

The time trend is included to allow for any capital-augmenting technical progress and the equation also includes quarterly dummies since the data is seasonally unadjusted. Lags up to ten quarters are allowed to ensure that the full distribution is included. Data-based simplification is now performed along the lines suggested by economic theory. That is, the precise specification of the equation, including its lag structure, is determined largely by the data except that any simplifications of the equation have to be consistent with theory. Any simplifications (which involve parameter restrictions) are only adopted provided they are not rejected by the data.

The underlying theory adopted by Bean is the neo-classical model. Assuming profit maximisation, and a CES production function with constant returns to scale, optimal capital stock is given by[18]

$$K = AQC^{-\sigma} \qquad [9.57]$$

where $C = c/p$ is the real user cost of capital, σ is the elasticity of substitution and A is a constant. Consider now the basic identity

$$GI_t = \dot{K}_t + \delta K_t \qquad [9.58]$$

where $\dot{K}_t$ is the change in capital stock and δ the depreciation parameter. Suppose that in long-run equilibrium the actual and desired capital stock are equal, with K and Q growing at the same constant rate, g. From [9.58] we then have

$$\frac{GI_t}{K_t} = \frac{\dot{K}_t}{K_t} + \delta = g + \delta \qquad [9.59]$$

and hence

$$GI_t = (g + \delta)K_t = A(g + \delta)C_t^{-\sigma}Q_t = BQ_t$$

where $B = A(g + \delta)C_t^{-\sigma}$ or in log form

$$\log GI_t = \log B + \log Q_t \qquad [9.60]$$

Thus in long-run equilibrium there is a constant ratio between gross investment and output, that ratio depending, among other things, on the growth rate and the real user cost of capital. This suggests, in disequilibrium, an equation of the form

$$\Delta_4 \log GI_t = \alpha + \beta(L)\Delta_4 \log Q_t + \eta(\log GI_{t-4} - \log Q_{t-4}) \qquad [9.61]$$

where $\beta(L)$ is a polynomial in the lag operator. Thus changes in gross investment depend not only on changes in output but on the extent of previous disequilibrium in the levels of GI_t and Q_t. Notice that [9.61] is based on the notion of an equilibrium ratio between *investment* and output and not between capital stock and output as in accelerator-type models. This has the advantage of side-stepping any need for data on capital stock.

Equation [9.56] was now estimated in unrestricted form using quarterly data for 1957–75 on UK manufacturing investment. Restrictions suggested by the data were then imposed provided they were consistent with equation [9.61], suggested by theory. Such restrictions were F-tested for compatibility with the data by comparing residual sums of squares, with and without the restrictions imposed, in the manner of Section 5.4. Bean eventually selected the following model

$$\Delta_4 \log GI_t = 0.62\Delta_4 \log Q_t + 1.14\Delta_4 \log Q_{t-5} + 0.35\Delta_4(\log GI_{t-1} - \log Q_{t-6})$$
$$\quad (5.1) \qquad\qquad\qquad (7.8) \qquad\qquad\qquad (4.2)$$

$$+ 0.23\sum_{i=1}^{4}(\log GI_{t-i} - \log Q_{t-i-5}) - 1.03(\log GI_{t-4} - \log Q_{t-9})$$
$$\quad (5.1) \qquad\qquad\qquad\qquad\qquad\qquad (6.6)$$
$$\qquad\qquad\qquad\qquad\qquad\qquad\qquad\qquad\qquad [9.62]$$

A constant-term and seasonal dummies are also included in the equation. Figures in parentheses are t-statistics so the equation is well determined. Moreover, when re-estimated for 1957–77 it passes the second of the Chow tests for parameter stability described in Section 5.3. The results indicated a five-quarter lag between decisions to invest and realisation, although this may be modified by short-run effects. The final term in [9.62] represents previous disequilibria in the levels of the variables while the two previous terms are held to represent a production-smoothing response by capital goods suppliers. This is likely if capacity shortages in the capital goods industries lead to the satisfaction of demand being spread out over time. The lag distribution implied by [9.62] is shown to be bimodal with a minor peak after three quarters and a major peak after seven quarters. This is attributed to aggregation over different types of investment, not all of which involve long gestation lags.

The factor of proportionality, B in equation [9.60], depends on the real user cost of capital, so that changes in user cost are likely to appear in the disequilibrium equation [9.61] as well as changes in output. Accordingly, a Jorgenson-type after-tax user-cost variable is introduced into the equation although, following Feldstein and Flemming (1971), its components are initially included separately. Bean's final preferred equation, estimated subject to a fourth-order autoregressive process, is

$$\Delta_4 \log GI_t = 0.82\Delta_4 \log Q_t + 1.33\Delta_4 \log Q_{t-5} + 0.40\Delta_4(\log GI_{t-1} - \log Q_{t-6})$$
$$\quad (6.2) \qquad\qquad (8.6) \qquad\qquad (4.7)$$

$$+ 0.19 \sum_{i=1}^{4} (\log GI_{t-i} - \log Q_{t-i-5}) - 1.03(\log GI_{t-4} - \log Q_{t-9})$$
$$\quad (3.4) \qquad\qquad\qquad\qquad\qquad (5.1)$$

$$- 0.25\Delta_4 \log R^*_{t-5} - 0.04\Delta_4 \log C_{t-5} - 0.11(CA)_{t-6} + 0.07\Delta_4 D_t$$
$$\quad (3.4) \qquad\qquad (2.0) \qquad\qquad (2.1) \qquad\qquad (3.6)$$
$$\tag{9.63}$$

R^*_t is the nominal rate of interest so that a role is found for this variable as well as C_t, the real after-tax user cost of capital. D_t is a dummy variable introduced to capture the effects of the anticipated removal of certain investment grants at the end of 1968. CA_t is the difference between the proportion of firms with adequate capacity to meet demand and the proportion of firms suffering shortages of capacity. It reflects cumulative past errors in investment policy and has the expected negative sign. The t-values in equation [9.63] are larger than in [9.62] so the coefficients are better determined while the standard error of the residuals, in fact, falls from 0.046 to 0.036.

Bean finally compares his model with four alternative models – a flexible accelerator model, a neo-classical putty–putty model with elasticity of sub-stitution set equal not to unity but to 0.5, as suggested by the work of Boatwright and Eaton (1972), an interrelated factor demand model of the Nadiri–Rosen (1969) type, and the Hines and Catephores (1970) model described at the beginning of Section 9.3. Since the competing models cannot all be expressed as special cases of a general model (i.e. they are not 'nested' hypotheses), it is not possible to distinguish between them using the usual F-tests. However, using a technique developed by Pesaran and Deaton (1978) for testing pairs of non-nested hypotheses, Bean claims that the only serious contender to his own model is that based on the Nadiri–Rosen model. This suggested that equation [9.63] should be extended in some way to incorporate interrelated factor demands and that this would improve explanatory power.

9.6   Outstanding issues and likely areas of future research

The *ad hoc* nature of most empirical models of investment behaviour has, necessarily, meant that relatively few consistent findings have emerged from the vast quantity of econometric work carried out over the past two decades. There has been little attempt at a systematic testing of hypotheses with a given data-set such as that performed by Bean in the study considered in the last section. As a result different investigators have tended to reach different conclusions often without even considering why this should be so. However, one point on which agreement does exist is over the importance of lags in the adjustment of actual capital stock to its desired level. The lag structure is generally accepted as being normally of the pattern illustrated in Fig. 9.1, but there is unfortunately little agreement over the best procedure for estimating this structure. Moreover, the theoretical underpinning of adjustment processes is uncertain with most empirical studies simply attaching *ad hoc* adjustment processes to theoretical models.

There is still much disagreement over the factors which determine the desired capital stock. The one consistent finding is that, not surprisingly, some measure of output change is an important determinant of investment. However, there is no general agreement whether this measure should refer to sales or output or whether expected sales or expected output should replace their actual values. *A priori* considerations suggest that desired capital stock depends on expected measures of output, but there are problems in specifying how expectations are determined and deciding on the length of the period to which expected output should refer.

The major area of disagreement is over the importance of financial variables in general, over whether it is cost of capital or liquidity variables that matter, and whether financial factors are important in determining desired capital stock or merely in affecting the speed of adjustment of actual stock to its desired level. The investigation of the interest elasticity of investment has proceeded either via the *ad hoc* addition of interest rate variables to accelerator-type equations, or through the neo-classical approach in which the interest rate is one element in the user cost of capital. A rather striking difference has emerged over results obtained with UK as opposed to US data. With the exception of the studies by Hines and Catephores (1970) and Bean (1981), hardly any UK work has suggested that interest rates are an important determinant of investment. For example, Feldstein and Flemming, using the neo-classical approach, found their composite user cost variables were significant but that it was the tax allowance element, rather than any interest rate effect, that was the important factor. In contrast, US investment has generally been found to be interest-elastic. Such a finding is a feature both of studies using an *ad hoc* approach, e.g. de Leeuw (1962) and Evans (1967a), and of the neo-classical studies. Even when the Jorgenson assumption of a unit-relative price elasticity is relaxed, the real user cost variable remains generally significant.

A number of possible reasons can be advanced for the apparent lack of an interest rate effect for the UK. In the *ad hoc* 'accelerator-type' studies nominal rates of interest rather than real rates have almost invariably been used and it may be that nominal rates do not reflect adequately the expected rate of price inflation. This is especially likely to have been the case when nominal rates have been pegged by the authorities as has occurred for long periods in the UK. Also, when rates are pegged they show little variability so any relationship with investment becomes difficult to pick up. Alternatively, it may be that a more appropriate interest variable to use is some expected own rate of return on capital expenditure rather than returns on alternative (financial) assets.

The relative size of desired capital stock elasticities with respect to output and to relative prices has been the subject of much debate. It appears that estimated relative price elasticities tend to be significantly less than the unity originally imposed by Jorgenson. However, they appear to be non-zero, at least for US data. The output elasticity also tends to be estimated as slightly less than the unity suggested by the accelerator models. It also seems that the lag distributions with respect to output and relative prices do differ. As predicted by the putty–clay models the response to output changes appears generally quicker than that to relative price changes.

The neo-classical models, as originally formulated, failed to incorporate profit or liquidity variables and it is of interest that estimates of relative price elasticities tend to be smallest when account is also taken of such variables. For example, Coen (1971) found a smaller elasticity for the case where speed of adjustment depended on liquidity factors than for the case of constant adjustment lags. Similarly, Feldstein and Flemming, as we have noted, found that the availability of internally generated funds, when allowed for separately, reduced relative price effects to insignificance. Such findings suggest the cost of capital effects of the availability of funds are of considerable importance. However, whether such effects are of long-run importance or merely affect the speed of adjustment is unclear. The two mechanisms unfortunately give rise to very similar estimating equations so that it is difficult to discriminate statistically between them.

Increased attention is now being paid in empirical work to the effectiveness of tax incentives in stimulating investment. Government measures to affect the distribution of profit between retained earnings and dividends have received particular attention. Changes in the tax system can affect speeds of adjustment to the extent that such speeds are influenced by cost of capital and liquidity factors. More importantly, tax changes can influence the desired level of capital stock. For example, in the neo-classical models variations in the tax parameters u, v, and y of equation [9.20] lead to changes in the after-tax user cost of capital. Furthermore, differential tax rates between retained earnings and dividends are aimed at influencing internal cash flows and this can also affect user cost in the way suggested by Feldstein and Flemming. Finally, expectations of changes in tax parameters may have effects on the timing of investment decisions and information on the quantitative importance of such effects is of interest for counter-cyclical economic policy.

A major attempt at assessing the importance of US tax changes was that of Hall and Jorgenson (1967). However, the only mechanism by which tax changes were held to influence investment in this work was through the Jorgenson after-tax user cost variable. Since the original neo-classical model constrained the elasticity of desired capital stock with respect to user cost to be unity, it could be argued that the Jorgenson model built-in substantial tax effects by assumption. Nevertheless, the later Bischoff (1971), work with US data seemed to confirm the importance of tax variations even when the more restrictive Jorgenson assumptions were dropped. Eisner (1969), however, argued that tax changes resulted in intertemporal shifts in investment rather than long-run changes in levels which he regards as being determined primarily by output.

Increasing use is likely to be made of 'vintage models' to investigate both the putty–clay hypothesis and the effectiveness of government tax incentives. The major advantage of introducing machines of different vintages into investment models is that it makes possible the relaxation of the neo-classical assumptions of capital homogeneity and malleability. However, once it is accepted that firms cannot hire and fire machines at will, it becomes clear that in calculating such variables as user cost it is no longer sufficient simply to use the current value of its various components. Variables like Feldstein and Flemming's A in equation [9.53] have to be constructed measuring the present value of tax savings from depreciation allowances and investment credits, etc. received over the lifetime of the machine. It appears that the choice of discount rate used to obtain such present values is important in deciding which form of incentive is most effective in encouraging investment. For example, both King (1972) and Sumner (1974) found that, in evaluating the relative merits of systems of cash grants and investment allowances, choice of the relevant discount rate was a crucial factor. In a later paper, again using vintage models, Sumner (1981) comes down firmly in favour of the putty–clay model as opposed to a putty–putty model.

Another area of some dispute is that of replacement investment. In all the empirical studies considered in this chapter, replacement investment was assumed to equal a constant proportion of existing capital stock. This requires, firstly, that capital stock decay at a constant exponential rate, so that depreciation equals a constant proportion of stock in any period,[19] and, secondly, that replacement investment automatically equals depreciation.

Several investigators have questioned the assumption of exponential decay. Coen (1975) tested five alternative forms of decay in investment equations for structures and equipment in twenty-one US industries. In only one case did the standard exponential decay assumption prove the best. In most cases, exponential decay was either too rapid in the initial stages or needed to be cut off at some point. This suggests that the 'scrapping' of machines before they depreciate to zero was, not surprisingly, an important phenomenon.

Other evidence suggests that replacement investment is dependent on economic factors rather than being determined mechanistically by such a process as exponential decay. Feldstein and Foot (1971) made use of questionnaire data about the division of expenditure between expansion and replacement. They found significant roles for both changes in demand and capital costs in the determination of replacement investment and concluded that the assumption of proportional replacement was invalid. However, it can be argued that replacement investment is a strange variable to attempt to explain since its level is a residual of a firm's true decision variables which include gross investment and the rate at which machines are scrapped. For this reason, Bitros and Kelejion (1974) study the scrapping rate itself in the electric utilities industry and conclude that this, too, is dependent on economic factors.

Other investigators have questioned the distinction between expansion investment and replacement investment. For example, Helliwell and Glorieux

(1970) argue that models should attempt simply to explain gross investment and that a split between replacement investment, performed automatically and immediately, and expansion investment, occurring subject to lags, is unacceptable. It requires, at least, that equipment failures should be foreseen and replacement investment planned to coincide. During times of falling demand for capital stock standard neo-classical-type equations still suggest positive replacement investment counterbalanced by net disinvestments occurring with a distributed lag. A more acceptable model would show no new projects either for expansion *or* replacement with capital stock falling at a rate determined by physical depreciation. Even during periods when the aggregate demand for capital stock is rising this may be the result of large increases in certain sectors combined with decreases in others. Standard investment equations treat a proportion of the investment for expansion in the expanding sector as replacement for depreciating stock in the contracting sector. Such a proportion should clearly be regarded as dependent on economic factors rather than be treated as mechanistic replacement investment.

Another area in which there is much scope for further development is in the determination of appropriate lag structures for investment equations. The lag structures in the neo-classical studies are of an obviously *ad hoc* nature and the models of, for example, Eisner and Strotz and Coen in which lagged adjustment is a direct consequence of the optimising behaviour of firms seems a more promising and satisfactory approach. Such models have as yet provided few useful restrictions on the form of estimating equations. However, it is in this area, together with the further development of vintage models and a more plausible attitude to replacement investment, that much future empirical effort is likely to be made.

APPENDIX
Empirical exercise

We shall concentrate in this exercise on the influence of output changes on net investment. Because of lack of space and the difficulties of constructing after-tax user cost variables we shall not attempt to estimate neo-classical-type models. We shall use annual data because capital stock data is generally available only on an annual basis. To obtain a quarterly series would have meant constructing it using, for example, equation [9.21]. We shall concentrate on fixed investment in plant and machinery in the UK manufacturing sector and therefore begin by defining the variables

Q_t = index of industrial production for manufacturing industry
GI_t = gross fixed investment at 1975 prices in plant and machinery by manu- facturing industry
K_t = gross capital stock, at 1975 replacement cost, of plant and machinery in manufacturing industry

We begin by attempting the estimation of a flexible-accelerator model. Since a major criticism of this type of model is that it cannot be applicable during periods of declining output, we shall use annual data for 1959–78, thus omitting the recent recession years from 1979 on. Data on Q_t and GI_t are available in *ETAS* 1983 on pages 80 and 56 respectively. Data on K_t can be obtained from Table

11.10 in *BB* 1982, and earlier editions. The earlier data is at 1970 and 1963 replacement cost so, in obtaining a consistent series, you will face the same problems as in the last exercise.

Estimation of equations [9.4A] and [9.8] by OLS should yield, (attempt to duplicate them)

$$\hat{K}_t = -0.204 + 0.0283Q_t + 0.984K_{t-1} \qquad R^2 = 0.9998 \quad h = 1.30 \quad [A9.1]$$
$$\quad\;\;(0.356) \quad (0.0080) \qquad (0.010)$$

$$\hat{GI}_t = -0.094 + 0.0276Q_t - 0.00046K_{t-1} \qquad R^2 = 0.783 \quad d = 1.27 \quad [A9.2]$$
$$\quad\;\;(0.428) \quad (0.0096) \qquad (0.01201)$$

The very high R^2 in [A9.1] partly results from the presence of the lagged dependent variable on the right-hand side. Notice also that the Durbin h-statistic rather than the Durbin–Watson statistic is quoted for this equation, again because of the presence of K_{t-1}. While the hypothesis of no autocorrelation cannot be rejected for [A9.1], the d-statistic in [A9.2] is in the inconclusive range at the 5 per cent level of significance. The smallness and non-significance of K_{t-1} in [A9.2] implies, in the context of the accelerator model, that depreciation and adjustment parameters (see equation [9.8]) are approximately equal.

Comparison of [A9.1] and [A9.2] with [9.4] and [9.8] yields estimates of the parameters of the accelerator model as $\hat{\lambda} = 0.016$ for the adjustment parameter and $\hat{\delta} = 0.0155$ for the depreciation parameter. These values are highly implausible, implying, for example, that only 1.6 per cent of any discrepancy between actual and desired capital stock is made up each year. Equation [A9.1] also yields an estimate $\hat{v} = 1.75$ of the capital/output ratio. While this number has no absolute meaning since output has been measured in index number terms, it compares unfavourably with a mean K/Q ratio of about 0.5 for the twenty years of the sample period.

It is conceivable that the unsatisfactory results just obtained are a consequence of deficiencies in the capital stock series. This is probably the least reliable of the data series used. Also, as we saw in the last exercise, two measures of capital stock exist: net and gross capital stock. We have used gross capital stock because only this measure is available for plant and machinery in manufacturing industry but net capital stock would have been a more appropriate choice.[20] We can avoid having to use capital stock data by instead estimating [9.9]

$$\hat{GI}_t = 0.058 + 0.00076Q_t + 0.0194Q_{t-1} + 0.232GI_{t-1} \quad R^2 = 0.852 \quad [A9.3]$$
$$\quad\;\;(0.282) \quad (0.0127) \qquad (0.0144) \qquad (0.216) \qquad\qquad h = 6.22$$

Equation [A9.3] provides a fairly clear case of multicollinear explanatory variables. Although between them Q_t, Q_{t-1} and GI_{t-1} can explain 85.2 per cent of variations in GI_t, none of these variables have significant coefficients. t-ratios are 0.060, 1.35 and 1.07 respectively, whereas with $n - k = 16$ d.f. critical t-values are $t_{0.05} = 1.75$ and $t_{0.01} = 2.58$. Although multicollinearity alone provides no reason to doubt the specification of the model, the h-statistic suggests strong positive autocorrelation and the coefficient on Q_t is extremely small. The implied values for some of the underlying parameters are also totally unacceptable. Comparison with [9.9] yields $\hat{\lambda} = 0.768$ for the adjustment parameter – not too unreasonable for annual data, but $\hat{\delta} = 26.5$ and $\hat{v} = 0.001$. A depreciation rate of 2,650 per cent per annum hardly needs commenting on!

You should now re-estimate equations [A9.1–A9.3] with Q_{t-1} replacing Q_t and Q_{t-2} replacing Q_{t-1}. Such equations arise if we replace equation [9.3] for desired capital stock by

$$K^* = vQ_{t-1}$$

You should obtain slightly better results, although autocorrelation remains a problem and parameter estimates are only a little less implausible.

The results obtained thus far are not untypical of those normally obtained with simple accelerator models. One reason for the poor performance of such models is the geometric lag structure implied. As we have seen, an inverted V-type lag profile is often more appropriate for investment equations. One way of permitting such a profile is to use the Almon-type polynomial lags described in Section 5.1. Suppose we specify an equation

$$\hat{GI}_t = \alpha + \beta_0 \Delta Q_t + \beta_1 \Delta Q_{t-1} + \beta_2 \Delta Q_{t-2} + \beta_3 \Delta Q_{t-3} + \beta_4 \Delta Q_{t-4} + \delta K_{t-1} + \varepsilon_t$$

$$[A9.4]$$

In [A9.4], net investment depends simply on present and past output changes with the maximum lag, m, fixed as four years. Replacement investment is again given by δK_{t-1}. If we approximate the coefficients on the output change variables by a third-degree polynomial, then we have

$$\beta_i = a_0 + a_1 i + a_2 i^2 + a_3 i^3 \qquad i = 0, 1, 2, 3, 4 \qquad [A9.5]$$

Following the same procedures as in Section 5.1 we can then replace [A9.4] by

$$GI_t = \alpha + a_0 Z_{0t} + a_1 Z_{1t} + a_2 Z_{2t} + a_3 Z_{3t} + \delta K_{t-1} + \varepsilon_t \qquad [A9.6]$$

where

$$Z_{0t} = \Delta Q_t + \Delta Q_{t-1} + \Delta Q_{t-2} + \Delta Q_{t-3} + \Delta Q_{t-4}$$
$$Z_{1t} = \Delta Q_{t-1} + 2\Delta Q_{t-2} + 3\Delta Q_{t-3} + 4\Delta Q_{t-4}$$
$$Z_{2t} = \Delta Q_{t-1} + 4\Delta Q_{t-2} + 9\Delta Q_{t-3} + 16\Delta Q_{t-4}$$
$$Z_{3t} = \Delta Q_{t-1} + 8\Delta Q_{t-2} + 27\Delta Q_{t-3} + 64\Delta Q_{t-4}$$

Your program may enable you to estimate [A9.6] directly together with the implied β's, otherwise you will have to construct the Z variables for yourself. Either way you should obtain

$$\hat{GI}_t = 0.313 + 0.0125 Z_{0t} + 0.0639 Z_{1t} - 0.0322 Z_{2t} + 0.00404 Z_{3t}$$

$$(0.264) \quad (0.0153) \qquad (0.0342) \qquad (0.0212) \qquad (0.00355)$$

$$+ \ 0.0410 K_{t-1}$$

$$(0.0047) \qquad\qquad\qquad\qquad\qquad R^2 = 0.875 \quad d = 0.85 \quad [A9.7]$$

Using [A9.5], the implied values for the β's in [A9.4] are

$$\beta_0 = 0.0125, \quad \beta_1 = 0.0483, \quad \beta_2 = 0.0442, \quad \beta_3 = 0.0244 \quad \text{and} \quad \beta_4 = 0.0131$$

Thus, we do, indeed, obtain an inverted V-type lag distribution as illustrated in Fig. A9.1.

However, although R^2 has risen compared with our previous equations for GI_t, the Durbin–Watson statistic is now very low although still just in the inconclusive zone at the 5 per cent level of significance. A value of 0.041 for δ

285

A9.1 Alternative estimated lag distributions.

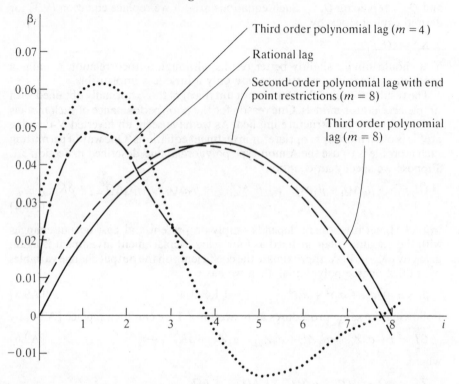

implies a depreciation rate of 4.1 per cent per annum – rather low, possibly because of the capital stock series used. One might not normally adapt the Almon lag procedure if we believed the maximum lag length was only four periods. Indeed because we have adopted a third-order polynomial, the number of parameters to be estimated in [A9.6] is only one less than for [A9.4]. It would have been almost as efficient to apply OLS to [A9.4] directly. You should try this and compare the lag distribution obtained with that implied by [A9.7].

When using Almon lags it is always important to try alternative maximum lag lengths. With $m = 8$, the equivalent equation to [A9.4] will have eleven parameters, but by again adopting a third-order polynomial we can reduce this number to six. Work out for yourself how the Z-variables are defined in this case. Estimation should then yield

$$\hat{GI}_t = 0.259 + 0.0061Z_{0t} + 0.0214Z_{1t} - 0.00299Z_{2t} + 0.0000174Z_{3t}$$
$$\quad\;\; (0.281) \quad (0.0147) \quad\;\; (0.0229) \quad\;\;\; (0.00909) \quad\;\;\; (0.000792)$$

$$+ \; 0.0369K_{t-1}$$
$$\quad (0.0063) \hspace{4.5cm} R^2 = 0.850 \quad d = 1.23 \qquad [A9.8]$$

Use equation [A9.5] to calculate the implied β's for this equation. You will again obtain an inverted V distribution which is illustrated in Fig. A9.1. The Z-variables in [A9.8] are clearly multicollinear, while the coefficient on Z_3 is very small with a t-ratio of only 0.02. This suggests we set $a_3 = 0$ thus reducing the polynomial [A9.5] to one of the second order. We can further reduce the multicollinearity problem by imposing the 'end-point restrictions' $\beta_0 = \beta_8 = 0$. An examination of the lag profile in Fig. A9.1 suggests these restrictions to be reasonable, so our estimates of the remaining β's should not be seriously biased. You should verify that with a second-order polynomial, imposing these restrictions involves not only setting $a_4 = 0$ but also $a_0 = 0$ and $a_1 = -8a_2$. This reduces equation [A9.6] to

$$GI_t = \alpha + a_2 W_t + \delta K_{t-1} + \varepsilon_t \qquad [A9.9]$$

where

$$W_t = Z_{2t} - 8Z_{1t}$$

Estimation of [A9.9] should yield

$$\hat{GI_t} = 0.323 - 0.00286 W_t + 0.0351 K_{t-1} \qquad R^2 = 0.846 \quad d = 1.23 \quad [A9.10]$$
$$\quad (0.228) \quad (0.00066) \quad\quad (0.0037)$$

The W variable is now significant with a t-ratio of 4.33. Calculate a_2 and hence the β's implied by [A9.10]. The lag profile for this equation is shown in Fig. A9.1 and is very similar to that for equation [A9.8] expect that it is 'tied down' at the end-points.[21]

Notice that the lag structures obtained for $m = 8$ are, not surprisingly, rather different from $m = 4$. This well illustrates the need to try different maximum lag lengths when using the Almon technique. You should now experiment with values of m equal to 3, 5 and 6, for example. Normally, a choice between different values of m is made on the basis of goodness-of-fit comparisons combined with a priori considerations. In this case we obtain better fits with $m = 4$ than with $m = 8$, although the Durbin–Watson statistic is lower in the former case. Also, with annual data, a lag of eight periods before the full effect of output changes is felt on capital stock seems rather long, so we should not be surprised that the shorter maximum lag works rather better.

An alternative method of obtaining the typical inverted V-type lag structure is to use the rational lags also described in Section 5.1. In this case we specify a relationship

$$GI_t - \delta K_{t-1} = \mu(L)\Delta K_t^* = \mu(L)v\Delta Q_t \qquad [A9.11]$$

where

$$\mu(L) = \mu_0 + \mu_1 L + \mu_2 L^2 + \mu_3 L^3 \ldots$$

Thus net investment is determined by a distributed lag of past changes in desired capital stock, as in Jorgenson's equation [9.36], but ΔK_t^* is here simply proportional to output change ΔQ_t. If we approximate $\mu(L)$ by

$$\mu(L) = \frac{\gamma_0 + \gamma_1 L + \gamma_2 L^2}{1 + w_1 L + w_2 L^2} \qquad [A9.12]$$

then we eventually obtain the estimating equation

$$GI_t = \gamma_0 v\Delta Q_t + \gamma_1 v\Delta Q_{t-1} + \gamma_2 v\Delta Q_{t-2} - w_1(GI_{t-1} - \delta K_{t-2})$$
$$\quad - w_2(GI_{t-2} - \delta K_{t-3}) + \delta K_{t-1} \qquad [A9.13]$$

Estimation of [A9.13] requires prior knowledge of the depreciation parameter, δ, for the construction of the variables

$$GI_{t-1} - \delta K_{t-2} \quad \text{and} \quad GI_{t-2} - \delta K_{t-3}$$

In the following equation we have used the value $\delta = 0.041$, obtained from equation [A9.7]

$$GI_t = 0.065 + 0.0320\Delta Q_t + 0.0307\Delta Q_{t-1} + 0.0174\Delta Q_{t-2}$$
$$\quad\;\; (0.220)\;\;\; (0.0163) \qquad\;\; (0.0099) \qquad\qquad (0.0133)$$

$$\quad + 0.929(GI_{t-1} - \delta K_{t-2}) - 0.477(GI_{t-2} - \delta K_{t-3}) + 0.0434K_{t-1}$$
$$\quad\;\; (0.278) \qquad\qquad\qquad (0.286) \qquad\qquad\qquad (0.0038)$$

$$R^2 = 0.930 \tag{A9.14}$$

The coefficient on K_{t-1} in [A9.14] suggests a value for the depreciation parameter, δ, of 0.043, close to the value assumed in computing values for the right-hand-side variables. We can also obtain an estimate of the capital/output ratio by using

$$\hat{v} = \frac{\gamma_0 + \gamma_1 + \gamma_2}{1 + w_1 + w_2} = \frac{0.0320 + 0.0307 + 0.0174}{1 - 0.929 + 0.477} = 0.146$$

This estimate is low compared with a mean K/Q ratio of about 0.5 for the sample period but is at least closer than the estimates obtained with, for example, the accelerator model.

We can obtain the lag structure implied by [A9.14] by rewriting [A9.12] as

$$(\mu_0 + \mu_1 L + \mu_2 L^2 + \mu_3 L^3 \ldots)(1 + w_1 L + w_2 L^2) = \gamma_0 + \gamma_1 L + \gamma_2 L^2$$

Comparing coefficients on the various powers of L yields the sequence of equations

$$\gamma_0 = \mu_0$$
$$\gamma_1 = \mu_1 + \mu_0 w_1$$
$$\gamma_2 = \mu_2 + \mu_1 w_1 + \mu_0 w_2$$
$$0 = \mu_j + \mu_{j-1}w_1 + \mu_{j-2}w_2 \qquad j = 3, 4, 5, \ldots$$

We can obtain estimates of the γ's by dividing the coefficients of the ΔQ's in [A9.14] by the above estimate of v Estimates of the w's can be obtained directly from [A9.14]

$$\hat{\gamma}_0 = 0.219, \quad \hat{\gamma}_1 = 0.210, \quad \hat{\gamma}_2 = 0.119, \quad \hat{w}_1 = -0.929 \quad \text{and} \quad \hat{w}_2 = 0.477$$

We can now solve the above equations recursively for the μ's to obtain

$$\hat{\mu}_0 = 0.219, \quad \hat{\mu}_1 = 0.413, \quad \hat{\mu}_2 = 0.399, \quad \hat{\mu}_3 = 0.173, \quad \hat{\mu}_4 = -0.029,$$
$$\hat{\mu}_5 = -0.110, \quad \hat{\mu}_6 = -0.088, \quad \hat{\mu}_7 = -0.029, \quad \hat{\mu}_8 = 0.014, \ldots$$

The lag profile implied by these values is illustrated in Fig. A9.1. Notice that to obtain the equivalents of the β's in equation [A9.4] each estimated μ has to be multiplied by $\hat{v} = 0.146$.

Figure [A9.1] well-illustrates how the lag profiles obtained will depend to a large extent on the procedures followed and assumptions made. However, our analysis does suggest that the full effect of an output change on investment is completed within three to four years with an average lag of about eighteen months. Such a conclusion is suggested both by our rational lag equation and the fact that, with polynomial lags, a better fit was obtained with $m = 4$ than with $m = 8$. Remember, though, that we have made no attempt to allow for financial variables in our equations. The exclusion of such may have influenced our findings and could be the cause of the rather dubious values we have obtained for autocorrelation statistics.

You should now attempt to estimate investment equations for industry groupings within and outside the manufacturing sector. Data can be found in the *National Income and Expenditure Blue Books*. Output data is in Table 2.4 of *BB* 1982, and data on gross capital stock (plant and machinery) in Table 11.10 of the same. Figures on gross fixed investment in plant and machinery are given in current prices only (see Table 10.8 of *BB* 1982), so you will have to deflate this series by a price index for such investment goods. You can construct such an index using the data on page 56 of *ETAS* 1983. Divide the figures for plant and machinery in current prices by those in 1975 prices.

Notes

1. Notice, however, that if K_t^* is dependent on more than one variable, e.g.

   $$K_t^* = v_1 Q_t + v_2 P_t$$

   where P_t is some price index for capital goods, then the parameters become overidentified if the corresponding version of [9.9] is estimated.
2. See Section 8.1.
3. Perfect markets for new and second-hand capital goods ensure malleability for the individual firm since, under such conditions, a firm by buying and selling machines at will can achieve any capital/labour ratio it wishes. Such an argument will not, of course, hold for the whole economy. For a fuller discussion of malleability, see Section 8.6, p. 243–244.
4. See equations [8.13].
5. Equation [8.41] is, in fact, a logarithmic version of this equation.
6. In an attempt to stimulate investment expenditure this percentage has sometimes exceeded 100 per cent.
7. That is, capital equipment constructed at different dates is therefore of different design and, almost certainly, of different efficiency.
8. Equation [9.2] might be rewritten as

   $$K_t - K_{t-1} = \lambda(K_{t-1}^* - K_{t-2})$$

   which implies

   $$K_t = v[\lambda Q_{t-1} + \lambda(1 - \lambda)Q_{t-2} + \lambda(1 - \lambda)^2 Q_{t-3}, \ldots,]$$

9. That is, if a disturbance, ε_t, is added to [9.5], then application of the Koyck transformation yields [9.4A] as

   $$K_t = v\lambda Q_t + (1 - \lambda)K_{t-1} + \varepsilon_t - (1 - \lambda)\varepsilon_{t-1}$$

Notice, however, that if the disturbance simply appears in [9.2] instead, then there are no autocorrelation problems.

10. Overidentification means it is not possible to obtain unique estimates of v_1, v_2, λ, and δ from [9.23A] (see note 1).

11. If

$$K_t = vQ_t \quad \text{and} \quad I_t = v(Q_t - Q_{t-1})$$

then

$$\frac{I_t}{K_t} = \frac{Q_t - Q_{t-1}}{Q_t}$$

12. Given K_t, the equations

$$Q_t = AK_t^\alpha L_t^\beta \quad \text{and} \quad \beta\left(\frac{Q_t}{L_t}\right) = \frac{w_t}{p_t}$$

can be solved for Q_t and L_t if w_t/p_t is determined exogenously.

13. The special case of [9.46] which occurs when $v = 1$ can be obtained on rearrangement of the first of equations [8.20]. In this case

$$A = (\delta/\gamma^\theta)^\sigma.$$

Equation [9.46] itself is obtained using the general CES function [8.24].

14. See also Section 8.6.

15. Thus current output Q_t is replaced by

$$(1 + g^*)^a (1 + g_t)^{a_0} (1 + g_{t-1})^{a_1} \dots (1 + g_{t-m})^{a_m} Q_t,$$

where g^* is the expected long-run growth rate and g_t is the actual growth rate in quarter t. The implication is that the output level to which the firm adjusts K, reflects recent growth rates as well as current output.

16. Equation [9.53] may be obtained from [9.20] by setting $\dot{q}_t = 0$, letting $v = w$ and writing

$$A = uv = uw.$$

17. θ is, in fact, defined as

$$\theta = (1 - t_y)(1 + t_d - t_y - t_u)^{-1}$$

where t_y is the standard rate of income tax and t_d and t_u are the tax rates on distributed and undistributed profits respectively.

18. Equation [9.57] can be derived by rearrangement of the first equation in [8.20]. The constant $A = (\delta/\gamma\theta)^\sigma$

19. Constant exponential decay implies that

$$K_t = (1 - \delta)K_{t-1}$$

or

$$K_t = (1 - \delta)^i K_{t-i}$$

If decay is non-exponential, then for depreciation to equal a constant proportion of capital stock requires the implausible assumption that the age structure of capital stock should remain constant over time (see, for example, Nickell 1978: Ch. 7).

20. The difference between the two measures is that, whereas the gross capital stock data are constructed by assuming that the full original value of an item of equipment remains in stock throughout its service life, for net capital stock its original value is deemed to decline linearly over its service life. Although service lives are assumed to differ for different kinds of equipment, it should be clear that the assumption of exponential depreciation is better suited to the net than the gross capital stock concept.
21. Tie down the lag distribution for [A9.7] and see what happens.

10 The demand for money

Empirical interest in demand for money functions arises because the stability and interest elasticity of such functions are of crucial importance for the relative effectiveness of monetary and fiscal policy. The smaller is the interest elasticity of the demand for money the greater are the sizes of monetary multipliers relative to fiscal multipliers. Monetarists also claim that monetary multipliers are far more stable than fiscal multipliers. That is, it is much easier to predict the effect on aggregate money income of a given increase in the money supply than of a given increase in government expenditure. A necessary condition for a stable money multiplier is a stable demand for money function. An unstable (shifting) demand for money function would make it impossible to predict the effect on interest rates and, hence, on aggregate expenditure, of a given increase in the money supply. Notice, however, that for a stable money multiplier, a stable relationship between interest rates and aggregate expenditure is also necessary although we are not concerned with such relationships here.

It is important, at this point, to consider in detail what is meant by a 'stable' demand for money function. Suppose the function is given by

$$M_D = \alpha + \beta R + \gamma Y + \varepsilon \qquad [10.1]$$

where M_D, R and Y are suitably defined measures of the 'real demand for money', 'the rate of interest' and 'real income' – we shall consider the question of appropriate measures and definitions later. ε is a disturbance with zero mean and constant variance. Stability in the function [10.1] implies that given values of R and Y always result in the same, or a least very similar, values for M_D, the demand for money. This requires, firstly, that the 'parameters' α, β, and γ should remain constant over time. It also requires that the variance of the disturbance ε should be small. Otherwise, large changes in ε could lead to large changes in M_D even for constant values of R and Y. Note that this second requirement implies that no other variables apart from R and Y have important influences on the demand for money. If no other variables are specifically included in [10.1] then their influence must be represented by the disturbance. But since the variance of ε is small this rules out the possibility of other variables seriously affecting the demand for money. Of course, if a third variable (maybe the expected rate of price change) were important in the determination of M_D, then it is possible that a stable relationship might exist between M_D, R, Y and this third variable. However, when we refer to a stable demand for money function, we normally mean a stable relationship between just the demand for money, some 'scale' variable such as income, and some rate of interest variable. The importance of a third variable would rule out a stable relationship in this sense.

Empirically, two findings are necessary if it is to be maintained that a stable demand for money function has been found. Firstly, the constancy of α, β and γ over time requires that versions of [10.1] estimated over different time periods should yield non-significantly different estimates of these parameters. Secondly, a low variance for ε should be reflected in small residuals from fitted equations and, hence, high values for the coefficient of multiple determination.[1] If these conditions are met, then equations such as [10.1] should yield accurate predictions for the demand for money. Alternatively, the forecasting performance of such equations can be assessed directly by using them to predict the demand for money over data periods not available when the equations were estimated.

10.1 Alternative specifications of the demand for money function

The Keynesian view of the demand for money function split the demand for real balances into two parts – a demand for transactionary and precautionary balances, assumed to be proportional to the level of real income, Y, and a demand for speculative balances assumed to vary inversely with the rate of interest, R. However, it was always clear that such a split was little more than a convenient simplification. Later, for example, Baumol (1952) and Tobin (1956) suggested that the transactionary demand for money may also depend on, at least, short-run interest rates since firms can earn interest by holding transactions balances in the form of short-term liquid assets other than money. Their 'inventory–theoretic' approach leads to the following demand function for transactionary balances

$$\frac{M_{DT}}{P} = \frac{1}{2}\sqrt{\frac{2bY}{R}} \qquad [10.2]$$

where M_{DT} is the demand for nominal transactionary balances, P is the price level and b is a 'brokerage' fee payable every time a firm converts short-term interest-bearing assets into cash. Notice that equation [10.2] implies that transactionary demand is negatively related to the interest rate with an elasticity of -0.5 and positively related to real income with an elasticity of only $+0.5$. This implied income elasticity contrasted with the proportional relationships previously suggested. It has the important policy implication that a given increase in the money supply might have a more than proportionate rather than a proportionate effect on money income. When the income elasticity is less than unity, there are said to be '*economies of scale*' in the holding of money since a proportionate change in income requires a less than proportionate change in money balances to sustain it. Equation [10.2] also suggests that another variable 'the brokerage fee' may be of relevance in the determination of transactionary demand.[2]

The possibility that the demand for transactionary as well as speculative balances might be interest-elastic, plus the fact that with most data sources it is virtually impossible to distinguish one type of balance from the other, meant that demand for money functions began to be formulated simply as

$$\frac{M_D}{P} = AR^\beta Y^\gamma \qquad [10.3]$$

where M_D is now the *total* demand for nominal balances.

The logarithmic formulation was adopted not from any theoretical considerations but simply for convenience since it is then possible to interpret β and γ as elasticities. Some empirical studies (for example, Bronfenbrenner and Mayer

1960) restricted γ to unity, implying a demand for real balances that is exactly proportional to the level of real income at a given interest rate.[3] Such a formulation, of course, ruled out the possibility of 'economies of scale' in moneyholding as implied by the Baumol–Tobin approach, while the omission of any variable representing the brokerage fee provides a possible reason for instability arising in a relationship such as [10.3].

The Keynesian analysis of the speculative demand for money laid greatest stress on the asset holder who has definite ideas about what constitutes a 'normal' rate of interest. Provided different assetholders have different ideas about the level of such a normal rate, this analysis leads, for the *aggregate* of the assetholders, to a negative relationship between the current interest rate and the demand for money. However, it also implies that the *individual* assetholder holds either 'all bonds' or 'all money'. This is at variance with the commonly observed phenomenon of 'portfolio diversification – individuals typically hold both 'bonds' and money. Tobin (1958) hypothesised that while utility derived by the individual from his portfolio of assets depends positively on the expected return from the portfolio, it also varies inversely with the risk (resulting from possible capital loss) attached to the portfolio.[4] This yielded the result that the proportion of the *individual's* non-human wealth held in the form of money varies inversely with the rate of interest but increases as the 'riskiness' of bonds increases. Thus Tobin was able to explain the phenomenon of portfolio diversification. Such analysis implied a demand for money function of the form

$$\frac{M_D}{P} = f(R, \sigma)W \qquad [10.4]$$

where W is the individual's real non-human wealth and σ is a measure of the riskiness of bonds. Equation [10.4] led to empirical specifications (see, for example, Meltzer 1963) of the form

$$\frac{M_D}{P} = AR^\beta W^\gamma \qquad [10.5]$$

Notice that the Tobin analysis suggests the wealth-elasticity of the demand for money, γ, should be unity. Equation [10.5] also differs from equation [10.3] in that a different 'scale variable' is included – the Tobin analysis suggests that it is real non-human wealth rather than real income that influences the demand for money. Finally, [10.4] suggests that the riskiness of bonds may be an additional determinant of M_D/P so that changes in such a variable may make it impossible to isolate stable functions of the form [10.5] unless this variable is taken into account.

Friedman (1956), in his restatement of the quantity theory of money, regards money as being held because an individual receives services from it as he would from any other durable good. A diminishing MRS is assumed between the services yielded by money and those by other assets. The demand for money therefore depends on the rates of return on all assets (including money) and also on the individual's wealth which limits the total value of the portfolio. Friedman's wealth variable, however, includes both human and non-human wealth since an individual may borrow on the strength of his expected future earned income and hold such extra assets as money. Friedman's demand for money function takes the form

$$\frac{M_D}{P} = f(R_b, R_e, P^e, W, h) \qquad [10.6]$$

where R_b and R_e are the expected rates of return on bonds and equities (including durable goods), $\dot{P}^e$ is the expected rate of change in the price level, W is Friedman's wealth concept and h is the ratio of human to non-human wealth. R_b and R_e are defined so as to include any expected capital gain or loss on bonds or equities. $\dot{P}^e$ is included because the expected change in prices is an obvious determinant of the expected *future* real value of money balances and, hence, of the services likely to be yielded. $\dot{P}^e$ is therefore to be regarded as an important determinant of the expected rate of return on money itself. The variable h is included to allow for the fact that, because of the non-marketability of human wealth, the greater is the proportion of total wealth held in human form the greater is the demand for money. Equation [10.6] determines the demand for real rather than nominal balances (i.e. the demand for nominal balances is homogeneous of degree unity in the price level), because it is holdings of *real* balances which determine the magnitude of the flow of services from which the assetholder derives utility.

Since R_b and R_e tend to move together over time, they are generally replaced by a single interest rate variable, R, in empirical versions of Friedman's equation. Measurement problems have led to total wealth, W, being replaced by permanent income Y^p, to which it is directly proportional provided the rate at which future income is discounted remains constant over time. Finally, the ratio of human to non-human wealth, h, is generally also taken as constant over time so that empirical versions of equation [10.6] take the form

$$\frac{M_D}{P} = f(R, Y^p, \dot{P}^e) \qquad [10.7]$$

Notice, however, that if [10.7] is cast in the form of [10.3] and [10.5]

$$\frac{M_D}{P} = AR^\beta (Y^p)^\gamma \qquad [10.8]$$

then we have another possible choice for the 'scale variable' in the demand for money function – permanent income as opposed to measured income or non-human wealth. Furthermore, insofar as the expected rate of price change influences the demand for real balances, this is a further reason for expecting instability in functions such as [10.8] involving only a scale variable and an interest rate variable.

10.2 Problems of estimation

Before we turn to specific empirical studies of the demand for money function, it will be helpful to consider, in a general way, some of the problems that are likely to be met once an attempt is made at estimation.

Data problems and the definition of variables

While at a theoretical level it may be quite appropriate to talk about 'money' in a very general sense, for empirical work a precise definition is obviously necessary if required data series are to be obtained. Unfortunately, in practice it is unclear which assets should be classified as money and which not. A spectrum of assets exists, of varying acceptability as a medium of exchange and of varying suitability as a store of value. These range from currency in circulation, through various types of bank and saving deposits, to highly illiquid securities unacceptable as a medium of exchange and on which there would be a considerable risk of capital loss if they were sold. If it were possible to concentrate on transactionary or speculative balances alone, it might be clearer which assets should be classified as money, but in practice functions often have to be estimated for the total demand for money, so that any division of the spectrum of assets between 'money' and 'non-money' becomes essentially arbitrary. A procedure frequently adopted is to 'let the data decide'. Alternative definitions of money are tried – the most common being a 'narrow' definition, including just currency in circulation and current accounts or 'demand deposits' at commercial banks, and a 'broad' definition, including also deposit accounts or 'time deposits' and maybe certain other saving accounts. That definition which results in the most stable demand for money function may then be regarded as the most appropriate. Fortunately, a number of the properties of estimated demand for money functions (e.g. their interest elasticity) seems not to depend on the precise definition of money adopted.

A further problem is whether money should be measured in nominal terms, in real or constant price terms or in real per capita terms. As already noted, theoretical considerations suggest that at the individual level it is the demand for real money balances which we should be concerned with although, as we shall see (p. 300–1) it is possible to test this proposition. For aggregate data, dealing in per capita quantities at least represents a token attempt to deal with aggregation problems. Unfortunately, most demand for money functions are formulated in logarithmic terms and, as we have seen in Chapters 6 and 8, proper handling of the aggregation problem would require at least dealing in terms of geometric rather than arithmetic means. However, during periods of large population change, working with per capita variables (i.e. arithmetic means) is probably an advance on the use of simple aggregates.

Just as problems arise in *a priori* attempts to decide on an appropriate definition of money, there are difficulties in selecting which interest rate variables should be included in a demand for money function. While the speculative motive suggests that a long-term rate should be included, if the transactionary motive predominates then a short-term rate may be the more appropriate. On the other hand, Friedman's analysis suggests that rates of return on *all* alternative assets are relevant. However, since all rates are likely to move together closely over time, multicollinearity problems normally make the inclusion of more than one interest rate variable impractical. Investigators have usually adopted a pragmatic approach, experimenting with either a long-term rate of interest or a short-term rate, occasionally trying both together. For example, in the UK the yield on $2\frac{1}{2}$ per cent consolidated government stock and the three-month local authority rate are normally used as long-term and short-term rates. In the US, favourites are the yield on twenty-year corporate bonds for the long-term rate and that on four to six month commercial bills for the short. Such measures have the advantage that they are calculated so as to allow for any capital gain or loss on the assets concerned.

In most theoretical work money is regarded as yielding a zero return. However, in practice, the deposit account or time deposit component of 'broad money' is clearly interest-bearing and even narrowly defined money is implicitly interest-bearing in the sense that banks may give preferential treatment or reduce service charges to large depositors. The Friedman approach clearly specifies that the own rate of return on money should be a variable in the demand for money function. Also, in all the other approaches to the demand for money, the interest rate of theory is to be interpreted as the opportunity cost of holding money. The own rate of return on money is an important determinant of this opportunity cost. For example, in a two-asset world of money and 'bonds' the true opportunity cost of holding money is not simply the yield on bonds but the difference between that yield and the own rate of return on money. It is therefore clear that the rate of return on money itself may be a relevant variable as far as the demand for money is concerned. Unfortunately, calculating such implicit interest rates is not a straightforward matter although one possibility, adopted by, for example, Barro and Santomero (1972), is to consider how *remitted* service charges vary with the size of a customer's account.

Another factor relevant to the own rate of return on money is the expected rate of inflation. In particular, this needs to be considered during times of rapid and highly variable rates of inflation since it is then that expectations are likely to change most quickly. Since Cagan (1956), the most common way of representing this variable has been by an adaptive-expectations hypothesis of the kind described in Section 5.1. This implies that expected inflation is measured by a distributed lag function of current and past inflation rates, similar to equation [5.9], with geometrically declining weights.

For selection of the most appropriate scale variable to be included in a demand for money function, we have seen that there are three main candidates – income, non-human wealth and permanent income. *A priori* arguments can be put forward in favour of each of these variables. Indeed, insofar as all the motives for holding money discussed above are relevant, a case can be made for including at least two, and may be all three, in an estimating equation. However, since all these potential scale variables tend to move together over time, multicollinearity problems have generally resulted in their being tried one at a time with the selection of the most appropriate again being regarded as mainly an empirical matter. Only if it were believed that one motive for holding money predominates, would theory be of much help here. For example, with a very narrow definition of money, it could be argued that the transactions motive was predominant and that, hence, income was the appropriate scale variable.

In empirical work, 'income' is generally defined as net or gross national product in real constant price terms, and is expressed in per capita terms if there has been substantial variation in population during the sample period. Non-human wealth is most appropriately measured by the aggregate net worth of the private sector.[5] However, except for the US, such data is generally hard to come by so that this variable has been little used in empirical work.

Permanent income variables are constructed using the adaptive expectations hypothesis exactly as in empirical work on the consumption function, except that in this case variables are frequently defined in logarithmic terms. Unfortunately, estimation problems now arise, essentially similar to those encountered in PIH versions of the consumption function. Letting lower-case letters represent the logarithms of variables, and letting $\bar{M}_D$ refer to real balances as opposed to nominal balances, M_D, suppose the demand for money function is given by

$$\bar{m}_{DT} = \alpha + \beta r_t + \gamma y_t^P + \varepsilon_t \qquad [10.9]$$

where ε_t is a disturbance. The logarithmic equivalent of the adaptive expectations equation [7.35] (p. 179) is

$$y_t^P = \lambda y_t + (1 - \lambda)y_{t-1}^P \qquad [10.10]$$

Substituting [10.10] into [10.9] and applying the Koyck transformation then yields

$$\bar{m}_{Dt} = \lambda\alpha + \beta r_t - (1 - \lambda)\beta r_{t-1} + \lambda\gamma y_t + (1 - \lambda)\bar{m}_{Dt-1} + \varepsilon_t - (1 - \lambda)\varepsilon_{t-1}$$

$$[10.11]$$

Notice, firstly, that [10.11] is overidentified since four parameters have to be obtained from five estimated coefficients – the estimate of λ obtained from the coefficient on the $\bar{m}_{Dt-1}$ variable is unlikely to coincide with that obtained from the ratio of coefficients on the interest rate variables.

Secondly, just as in the PIH time series estimating equation [7.38], if ε_t is non-autocorrelated then [10.11] presents the combination of an autocorrelated disturbance term plus a lagged dependent variable among the explanatory variables. We know from Section 3.2 that under such conditions, OLS estimators will be biased and inconsistent. Finally, as we shall see in a moment, lagged dependent variables may appear in a demand for money function for other reasons and their observed importance cannot necessarily be taken as evidence in favour of adopting permanent income as the appropriate scale variable.

Desired balances versus actual balances

Just like any other demand equation, a demand for money function tells us about the individual's wants. Equation [10.3], for example, yields *desired* real balances for given values of income and interest rate. However, actual data on the money stock, however defined, necessarily refer to money balances actually in existence rather than balances which individuals in aggregate would like to hold. There can be no guarantee that the two quantities are the same and, certainly with quarterly data, it is doubtful whether assetholders have time to adjust actual balances to the desired level within such a short interval. Feige (1967) suggested a model in which the individual assetholder seeks to minimise the sum of 'adjustment costs' and 'disequilibrium costs'. Adjustment costs are assumed to vary with the square of the change in *actual* real balances held, $\bar{m}_t - \bar{m}_{t-1}$, while disequilibrium costs are assumed proportional to the square of the difference between *actual* real balances $\bar{m}_t$ and *desired* real balances $\bar{m}_{Dt}$. This leads to an equation of the form

$$\bar{m}_t - \bar{m}_{t-1} = \mu(\bar{m}_{Dt} - \bar{m}_{t-1}) \qquad 0 < \mu < 1 \qquad [10.12]$$

Equation [10.12] is an example of the partial adjustment hypothesis described in Section 5.1. Since $0 < \mu < 1$ only a proportion of any difference between actual and desired balances is made up during any one period.

Suppose, now, that desired real balances are determined by an equation similar to [10.9] except that real measured income rather than real permanent income is the scale variable

$$\bar{m}_{Dt} = \alpha + \beta r_t + \gamma y_t + \varepsilon_t \qquad [10.13]$$

Substituting [10.13] into [10.12] yields

$$\bar{m}_t = \mu\alpha + \mu\beta r_t + \mu\gamma y_t + (1 - \mu)\bar{m}_{t-1} + \mu\varepsilon_t \qquad [10.14]$$

Notice that, apart from the disturbance term, equation [10.14] is of very similar form to the estimating equation [10.11] which arose from combining a permanent income scale variable with the assumption that actual money balances are always fully adjusted to their desired level. Both types of equation contain the lagged money stock as an explanatory variable. The only difference is that the lagged rate of interest, r_{t-1}, appears as an additional explanatory variable in equation [10.11]. In practice, however, r_t and r_{t-1} are likely to be highly correlated so it may be difficult to determine statistically whether or not r_{t-1} should be included in estimating equations. This is a potentially serious matter since equation [10.11] arises from a totally different idea about factors underlying demand for money equations than that implied by [10.14]. The practical importance of this is that the two approaches imply a clearly different response for $\bar{m}_t$ over time to changes in real income and the rate of interest. For example, successive substitution for $\bar{m}_{t-1}$ in equation [10.14] leads, ignoring disturbance terms to

$$\bar{m}_t = \alpha + \beta[\mu r_t + \mu(1 - \mu)r_{t-1} + \mu(1 - \mu)^2 r_{t-2}\ldots]$$
$$+ \gamma[\mu y_t + \mu(1 - \mu)y_{t-1} + \mu(1 - \mu)^2 y_{t-2}\ldots] \qquad [10.15]$$

On the other hand, substituting for permanent income in equation [10.9] yields

$$\bar{m}_t = \alpha + \beta r_t + \gamma[\lambda y_t + \lambda(1 - \lambda)y_{t-1} + \lambda(1 - \lambda)^2 y_{t-2}\ldots] \qquad [10.16]$$

Thus the partial adjustment approach implies an *identical* geometric distributed lag for *all* explanatory variables whereas the permanent income hypothesis implies such a lag *only* for the income variable. In the latter case responses to changes in the rate of interest are completed within one period.

As we shall see, many investigators have found the lagged money stock $\bar{m}_{t-1}$ to be a significant variable in demand for money functions. Unfortunately, the above problems make it very difficult to tell whether its importance is the result of permanent income being the correct scale variable or the result of a non-instantaneous adjustment of actual to desired balances. This difficulty stems from our inability to measure directly such concepts as 'permanent income' and 'desired balances'. Assumptions therefore have to be made which lead to essentially similar estimating equations.

Feige (1967) was the first to suggest a model of the demand for money involving *both* lagged adjustment and the use of permanent income as the scale variable. The desired level of balances is given by [10.9], permanent income again being determined by the adaptive equation [10.10]. Partial adjustment of actual to desired balances is also introduced via equation [10.12].

Substituting [10.9] and [10.10] into [10.12] yields firstly

$$\bar{m}_t = \mu\alpha + \mu\beta r_t + \mu\gamma y_t^P + (1 - \mu)\bar{m}_{t-1} + \mu\varepsilon_t \qquad [10.17]$$

and then

$$\bar{m}_t = \mu\alpha + \mu\beta r_t + \mu\lambda\gamma y_t + \mu(1 - \lambda)\gamma y_{t-1}^P + (1 - \mu)\bar{m}_{t-1} + \mu\varepsilon_t \qquad [10.18]$$

Multiplying [10.17] by $1 - \lambda$ and lagging by one period gives

$$(1 - \lambda)\bar{m}_{t-1} = \mu(1 - \lambda)\alpha + \mu(1 - \lambda)\beta r_{t-1} + \mu(1 - \lambda)\gamma y_{t-1}^P$$
$$+ (1 - \mu)(1 - \lambda)\bar{m}_{t-2} + \mu(1 - \lambda)\varepsilon_{t-1} \qquad [10.19]$$

Finally, subtracting [10.19] from [10.18], we eventually obtain an equation which does not involve the unobservable permanent income variable

$$\bar{m}_t = \mu\lambda\alpha + \mu\beta r_t - \mu(1 - \lambda)\beta r_{t-1} + \mu\lambda\gamma y_t + (2 - \mu - \lambda)\bar{m}_{t-1}$$
$$- (1 - \mu)(1 - \lambda)\bar{m}_{t-2} + \mu\varepsilon_t - \mu(1 - \lambda)\varepsilon_{t-1} \qquad [10.20]$$

Straightforward estimation of [10.20] by OLS is not feasible however, firstly because of the familiar problem of an autocorrelated disturbance term combined with lagged dependent variables on the right-hand side, and secondly, because, as with equation [10.11], its parameters are overidentified. However, provided appropriate estimation techniques are used, the model does, in theory, seem to provide a way of distinguishing the relative importance of general adjustment-type lags and expectational lags which are specific to the income variable. In practice, however, multicollinearity between r_t and r_{t-1}, and between m_{t-1} and m_{t-2} is likely to lead to some imprecision in estimators of the parameters of [10.20]. Since the relative importance of the types of lags is assessed by comparing the estimates of μ and λ, such imprecision may make it difficult to reach any firm conclusion on this matter.

Real versus normal balances

It has been implicitly assumed in the above discussion that, as theory suggests, the appropriate dependent variable was the demand for real rather than nominal balances, i.e. that, at least in the long run, the demand for nominal balances was unit-elastic with respect to the price level. However, if it is felt necessary to test this assumption, then equations such as [10.13] must be rewritten as

$$m_{Dt} = \alpha + \beta r_t + \gamma y_t + \delta p_t + \varepsilon_t \qquad [10.13A]$$

with m_{Dt} refering to nominal balances and equation [10.12] also re-interpreted in nominal terms. Substitution of [10.13A] into [10.12] then yields

$$m_t = \mu\alpha + \mu\beta r_t + \mu\gamma y_t + \mu\delta p_t + (1 - \mu)m_{t-1} + \mu\varepsilon_t \qquad [10.14A]$$

Notice that, if we restrict δ to unity in [10.14A], rearrangement gives

$$\bar{m}_t - p_t = \mu\alpha + \mu\beta r_t + \mu\gamma y_t + (1 - \mu)(m_{t-1} - p_t) + \mu\varepsilon_t \qquad [10.14B]$$

This is not quite the same as [10.14] since in that equation $\bar{m}_{t-1}$ represents lagged nominal balances deflated by the *lagged* price level, whereas in [10.14B] deflation is by the current price level.[6]

Hence, deflation of lagged nominal balances by the lagged price level as in [10.14] implies an instantaneous adjustment of the demand for nominal balances to changes in the price level. However, deflation by the current price level as in [10.14B] implies a lagged adjustment to price level changes identical to the response to changes in y_t or r_t.

The simultaneity problem

So far we have treated the demand for money function as if it were an isolated relationship, paying no attention to which variables in the function are endogenous and which can be treated as predetermined. In reality any demand for money function can only be one of a set of simultaneous relationships, also containing at least a simple supply of money function and some equation describing how quickly and in what manner the money market is cleared. What estimation procedures should be used to estimate a demand for money function will depend very much on the characteristics of the simultaneous system in which the function is embedded.

To illustrate the problems involved, we consider two simple stylistic models of the market for money. The price level is assumed constant so that we need not distinguish between real and nominal money balances. Both models have a simple and more general version. In both models the level of income is treated as exogenous, whereas in an economy-wide model account would have to be taken of the influence of the money supply both directly and via interest rates, on income.

The simplest version of the first model, which we shall call model IA, has the following three equations (lower case letters as usual denoting the logarithms of variables).

$$m_D = \alpha + \beta r + \gamma y + \varepsilon_1 \qquad\qquad\qquad [10.21]$$

$$m_S = \lambda + h \qquad \text{where } \lambda = \log \theta \qquad\qquad\qquad [10.22]$$

$$m_S = m_D \qquad\qquad\qquad [10.23]$$

Equation [10.21] is a normal demand for money function, although a scale variable other than income could have been selected without affecting the following arguments. Equation [10.22] is a very simple supply of money function in logarithmic form, giving the money supply in non-logarithmic form as

$$M_S = \theta H$$

where H is the stock of 'high powered' money or eligible reserve assets. The multiplier θ, assumed constant, will depend on the reserve asset ratio adhered to by commercial banks and on the proportion of their money holdings that the public wish to hold in the form of currency. Equation [10.23] is a simple market-clearing assumption. Since income is assumed exogenous, the implicit assumption is that the rate of interest adjusts instantaneously to bring the demand and supply of money into equilibrium. M_S and M_D are therefore always identical to M, the actual stock of money in existence, so that we are assuming away any of the adjustment problems discussed in the last two subsections.

In model IA the endogenous variables are assumed to be M_S and M_D and the rate of interest, R. In addition to income, the stock of high-powered money, H, controlled by the monetary authorities, is also assumed to be exogenous. Given these assumptions the reduced form of the model is given by

$$m_D = \lambda + h$$
$$m_S = \lambda + h$$
$$r = \frac{1}{\beta}(\lambda - \alpha) - \frac{\gamma}{\beta}y + \frac{1}{\beta}h - \frac{\varepsilon_1}{\beta} \qquad \text{[10.24]}$$

Notice from equation [10.24] that the rate of interest variable, r, is positively correlated (since $\beta < 0$) with the disturbance ε_1. Thus, in attempting to estimate the demand for money function [10.21], we are faced with the familiar consequence of simultaneity – correlation between an explanatory variable (r in this case) and the disturbance. We know from our discussion in Section 3.1 that the application of OLS to equation [10.21] therefore yields, *under the present assumptions*, biased and inconsistent estimators of demand for money elasticities.

For model IA the solution to the estimating problem is relatively simple. Ordinary least squares can be directly applied to the reduced-form equation [10.24]. Moreover, since $\lambda + h = m$, the log of the actual money stock, [10.24], can be rewritten as

$$r = -(\alpha/\beta) - (\gamma/\beta)y + (1/\beta)m - (\varepsilon_1/\beta) \qquad \text{[10.25]}$$

Ordinary least squares may therefore also be used to regress r on y and m to yield unbiased and consistent estimators of the coefficients in equation [10.25]. Estimators of α, β and γ, the parameters in the demand for money function [10.21] may then be obtained but these will retain only the property of consistency. Notice that this procedure merely involves 'turning round' the demand for money function [10.21], expressing r as a function of y and m.

The simple solution to the estimating problem in model IA stems from the very simple supply of money function assumed. Since the supply of money is assumed to be a constant multiple of the exogenously determined high-powered money stock, H, we have effectively assumed that the money supply itself is exogenous. In model IB we generalise this situation by making the money supply, as well as the demand for money, dependent on the rate of interest. The higher are interest rates the more inclined are the banks to make advances and loans so that the multiplier in equation [10.22] is likely to be a positive function of the rate of interest. Thus we have

$$M_S = \theta R^\mu H$$

rather than

$$M_S = \theta H.$$

In logarithmic terms this involves replacing equation [10.22] in model IA by

$$m_S = \lambda + \mu r + h + \varepsilon_2 \qquad \text{[10.26]}$$

where ε_2 is a disturbance introduced into the supply function.

Model IB is given by equations [10.21], [10.26] and [10.23]. The level of income and the high-powered money stock are still assumed exogenous. Notice that there is still no *identification* problem despite the fact that the rate of interest now appears in both the demand and the supply function. A variable – income – appears in the demand function but not in the supply function, while another variable – high-powered money – appears in the supply function but not in the demand function. The consequences of *simultaneity*, however, must still be considered and for this we turn to the reduced form which for model IB is

$$r = \frac{\lambda - \alpha}{\beta - \mu} - \left(\frac{\gamma}{\beta - \mu}\right)y + \left(\frac{1}{\beta - \mu}\right)h + \frac{\varepsilon_2 - \varepsilon_1}{\beta - \mu} \qquad [10.27]$$

$$m_D = \frac{\lambda\beta - \mu\alpha}{\beta - \mu} - \left(\frac{\mu\gamma}{\beta - \mu}\right)y + \left(\frac{\beta}{\beta - \mu}\right)h + \frac{\beta\varepsilon_2 - \mu\varepsilon_1}{\beta - \mu} \qquad [10.28]$$

Because $m_S = m_D$, the reduced-form equation for m_S is identical to that for m_D. Since $\beta < 0$ and $\mu > 0$ the rate-of-interest variable is again positively correlated with ε_1, so that the application of OLS to the demand for money function [10.21] will again result in biased and inconsistent estimators. Now, however, no simple solution to the problem of simultaneous equation bias is available since it is no longer possible to make the simple substitution for h in equation [10.27] as was done in equation [10.24]. Neither is it possible to turn the demand for money function round as in equation [10.25] and regress the rate of interest on income and the money stock. Since m_S, m_D and m are, by assumption, identical, equation [10.28] implies that the money stock is also correlated with ε_1. Thus, under the assumptions of model IB, the application of OLS to equation [10.25] will also yield inconsistent estimators.

Obtaining consistent estimates of the demand for money function in model IB requires a fully-fledged simultaneous estimating procedure. Under the present assumptions, the demand for money function is exactly identified so that the obvious method would be ILS. Estimates of the reduced-form parameters of equation [10.27] may be obtained by using OLS to regress r on y and h, and estimates of the parameters of [10.28] by using OLS to regress the log of the actual money stock, m, on y and h. Unique and consistent estimators of α, β and γ can then be obtained from the reduced-form parameters.

In the second type of money market model we abandon the assumption of an exogenous stock of high-powered money. Instead, it is the rate of interest that is treated as exogenous together with the level of income. The assumption, implicit in the model, is that the authorities decide on an appropriate rate of interest and are able to adjust the high-powered money stock, and hence the total money supply, so as to attain this desired interest rate. The high-powered money stock thus becomes an endogenous variable together with the demand for, and supply of, money.

In model IIA the structural equations are identical to model IA, that is equations [10.21–10.23]. The difference, of course, is that the exogenous variables are now y and r rather than y and h. Under these conditions the problem of estimation becomes straightforward. Since y and r are exogenous they can be regarded as independent of the disturbance in equation [10.21]. Thus we can obtain unbiased and consistent estimators of α, β and γ, the demand for money parameters, by simply applying OLS to equation [10.21]. Equation [10.21] is, in fact, the first equation in a very simple recursive system of the type discussed in Chapter 4.

In the more general model IIB the structural equations are identical to those of model IB, i.e. equations [10.21], [10.26] and [10.23]. Again, the exogenous variables are r and y rather than y and h. Fortunately, the replacement of equation [10.22] by [10.26] does not complicate the estimation problem. As in model IB, the appearance of the rate of interest in both demand and supply

303

functions causes no identification problem so that, since y and r are again independent of ε_1, the application of OLS to the demand for money function will yield unbiased and consistent estimators of its parameters. Models IIA and IIB are sometimes referred to (see, for example, Artis and Lewis 1976; Laidler 1980), as models in which the money stock is 'demand-determined'. That is, predetermined values of the exogenous variables (r and y in model II) determine the demand for money. The stock of money then adjusts passively (with the acquiescence of the monetary authorities), so as to satisfy the ongoing demand. This adjustment may either occur instantaneously as is implied by models IIA and IIB or, more realistically, via some form of partial adjustment process similar to that described previously. In either case, however, the long-run or equilibrium value of the money stock is essentially determined by demand factors.

At this point it should be noted that, while the partial adjustment process referred to above fits relatively easily into frameworks similar to those of model II, such a process is, at least at the aggregate macro-level, basically inconsistent with models such as IA and IB. In both these models the *aggregate* money supply, or at any rate the high-powered money stock, is exogenous and, hence, cannot be regarded as being determined by demand factors. It is outside the control of assetholders. Under such circumstances it may be reasonable to regard the *individual* assetholder as gradually, and over time, adjusting his actual money balances until they equal a desired level determined by demand factors such as r and y. However, it is not reasonable to treat the economy as a whole (i.e. the *aggregate* of assetholders) as adjusting the aggregate money supply to some desired level. The aggregate money supply is by assumption outside the control of the aggregate of assetholders. Thus, as noted by Laidler (1977), to apply the partial adjustment model to the economy as a whole in such circumstances involves committing a fallacy of composition. This point was originally made by Walters (1965) and is equally valid if we relax the assumption of constant prices so far made in this subsection. Even if it is the nominal money supply rather than the real money supply that is exogenous, adjustments of aggregate real balances to their desired level can then only occur through changes in the aggregate price level. Such an adjustment process is totally different from that underlying equations [10.14] and [10.14A] which arose from individual assetholders attempting to minimise the costs of portfolio adjustment.

Apart from the adjustment problems discussed, the lessons of this section may appear straightforward. Provided we can decide on the correct variables to treat as exogenous then the appropriate estimation procedure can be selected. Unfortunately, matters are never as simple as this in practice. Firstly, it is highly unlikely that we will ever find, for estimating purposes, a data period of sufficient length in which the monetary authorities consistently followed a policy of controlling the same policy variable, whether that variable be the money supply or the rate of interest. Rather, we are likely to find periods of a few years when attention was focused on money supply targets followed by similarly short periods when attempts were made to control interest rates. Indeed, there are very likely to be some years when the aim of the monetary authorities was unclear or ambivalent so that we would be uncertain as to which of our two models represented the closest approximation to reality.

Secondly, it may well be the case that variables which we might like to treat as exogenous are not truly under the control of the monetary authorities. For example, in the UK during the 1970s the stock of high-powered money, which in

304

the UK context is to be interpreted as the stock of eligible reserve assets, was partly outside the control of the Bank of England. Thus during this period, even if some version of model I was deemed most appropriate, the money supply can at best be regarded as being only partly exogenous. Similarly, in model IIB it is not necessarily the case that the monetary authorities will be able to select the correct stock of high-powered money so precisely as to obtain, exactly, the desired rate of interest. This would require a very accurate knowledge of the demand for, and supply of, money functions and no unforeseen variations in the level of income. Under such circumstances it is debatable whether it is the rate of interest that could be regarded as exogenous.

Finally, even if it were true that the authorities are able to control either H or R, these variables may be no more than policy instruments and still not genuinely exogenous. That is, the level at which the authorities wish to fix their policy instruments may itself be influenced by economic variables and even by variables within the monetary sector. For example, although the authorities may be controlling H, an increase in the stock of high-powered money might be made *in response to* a rise in income which would otherwise result in rising interest rates. Similar considerations apply when it is the rate of interest which is the chosen policy instrument. When the setting of policy instruments is influenced by economic conditions in this way, there is a limit to the extent to which they can be regarded as exogenous variables.

The implication of the above discussion is that the selection of an appropriate method of estimation for a demand for money function is rarely likely to be a clear-cut matter. However, a few rough-and-ready guidelines may be discerned. As a crude approximation it is probably true to say that, prior to 1970 in both the UK and the US, it was the rate of interest rather than the supply of money which was generally the policy target. To the extent that this was the case, the estimation of demand for money functions as in model II appears to be most appropriate for pre-1970 data. That is, OLS may be applied directly to the demand for money function. This, in fact, was how most pre-1970 demand for money functions were estimated – although not necessarily because any thought had been given to simultaneity problems.

As an equally rough generalisation it might be said that since the early 1970s, in both the UK and the US, it is money supply aggregates rather than interest rates that have been the main policy target. Given such an assumption, the best way to estimate demand for money elasticities from post-1970 data may well be as in model I. In particular, suppose it is believed that interest rates have little influence on the *supply* of money and that model IA is a reasonable approximation to reality. It is then probably better to reverse the causation in the demand for money function and apply OLS to equations such as [10.25] rather than apply OLS directly to demand for money functions such as equation (10.21).

 ## Empirical studies of the demand for money – a general overview

We saw at the outset that two of the major reasons for interest in demand for money functions were the questions of their elasticity and their stability. Associated with the former question is the problem of whether there exists a Keynesian-type 'liquidity trap' or a rate of interest sufficiently low for the demand for money to become infinitely elastic. In fact, if such a rate of interest existed, this would be a factor contributing to instability in the demand for money function, since it would then be possible for a changing money supply to be matched by a change in the demand for money without there being any change in income or the rate of interest. Normally, however, we would expect instability to occur because of a failure to take account of factors, other than variations in scale and rate of interest variables, which might influence demand. Hence, another aim of empirical work is to examine, firstly, whether variables such as the expected rate of inflation or the riskiness of bonds are of quantitative importance in determining the demand for money and, secondly, whether institutional factors can alter responses to the scale and interest rate variables.

Our discussion in Section 10.1 suggested some additional problems which are mainly empirical. Quantitative studies could be expected to answer such questions as whether a short-term or a long-term interest rate is best included in a demand for money function and whether a 'narrow' or a 'broad' definition of money is most appropriate. A further question is whether money balances should be expressed in nominal terms or as theory suggests in real terms. Finally, and perhaps more fundamentally, empirical work may help in deciding which is the appropriate scale variable – measured income, permanent income, or non-human wealth, to be included in a demand for money equation. Once this question is answered attention may then be turned to whether there exist economies of scale in the holding of money, i.e. whether the elasticity of demand for money with respect to the appropriate scale variable is less than unity.

Rather than concentrating on any particular empirical studies, the next three sections will consider the extent to which empirical work on the demand for money has been successful in answering the questions posed in the previous two paragraphs.

10.3   The interest elasticity of the demand for money

Of all the above issues, the question of the interest elasticity of the demand for money is the one on which empirical studies have led to the greatest agreement. Almost without exception investigators have found a non-zero interest elasticity, although the absolute size of this estimated elasticity is virtually always less than unity. Moreover, a non-zero elasticity is found no matter what definition of money is used, whatever the scale variable included in the function, and whether elasticity is measured with respect to short-term interest rates or long-term interest rates. For example, Meltzer (1963), in one of the most comprehensive of earlier studies, fitted logarithmic functions of the kind [10.3], [10.5] and [10.8] to annual US data for the period 1900–58, using three alternative definitions of the money stock – M1 including currency and demand deposits, M2 including, as well, time deposits, and M3 including also deposits at mutual savings banks. In all cases he found a significant negative elasticity with respect to the long-term rate of interest (defined as the yield on twenty-year corporate bonds). While the absolute size of the interest elasticity varied with the definition of money used, all estimates were in the range 0.5–0.95 and the evidence suggested that the size of the elasticities remained relatively constant decade by decade. The following result based on equation [10.5] for Meltzer's full sample period is fairly typical of results obtained for the US at that time. Figures in parentheses are t-statistics.

$$\bar{m}_{2t} = -1.98 - 0.50r_t + 1.32w_t \qquad \bar{R}^2 = 0.994 \qquad [10.29]$$
$$\qquad\qquad (10.8) \quad (53.2)$$

The coefficient on the rate of interest was clearly highly significant in the statistical sense.

The interest elasticity of the UK demand for money was first confirmed by Kavanagh and Walters (1966) using annual data for 1877–1961. During the decade after this, non-zero interest elasticities for either short-term or long-term rates were confirmed for a wide variety of economies. For a summary of some of these results, see Fase and Kune (1975) and for a more detailed discussion than there is room for here, see Laidler (1977: 122–30).

In general the size of estimated interest elasticities has depended on whether a short- or long-run interest rate variable has been included and to a lesser extent on the definition of money used. For example, in the US, when a narrow definition of money is used, the elasticity with respect to the long-term rate has been found to be about -0.7 but for a short-term rate only -0.2. The figures are slightly less for broader definitions of money. Similar values are found for most other countries. These variations are not difficult to explain. Long-term rates vary less than short-term rates although the two tend to be highly correlated. Hence, for a given degree of variation in a money stock series, the long-term rate is always likely to yield the higher elasticity. Also, when a broad definition of money is used, part of the substitution effects caused by changes in the rate of interest are hidden within the composition of money itself. Hence, a smaller elasticity is obtained than when a narrower definition is employed.

Of all the empirical studies of interest elasticities very few have failed to find a significant role for interest rates. The most well-known example is probably the early study by Friedman (1959). However, Friedman's failure appears to be the result of his rather unusual estimation and prediction procedures. More orthodox methods employed by Laidler (1966) yielded interest elasticities of the usual size and significance over a similar sample period to Friedman's. Laidler and Parkin (1970), using UK quarterly data for 1955–67, also found the rate of interest to be insignificant in their demand for money function. However, in this study a broad definition of money was used together with the short-term Treasury bill rate and, as we have already seen, such a combination is the least likely to yield a large interest elasticity. Furthermore, Laidler and Parkin themselves suggest that since the Treasury bill rate was subject to artificial smoothing operations by the authorities, their choice of interest rate variable may not have adequately reflected the real opportunity cost of holding money at that time. The Bank of England (1970), using a similar sample period, found a clear role for alternative interest rate variables.

All the studies referred to above based their conclusions on the straightforward application of OLS to the demand for money function, making no attempt to allow for the presence of supply of money relationships. However, as we noted in the last section, this is in fact the most appropriate procedure provided it is reasonable to regard the rate of interest as an exogenous variable. If this is not the case then both versions of model I suggest that the rate of interest will be positively correlated with the disturbance in a demand for money function. Under such circumstances OLS is likely to *underestimate* rather than overestimate the absolute size of interest rate elasticities. Hence, any bias due to simultaneity in the estimates described above is in a downwards direction, with true elasticities if anything being larger than those estimated. In the rare cases where simultaneous equation estimating methods have been employed, estimates of interest elasticities have generally confirmed estimates obtained by OLS. For example, Teigen (1964) constructed a structural model of the US monetary sector which contained not only a supply of money function but also an income relationship. Thus both the rate of interest and the level of income were treated as endogenous variables. Two-stage least squares estimation of the model yielded a short-term interest elasticity in steady state of about -0.15 – very similar to most OLS estimates.[7]

Although empirical work has established the interest elasticity of money demand beyond much doubt it has not generally suggested the existence of a Keynesian liquidity trap. Studies from Laidler (1966) onwards have found no evidence of higher, let alone infinite, elasticities when attention is confined to periods of low interest rates. It should be remembered that the idea of a trap arose because of a belief that some 'normal' rate of interest might be important in the demand for money function. Keynes suggested that, if the rate of interest was sufficiently low, all assetholders would expect it to rise and, hence, the demand for money would be unlimited. Attempts dating back to Starleaf and Reimer (1967) to find a role for such a normal rate in demand for money functions have proved largely unsuccessful. For this reason, plus the general lack of evidence in its support, the majority of econometricians would nowadays doubt the existence of a 'liquidity trap'.

10.4 The stability of the demand for money function

Up until a decade ago the general consensus of opinion concerning stability was that, since the beginning of the century, demand for money functions had been stable in the sense described at the start of this chapter. To quote Laidler (1971: 99), *For the United States, the evidence is overwhelming and for Britain it is at the very least highly suggestive.* Little attempt had been made at that time to test rigorously for stability, and this conclusion was based mainly on rough comparisons of scale variable and interest rate elasticities obtained from equations estimated for various subperiods within full sample periods of from thirty to seventy years. Such comparisons (see, for example, Laidler 1966; 1971) suggested fairly constant interest rate elasticities but provided some evidence that scale variable elasticities were declining over time. However, it was felt that these changes were gradual and predictable, reflecting long-run institutional changes rather than short-run unpredictable shifts in income velocity that might offset any changes in the money supply.

During the last ten years the stability of demand for money functions has begun to be subjected to more rigorous statistical tests. We lack the space to describe the theoretical basis of these tests but their application by, for example, Kahn (1974), Laumas and Mehra (1976) and Laumas (1978) tended to confirm previous findings for pre-1970 data.

By the mid-1970s however, doubts began to be cast on the stability of both the

UK and the US demand for money functions. In the UK, Hacche (1974) found that equations estimated from quarterly data for 1963–71 severely underestimated M3, the UK broad money aggregate during 1972–74. This was especially the case for that portion of M3 held by the company sector. Hacche argued that the major reform of the UK monetary system in 1971 (the new Competition and Credit Control system) had led to competition by the clearing banks for large wholesale deposits in parallel money markets that had previously been dominated by the secondary banking system. The clearing banks also began issuing their own certificates of deposit at this time. These developments increased the attractiveness of M3 (which includes wholesale time deposits and certificates of deposit) to assetholders and hence led to an upward shift in the demand for M3 function.

Hacche's work was rather severely criticised by Courakis (1978) and Hendry and Mizon (1978), (see Section 10.6). However, it appeared fairly clear that the type of demand for money equations normally estimated prior to 1971 (i.e. those with the money stock as the dependent variable) were not capable of satisfactorily explaining post-1971 data. Rather than any general instability there appeared to be a distinct shift in the relationship occurring in the early 1970s. For example, Artis and Lewis (1974), using the Chow tests described in Section 5.3 found evidence of a definite shift in demand for money functions for *both* M3 *and* M1 at the time of the introduction of the new Competition and Credit Control system.

Artis and Lewis (1976) suggested a very different reason from that of Hacche for the apparent breakdown in previous relationships. They argued that it was no longer reasonable, during the post-1971 period, to treat the supply of money as endogenous or 'demand-determined'. Roughly, this is equivalent to saying that model I of Section 9.2 is a closer approximation to reality than is model II. The gradually increasing influence of 'monetarism' on successive UK governments meant that it had become more and more appropriate to treat the money supply rather than the rate of interest as the exogenous variable. Artis and Lewis went further, however, and argued that there was at least some ground for doubting the endogeneity of the money supply even before 1971. They argued that the money supply cannot be fully endogenous in an open economy with fixed exchange rates and that, although interest rates may have appeared to be administered in the earlier period, this did not mean that rates were set without regard for market conditions. There was, at least, sufficient doubt about the endogeneity of the money supply in the 1960s to justify experimenting with something akin to model I for the whole sample period 1963(ii)–1973(i).

As we have seen, under model I, provided the market clears instantaneously and we can identify both supply and demand for money with the existing stock, demand for money parameters are best estimated with the rate of interest as the dependent variable. Artis and Lewis, however, consider models where the market only partially clears in each quarter, and where adjustment of money demand to money supply can be brought about, not only via interest rate changes, but also through changes in the level of income.

Their first model is a simple income adjustment model in which the supply of money, M_S, is given as identical with the existing stock, i.e. $M_S = M$, but where the demand for money, M_D, adjusts to M via a simple quantity theory mechanism. The desired ratio of money to income depends on the rate of interest and the level of income plus a disturbance u_t

$$\left(\frac{M}{Y}\right)_t^D = \alpha_0 + \alpha_1 Y_t + \alpha_2 R_t + u_t \qquad\qquad [10.30]$$

Discrepancies between the desired and actual money/income ratios are eliminated by changes in income but a partial adjustment process is assumed, i.e.

$$\left(\frac{M}{Y}\right)_t - \left(\frac{M}{Y}\right)_{t-1} = \theta\left\{\left(\frac{M}{Y}\right)_t^D - \left(\frac{M}{Y}\right)_{t-1}\right\} + \beta C_t + v_t \qquad [10.31]$$

where $0 < \theta < 1$ is an adjustment parameter which determines the speed of the process and v_t is a disturbance. The variable C_t in equation [10.31] represents factors which generate changes in the actual money/income ratio independently of the adjustment process. The adjustment of the actual money/income ratio to its desired level may be disturbed by sudden increases in the actual money stock. It is these 'supply constraints' on moneyholders' ability to bring the money/income ratio to its desired level which lie at the root of the Artis–Lewis explanation of apparent instability in the demand for money function. Substituting [10.30] into [10.31] yields the estimating equation

$$\left(\frac{M}{Y}\right)_t = \theta\alpha_0 + \theta\alpha_1 Y_t + \theta\alpha_2 R_t + \beta C_t + (1-\theta)\left(\frac{M}{Y}\right)_{t-1} + \theta u_t + v_t \qquad [10.32]$$

The model is estimated from quarterly UK data for 1963–73 using both M1 and M3, the yield on $2\frac{1}{2}$ per cent consols for R and GDP as the income variable. C_t is represented by the domestic borrowing requirement, an index of Bank of England restraint on bank lending and the high-powered money stock. The first two of these measures proved to be important influences on the M1 ratio and the third on the M3 ratio. When post Competition and Credit Control data is included in the sample, not only are these influences most marked but equation [10.32] exhibits much greater parameter stability than do normal demand for money equations excluding constraint variables. Unlike Hacche, Artis and Lewis do not claim that the demand for money function shifted; rather the economy has been pushed off a stable demand for money function because the supply of money expanded too rapidly for demand to adjust to it. The money stock could no longer be regarded as demand-determined.

The difficulty with the above model is that, since adjustment is brought about by changes in income, interest rates as well as the money supply have to be treated as predetermined. However, adjustment can also come about via rate of interest changes, so that the appearance of R_t on the right-hand side of [10.32] may lead to OLS bias as in model I of Section 10.2. Artis and Lewis's second model is, in fact, a development of model I, since now the level of income is treated as predetermined and an equation identical to [10.25] is held to determine the equilibrium or market clearing rate of interest R^*. In log-linear terms

$$r_t^* = -\frac{\alpha}{\beta} - \frac{\gamma}{\beta} y_t + \frac{1}{\beta} m_t - \frac{\varepsilon_t}{\beta} \qquad\qquad [10.33]$$

It is again assumed that market clearing is non-instantaneous but it is now changes in the rate of interest which are the equilibrating mechanism. Again, a partial adjustment mechanism is assumed

$$r_t - r_{t-1} = \lambda(r_t^* - r_{t-1}) \qquad 0 < \lambda < 1 \qquad\qquad [10.34]$$

Substitution of [10.33] into [10.34] yields the estimating equation

$$r_t = -\frac{\lambda\alpha}{\beta} + \left(\frac{\lambda}{\beta}\right)m_t - \left(\frac{\lambda\gamma}{\beta}\right)y_t + (1 - \lambda)r_{t-1} - \left(\frac{\lambda}{\beta}\right)\varepsilon_t \qquad [10.35]$$

Versions of [10.35] estimated over the same sample periods exhibit even greater coefficient stability than for [10.32]. The speed of adjustment implied by these equations is noticeably faster than that exhibited by the money/income ratio equations. This is consistent with a sequence whereby in the short run the market clearing function is borne by the interest rate, but where income adjustments make their presence felt in the longer run.

The belief that there had been a general breakdown in all UK demand for money functions was first seriously questioned by Coghlan (1978). Coghlan starts from the very reasonable proposition that no general theory of the demand for money could be applicable regardless of the definition of money applied. Factors influencing the demand for M1 are likely to differ from those determining the demand for M3. Since the demand for M1 is primarily a transactions demand, its most likely determinants are the level of income (rather than a wealth variable) and short- (rather than long-term) rates of interest. Furthermore, there is a much greater likelihood that M1 balances (unlike M3 balances) were demand-determined even during the post-1971 period. It is certainly true that the supply of currency is determined by the public's demand for it, and demand deposits can also be regarded as largely determined in this way since individuals can switch, relatively easily, between these and interest-bearing time deposits.

Since M1 can be regarded as demand-determined throughout the 1960s and 1970s, Coghlan retains the money stock as the dependent variable throughout his empirical work. Equations incorporating both adjustment and expectational lags are estimated from quarterly data for 1964–76. The results revealed two facts. When data for the 1970s are included the overall fit of the equations deteriorates badly. However, when the later data is excluded, estimated coefficients become highly variable and often implausible – the income elasticity at one point becomes negative.

Coghlan argues that, not only are these results unsatisfactory for the longer data period, but they also cast doubt on whether a stable demand for money function had been isolated even for the pre-1971 years. This was not to imply that such a stable function had not existed, but that lack of variation in the data had prevented its precise estimation. Previous studies based on pre-1971 data invariably obtained excellent 'fits' but, as Coghlan illustrates in his appendix 3, yielded widely varying estimates of income and interest rate elasticities.

The deterioration in explanatory power as the sample period is lengthened, plus the fact that it appears unreasonable to impose, a priori, an identical lag pattern of adjustment on all explanatory variables, leads Coghlan to experiment with rational distributed lags of the kind described in Section 5.1. In this case

$$P(L)m_t = Q(L)y_t + R(L)r_t + u_t$$

where $P(L)$, $Q(L)$ and $R(L)$ are polynomials in the lag operator L. The best-fitting equation for the full sample period proved to be (figures in parentheses are t-

statistics)

$$m_t = \text{const} + 0.405y_t - 0.233y_{t-1} + 1.430p_{t-1} - 2.282p_{t-2} + 1.813p_{t-3}$$
$$(3.95) \quad (2.16) \quad\quad (6.00) \quad\quad\quad (5.81) \quad\quad\quad (4.60)$$
$$- 0.836p_{t-4} - 0.053r_t + 0.830m_{t-1}$$
$$(3.37) \quad\quad (5.29) \quad\quad (14.41)$$
$$\bar{R}^2 = 0.998 \quad\quad d = 2.142 \quad s = 0.0131$$

This time, there was no deterioration in the fit of the equation as the sample period was lengthened. The estimated coefficients become very stable once data for later years is included. This reflects the greater variability in the 1970s data which enables parameters to be more precisely estimated. The lag structure of the equation is quite complex and is *not the same for each explanatory variable*. While adjustment to real income and prices is rapid, being complete in less than a year, there appears to be a geometric lag on the rate of interest variable with little more than half of the adjustment complete within a year.

Coghlan used both the more traditional type of equation and equations such as the above to forecast the money stock during 1976 and 1977. His preferred equations forecast considerably the better and, in particular, correctly predict the rapid growth of M1 during 1977.

Coghlan's study suggests that provided lag structures are not imposed *a priori*, there is no real evidence of a breakdown in the UK demand for narrow money function even during the post-1971 period. In contrast, Rowan and Miller (1979) deliberately eschew the use of more complicated lag structures, since they doubt that sophisticated lag patterns such as that in Coghlan's equation can possibly remain unchanged over time. However, they also reach the conclusion that it is possible to isolate a stable demand for M1 function over the period 1964–76. Stability in their function, and post-sample forecasts for 1976–77 of comparable accuracy to those of Coghlan's equations, are obtained either by omitting from the data the period covering the introduction of Competition and Credit Control (1971(iii)–1973(iv)), or by introducing a dummy variable to account for distortions during these quarters. Rowan and Miller argue that, while the introduction of Competition and Credit Control ought to have no permanent effect on the demand for transactionary balances, some temporary increase in the demand for M1 was to be expected because of increased uncertainty during the transition to the new system. The Competition and Credit Control dummy does, in fact, prove to have a statistically significant positive sign.

The work done during the past decade on UK demand for money functions has left the stability question less than completely resolved. However, the emerging consensus appears to be that while it is possible to isolate a stable M1 function – either by introducing a more complex lag structure or by making merely temporary allowance for the introduction of Competition and Credit Control, the conventionally estimated demand function for M3 has been subject to considerable instability since the early 1970s. Whether this instability in the M3 function is a temporary affair or reflects a permanent shift is the subject of much disagreement. The arguments of Artis and Lewis suggest an *apparent* temporary instability brought about by increases in the money supply too rapid for demand to adjust to. That is, we are in a 'disequilibrium situation' with recent data providing observations representing points lying 'off' a *stable* demand function. This suggests that, given time for demand to adjust to supply, a stable M3

312

function should re-emerge. The arguments originally stressed by Hacche, however, suggest that the introduction of Competition and Credit Control has led to a *permanent* upward shift in the M3 demand function. Both these arguments are plausible, in particular, because they are consistent with the findings of a stable M1 function. M1 is to a large extent demand-determined and the demand for transactionary balances has been unlikely to have been permanently influenced by Competition and Credit Control. Clearly, which of the competing explanations has most contributed to the observed instability in the conventional M3 function is a matter that can only be resolved by time and the availability of data from future years.

Doubts about stability in the UK context have coincided with similar doubts about the stability of the US demand for money functions. However, the problem with US functions is that, in contrast to the UK findings, instability has occurred in *the demand for narrow rather than that for broad money* while the tendency has been to *underpredict rather than overpredict* the actual money stock.

United States instability was originally discovered in a particular version of the demand for narrow money function – that contained in the MIT–Penn Social Science Research Council (MPS) econometric model. This demand for money function is of the form

$$m_t - y_t = \alpha_0 + \alpha_1 r_t + \alpha_2 \bar{y}_t + \alpha_3 (m_{t-1} - y_t) \quad \alpha_1 < 0, \quad \alpha_2 < 0, \quad \alpha_3 > 0 \quad [10.36]$$

where y_t now represents the logarithm of nominal income and $\bar{y}_t$ that of real income. The equation reflects a fairly orthodox 'inventory–theoretic' approach to the demand for transactionary balances, with the negative coefficient on the real income variable implying economies of scale in the holding of real money balances.[8] Its only unconventional aspect is the use of

$$m_t - y_t = \log \frac{m_t}{y_t} = -\log \frac{y_t}{m_t}$$

i.e. income velocity, rather than money balances as the dependent variable. This, together with the lagged independent variable on the right-hand side (where the lagged money stock is deflated by *current* income), implies identical distributed lag adjustment patterns with respect to real income, interest rates and prices and, moreover, constrains the long-run price elasticity to unity.[9] The MPS equation uses GNP as the income variable and various *short-term interest rates* – the argument being that it is these rates on near money substitutes which are most relevant for transactionary demands.

Instability in the MPS function was observed by Goldfeld (1976) and Enzler, Johnson and Paulus (1976) who found that versions of [10.36], estimated from quarterly data for 1955(ii)–1972(iv), seriously overpredicted the money stock by as much as 10 per cent by 1976(ii). The forecasting procedure used was 'dynamic' in the sense that the forecast value for m_t obtained for any given quarter was used as the m_{t-1} value needed to obtain a forecast for the next quarter. This naturally leads to forecast errors becoming cumulatively larger once the equation begins to overpredict.

Hamburger (1977b) attempted to resolve the overprediction problem by making two major respecifications of equation [10.36]. Firstly, long-term interest rates as well as short- are included in the equation. This is justified by the monetarist argument that money is a substitute for a wide range of assets, both real and financial, and not merely for short-term financial assets. Secondly, the real income variable on the right-hand side of equation [10.36] is suppressed, which has the effect of restricting the real income elasticity of the demand for narrow money balances to unity. Hamburger's equation, estimated using the simple Cochrane–Orcutt (Cochrane and Orcutt 1949) two-stage procedure described in Section 3.2, and again estimated for 1955(ii) to 1972(iv) is as follows

$$m_t - y_t = -\ 0.051 - 0.022r_E - 0.028r_{Lt} - 0.024r_{St} + 0.89(m_{t-1} - y_t)$$
$$(1.88) \quad (2.45) \quad\quad (2.39) \quad\quad (2.30) \quad\quad (29.7)$$

$$\bar{R}^2 = 0.9953 \quad d = 1.90 \quad \rho = 0.52 \qquad\qquad\qquad [10.37]$$

The figures in parentheses in this equation are t-ratios. r_{Et} is the dividend price ratio on equities which is regarded by Hamburger as an indicator of the yield on all physical capital. r_{Lt} is the yield on long-term US government bonds while r_{St} is a short-term interest rate (the rate on commercial bank passbooks). It is noticeable that all the interest rate elasticities in the equation are of very similar magnitude, suggesting that time and savings deposits, long-term bonds and equities, are all almost equally effective substitutes for narrow money. This equation also overpredicts during the post-sample forecast period, but the percentage overprediction is reduced to a maximum of 3 per cent and deterioration in the forecasts does not occur seriously until 1976, whereas in the previous studies it began much earlier. Hamburger maintains that the 1976 overprediction can be attributed to changes in bank regulations made at that time which led to a sudden substitution of savings deposits for demand deposits.

Laidler (1980), however, concluded that the problem required further investigation. Hamburger's equation, without *a priori* justification, constrained the income elasticity of the demand for money to unity and also, like the MPS equation, implied identical lagged response patterns for the demand for money with respect to all arguments in the function. Such constraints on adjustment processes might themselves be, at least partly, the cause of the overprediction problem.

Laidler uses quarterly data for 1953(i)–1972(iv) to estimate equations which are then used to forecast for the period 1973(i)–1978(i). He first presents a simple partial adjustment model, of the kind described by equations [10.12]–[10.14], with real money balances rather than the money/income ratio as the dependent variable. A disturbance term is added to [10.12] and this disturbance hence also appears in the estimating equation [10.14]. The possibility that this disturbance may follow a first-order autoregressive scheme is allowed for, so equations are estimated by OLS with the usual Cochrane–Orcutt adjustments described in Section 3.2.

Laidler, like Hamburger, uses GNP as the real income variable and experiments with long- and short-run nominal interest rates and also the dividend/price ratio as representing the yield on physical capital. His results with this model to a large extent confirm Hamburger's findings. However, estimates of the adjustment parameter (μ in equation [10.12]), are as low as 0.05 suggesting an implausibly low rate of adjustment of actual to desired cash balances. Estimates of the long-run elasticity with respect to real income are, indeed, close to unity, suggesting that Hamburger's equation was not, after all, seriously mis-specified in this respect. Laidler also estimates the partial adjustment model with the US broad money stock (M2) as the dependent variable. For this definition of money, overprediction problems for 1973–78 are much less severe and are virtually eliminated when both the long-run rate of interest and the dividend/price ratio are included in the equation. This suggests that as far as instability in the US demand for money function is concerned, the problem may be limited to M1, i.e. narrow money.

Laidler next considers the possibility that problems with the narrow money equations may have arisen because 'demand-determined' models similar to models IIA and IIB in Section 10.2 may be inappropriate for the US economy. Similar arguments had, of course, been used by Artis and Lewis to explain UK instability. As we noted at the end of our discussion of simultaneity, if it is the money supply that is exogenous then traditional partial adjustment models are likely to represent a serious mis-specification of the short-run dynamics involved in demand for money functions. Laidler first considers an 'Artis–Lewis'-type model in which the brunt of short-run adjustment to exogenous shocks to the money supply is borne by interest rates. This model is very similar to that represented by equations [10.33] to [10.35] except that permanent real income was used as the scale variable. However, unlike for the UK, parameters of the demand for M1 function were invariably badly determined for this model. Next, a more complicated model is presented in which real income bears the burden of adjustment, i.e. expenditure flows brought about by a 'disequilibrium real balance effect' lead to changes in output which eventually restore equilibrium. This involves the construction of a simple aggregate demand function containing as one of its arguments the excess of money supply over money demand. Again, though, it proves impossible to obtain sensible and well-determined estimates of the demand for M1 parameters. It is noticeable, however, that, for both the interest-adjustment and income-adjustment models, much better fits are obtained for the broad money aggregate M2.

Finally, Laidler considers a model based on the work of Carr and Darby (1981) in which 'unanticipated' changes in the money supply lead, firstly to an excess of actual money holdings over their desired long-run level, and then to a slow adjustment in prices and, hence, of real balances to their desired level. The addition of an 'unanticipated' money supply variable to equation [10.14] using, this time, annual data, generally improves forecasting performance and sensible well-determined estimates of the demand for M1 parameters are this time obtained. This latter performance is not too surprising given the orthodox form of the equation, but at least it is now possible to attribute low values for the adjustment parameter, μ, not to an implausibly slow portfolio adjustment, but to a very gradual price level adjustment.

Laidler sees the relative robustness of the demand for *broad* money parameters as the most interesting feature of his results. In contrast to narrow money, the size and statistical significance of these parameters vary little no matter what form of short-run dynamic adjustment processes are hypothesised. To this extent, Laidler's work suggests that M2 may be the best choice of US monetary aggregate for policymaking purposes. The adoption of alternative forms of short-run dynamics do not, however, solve the instability problem as far as M1 is concerned. Some systematic forecasting errors remain even when the Carr–Darby formulation is adopted. However, Laidler points out that the shift in the demand for money function is less dramatic than the work of Goldfeld, and of Enzler, Johnson and Paulus originally seemed to imply. Laidler uses a 'static' rather than a 'dynamic' forecasting procedure, i.e. the *actual* rather than the

315

forecast value of the lagged money stock is used to generate each forecast. This procedure suggests, not the cumulative overpredictions of previous studies, but a single once-and-for-all shift in the demand for money function.

The importance of further variables in demand for money functions

Another issue relevant to the question of stability in demand for money equations is the possibility that other variables may be important in the function. Variations in such variables can lead to instability if the demand for money is specified as depending on scale and interest rate variables only. Of the various additional factors discussed in Section 10.1, which have been suggested as having a likely influence on the demand for money, the expected rate of inflation is the variable for which most empirical evidence is available. This variable is an important determinant of the opportunity cost of holding money. While theoretically one might expect its influence to be reflected in the nominal rates of interest usually included in demand for money functions, the evidence does suggest that expected inflation rates affect the demand for money directly in a manner over and above their indirect influence via nominal interest rates. That this is so during periods of rapid inflation has been established reasonably clearly in a series of studies dating back as far as Cagan's (1956) work on European hyperinflations. More recent studies of high inflation economies which have found a statistically significant role for an expected inflation variable include Vogel's (1974) study of sixteen Latin American republics and Frenkel's (1977) work on the German economy in the 1920s. The role of inflation rates during periods of relatively moderate inflation is far less clear, although Shapiro (1973) and Goldfeld (1973) found such a variable to be significant in demand for money functions estimated for postwar US data.

Less work has been done on other possible factors influencing the demand for money. The possible importance of the 'riskiness' of bonds was emphasised by Tobin as early as 1958 but has received virtually no attention in empirical work. Finally, both the inventory–theoretical approach to the demand for transactionary balances and later work on the precautionary motive draw attention to the 'brokerage fee' involved in selling bonds. Proxied by the real wage rate, such a fee has been successfully included in US demand for money functions by, for example, Dutton and Gramm (1973) and Karni (1974). However, the general importance of such variables is as yet unclear and the chain of theoretical arguments leading to the inclusion of the real wage rate does seem somewhat tenuous.

10.5 Choice of variables in demand for money functions

The choice of scale variable

The most fundamental question concerning the variables to be included in demand for money functions is the choice of the scale variable. Empirical work on this problem has revealed, fairly conclusively, that the most appropriate choice is some measure of wealth rather than current measured income. It is less clear whether this measure should consist solely of non-human wealth or whether total wealth (proxied by permanent income), should be included in the function. However, few investigators would nowadays limit themselves to income as the scale variable, unless it was strongly believed that the transactions motive for holding money was dominant – as might be the case for very narrowly defined money aggregates.

The likely superiority of wealth measures as scale variables was demonstrated as early as 1963 by Meltzer who, using US annual data for 1900–58 compared the stability over different decades of equations similar to [10.5] but containing alternative scale variables: non-human wealth, permanent income and measured income. He found that the wealth variables produced stabler demand for money functions than the income variable no matter what definition was used for money. Such a conclusion was supported by Brunner and Meltzer (1963), Chow (1966) and Laidler (1966).

The lack of data on private-sector financial wealth for most economies apart from the US has meant that in many cases the choice of scale variable in practice lies between measured and permanent income. Choice has most frequently been made on the basis of equations such as [10.11], the underlying implication being that permanent income can be regarded as the usual distributed lag function of present and past measured income levels. Estimated versions of [10.11] have, almost invariably, confirmed the importance of lagged as well as current income levels as determinants of the demand for money. While it is tempting to interpret this as support for permanent income as the appropriate scale variable, we have already observed in Section 10.2 that the issue is not as simple as that. Equation [10.14], obtained by using measured income as the scale variable and postulating only a gradual adjustment of actual to desired balances, is very similar to [10.11]. Thus, the importance of past income values may arise from adjustment rather than expectational lags, so that measured income rather than permanent income could still be the appropriate scale variable.

The first serious attempt to resolve this problem was by Feige (1967) who attempted the estimation of an equation similar to [10.20], using US data for 1915–63. Feige found that estimates of the partial adjustment parameter, μ, in [10.20] were not significantly different from unity, whereas estimates for λ, the permanent income or expectational parameter, were 0.37 for narrow money and 0.30 for broad money. These results suggested that, at least for annual data, the adjustment of actual to desired balances could be treated as instantaneous. Thus, the importance of lagged income variables indeed appeared to be the result of permanent income being the appropriate scale variable. Moreover, the estimates of λ were close to those obtained by Friedman in his time series work on the consumption function (see Section 7.4). More recently, Feige's findings concerning the relative importance of adjustment and expectational lags have been replicated for other countries, notably by Khoury and Myhrman (1976) for Sweden and by Spinelli (1978) for Italy. Like Feige's, these studies are based on long runs of annual data.

While with annual data there may appear no place for adjustment lags once the scale variable has been properly specified as permanent income, it is still conceivable that such lags could have a role to play over shorter time periods. A natural extension of Feige's work is therefore to estimate equations such as [10.20] from quarterly data. Laidler and Parkin (1970) attempted this using UK quarterly data for 1955–67. Using real per capita broad money, real per capita GDP as the income variable, and the three month Treasury bill rate for the interest rate variable, their investigations were handicapped by the fact that the coefficients on the interest rate variables in equation [10.20] proved insignificantly different from zero. The probable reasons for this finding have already been discussed and its consequences in the present context are easily demonstrated. If we set the long-run interest rate elasticity, β, equal to zero in equation [10.20] we obtain (ignoring any disturbance term)

$$\bar{m}_t = \mu\lambda\alpha + \mu\lambda\gamma y_t + (2 - \mu - \lambda)\bar{m}_{t-1} - (1 - \mu)(1 - \lambda)\bar{m}_{t-2} \qquad [10.38]$$

The parameters λ and μ enter the above equation in a perfectly symmetric manner and hence, in the absence of the interest rate variables, they become *under-identified*. The consequence of this was that Laidler and Parkin found two optimal sets of values for λ and μ between which it was not possible to discriminate on statistical grounds. These were $\lambda = 0.8$, $\mu = 0.2$ and $\lambda = 0.2$, $\mu = 0.8$. Since for quarterly data a value for the partial adjustment parameter, μ, of only 0.2 seemed on *a priori* grounds to be unreasonably small (it implies that only 20 per cent of any discrepancy between desired and actual balances are made up during any quarter) Laidler and Parkin opted for $\mu = 0.8$ and $\lambda = 0.2$ as the most likely estimates. The value $\mu = 0.8$ for quarterly data was consistent with Feige's US finding that the adjustment of actual to desired balances was complete within a year. The low value for λ, the expectational parameter, confirmed that for UK data, also, the importance of past income values on the demand for money was a reflection, not so much of lags in adjustment, but of permanent income being the appropriate scale variable.

The general consensus that appears to have emerged over the relative importance of adjustment and expectational lags may require some reappraisal in the light of the point made earlier that the conventional partial adjustment-type model cannot adequately portray short-run dynamics when the money supply is exogenous. We have already noted that Carr and Darby (1981) suggested that under such conditions movements to equilibrium may be brought about by gradual adjustments in the general price level. It is on such alternative modelling of partial adjustment processes that future work is likely to be concentrated. For example, the general preference for expectational-type models seems, to a large extent, to stem from the fact that results almost invariably imply an implausibly low rate of portfolio adjustment which can only be rationalised by re-interpreting them as reflecting expectational lags. However, once alternative partial adjustment processes are envisaged, it becomes at least possible to attribute low values for adjustment parameters to, for example, slow adjustments in the price level to an excess of money supply over demand.

Economies of scale
Associated with the problem of deciding on the appropriate scale variable is the question of whether or not there exist economies of scale in the holding of money balances. That is, does, for example, a doubling in the magnitude of the scale variable necessarily lead to a doubling in the demand for money balances? We have seen that the Baumol (1952)–Tobin (1956) inventory–theoretic approach implies that such economies of scale should exist, at least for transactionary balances. However, although estimates of scale variable elasticities did tend to be somewhat lower for narrow as opposed to broad definitions of money, long runs of annual data, both for the US (see, for example, Meltzer 1963; Laidler 1971), and for the UK (see, for example, Kavanagh and Walters 1966; Laidler 1971) tended

to produce elasticities generally in excess of unity. Such findings appeared to hold no matter what scale variable was used. There does, however, appear to be a tendency for such elasticities to decline over time, becoming less than unity in the postwar period. For example, Laidler (1971), estimated the permanent income elasticity of demand for US broad money as 1.39 for 1900–16, 1.28 for 1919–40 but only 0.65 for 1946–65.

Quarterly postwar data have tended to confirm the existence of economies of scale for this period. Goldfeld's 1973 study of US data suggested a long-run income elasticity of significantly less than unity, its value remaining remarkably stable over a variety of alternative lag structures. For the UK the study by Laidler and Parkin already referred to also found a long-run income elasticity of less than unity, and this was confirmed more recently by Rowan and Miller (1979) However, Coghlan (1978), using the rational distributed lag approach described in Section 10.4, estimated the long-run elasticity as very close to unity. For other economies the survey by Fase and Kure (1975) suggested fairly consistent evidence of economies of scale.

The definition of money

As far as the most appropriate definition of money was concerned, while no conclusive evidence had emerged in favour of any particular definition, it did appear by the early 1970s that it was possible to isolate stable demand functions for both narrow and broad definitions of money. Moreover, these functions appeared to have similar properties, e.g. with respect to interest elasticity, no matter what definition of money was adopted. Since that time, however, as we have seen, instability has emerged in functions for the broad money aggregate M3, in the UK and for the narrow money aggregate, M1, in the US.

The emerging consensus now appears to be that different behavioural relationships must be expected to hold for different components of the money stock. This approach has been stressed in the UK by Coghlan who argued that 'there is no general theory of the demand for money which is applicable regardless of the definition of money adopted' (Coghlan 1978: 48) If this is so, we cannot expect to isolate stable demand functions for broad money aggregates involving components as different as, for example, currency and time deposits. Hence, Coghlan's concentration on the demand function for M1 transactionary balances which he found to be stable.

This approach had been advanced rather earlier in the US particularly by Goldfeld (1973). Goldfeld, in fact, used his quarterly data to estimate equations similar to [10.14], both for the broad money aggregate M2 as a whole and for its two components, M1 = currency plus demand deposits, and the time deposits component. He found that, as expected, the rate of interest on time deposits was negatively related to M1 but positively related to the time deposits component itself. This well illustrates the danger of aggregating over different components. Indeed, in the aggregate equation for M2, the rate on time deposits proved insignificant. More seriously, post-sample predictions for the M2 equation were far worse than those for M1 and inferior to those obtained by aggregating forecasts for the two component equations.

Goldfeld's 1973 conclusion, that it is advisable to disaggregate the broad money stock, may seem somewhat discredited in the light of the apparent instability that has appeared in US demand for M1 functions since that date. This may appear particularly so when it is remembered that Laidler (1980) was able to isolate a far more robust relationship for M2 than he could for M1 once post-1972 data was used. Laidler, however, maintains that his findings are not necessarily in conflict with the idea that time deposits are a distinct entity needing separate treatment from other components of M2. As Cagan and Schwartz (1975) have emphasised, as the US financial system has developed M1 has increasingly satisfied a specialised transactionary demand for money. On the other hand, asset motives, previously satisfied by M1, have become increasingly satisfied by interest-bearing time deposits. Thus, while the motives for holding M1 may have changed over time to a greater extent than the motives for holding M2, important information may still be lost if the different components of M2 are not considered separately.

Our discussion of the appropriate definition of money has so far ignored the question of whether demand functions should be formulated in terms of real or nominal balances, i.e. whether, as theory predicts, the demand for real balances is homogeneous of degree zero in the price level. Early studies based on annual data, particularly for the US, did, in fact, suggest homogeneity of degree zero or, what amounts to the same thing, that the demand for nominal balances has unit elasticity with respect to the price level. However, most of these early studies failed to distinguish between short- and long-run elasticities. This is, of course, particularly important for dealing with quarterly data. As we have seen, a more appropriate procedure is to attempt the estimation of equations such as [10.14A] and to test whether the *long-run* price elasticity, δ, is significantly different from unity.

Some evidence on price elasticities is available for UK quarterly data. Hacche (1974) specified an equation of the form [10.14A] but arbitrarily set the long-run price elasticity, δ, equal to unity, thus actually estimating equation [10.14B]. While such *a priori* restriction may appear to be in accordance with theory, as Courakis (1978) points out we can have no way of knowing what is the precise measure of prices to which unitary elasticity is expected to refer. Hacche uses the current value of the implicit deflator for final expenditure in his equation concerning personal sector M3 holdings, but there is no reason why this should be the appropriate price variable. Indeed, Courakis, using identical data to Hacche, finds that a unitary price elasticity is at variance with the data. It is also notable that both Coghlan (1978) using his more flexible lag structure, and Rowan and Miller (1979) adopting a simpler lag specification, obtain an unrestricted estimate for the same long-run price elasticity in the neighbourhood of 0.7 for narrow money. This suggests that, at least as far as the implicit deflator of final expenditure is concerned, a unitary price elasticity is not a property of UK demand for money functions.

The choice of interest rate variables

A priori preferences as to the appropriate opportunity cost variables to be included in demand for money functions have depended on investigators' theoretical persuasions. 'Neo-Keynesian' research workers tend to regard short-term interest rates as most relevant for narrow definitions of money when transactionary motives are dominant, and only consider longer-term rates in the context of broad money aggregates. Monetarists, however, have always maintained that rates of return on *all* alternative assets are relevant even for narrow money. For the monetarist, money is an effective substitute for all assets – both financial and physical.

Empirical clarification of which are the most appropriate interest rate variables is bedevilled by multicollinearity problems since most rates tend to move together over time. For example, Laidler, in his 1980 paper experiments with alternative interest rates using narrow money for US quarterly data (1953–78). Some of his estimates of versions of the partial adjustment equation [10.14] are shown in Table 10.1. Figures in parentheses are t-ratios. r_1 is a short-term and r_2 a long-term interest rate. The method of estimation is OLS, using the Cochrane–Orcutt procedure for dealing with autocorrelation described in Section 3.2.

The typical multicollinearity problem is well illustrated by the fact that the estimates of both interest rate elasticities lose precision when r_1 and r_2 are included together. Notice also that, when r_1 is added to the equation already containing r_2, its coefficient proves insignificantly different from zero despite the fact that s, the standard error of the residuals, falls, i.e. despite the fact that the 'fit' of the equation is improved.

Laidler also found that there was 'room' in his equation for either r_1 or r_2 plus the dividend/price ratio variable used by Hamburger (see equation [10.37]) as a measure of the 'real rate' on all equities including durable goods. There is, in fact, increasing evidence, particularly for the US economy, that rates of return on equities as well as more traditional interest rate variables are important determinants of the demand for money even when a narrow definition of money is adopted. For example, in addition to Hamburger, Alchian and Klein (1973) and Thompson, Pierce and Parry (1975) found an empirical role for such variables. Few investigators have examined the role of the rate on equities in the demand for money functions for other economies, but Hamburger (1977a) found his variable to be significant in a UK demand for money function although not significant in a similar equation estimated for the West German economy.

There is also some evidence that, in more open economies, interest rates ruling in international capital markets should be regarded as relevant opportunity-cost variables. For example, Hamburger and Wood (1978) found the uncovered 3-month rate on Eurodollar deposits to be a significant variable in the UK demand for money function. Hamburger (1977b) and Rowan and Miller (1979) had similar success with such a variable, thus confirming the openness of the UK economy

10.1 Demand functions for US narrow money

Constant	r_1	r_2	y	$\bar{m}_{-1}$	s
−0.148	−0.011		0.030	0.949	0.0097
(3.01)	(3.13)		(3.25)	(29.6)	
−0.320		−0.043	0.067	0.913	0.0095
(3.69)		(3.60)	(3.95)	(28.3)	
−0.307	−0.006	−0.031	0.062	0.928	0.0092
(3.67)	(1.57)	(2.29)	(3.73)	(28.9)	

Source: Laidler (1980), Table 1

and the close substitutability between UK domestic money and Eurodollar deposits. Hamburger (1977b) also provides evidence that the Eurodollar rate may be important in the West German demand for money function.

The above survey, although selective, gives some idea of the great extent of recent work on the determination of appropriate interest rate variables. However, mainly because of the multicollinearity problem, it cannot be maintained that many issues have been fully resolved. In particular it is still unclear, when there is 'room' for only one interest rate variable in an estimating equation, whether this variable should be a shorter- or a longer-term rate.

10.6 A controversy over the UK demand for money function

In this section we shall consider in some detail two of the more recent studies concerning the UK demand for money function. We have already referred to the Hacche (1974) paper in Section 10.4. While Hacche's finding concerning the stability of pre-1971 estimated UK functions is hardly in dispute, his methodology has come under considerable criticism in two complementary papers by Courakis (1978) and Hendry and Mizon (1978). Hacche's model is as specified in equation [10.14B]–a partial adjustment-type equation in which the long-run price elasticity is restricted to unity. However, the model actually estimated by Hacche is somewhat different. Firstly, equation [10.14B] is 'first differenced' to remove any possibility of 'spurious correlations' caused by common trends in the data.[10] It therefore becomes

$$m_t - p_t - (m_{t-1} - p_{t-1}) = b_1(r_t - r_{t-1}) + c_1(y_t - y_{t-1})$$
$$+ e_1[m_{t-1} - p_t - (m_{t-2} - p_{t-1})] + v_t \qquad [10.39]$$

where $b_1 = \mu\beta$, $c_1 = \mu\gamma$, $e_1 = 1 - \mu$ and $v_t = \mu(\varepsilon_t - \varepsilon_{t-1})$. Next, the disturbance, v_t, is assumed to follow a first-order autoregressive scheme $v_t = \rho v_{t-1} + u_t$ so that, before estimation, [10.39] is further transformed in the manner described in Section 3.2 for dealing with such schemes. Since [10.39] can be rearranged as

$$m_t = b_1 r_t - b_1 r_{t-1} + c_1 y_t - c_1 y_{t-1} + (1 - e_1)p_t - (1 - e_1)p_{t-1}$$
$$+ (1 + e_1)m_{t-1} - e_1 m_{t-2} + v_t \qquad [10.40]$$

this second transformation means that the equation eventually estimated by Hacche is[11]

$$m_t = b_1 r_t - b_1(1 + \rho)r_{t-1} + b_1\rho r_{t-2} + c_1 y_t - c_1(1 + \rho)y_{t-1}$$
$$+ c_1\rho y_{t-2} + (1 - e_1)p_t - (1 - e_1)(1 + \rho)p_{t-1} + (1 - e_1)\rho p_{t-2}$$
$$+ (1 + e_1 + \rho)m_{t-1} - (\rho + e_1 + e_1\rho)m_{t-2} + e_1\rho m_{t-3} + u_t \qquad [10.41]$$

As pointed out by both Courakis and Hendry–Mizon, equation [10.41] implies a whole series of restrictions on the lag structure of the demand for money equation which are, in principle, testable hypotheses which may well not be valid. For example, [10.41] implies that the ratios of the coefficients on r_t and r_{t-1}, on y_t and y_{t-1} and on p_t and p_{t-1} are *all* equal to $-(1 + \rho)$. Such restrictions arise because Hacche *assumes* that first differencing is an appropriate procedure and then *assumes* that the disturbance in the first-differenced equation [10.39] follows a first-order autoregressive scheme. However, while differencing may remove any spurious correlation problems, it can also *cause* other problems. For example, if a non-autocorrelated disturbance is present in equation [10.14B] then v_t in the first-differenced equation [10.39] will indeed be autocorrelated, i.e. one problem will have been exchanged for another. Moreover, residual autocorrelation may reflect no more than a mis-specification of the lag structure in the equation (e.g. Hacche specifies no expectational lags but takes first differences), and its approximation by a first-order scheme may be quite inadequate[12] and can lead to considerable biases in estimated coefficients and implied long-run elasticities. For this reason it becomes important specifically to *test* the assumptions made by Hacche and to consider the effect on estimated elasticities of alternative specifications.

Courakis uses maximum likelihood methods to estimate a series of equations for the overlapping sample periods 1963(iv)–1971(iii), 1963(iv)–1973(iv) and 1963(iv)–1975(ii). The post-1974 data was not available to Haache. Courakis defines his variables identically to Haache but concentrates solely on personal sector holdings of M3. His estimated equations consist of a sequence of 'nested' hypotheses, i.e. the earlier equations may be derived from the later ones by the imposition of restrictions on the coefficients of the latter. Courakis's estimation method enables him, by comparing these equations, to test whether any of the restrictions necessary to move from one such equation to another are rejected by the data.

We have already noted, in the previous section, that Courakis found a unit long-run price elasticity to be rejected by the data. In addition, it could also be seen that a model in the *levels* of the variables such as [10.14B] with an autocorrelated disturbance term is preferable to a model in *differences* with an autocorrelated disturbance term such as that estimated by Hacche. In fact, the restrictions implicitly imposed by Hacche were rejected by the data.

Courakis's most striking result is the clear rejection of Hacche's specification, but even the alternative equations considered perform with only varying degrees

10.2 Estimates of long-run income and interest rate elasticities

Model	Sample period	Long-run Y elasticity	Long-run R elasticity
[10.14B]	1963(iv)–1971(iii)	1.921	−3.475
	1963(iv)–1973(iv)	4.015	−8.409
	1963(iv)–1975(ii)	*	*
[10.14B] with first-order scheme	1963(iv)–1971(iii)	2.141	−4.165
	1963(iv)–1973(iv)	3.985	−8.136
	1963(iv)–1975(ii)	0.112	−0.488
[10.41]	1963(iv)–1971(iii)	0.823	−0.504
	1963(iv)–1973(iv)	2.067	−0.321
	1963(iv)–1975(ii)	0.173	−0.176

Source: Courakis (1978). For [10.14B] the partial adjustment coefficient lay outside the range zero to unity for the last sample period. Long-run elasticities were therefore not calculated.

of success for the different sample periods. Since no alternative is clearly to be preferred, Courakis considers the effects on estimated elasticities of varying specifications of the demand for money function. He presents results obtained for three such specifications. These are shown in Table 10.2 and exhibit quite alarming variation.

Such is the variation in the estimated elasticities that Courakis calls into question whether it is at all possible to obtain sufficiently reliable estimates of demand for money parameters to resolve *any* of the outstanding issues in this area.

Hendry and Mizon (1978) estimate a general equation of the form

$$m_t = a + \sum_{j=1}^{5} b_j r_{t-j+1} + \sum_{j=1}^{5} c_j y_{t-j+1} + \sum_{j=1}^{5} d_j p_{t-j+1} + \sum_{j=1}^{5} e_j m_{t-j} \qquad [10.42]$$

The maximum lag is increased to four quarters in [10.42] compared with [10.41] because quarterly data is being used. To derive Hacche's equation [10.41] it is necessary to impose, in all, sixteen restrictions (we shall not list them) on the coefficients of [10.42]. Unrestricted estimation of [10.42] for the period 1963(i)–1975(ii) yields the values shown in Table 10.3. Figures in parentheses are standard errors.

While, in part because of multicollinearity, few of the individual coefficients in Table 10.3 are significantly different from zero, it is still the case that some of Hacche's restrictions are rejected by the data. In particular, Hacche's first differencing transformation is rejected. In fact when Hacche's equation [10.41] is estimated with restrictions imposed the coefficients are as shown in Table 10.4. It can be seen that these numbers differ considerably from those in Table 10.3.

Hendry and Mizon are not surprised that an equation in *differences* alone should be rejected by the data, since, for reasons similar to those outlined by

10.3 Unrestricted estimation of equation [10.42]

j	b_j	c_j	d_j	e_j	
1	0.90	0.22	0.59	0.92	$a = 2.40$ $R^2 = 0.9995$
	(0.39)	(0.13)	(0.25)	(0.22)	$s = 0.0096 \,(3.63)$
2	−0.82	0.05	−0.71	−0.05	
	(0.66)	(0.15)	(0.42)	(0.28)	
5	−0.99	0.14	0.94	−0.17	
	(0.76)	(0.15)	(0.59)	(0.28)	
4	1.28	0.01	−0.99	−0.22	
	(0.81)	(0.15)	(0.60)	(0.29)	
5	−0.63	0.20	0.24	0.30	
	(0.68)	(0.13)	(0.39)	(0.23)	

Source: Hendry and Mizon (1978)

10.4 Restricted estimation of equation [10.41]

j	b_j	c_j	d_j	e_j
1	0.89	0.13	0.67	1.53
2	-1.07	-0.16	-0.80	-0.46
3	0.18	0.03	0.13	-0.07

Source: Hendry and Mizon (1978)

DHSY (1978), (see Section 7.6) they believe that such equations must also allow for mechanisms by which previous disequilibria in the *levels* of the variables are permitted to affect their rate of change. As an analogue to the model used by DHSY, which cannot be rejected against [10.42], they estimate the equation

$$m_t - p_t - (m_{t-1} - p_{t-1}) = 1.61 + 0.21(y_t - y_{t-1}) + 0.81(r_t - r_{t-1})$$
$$(0.65) \quad (0.09) \qquad\qquad (0.31)$$
$$+ \ 0.26[m_{t-1} - p_{t-1} - (m_{t-2} - p_{t-2})] - 0.40(p_t - p_{t-1})$$
$$(0.12) \qquad\qquad\qquad\qquad (0.15)$$
$$- \ 0.23(m_{t-1} - p_{t-1} - y_{t-1}) - 0.61r_{t-4} + 0.14y_{t-4}$$
$$(0.05) \qquad\qquad\qquad (0.21) \qquad (0.04)$$
$$R^2 = 0.69 \quad s = 0.0091 \qquad\qquad\qquad\qquad [10.43]$$

The major difference between [10.43] and Hacche's specification is that it contains *both* levels *and* differences, hence providing the mechanisms mentioned above. Previous disequilibria in the relationship between the levels of 'real' money and 'real' income affect changes in real demand through the variable

$$(m_{t-1} - p_{t-1} - y_{t-1})$$

which is the ratio of lagged real balances to lagged real income. The coefficient on $p_t - p_{t-1}$ reflects a negative influence for the inflation rate in the short run, although the long-run price elasticity of the demand for money is still constrained to be unity. Equation [10.43] can, in fact, be 'solved' for the resultant coefficients on m_t, y_t, r_t and m_{t-1}. These are shown in Table 10.5 and demonstrate that [10.43] in effect omits the unsuccessful variables in [10.42] and rearranges the remainder such that they represent '*separate decision variables with sensible economic interpretations*' (Hendry and Mizon 1978: 561).

The above criticisms of Hacche well illustrate the dangers of the mechanical use of 'standard' econometric techniques. Much recent US work (e.g. Laidler 1980; Hamburger 1977a) is equally free with the automatic use of 'OLS with Cochrane–Orcutt adjustment'. The work of Courakis in particular suggests that much greater attention needs to be paid to the dynamic structure and/or autocorrelation properties of demand for money equations.

10.5 Solved version of equation [10.43]

j	b_j	c_j	d_j	e_j
1	0.81	0.21	0.60	1.03
2	−0.81	0.02	−0.63	−0.26
3	0	0	0.26	0
4	0	0	0	0
5	−0.61	0.14	0	0

Source: Hendry and Mizon (1978)

10.7 Conclusions

It would be idle to pretend that the vast amount of empirical work performed during the last two decades has been successful in resolving all the outstanding issues concerning the demand for money. Nevertheless, one or two propositions seem to be established beyond reasonable doubt. Few economists would now deny that the demand for money is to some extent interest-elastic. The elasticity, however, appears to lie between zero and unity – for less than originally suggested by 'Keynesian' economists, and there appears very little evidence in favour of a 'liquidity trap'. The problem of whether long- or short-term interest rates are most relevant remains largely unresolved, mainly because of the multicollinearity problem. However, evidence is beginning to emerge, particularly for the US economy, in favour of the monetarist thesis that money, however narrowly defined, is a substitute for all assets – both liquid and non-liquid and even physical. This implies that rates of return on *all* assets are relevant opportunity cost variables.

A second issue on which there is a large measure of agreement is that the appropriate scale variable, particularly for broad money functions, is some measure of wealth rather than measured income. Choosing between non-human wealth and permanent income for this measure is less easy, and is handicapped for most economies by a general lack of data on the net worth of the private sector. For narrow money it is still possible to argue that measured income is the appropriate scale variable. The inventory theoretic approach suggests this, and simple partial adjustment models have in the past worked well for this definition of money. Implausibly low estimates of the rate of adjustment may simply reflect a mis-specification of short-run dynamics. We have seen that under conditions where the money stock cannot be regarded as demand-determined, the traditional type of partial adjustment model is almost certainly inappropriate.

The general belief in the stability of demand for money functions regardless of definitional problems has obviously been eroded during the past decade, both by the behaviour of M3 in the UK and M1 in the US. An emerging attitude seems to be that the diverse components of broad money aggregates should be considered separately. This implies that while it may be possible to isolate (at least for short periods), a stable demand for M1 function, problems are likely to occur for broader definitions of money. Also, as the motives for holding M1 change over time, we should expect gradual long-run shifts even in the demand equation for this narrow money aggregate.

It is also becoming clearer that long-run demand for money elasticities, with respect both to real income and to the price level, tend nowadays to be less than unity. The presence of economies of scale in the holding of money balances has, from the outset, been regarded as a matter for empirical testing. However, until more recently, a unit price elasticity tended to be implicitly assumed, attention being concentrated on real rather than nominal balances. Recent findings, particularly for the UK economy, suggest that in future empirical work money balances will be defined in nominal terms, with no attempt being made to impose unitary values on price elasticities.

Future empirical research will obviously tend to concentrate on those issues which remain unresolved. In particular, much consideration is likely to be given to the modelling of short-run adjustment mechanisms under conditions when it is no longer appropriate to regard the money stock as demand-determined. Finally, more attention will probably be paid to the extent to which the 'open-ness' of an economy influences the behaviour of assetholders. As areas of the world-economy become more integrated, then provided exchange rates remain relatively stable, an increasing substitutability between 'domestic' and 'foreign' money is to be expected.

APPENDIX
Empirical exercise

In this exercise we shall estimate demand functions for the UK narrow money aggregate, M1. We concentrate on M1 since it is not unreasonable to regard this quantity as 'demand-determined' throughout the postwar period. As Section 10.2 indicates, this means that we can hope to obtain consistent estimators of demand for M1 parameters by the straightforward application of OLS.

We begin with annual data for 1964–78, defining the following variables.

M = nominal M1 money balances held by the private sector (average of quarterly figures).

Y = total personal disposable income in 1975 prices.

R^S = 3-month local authority rate (i.e. a short-term interest rate),

R^L = yield on 20-year British government securities (i.e. a long-term interest rate),

P = implied consumers' expenditure deflator.

Data on all variables can be found in *ETAS* 1983. That for M is on pages 146–47, for Y on page 18, and for R_S and R_L on page 194. The series for P is obtained by dividing the figures for total personal disposable income in current prices on page 18 by those for the Y variable. Note that the coverage of the money series varies so that you will have to take care in obtaining a consistent series. Using your OLS program to estimate equation [10.13A] you should obtain, using lower-case letters to denote the natural logarithm of variables,

$$\hat{m}_t = -0.941 - 0.298r_t^L + 1.022y_t + 0.832p_t$$
$$\quad (1.032) \quad (0.035) \quad (0.097) \quad (0.022)$$
$$R^2 = 0.999 \quad d = 2.23 \qquad [\text{A}10.1]$$

While it is not unreasonable to use measured income rather than a wealth measure as our scale variable in a demand for narrow money function, you will find that the long term interest rate works better than the short rate. This is contrary to what we would expect on a strict Keynesian interpretation, but try replacing R^L by R^S in equation [A10.1].

Even with annual data, we cannot assume an instantaneous adjustment of actual to desired money balances, so we add the lagged money stock to our equation

$$\hat{m}_t = -1.464 - 0.262r_t^L + 0.842y_t + 0.654p_t + 0.254m_{t-1}$$
$$\quad (0.944) \quad (0.036) \quad (0.123) \quad (0.089) \quad (0.124)$$
$$R^2 = 0.999 \quad h = -0.01 \qquad [\text{A}10.2]$$

Do not be impressed by the high R^2's in equations [A10.1] and [A10.2]. Notice that M, P, and to a lesser extent Y, all show strong upward trends during the sample period and, of course, [A10.2] contains m_{t-1} among its explanatory variables. However, there is no suggestion of autocorrelation, all variables are significant and the t-ratio on m_{t-1} is 2.05 (critical t-values, with $n - k = 10$ d.f., are $t_{0.05} = 1.812$ and $t_{0.01} = 2.764$). There is therefore some evidence of partial adjustment of actual balances to desired levels. Equation [A10.2] implies values for the parameters in [10.14A] of $\mu = 0.746$, $\beta = -0.351$, $\gamma = 1.129$ and $\delta = 0.877$. Notice that the elasticities with respect to real income and the price level are reasonably close to unity, whereas the interest rate elasticity is negative as expected and of similar size to that normally found. The value for μ implies that about 75 per cent of any difference between desired and actual balances is eliminated each year.

We can test the theoretical prediction that the demand function is homogeneous of degree unity in the price level by imposing the restriction $\delta = 1$ and estimating equation [10.14B]. This yields

$$\hat{m}_t - p_t = -1.513 - 0.239r_t^L + 0.644y_t + 0.495(m_{t-1} - p_t)$$
$$\quad (1.096) \quad (0.040) \quad (0.091) \quad (0.068)$$
$$R^2 = 0.957 \quad h = 0.71 \qquad (\text{A}10.3]$$

We can now test the restriction $\delta = 1$ by using the F-test described in Section 5.4 and comparing the residual sum of squares, SSR_U, in the unrestricted equation [A10.2] with the residual sum of squares, SSR_R, in the restricted equation [A10.3]. Since

$$\text{SSR}_u = 1.72 \times 10^{-3} \quad \text{and} \quad \text{SSR}_R = 2.55 \times 10^{-3}$$

we obtain, using [5.81], a value for the test statistic of 4.83. With (1, 10) d.f., critical F-values are $F_{0.05} = 4.96$ and $F_{0.01} = 10.04$. The theoretical restriction is therefore not rejected by the data – the function does appear to be homogeneous of degree unity in the price level. You should now try imposing the restriction $\gamma = 1$ by the same procedure. What does such a restriction imply in economic terms?

328

We shall now re-estimate equation [A10.3] using data for 1964–81. We can then use the second of the Chow tests described in Section 5.3 to see whether the 'new' 1979–81 observations can be regarded as generated by the same relationship. For 1964–81

$$\widehat{m_t - p_t} = 2.437 - 0.096r_t^L + 0.178y_t + 0.576(m_{t-1} - p_t)$$
$$(2.170) \quad (0.083) \quad\quad (0.156) \quad\quad (0.158)$$
$$R^2 = 0.779 \quad h = 2.53 \qquad [A10.4]$$

There appears to be a clear change in parameter values between [A10.3] and [A10.4] and a general deterioration in the fit of the equation. Also, [A10.4] implies a value for μ of 0.424, implying an implausibly slow adjustment process for annual data. The residual sum of squares for [A10.3] is, as we have seen, 2.55×10^{-3}. For equation [A10.4] it is 18.48×10^{-3}. Hence, the Chow test statistic [5.62] (p. 117) takes the value

$$\left\{ \frac{\sum e_p^2 - \sum e_1^2}{\sum e_1^2} \right\} \left\{ \frac{n_1 - k}{n_2} \right\} = \left\{ \frac{18.48 - 2.55}{2.55} \right\} \left\{ \frac{15 - 4}{3} \right\} = 22.91$$

With (3,11) d.f. critical F-values are $F_{0.05} = 3.59$ and $F_{0.01} = 6.22$, so we must clearly reject the hypothesis of parameter stability. If you re-estimate [A10.2] for 1964–81 you will find you reach a similar conclusion.

It is clear that we have failed to isolate a stable demand for money function for our sample period. A possible reason for our failure may be the simplicity of the lag structure implied by the partial adjustment model adopted. Remember, for example, that the significance of m_{t-1} in [A10.2] could also be the result of permanent rather than measured income being the appropriate scale variable. Before considering this possibility further we will resort to quarterly data.

Firstly, we will use seasonally adjusted data for 1964–71, thus limiting ourselves to a timespan prior to the introduction in late 1971 of the, possibly disrupting, new system of Competition, Credit and Control. Quarterly data on M can be found on pages 146–47 of ETAS 1983 and on Y and P on pages 21–22. To find quarterly data on R^L, however, you will have to resort to Table 30 of the Bank of England Statistical Abstract No. 1 (1970), as well as ETAS 1983, p.195 (you will have to take the average of monthly figures). Estimation of [10.14A] for this period should yield

$$\hat{m}_t = 1.332 - 0.101r_t^L + 0.282y_t + 0.381p_t + 0.609m_{t-1}$$
$$(2.473) \quad (0.043) \quad (0.184) \quad (0.185) \quad (0.158)$$
$$R^2 = 0.981 \quad h = 1.35 \qquad [A10.5]$$

Equation [A10.5] implies values for the parameters in [10.14A] of $\mu = 0.391$, $\beta = -0.258$, $\gamma = 0.721$, $\delta = 0.974$. Notice that the price elasticity of the demand for nominal balances is now very close to unity. In fact, enforcing the restriction $\delta = 1$ yields

$$\widehat{m_t - p_t} = 1.502 - 0.103r_t^L + 0.267y_t + 0.608(m_{t-1} - p_t)$$
$$(1.809) \quad (0.037) \quad\quad (0.104) \quad\quad (0.150)$$
$$R^2 = 0.708 \quad h = 1.28 \qquad [A10.6]$$

Don't be misled by the reduction in R^2 in [A10.6]. We are now attempting to

329

explain variations in *real* balances, M/P, whereas in [A10.5] the dependent variable was *nominal* balances. The 'superior' R^2 in [A10.5] is chiefly the result of the common upward trend in the M and P variables. A better comparison of 'fits' in this case is provided by s, the standard deviation of the residuals (see Section 2.4). In [A10.5] $s = 1.485 \times 10^{-2}$, whereas in [A10.6] s falls to 1.459×10^{-2}. You should now test the restriction $\delta = 1$ in the same manner as we tested it for annual data. You will again find that the restriction cannot be rejected. Thus our first quarterly sample also supports the theoretical prediction that demand for money functions are homogeneous of degree unity in the price level.

Equation [A10.6] implies underlying parameter values of $\mu = 0.392$, $\beta = -0.263$, $\gamma = 0.681$. The value of μ suggests that some 39 per cent of any discrepancy between actual and desired balances is eliminated *per quarter*. This is a somewhat faster and more plausible rate of adjustment than that implied by our annual equations. The interest elasticity, β, is again in line with usual findings, while an income elasticity, γ, of less than unity suggests economies of scale in the holding of money balances, (as predicted for transactions balances by the Baumol–Tobin inventory–theoretic approach).

We shall now take the opportunity of applying the first of the Chow tests for parameter stability described in Section 5.3. For our second sample we shall use quarterly data for 1974–81. This covers a period after the introduction of the new Competition, Credit and Control system. All data can be obtained from the sources already given in *ETAS* 1983. Equivalent versions of [A10.6] for 1974–81 and for the pooled sample period are

1974–81 $\quad \widehat{m_t - p_t} = 2.201 - 0.083r_t^L - 0.106y_t + 0.906(m_{t-1} - p_t)$
$$\qquad\qquad\quad (0.733)\quad (0.037)\qquad (0.048)\qquad (0.060)$$
$$R^2 = 0.904 \quad \textstyle\sum e_2^2 = 0.843 \times 10^{-2}$$

pooled $\quad \widehat{m_t - p_t} = 1.544 - 0.064r_t^L - 0.00085y_t + 0.846(m_{t-1} - p_t)$
$$\qquad\qquad\quad (0.670)\quad (0.020)\qquad (0.0385)\qquad (0.057)$$
$$R^2 = 0.934 \quad \textstyle\sum e_p^2 = 1.941 \times 10^{-2}$$

A comparison of the above equations with [A10.6] again suggests considerable parameter instability. For the later 1964–71 period, the coefficient on the income variable has the wrong sign with a t-ratio of 2.21, while for the pooled sample period it is insignificantly different from zero. The coefficient on $m_{t-1} - p_t$ is also much higher for the later period, suggesting an implausibly slow adjustment process. Applying the first Chow test statistic [5.60] yields, since the residual sum of squares in [A10.6] is $\sum e_1^2 = 0.596 \times 10^{-2}$

$$\left\{ \frac{\sum e_p^2 - (\sum e_1^2 + \sum e_2^2)}{(\sum e_1^2 + \sum e_2^2)} \right\} \left\{ \frac{n_1 + n_2 - 2k}{k} \right\}$$

$$= \left\{ \frac{1.941 - (0.596 + 0.843)}{0.596 + 0.843} \right\} \left\{ \frac{56}{4} \right\} = 4.88$$

With (4, 56) d.f. critical F-values are $F_{0.05} = 2.55$ and $F_{0.01} = 3.68$, so that, as with our previous Chow test, we have to reject the hypothesis of parameter stability.

Quite clearly we have failed to isolate a stable demand for narrow money function. As suggested earlier, this may be because of the very simple lag structure we have experimented with. One possibility we can investigate is whether permanent income, (as determined by an adaptive expectations hypothesis), is preferable to measured income as the scale variable. Rather than face the technical problems (what are they?) of estimating equations such as [10.11], we shall construct permanent income series directly using a generalisation of [7.35]

$$Y_t^P = \lambda Y_t + (1 + g)(1 - \lambda)Y_{t-1}^P \qquad\qquad [A10.7]$$

In [A10.7] a secular long-run permanent income growth rate, g, has been built into the standard adaptive expectations equation. Given an estimate of g plus a starting value, Y_0^P, for permanent income, we can use [A10.7] to generate a series for Y_t^P for any given value of λ. We shall estimate g by the growth rate in measured income over our sample period. If measured income grows exponentially, then

$$Y_t = Y_0 e^{gt}$$

or, taking logarithms

$$\log Y_t = \log Y_0 + gt,$$

where t is time and Y_0 is income at time $t = 0$. Estimating such an equation over our earlier sample period, 1964–71 yields

$$\widehat{\log Y_t} = 9.53 \quad + 0.00472t \qquad R^2 = 0.877 \quad d = 1.93 \qquad [A10.8]$$
$$\quad\quad (0.006) \quad (0.00032)$$

In [A10.8] the time trend t simply takes the values $1, 2, 3, \ldots, 32$. The equation implies a growth rate for real measured income of 0.472 per cent per quarter or $g = 0.00472$. It also gives a value for Y_0, the 'trend' value of income at $t = 0$, that is during 1963(iv). We can obtain this by taking the antilog of the intercept which yields $Y_0 = £13,845$ million. We shall regard this trend value as an estimate of permanent income during 1963(iv). Using [A10.7], we can now, for any given value of λ, generate a data series for Y_t^P and then estimate equations such as [10.9] directly. For example, taking $\lambda = 0.5$ yields

$$\hat{m}_t = -0.011 - 0.111r_t^L + 0.449y_t^P + 0.351p_t + 0.580m_{t-1}$$
$$\quad (3.041) \quad (0.043)(0.274) \qquad\quad (0.190) \quad (0.152)$$
$$R^2 = 0.982 \quad h = 1.47 \qquad [A10.9]$$

Equation [A10.9] is the estimating equation obtained if measured income is replaced by permanent income in equation [10.14A].

Notice that [A10.9] is very little different in terms of overall fit from equation [A10.5] in which measured income is used as the scale variable. You will also find little change in equation [A10.6] if you replace y_t by y_t^P. However, $\lambda = 0.5$ may not, of course, be the appropriate value for generating the permanent income series. You should now use [A10.7] and [A10.8] to generate series for Y_t^P for values of λ equal to $0.1, 0.2, 0.3, \ldots, 0.9$. You can then try each series as the scale variable in your demand for money function and find the value of λ which results in the smallest residual sum of squares. Repeat this procedure for the later sample period 1974–81 and see whether you can isolate a stable demand for money function with permanent income as the scale variable. Don't expect to be oversuccessful!

You should now repeat the above analysis for the UK broad money aggregate M3. The required data sources are the same as those for M1. Re-read the last part of Section 10.2 to see if it gives you any ideas for alternative ways of estimating demand for M3 parameters using an OLS program. Remember also, that we have so far adopted only the simplest of lag structures in our equations. You could try fitting polynomial or rational lag functions for both M1 and M3.

Finally, now you have found a way of generating data on permanent income, you can refer back to the exercise at the end of Chapter 7 and re-estimate equation [A7.8] using alternative series for permanent income. Remember, though, that you will first have to re-estimate [A10.8] to obtain a value of g over the period 1966–75. Compare your best-fitting permanent income equation with those obtained for the RIH.

Notes

1. A high coefficient of determination is, in fact, a necessary but not sufficient condition. If a third variable were important, but during the sample period happened to be highly correlated with R and Y, a high coefficient of determination could still be obtained if the effect of the third variable is captured by the R and Y variables.
2. Much later work by, for example, Weinrobe (1972), has suggested that the precautionary demand for money may also be dependent on 'the brokerage fee' and on the rate of interest.
3. The resultant function is that implied by the old 'Cambridge version' of the quantity theory of money, i.e. $M_D/P = kY$ where k depends on the level of interest rates.
4. In the Tobin analysis risk is measured by the standard deviation of the possible rates of return on the portfolio.
5. The variable most commonly used is the 'consolidated' net worth of the private sector including ownership of government debt. It is consolidated in the sense that 'double-counting' is avoided so that in cases where, for example, households own firms, the value of firms' wealth is counted only once despite the fact that it also forms part of household wealth. Such empirical evidence as exists (see, for example, Meltzer 1963) suggests that the extent of consolidation makes little difference to results. The inclusion of government debt implies that the private sector does not regard future tax liabilities as reducing its net worth.
6. Hence, deflation of lagged nominal balances by the lagged price level as in [10.14] implies an instantaneous adjustment of the demand for nominal balances to changes in the price level. However, deflation by the current price level as in [10.14B] implies a lagged adjustment to price level changes identical to the response to changes in y_t or r_t.
7. Teigen's demand for money equation included a lagged money stock variable m_{t-1} to allow for partial adjustment of actual to desired balances.

The steady state elasticity is found by setting $m_t = m_{t-1}$ in his estimated equation.

8. Equation [10.36] can be written as

$$\frac{M_t}{Y_t} = AR_t^{\alpha_1} \bar{Y}_t^{\alpha_2} \left(\frac{M_{t-1}}{Y_t} \right)^{\alpha_3}$$

or

$$\frac{M_t}{P_t} = AR_t^{\alpha_1} \bar{Y}_t^{1+\alpha_2-\alpha_3} \left(\frac{M_{t-1}}{P_t} \right)^{\alpha_3}$$

where $\alpha_0 = \log A$ and $1 + \alpha_2 - \alpha_3 < 1$.

9. Equation [10.36] may also be rewritten as

$$m_t - p_t = \alpha_0 + \alpha_1 r_t + (1 + \alpha_2 - \alpha_3)\bar{y}_t - \alpha_3(m_{t-1} - p_t)$$

and, hence, implies the same adjustment processes as do equations [10.14A] and [10.14B] and is the same as [10.14B] as far as the long-run price elasticity is concerned.

10. If two variables are 'trending' over time, they will necessarily be highly correlated even if there is no *causal* relationship between them.

11. Equation [10.41] is obtained in the usual manner. First lag equation [10.40] by one period and multiply throughout by $1 - \rho$. Then subtract the equation thus obtained from [10.40]. On rearrangement, the equation eventually obtained becomes [10.41].

12. Hacche's assumption that v_t in [10.39] follows a first-order scheme, implies that, for some unstated reason, the disturbance $\mu\varepsilon_t$ in equation [10.14B] follows the second-order scheme

$$(\mu\varepsilon)_t = (1 + \rho)(\mu\varepsilon)_{t-1} - \rho(\mu\varepsilon)_{t-2} + u_t$$

11 Macroeconomic models

The history of macroeconomic model-building stretches back to the early business cycle models of Tinbergen (1939; 1951). During this time the size of macroeconomic models has grown considerably – whereas in the early 1950s the largest was the Klein–Goldberger annual model of the US economy with twenty-two structural equations, the largest models currently in use are quarterly models and contain many hundreds and occasionally thousands of equations.

Macro-models have come increasingly into use as aids to government policymaking. Forecasts from models are published regularly and are of use not only to governments but also to private firms in the planning of their investment programmes. However, the provision of forecasts is not the only use to which, ideally, macro-models can be put. As we shall see, 'simulation' of macro-models can increase understanding about the workings of an economy and, in addition, they can be used to assess the likely effect of alternative government policy measures.

Different theoretical perspectives have led to two different approaches to model-building. Since Keynesians believe that disaggregation both by sector and expenditure category is necessary for a proper understanding of a complex modern economy, they tend to favour large structural models. Monetarists, on the other hand, tend to bypass the detailed structure of an economy and stress the effect of monetary changes on aggregate money income, ignoring individual expenditure categories. This naturally leads to smaller-scale models. However, most of the macro-models now in use, particularly in the UK, have been developed out of earlier models constructed at a time when 'Keynesianism' dominated the thinking of most economists. They have therefore tended to retain a basic Keynesian income–expenditure structure, although in recent years far more attention has been given to the modelling of monetary variables and to the channels by which these variables may influence the real economy.

We begin this chapter by introducing some basic ideas about macro-models, illustrating them by means of an early six-equation model. Next, we compare in a general manner the structure of the major present-day UK models. Finally, we describe how, in practice, these models are used for making forecasts and also consider the use of models in their so-called 'simulation mode'.

11.1 Some basic ideas

Consider the following very simple model of an economy

$$C_t = \alpha + \beta Y_t \tag{11.1}$$

$$I_t = \gamma (Y_t - Y_{t-1}) \tag{11.2}$$

334

$$Y_t = C_t + I_t + G_t \qquad [11.3]$$

Equation [11.1] is a simple Keynesian consumption function relating consumption, C_t, to income, Y_t. I_t is investment which is determined by a simple accelerator mechanism and G_t is government expenditure. The model is a three-equation system in three endogenous variables C_t, Y_t and I_t, with two predetermined variables, Y_{t-1} and G_t. Y_{t-1} is, of course, a lagged endogenous variable and G_t is exogenously determined. The system is, in fact, a version of the famous Samuelson–Hicks multiplier–accelerator model.

Notice firstly that, if we wish to assess the immediate current period effect of a change in G_t on the endogenous variables, we must consider both direct and indirect effects. For example, there will be a direct effect on Y_t because of the appearance of G_t in the income identity [11.3]. But there will also be indirect effects because any rise in Y_t leads to increases in C_t and I_t via equations [11.1] and [11.2]. These increases lead to further increases in Y_t via equation [11.3]. To obtain the overall effect within the current period of a change in G_t it is simplest to consider the reduced form which for the above model is

$$C_t = a_1 + b_1 Y_{t-1} + c_1 G_t \qquad [11.4]$$

$$Y_t = a_2 + b_2 Y_{t-1} + c_2 G_t \qquad [11.5]$$

$$I_t = a_3 + b_3 Y_{t-1} + c_3 G_t \qquad [11.6]$$

The reduced form gives the endogenous variables as functions of the predetermined variables, Y_{t-1} and G_t, alone. The a's, b's and c's are, of course, functions of the parameters in the original structural equations. In fact, for example

$$c_1 = \frac{\beta}{1 - \beta - \gamma}, \quad c_2 = \frac{1}{1 - \beta - \gamma}, \quad c_3 = \frac{\gamma}{1 - \beta - \gamma}$$

We can now see that the overall *immediate* effects of a unit increase in G_t on C_t, Y_t and I_t are given by c_1, c_2 and c_3 respectively. The quantities c_1, c_2 and c_3 are known as *impact multipliers*.

However, the impact multipliers do not give the total effect of a change in government expenditure on the endogenous variables but only the effect within the same time period. The appearance of the lagged endogenous variable, Y_{t-1}, in the model means that our model is *dynamic* and that a change in G_t has further effects after the current period. The impact effect leads to an immediate increase in Y_t, but the appearance of Y_{t-1} in all the reduced-form equations [11.4–11.6] ensures that there are further changes in C, Y and I during period $t + 1$.[1] This change in Y_{t+1} then leads to further changes in C, Y and I during period $t + 2$, etc., etc.

We can examine these long-run effects on, for example, consumption by successively substituting for $Y_{t-1}, Y_{t-2}, Y_{t-3}$, etc. in equation [11.4]

$$
\begin{aligned}
C_t &= a_1 + b_1(a_2 + b_2 Y_{t-2} + c_2 G_{t-1}) + c_1 G_t \\
&= a_1 + a_2 b_1 + b_1 b_2 (a_2 + b_2 Y_{t-3} + c_2 G_{t-2}) + c_1 G_t + b_1 c_2 G_{t-1} \\
&= a_1 + a_2 b_1 (1 + b_2) + b_1 b_2^2 (a_2 + b_2 Y_{t-4} + c_2 G_{t-3}) + c_1 G_t \\
&\quad + b_1 c_2 G_{t-1} + b_1 c_2 b_2 G_{t-2}
\end{aligned}
$$

......

335

$$\begin{aligned} \ldots\ldots \\ = a_1 + a_2 b_1 (1 + b_2 + b_2^2 + b_2^3 \ldots) + c_1 G_t + b_1 c_2 G_{t-1} \\ + b_1 c_2 b_2 G_{t-2} + b_1 c_2 b_2^2 G_{t-3} + \cdots \end{aligned}$$

That is, provided $b_2 < 1$

$$C_t = a_1 + \frac{a_2 b_1}{1 - b_2} + c_1 G_t + b_1 c_2 (G_{t-1} + b_2 G_{t-2} + b_2^2 G_{t-3} \ldots) \qquad [11.7]$$

Similarly, successive substitution for Y_{t-1} in equations [11.5] and [11.6] yields eventually

$$Y_t = \left(\frac{a_2}{1 - b_2} \right) + c_2 (G_t + b_2 G_{t-1} + b_2^2 G_{t-1} \ldots) \qquad [11.8]$$

and

$$I_t = a_3 + \frac{a_2 b_3}{1 - b_2} + c_3 G_t + b_3 c_2 (G_{t-1} + b_2 G_{t-2} + b_2^2 G_{t-3} \ldots) \qquad [11.9]$$

Equations [11.7–11.9] represent the *final form* of the system. They express the endogenous variables in terms of the exogenous levels (both current and past) of government expenditure only. To obtain the long-run final effect of a sustained change in government expenditure, suppose such expenditure remains constant at a level $G_t = \bar{G}$. The final-form equation for C_t then becomes

$$C_t = a_1 + \frac{a_2 b_1}{1 - b_2} + \{ c_1 + b_1 c_2 (1 + b_2 + b_2^2 + b_2^3 \ldots) \} \bar{G}$$

or, again assuming $b_2 < 1$,

$$C_t = a_1 + \frac{a_2 b_1}{1 - b_2} + \left\{ c_1 + \frac{b_1 c_2}{1 - b_2} \right\} \bar{G} \qquad [11.10]$$

Similarly, equations [11.8] and [11.9] become

$$Y_t = \frac{a_2}{1 - b_2} + \left\{ \frac{c_2}{1 - b_2} \right\} \bar{G} \qquad [11.11]$$

and

$$I_t = a_3 + \frac{a_2 b_3}{1 - b_2} + \left\{ c_3 + \frac{b_3 c_2}{1 - b_2} \right\} \bar{G} \qquad [11.12]$$

We can now see that the *long-run effect* of a *sustained* unit increase in government expenditure on consumption, income and investment is given by the coefficients of $\bar{G}$ in equations [11.10–11.12]. These quantities are known as *equilibrium dynamic multipliers*. Notice that the change in government expenditure we are talking about here is a change from one continually recurring level to another continually recurring level.

The equilibrium multipliers may also be obtained by setting $Y_t = Y_{t-1}$ in the reduced-form equations and solving for C_t, Y_t and I_t in terms of G_t. The advantage of deriving the final-form equations first is that this enables us to derive the time paths of C_t, Y_t and I_t after the change in government expenditure. Given values for the exogenous G's we can use [11.7–11.9] to obtain the values of

C, Y and I for any time period. Also, it may not be the case that the model converges to a new equilibrium after a disturbance or, alternatively, if it does, convergence may take many years. The long-run equilibrium multipliers will then have no useful meaning and we may be more interested in the effects of a change in G after two or three years.

The condition for convergence in the above model is $b_2 < 1$ [2] and, in fact, substitution of typical values for the MPC, β, and the capital/output ratio, γ, into the expression for b_2 suggest that the condition is not met.[3] To obtain the effect of a sustained increase in government expenditure after, for example, two years, it is simply necessary to add the additional effects one year and two years hence to the impact effect. For example, the effect on consumption one year hence of a unit increase in G is given by the coefficient of G_{t-1} in equation [11.7] and the effect two years hence by the coefficient of G_{t-2}. These coefficients are, in fact, known as *interim multipliers*. The total effect in two years time is therefore given by

$$c_1 + b_1 c_2 + b_1 c_2 b_2$$

In general, the total effect, n years hence, of a sustained unit change in government expenditure on consumption is

$$c_1 + b_1 c_2 (1 + b_2 + b_2^2 + b_2^3 + \ldots + b_2^{n-1}) \tag{11.13}$$

On income it is

$$c_2 (1 + b_2 + b_2^2 + b_2^3 + \ldots + b_2^n) \tag{11.14}$$

and on investment

$$c_3 + b_3 c_2 (1 + b_2 + b_2^2 + b_2^3 + \ldots + b_2^{n-1}) \tag{11.15}$$

As has been already pointed out, the expressions [11.13–11.15] may have more operational content than the equilibrium multipliers and hence be of more interest for policy purposes. Notice that if the condition for convergence is met, i.e. if $b_2 < 1$, then the additional effects of the increase in G become less and less over time and, as n increases, the expressions [11.13–11.15] approach the equilibrium multipliers given by [11.10–11.12].

Klein model I

To illustrate the above ideas we shall use the six-equation model of the US economy constructed by Klein (1950) and generally referred to as Klein model I. Although a small model by present standards, it has been extensively examined and we can take advantage of the fact that values for the various impact, interim and equilibrium multipliers are readily available. The model has, in fact, been used as a testing ground for many of the new estimation techniques that have since been developed.

The model contains three behavioural equations and three identities. The first equation is a consumption function which allows for different MPC out of profits and wage income

$$C_t = \alpha_0 + \alpha_1 \Pi_t + \alpha_2 \Pi_{t-1} + \alpha_3 (W_{1t} + W_{2t}) + \varepsilon_{1t} \tag{11.16}$$

where C_t is aggregate consumption, Π_t profits, and W_{1t} and W_{2t} are the private industry and government wage bills.

Investment is determined by a profits rather than an accelerator theory so that the second equation is

$$I_t = \beta_0 + \beta_1 \Pi_t + \beta_2 \Pi_{t-1} + \beta_3 K_{t-1} + \varepsilon_{2t} \qquad [11.17]$$

where I_t is aggregate net investment and K_{t-1} is the beginning of period capital stock.

The third equation is an employment equation. The private wage bill (as an indicator of employment) is related to current and previous period total private product and a time trend. Total private product is measured as net national product, Y_t, plus business taxes, T_t, minus the government wage bill.

$$W_{1t} = \gamma_0 + \gamma_1(Y_t + T_t - W_{2t}) + \gamma_2(Y_{t-1} + T_{t-1} - W_{2t-1}) + \gamma_3 t + \varepsilon_{3t} \qquad [11.18]$$

The time trend t is included to account for the effect of growing trade union strength on the private wage bill.

The above three equations contain disturbances $\varepsilon_{1t}, \varepsilon_{2t}$ and ε_{3t} respectively but the remaining three equations are definitional identities

$$Y_t = C_t + I_t + G_t - T_t \qquad [11.19]$$

$$Y_t = \Pi_t + W_{1t} + W_{2t} \qquad [11.20]$$

$$I_t = K_t - K_{t-1} \qquad [11.21]$$

The first identity expresses net national product as the sum of all expenditures less taxes. The second defines net national income as the sum of profits and wages while the third simply states that net investment equals the change in capital stock. Equations [11.16 − 11.21] represent a six-equation income–expenditure model in six endogenous variables $C_t, I_t, W_{1t}, Y_t, \Pi_t$ and K_t. There are four exogenous variables – the government sector variables W_{2t}, G_t and T_t plus the time trend and three lagged endogenous variables Y_{t-1}, Π_{t-1} and K_{t-1}. Lagged values of two of the exogenous variables W_{2t-1} and T_{t-1} also appear.

Since there are fifteen variables in the model altogether, the first three equations are clearly overidentified. Klein estimates their parameters by three different methods – OLS, limited information maximum likelihood (LIML) and full information maximum likelihood (FIML). Alternative two-stage and three-stage least squares estimates were later provided by Zellner and Theil (1962). Klein's FIML estimates are presented in Table 11.1.

11.1 Full information maximum likelihood estimates of parameters in Klein model I.

i	0	1	2	3
α_i	16.78	0.020	0.235	0.800
β_i	17.79	0.231	0.546	−0.146
γ_i	1.60	0.420	0.164	0.135

Source: L.R. Klein (1950)

11.2 Reduced-form parameters for Klein model I.

Endo-genous variable	Reduced-form coefficient of								
	Y_{t-1}	Π_{t-1}	K_{t-1}	W_{2t}	G_t	T_t	t	W_{2t-1}	Y_{t-1}
C_t	0.189	0.743	−0.098	0.666	0.671	−0.188	0.155	−0.189	0.189
I_t	−0.015	0.746	−0.184	−0.052	0.259	−0.296	−0.012	0.015	−0.015
W_{1t}	0.237	0.626	−0.119	−0.162	0.811	−0.204	0.195	−0.237	0.237
Y_t	0.174	1.489	−0.283	0.614	1.930	−1.484	0.143	−0.174	0.174
Π_t	−0.063	0.363	−0.164	0.224	1.119	−1.281	−0.052	0.063	−0.063
K_t	−0.015	0.746	0.816	−0.052	0.259	−0.296	−0.012	0.015	−0.015

Source: Theil and Boot (1962)

The reduced-form for this set of estimates has been calculated by Theil and Boot (1962) and is given in Table 11.2.

The impact multipliers defined in the previous section are shown in the columns underneath the policy instrument variables W_{2t}, G_t and T_t in Table 11.2. Thus the immediate current period impact of a $1 million increase in taxation is a reduction of $0.188 million in consumption, a reduction of $0.296 million in investment, etc., etc. The impact effect of a $1 million increase in government expenditure on, for example, income, is an increase of $1.930 million. Since the tax-multiplier in this case is − 1.484 we can obtain a value for the balanced budget impact multiplier of $1.930 − 1.484 = 0.446$ for income. Similarly, the balanced budget multiplier for the private wage bill is 0.607 while for profits it is − 0.162. Thus balanced increases in government expenditure and taxation initially benefit wages rather than profits.

Theil and Boot also calculate long-run equilibrium multipliers (of interest provided the process is convergent) for the three-policy instruments. These are shown in Table 11.3.

The long-run dynamic multiplier effects on investment are zero because, in equilibrium, capital stock is constant so that no investment takes place. The long-run effect of a $1 million increase in G is a rise of $2.323 million in income, while that of a similar increase in T is a fall of $1.569 million. Thus the long-run balanced budget multiplier effect on income is $2.323 − 1.569 = 0.754$. This compares with an impact multiplier of 0.446, so that roughly 60 per cent of the effect of a balanced increase in government expenditure and taxation is felt immediately. Similarly, the long-run balanced budget multiplier effect on W_1 is $1.358 − 0.333 = 1.025$ while on Π it is $0.965 − 1.237 = − 0.272$. Thus the long-run effect as well as the impact effect of such a policy is to benefit wages rather than profits.

11.3 Long-run multipliers for Klein model I.

	C	I	W_1	Y	Π	K
W_2	0.536	0	−0.271	0.536	−0.192	−1.024
G	1.323	0	1.358	2.323	0.965	5.123
T	−0.569	0	−0.333	−1.569	−1.237	−6.564

Source: Theil and Boot (1962)

Theil and Boot also compute interim multipliers which measure the effect of a change (not sustained) in one of the exogenous variables on the endogenous variables a finite number of periods j later. These are, in fact, equivalent to the coefficients on the current and lagged G variables in equations [11.7–11.9]. These multipliers, in fact, change sign as j increases, indicating that the system oscillates after an external shock. By adding these interim multipliers together we can find the effect of a sustained change in any of the exogenous variables as was done to derive equations [11.13–11.15]. It is then possible to plot the time paths of the endogenous variables after a disturbance. Such time paths are shown in Fig. 11.1 for a sustained increase of $1 million in government expenditure.

It can be seen from Fig. 11.1 that the first-period impact effects of the change in G give little indication of what the long-run equilibrium effects will be. While this is already apparent from study of the impact and equilibrium multipliers in Tables 11.2 and 11.3, what Fig. 11.1 also illustrates is that neither impact nor equilibrium multipliers give any indication of the effect of the change after, for example, two to three years. As already noted, for policy purposes we are often more interested in such effects as these than in the final long-run effects.

The time paths of Fig. 11.1 also confirm that Klein model I is, in fact, a stable system.[4] The endogenous variables do eventually converge on their long-run equilibrium values after the change in G, although clearly the system oscillates on its way to its new equilibrium. The long-run equilibrium multipliers of Table 11.3 do then have some operational meaning although, since the system only begins to converge on its equilibrium after fifteen to twenty years, they have limited practical significance.

Before leaving the Klein model it is worth asking why, since all the use we have made of that model has involved only the reduced-form parameters, so much effort was put into estimating the structural parameters? Why not simply estimate the reduced-form directly, thus bypassing the problems of simultaneity

11.1 Time paths for the endogenous variables in Klein model I.

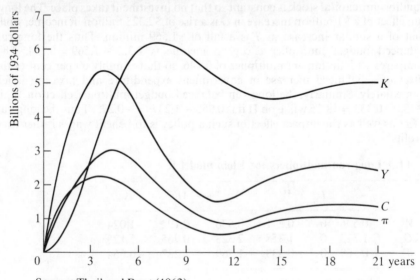

Source: Theil and Boot (1962)

and overidentification? The reason is that any *a priori* information about the sign and maybe size of parameters provided by economic theory almost always refers to the structural parameters. Hence, the plausibility of estimates can be best assessed when they refer to the structural equations. Furthermore, suppose we have reason to believe that one of the parameters in the model is likely to change during the forecast period. If the parameter is a reduced-form parameter there is no problem, but it is much more likely to be a structural parameter, e.g. the MPC wage income in Klein model I. If we only have estimates of the reduced-form parameters it becomes far more difficult to adjust forecasts to allow for the suspected change.

11.2 United Kingdom macro-models

As noted at the outset all the major macroeconometric models of the UK economy were originally based on essentially Keynesian ideas. However, it needs no more than a moment's reflection to realise that the standard textbook version of the 'Keynesian model' is likely to be an inadequate representation of a real world economy. While it is easy to broaden the simple model given by equations [11.1–11.3] into a 'full blown' IS-LM model complete with production function and labour market, it is clear that even this falls well short of a realistic model. At the very least, in an economy as 'open' as the UK, a foreign sector has to be included and if the model is to be used to analyse fiscal and monetary policies then the government sector has to be modelled also. Hence, instead of [11.3] we need to write

$$Y_t = C_t + I_t + G_t + X_t - M_t - T_t \qquad [11.22]$$

where X_t and M_t represent exports and imports of goods and services and T_t refers to indirect taxes net of expenditure subsidies.

Disaggregation is also likely to be necessary in terms of income and output. Income is the sum of the various factor shares so we may also therefore have

$$Y_t = W_t + (RP)_t + D_t + (TY)_t \qquad [11.23]$$

where W_t is disposable wage income, $(RP)_t$ represents retained profits, D_t dividends, and $(TY)_t$ taxes on income. The consumption function [11.1] might then be respecified to allow for different propensities to consume wage and non-wage income, as in Klein model I, and/or by replacing total income, Y_t, by personal disposable income, $Y_t - (TY)_t - (RP)_t$.

Output may need to be disaggregated into at least the major sectors of the economy, so we might also have, for example

$$Y_t = A_t + N_t + S_t \qquad [11.24]$$

where A_t, N_t and S_t are the outputs of the agricultural, manufacturing and service sectors.

The three identities [11.22–11.24] all introduce additional variables, most of which cannot be treated as exogenous, and which therefore imply a need for additional equations. For example, imports in [11.22] and taxes on income in [11.23] are obviously going to depend on income Y_t and, to explain any split

341

between retained profits and dividends, it is likely to be necessary to introduce the yield on equities and the return to capital.

When it is also realised that the major expenditure components in the textbook Keynesian model will also need to be split up – consumption into its durable and non-durable components, investment at least into fixed investment and inventories – it is not difficult to understand how we can soon find ourselves with a very large simultaneous equation model indeed.

Another important manner in which the econometric models differ from those of the textbook is in the attention paid to the dynamic structure of equations. The typical textbook model is entirely static in nature, yielding equilibrium solutions but having nothing to say about the time path by which an economy moves to such an equilibrium. While such models, suitably disaggregated, may be satisfactory for the analysis and forecasting of long-run developments in an economy, most macroeconomic models are built for short-term forecasting and policy analysis. Since initial changes in response to any disturbance are likely to be significantly less than the overall long-run effects, the manner in which an economy approaches its long-run position becomes of overriding importance. As in our discussion of Klein model I, we are interested in impact and interim multipliers rather than long-run multipliers. This requirement necessitates careful specification of the lag structures in the behavioural relationships since it is through such lagged responses that the models link one period to the next.

There are six major macroeconometric models of the UK – those of the Bank of England, Her Majesty's Treasury, the National Institute (NI), the London Business School (LBS), the Cambridge Economic Policy Group (CEPG) and Cambridge Econometrics (CE). Since all the models developed out of orthodox 'Keynesian' ideas, they adopt an income–expenditure approach with effective demand and hence GNP determined by the expenditures of private, government and overseas sectors. The degree of disaggregation and, hence, the size of the models varies, however. For example, the CE model contains as many as 3,000 equations, whereas the NI contains only about 150. The equations in all the models are continually being revised so it is pointless to describe them in detail.[5] We shall therefore concentrate on the general structure and underlying ideas of the models, paying some attention to those aspects that have been covered in detail in earlier chapters. For a more detailed comparison of the various models see the survey by Thompson (1984).

The real sector

Since all models adopt an income–expenditure approach, most analyse the major components of total expenditure – consumption, investment, stockbuilding, exports and imports. The exception is the CEPG model which has an equation for aggregate private sector expenditure – both consumption and investment, and another equation for private fixed investment. Consumption in this model is then determined by the difference between the two.

Consumption
Apart from the CEPG model, all models disaggregate consumption into its durable and non-durable components and in some cases separate equations are estimated for individual items within these categories. For non-durable con-

sumption, equations of a general nature, consistent with any of the standard theories of consumption behaviour outlined in Chapter 7, are estimated in real terms with lagged consumption and current and lagged income among the explanatory variables. The DHSY (1978) methodology has recently been adopted by the Treasury and LBS models so that non-durable consumption equations in these models have a form similar to equation [7.67]. The Treasury model adds the change in unemployment as a proxy for uncertainty to the variables explaining changes in consumption. The Treasury model also adopts the DHSY approach in the estimation of consumer durable equations. Other models, however, tend to use the conventional stock adjustment formulation described in Section 6.5.

All the models now include some form of wealth or liquid asset variables. The Bank of England model uses liquid asset-type variables in both its durable and non-durable equations, whereas the Treasury model includes net-financial wealth (liquid and non-liquid) in its equations for durables but not for non-durables. Moreover, as we saw in Chapter 7, the DHSY type terms when combined with inflation variables can also be interpreted as representing a classical wealth effect operating via money-fixed assets, and such an interpretation is adopted in the Treasury model. Inflation effects are also included in the non-durables equations of the LBS model.

Credit availability effects on consumption dominate cost of credit or interest rate effects in most models, although the Treasury equations for durables include a real interest rate variable. Credit availability effects on the consumption of durable goods are allowed for, both through the inclusion of policy variables and via variables reflecting the level of outstanding credit. For example, in the Bank of England and LBS models the minimum deposit rate on durables is included as a policy variable, while the NI model includes a variable constructed from the stock of non-householding loans to the personal sector and the change in outstanding hire purchase debt.

Investment in plant and equipment
Fixed investment is generally analysed by sector rather than by type of asset. For example, in the Treasury model there are two main categories: investment in manufacturing and investment in other industries. A single equation is always used to determine both replacement and net investment. In most models private investment in housebuilding is considered separately, as is public sector investment which is typically regarded as exogenously determined.

Most investment equations are based on some form of accelerator-type relationship so that terms in the change in output are important explanatory variables. However, both the LBS and Treasury models adopt the DSHY approach in the manner of Bean (1981), as described in Section 9.5. This approach, of course, implies an equilibrium relationship between investment and output rather than between capital stock and output. None of the UK models follow the neo-classical approach of Jorgenson and his associates. Interest rate effects have therefore been searched for in a relatively *ad hoc* manner and with little success. As observed in Chapter 9, this is consistent with UK research generally. However, availability rather than cost of funds may be of more relevance and the main investment equations of both the LBS and NI models include profit variables while the Treasury model at one time included company cash flow variables.

Other forms of investment

All the models contain equations explaining *stockbuilding* by firms, although the degree of disaggregation varies. For example, the Treasury model contains six equations for various kinds of stock, while the LBS and CEPG models each contain only one aggregate equation. Most models use a stock adjustment mechanism with desired stocks dependent on expected output or sales. The LBS model, however, adopts the DHSY approach. None of the stockbuilding equations have proved particularly successful, mainly because such stockbuilding is unplanned and, hence, difficult to model.

Whereas financial factors play a fairly minor role in the stockbuilding equations they are of overriding importance in equations explaining *private sector investment in housing*. With the exception of the CEPG model, all the models contain a separate equation for housebuilding and the behaviour of building societies is modelled in detail in the Treasury, Bank of England and LBS models. Both interest rate and credit availability effects on housebuilding are considered, operating either via the demand side or via the supply side of the market and sometimes both. Indeed, in UK macro-models it is through private spending on housebuilding that interest rates have their greatest effect on expenditure.

Imports and exports

All the models specify equations for various categories of imports and exports. Explanatory variables in both types of equation include both measures of competitiveness and measures of demand. Thus imports generally depend on UK output and expenditure and on the relationship between UK and overseas costs and prices. Exports equations include as explanatory variables some measure of world trade and production plus the relative cost/price measures.

Government income and expenditure

Government expenditure on goods and services is treated as mainly exogenous. However, other categories of government expenditure such as unemployment benefit and social security payments are endogenously modelled in some cases. All models consider government income arising from taxes, both direct and indirect. While the various tax rates are assumed to be exogenous, such income is determined by applying these rates to the endogenous income and expenditure flows.

Given the above modelling of real flows in the economy, plus a set of identities, current values of income, output and expenditure for each sector of the economy are determined. Equations for *employment* levels are then related to these output levels, although productivity trends are included as separate explanatory variables in the employment equations of the Bank of England, Treasury and LBS models. The level of *unemployment* is generally determined from the employment equation and an exogenous estimate of labour supply. Only in the Treasury model has any attempt been made to model the labour supply.

The wage–price sector

Wages per head are either determined by an expectations-augmented Phillips curve relationship as in the Treasury, NI and CE models, or seen as the outcome of institutionalised bargaining between unions and employers as in the Bank of

England and CEPG models. Some models include income policy dummy variables but in the Treasury model exogenous estimates of wage change are made during periods of incomes policy, the size of these changes depending on the guidelines in force.

Domestic prices are determined by markup equations – markups on labour cost, import prices and indirect taxes, with allowance made for changes in labour productivity in the price equations of some models. A wage–price spiral is therefore built into all the models but, except in the NI model, there is no provision for demand pressures to influence prices directly. However, indirect effects make themselves felt via the labour market in those models that contain a Phillips curve relationship.

Price equations are also estimated for various categories of imported and exported goods such as finished manufactured goods and raw materials. For manufactured goods, prices of imports and exports are generally influenced both by the world price and by UK costs. However, for non-manufactures the UK is regarded as a price-taker in both foreign and domestic markets. The LBS model also adopts this approach in its treatment of manufactured imports. In most models world prices are expressed in sterling and hence vary with the exchange rate which is determined in the external monetary sector.

The domestic monetary sector

None of the models base their monetary sectors on the IS-LM model. Thus, rather than explicitly considering demand for and supply of money functions, they are built round the balance sheet identities of the banking and non-banking private sectors and the government's budget constraint. However, decision-making is dichotomised between real expenditure decisions and the purchase and sale of financial assets. We have seen that the real sector in the models determines income and expenditure flows in the various sectors of the economy. In this way financial surpluses and deficits are generated for each sector (including the government) and this creates demand for, and supplies of, various financial assets including money. The split in decision-making means that, in orthodox Keynesian fashion, an excess demand for one financial asset implies excess supplies for other assets but not an excess supply of goods.

The extensiveness of the modelling of portfolio behaviour varies, the most disaggregated treatment being that of the Treasury model. Because of the existence of the balance sheet identities it is not necessary to specify sector equations for all assets and liabilities. Once equations are estimated for $n-1$ of the items in the balance sheet, the nth can be deduced from the balance sheet identity. In many of the models no explicit demand for money functions of the kind described in Chapter 10 appear. Typically, the demand for money is determined as the residual after the other asset allocation decisions of the non-bank private sector have been made. For example, in the Treasury model, non-bank holdings of liquid assets are obtained as the residual and this largely determines the demand for M3. An exception is the NI model which contains a demand for M1 equation, although not a demand for M3 equation. Others such as the LBS and CEPG models contain equations for the money stock or its rate of change, but these include both demand and supply influences.

Interest rates tend to be determined endogenously with representative short-term and long-term rates being specified. In the Treasury model, although the long-term rate is treated as exogenous, the short rate is set so as to ensure market clearing and hence is determined by all participants in the market. The other models generally contain explicit equations for the representative short-term rate that take into account the policy goals of the authorities. The representative long-term rate is then obtained from a term–structure relationship typically including a variable representing the rate of change of prices.

The external monetary sector

Most of the models attempt to estimate explicit exchange rate equations, the rate normally being defined as that for sterling relative to a weighted average of other countries' currencies. The Treasury model, however, has a more complex approach in which the exchange rate is determined by a market-clearing mechanism. In this model the long-run exchange rate is determined by the maintenance of purchasing power parity as determined by trends in relative costs and relative money supply growth rates in the UK and in overseas economies. In the short run the exchange rate also reflects short-term capital flows which are in turn influenced by exchange rate expectations and interest rates.

Although the CEPG model adopts a similar, if less detailed structural approach, all the other models estimate single 'reduced-form' equations to determine exchange rates. The Bank of England and LBS models distinguish between factors, such as the ratios of world money supply to domestic money supply and world output to UK output, which affect equilibrium rates, and other factors, such as interest differentials and relative price inflation between the UK and overseas countries, which are held to determine the actual exchange rate.

The fact that in nearly all the models the exchange rate is influenced by the money supply and by interest rates provides an important potential link between the monetary sectors and the rest of the respective models. Changes in the exchange rate affect competitiveness and hence import and export flows while changes in the level of import prices have a direct effect on the domestic price level.

11.3   Two monetarist models

While the size of the models discussed above stems from their essentially Keynesian origin, monetarists tend to prefer much smaller models, stressing the link between monetary aggregates and money income. The best-known 'monetarist' model of the UK economy is probably that developed at Liverpool University.[6] The Liverpool model is an annual model of just twenty equations. It differs from the UK models just described not only because of its size and the stress it places on monetarist transmission mechanisms but also because of the important role it gives to expectations. In the Liverpool model expectations are not generated by past observations on variables as in other UK models, but by the so-called rational expectations hypothesis. Expectations are, in fact, based on the model's own predictions of the future values of variables. This has the effect that anticipations of government policy even beyond the forecasting horizon are capable of influencing model behaviour within the horizon itself.

Another unusual feature of the Liverpool model is that it is an equilibrium model in the sense that a full rather than any partial adjustment of prices to expected changes in supply and demand is assumed in every period. The model contains a significant 'supply side' determining equilibrium unemployment.

Whereas in most UK macro-models monetary influences on the real sector are felt mainly via the exchange rate, the monetarist aspect of the Liverpool model is seen strongly in the importance it attaches to real balance effects. The level of real wealth (both financial and physical) held by decision-makers plays a key role in the determination of both their investment and consumption expenditures. Since real wealth levels are influenced by changes in the price level and because nominal long-term interest rates are an important factor in determining the market value of financial wealth, money has a more direct impact on aggregate demand than in most other UK models. Uncertainty about future inflation rates is also held to influence expenditure decisions.

The Liverpool model also contains an explicit demand for money function in which the ratio of money demanded to total financial wealth is made dependent on interest rates, total wealth and the measure of future uncertainty about inflation. While under fixed exchange rates the money supply is assumed to be demand-determined, under flexible exchange rates it is regarded as determined by the government via such factors as its long-run budget deficit. Given the demand for money equations, variations in the money supply are therefore transmitted to the real sector via the effect of interest rate changes on the level of real wealth and through changes in the expected rate of inflation.

An even greater contrast to the large-scale Keynesian models is the so-called *St Louis model*, which we shall also describe briefly. The model is named after the link between its builders and the Federal Reserve Bank of St Louis in the US, but has also been estimated from UK data. As presented by Anderson and Carlson (1970) it is an eight-equation model with just five behavioural relationships and three identities. The equation of most interest, however, is one determining changes in total spending $\Delta(YP)_t$

$$\Delta(YP)_t = g(\Delta M_t, \Delta M_{t-1}, \Delta M_{t-2}, \ldots, \Delta M_{t-k}, \Delta E_t,$$
$$\Delta E_{t-1}, \Delta E_{t-2}, \ldots, \Delta E_{t-l}) \tag{11.25}$$

where ΔM_t is the change in the money supply and ΔE_t the change in 'high unemployment' government expenditure (both assumed exogenous). Equation [11.25] is very much a monetarist equation. Since the cumulative effect of the government expenditure variable is expected to be zero, it implies that in the long run changes in spending depend solely on changes in the money supply. Changes in total spending are defined as identically equal to changes in output, ΔY_t, plus changes in prices ΔP_t

$$\Delta(YP)_t = \Delta Y_t + \Delta P_t \tag{11.26}$$

Changes in prices depend on expected price changes and demand pressure (itself partly dependent on $\Delta(YP)_t$). Once $\Delta(YP)_t$ and ΔP_t are determined, changes in output are determined by the identity [11.26]. The rest of the model is concerned with determining the expected rate of price change, the rate of interest (assumed endogenous) and the level of unemployment.

Equation [11.25] is usually estimated from quarterly data using the Almon lag technique described in Section 5.1. Anderson and Carlson use a fourth-order polynomial with β_{-1} and β_5 pegged to zero. The sum of the coefficients on the ΔE

variables is, indeed, zero while changes in the money supply have a rapid effect on changes in total spending. The equation forecasts nominal GNP very well – over 1963–64 its forecasts have a root mean square error of 1.49 per cent.[7] This compares with 2.00 per cent of nominal GNP for the much larger 'Wharton model' of the US over the same period.

Matthews and Ormerod (1978) have obtained similar results with the St Louis model for the UK. The sum of the coefficients on the ΔE variables in [11.25] is again insignificantly different from zero, although the effect of changes in the money supply is less rapid. The UK version of the model also forecasts well with a root mean square error of 4.16 per cent of nominal GDP over 1975(i) to 1976(ii). This compared with a root mean square forecast error of 3.14 for the NI model over the same period. Matthews and Ormerod, however, find that, for the UK, the equation is far less robust to changes in the definition of the money stock.

The forecasts obtained with the St Louis model illustrate the fact that it is by no means clear that large models forecast more accurately than small ones. The advantage of the large model, however, lies in the detail of the forecasts they produce and their ability adequately to represent the many different channels through which various policy instruments can influence the economy.

11.4 Forecasting in practice

In theory the procedure for obtaining a one, or more generally, a k period ahead forecast is simple. If data is available up to period t, the model can be estimated using this data. Forecasts for period $t + 1$ are then obtained by substituting into the model the period $t + 1$ values of the predetermined variables and solving for the endogenous variables. If the reduced-form is easily obtained then the values for the predetermined variables can simply be substituted into the reduced-form equations. Similarly, forecasts for period $t + k$ are obtained on substitution of the period $t + k$ values of the predetermined variables. In practice, however, the procedure is far more complicated with judgement playing as important a part as standard statistical procedures. For example, it should immediately be obvious that future values for the exogenous variables will not be available at the time of making the forecast. It is true that future values of lagged endogenous variables will be generated by the forecasts themselves, but any errors in forecasting these variables will have a cumulative effect in subsequent periods because of the dynamic structure of the model.

Osborne and Teal (1979) have summarised the procedure by which the quarterly forecasts of the NI model are prepared. The procedure consists of five main steps:

1. Firstly, the data base is updated, making use of all new quarterly observations on variables and any revisions to past data. Values in the most recent quarter may have to be estimated for variables on which data are not available. When making the February forecast, for example, National Accounts are not yet available for the fourth quarter of the previous year and have to be estimated using data on such variables as industrial production and retail sales.

2. Predictions are now made for values of the exogenous variables during the forecast period. This involves considerable background work in assessing recent trends and likely future developments. The exogenous variables mainly

concern the world economy and government policy. For example, projections have to be made about the future path of commodity prices – particularly that of oil. Variables influenced by government policy, e.g. public expenditure and tax rates, are forecast under the assumption of unchanged government policies.

3. Making use of the latest data, residuals for the past two or three years are obtained for each of the structural equations in the model. These residuals are the differences between the actual and predicted values of the endogenous variables when actual values of all variables, both endogenous and exogenous, are used on the right-hand side. For equations estimated on the basis of random disturbances one would not expect to find any systematic pattern in such residuals. However, since in practice the model is neither respecified nor re-estimated every quarter, it is possible that a sequence of, for example, positive residuals might be obtained for an equation during the past, say, four to six quarters.

4. Any systematic pattern found in the residuals for any equation is next extrapolated into the forecast period. The extrapolation is performed subjectively and not by some mechanical rule. This judgemental procedure enables other factors not explicitly allowed for in the model to be incorporated into the forecast via these residual terms. For example, it may be necessary to allow for the effect of North Sea oil on imports or for the possibility that a pre-Budget spending spree may have an offsetting effect on expenditure during the quarter after the Budget.

5. The predictions for the exogenous variables and extrapolations of the residuals are combined throughout the model to provide forecasts of all the endogenous variables.

Steps (4) and (5) above are, in fact, iterative. Initial forecasts of the endogenous variables are assessed for plausibility and consistency in the light of expected developments in the economy. If the forecasts are considered to be implausible in any sense, some of the predictions for the exogenous variables may be altered or the values for the residuals revised and the forecasting redone. Several 'runs' of the model may be necessary before the forecasters are satisfied, and the final forecasts are as much the product of judgement as of the econometric model. Such a procedure is, in fact, typical of all macroeconomic forecasting not merely that with the NI model.

The forecasts of all macroeconomic models are continually checked for their accuracy. Osborne and Teal (1979) decompose the error that can be observed between the forecast value of an endogenous variable and the actual outcome into four parts: (a) that due to errors in predicting the values of exogenous variables; (b) that due to errors in the specification of the model; (c) that due to judgemental errors in the extrapolation of residuals; and, (d) that due to revisions to published data used in making the forecast. These sources of error are not independent, however. For example, revisions to data, had they been known at the time of the forecast, might have affected the predictions made for the exogenous variables.

Osborne and Teal consider the NI forecasts for the UK economy made in February of 1975 and 1976. Firstly, they compare the published *ex ante* forecasts with the actual outcome. Next they calculate the forecasts that would have been made had the 'actual' values of exogenous and lagged endogenous variables been available at the time of the actual forecast. These *ex post* forecasts are also compared with the actual outcome. For 1975 in six out of nine categories the *ex post* forecast proves more accurate than the *ex ante* forecast. However, more interestingly, for 1976 the forecasts using revised data are less accurate in six out of the nine cases. This illustrates that not having access to final revised data does not necessarily increase forecast errors but can sometimes fortuitously reduce them. Osborne and Teal also find that the relative importance of data revisions and errors in predicting the exogenous variables is different in the two years. In 1975 data revisions are the more important but for the 1976 forecast the effect of the two is very similar.

A comparison of *ex ante* forecasts has recently been made by Artis (1982). He compares the October–November 1981 forecasts for the period 1981–83 of five models: the NI, Treasury, LBS, CEPG and Liverpool models. The forecast made with the Treasury model is that of the Economist Intelligence Unit (EIU) (published in *The Economist*) and not that of the Treasury itself. The aim of this work is not to compare the *ex ante* forecasts with the actual outcome but to examine the reasons why the ex ante forecasts themselves should differ.[8]

There is, in fact, a wide variation in the forecasts of the five models. For example, whereas the CEPG model predicts a fall in GDP of $7\frac{3}{4}$ per cent between 1980–83, the Liverpool model forecasts a rise of $5\frac{3}{4}$ per cent. The remaining three models present more consistent forecasts giving output predictions ranging from an increase of $1\frac{1}{2}$ per cent over the period to a fall of $1\frac{1}{4}$ per cent. The suggested reasons for these differences reflect the stages of the forecasting procedure outlined at the beginning of this section. Differences in the information and data series available to the forecasters were unimportant, since all the forecasts were prepared at roughly the same time. The remaining possible reasons for the variation in forecasts were therefore:

(a) differences in the predicted paths of exogenous variables;
(b) differences in the way residuals were extrapolated into the future, i.e. in the way 'judgement' is applied; and
(c) differences in model structure

Differences due to (a) above were isolated by comparing the actual or 'base' forecasts with 'common assumptions' forecasts commissioned by a House of Commons select committee. These forecasts were generated by feeding into the models a *common set of exogenous variable paths*. These common assumptions forecasts were, unfortunately, only available for three of the models: those of the Treasury, LBS and NI, so that a detailed breakdown of the reasons for the variability in forecasts was only possible for these models.[9] The comparison of base and common assumptions forecasts did not suggest that differences in the predicted paths of the exogenous variables were a major factor in causing GDP forecasts to differ. The common assumptions forecasts for the three models were, if anything, wider apart than the base forecasts.

In the common assumptions forecasts, forecasters had been permitted to use 'judgement' in the extrapolation of residuals in the same manner as they had for the base forecasts. Differences in forecasts because of (b) above were isolated by securing from the forecasters a third forecast – this time based on the setting of a mechanical rule for the extrapolation of equation residuals. It was suggested that all forecasters followed the rule of setting residuals to zero in first-differenced equations and setting residuals equal to the average of the previous known four quarters for equations in levels. In this way variations in the forecasts arising from the different 'judgements' of the forecasters could be largely eliminated. The removal of judgement resulted in a much greater variation in the forecasts than for the base forecasts. 'Judgemental' intervention in the NI model, for example, reduced forecasts of output, while intervention in the Treasury model had increased them. Overall, the exercise of judgement appeared to have led to much greater uniformity in the GDP forecasts of the three models than would otherwise have been the case.

Provided that the contributions of (a), (b) and (c) above to forecast differences are strictly additive, it was now possible to isolate the contribution of (c). The difference between the base forecasts of any pair of the models is the result of all the factors (a), (b) and (c). The difference between the common assumptions forecasts is, however, due to only (b) and (c). Hence, by subtracting the latter difference from the former, the difference due to factor (a) alone is obtained. Finally, because the difference between any pair of constant residual forecasts is the result of factors (a) and (c) alone, the contribution of model difference may be isolated by subtracting the difference due to factor (a) from the difference in constant residual forecasts.

When comparing the NI and LBS forecasts, Artis found that the small difference in 1981 output forecasts could be attributed to differences in exogenous variable values but with large model differences being offset by equally large judgemental intervention. In 1982, exogenous variable differences are unimportant but model differences are not completely offset by judgement. Similarly, when comparing the NI forecast with the EIU forecast obtained with the Treasury model, it was again found that judgemental intervention counteracted model difference with exogenous variable differences playing a minor role. These results confirm a general belief among forecasters concerning the importance of judgement in modifying model outcome and causing forecasts to converge.

The remaining forecasts – of the CEPG and Liverpool models are considered in less detail. The extremely low output forecasts for CEPG are found to be the result of pessimistic assumptions concerning future UK competitiveness. The Cambridge group's indices of competitiveness are predicted to decline throughout the forecast period. In contrast the NI–LBS–EIU forecasters tended to assume a slight improvement in competitiveness. The very optimistic output forecasts of the Liverpool model are the result of a dramatic improvement in the trade balance during 1982 and a large increase in stockbuilding reflected in a massive increase in private investment during 1982–84. The improvement in the trade balance appears to be at least partly the result of the residual-adjustment procedure used, while the increased stockbuilding is the result of the impact of reduced inflation in raising private sector net worth. The reduced inflation forecast stems from expectations about inflation, arising simply from assumed government adherence to the 'medium-term financial strategy' of that time. The optimistic Liverpool forecast is therefore partly due to judgemental intervention and partly to the major differences between this model and the others considered.

11.5 The simulation of macro-models

In Section 11.1 we analysed the impact and long-term effects of changes in the values of the exogenous variables in Klein model I. This involved the derivation of the reduced-form and final-form of the model and the calculation of impact and dynamic multipliers. Clearly, if the far more complicated macro-models of the succeeding sections are to be used to provide information on the likely effect of policy changes, e.g. in taxation or public expenditure or in monetary policy, then some similar form of analysis has to be performed. Unfortunately, such is the complexity of most recent macro-models that calculation of reduced-forms is rarely feasible and the elaborate lag structures in many of the equations make *analytical* study of the dynamic properties of the model impossible. That is, we cannot determine, analytically, whether the system returns to equilibrium after an exogenous 'shock'. Neither, if the system is, in fact, stable, can we derive the time paths of the endogenous variables as they move to their new equilibria or, for that matter, determine at what levels equilibrium is again reached. The answer to these difficulties is to run the model in what is known as 'simulation mode'.

Simulation is a purely numerical technique which is possibly the closest we can get to an experimental situation in the social sciences. A simulation may be performed either over the sample period used for estimation or over any future period. The procedure followed is to run the model, firstly with one set of values for the exogenous variables (probably actual present values) and then re-run it with an alternative set of values. The changes could involve merely a single change in one exogenous variable for just one period, or a change in more than one maybe sustained indefinitely.

A further important use of simulation is that it enables the model builders to check whether the time paths for the endogenous variables generated by the model approximate the actual time paths. The properties of a model are analysed in this way since an obviously important criterion for judging a model is whether its behaviour resembles adequately the behaviour of the economy it is supposed to represent. For example, does the model generate the 'cycles' characteristic of most modern industrial economies?

Let us illustrate the simulation technique by considering again Klein model I, introduced in Section 11.1. Klein estimated this model from annual data for 1921–41 and we consider how a simulation over the actual sample period would be performed. We have available actual 1921 values for the exogenous variables W_2, G, T and t and also 1921 values for the lagged endogenous variables Y_{-1}, Π_{-1} and K_{-1} (these will be actual values for 1920). We can therefore substitute these initial values into the estimated versions of equations [11.16–11.21] and solve to obtain 'simulated' 1921 values for all the endogenous variables $C, I, W_1, Y,$ Π and K. These values form the first points in our simulated time paths for these variables. To obtain simulated 1922 values for the endogenous variables, we again substitute into the model actual (this time 1922) values for the exogenous variables, but instead of using actual (1921) values for the lagged endogenous variables, we use the simulated values for these variables obtained in the 1921 calculations. For all successive years we proceed in this way, using actual values for exogenous variables but simulated values for lagged endogenous variables. Eventually we obtain simulated time paths for 1921–41 for all the endogenous variables which may then be compared with the actual time paths. Such a comparison is, in fact, made by Desai (1982: Ch. 8) and it is immediately clear that the simulated time paths differ significantly from the actual time paths. They show no sign of the large cyclical fluctuations characteristic of the inter-war US economy. This, of course, is not particularly surprising, since Klein model I is a very simple model which can hardly be expected to capture adequately the workings of such a complex economy as the US, particularly during the traumatic inter-war years.

Notice that the use of simulated values for lagged endogenous variables after the initial period means that divergences of simulated from actual time paths are likely to be compounded as we move through the sample period. This is because differences between actual and simulated values are incorporated into subsequent calculations. However, the simulation has to be performed in this way, since we wish the system to be moved ultimately only by the exogenous variables. We do not wish the simulated time paths for the endogenous variables to be influenced by their actual time paths because we wish to compare the two. Notice also that in simulation exercises we are analysing the properties of the model alone – the time paths are generated by the model alone, unmodified by the 'judgement' described in the previous section and necessarily a part of published forecasts.

It should be clear that, given initial values for the lagged endogenous variables, simulation exercises, such as that described above for Klein model I, can be performed over any time period for given paths of the exogenous variables. They need not necessarily be restricted to the sample period over which the model was estimated. The technique therefore provides a valuable method of assessing various policy options. Simulations obtained by use of values of the exogenous variables forecast under the assumption of unchanged policies can be compared with simulations arising when various policy changes are assumed. In each case the initial values for the lagged endogenous variables will be their current or latest available values.

An example of this type of exercise is the analysis in the *National Institute Economic Review* for November 1981 of the effects on the UK economy of alternative reflationary fiscal policies each costing £5 billion (gross) in 1981 prices. The results of the simulations made using the NI model are shown in Table 11.4.

The simulations suggest that an increase in government spending on goods and services is the most potent way of increasing output and the effects are felt immediately. This form of stimulus also causes the most inflation, although the effect on prices is relatively small. The effect of a reduction in income tax on both output and employment is much weaker and takes longer to be felt. On the other hand, the effect on prices is such that the rate of inflation is reduced from what it otherwise would have been. Cuts in indirect taxes and in the National Insurance Surcharge have similar effects on output and employment as an income tax cut, although the insurance surcharge cut takes longer to work. These latter two forms of fiscal stimulus have, however, a distinctly better effect on the price level than the income tax cut.

The National Insurance concludes that the most important result yielded by the simulations is that it is possible simultaneously to reduce both unemployment and inflation. This is true in both the short run and the medium term. (The figures in Table 11.4 refer to a version of the NI model which contains a Sargan (1964)-type 'real-wage' equation. Effects on prices are greater when this is replaced by an 'expectations-augmented Phillips curve' but it still remains possible to reduce unemployment and prices at the same time.)

A more extensive description of fiscal policy simulations, using both the NI and Treasury models is provided by Lewis and Ormerod (1979). While over short periods of two to three years there was little difference between the two models as

11.4 Effects of alternative reflationary policies each costing £5 billion.

| Policy | Effect in first year | | Cumulative effect after 5 years | | | |
	Output (%)	Price level (%)	Output (%)	Price level (%)	Unemploy- ment ('000's)	Budget deficit (% of GNP)
Increase in government spending on goods and services	1.8	0.0	1.7	1.1	− 330	1.0
Income tax cut	0.5	− 0.2	1.1	− 0.2	− 190	1.5
Indirect tax cut	0.6	− 2.6	1.0	− 6.6	− 180	1.2
National insurance surcharge cut	0.3	− 0.7	1.2	− 5.4	− 190	1.0

Source: National Institute Economic Review, Nov. 1981

far as the effects of the various policy options were concerned, over longer periods multipliers differed quite considerably. Lewis and Ormerod attempt to explain what particular characteristics of the models are the cause of the divergency.[10]

Limitations of simulation studies

While the use of macro-models in their simulation mode has obviously many attractions, the models also have important limitations when used to analyse the effects of changes in policy. We therefore close this section by considering some of these limitations.

Simulations are almost always performed under the implicit assumption that the estimated coefficients of a model are fixed and unchanging constants. In fact, there is always a margin of error associated with point estimates – sampling variability means that parameters cannot be determined precisely and estimates will always have standard errors associated with them. Since even slight changes in parameters can have considerable effects on the simulation properties of models, it is clearly desirable that all predictions should have confidence intervals attached to them. Unfortunately, the computational burden of calculating such intervals for the larger macro-models of the present day is a heavy one. However, if such confidence intervals were known it could well be the case that apparent large differences between the effects of different policies could simply be accounted for by sampling variability. For example, the appearance of confidence intervals on the numbers in Table 11.4 might well have served to reduce any belief in the differences between predictions for the first policy option compared with the other three.

Even if it were possible to estimate parameters with complete precision there are additional reasons why impact and long-run multipliers should not be regarded as unchanging constants. Most macro-models contain some non-linearity in their variables, e.g. deflation of monetary variables by price indices to produce real variables involves introducing the ratio of two variables. The existence of non-linearities is one of the reasons why the derivation of reduced- and final-forms for large models is so difficult and, hence, why the analysis of the effects of changes in exogenous variables is undertaken through simulation. However, non-linearities can also result in the size of multipliers being itself dependent on the values of variables in the models (see Wallis 1979: 152 for an example of this). This means that the results of simulations may vary depending on the initial conditions of the simulation run. Laury, Lewis and Ormerod (1978) provide an example of this using the NI model. When the base set of data began with the first quarter of 1972, simulation of the effects of a 5 per cent sterling devaluation suggested that such a devaluation would not improve the balance of payments until more than three years later. However, for a base data set beginning in the first quarter of 1976, simulation suggested an improvement after only one year. Thus conclusions drawn from simulations performed with the economy assumed to be in one state can by no means necessarily be assumed to apply when the economy is in some other state.[11]

Perhaps the most fundamental criticism of simulation studies is that of Lucas (1976). Lucas argues that parameters in a macro-model may well vary with the policy in operation. Thus, while the forecasting accuracy of a macro-model may be good, it may be of little use for comparing the effects of alternative policies. Parameters may vary because, if a policy remains in force long enough or has been tried on a number of occasions before (e.g. successive 'incomes policies' or repeated devaluations), then rational individuals may learn how the policy affects the economy and hence adjust their behaviour to allow for it. However, while this is clearly a potentially serious problem, fortunately it is doubtful whether actual policies during the past few decades have ever been followed with sufficient consistency or continuity for such behaviour to be widespread.

11.6 Some outstanding issues

The last two decades have seen an increase both in the number of full-scale macro-models in the UK and the US and in the average size of these models. More rapid and sophisticated computing facilities together with greater disaggregation in data series have made this possible and maybe inevitable. However, there remain a number of unresolved issues. For example, it is still be no means proven that large models forecast better than small models. We have seen that small monetarist models such as the St Louis model can provide forecasts comparable in accuracy with large Keynesian-type models. It is also the case that far less disaggregated Keynesian models also provide equally adequate forecasts, at far less cost in time and effort, of broad aggregate measures such as GDP and total consumer expenditure. Where the large models score, of course, is in the range of information that they provide. The separate effects of many variables can be allowed for and detailed questions about the alternative effects of the many policy instruments available to governments can be tackled. It is not often that complex policy measures can be translated adequately into, for example, broad changes in G or T as would be required by Klein model I. Maybe the ideal solution is for model-builders to maintain small models for forecasting purposes side by side with large disaggregated models to be used for simulation and detailed policy analysis. Re-estimation of the smaller model using latest available data series then takes place at more frequent intervals than does that of the larger model.

One issue concerning the structure of the main UK models over which there has been much debate has been the nature of links between monetary and real variables. In contrast to the situation in the US, there has been little success in the UK in establishing significant interest rate effects on expenditure – the traditional Keynesian transmission mechanism. Neither have UK models permitted any significant real balance effects, the orthodox short-run monetarist channel of influence. Rather than working through domestic demand, changes in the money supply affect prices more directly. For example, in the Treasury and particularly the LBS models, the effect is felt via the exchange rate. In the NI model, on the other hand, the link comes about through changes in interest rates affecting the exchange rate via domestic demand and capital flows.

A practical issue which causes some argument concerns the extent to which judgement should be allowed to influence forecasts. Forecasts are adjusted by projecting residuals from estimated equations into the future and also to allow for any recognised events during the forecast period, e.g. the imposition of an incomes policy. All forecasters make such residual adjustments. There is no disagreement about making such extrapolations *before* the first forecast is made. The controversial issue is whether forecasters should be prepared to modify forecasts to make them conform to intuitive ideas of how the economy should behave. Adjustments made *after* the forecast to ensure internal consistency of the forecast values for different variables obviously make sense. The important question is the extent to which *a priori* notions should be allowed to influence the forecast.

A methodological issue which has caused some controversy is that of whether data should be allowed to determine the parameters of a model quite freely or whether *a priori* constraints should be built into equations to ensure that they meet consistent theoretical criteria. For example, it could be the case that, while individual equations appear quite plausible, when they are combined together in the model their overall properties appear totally implausible. Indeed, one of the most useful purposes of simulation studies is to determine whether the properties of the model conform to *a priori* ideas about the economy. If not, one might wish to impose certain properties before estimation. The danger of building theoretical properties into the model is, of course, that users can be misled into believing that they have obtained empirical support for hypotheses that are a necessary consequence of the model. The general tendency among UK model-builders is to allow *a priori* notions to influence the long-run properties of equations – if only to rule certain specifications out because of their undesirable properties. However, it is generally agreed that short-run dynamic behaviour should not be imposed but that precise lag structures should be allowed to emerge during the estimation process. In effect, an approach closely related to the DHSY methodology referred to at a number of points in this book, is being adopted.

Notes

1. For example [11.5] may be rewritten as

$$Y_{t+1} = a_2 + b_2 Y_t + c_2 G_{t+1}$$

2. This can easily be seen if we regard equation [11.5] as a simple first-order difference equation. The single root of its characteristic equation is b_2 which must be less than unity for stability.

3. b_2 is in fact given by $b_2 = -\gamma/(1 - \beta - \gamma)$. Substituting in typical values for β, the MPC, e.g. $\beta = 0.8$, gives $b_2 = \gamma/(\gamma - 0.2)$ which exceeds unity for any value of γ the capital-output ratio.

4. The stability or instability of a dynamic equation system can, in fact, be determined analytically (see, for example, Baumol 1970: Ch. 10).

5. These models are described in great detail in their respective technical manuals. At the time of writing the current versions of the models were described in HM Treasury (1980), National Institute of Economic and Social Research (1979), London Business School (1981), Bank of England (1979), Coutts, et al. (1980) and Barker, et al. (1980).

6. For a detailed description of the model see Minford (1980).

7. If there are n forecast errors, e, then the root mean square error is $\sqrt{(\sum e^2/n)}$.

8. *Ex post* evaluations of comparative forecasts are rare, although the *National Institute Economic Review* now regularly publishes a comparison of Treasury, LBS and National Institute forecasts with actual outcomes, decomposing forecast errors in the manner of Osborne and Teal in the article just discussed.

9. Clearly 'common assumptions' forecasts can only be made for models in which the exogenous variables are broadly similar. This limited comparison to the models mentioned.

10. For a more lengthy description of the simulation performance of UK models see Holden, Peel and Thompson (1982).

11. In the devaluation example the difference between the two simulations arose because capacity utilisation was high and rising sharply during 1972–73 but very low during 1976–77.

References

Alchian, A.A. and Klein, B. (1973) On the correct measure of inflation, *Journal of Money Credit and Banking*, **5**, 173–91.

Allen, R.G.D. and Bowley, A.L. (1935) *Family Expenditure*. Staples Press.

Almon, S. (1965). The distributed lag between capital appropriations and expenditures, *Econometrica*, **33**, 178–96.

Anderson, L.C. and Carlson, K.M. (1970). A monetarist model for economic stabilisation, *Federal Reserve Bank of St Louis Review*, **52**, 7–25.

Ando, A. and Modigliani, F. (1963) The life-cycle hypothesis of savings, *American Economic Review*, **53**, 55–84.

Ando, A.K., Modigliani, F., Rasche, R. and Turnovsky, S.J. (1974) On the role of expectations of price and technological change in an investment function, *International Economic Review*, **15**, 384–414.

Arrow, K.J. (1962) The economic implications of learning by doing, *Review of Economic Studies*, **29**, 155–73.

Arrow, K.J., Chenery, H.B., Minhas, B.S. and Solow, R.M. (1961) Capital–labour substitution and economic efficiency, *Review of Economics and Statistics*, **43**, 225–50.

Artis, M.J. (1982) *Why Forecasts Differ*. Bank of England Panel of Academic Consultants, Panel Paper 17.

Artis, M.J. and Lewis, M.K. (1974) The demand for money–stable or unstable, *The Banker*, **124**, 239–43.

Artis, M.J. and Lewis, M.K. (1976) The demand for money in the United Kingdom: 1963–73, *Manchester School*, **43**, 147–81.

Ball, R.J., Boatwright, B.D., Burns, T., Lobban, P.W.M. and Miller, G.W. (1975) The London Business School quarterly econometric model of the UK economy, in: Renton. G.A. (ed.), *Modelling the Economy*. Heinemann Educational Books.

Ball, R.J. and Drake, P.S. (1964) The relationship between aggregate consumption and wealth, *International Economic Review*, **5**, 63–81.

Bank of England (1970) The importance of money, *Bank of England Quarterly Bulletin*, **10**, 159–98.

Bank of England (1979) *Bank of England Model of the UK Economy*. Bank of England Discussion Paper 5.

Barker, T., Borooah, V., van der Ploeg, R. and Winters, A. (1980) *The Cambridge Multisectoral Dynamic Model: an instrument for national economic policy analysis.* Department of Applied Economics, University of Cambridge.

Barro, R.J. and Santomero, A.J. (1972) Household money holdings and the demand deposit rate, *Journal of Money, Credit and Banking*, **4**, 397–413.

Barten, A.P. (1964) Family composition, prices and expenditure patterns, in Hart P.E., Mills G. and Whitaker J.K. (eds.), *Econometric Analysis for National Economic Planning*, Butterworth.

Barten, A.P. (1966) Therie en empirie van een volledig stelsel van vraagvergelijkingen, doctoral dissertation, University of Rotterdam.

Barten, A.P. (1969) Maximum likelihood estimation of a complete system of demand equations, *European Economic Review*, **1**, 7–73.

Baumol, W.J. (1952) The transactions demand for cash: an inventory theoretic approach, *Quarterly Journal of Economics*, **66**, 545–56.

Baumol, W.J. (1970) *Economic dynamics – an introduction*. Macmillan, New York.

Bean, C.R. (1978) *The Determination of Consumers' Expenditure in the UK*. Treasury Working Paper 4.

Bean, C.R. (1981) An econometric model of manufacturing investment in the UK, *Economic Journal*, **91**, 106–21.

Bhatia, K.B. (1972) Capital gains and the aggregate consumption function, *American Economic Review*, **62**, 866–79.

Bhatia, K.B. (1979) Corporate taxation, retained earnings and capital formation, *Journal of Public Economics*, **11**, 123–34.

Bird, R. and Bodkin, R.G. (1965) The National Service Life Insurance Dividend of 1950 and consumption: a further test of the strict permanent income hypothesis, *Journal of Political Economy*, **73**, 499–515.

Bischoff, C.W. (1969) Hypothesis testing and the demand for capital goods, *Review of Economics and Statistics*, **51**, 354–68.

Bischoff, C.W. (1971) The effect of alternative lag distributions, in: Fromm, G. (ed.), *Tax Incentives and Capital Spending*. Brookings Institution, North Holland, Amsterdam.

Bitros, G.C. and Kelejian, H.H. (1974) On the variability of the replacement capital stock: some evidence from capital scrappage, *Review of Economic Statistics*, **56**, 270–78.

Boatwright, B.D. and Eaton, J.R (1972) The estimation of investment functions for manufacturing industry in the UK, *Economica*, **39**, 403–18.

Bodkin, R.G., (1959) Windfall income and consumption, *American Economic Review*, **49**, 602–14.

Box, G.E.P. and Pierce, D.A. (1970) Distribution of residual autocorrelations in autoregressive–integrated moving average time series models, *Journal of the American Statistical Association*, **65**, 1509–26.

Brady, D. and Friedman, R. (1947) Savings and the income distribution, *Studies in Income and Wealth*, **10**, National Bureau of Economic Research, New York.

Branson, W.H. and Klevorick, A.K. (1969) Money illusion and the aggregate consumption function, *American Economic Review*, **59**, 832–49.

Bronfenbrenner, M. and Mayer, T. (1960) Liquidity functions in the American economy, *Econometrica*, **28**, 810–34.

Brown, T.M. (1952) Habit persistence and lags in consumer behaviour, *Econometrica*, **20**, 355–71.

Brunner, K. and Meltzer, A.H. (1963) Predicting velocity: implications for theory and policy, *Journal of Finance*, **18**, 319–54.

Byron, R.P. (1970a) A simple method of estimating demand equations under separable utility functions, *Review of Economic Studies*, **37**, 261–74.

Byron, R.P. (1970b) The restricted Aitken estimation of sets of demand relations, *Econometrica*, **38**, 816–30.

Cagan, P. (1956) The monetary dynamics of hyperinflation, in: Friedman, M. (ed.), *Studies in the Quantity Theory of Money*. University of Chicago Press.

Cagan, P. and Schwartz, A.J. (1975) Has the growth of money substitutes hindered monetary policy? *Journal of Money, Credit and Banking*, **7**, 137–60.

Carr, J. and Darby, M.R. (1981) The role of money supply shocks in the short-run demand for money, *Journal of Monetary Economics*, **8**, 183–200.

Central Statistical Office (1978) Personal sector balance sheets, *Economic Trends*, **291**, 97–107.

Chow, G. (1957) *Demand for automobiles in the U.S.: a study of consumer durables*. North Holland, Amsterdam.

Chow, G. (1960a) Statistical demand functions for automobiles and their use for forecasting, in: Harberger A.C. (ed.), *The Demand for Durable Goods*. University of Chicago Press.

Chow, G. (1960b) Tests of equality between sets of coefficients in two linear regressions, *Econometrica*, **28**, 591–605.

Chow, G. (1966) On the long-run and short-run demand for money, *Journal of Political Economy*, **74**, 111–31.

Christensen, L.R., Jorgenson, D.W. and Lau, L.J. (1973) Transcendental logarithmic production frontiers, *Review of Economics and Statistics*, **55**, 28–45.

Christensen, L.R., Jorgenson, D.W. and Lau, L.J. (1975) Transcendental logarithmic utility functions, *American Economic Review*, **65**, 367–83.

Clark, J.M. (1917) Business acceleration and the law of demand, *Journal of Political Economy*, **25**, 217–35.

Clower, R.W. and Johnson, M.B. (1968) Income, wealth and the theory of consumption, in: Wolfe, N. (ed.), *Value, Capital and Growth*. Edinburgh University Press.

Cochrane, E. and Orcutt, G.H. (1949) Application of least squares regressions to relationships containing autocorrelated error terms, *Journal of the American Statistical Association*, **44**, 32–61.

Coen, R.M. (1968) The effects of tax policy on investment in manufacturing, *American Economic Review*, **58**, 200–11.

Coen, R.M. (1971) The effect of cash flow on the speed of adjustments, in: Fromm, G. (ed.), *Tax Incentives and Capital Spending*. Brookings Institution, North Holland, Amsterdam.

Coen, R.M. (1975) Investment behavior, the measurement of depreciation and tax policy, *American Economic Review*, **65**, 59–74.

Coghlan, R.T. (1978) A transactions demand for money, *Bank of England Quarterly Bulletin*, **18**, 48–60.

Courakis, A.S. (1978) Serial correlation and the Bank of England's demand for money function: an exercise in measurement without theory, *Economic Journal*, **88**, 537–48.

Coutts, K.J., Cripps, T.F., Fetherston, M.J. and Anyadike-Danes, M.K. (1980) *CEPG Model of the UK Economy Technical Manual* (6th edn). Department of Applied Economics, University of Cambridge, Cambridge.

Darby, M.R. (1972) The allocation of transitory income among consumers' assets, *American Economic Review*, **72**, 928–41.

Darby, M.R. (1974) The permanent income theory of consumption – a restatement, *Quarterly Journal of Economics*, **88**, 228–50.

Davidson, J.E.H., Hendry, D.F., Srba, F. and Yeo, S. (1978) Econometric modelling of the aggregate time series relationship between consumers' expenditure and income in the UK, *Economic Journal*, **88**, 661–92.

Davis, T.E. (1952) The consumption function as a tool for prediction, *Review of Economic Statistics*, **34**, 270–7.

Deaton, A.S. (1974) The analysis of consumer demand in the United Kingdom 1900–1970, *Econometrica*, **42**, 341–67.

Deaton, A.S. (1975) *Models and Projections of Demand in Postwar Britain*. Chapman and Hall.

Deaton, A. (1978) Involuntary saving through unanticipated inflation, *American Economic Review*, **68**, 899–910.

Deaton, A.S. and Muellbauer, J. (1980) *Economics and Consumer Behaviour*. Cambridge University Press.

Desai, M. (1982) *Applied Econometrics*. Phillip Allen.

De Leeuw, F. (1962) The demand for capital goods by manufacturers: a study of quarterly time series, *Econometrica*, **30**, 407–23.

Dhrymes, P. (1965) Some extensions and tests for the CES class of production functions, *Review of Economics and Statistics*, **37**, 357–66.

Diewart, W.E. (1974) Applications of duality theory, in: Intriligator, M.D. and

Kendrick, D.A. (eds), *Frontiers of Quantitative Economics, Vol II*. North Holland/American Elsevier, Amsterdam.

Douglas, P. (1948) Are there laws of production? *American Economic Review*, **38**, 1–41.

Duesenberry, J.S. (1949) *Income, Savings and the Theory of Consumer Behaviour*. Harvard University Press.

Duesenberry, J.S. (1958) *Business Cycles and Economic Growth*. McGraw-Hill, New York.

Durbin, J. (1953) A note on regression when there is extraneous information on one of the coefficients, *Journal of the American Statistical Association*, **48**, 799–808.

Durbin, J. (1970) Testing for serial correlation in least squares regression when some of the regressors are lagged dependent variables, *Econometrica*, **38**, 410–21.

Durbin, J. and Watson, G.S. (1950; 1951) Testing for serial correlation in least squares regression, *Biometrika*, **37**, 409–28; **38**, 159–78.

Dutton, D.S. and Gramm, W.P. (1973) Transactions costs, the wage rate, and the demand for money, *American Economic Review*, **63**, 652–65.

Eisner, R. (1960) A distributed lag investment function, *Econometrica*, **28**, 1–30.

Eisner, R. (1967) A permanent income theory of investment: some empirical explorations, *American Economic Review*, **57**, 363–90.

Eisner, R. (1969) Tax policy and investment behaviour: comment, *American Economic Review*, **59**, 379–88.

Eisner, R. and Nadiri, M.I. (1968) Investment behaviour and neo-classical theory, *Review of Economics and Statistics*, **50**, 369–82.

Eisner, R. and Strotz, R.H. (1963) Determinants of business investment, in: Commission on Money and Credit, *Impacts of Monetary Policy*. Prentice-Hall, Englewood Cliffs, New Jersey.

Enzler, J., Johnson, L. and Paulus, J. (1976) Some problems of money demand, *Brookings Papers on Economic Activity*, **6**, 261–80.

Evans, M.K. (1967a) A study of industry investment decisions, *Review of Economics and Statistics*, **49**, 151–64.

Evans, M.K. (1967b) The importance of wealth in the consumption function, *Journal of Political Economy*, **75**, 335–51.

Evans, M.K. (1969) *Macroeconomic Activity*. Harper and Row, New York.

Farrar, D.E. and Glauber, R.R. (1967) Multicollinearity in regression analysis: the problem revisited, *Review of Economics and Statistics*, **49**, 92–107.

Fase, M.M.G. and Kure, J.B. (1975) The demand for money in thirteen European and non-European countries: A tabular survey, *Kredit und Kapital*, **3**, 410–19.

Feige, E. (1967) Expectations and adjustments in the monetary sector, *American Economic Review*, **57**, 462–73.

Feldstein, M.S. (1973) Tax incentives, corporate saving and capital accumulation, *Journal of Public Economics*, **5**, 159–71.

Feldstein, M.S. and Fane, G. (1973) Taxes, corporate dividend policy and personal saving: the British postwar experience, *Review of Economics and Statistics*, **55**, 399–411.

Feldstein, M.S. and Flemming, J.S. (1971) Tax policy, corporate savings and investment behaviour in Britain, *Review of Economic Studies*, **38**, 415–34.

Feldstein, M.S. and Foot, D.K. (1971) The other half of gross investment: replacement and modernisation expenditure, *Review of Economics and Statistics*, **53**, 49–58.

Fisher, F.M. and Kaysen, C. (1962) *The Demand for Electricity in the United States*. North Holland, Amsterdam.

Fisher, I. (1907) *The Theory of Interest*. Macmillan, New York.

Fox, K.A. (1958) *Econometric Analysis for Public Policy*. Iowa State College Press.

Frenkel, J. (1977) The forward exchange rate, expectations and the demand for money: the German hyperinflation, *American Economic Review*, **67**, 653–70.

Friedman, M. (1956) The quantity theory of money, a restatement, in: Friedman, M. (ed.), *Studies in the Quantity Theory of Money*. University of Chicago Press.

Friedman, M. (1957) *A Theory of the Consumption Function*. Princeton University Press.

Friedman, M. (1959) The demand for money – some theoretical and empirical results, *Journal of Political Economy*, **67**, 327–51.

Friedman, M. (1963) Windfalls, the horizon, and related concepts in the permanent income hypothesis, in: Christ, C. (ed.), *Measurement in Economics*, Stanford University Press.

Fuchs, V.R. (1963) Capital–labour substitution: a note, *Review of Economics and Statistics*, **45**, 436–8.

Glaister, S. (1972) *Mathematical Methods in Economics*. Gray-Mills.

Goldberger, A.S. and Gamaletsos, T. (1970) A cross-country comparison of consumer expenditure patterns, *European Economic Review*, **1**, 357–400.

Goldfeld, S.M. (1973) The demand for money revisited, *Brookings Papers on Economic Activity*, **3**, 577–638.

Goldfeld, S.M. (1976) The case of the missing money, *Brookings Papers on Economic Activity*, **6**, 683–739.

Goldsmith, R.W. (1955) *A Study of Savings in the United States*. Princeton University Press.

Gould, J.P. (1968) Adjustment costs in the theory of investment of the firm, *Review of Economic Studies*, **35**, 47–55.

Green, H.A.J. (1964) *Aggregation in economic analysis, an introductory survey*. Princeton University Press.

Greenberg, E. (1964) A stock adjustment investment model, *Econometrica*, **32**, 339–57.

Griliches, Z. (1967) Distributed lags: a survey, *Econometrica*, **35**, 16–49.

Griliches, Z. and Ringstad, V. (1971) *Economies of Scale and the Form of the Production Function*. North Holland, Amsterdam.

Grunfeld, Y. (1960) The determinants of corporate investment, in: Harberger, A.C. (ed.), *The Demand for Durable Goods*. University of Chicago Press.

Hacche, G. (1974) The demand for money in the United Kingdom: experience since 1971, *Bank of England Quarterly Bulletin*, **14**, 284–305.

Hadley, G. (1965) *Linear Algebra*. Addision-Wesley, Reading, Mass.

Hall, R.E. and Jorgenson, D.W. (1967) Tax policy and investment behaviour, *American Economic Review*, **57**, 391–414.

Hamburger, M.J. (1977a) The demand for money in an open economy: Germany and the United Kingdom, *Journal of Monetary Economics*, **3**, 25–40.

Hamburger, M.J. (1977b) Behaviour of the money stock. Is there a puzzle?, *Journal of Monetary Economics*, **3**, 265–88.

Hamburger, M.J. and Wood, G.E. (1978) Interest rates and monetary policy in open economies, Federal Reserve Bank of New York Working Paper, May.

Harrod, R. (1948) *Towards a Dynamic Economics*. Macmillan.

Heathfield, D. (1971) *Production Functions*. Macmillan.

Helliwell, J.F. and Glorieux, G. (1970) Forward-looking investment behaviour, *Review of Economic Studies*, **37**, 499–516.

Henderson, J.M. and Quandt, R.E. (1971) *Microeconomic Theory: a mathematical approach*. McGraw-Hill.

Hendry, D.F. (1974) Stochastic specification in an aggregate demand model of the UK, *Econometria*, **42**, 559–78.

Hendry, D.F. and Mizon, G.E. (1978) Serial correlation as a convenient simplification, not a nuisance: a comment on a study of the demand for money by the Bank of England, *Economic Journal*, **88**, 549–63.

Hendry, D.F. and Ungern-Sternberg, T. von (1980) Liquidity and inflation effects on consumers' expenditure, in: Deaton, A.S. (ed.), *Essays in the Theory and*

Measurement of Consumers' Behaviour. Cambridge University Press.

Hicks, J.R. (1956) *A Revision of Demand Theory.* Oxford University Press.

Hildebrand, G.H. and Liu, T.C. (1965) *Manufacturing Production Functions in the United States* 1957, New York State School of Industrial Relations, Ithaca.

Hildreth, C. and Lu, J.Y. (1960) *Demand Relations with Autocorrelated Disturbances.* Michigan Agricultural Experiment Station Technical Bulletin 276, Michigan State University.

Hines, A.G. and Catephores, G. (1970) Investment in UK manufacturing industry, in: Hilton, K. and Heathfield, D. (eds), *The Econometric Study of the UK.* Macmillan.

Holden, K., Peel, D.A. and Thompson, J. (1982) *Modelling the UK Economy – an introduction.* Martin Robertson.

Houthakker, H. (1960) Additive preferences, *Econometrica,* **28**, 244–56.

Houthakker, H. and Taylor, L.D. (1970) *Consumer Demand in the United States* 1929–1970 (2nd edn). Harvard University Press, Cambridge, Mass.

Johnston J. (1972) *Econometric Methods* (2nd Edition). McGraw-Hill.

Johnston, J. (1984) *Econometric Methods* (3rd Edition). McGraw-Hill.

Jones, H. (1975) *An Introduction to Modern Theories of Economic Growth.* Nelson.

Jorgenson, D.W. (1963) Capital theory and investment behaviour, *American Economic Review,* **53**, 247–59.

Jorgenson, D.W. (1965) Anticipations and investment behaviour, in: Duesenberry, J.S., From, G., Klein, L.R., Kuh, E., (eds), *The Brookings Quarterly Model of the United States,* Rand McNally, Chicago.

Jorgenson, D.W. and Siebert, C.D. (1968) A comparison of alternative theories of corporate investment behaviour, *American Economic Review,* **58**, 681–712.

Jorgenson, D.W. and Stephenson, J.A. (1967) Investment behaviour in US manufacturing, 1947–60, *Econometrica,* **35**, 169–220.

Juster, F.T. and Wachtel, P. (1972) *Inflation and the Consumer.* Brookings Papers on Economic Activity 1, pp. 71–114.

Kahn, M. (1974) The stability of the demand for money function in the US, 1901–1965, *Journal of Political Economy,* **82**, 1205–1220.

Karni, E. (1974) The value of time and the demand for money, *Journal of Money, Credit and Banking,* **6**, 45–64.

Kavanagh, N.J. and Walters, A.A. (1966) The demand for money in the United Kingdom, 1877–1961: preliminary findings, *Bulletin of the Oxford University Institute of Economics and Statistics,* **28**, 93–116.

Kelejian, H.H. and Oates, W.E. (1981) *Introduction to Econometrics – principles and applications.* Harper and Row, New York.

Khoury, M. and Myhrmon, J. (1976) Econometric analysis of the demand for money in Sweden, 1909–1968. University of Stockholm (mimeo.).

King, M.A. (1972) Taxation and investment incentives in a vintage investment model, *Journal of Public Economics,* **1**, 121–47.

Klein, L.R. (1950) *Economic Fluctuations in the United States,* 1921–1941. Cowles Commission Monograph 11.

Klein, L.R. (1953) *A Textbook of Econometrics.* Row Peterson, Evanston, Ill.

Klein, L.R. (1958) The estimation of distributed lags, *Econometrica,* **26**, 559–65.

Kmenta, J. (1967) On the estimation of the CES production function, *International Economic Review,* **8**, 180–9.

Kmenta, J. (1971) *Elements of Econometrics,* Macmillan.

Koyck, L.M. (1954) *Distributed Lags and Investment Analysis.* North Holland, Amsterdam.

Kreinin, M. (1961) Windfall income and consumption – additional evidence, *American Economic Review,* **51**, 388–90.

Kuznets, S. (1942) *Uses of National Income in Peace and War.* National Bureau of Economic Research Occasional Paper 6.

Laidler, D. (1966) Some evidence on the demand for money, *Journal of Political Economy*, **74**, 55–68.

Laidler, D. (1971) The influence of money on economic activity: a survey of some current problems, in: Clayton, G. Gilbert, J.C. and Sedgwick, R. (eds), *Monetary Theory and Policy in the 1970s*. Oxford University Press.

Laidler, D. (1977) *The Demand for Money: theories and evidence*. Harper and Row, New York.

Laidler, D. (1980) The demand for money in the United States yet again, in: *On the State of Macroeconomics*. Carnegie–Rochester Conference Series on Public Policy, 12, pp. 219–71.

Laidler, D. and Parkin, J.M. (1970) The demand for money in the United Kingdom, 1956–1967: preliminary estimates, *Manchester School*, **38**, 187–208.

Laumas, G.S. (1978) A test of the stability of the demand for money, *Scottish Journal of Political Economy*, **25**, 239–51.

Laumas, G.S. and Mehra, Y.P. (1976) The stability of the demand for money function: The evidence from quarterly data, *Review of Economics and Statistics*, **58**, 463–8.

Laury, J.S.E., Lewis, G.R. and Ormerod, P.A. (1978) Properties of macroeconomic models of the UK economy: a comparative study, *National Institute Economic Review*, **83**, 52–72.

L'Esperance, W.L. (1964) A case study in prediction: the market for water-melons, *Econometrica*, **32**, 163–73.

Lewis, G.R. and Ormerod, P. (1979) Policy simulations and model characteristics, in: Cook, S.T. and Jackson, P.M. (eds), *Current Issues in Fiscal Policy*. (Ch. 8) Martin Robertson.

Liu, T.C. (1960) Underidentification, structural estimation and forecasting, *Econometrica*, **28**, 855–65.

Liviatan, N. (1963) Tests of the permanent income hypothesis based on a re-interview savings survey, in: Christ, C. (ed.), *Measurement in Economics*. Stanford University Press.

Lluch, C. (1971) Consumer demand functions, Spain 1958–64, *European Economic Review*, **2**, 277–302.

London Business School (1981) *Quarterly Econometric Model of the UK Economy*. London Business School Econometric Forecasting Unit.

Lucas, R.B. (1976) Econometric policy evaluation: a critique, in: Brunner, K. and Meltzer, A.N. (eds), *The Phillips Curve and Labour Markets*. North Holland, Amsterdam.

Maddala, G.S. and Kadane, J.B. (1966) Some notes on the estimation of CES production functions, *Review of Economics and Statistics*, **48**, 340–4.

Malcomson, J.M. and Prior, M.J. (1979) The estimation of a vintage model of production for UK manufacturing, *Review of Economic Studies*, **46**, 719 – 33.

Matthews, K.G.P. and Ormerod, P.A. (1978) St Louis models of the UK economy, *National Institute Economic Review*, **84**, 65–9.

Mayer, T. (1972) *Permanent Income, Wealth and Consumption*. University of California Press.

Meltzer, A.H. (1963) The demand for money: the evidence from the time series, *Journal of Political Economy*, **71**, 219–46.

Meyer, J.R. and Kuh, E. (1957) *The Investment Decision: an empirical study*. Harvard University Press, Cambridge, Mass.

Minford, A.P.L. (1980) A rational expectations model of the UK under fixed and floating exchange rates, in: Brunner, K. and Meltzer, A.H. (eds), *On the State of Macroeconomics*. Carnegie-Rochester Conferences on Public Policy 12, pp. 293–355.

Mizon, G.E. (1974) The estimation of non-linear econometric equations: an application to the specification and estimation of an aggregate putty–clay relation for the UK, *Review of Economic Studies*, **41**, 353–69.

Modigliani, F. (1949) Fluctuations in the savings income ratio: a problem in economic forecasting, *Studies in Income and Wealth*, **11**, National Bureau of Economic Research, New York.

Modigliani, F. (1966) The life cycle hypothesis of saving, the demand for wealth and the supply of capital, *Social Research*, **33**, 160–217.

Modigliani, F. and Brumberg, R. (1954) Utility analysis and the consumption function: an interpretation of cross-sectional data, in: Kurihara, K. (ed.), *Post-Keynesian Economics*. Rutgers University Press.

Moore, H.L. (1914) *Economic Cycles: their law and cause*. Macmillan, New York.

Muellbauer, J. (1974) Household composition, Engel curves and welfare comparisons between households: a duality approach, *European Economic Review*, **6**, 103–122.

Muellbauer, J. (1980) The estimation of the Prais-Houthakker model of equivalence scales, *Econometrica*, **48**, 153–76.

Nadiri, M.I. and Rosen, S. (1969) Inter-related factor demand functions, *American Economic Review*, **59**, 457–71.

National Institute of Economic and Social Research (1979) *Listing of the Interim NIESR Model IV*, Discussion Paper 38.

Nerlove, M. (1958) *Distributed Lags and Demand Analysis*. Agricultural Handbook 141, US Department of Agriculture, Washington.

Nerlove, M. (1963) Returns to scale in electricity supply, in: Christ, C. (ed.), *Measurement in Economics*. Stanford University Press.

Nerlove, M. (1967) Recent empirical studies of the CES and related production functions, *Studies in Income and Wealth*, **31**, 55–122 National Bureau of Economic Research, New York.

Nickell, S.J. (1978) *The Investment Decision of Firms*. Cambridge University Press.

Osborne, D. and Teal, F. (1979) An assessment and comparison of two NIESR econometric model forecasts, *National Institute Economic Review*, **88**, 50–62.

Pesaran, M.H. and Deaton, A.S. (1978) Testing non-nested, non-linear regression models, *Econometrica*, **46**, 677–94.

Phlips, L. (1974) *Applied Demand Analysis*. North Holland, Amsterdam.

Pollock, R.A. and Wales, T.J. (1969) Estimation of the linear expenditure system, *Econometrica*, **37**, 611–28.

Prais, S.J. and Houthakker, H.S. (1955) *The Analysis of Family Budgets*. Cambridge University Press.

Revankar, N.S. (1971) A class of variable elasticity of substitution production functions, *Econometrica*, **39**, 61–71.

Rowan, D.C. and Miller, J. (1979) *The Demand for Money in the UK, 1963–1977. University of Southampton Discussion Paper 7902, University of Southampton*.

Sargan, J.D. (1964) Wages and prices in the United Kingdom, in Mort P.E., Mills G. and Whitaker J.K. (eds.), *Econometric Analysis for National Economic Planning*. Butterworth.

Sato, R. and Hoffman, R.F. (1968) Production functions with a variable elasticity of factor substitutions some analysis and testing, *Review of Economics and Statistics*, **50**, 453–60.

Schmidt, P. (1976) On the statistical estimation of parametric frontier production functions, *Review of Economics and Statistics*, **58**, 238–9.

Schultz, H. (1938) *The Theory and Measurement of Demand*. Chicago University Press.

Shapiro, A.A. (1973) Inflation, lags and the demand for money, *International Economic Review*, **14**, 81–96.

Smith, R.P. (1975) *Consumer Demand for Cars in the USA*. Cambridge University Press.

Solow, R.M. (1957) Technical change and the aggregate production function, *Review*

365

of Economic Statistics, **39**, 312–20, reprinted in: Meuller, M.G. (1969), *Readings in Macroeconomics*. Holt, Rinehart and Winston.

Solow, R.M. (1960) Investment and technical progress, in: Arrow, K., Karlin, S. and Suppes, P. (eds), *Mathematical Methods in the Social Sciences*. Stanford University Press.

Spinelli, F. (1978) *The Demand for Money in Italy*. University of Western Ontario, (Mimeo.).

Spiro, A. (1962) Wealth and the consumption function, *Journal of Political Economy*, **70**, 393–54.

Starleaf, D.R. and Reimer, R. (1967) The Keynesian demand for money function: some statistical tests, *Journal of Finance*, **22**, 71–6.

Stewart, J. (1976) *Understanding Econometrics*. Hutchinson.

Stewart, J. (1984) *Understanding Econometrics* (2nd edition), Hutchinson.

Stewart, M.B. and Wallis, K.F. (1981) *Introductory Econometrics*. Blackwell.

Stone, J.R.N. (1954) Linear expenditure systems and demand analysis – an application to the pattern of British demand, *Economic Journal*, **64**, 511–27.

Stone, J.R.N. (1964) Private saving in Britain, past, present and future, *Manchester School*, **32**, 79–112.

Stone, J.R.N. (1973) Personal spending and saving in postwar Britain, in: Bos, H.C. Linneman, H. and De Wolff, P., (eds), *Economic Structure and Development*. North Holland, Amsterdam.

Stone, J.R.N., Brown, J.A.C. and Rowe, D.A. (1964) Demand analysis and projections for Britain, 1900–1970: a study in method, in: Sandee, J. (ed.), *Europe's Future Consumption*. North Holland, Amsterdam.

Stone, J.R.N. and Rowe, D.A. (1957) The market demand for durable goods, *Econometrica*, **25**, 423–43.

Suits, D.B. (1955) An econometric analysis of the water-melon market, *Journal of Farm Economics*, **37**, 237–51.

Sumner, M.T. (1974) Taxation and investment incentives in a vintage investment model: a comment, *Journal of Public Economics* **3**, 185–94.

Sumner, M.T. (1981) Investment grants, in: Currie, D. and Peters. W. (eds), *Microeconomic Analysis: essays in microeconomics and economic development*. Croom Helm.

Teigen, R. (1964) Demand and supply functions for money in the United States, Econometrica, **32**, 477–509.

Theil, H. (1965) The information approach to demand analysis, *Econometrica*, **33**, 67–87.

Theil, H. (1975) *Theory and Measurement of Consumer Demand*. North Holland, Amsterdam.

Theil, H. and Boot, J.C.G. (1962) The final form of econometric equation systems, *Rev. Int. Statist. Inst.*, **30**, 136–52, reprinted in: Zellner, A. (ed.) (1968), *Readings in Economic Statistics and Econometrics*. Little and Brown, Boston.

Thomas, R.L. (1981) Wealth and aggregate consumption, *Manchester School*, **49**, 129–52.

Thompson, W.N. (1984) Money in UK macromodels, in: Demery et al. *Macroeconomics*, Surveys in Economics, Longmans.

Thompson, T.D., Pierce, J.L. and Parry, R.T. (1975) A monthly money market model, *Journal of Money, Credit and Banking*, **7**, 411–31.

Tinbergen, J. (1939) *Statistical Testing of Business Cycle Theories, II: business cycles in the USA*, 1919–1932, League of Nations, Geneva.

Tinbergen, J. (1951) Business cycles in the United Kingdom, 1870–1914, North Holland, Amsterdam.

Tobin, J. (1956) The interest elasticity of the transactions demand for cash, *Review of Economics and Statistics*, **38**, 241–7.

Tobin, J. (1958) Liquidity preference as behaviour towards risk, *Review of Economic Studies*, **25**, 65–86.

Townend, J.C. (1976) The personal savings ratio, *Bank of England Quarterly Bulletin*, **16**, 53–61.

Treasury (1980) *Macroeconomic Model Equation and Variable Listing*, H.M. Treasury, London.

Ungern-Sternberg, T. von (1981) Inflation and savings: international evidence on inflation-induced income losses, *Economic Journal*, **91**, 961–76.

Vogler, R.C. (1974) The dynamics of inflation in Latin America, 1950–1969, *American Economic Review*, **64**, 102–14.

Wall, K.D., Preston, A.J., Bray, J.W. and Peston, M.H., (1975) Estimates of a simple control model of the UK economy, in: Renton, G.A. (ed.), *Modelling the Economy*. Heinemann Education Books.

Wallis, K.F. (1979) *Topics in Applied Econometrics*. Blackwell.

Walpole, R.E. (1982) *Introduction to Statistics*. Macmillan.

Walters, A.A. (1965) Professor Friedman on the demand for money, *Journal of Political Economy*, **73**, 545–51.

Walters, A.A. (1970) *An Introduction to Econometrics*, (2nd edn). Macmillan.

Weinrobe, M.D. (1972) A simple model of the precautionary demand for cash, *Southern Economic Journal*, **39**, 314–24.

Westin, R.B. (1975) Empirical implications of infrequent purchase behaviour in a stock adjustment model, *American Economic Review*, **65**, 384–96.

Wright, C. (1969) Estimating permanent income: a note, *Journal of Political Economy*, **77**, 845–50.

Wold, H.D.A. (1958) A case study of interdependent versus causal chain systems, *Review of the International Statistical Institute*, **26**, 5–25.

Zellner, A. and Geisel, M.K. (1970) Analysis of distributed lag models with applications to consumption function estimation, *Econometrica*, **38**, 865–88.

Zellner, A., Huang, D.S. and Chau, L.C. (1965) Further analysis of the short-run consumption function with emphasis on the role of liquid assets, *Econometrica*, **33**, 571–81.

Zellner, A. and Theil, H. (1962) Three stage least squares: simultaneous estimation of simultaneous equations, *Econometrica*, **30**, 54–78.

Index

absolute income hypothesis, 160–3, 168, 178–9, 182, 197, 199, 200–1
accelerator models, 251–4, 262–4, 271, 273, 278, 280–1, 288, 338, 343
  naive, 251–3, 255, 335
  flexible, 252–5, 260, 262–4, 273, 276, 279, 283–5
accounting identity, 220, 223–4, 228, 235
adaptive expectations, 45, 61, 103–5, 178–9, 185–7, 263, 297–8, 331
adding-up criterion, 135, 138
additivity, 145–7, 149
adjustment, 252, 280
  costs of, 252, 254–5, 257–8, 298
  coefficient, *see* parameter
  speed of, 254–5, 264, 276, 280–1, 310–11
  parameter, 103–4, 139–40, 179, 262–4, 275, 284–5, 310, 314–15, 317–18, 328–31
aggregation, 127–9, 153, 234, 239, 259, 296, 319
  convergence approach to, 128–9, 162, 218
  for non-linear functions, 129
  over commodities, 127
  over consumers, 127–9, 162, 188
  over factors of production, 216
  over firms, 217–18, 233–4
  over industries, 218
  restrictions, 144–5, 151
almost ideal demand system (AIDS), 153
assets
  financial, 170, 281, 314, 321, 343, 345
  liquid, 2–3, 11, 66–7, 95, 185–92, 196–7, 204, 326, 343, 345
  physical, 170
  real financial, 314
  see also wealth
asymptotic distribution, 21, 24
autocorrelation, 59–60, 67, 69, 143, 199, 202, 261, 268, 284–5, 289, 320, 328
  fourth order, 57, 59, 203, 279
  negative, 56–9
  positive, 56–9, 156, 284
  sample, 60
  see also disturbances, autocorrelated
average propensity to consume (APC), 55, 160, 162, 164–7, 179, 185, 188, 197–8
  permanent income, 174
average propensity to save (APS), 55, 166, 171, 188, 192, 198
  see also saving ratio

Ball-Drake model, 187–90
Bank of England, 305, 307, 310
  model, 342–6
best linear unbiasedness, 20
  see also OLS estimators, best linear unbiasedness of bonds, 294–297, 314–16
  rate of return on, 295, 297
  riskiness of, 294, 306, 316
Box-Pierce test, 60, 195
brokerage fee, 293–4, 316
budget constraint, 144, 146, 150–2, 154, 168–9, 187, 189, 196
  government, 345
  lifetime, 170, 205
budget, share, 147, 151, 153
budget surveys, 127, 162–3

Cambridge Econometrics (CE) model, 342, 344
Cambridge Economic Policy Group (CEPG), 342. 344–6, 350–1
capital
  cost of, 254, 258, 280, 282–3
  equipment, 104, 232, 253, 258, 265–7, 274–5
  gains, 185, 189–91, 220, 257–8, 268, 271, 276, 295, 297
  goods industry, 106, 252, 254, 261, 278
  intensity, 213, 218, 230, 234, 238, 241
  —labour ratio, 211–16, 241–4, 274–5
  —labour substitution, 255, 258
  marginal product of, 209–15, 221, 255–6, 266
  —output ratio, 251–5, 263, 284, 288, 337
  rental price of, 211–2, 220, 223–9, 253–7
  real price of, 211, 222, 255
  services, 208–21, 255–7, 260
  stock, 104, 106, 208, 220, 232, 243–8, 251–72, 275–8, 280–9, 338–9, 343
  user-cost of, 257–60, 268, 271, 275–82
  utilisation, 208, 220, 246, 260–1, 264
ceteris paribus assumption, 16–17, 79
X^2 distribution, 60
Chow tests, 309, *see also* parameter stability
classical multiple regression model, 5, 27–38
Cochrane–Orcutt
  coefficient, 62, 247
  two stage procedure, 62, 314
  iterative procedure, 62–3, 156, 247–8, 314, 321
coefficient of multiple determination, 35–8, 66,

permanent income, 181, 183
profits, 337
transitory income, 181–2
wage income, 337, 341
windfalls, 181
marginal rate of substitution of capital for labour, 210–12, 230, 239, 294
maximum lag length, 101, 109–111, 265–6, 285–7, 324
maximum likelihood estimators (MLE), 24–6, 32, 95–7, 103, 123, 141, 149, 151, 180, 185, 243, 274, 323
measurement errors, 47–9, 175, 269
monetarist models, 346–8
money
    broad, 297, 306–7, 309, 312–15, 317–320, 326–7, 332
    definition of, 296–7, 306–7, 311, 314, 317–22, 326
    high powered, 301–5, 310
    —income ratio, 309–11, 314
    narrow, 296–7, 306–7, 312–5, 317–21, 326–31
    quantity theory of, 294, 309
    rate of return on, 295, 297
money-fixed assets, 196
money illusion, 191
mongrel equation, 79, 81–2, 85–6, 88–9
multicollinearity, 65–71, 101–2, 122, 133–5, 155–7, 230–2, 241, 246–7, 255, 260, 263, 287, 296–7, 300, 321–2, 324, 326
    complete (perfect), 14, 66, 94, 115
multiplier
    balanced budget, 339
    bank, 301–2
    dynamic or long run, 109, 336–7, 339–40, 342, 352, 355
    fiscal, 292
    impact, 335–7, 329–40, 342, 352, 355
    interim, 337, 340, 342
    Keynesian, 179
    monetary, 292
    tax, 339
multiplier-accelerator model, 334–5

National Institute (NI), 353–4
    model, 342–3, 348–51, 353, 355–6
necessities, 129, 136–7
negativity restrictions, 145
    see also Slutsky equation
neoclassical investment model, 253–4, 260, 266–71, 274, 276–81, 283, 343
nominal balances, 295, 298, 300–1, 306, 320, 327, 330
non-linear least squares, 123, 141, 186
normal distribution, 27, 29–30, 68

omitted variables, 71–72, 75, 154
open economy, 309, 321, 327, 341
opportunity cost of holding money, 297, 307, 316, 320–1

ordinary least squares (OLS), 3, 11, 12–17, 73, 82, 86, 89, 92, 94–5, 98, 102, 108, 110, 116–20, 123, 130–2, 136, 138, 141–3, 154, 162, 180, 182, 186, 199–201, 227, 232–3, 235, 237, 239, 248, 261–3, 273, 275, 284–6, 300, 302–5, 307–8, 310, 327, 338
    estimators, 14–7, 30–3, 42–57, 63–71, 75, 89, 118–9, 133–4, 162, 175, 180, 185, 199, 224, 228, 273, 298, 320
        best linear unbiasedness of, 31, 51, 55, 63, 67, 71, 101
        consistency of, 31, 51, 55, 63, 67, 71, 75, 89–90, 101, 105, 130–1, 184, 227, 302–4
        efficiency of, 31–2, 51, 55, 63, 71
        linearity of, 30
        normality of, 32, 63
        standard errors of, 31, 33–4, 51–2, 55–7, 66–70, 231, 248, 274
        unbiasedness of, 30–1, 51, 55, 63, 67, 71, 75, 89–90, 130–1, 227, 302–4
output, 251–5, 260–1, 270–2, 275, 278, 280–2
    constraint, 211
    elasticity of, 213, 227, 245–6, 248, 268
    of economy, 235–7, 341, 343–4, 347, 351, 353–4
    of firm, 104, 106, 118, 208–18, 220–9, 256–7, 259–60, 265–6, 275–6
    of industry, 218–20, 232–5, 239, 244–8, 262–3, 268, 273–4, 277–9, 283–9
    price of, 214, 217, 219, 223–5, 232–4, 255–6
overidentification, 119–20, 123, 186, 227, 341
overidentified equations, 93–8, 200–1, 298, 300, 338

parameter restrictions 117–123, 144, 150–1, 153, 231
    cross equation 145, 153
    linear, 118–22, 126, 148
    on intercept, 117
    non-linear, 122–4
    testing, 120–2, 147–9, 151, 153, 156, 246–7, 278, 323–4, 328, 330
parameter stability, 310
    testing for, 115–17, 158, 197, 204, 279, 329–331
partial adjustment, 45, 61, 104–6, 139, 180, 252, 275, 298–9, 304, 310, 314–5, 317–8, 321–2, 326, 328–9, 347
perfect competition, 214–5, 220
    in factor market, 211, 226, 240, 256, 258, 276
    in product market, 211, 233, 256
permanent income hypothesis (PIH), 126, 137–8, 172–185, 197, 202, 297–9
Phillips curve, 344–5, 353
policy
    economic, 160, 281
    fiscal, 292, 341, 353–4
    government, 143, 334, 346, 349
    instruments, 305, 339, 348, 355
    monetary, 115, 292, 341, 352